# APPLYING
# THE SCRIPTURES

# APPLYING
# THE SCRIPTURES

## Papers From ICBI Summit III

### Kenneth S. Kantzer

### Editor

Academie Books Grand Rapids, Michigan
Zondervan Publishing House

APPLYING THE SCRIPTURES
Copyright © 1987 by the International Council on Biblical Inerrancy

ACADEMIE BOOKS
is an imprint of
Zondervan Publishing House
1415 Lake Drive S.E.
Grand Rapids, Michigan 49506


**Library of Congress Cataloging in Publication Data**

ICBI Summit (3rd : 1986 : Chicago, Ill.)
   Applying the Scriptures.

   Papers from ICBI Summit III, held in Chicago, Dec. 10–13, 1986.
   Includes bibliographies.
   1. Bible—Theology—Congresses.    2. Evangelicalism—Congresses.
I. Kantzer, Kenneth S.    II. International Council on Biblical Inerrancy.
III. Title.

BS543.I32   1986     230     87–1455

ISBN    0–310–25151–6

*Printed in the United States of America*

87  88  89  90  91  92  93  94  95 / MG / 10  9  8  7  6  5  4  3  2  1

# CONTENTS

# ABOUT THE CONTRIBUTORS

**Edmund P. Clowney** is associate pastor/teacher-in-residence at Trinity Presbyterian Church, Charlottesville, Virginia. He is a graduate of Westminster Theological Seminary, Th.B., and Yale Divinity School, S.T.M. He has served as president and as professor of practical theology at Westminster Theological Seminary and has been on the theological commission of the executive committee for World Evangelism Fellowship. He is a member of the ICBI Council. Books authored by Dr. Clowney include *Preaching and Biblical Theology, Called to the Ministry*, and *Christian Meditation*.

**Charles W. Colson** is the chairman of the board of Prison Fellowship Ministries, which he founded in 1976. A graduate of Brown University, B.A., and George Washington University, J.D., Mr. Colson has served as assistant to the assistant secretary of the Navy (1955–56) and as an administrative assistant in the United States Senate (1956–61). He was a partner in a Washington, D.C., law firm (1961–69) and special counsel to President Richard M. Nixon (1969–73). He is the author of four best-selling books: *Born Again, Life Sentence, Loving God*, and *Who Speaks for God?* He is a contributing editor for *Christianity Today* and a fellow of Christianity Today Institute.

**Norman L. Geisler** is professor of systematic theology, Dallas Theological Seminary, Dallas, Texas. He is a graduate of Loyola University, Ph.D. He has also done graduate study at Wayne State Graduate School, University of Detroit Graduate School, and Northwestern University. Dr. Geisler is an ordained minister and has served as chairman and professor of Philosophy and Religion at Trinity Evangelical Divinity School, has lectured throughout the

United States and abroad, and is a member of the ICBI Council. He has authored over thirty books, among which are *General Introduction to the Bible* (coauthored by William Nix), *Biblical Errancy, What Augustine Says*, and *Cosmos: Carl Sagan's Religion for the Scientific Mind.*

**Walter A. Henrichsen** is an associate at Leadership Foundation, Inc., Colorado Springs, Colorado. He is a graduate of Western Theological Seminary, Holland, Michigan, M.Div. He is an ordained minister in the Reformed Church in America and has served the Navigators for twenty years as area, deputy, personnel, and regional director. Mr. Henrichsen has authored *Disciples Are Made—Not Born, Understand, A Layman's Guide to Interpreting the Bible, After the Sacrifice, How to Discipline Your Children,* and *Laymen, Look Up! God Has a Place for You* (coauthored with William Garrison).

**Carl F. H. Henry** is lecturer-at-large for World Vision International. He is a graduate of Boston University, Ph.D., and Northern Baptist Seminary, Th.D. He has served as visiting professor of Christian studies, Hillsdale College, and visiting professor of theology, Calvin Theological Seminary. Dr. Henry has authored over twenty-five books, among which are his six volumes on *God, Revelation and Authority.*

**William A. Heth** is instructor of New Testament literature and exegesis at Dallas Theological Seminary. He is a graduate of Dallas Theological Seminary, Th.M., Th.D. Dr. Heth has served as campus director on the staff of Campus Crusade for Christ, field instructor in training seminary students in evangelism at Southern Methodist University, seminar leader for the Texas Sunday School Association, and teaching assistant and tutor for Greek exegetical courses at Dallas Theological Seminary. He has authored "A Critique of the Evangelical Protestant View of Divorce and Remarriage," "Another Look at the Erasmian View of Divorce and Remarriage," "The Meaning of Divorce in Matthew 19:3–9," *Jesus and Divorce* (with Gordon J. Wenham), and "Unmarried 'for the Sake of the Kingdom' in the Early Church."

**Gretchen Gaebelein Hull** is an author and lecturer. She is a graduate of Bryn Mawr College, B.A., and has done graduate study at Columbia University. She has served as a member and editor for the board of the Women's Union Missionary Society of America and on the executive committee of Presbyterians United for Biblical Concerns. She is an ordained elder in the Presbyterian Church, U.S.A. Mrs. Hull has lectured throughout the United States and abroad on "Authenticity, Inspiration, and Authority of Scripture," "Biblical Feminism Within the Context of a High View of Scripture," "Promoting a Christian Ministry to the Handicapped," and "Supporting Programs Working to Alleviate World Hunger." She has written several articles on Christian topics and is in the process of writing a book to be published by Revell in 1987.

**Kurt E. Marquart** is associate professor of systematic theology, Concordia Theological Seminary, Fort Wayne, Indiana. He is a graduate of Concordia Theological Seminary, M.Div., and the University of Western Ontario, M.A. He is an ordained minister in the Lutheran Church—Missouri Synod, and he served for fourteen years as pastor of Redeemer Lutheran Parish in Australia. Mr. Marquart is the author of *Anatomy of an Explosion*, "The Incompatibility Between Historical-Critical Theology and the Lutheran Confessions," and *Studies in Lutheran Hermeneutics*.

**John Warwick Montgomery** is dean and professor of Jurisprudence at the Simon Greenleaf School of Law, Anaheim, California, and director of its annual summer program at the International Institute of Human Rights, Strasbourg, France. He holds eight earned degrees besides the LL.B.: the A.B. with distinction in philosophy (Cornell University; Phi Beta Kappa), B.L.S. and M.A. (University of California at Berkeley), B.D. and S.T.M. (Wittenberg University, Springfield, Ohio), M.Phil. in law (University of Essex, England), Ph.D. (University of Chicago), and the *Doctorat d'Université* from Strasbourg, France. He is author of over one hundred scholarly journal articles and more than thirty-five books in English, French, Spanish, and German. He is internationally regarded both as a theologian (his debates with the late Bishop James Pike, death-of-God advocate Thomas Altizer, and situation-ethicist Joseph Fletcher are historic) and as a lawyer (barrister-at-law of the Middle Temple and Lincoln's Inn, England; member of the California, Virginia, and District of Columbia Bars and the Bar of the Supreme Court of the United States).

**Ronald Nash** is professor of philosophy and religion at Western Kentucky University. He holds degrees from Brown University (M.A.) and Syracuse University (Ph.D.). Dr. Nash is the author or editor of close to twenty books including: *Evangelicals in America, Process Theology, Liberation Theology, Poverty and Wealth, Evangelical Renewal in the Mainline Churches, Social Justice and the Christian Church*, and *Christianity and the Hellenistic World*.

**Roger Nicole** is professor emeritus of theology at Gordon-Conwell Theological Seminary, where he served for forty-one years (1945–86). In addition to the D.D. (Wheaton College), he holds the following degrees: A.B. (the Gymnase Classique, Lausanne), M.A. (Sorbonne, Paris), B.D., S.T.M., and Th.D. (Gordon Divinity School, Boston), and Ph.D. (Harvard University). Besides a bibliographical volume on Moyse Amyraut, he has contributed many articles for quarterly reviews and symposia. He has taught as visiting professor in many seminaries around the world and has been a frequent contributor to the Philadelphia Conference on Reformed Theology. For sixteen years Dr. Nicole has pastored the Worcester and Manchaug First Baptist Churches in Massachusetts. He has served as charter member and president of the Evangelical Theological Society and is a member of the ICBI Council.

**James I. Packer** is professor of historical and systematic theology, Regent College, Vancouver, Canada. He is a graduate of Oxford University, D.Phil. He has served as associate principal of Trinity College, Bristol, England, and is a member of the ICBI Council. Dr. Packer has authored several books, among which are *Fundamentalism and the Word of God, Evangelism and the Sovereignty of God, God Speaks to Man, Knowing God, I Want To Be a Christian,* and *Your Father Loves You.*

**John M. Perkins** is president and founder of the John M. Perkins Foundation for Reconciliation and Development and the Harambee Christian Family Center, Pasadena, California. He holds honorary degrees from Wheaton College, Gordon College, and Huntington College. He has served as president and founder of Voice of Calvary Ministry, as a board member for World Vision U.S.A., and has lectured throughout the United States and abroad. Dr. Perkins has authored *Let Justice Roll Down, A Quiet Revolution, Call to Wholistic Ministry, With Justice for All,* and articles for several leading magazines.

**Robert D. Preus** serves as president and professor of systematic theology at Concordia Theological Seminary, Fort Wayne, Indiana. He is a graduate of Edinburgh University, Ph.D., and Strasbourg University, Th.D. He is an ordained minister in the Lutheran Church—Missouri Synod, has served as professor at Concordia Theological Seminary, St. Louis, Missouri, and is a member of the ICBI Council. He is the author of *The Inspiration of Scripture, The Theology of Post-Reformation Lutheranism* (2 vols.), *Getting into the Theology of Concord,* and *A Contemporary Look at the Formula of Concord* (edited with Wilbert Rosin).

**Mary Pride** is an author, vice president of Missouri Parents and Children, and president of Home Life. She is a graduate of Rensselaer Polytechnic Institute, B.S., and has her M.S. in engineering. Mrs. Pride is the author of *The Way Home: Beyond Feminism, Back to Reality, Big Book of Home Learning,* and *Child Abuse Industry.*

**William Pride** is a senior systems programmer analyst for the Brown Group and president of Missouri Parents and Children. He is a graduate of Covenant Theological Seminary, M.A., M.Div. Mr. Pride has served as systems programmer for Raytheon Corporation, a systems associate for Travellers Insurance Company, and as an instructor of business data processing at Orange County Community College.

**John White** was, until his retirement, associate professor of psychiatry at the University of Manitoba, Canada. A former president of the Provincial Psychiatric Association and board member of the National Association, he served on numerous boards and committees, both professional and academic. He is a graduate in Medicine of the University of Manchester, England, M.D., the University of Manitoba in Psychiatry, and a fellow of the Canadian Psychiatric Association and of the Royal Society of Medicine of Great Britain. Dr. White is the author of fifteen books and numerous articles both professional and popular.

**Gleason L. Archer,** Ph.D. Professor of Old Testament and Semitic Languages, Trinity Evangelical Divinity School.

**W. David Beck,** Ph.D. Director, Graduate School of Religion and Chairman, Department of Philosophy, Liberty University.

**David Breese,** Th.B. President, Christian Destiny.

**Eugene W. Bunkowske,** Ph.D. Professor and Director of Missions, Concordia Theological Seminary.

**Lawrence Crabb,** M.A., Ph.D. President, Institute of Biblical Counseling.

**Ted W. Engstrom,** Lh.D., Ll.D., Litt.D. President, World Vision.

**Anthony T. Evans,** Th.D. Senior Pastor, Oak Cliff Bible Fellowship

**Richard B. Gaffin,** Th.D. Professor of Systematic Theology, Westminster Theological Seminary.

**William N. Garrison,** J.D. Attorney at Law, Fort Worth, Texas.

**S. Craig Glickman,** Th.D. Adjunct Teacher is Systematic Theology, Dallas Theological Seminary.

**Michael E. Haynes,** Th.B. Pastor, Twelfth Baptist Church.

**Harold W. Hoehner,** Th.D., Ph.D. Chairman and Professor of New Testament Literature and Exegesis, Dallas Theological Seminary.

**Robert T. Jensen,** M.D. Associate Professor for Clinical Family Practice, University of Texas at San Antonio.

**Wallace E. Johnson,** B.A. President, Computer Code Consultant, Incorporated

**Walter C. Kaiser, Jr.,** Ph.D. Professor of Semitic Languages, Trinity Evangelical Divinity School

**Kenneth S. Kantzer,** Ph.D. Chancellor, Trinity College.

**John W. Klotz,** Ph.D. Director of the Graduate School and Professor of Practical Theology, Condordia Theological Seminary.

**Everett Koop,** M.D., Sc.D. Surgeon General, U.S. Public Health Service.

**Gordon Mac Donald,** B.A., M.Div. President, InterVarsity Christian Fellowship in the United States.

**Earl D. Radmacher,** Th.D. President, Western Conservative Baptist Theological Seminary.

**Frederic R. Schatz,** M.B.A. President, Creative Water Works.

**Herbert Schlossberg,** Ph.D. Free-lance writer and editor, Minneapolis, Minnesota.

**Jay Alan Sekulow,** J.D. Attorney at Law, Atlanta, Georgia.

**Ray C. Stedman,** D.D. Pastor, Peninsula Bible Church.

**Paul E. Steele. Senior Pastor, The Valley Church.**

**Bruce K. Waltke,** Th.D., Ph.D. Professor of Old Testament, Westminster Theological Seminary.

**Michael D. Warner,** Ph.D. Pastor, Grace Lutheran Church

**William C. Weinrich,** Th.D. Associate professor of Early Church History and Patristic Studies, Concordia Theological Seminary.

**John W. Whitehead,** J.D. President and Founder, The Rutherford Institute.

**Loren Wilkinson,** Ph.D. Associate Professor of Interdisciplinary Studies and Philosophy, Regent College.

**Earl D. Wilson,** Ph.D. Associate Professor of Psychology, Western Conservative Baptist Theological Seminary.

**Ralph D. Winter,** Ph.D. General Director, U.S. Center for World Missions.

**Curtis J. Young,** M.Div. Executive Director, Christian Action Council.

**Thomas F. Zimmerman,** D.D. General Superintendent, The General council of the assemblies of God.

# FOREWORD

The inerrancy of the Bible is an intensely practical doctrine. Its purpose is not to make us capable of building an infallible systematic theology or a perfect system of ethics. This book will demonstrate, if we did not already know it, that such a "theology of glory" lies far beyond us during our life here below. For that, we must wait until heaven, where the Lord of glory will meet us face to face and we shall finaly know as we are known by our divine Redeemer (1 Cor. 13:12).

What an inerrant Bible does is to provide us with an objective authority outside ourselves, and over ourselves, by which we must judge ourselves. No matter how much we may twist and pull its teaching (and sometimes, it is true, we treat it like a wax nose and push it into all sorts of impossible and grotesque shapes) it still stands there written. We can't rewrite the Bible. Its letters stand there, awesomely silent, spelling out their words of condemnation and forgiveness and guidance. And when the Holy Spirit takes those words and writes them upon our hearts and minds and consciences, we find ourselves face to face with the living God. "It is written inerrantly" becomes then, "Speak, Lord, for thy servant heareth."

If someone objects: "But how do you know you have the right text," we respond: "We don't choose a text because we happen to like it. Or because it makes us feel good. Or because it fits our pre-conceived theological or ethical system. We accept the text because of the history of the textual data. We have objective textual data that show what is the right text."

The proof that the text is not determined by our theology is the fact that radicals, liberals, neo-orthodox, evangelicals and fundamentalists all use the same texts. In fact, the Greek text of the New Testament most widely used in evangelical colleges and seminaries is a text produced by radical liberals—Nestle's twenty-fourth edition. No single doctrine in dispute between radicals and fundamentalists turns on a battle over what is the correct text. The issue that divides them is: Is the text telling the truth? Here evangelicals and fundamentalists are united: We stand under the infallible judgment of the written Word of God. By its teaching our thought and life must be guided. What the Bible says about God and man and all else on which it speaks, we accept as truth from the sovereign God of the universe and as binding on our conscience.

The purpose of this volume is to thresh out ethical guidelines for the public and institutional life of the church from this perspective of the inerrant truth and divine authority of the Bible. Here some of the finest minds among evangelical leaders of our generation have set themselves to this task.

The articles were prepared for a four-day summit meeting (Summit III) held near Chicago, Illinois, during December 1986. Papers were circulated before the conference; and at the meeting, discussion was hot and heavy. It would be difficult to find a group more dedicated to conservative orthodox protestant theology. Yet evangelicals are an independent lot. No one seemed to agree with anybody. Every issue became a battle ground.

This wide divergence in viewpoint was absolutely amazing. To some it was also very disconcerting. All were committed to an inerrant Bible and accepted it as their final guide on matters of faith and practice. To many, radical disagreement as to how the Bible should be interpreted and applied seemed to pose a flat contradiction to their united commitment to an inerrant Bible. If all really accepted the Bible as their guide for life, how could they disagree so as to what is required of them. Inerrancy should bring uniformity of doctrine and ethics.

Yet of disagreement there was a plenty, and not just on trivial matters. On war and peace, for example, some were pacifists (and not all the same kind of pacifist either), others were nuclear pacifists, and still others defended a just war. Those espousing the last position disagreed on whether Christians ought to urge the American government to cut its armaments back to bare minimum or maintain a position of great strength.

On social justice, likewise, some argued that God is on the side of the poor. Others hesitated even to use such words as injustice or repression on the grounds that these were code words for an anti-christian "liberation theology."

On the sanctity of life, some argued that all abortions represented murder. Others were quite willing to grant that it was appropriate to destroy the fetus in order to save the life of the mother or even in the case of rape and incest. And each of these positions disagreed as to how much of what he himself believed to be right the Christian should seek to make into laws binding on a non-Christian society.

On marriage and the family, some were adamant that the place of the wife is in the home. The husband is the head of the family, and a wife is to submit herself to her husband in all things not requiring disobedience to God. Others argued for a basic equality of rights *and roles* in society, including the freedom of women to be ordained to the Christian ministry and to teach and exercise authority over men.

On divorce and remarriage, some were convinced that the Bible simply does not allow for divorce on any grounds. Others would permit divorce but without the right to remarry, irrespective of the grounds on which the divorce was secured. Others allow for divorce on certain limited grounds with the right to remarry on the part of the innocent partner. And some even granted the right to remarry in the case of the guilty party if the original marriage covenant had been finally broken.

And so it went on and on and on. Some of those attending the conference experienced a severe case of shock. How could Christians, all of whom believed the Bible to be the infallible guide for faith and life, find themselves in such chaotic disagreement?

The printed papers, including responses, do not by any means reflect the full spread of viewpoints represented in the discussion groups. The writers of the position papers were not chosen in order to provide a fair spectrum of divergent evangelical views but rather were selected because they had written authoritative and influential pieces on the topics assigned to them and were committed to the inerrancy of Scripture. Even responders did not in every case cover the entire waterfront but represented rather viewpoints differing in some significant way from those put forth in the position papers.

Discussion ranged freely over the topics presented, and it very quickly became apparent that scholars committed to inerrancy do not necessarily agree on how that inerrant Bible should be applied to the practical issues of living the Christian life.

Most of the evangelicals present realized that such wide disagreement was not so surprising as they had first assumed. During two thousand years of church history in which the church has adhered to an inerrant Bible, it has not arrived at a consensus on many doctrines. Since its early days, the church has divided over the mode and meaning of baptism, the nature and significance of the Lord's supper, predestination, perseverance of the saints, the nature of sanctification, the possibility of freedom from sin in this life, the promise of a millennium, the relationship between the millennium and the second coming of Christ, and a host of other doctrines.

If on these broader doctrinal issues the church has been unable to agree, is it so surprising that we were at loggerheads in trying to apply the biblical teaching to social issues troubling our world today? It is one thing to interpret the meaning of relevant scriptural passages. It is quite a different matter to explain how one should *apply* those biblical principles to another day and age.

It would be putting the matter too simply, perhaps, to say that on these doctrinal issues the church had the task of merely interpreting the meaning of the whole of the relevant Scriptures and of showing their relationship to each other. And even this task proved too much for the church. It found itself quite unable to arrive at any complete agreement in doctrine. It had to learn to live together as Christians without a consensus of doctrine.

Application, moreover, adds at least two new factors beyond those involved in the interpretation of the text. First, the Bible does not purport to give specific guidance on all issues for Christians living in every age. Second, the world is constantly changing. Even if the Bible were to give us explicit directions for one situation, a new day with new structures of society and new problems would require continuous re-adaptation and re-application of the Scriptures, to apply them fairly to the changing world about us. It is not surprising therefore, and we should not be unduly discouraged, when we do not find ready answers as to how we can most faithfully apply Scripture to all the perplexing and disturbing questions raised for us in today's world.

Yet if Scripture details no clear and specific guidance for our problems, how can evangelicals become salt and light in our society as Jesus has commanded us? The world is not interested in our pious guesses; it has quite enough of its own, though they are usually not very pious. The world will simply set one evangelical opinion against another and blithely ignore any evangelical contribution to the moral guidance of society. The evangelical impact will be totally lost in our day. Certainly it will be impossible for evangelicals to sound a powerful and effective moral note in contemporary society.

Yet there were some very encouraging aspects of Summit III, its position papers, and the discussions that grew out of them. First, evangelicals learned to argue heatedly about things on which they had strong convictions and felt very deeply. They found themselves arguing passionately and yet with civility and, indeed, with a love for those with whom they disagreed even in their most heated debate.

Second, the discussions clearly expanded the horizons of those evangelicals who participated in the free give and take of the disputes. Evangelicals recognized that other evangelicals were not arguing simply out of a careless attitude towards the Word of God or a mere desire selfishly and wickedly to escape from its force, but out of a strong commitment to the inerrant Word of God and the clear conviction that the Holy Spirit had led them in a right path.

Sometimes convictions were deepened. On other occasions, convictions were changed. Often the evangelical was forced to make distinctions. Some parts of what he stood for he continued to believe with stronger conviction than ever. Other aspects he might have to rethink or, at least, learn to tolerate even though he might not appreciate them.

Third, in this process one thing became very clear to many evangelicals. True tolerance is not a mere willingness to put up with viewpoints about which one is utterly indifferent. True tolerance requires a wrenching of soul in which one comes to respect another individual and chooses to put up with his views even though one is seriously and deeply in disagreement with them.

Fourth, inerrantists learned that their diversity is not so great as first appears. Commitment to the Bible as the infallible rule of faith and practice *does* make a difference. The Bible sets forth unmistakable teaching about the nature of God and of man and of the world. This framework gives shape and boundary to all other issues including troublesome applications to the highly mooted ethical problems of our day.

Even in those areas of sharpest contention, there was clear agreement as to the basic thrust of how the Bible is to be applied. This was evidenced by the willingness of the group, in spite of their sharp disagreements on many particulars, to sign a statement commiting themselves to the general thrust of the document produced at the conference.

For example, even those who allow for divorce and remarriage after divorce highly disapprove of divorce and reckon it to be a tragic breakdown in personal relationships and in society. They are unutterably opposed to the easy divorce and careless approach to remarriage so prevalent in contemporary American society.

Again, all are opposed to war and are convinced that peace is worth fighting for. They agree, too, that it is the duty of everyone to care for the poor who are willing to work or who have encountered poverty through no fault of their own. They argue, however, that it is wrong to do so in a way that only enslaves individuals and locks them into permanent poverty.

Fourth, perhaps, the best thing to be observed from evangelical attitudes is their almost universal recognition of servant leadership. Every Christian, because he is a follower of Christ, is called to serve others. Leadership is not an opportunity to lord it over lesser mortals but an opportunity to serve and minister to fellow humans so as to bring to them the highest possible level of justice, freedom, and opportunity for all mankind.

How, then, can evangelicals serve our generation? Not all agree as to exactly what is the answer to every question troubling modern society. Holy Scripture is, indeed, infallible, but our interpretations and our applications are not. And to confuse Scriptural infallibility with our own fallibility is not becoming to a Christian and robs him of his ability to work effectively either with his fellow Christians for the Kingdom of God or with unbelievers for the good of human kind.

Yet neither is the inerrantist adrift on a vast sea of skepticism so that, at best, he can only offer to a troubled and uncertain world, bits of human advice which even he only half believes. The evangelical with his inerrant Bible knows that he has a sure and certain Word of God written.

In our sensate twentieth-century culture the significance of this objective written Word cannot be overestimated. All too often the final justification for our conduct becomes: "It feels so good, it must be right." For the evangelical inerrantist, the last word is not how it feels, but: "It stands written." And that written Word of God stands there unmoved by the surging tide of the current events or the passions that sway mens' minds. It stands unmoveable and sharp as a two-edged rapier to cut and mold the conscience. Of course, it can be misunderstood and misapplied. But the Word of God remains as one still point by which to set the compass of one's life. It is a measuring stick that does not shrink or stretch.

Like Jesus Christ, the Lord of the church, Christians are servants in a needy world. They must immerse themselves in the world in order to serve it. Yet they dare not merely acquiesce to the values of those who have neither a fixed point by which to set the course of their lives nor a reliable measuring stick by which to set their consciences. At one and the same time, they must seek to identify with the society they wish to serve and yet not be pressed into its mold. In appropriate humility, because they, too, are finite and sinful humans, they do not simply tell others what is best for them. In the light of the revelation God has graciously provided, they seek to work out with others, many of whom will not recognize that revelation, what are the best ways to meet the problems of our day. They choose to give themselves and their lives to secure what they believe to be the best solutions for the good of humankind.

That was the goal of Summit III. And that is the goal for which these papers were prepared as well as of the discussion that followed. We invite the readers of [Applying the Scriptures] to share with us in the fruit of our labors. But that fruit can only be shared by those who are willing to share also in the process by which that fruit is produced.

So we invite you to read these articles and to interact with them. Share them with your friends. Then in turn, discuss them with your friends and, like the wise Bereans of Acts 17, search the Holy Scriptures for they alone are infallible and give us the divine guidance for which our world cries out so desperately in our day.

And the rigorous process of examining the objective written Word of God with other deeply committed believers, the resultant wrestling with the diverse interpretations set forth reverently and earnestly by those seeking to apply its truths to the world of the twentieth century, and the mutual support of one another in Christian love as to the importance of the task will nudge us all nearer to what is truly right and just and thus will strengthen the community of faith.

\* \* \*

The articles in this volume—both position papers and responses—are here reproduced pretty much as they were originally circulated. Duplications, inconsistences, sharp contradictions—all remain as they were presented with only the lightest of editing. A few authors sent along later addenda or corrections, but most did not. In spite of the rush to get this into print as quickly as possible, we believe we were able to incorporate most such last minute changes.

It is the sincere hope of the publishers and the editor, speaking for the International Council on Biblical Inerrancy, that the readers of this volume can, in some measure, share in the excitement and joy of Summit III.

# THE LIVING GOD

## Robert D. Preus

## I. INTRODUCTION

All of Scripture is theology—that is, language or talk about God. Whether we are talking about the Trinity, as I propose to do in this chapter; or about justification by grace; the Lord's Supper; eternal life; or the life of Abraham, Isaac, or Jacob, we are always and preeminently talking about God. Please bear this fact in mind as you read this chapter, for there are many important and essential topics we cannot discuss in this chapter, and so even our treatment on the subject of "The Living God" will seem—and will be—inadequate and incomplete. In this chapter we will discuss and attempt to answer three basic questions about God: (1) How do we know him? (2) What is he like? and (3) Who is he? Our answers to these questions will serve as an introduction and basis to everything else that can be said about God in later chapters, for everything discussed will be theological.

Another word of introduction: Our entire discussion will be on the basis of Scripture. This procedure is based on the principle that God is a living and speaking God, that he has made himself known to fallen mankind in various ways—through prophets and Old Testament Scriptures before the advent of his Son (Heb. 1:1) and through the apostolic Scripture of the New Testament after the death and resurrection of Christ.

## II. HOW DO WE KNOW GOD?

To know God means not merely to know things about him—that he is Father, Son, and Holy Spirit; that he is righteous, almighty, wise, good, and loving—important and fundamental as

1

such knowledge is. According to Scripture, our knowledge of God is similar to our knowledge by acquaintance. It is a knowledge of the heart which results in love (Deut. 6:13). Such knowledge is not merely factual but involves a relationship, a walking with God in communion (Mic. 6:8). It is personal and intimate like our knowledge of a dear friend, and it affects our lives. Where there is no knowledge of God there is neither truth nor mercy (Hos. 4:1), neither obedience nor sacrifice to him (Matt. 9:13). "I know whom I have believed," Saint Paul says, "and am persuaded that he is able to keep that which I have committed unto him against that day" (2 Tim. 1:12 KJV; cf. Rom. 8:38). Here we see that knowing God always involves personal trust and confidence. Christ knows his sheep, and his sheep know him (John 10:14). When Peter denies Christ and says, "I know him not" (Luke 22:57 KJV), he cuts himself off from God and his grace and loses everything. When Jesus says, "This is life eternal, that they might know thee the only true God, and Jesus Christ whom thou hast sent" (John 17:3 KJV), he declares that salvation and life eternal are the results of knowing God and what he in his grace has done for sinners (cf. 20:31; 1 Tim. 1:15). The basic theme of the Old Testament is that one knows God only when one recognizes his redemptive activity. Philip Melanchthon echoes this truth when he says, "To know Christ is to know His benefits."[1]

Modern existential theology and neoorthodoxy (Martin Buber, Søren Kierkegaard, Emil Brunner, John Baillie, et al.) have emphasized the personal, experiential, and relational aspect of our knowledge of God to the virtual exclusion of revealed facts and information about God and what he has done to save us. They tend to ignore, pooh-pooh, and deny the historicity of the mighty acts of God and the redemptive acts of Jesus as well as the pure doctrine of the biblical gospel which recounts these acts and interprets them for us. This neomysticism and enthusiasm are not only contrary to every page of the Bible, which gives us facts and information about God, but are nonsensical. How can one know God without knowing anything about God?

In the Scriptures the existence of God is never questioned. The prophets and apostles and the saints of the Old and New Testaments take the existence and power of God for granted. They may deny God, defy him, and rebel against him, but they do not question his existence. When the house of Israel and of Judah dealt treacherously against the Lord, and the prophet says, "They have belied the Lord, and said, "It is not he [literally, he is not]; neither shall any evil come upon us," they have not denied God's existence but have become *practical* atheists, i.e., living as though there were no God, not bothering about him or his commands (Jer. 5:12; cf. Ps. 14:1).

According to Scripture, the knowledge of God is everywhere.

"The heavens declare the glory of God and the firmament sheweth his handywork" (Ps. 19:1 KJV). The glory and power of God are in nature and in history to be seen by all (Ps. 8:29; Isa. 40; Jer. 10). But only God's people know him and worship him aright. In a sense, even sin proclaims God, for sin is, above all, rebellion against God. The polemics in the Old and New Testament are directed in favor of monotheism, the superiority of Christianity over other religions, and the pure doctrine of the gospel.

It must go without saying that there is no speculation in the Bible about the origin or development of God, although this was quite common in ancient heathen religions. God does not evolve or emerge from something. The Bible does not give us a "history" of Yahweh. He does not change or develop as Alfred North Whitehead and modern process theologians would have us believe. Neither is God a god among many as in modern Buddhism and Mormonism. He is always portrayed in Scripture as the eternal and unchangeable God and Lord of all.

How, then, do we know God? The ready answer of Scripture is that we do not know him by our ratiocinations and investigations of his essence and attributes; rather he reveals himself to us. How does he do this? In two ways. First, through the natural course of his created order (nature) and of human events (history); and second, through special acts of revelation.

God's creation bespeaks the goodness and wisdom of God (Job 38:41; Ps. 19:1). The mountains, sea, and waves are witness to the power and majesty of God; the seasons testify to his goodness (Ps. 65). His revelation in nature as a creator God who is personal and providential is in contrast to the idols of the heathens and the false gods of deists and the philosophers (Isa. 40; Jer. 10:11–15). This "natural knowledge" of God is very clearly addressed by Paul in Romans 1:19–20: "Because that which is known [knowable] of God is manifest in [to] them; for God manifested it unto them. For the invisible things of him from the creation of the world are clearly seen, being perceived through the things that are made, even his everlasting power and divinity; that they may be without excuse" (ASV). Paul tells us here that "the things that are made" give evidence to all that there is a God who is highly exalted above the world and time, an eternal God who has created the ends of the earth (cf. Isa. 40). The evidence is so clear that anyone may "see"—that is, know—that there is an invisible God who is all powerful and has created this visible order. But from this created order anyone can also know of God's divinity; his Godhead; his incomprehensible, incomparable, and glorious nature—what Luke calls the "majesty" or mighty power of God when he describes Jesus' divine healing miracles (Luke 9:43). He who does not recognize all this is "without excuse"; for it is there to be known.

But all the knowledge that the unconverted sinner can gain from God's creation and his providence in nature and human events can never save a person. In nature is revealed God's power and majesty and wisdom, even benevolence, but not his love that saves lost and condemned sinners and grants them eternal life. Our old theologians used to say that God's revelation in nature can bring us to a knowledge that there is a God with magnificent attributes but not of who God is—namely, Father, Son, and Holy Spirit, triune in his very essence, who is a gracious Savior, God, and Lord. That is revealed only in the gospel of Jesus Christ, Paul says (Rom. 1:17). And even the godhead, majesty, and wrath revealed from heaven man persistently and always distorts (Rom. 1:18, 21ff.). All heathen and unbelievers, according to Scripture, may well know God in the sense that they have an awareness of his existence and presence and power. But, at the same time, they do not know him (Gal. 4:8; 1 Thess. 4:8)—not in the sense that they have an absolute ignorance of him as Karl Barth says but in the sense that they are without him. Paul calls them *atheoi:* atheists in the practical sense of having no God (Eph. 2:12).

But if man cannot know God from the created order and from his own futile searchings after the Deity (1 Cor. 1:21), how can he know him, who he is and what he is really like? We know him only when we are known by him, Paul says (Gal. 4:9), when he chooses to disclose himself to us not generally (as in nature) but specifically and specially in his Son and through his gospel Word, which today comes to us in the sacred Scriptures. Knowledge of salvation is only through Christ and the gospel (John 1:18; Acts 4:12; Rom. 10:17; cf. also John 3:18, 36).

It is important for us to emphasize this basic fact today because it goes against the hubris of our fallen sinful nature and our *Zeitgeist.* Today in our Western world our primary concern, as we seek to follow ancient Greek thought, is to understand, explain, and comprehend reality around us (including God), and this presumably for practical purposes, if there are any. Coupled with this concern is the desire to control environment and to escape the frustration of not understanding nature and everything about us. Such an attitude and approach to life is based on the assumption that the principles of the universe and of all reality can be grasped by the human intellect. In the area of modern science such a procedure has proved to be very fruitful. But where God and religion are concerned, such an attitude turns man in the wrong direction. For God cannot be found, analyzed, and understood by the speculative mind of finite and sinful man. He is simply not the object of speculation. And no speculation from Plato to Whitehead has produced any concept of God even approaching reality, the reality made so clear to all in God's own Word, that God is not merely some sort of numen or pancreator or "ground of being." No speculation can develop the notion that God is a loving, personal creator God, Maker and Sustainer of "all things visible and invisible," a redeemer God, "begotten of his Father before all worlds . . . who for us men, and for our salvation came down from heaven, and was incarnate by the Holy Ghost of the Virgin Mary, and was made man, and was crucified also for us under Pontius Pilate"; and that he is a comforter and sanctifier who is the Lord and Giver of life and thus creates and sustains Christ's church on earth. Only the revelation in Scripture shows us the true God, God as he really is and as he has really declared himself in Christ, a Savior God.

In the Scriptures the knowledge of God and the knowledge of salvation are inextricably linked. And who brings us salvation? Jesus. The priest Zacharias sings by inspiration that Jesus brings "the knowledge of salvation" to God's people by procuring the remission of sins (Luke 1:77). Peter says that we grow in grace when we grow in the knowledge of our *Savior* Jesus Christ (2 Peter 3:18). According to the apostle Paul, to be saved and to come to the knowledge of the truth (of God) are inseparable, and this is all because our Mediator, the God-man Jesus Christ, gave himself as a ransom for us (1 Tim. 2:4–6).

To know our Savior Christ, therefore, is to have salvation and to know God (Eph. 4:13; Phil. 3:8, 10; 1 John 4:9; 5:20); and there is no other way to know God. "No man hath seen God at any time; the only begotten Son [better texts say "God"], which is in the bosom of the Father, he hath declared him" (John 1:18 KJV). Just prior to this text John has spoken of the Incarnation (v. 14) and said that divine grace and truth are gained only through Christ. No man can see God and live. Yet the Son declares that God makes him known to all who know and believe in the Son. So Jesus can say that one who has seen him, the incarnate Son, has seen the Father (John 14:9). In fact, he can assure believers in him of eternal life because he and the Father are one in essence (John 10:30) and because he and the Father work in intimate union as he carries out the works of salvation (John 10:38). In Hebrews we are told that Jesus is the "very image of [God's] substance" (Heb. 1:3 ASV), and Saint Paul says that the "light of the knowledge of the glory of God" is revealed "in the face of Jesus Christ" (2 Cor. 4:6 KJV). Thus, when the evangelist says that the Son, Jesus, "is" (ever existing) in the bosom of the Father (John 1:18), he is speaking of a direct seeing, or knowledge, of God which we have through Jesus. To know Jesus is to know God *himself*. Jesus is not a mere reflection of God. Christ witnesses of the Deity, he declares God to us because he *is* God. We have a knowledge of God and eternal life only when we know Christ (1 John 5:20).[2]

But how do we know Christ? Not by a heroic act of faith, leaping blindly into the dark. Not by historic research. Certainly we cannot turn back the clock and walk with him and talk with him as the disciples did. We know him and receive his grace through his Word, the informative and powerful gospel word of Scripture. And this written word of the Old Testament which Christ fulfilled (Matt. 5:17ff.; John 5:39) and of the New Testament which he guaranteed by the gift of the Holy Spirit to his apostles (John 14:26; 15:26–27; 16:13), this revelatory word, affords *knowledge*, knowledge of God, divinely revealed information about God.

Promoters of neoorthodoxy (Karl Barth, Andrew Nygren, John Baillie, Emil Brunner, et al.) deny that Scripture provides such cognitive knowledge about God: pure doctrine does not exist, according to these theologians. And scholars of modern logical positivism and its many theological satellites posit that all theology—language about God in Scripture or elsewhere—is nonsense, neither true nor false, incapable of conveying information. Thus all theological assertions are outlawed by definition and are reduced to mere "metaphysical" or aesthetic or emotive utterances like "Ouch!" or "Oh!" or "Look!" which tell us only about ourselves, not about God. We do not have time to refute these two ideologies in this short chapter.[3] Suffice it to say that such viewpoints spring from the matrix of secular materialism. And whether these ideologists believe in a transcendent God or in no God, they operate from the principle, *finitum non est capax infiniti*, the finite is not capable of conveying or containing the infinite, whether we are speaking of the human Jesus or the human Scriptures.

## III. WHAT IS GOD LIKE?

The Bible speaks less about the essence and attributes of God than about his works in history and in the lives of believers. One simply cannot get at the essence of God by speculation or by depicting him in stone or wood, which was strictly forbidden in the Old Testament. God is holy and transcendent. He is the living God who cannot be caught by static images or conceptions. The emphasis throughout Scripture upon the actions of God, upon his intervention in history and his dealings with people, shows us that he is a living God. He fights for them and guides them (1 Sam. 17:26, 36); he loves his people and comforts them, and when they thirst after him he fills them (Ps. 42:3) and they find rest in him (Ps. 84:3; Matt. 11:28–29). The living God is utterly dependable.

The living God is Author and Sustainer of all life: "In him we live and move and have our being" (Acts 17:28). It is significant that in the New Testament Christ is called life and is the source of all life and all that is (John 1:1–2; Col. 15:17), thus showing that he is God. A central motif of Scripture is that God is the origin of life

and all life springs from him (Ps. 36:9). All life is a gift from him
(Ps. 104), and this is because God himself is living. Life, activity,
*presence for us* are fundamental to God's nature; he is not some
pantheistic "ground of being." As the living God he is *personally*
concerned about the world and his people (Ps. 18:47; Jer. 10:9–10;
Hos. 1:10).

The living God is a *personal* God. The personal nature of God
is brought out in many ways. Second Corinthians 4:6 speaks of the
"face" of Jesus Christ—that is, his personality. We pray to God,
and he answers. We trust him as we trust a person. We say
"thou" to him and he to us. Throughout Scripture our relationship
with him is always personal. God has a will; he makes decisions.
All his actions—*all* his actions—toward us are personal (see
1 Cor. 1). His grace and love and goodness, as well as his wrath
and judgment, are personal actions (Rom. 2:4; 11:22; Titus 3:4).
And when Scripture describes God as wise and true and good
(John 3:33; Rom. 2:4; 16:27), it ascribes eminently personal
attributes to God. Stauffer says, "Love is not the essence of deity,
but rather the personal God is love in all His will and work, and
this expressly in the work of Christ (John 3:16)."[4]

Biblical anthropomorphisms (ascribing human parts to God)
and anthropopathisms (ascribing human affections or feelings or
reactions to God) emphasize in a striking way his personal nature.
In fact, the very transcendence of God is expressed by some
anthropomorphisms, thus showing that even though God is one
who is personally related to man, nevertheless, there is no
common measure between God and man (Num. 23:19; Isa. 43:13;
45:12, 23; Hos. 11:9). The anthropomorphisms bring out the
uniqueness of God and at the same time tell us about him
cognitively. They are not mere naïve thoughts of primitive people
concerning God but are God's own revealed descriptions of
himself and his actions in human terms which finite and sinful
men can understand. These and other figures of speech must be
taken therefore in all seriousness, for they tell of God as he really
is and as he really acts.

The personal nature of God is brought out in Scripture also by
the intimate relationship and dealings of God with man. This
personal fellowship is expressed often by the verb "walk" in
Scripture (Mic. 6:8). Adam walked with God in the Garden (Gen.
3:8). Enoch walked with God (Gen. 5:24). This means that Adam
and Enoch had intimate communion with him; no estrangement
or disrupting factors broke the fellowship. A different but related
word is used by Jesus and the New Testament, the word "love"
which expresses the intimate relationship of husband and wife.
Jesus says, "If a man love me, he will keep [cling to] my words:
and my Father will love him, and we will come unto him, and
make our abode [dwelling place] with him" (John 14:23 KJV; cf.

John 3:16; Eph. 5:25; 1 John 4:7–21). Love is a personal act. The God who loves our fallen race is a personal God.

God's intimate personal association with men is seen also in the term "know" in Scripture. "I am the good shepherd, and know my sheep, and am known of mine" (John 10:14 KJV; cf. 10:27; 2 Tim. 2:19). Jesus knows us with the same intimacy that he knows the Father and the Father knows him (John 10:14–15a). Such personal knowledge and love (communion) between God and man is unique to the Christian religion (Isa. 52:6; Jer. 31:1ff., 31ff.; Hos. 2:23; John 17:3).

Still another attribute and activity ascribed to God tells of his personal relationship with mankind: his presence among us. We are speaking here not so much of his immensity, his repletive presence whereby he fills and sustains and upholds all things, as of his gracious personal presence. God's repletive omnipresence (2 Chron. 2:6; Ps. 113:4–7; Prov. 15:3; Jer. 23:24) declares clearly that he is a personal God but primarily in terms of his sovereignty, his utter transcendence, and his awesome majesty and wrath. It is a preachment of Law in the main. We are thinking more of God's gracious and loving presence with believers (Isa. 57:15), his evangelical presence, the presence which is marked by his promises to come to us who call upon him for help and to save us, by the promises of Jesus that he will be with us, and by his promises of the presence of the Holy Spirit to guide and comfort us (Pss. 23:4; 91:14–16; 145:18–19; Isa. 43:1–7; Matt. 18:10, 20; 28:20; John 14:23, 25–26; 15:26; 16:13–14). This personal presence of God in and with believers is not some vague ubiquity, "thereness," but a dynamic, gracious, real presence of our God himself in his very essence, analogous to an eternal marriage (Hos. 2:19) or to a vine giving life to branches (John 15:1) or to a head and a body (Eph. 5:23). God himself, not just his gifts, lives and is in the believer in a union whereby we become partakers of the divine nature (2 Peter 1:4). The Holy Spirit dwells in all believers in Christ, not merely figuratively through his gifts, but personally (1 Cor. 3:16–17). And this means that the very Godhead dwells in believers in what our church fathers have called a mystical union with all the fullness of his wisdom, holiness, power, and other divine gifts (Eph. 3:18).

The personal God who is present for us through the atoning work of Christ and present in us through the sanctifying work of the Holy Spirit is an omniscient God. He has a perfect knowledge of his creatures and of his people. He knows perfectly our weaknesses, our needs, and the secrets of our hearts (Ps. 44:21). No desire for peace or forgiveness, no groaning is hidden from him (Ps. 38:9). This knowledge is both personal and intimate, and this is of great comfort to us who trust in him (Ps. 103:14; Matt. 6:32; 10:30; 1 John 3:20).

Every attribute and action ascribed to God in Scripture testifies that our God is personal. This is what God is truly like. God is as he has acted and revealed himself. We know him by his works. Werner Elert says, "The question to what degree God is personality or how His personality as such is to be described can be answered in no other way than through the consideration of His works."[5]

A fundamental fact of God's revelation of himself in Scripture is that he, the Lord, is one and undivided in essence. A correlate of this fundamental truth is the biblical teaching of the uniqueness of God, that he alone is God and there are no other gods besides him. The one truth involves the other. This unity and unicity of God (monotheism) is the foundation stone of the Christian religion. From the time of our first parents in the Garden, God has always revealed himself as one God who is utterly unique. The unity of God is expressed by the great schema of the Israelites' morning and evening prayer, "Hear, O Israel: The LORD our God, is one LORD . . ." (Deut. 6:4ff. KJV). And this oneness of God demands that we worship him in our whole heart and being. For the schema goes on to say: "And thou shalt love the LORD thy God with all thine heart, and with all thy soul, and with all thy might" (v. 5 KJV). The unity of God implies and demands unity of worship and doctrine. He cannot be worshiped in one way at one place and in another way at another place. God cannot be divided (John 4:24).

That God is one and cannot be divided means that he is absolute unity, free from all composition, not consisting of parts. When Jesus says he comes from God and is God, he does not deny or vitiate the unity of God. Schlater says, "The early Christian monotheism is not threatened by the Christology of the New Testament, but made secure."[6] Christ himself speaks about only one God. He repeats the schema (Mark 12:29, 32) and remarks that there "is none good but one, that is, God" (Mark 10:18 KJV; cf. John 4; 1 Cor. 8:4; Eph. 4:5–6; 1 Tim. 1:17; 2:5; 6:15–16), and this even though he claimed to be one with God the Father (John 10:30; 17:21).

What about the fact that the Scriptures call the Son and the Holy Spirit God as well as the Father (e.g., Isa. 9:6; 11:2ff.; 61:1; Jer. 23:6; Matt. 12:28; John 1:1; 1 Tim. 3:15; Titus 3:5)? We can only reply that there can be no contradiction here but rather a mystery which transcends our understanding. We must simply hold to all the revealed data made known to us in Scripture.[7]

Neither does the unity of God conflict with the many, sometimes seemingly contradictory attributes and actions Scripture ascribes to God, such as his wrath and his love, his judgment and his grace, his word of law and his word of gospel. Our infinite and transcendent God cannot be caught within the categories of our finite and fallen reason. Our minds cannot set limits to his being and works (Isa. 40:18ff.; Rom. 11:33); God cannot be defined.

Like the unity of God, monotheism is a fundamental premise of all biblical theology. There is no suggestion anywhere in Scripture of gods besides the one true God; throughout the history of God's people recorded in the Pentateuch Yahweh reveals himself as the only God. The first commandment of the Decalogue forbids worshiping or recognizing other gods (Exod. 20:2–3); and the punishment is imposed: "He that sacrificeth unto any god, save unto the LORD only, he shall be utterly destroyed" (22:20 KJV). The implication of some scholars that such prohibitions indicate monolatrous or henotheistic belief on the part of Moses is untenable. The first commandment indicates not the existence but the nonexistence of other gods. Only the Lord is the *living* God; the very name Yahweh is taken from the word "to be, to exist." When in Exodus 2:4 graven images are forbidden, no one would assume that Scripture thereby attributes divine existence to graven images. No, only the Lord is God, and "there is none else beside him" (Deut. 4:35 KJV, 39; 32:39); all idols are "things of naught, worthless gods" (Lev. 19:4; 26:1), no gods at all, "vanities," "nothing," "wind" (1 Kings 16:13; Isa. 41:29; Jer. 8:19 KJV). God is transcendent, and his transcendence is his uniqueness (Isa. 40:18; 45:5–6).[8]

All the attributes ascribed to God in the biblical revelation tell us what God is like. He is holy, separated from all that is not God (Isa. 1, 6, 10, 40, 41, 43, 45, 48ff.). Holiness denotes God's radiance and purity, his absolute moral perfection in every direction (Job 15:15; Isa. 1:4; Luke 5:8). It denotes his absolute transcendence and otherness (Hos. 11:9). Therefore his actions are a wonder to behold (Isa. 29:14). Holiness denotes God's absolute power; what he does, only he can do (Isa. 40:25–27; 41:1ff.). But God's holiness also marks his goodness, mercy, grace (Exod. 15:11; 1 Sam. 2:2), and glory.

God's glory is the manifestation of his holiness, of his absolute majesty (Exod. 33:18). And this glory fills men's hearts with wonder, fear, and confusion (Isa. 6:5; Luke 5:8); but also with joy, peace, and anticipation (Isa. 6:5; Luke 2:8, 14; 5:8; cf. also Exod. 3; John 1:14; Eph. 1:17–18; 1 Peter 1:17). The Holy One of Israel *is* the Redeemer, the Savior (Heb. *goel*) of Israel (Isa. 41:14; 43:3, 14; 49:7; 54:5), and his holiness or his "holy name" "always has its basis in His saving work."[9] When Jesus is called Savior or Redeemer in Scripture, when he is called "the holy one of God" (Luke 1:35; John 6:69; Acts 4:27, 30), when he is said to manifest his glory (John 1:14), he himself is declared to be God (cf. Isa. 42:8). It is significant that the glory of God in the New Testament is always associated with Christ, the man (John 1:14), either in his birth (Luke 2:9), his activities (John 2:11), his transfiguration, his ascension, or even his death (John 16–17).

Like his holiness, omnipresence, and knowledge which we have spoken of before, God's omnipotence embraces the whole spectrum of God's attributes and actions and reveals to us what kind of God he is, a living and personal God, a free God who does what he pleases and who can do anything (Gen. 18:14; Ps. 115:3; Jer. 32:17; Matt. 3:9). God's power embraces his justice, his wrath against sin, his control of all things, his benevolence, and his saving grace (Eph. 1:19), even his eternity. His omnipotence may well frighten us because of our sins, but it also assures us that he is our God and that he is able to care for us in every way and to save us (Isa. 50:2–3; Rom. 8:32ff.; Eph. 1:18f.; 3:20ff.; cf. also Gen. 15:1; 17:1).

God's power is eternal, and his eternity is omnipotent. There is an inextricable nexus between all the attributes of God. All the attributes of God, however we might classify them, ascribed in Scripture to God and his works are really one with the divine essence, for God is absolutely one and undivided, as we have seen. There can be no confusion or contradiction between the different attributes and works of God. As Scripture tells us that he is just, transcendent, good, righteous, immutable, truthful, omniscient in himself and in all his works and ways, it tells us the truth about God and what he is really like.

## IV. WHO IS GOD?

### A. The Trinity

As we have searched the Scriptures to learn what God is like, we have also learned his identity, who he is: Father, Son, and Holy Spirit. That is to say, he who has revealed himself to be Creator of all things and is the Father of our Lord Jesus Christ from eternity is called and is God; he who existed with God from eternity and has revealed himself to be the only begotten Son of God and Savior of the world is called and is God. He who revealed himself to be the Spirit of God proceeding of eternity from the essence of God, who came upon the Virgin Mary so that she became pregnant with the Son of the Highest, who anointed the Son of God to his ministry of redemption, and who calls, gathers, and enlightens Christ's church on earth through the Word of God is called and is God.

Here we stand on holy ground. We are confronted with the divine mystery of the Holy Trinity. The absolute unity of the divine essence is affirmed everywhere in Scripture, yet he is three distinct persons—Father, Son, and Holy Spirit. And these identifying names are never used in Scripture metaphorically, never used to denote a mere attribute or activity or emanation of God or a mere relation or force or mode of divine being. They denote always specific, concrete, real, distinct, identifiable, individual, conscious persons.

The term *person* (Greek *hypostasis*, Latin *persona*) as it was used in the early church and to this very day by Christians is not explicitly found in the Old or New Testaments. But the idea which Christians have attempted to convey by this term, which was used and defined to combat misunderstanding and heresy, is certainly biblical.

According to the Augsburg Confession, the Magna Charta of the Reformation, the three persons of the Godhead are "of the same essence and power, who also are co-eternal, the Father, the Son and the Holy Ghost. And the term 'person' they [the Reformers] use as the Fathers have used it, to signify, not a part of quality in another, but that which subsists of itself."[10] This is what the church fathers taught in accordance with Scripture.[11]

And this is precisely the unsophisticated and clear teaching of Scripture. Everywhere in the Old and New Testaments where the Father or Christ, the Son, or the Holy Spirit is spoken of individually, a conscious, real, individual, and distinct person is referred to, a person who creates, who wills, who loves, who judges, who has compassion, who comforts, who inspires prophets, etc. This is true also when one person of the Godhead is spoken of in Scripture in relation to another; a relationship of persons is always evidenced. The personal relationship and thus the personal characteristics of the Father, Son, and Holy Spirit have been revealed most concretely in the ministry of Jesus, God's only Son. The Father and the Holy Spirit are intimately and personally involved in his incarnation, conception, and birth (Matt. 1:18–24; Luke 1:26–35), in his baptism and anointment into his redemptive ministry (Matt. 3:13–17; cf. Isa. 61:1–3; Matt. 12:18ff.; 4:1ff.; cf. Gen. 3:16), in his transfiguration (Matt. 17:8) and crucifixion. Jesus obeys (a personal act) the will of the Father; he promises and sends (personal acts) the Spirit. Throughout Scripture only masculine personal pronouns are used to denote Father, Son, and Holy Spirit.

The personal nature of Father, Son, and Spirit are most emphatically evidenced in Jesus' discourses in John 14–16. He urges his disciples to believe in the Father and in him. If we know him, we know the Father. If we have seen him, we have seen the Father. He is in the Father, and the Father is in him—in him in the most unique and divine communion and interpenetration (what the Greek fathers called *perichoresis*) but without any confusion of the identity of the persons. The Father sends another Comforter, the Spirit of truth, who abides with the disciples and with his church. The world does not see him or know him, but we know

him. He is loved by all who love the Father. The Father sends the
Holy Spirit in Jesus' name. Jesus, too, sends the Comforter from
the Father, and the Comforter testifies of him. The Comforter
comes and testifies and leads us into all truth. Now, it is
persons—individual, intelligent centers of consciousness, "I[s],"
"you[s]," "he[s]"—who are spoken of in this discourse of our
Lord, not principles, relationships, events, attributes, or modes of
being.

Just as Scripture witnesses to the fact that the names,
activities, and attributes ascribed to the Father, Son, and Holy
Spirit indicate that each is a true and individual person, so the
testimony of Scripture teaches that each of the three persons is
true God, that the Son and the Holy Spirit possess the fullness of
the deity with the Father. Divine names are ascribed to Christ, the
Son, throughout the Old Testament (*Yahweh* [Ps. 68:17; Isa. 6:1;
Jer. 23:6; Hos. 1:7; Zech. 2:8ff.], *Adonai* [Ps. 110:1; Mal. 3:1], *El* [Ps.
95:7; Isa. 7:14; 9:6; 35:4–6]). In the New Testament he is called
both Lord and God in the absolute sense without any limitations
(John 1:1; 20:28; Acts 20:28; Rom. 10:13; 1 Cor. 1:31; 2:8; 8:6; Col.
2:2; 1 Tim. 3:15; 6:14–16; Titus 2:13; Heb. 1:8; 1 John 5:20). To him
is ascribed the creation of all things (Col. 1:14–16). His work of
redemption and everything pertaining to it is a work that only
Almighty God can carry out. He is eternal with God (John 1:1) and
is called "the only begotten Son" (v. 18 KJV), or the only begotten
*God*, of God. He possesses all the attributes of God, "for in him
dwelleth all the fulness of the Godhead bodily" (Col. 2:9 KJV). He
is the effulgence of God's glory and the image of his substance
(Heb. 1:3). Therefore he is to be worshiped and believed just as
the Father is to be worshiped and believed (John 5:23; 6:29; 14:1;
Rev. 4:11).

The deity of the Holy Spirit is also clear from the witness of
Scripture. All personal characteristics ascribed to him in Scripture—that he proceeds from God, that he witnesses, that he gives
life, that he comforts, regenerates, forgives, and saves—are
characteristics and works of God alone. His very name "Spirit" as
ascribed to him in Scripture suggests deity, and the common
adjective "holy" is an essential attribute only of God. The gifts of
the Spirit to the church—confession of Christ, prophecy, inspiration, tongues and the interpretation of tongues, faith, love, unity,
hope, baptism, etc. (Rom. 12:6ff; 1 Cor. 12; Gal. 5:22–25; Eph.
4:3ff.) are all divine gifts, even as they are personal gifts. All that
pertains to the Christian's spiritual existence has its origin in the
Holy Spirit. There would be no church, no faith, no baptism, no
forgiveness, no conferral of divine grace, and no enjoyment of
salvation apart from the Holy Spirit and his work. That is why it is
so important for us to believe that, as the Holy Spirit works, God
is graciously and mightily at work with us and in us and for us,

just as it is utterly crucial for us to know and believe that Christ's
work of redemption is nothing else but the work of God himself.
Luther says:

> For neither you nor I could ever know anything of Christ or
> believe on Him and have Him for our Lord, except as it is
> offered to us and granted to our hearts by the Holy Ghost
> through the preaching of the gospel. The work is finished and
> accomplished; for Christ, by His suffering, death, resurrection,
> etc. has acquired and gained the treasure for us. But if the work
> remained concealed, so that no one knew of it, then it were in
> vain and lost. That this treasure therefore might not lie buried,
> but be appropriated and enjoyed, God has caused the Word to
> go forth and be proclaimed, in which He gives the Holy Ghost
> to bring this treasure home and apply it to us. Therefore
> sanctification is nothing else but bringing us to Christ to receive
> this good, to which, of ourselves, we could not attain.[12]

What Luther has just said is eminently biblical and of decisive
importance. If Christ our Savior is not God, if the Holy Spirit our
Sanctifier is not God, then there is no atonement, no salvation, no
life after death, and no faith or hope for the Christian.

But is God really three divine persons, or does he only reveal
himself to be so? Christian theologians have distinguished between the eternal works or inner relations of the Father, Son, and
Holy Spirit within the Trinity and those works which Father, Son,
and Holy Spirit do in relation to creation and mankind. When we
refer to the former—i.e., the Father begets his own Son from
eternity, the Son is eternally begotten of the Father and is identical
with him and is Light of Light, the Spirit proceeds from the Father
and the Son (Pss. 2:7; 96:6; 110:4; John 1:1, 9, 18; 3:16; 5:18; 8:29;
10:30; 12:40–41; 15:26; Rom. 8:32; Phil. 2:6; Col. 1:15; Heb. 1:3)—
we speak of the *immanent* Trinity. When we refer to the actions of
the persons of the Godhead in relation to us, we commonly speak
of the *economic* Trinity. The eternal intertrinitarian works of the
Godhead are no less real than his external and sometimes
historical works toward his fallen creation. Our one God is triune,
three divine persons sharing the one divine essence, immanently
as well as economically. "For," as Werner Elert says, "God cannot
be anything else than what He has revealed Himself to be. If He
has revealed Himself as three in one, then He is three in one."[13]

It is significant to note that throughout the history of doctrine
when theologians have denied that the Father, Son, and Holy
Spirit are persons, they have also lost the doctrine of the
immanent Trinity just as surely as when they deny the deity of the
three persons. But they have lost more than what they think is just
a relic of antiquated medieval metaphysics: they have lost the
economic Trinity as well; they have lost God's mighty acts or
muddled them beyond recognition. No longer do these theolo-

gians believe in a creation of all things, a redemption of the human race, and a sanctification of God's own people, all carried out by the living God himself. And so they have lost God.

Who am I talking about here? Not just relationalistic or Romantic theologians and philosophers of the so-called European Enlightenment; not just Socinians, Jehovah's Witnesses, and modern Unitarians of recent generations who called themselves Modernists; not just *Ichtheologen* (Subjectivists) and classical liberals of the nineteenth century (Schleiermacher, Ritzschl, Harnack, et al.),[14] but also contemporary theologians from a veritable welter of ideologies and schools, such as process theology, existentialism, theology of hope, liberation theology, neoorthodoxy, neoliberalism, *ad nauseam* . By rejecting the doctrine of the Trinity as unevangelical or unintelligible or for some other reason, by distorting or trying to "rehabilitate" the biblical doctrine, or by ignoring the doctrine altogether, these theological leaders of our day have given up the gospel which can only be proclaimed in a Trinitarian matrix and setting.[15]

The doctrine of God—that is, the Trinity—so firmly based on Scripture, is *the* fundamental article of the Scriptures and of the Christian faith in the sense that all biblical theology ought to be grounded upon and subsumed under this one article which tells us everything we should know and believe about who God is and what he is like and what he has done.[16]

The doctrine of the Trinity is necessary because it helps us to present the relationship between Father, Son, and Holy Spirit, and at the same time to maintain the monotheistic obligation which is every Christian's.[17] But the doctrine of the Trinity also forms the only possible theological context for presenting the gospel. For the gospel is nothing else than the proclamation of the external works of the economic Trinity, the Father, Son, and Holy Spirit. Really, it is all summed up beautifully by Luther in his commentary on the Apostles' Creed in his *Large Catechism*.

> In these three articles God Himself has revealed and opened to us the most profound depths of His fatherly heart, His sheer, unutterable love. He created us for this very purpose, to redeem and sanctify us. Moreover, having bestowed upon us everything in heaven and on earth, He has given us His Son and His Holy Spirit, through whom He brings us to Himself. As we explained before, we could never come to recognize the Father's favor and grace were it not for the Lord Christ, who is a mirror of the Father's heart. Apart from Him we see nothing but an angry and terrible Judge. But neither could we know anything of Christ, had it not been revealed by the Holy Spirit.
>
> These articles of the Creed, therefore, divide and distinguish us Christians from all other people on earth. All who are outside the Christian church, whether heathen, Turks, Jews, or

false Christians and hypocrites, even though they believe in and
worship only the one, true God, nevertheless do not know what
His attitude is toward them. They cannot be confident of His
love and blessing. Therefore they remain in eternal wrath and
damnation, for they do not have the Lord Christ, and, besides,
they are not illuminated and blessed by the gifts of the Holy
Spirit.[18]

# ENDNOTES

[1] *Apology of Augsburg Confession,* 4:101.

[2] Luther says: "Scripture begins tenderly and leads us to Christ as a man, then
to the Lord over all creatures and to a God. In this way I advance gently and learn
to know God. But philosophy and worldly-wise people desired to begin at the
top—and thereby they became fools" (WA 21:22). Cf. WA 1:362:

> It suffices and avails no one to know God in His glory and majesty,
> unless he knows Him in the humility and ignominy of the cross. Thus
> when Philip, in the spirit of a "theology of glory" said, "Show us the
> Father" (John 14:8), Christ immediately restrained His wandering
> thought which sought God elsewhere and directed it to Himself, saying:
> "Philip, he that seeth me seeth my Father also." Therefore the true
> theology and knowledge of God is to be found in the crucified Christ.

[3] I have attempted to analyze and evaluate these opinions in *Crisis in Lutheran
Theology,* ed. John Warwick Montgomery (Grand Rapids: Baker, 1967), 2:18–30.

[4] See Gerhard Kittel, ed., *Theologisches Woerterbuch zum Neuen Testament*
(Stuttgart: Verlag von W. Kohlhammer, 1933–79), 3:111.

[5] Werner Elert, *Der Christliche Glaube* (Hamburg: Furche-Verlag, 1956), p. 230.

[6] Adolf Schlater in *Theologisches Woerterbuch zum Neuen Testament,* 3:103.

[7] Christian theologians of all ages have struggled with this problem of
whether the Trinity militates against the unity of God. John Gerhard says:

> To the question whether the Trinity of Persons militates against the
> simplicity of God we reply in the following manner: 1. Different articles
> of faith are not to be opposed to each other. Both the simplicity
> [undivided unity] of the divine essence and the Trinity of the persons
> are set forth in the Word for our benefit. Hence we ought to accept both
> with obedience of faith. 2. We do not contend that the divine essence
> must be separated according to its actual existence. . . . But rather we
> affirm that the divine essence and three Persons of the Deity are in a
> most real and simple sense one. Therefore there is no composition [in
> God]. The personal characteristics [of the persons in the Godhead] do
> not multiply or compound the divine essence, since one and the same
> divine essence is in the Father unbegotten, in the Son begotten, and in
> the Holy Spirit as one who proceeds [from the Father and the Son].

---

Quoted in John William Baier, *Compendium Theologiae Positivae,* ed. C. F. W.
Walther (St. Louis: Concordia, 1879), 2:18.

[8] Among scholars who claim some allegiance to Scripture there have been
three main opinions concerning the origin and evolution of monotheism.
(1) Yahweh originally was one God among others; but he is not like others because
he is superior to them. See Jacob, *Theology of the Old Testament,* trans. Arthur H.
Heathcote and Philip J. Allcock (London: Hodder and Stoughton, 1985), pp. 66ff.
Henotheism verges into monotheism at the time of the so-called Second Isaiah.

(2) A more cautious view that is monotheism is implied at the time of Moses or even earlier; however, the uniqueness of Yahweh was not thought out theoretically until long after Moses. See Theodore Christian Vriezen, *An Outline of Old Testament Theology* (Oxford: Blackwell, 1958), pp. 175ff. (3) Full monotheism is taught throughout Scripture. God reveals himself originally to man as one and unique. This position, which is the doctrine we hold, is ably defended by Heinish, *Theology of the Old Testament*, English ed. (Collegeville: Liturgical, 1950), pp. 57ff. The reason even relatively conservative biblical scholars believe that there may be a trace of henotheism in Scripture is due to three factors: (1) They do not accept the biblical doctrine of revelation whereby God breaks in upon man's history and makes himself known as he really is. (2) They are committed to the theory that doctrine (cognitive information about God) is not revealed but evolves out of the treasures of the human heart. (3) They are committed to higher criticism, which has a propensity toward dating books of the Bible according to evolutionary hypothesis concerning the development of doctrine.

⁹August Pieper, "The Glory of the Lord," *Quartalschrift* (1955), p. 175.

¹⁰*Apology of Augsburg Confession*, 1:3–4.

¹¹G. L. Prestige, *God in Patristic Thought* (London: SPCK, 1956), pp. 161ff., *passim*. Melanchthon, the author of the Augsburg Confession, like the medieval scholastic theologians and other Reformers, uses and elaborates on the definition of *persona* given by the philosopher Boethius, *naturae rationalis individua substantia*. See Frederick Coppleston, *A History of Philosophy* (Westminster: Newman, 1952), 2:102. This is the understanding that orthodox Christians have had as they apply the term "person" to the Father, Son, and Holy Spirit.

¹²*Large Catechism*, 2:38–39.

¹³Elert, *Der Christliche Glaube*, p. 225.

¹⁴See Claude Welch, *In This Name, the Doctrine of the Trinity in Contemporary Theology* (New York: Scribner, 1952). With clarity, insight, and some pathos, Welch traces the understanding and treatment of the doctrine of the Trinity by leading theologians of the West through the nineteenth and twentieth century, including Karl Barth and Leonard Hodgson. No one has brought such a study up to date.

¹⁵It would require a large book to analyze and evaluate all the literature by unorthodox theologians of various traditions and stripes as they address themselves to the doctrine of the Trinity today. I offer two "Lutheran" examples that might serve to illustrate the utter confusion that reigns in Protestant and, I fear, also Roman Catholic circles. I mention first the so-called *Evangelical Catechism*, published in Germany (1979) by a number of prominent theologians and then revised for American consumption (Minneapolis: Augsburg, 1982). The significance of this little book, which was intended as a sort of modern rendition of Luther's *Large Catechism*, is marked by the fact that the volume was sent to every pastor and congregation of the American Lutheran Church. Yet this work of 399 pages does not even mention the doctrine of the Trinity or allude to it. So far does this highly touted theological piece, calculated to edify God's people, fail to come to grips with the biblical revelation of who God is.

Another more scholarly head-on discussion of the Trinity intended for a more sophisticated, elite audience, is presented by Robert Jenson in a book coedited with Carl E. Braaten entitled *Christian Dogmatics* (Philadelphia: Fortress, 1984). Jenson (p. 143), by a curious combination of the antimetaphysical notions of nineteenth-century liberalism, Hegelianism, positivistic linguistic analysis, and modern process theology, pokes fun repeatedly at the old Augustinian and creedal statements that God is one essence and three persons. The terms "communicate nothing whatsoever," Jenson avers. Dredging up a statement of Peter Lombard, of all people, and pushing the statement beyond its force, he proclaims the complete "bankruptcy of the Trinitarian meaning." With this kind of *tour de force* Jenson seems content to rest his case against the biblical doctrine of the Trinity. And what is Jenson's replacement for the biblical doctrine? "Truly, the Trinity is simply the Father and the man Jesus and their Spirit as the Spirit of the believing community"

(1:155). Jenson goes on, "This 'economic' Trinity is *eschatologically* God 'Himself,' an 'immanent' Trinity. And that assertion is no problem, for God *is* Himself only eschatologically, since He is Spirit." Here we see the pathetic results of a neologist who abandons the authority of Scripture and the clear categories of biblical language (person, tense, etc.) and thus the plain teachings of Scripture concerning who God is.

[16]This has been the procedure of great theologians through the centuries, such as Augustine, Luther, Calvin, and others as they structured their theology on the basis of the Apostolic or Nicene Creed. Jacob in his *Theology of the Old Testament* works with the same pattern as he subsumes all Old Testament theology under the single treatment of God.

[17]Elert, *Der Christliche Glaube*, pp. 217ff.

[18]*Large Catechism*, 2:64–66.

# A Response to
# The Living God

## Walter C. Kaiser, Jr.

The threefold division of Dr. Robert Preus's discussion of the doctrine of God is most helpful. In catechetical fashion he has set out to answer three basic questions about God: (1) How do we know him? (2) What is he like? (3) Who is he? Each section has a distinctive emphasis which makes a unique contribution to the doctrine of God.

While carefully circumscribing any knowledge of God that could be called "natural theology" or such traditional apologetical evidences for God's existence as the historical, experiential, or philosophical arguments, Dr. Preus makes it clear that what he is after is the knowledge of the heart: a knowledge that involves a relationship with the God who is Father, Son, and Holy Spirit, triune in essence and the one revealed in the gospel of Jesus Christ. Though some may express disappointment over the fact that not enough attention has been given to the arguments such as those in Psalm 19 or Romans 1–2, this respondent is not especially disappointed, since the most that those apologetical arguments can establish is the case for the existence of the God of creation. But the God who revealed himself in the Scriptures and in our Lord Jesus Christ must still be sought by means of the gospel itself.

Accordingly, everything hangs on what we mean by the word "know." There is a great difference between a cognitive cerebral knowledge of God and a personal, believing commitment to him. When this distinction is observed, then the emphasis of Preus's disclaimers are all the more apparent.

The opposite problem is faced in existential systems of theology that play up the experiential and relational sides of the knowledge of God but deny the historical, factual, and objective

19

nature of the revealed truth of Scripture on the doctrine of God. This modern trajectory was also wisely resisted in this essay.

In answer to his second question, "What is God like?" Preus answers with a brief survey of God's attributes (he is living, personal, intimate, present, unique, holy, omnipotent, eternal), work (especially his work of atonement), and nature (his unity or unicity). The highlight of this section is his definition of what it means to be a personal living God and what it means that God is absolute unity. We are properly assured, of course, that when we say that "God is one and cannot be divided," it means that he is "free from all composition, not consisting of parts." But how does Preus put this together with the fact that there are three who are called God in Scripture? Preus assures us once again that there is no contradiction here; rather it is "a mystery which transcends our understanding."

I am sure that is all correct as far as it goes, but perhaps we would be well advised to exegete John 10:34–39 with its dual emphasis: I and my Father are *one* and the Father has *sent* me. This is where Augustine and Calvin rested their case on this issue, and we would be well advised to do no less.

The final section, "Who Is God?" was perhaps the most creative in its simple statement of extremely profound truths such as the Trinity. While the argument tended to emphasize more the historical confessions and philosophical distinctions (as it always has and to some degree must), it underscored the true individuality of all three persons as well as their interpenetration, so as to form the unity of the Godhead. Preus's stress on an immanent Trinity (the inner relations of the Trinity and their works from eternity) and an economic Trinity (the works each person of the Godhead does in relation to us) underscores the deity of each of the Trinity as well as the distinctive work Scripture ascribes to each.

Truly, the doctrine of God is "*the* fundamental article of the Scriptures and of the Christian faith."

If there is anything lacking in this article, it is this: an identification of a major teaching passage (*sedes doctrinae*) in the Scripture for each of the major points made about God. What we call for here has not been done very frequently, if at all, in the history of theological development. But the time is long past when it should have been adopted as the only way to present Christian doctrines, especially for scholars and teachers who rightfully press the claims of *sola Scriptura* with its corollary of inerrancy.

What I mean is this: Prior to any discussion of a doctrine or any of its major constituent parts, the largest teaching block of biblical text ought to be identified and properly exegeted. The fortunes of systematic theology continue to dip lower each year even within the evangelical community of faith. This is not only due to the demise of interest in system building in philosophy and the utter rejection of all metaphysics; it is also due to the tremendous upsurge in interest and our evangelical success in more consistent exegesis of the text in Scripture.

There is a whole new generation of younger scholars who become tremendously uneasy when theological argumentation proceeds by means of a definition substantiated by a string of phrases, clauses, or a random sentence quickly identified with an allusion to a chapter and a verse number. Whether the context truly supported the notion for which it was cited is usually left up to the imagination of the listener/reader. How can we avoid the charge of "proof-texting" if we do not pause to show that the basic idea we are urging does have a "home base," a "chair location" with the exact teaching for which we are wanting that text? Only after we have carefully exegeted that "teaching text" in its context can we be free to use the method of the "analogy of Scripture" and allude to other better-known contexts whose phrases and clauses establish the same truth.

Based on our high view of Scripture, then, I call for a whole new method of teaching dogma or doctrine in our seminaries, in our Bible studies, and from our pulpits. In setting forth the attributes of God, I would first identify the key teaching passages for each main proposition in my doctrine of God. For example, here are some chair teaching passages on the doctrine of God: God's incomparable greatness (Isa. 40:9–31); God's aseity and communication of revelation (44:24–28); God's attributes—his omniscience, omnipresence, and omnipotence (Ps. 139); God's unity and distinction of persons (John 10:27–39); etc.

After an exegesis and exposition of each of these texts or ones like them had been completed, then a survey of additional texts in the progress of revelation (biblical theology) could be the second step in building a doctrinal statement. This must be followed by a third level of study which investigated what the Spirit of God had helped the church through the centuries (history of church doctrine) to understand on this theme. The fourth and final step would ask our contemporary philosophical and practical questions which would help us apply this doctrine of God to our lives today.

We believe such a fourfold program of study would restore to the church a greater confidence in the authority of what was being said on each doctrine. It would be a natural corollary of our high view of Scripture and attract students to the presently faltering fortunes of the discipline of systematic theology or church dogma. We urge Christ's church to put into action this important implication of *sola Scriptura* for building doctrine and making what has already served the church well, even better, to the glory of our great God and coming King.

# A Response to
# The Living God

**Bruce K. Waltke**

Dr. Robert D. Preus, after an introduction, divides his enlightening essay into three sections: "How Do We Know God?" "What Is God Like?" and "Who Is God?" I will follow his format.

## I. HOW DO WE KNOW GOD?

Our author rightly gives pride of place to the distinction between knowing about God and knowing God (pp. 1–2). In keeping with the intention of this summit, he incisively applies his insight. "A knowledge of the heart," Preus writes, "results in love." He adds, "Where there is no knowledge of God there is neither truth nor mercy (Hos. 4:1), neither obedience nor sacrifice to him" (Matt. 9:13).

Let me support from linguistics Preus's important differentiation, then underscore its importance to the gospel and apply it to hermeneutics and the teaching of theology. As the first sentence in the preceding paragraph illustrates, English discriminates "factual" knowledge from "relationship" knowledge by using a particle such as "that" or "about" with verbs of knowing for the former notion and omitting such for the latter. Hebrew makes a similar distinction by the particle *ki*.[1] For example, the Lord says to Cyrus, "I will give you . . . riches stored in secret places, so that you may *know that [teda ki]* I am the LORD" (Isa. 45:3), and then adds, "though you do not *know me [yedantani]*" (italics mine). Some professing Evangelicals think they are Christians because they know that Jesus is Lord, but they do not know the Lord Jesus. James cautioned: "You believe that [*su pisteueis hoti*] there is one God. Good! Even the demons believe that—and shudder" (James 2:19).

22

How does this distinction relate to hermeneutics and the teaching of theology? Immanuel Kant, it will be recalled, differentiated the way of knowing personal objects (that is, those possessing volition) from impersonal ones (that is, those lacking volition). For knowing the latter, he used the German word *Erklaerung;* for the former, he used *Verstehen.* He cogently argued that we "explain" impersonal objects, but we "know" personal objects. For the former the scientific method is appropriate; for the latter it is inappropriate. To understand objects that lack volition one distances oneself from them and attempts to be detached and as dispassionate as possible. On the other hand, to know a person one must commit oneself to her or him. The scientific method is appropriate for the text of Scripture and for systematic theology but inappropriate for the principal aim of Christian understanding of Scripture, the knowledge of God.

One time I was asked to teach a course on the Psalms at a state university. As I reflected on my assignment I contemplated how I could communicate the Psalter's highly devotional content to students schooled in the scientific method. In the first lecture I introduced the course by noting Kant's distinction. To get my point across, I asked one of the students to stand in a corner of the room. While the student stood there the class observed him, analyzed him, and systematically classified their information without talking to him or allowing him to talk to them. The point became quickly apparent to the students that by their method they had actually positioned themselves not to know their classmate. I drew the obvious conclusion that were I to teach the Psalms without commitment to God, the class could never understand the object of their content.

In contrast to "modern existential theology and neoorthodoxy," however, Preus adroitly does not pit the personal knowledge of God against revealed facts and information about God and what he has done (pp. 1–3). I applaud his balanced discussion. He overexaggerates the point, however, when he says, "The basic theme of the Old Testament is that one knows God only when one recognizes his redemptive activity" (p. 2). No contemporary biblical theologian of whom I am aware supports this theme as the center of biblical theology.[2]

Preus follows this discussion about epistemology with the sources of information about God and presents the position of the Reformers that God revealed himself in creation and in Scripture (pp. 2–4). Although the presentation is orthodox, it fails to satisfy the aim of this summit, "the application of Scripture to contemporary issues." For many thoughtful people Darwin's theory that organic structures developed from much simpler organisms by purely natural processes, and the biochemical possibility that life originated from lifeless matter undermines Paley's evidence for

God in creation and/or modifies man's understanding of God. The problems of evil, suffering, and frustration also affect the cogency of the Scriptures cited by Preus. Logicians argue that all cases of design are not necessarily due to one and the same designer. Even if there is only one designer, nothing is done to show that this being is predominantly good rather than evil, infinitely powerful or wise rather than limited in these qualities. A one-sentence shot at process theologians (p. 2) is no substitute for serious interaction with them.[3]

Preus once again returns to the subject of epistemology and argues that man cannot know God by assuming the posture of autonomous knower and God as the object to be known. Instead, he rightly argues that God, as subject, makes himself known to man, the object. He condemns modern man's hubris to speculate about God rather than to turn to Scripture for a revelation from him, more specifically God's revelation of himself in the gospel of Jesus Christ as mediated through the Word of Scripture (pp. 3–6). He "applies" this scriptural position by accusing neoorthodoxy and modern logical positivism of denying this doctrine.

Calling a spade a spade, however, does not effectively apply Scripture to contemporary theological issues. Our writer excuses himself from meaningful debate, saying, "We haven't time to refute these two ideologies. . . ." Let me supplement Preus here by reminding the reader of Carl F. H. Henry's *God, Revelation and Authority*, who, in a number of brilliant essays such as "The Ways of Knowing," "The Rise and Fall of Logical Positivism," "Empirical Verification and Christian Theism," does refute Neo-Protestantism and logical positivism.

Preus helpfully turns man back to Scripture and its gospel as the means of knowing God, but he stops too soon by failing to capitalize on his insight that the Cartesian way of knowing cannot lead to the knowledge of God even by means of Scripture. As God is not in our power, so also Scripture is not in our grasp. God is hidden in Scripture; the Spirit reveals truth to the childlike. Jesus Christ said, "I praise you, Father, Lord of heaven and earth, because you have hidden these things from the wise and learned, and revealed them to little children" (Matt. 11:25). David Steinmetz in a brilliant essay, "Hermeneutic and Old Testament Interpretation in Staupitz and the Young Martin Luther," summarized Luther's practical insights that flow from the truth that God is hidden in Scripture.

> Scripture is not at the disposal of our intellect and is not obliged to render up its secrets to those who have theological training, merely because they are learned. Scripture imposes its own meaning; it binds the soul to God through faith. Because the initiative in the interpretation of Scripture remains in the hands of God, we must humble ourselves in His presence and pray

that He will give understanding and wisdom to us as we meditate on the sacred text. While we may take courage from the thought that God gives understanding of Scripture to the humble, we should also heed the warning that the truth of God can never coexist with human pride. Humility is the hermeneutical precondition for authentic exegesis.[4]

## WHAT IS GOD LIKE?

Our author notes in the first place that God is living and active (pp. 6–7) with the correlative truths that he is personal (pp. 7–8), and graciously, evangelically present among us (vv. 11–12). He pastorally applies these truths: "He knows perfectly our weaknesses, our needs, the secrets of our hearts (Ps. 44:21). . . . No groaning is hidden from him (Ps. 38:9)" (p. 8). The discussion, however, focuses on what Scripture says, not on contemporary issues. Secular man believes that he lives in a closed universe and correlatively that his salvation lies in manipulating its laws to his advantage. Contemporary man wants to know how prayer, whose power seems less than verifiable, relates to technology, whose successes are all too apparent. Also, does not the fact that God is the Author and Sustainer of life have something to say about the current issue of abortion? In addition, does not the fact that he is living and eternal have something to say about man's not avenging himself but living by faith that in the future God will avenge wrongs (cf. Deut. 32:40–41)?

Preus now affirms that God is a unity (p. 9). He rests his case on Deuteronomy 6:4. (The other passages he cites teach that God is unique, not that he is undivided essence). His text, however, is less than convincing, for the Hebrew word *ehad*, traditionally translated "one," can also mean "alone," "unique" as in Song of Songs 6:9; Zechariah 14:9. Its cognates in Ugaritic and Akkadian also have this meaning. In fact, the Jewish interpreters before the third century A.D. did not understand *ehad* as "oneness."[5] The most recent translation of the Jewish Publication Society, *The Torah* (1962) returns to this ancient understanding, rendering "Hear, O Israel! The LORD is our God, the LORD alone."

Preus makes the helpful application from Deuteronomy 6:5 that "this oneness of God demands that we worship him." The relevance of this truth to materialism, which corrupts our entire society, should not be taken for granted, however.

Preus now turns his attention to monotheism (pp. 9–10). Here he underestimates the biblical data for the existence of other gods when he says, "There is no suggestion anywhere in Scripture of gods besides the one true God." Most modern commentators have taken passages such as Exodus 20:3; 22:20; 1 Samuel 26:19 as indications of an earlier stage of henotheism (the worship of one god without denying the existence of others) in the Israelite religion. Would it not be better to address these texts and note that they reflect not survival from earlier times but tacit recognition of religious practices and that theological statements such as Deuteronomy 4:35, 39 and 32:39 reflect the theological thought of God's elect community?

Preus draws this section to a conclusion by a succinct, enlightening summary of God's attributes (pp. 10–11). He does amazingly well in presenting these in the light of the breadth of subjects he has chosen to address. Nevertheless, a most important attribute, scarcely touched upon, is God's faithfulness [Hebrew *hesed*]. K. D. Sakenfeld has shown the relevance of this attribute; against self-actualization that ends in isolation and loneliness Sakenfeld shows ways in which serious, enduring, and life-giving interpersonal relationships may be produced.[6] Preus also mentions God's freedom but fails to drive home his elective purposes. God's role as creator is not distinct from his role as Lord of history, for both creation and history alike are expressions of his one will. Even false religions are taken up in the world plan of God (Deut. 4:19; 29:26; cf. 10:17).

## III. WHO IS GOD?

In his concluding section, Preus defends the doctrine of the Trinity by scriptural citations (pp. 11–16). Here we reach the high-water mark of the paper. He again applies the doctrine by naming many sorts of theologians who have lost God by denying it (p. 15). I find it difficult to interact or add to this animated, dogmatic, sweeping discussion. At times Preus prooftexts the position (e.g., Ps. 2:7), at other times, he fails to cite texts. If I understand him correctly, he argues that throughout the history of doctrine when theologians deny this doctrine they lose God (pp. 14–15). Recently, however, Charles Hummel reminded us that Isaac Newton became "convinced that a massive fraud had perverted the legacy of the Church and certain Scripture" and "adopted the Arian position. . . . During his lifetime, however, nobody cast aspersions on Newton's Anglican orthodoxy."[7] For the church fathers and for me the doctrine of the Trinity is of utmost practical importance. If Jesus Christ is not God, then he condemns men and cannot save them. If he achieved perfection as merely an earthly man, then by his moral achievement he only convicts the rest of mankind for their failure and cannot come to them as a heavenly Savior.

# ENDNOTES

[1] See now Anneli Aejmelaeus, "Function and Interpretation of KI in Biblical Hebrew," *Journal of Biblical Literature* 105/2 (1986): 193–209, esp. pp. 109–10.

[2] Cf. Samuel Terrien, "Biblical Theology: The Old Testament (1970–1984). A Decade and a Half of Spectacular Growth," *Biblical Theology Bulletin* 15/4 (October 1985): 127–35.

[3] Cf. R. Gillies, "A Little Known American," *Expository Times* 97/11 (1986): 323–28.

[4] David Steinmetz, "Hermeneutic and Old Testament Interpretation in Staupitz and the Young Martin Luther," *Archiv fuer Reformationsgeschichte* 70 (1979): 41–42.

[5] J. McBride, "The Yoke of the Kingdom," *Interpretation* 27 (July 1973): 243–306.

[6] Katherine Doob Sakenfeld, *Faithfulness in Action: Loyalty in Biblical Perspective* (Philadelphia: Fortress, 1985).

[7] Charles E. Hummel, *The Galileo Connection* (Downer's Grove: InterVarsity, 1986), p. 144.

# THE SAVIOR AND HIS WORK

## Roger R. Nicole

It is clear that the New Testament identifies the hope of salvation for anyone in the human race with the name of Jesus Christ. The apostle Peter stated it in Acts 4:12: "Salvation is found in no one else, for there is no other name under heaven given to men by which we must be saved."

Paul the apostle put it this way in Romans 10:9–15:

That if you confess with your mouth, "Jesus is Lord," and believe in your heart that God raised him from the dead, you will be saved. For it is with your heart that you believe and are justified, and it is with your mouth that you confess and are saved. As the Scripture says, "Anyone who trusts in him will never be put to shame." For there is no difference between Jew and Gentile—the same Lord is Lord of all and richly blesses all who call on him, for, "Everyone who calls on the name of the Lord will be saved."

How, then, can they call on the one they have not believed in? And how can they believe in the one of whom they have not heard? And how can they hear without someone preaching to them? And how can they preach unless they are sent? As it is written, "How beautiful are the feet of those who bring good news!"

Paul's argument is framed in the form of a series of questions to which the answer "In no way" is presupposed each time. The very same argument could be formulated in direct propositions as follows:

Unless God sends preachers, there will be no one to preach.

Unless there is someone preaching, no one will have a chance to hear.

> Unless there is hearing, no one will have a chance to believe.
>
> Unless there is belief in the Lord, no one will call upon his name.
>
> Unless a person calls on the Lord's name, there is no salvation.

The apostle does not envision any exception to this rule, at least with respect to people who have reached the age of accountability.

The apostle John said, "God has given us eternal life, and this life is in his Son. He who has the Son has life; he who does not have the Son of God does not have life" (1 John 5:11–12). To this may be added the statement, originating perhaps with John the Baptist, "Whoever believes in the Son has eternal life, but whoever rejects the Son will not see that life, for God's wrath remains on him" (John 3:36).

The Lord Jesus said, "I am the way and the truth and the life. No one comes to the Father except through me" (John 14:6). "If anyone does not remain in me, he is like a branch that is thrown away and withers; such branches are picked up, thrown into the fire and burned" (John 15:6). "No one knows the Father except the Son and those to whom the Son chooses to reveal him" (Matt. 11:27). "Now this is eternal life: that they may know you, the only true God, and Jesus Christ, whom you have sent" (John 17:3).

These are only some representative verses from some of the most highly accredited teachers in the New Testament. One could quote scores of other passages to the same effect. The sense of intense urgency which prompted our Lord to accomplish his work on earth and the apostles to proclaim the salvation which only he could secure for fallen human beings is in line with that same conviction. The centrality of Christ for salvation is not found in the New Testament alone, but it is envisioned in prophetic perspective in the Old Testament as well. This is implicit in the protevangel, Genesis 3:15:

> "And I will put enmity
>     between you and the woman,
>     and between your offspring and hers;
> he will crush your head,
>     and you will strike his heel."

The day of the Fall was thus the very day on which God revealed his redemptive purpose.

> The stone the builders rejected
>     has become the capstone; . . .
> O Lord, save us;
>     O Lord, grant us success.
> Blessed is he who comes in the name of the Lord (Ps. 118:22–26).

This was quoted by Jesus (Matt. 21:42; Mark 12:10; Luke 20:17) and by Peter (Acts 4:11; 1 Peter 2:7) and was fulfilled at least in part in Christ's triumphant entry into Jerusalem (Matt. 21:9; Mark 11:9; Luke 19:38; John 12:13).

"The Root of Jesse will stand as a banner for the peoples; the nations will rally to him" (Isa. 11:10; cf. Rom. 15:12).

Many people are shocked by this claim of exclusivity which appears to restrict the opportunity of salvation to a minority in the human race who may have contact with the gospel presented in the form of preaching. It is apparent, however, from the texts quoted and from others that could well be advanced, that this attitude was that of some of the most notable inspired writers, including some who have in the most moving manner spoken of God's immeasurable love. Isaiah should be remembered for his statements in 42:1–3; 49:15–16; and 6:1–3. Saint Paul is the one who penned the supreme hymn to love in 1 Corinthians 13. Saint John must be remembered in terms of the third and fourth chapters of his first epistle. As for Jesus Christ—who would question that he is the one who supremely manifested the love of God (John 13:15; Rom. 5:18; 1 John 4:10) and who gave expression to it in the most emphatic language (John 3:16; 10:11; 15:13)?

Anyone who seeks here to be more generous than God as stated in Scripture takes a stance which differs from that of these great exponents of revealed truth and exposes himself/herself to objections in two respects:

1. Those who assume that there are other remedies to sin than Jesus Christ tend to encourage people who are lost to seek salvation in places where it certainly may not—and probably cannot—be found. In doing this they are not exercising due diligence in commending the one remedy provided once for all for sinners. Such an attitude may well be compared to that of a physician who, knowing a fully effective remedy for cancer, would be satisfied to encourage people to rely on lesser medication. Such an attitude would be considered as malpractice in the medical profession, but there are those who think it should be a standard in Christian ministry. The net effect is to diminish the urgency of God's mandate to believers to evangelize and to those outside of Christ to seek salvation in him alone.

2. In assuming that there are other sources of salvation besides Jesus Christ made known to human beings through the gospel, these friends suggest by implication that the work of Christ is really not necessary. Indeed, if people can be saved otherwise than through a presentation and believing acceptance of Jesus Christ, why should it be necessary that Christ should come at all? It borders on the absurd to imagine that God would use an intervention as drastic as the incarnation, death, and resurrection of Christ if some other way of salvation were possible for

mankind. To propose such a notion is really in the highest degree injurious to the wisdom of God.

Some remarks may be necessary with respect to the salvation of believers before the resurrection of Christ and the destiny of those who die in infancy.

These are special applications of the same universal principle, and they do not constitute a legitimate exception to the rule so clearly set forth in Scripture.

1. Believers who lived and died before the resurrection of Christ are not lost. In fact, Abraham is called the Father of believers (Rom. 4:16; Gal. 3:7–9), and his faith was not independent of Jesus Christ; rather it was the fruit of the Spirit in one who saw Christ's day (John 8:56). The Old Testament provided a divinely instituted foreshadowing of Christ which could be the occasion of a faith in God that is really like the faith of New Testament people. This principle would not provide a proper ground for the expectation of salvation among the heathen apart from a special revelation, since the Scripture throughout views heathen religions as heinous and damning distortions of the truth rather than pedagogues leading us to Christ (Gal. 3:24).

2. The case of humans dying in infancy is in some respects more complex because the Scripture does not provide much information concerning their case. Let it suffice here to say that it appears clear that they could rightly be charged with the guilt of Adam, so that one could not insist that justice demands that they should be saved because of innocence (Rom. 5:12–21; 1 Cor. 15:22). It would appear from God's promises to believers and their offspring and from 2 Samuel 12:33 that believers' children dying in infancy are saved, and the bereaved may confidently expect this. One could also argue from passages like Matthew 18:3 and 19:14 and from the fact that the biblical picture of judgment always involved sinful actions committed by the individuals being judged, that infants dying in infancy may well be saved. This, however, would not be something that God owes them but a merciful provision by which he would automatically engraft them into Christ who were also automatically constituted sinners in Adam. One reason why this principle was not more clearly stated in Scripture is that there is nothing we can do to assist in God's saving purpose for those infants. God certainly does not want us to kill infants in order to ensure their salvation! We must be content therefore, to leave the matter fully in God's hands, knowing that "the Judge of all the earth [will] do right" (Gen. 18:25).

In view of the biblical emphasis upon the centrality of Christ for salvation, it is not surprising that we should note a corresponding emphasis on the question of who Christ was. The crucial significance of the doctrine of Christ's person is to be seen in its close interrelationship with Christ's work. A Christ who is less than the Scripture asserts could not perform what the Bible teaches he has accomplished; a Christ who is seen as the potential "savior of the world" (John 4:42; 1 John 4:14; 1 Tim. 4:10) must be such a superlative person as to be capable of this gigantic task.

The church was therefore on the right track when it made christological issues the major point of debate in the Conciliar period (A.D. 325–451 and later). Its judgment of heretics was somewhat harsh, but what was at stake was surely apparent, and we must admire the Fathers' insistence on securing a consensus of faith on the subject of Christ. The indifference and laxity which often prevail in modern times can scarcely be viewed as a virtue even by those who desire to promote charity and compassion at all times and toward everybody.

We must first of all emphasize the deity of Christ in order to provide a proper base for the Atonement. The Lord Jesus Christ took the place of a great number of guilty sinners, men and women drawn from all parts of the world and all periods of the life of humanity on this earth. In order that he could endure to the full the punishment due to their sins, it was necessary that he provide an offering of immense value. When the deity of Christ is asserted, this is strongly featured. When it is denied, the substitutionary penal character of his work is placed in jeopardy. This is a point which Anselm of Canterbury clearly saw in his work *Why Was God Made Human?* People who fail to acknowledge and even to emphasize the deity of Christ are grievously undermining the biblical doctrine of salvation.

If Christ were not God, it would follow that the supreme act of self-dedication which is at the basis of our salvation would be accomplished by another than God and that God himself would not share effectively in the work of our salvation, except by permitting this person to make an appropriate offering for us. The Father would be seen as the one who enforces the demands of justice and thereby threatens our lives by his wrath. The Son would be the one who delivers us from that predicament at the cost of his own life. But since we would owe our redemption to the work of Christ and the fact that he bore the condemnation for our sins, this would inevitably lead us to turn toward him and to worship him even more than we might worship the true God. Christ would therefore go beyond Christ in our conception; we would then be moving toward idolatry! The biblical view, however, makes it plain that the very one who took our place is God himself, and therefore we can offer him our complete consecration in response to his great work for us.

Jesus Christ is true God, and he is also true man. The full humanity of our Lord is an essential element of the salvific message. It is scarcely less important than his deity.

Surely if Christ is to take our place and be our representative as Adam once was it is imperative that he should be a human being. The redemption we need cannot be achieved extrinsically but must be worked organically from within the race as a suitable satisfaction of God's righteous demands. The reality of the connection with us of the saving work of Christ depends on the reality of his humanity.

"The Word became flesh and made his dwelling among us" (John 1:14).

> [He] made himself nothing,
>   taking the very nature of a servant,
>   being made in human likeness . . ." (Phil. 2:7).

"Since the children have flesh and blood, he too shared in their humanity. . . . For surely it is not angels he helps, but Abraham's descendants. For this reason he had to be made like his brothers in every way, in order that he might . . . make atonement for the sins of the people" (Heb. 2:14, 16–17).

"There is one God and one mediator between God and men, the man Christ Jesus, who gave himself as a ransom for all" (1 Tim. 2:5–6).

"Just as through the disobedience of the one man the many were made sinners, so also through the obedience of the one man the many will be made righteous" (Rom. 5:19; cf. also 14–17).

The need to retain a firm hold on Christ's real humanity must put us on guard against docetism in all its forms, which tends to obscure or erase the human in Christ. This is a very real danger which some strong supporters of the deity of Christ have not always been careful to guard against. We must accept without reservation the historical details of the life of Christ on earth as recorded for us in the Gospels. No ethereal Christ, however divine, could compensate for the loss of the real historical Jesus whom the New Testament presents to us. To lose Christ's humanity is to lose the relevancy of Christ's saving work to our race. We ought not therefore to favor a disjunction between the Christ of faith and the historical Jesus. The true historical Jesus Christ is both divine and human, and it is on him in the possession of the two natures that our faith is pitted.

Frequently people of various races of mankind, when attempting to represent Christ and his disciples, have not endeavored to portray Jewish Galileans of the first century, except perhaps in the clothing that they wore. What we see is a group of Chinese, Zulus, Eskimoes, Navahoes, Haitians, or Arabs, rather than Jews; and this may appear anomalous from a historical point of view. It may be good, however, that people of any human community could unmistakably recognize Jesus Christ as one of them, for the main thing he assumed is generic humanity, found alike in every member of the race, male or female, child or adult, great or small, Jew or Gentile. Historically, of course, he was a male Jewish person (Rom. 9:5) who died at the age of thirty-three, and we need to recognize that truth, but the representative character of Christ for the whole human race is perhaps even more important than the particularity of the circumstances of his incarnation.

The humility of our Lord's life on earth from his birth in a stable to his death on a cross ought to give great comfort to people of low estate, for they have the evidence that Christ enters into relation with them and not merely with some people of great eminence.

The incarnation of our Lord is presented as the pattern for the evangelical ministry: "As the Father has sent me, I am sending you" (John 20:21). We must ever learn again to go all the way, sin excepted, to make common cause with those to whom God sends us in order to lead them from where they are to the loving arms of the Savior.

Christology is essentially the study of a bridge—God's bridge, which crosses the immense chasm opened by sin between God and humanity. It is of the essence of a serviceable bridge that it should have a firm access on both sides and carry the traveler all the way across the gap. Christ, being true God and true man, has his moorings in the very nature of God and of humanity, and he is the "one mediator between God and men" (1 Tim. 2:5) who alone can lead us out of the estrangement and slavery of our sin into restored fellowship with the triune God and the glorious freedom of the children of God (John 8:36).

# A Response to
# The Savior and His Work

## William C. Weinrich

The paper by Professor Nicole, "The Savior and His Work," presents the three essential assertions of any good orthodox christology: the unity of Christ, the deity of Christ, and the humanity of Christ. This corresponds to the Definition of Faith of the Council of Chalcedon (A.D. 451): "Our Lord Jesus Christ is to be confessed as one and the same person. . . . This one and the same Jesus Christ, the only-begotten Son of God, must be confessed to be in two natures." That is, simply put, our Lord Jesus Christ is true God and also true man. Certainly, therefore, Professor Nicole is to be followed in rejecting any position which would compromise either the true deity or the true humanity of Christ (he mentions docetism explicitly).

But why the necessity of the confession that our Lord is true God and true man? Again, Professor Nicole points the way: "the crucial significance of the doctrine of Christ's person is to be seen in its close interrelationship with Christ's work." In terms of the Nicene Creed we confess: "Who *for us and for our salvation* came down from heaven and was incarnated by the Holy Spirit and was made man." These words of the Nicene Creed immediately lead us to a reflection of the relationship between Christ's person and his work and indeed in such a way that the doctrine of the person of Christ becomes itself an expression and proclamation of the gospel. That is, the true deity of Christ, his true humanity, and the indivisible unity of Christ's person are not merely bases or foundations upon which salvation rests but are themselves constitutive factors of what it means to be "saved." This "for us" of the creed is, if you will, the creedal fallout of the words of John: "As many as received him, to those who believe on his name, he gave the power to become the children of God; who were not born of blood, nor from the will of flesh, nor from the will of man, but from God" (John 1:12–13).

The gospel refers to the engendering of faith by God (in which we become "children of God") in terms of "virgin birth," that birth namely in which the "Word became flesh" (John 1:14). Our status as "children of God," therefore, has christological contours, and for this reason Martin Luther was quite on target when he wrote in explanation of the second article of the creed, "I believe that Jesus Christ, true God, begotten of the Father from eternity, and also true man, born of the Virgin Mary, is *my* Lord." As those who have been redeemed and delivered from sin, death, and the devil, we recognize and confess Jesus Christ to be what he in fact is, true God and true man. To know Jesus as true God is to know him as the one who forgives us our sin, as the one who frees us from Satan's bondage, as the one who gives us life to live in his name. For God alone can be the *subject* of salvation. He can alone forgive sin; only he can give victory over Satan; only he who has life in himself can bestow life.

By the same token, we know Jesus to be true man in that we know him to be *our* Savior. It is man who is the *object* of salvation, that is, who is the recipient of God's gracious coming. It is man who is the sinner; it is man who lives under the false lordship of the devil; it is man who is under the power of death and will in fact die. If Jesus is *our* Savior, he must be truly human even as we are human.[1] We confess Jesus to be true man, therefore, because *in our place* ("for us") he died for the forgiveness of *our* sin, because *in our place* he obeyed God in all things without fault, and because *in our place* he received the life of resurrection which *we* also shall receive and have ready in faith and hope.

When we proclaim, "Jesus saves us!" we proclaim at the same time, "Jesus is true God and true man." The true deity of Christ and his true humanity are not analytic truths but assertions of the gospel which proclaim our new status with God. In Christ we do not recognize God abstractly but *God for man*, and likewise in Christ we do not recognize man abstractly but *man for God*. That is, in Christ we recognize God and man as they, through the gospel, relate to one another. Perhaps it would be well to expand on this just a bit.

When we confess that Jesus is "true God" we do not think merely of his divine qualities or attributes. To be sure, Jesus is God, and for that reason is and has all that God is and has. Jesus is immortal, eternal, all-knowing, unchangeable. However, we cannot apprehend God directly but only in God's revelation of himself, that is, in his words and his works. But what is that most characteristic word and work of God by which God is revealed as God for man? Again, we take our clue from the prologue of John's Gospel, which begins the story of Jesus with the words, "all

things were made through him and . . . in him was life" (John
1:3–4). In the creation God was alone; no one nor anything existed
alongside of him. Solely through his almighty will did God create
all things including mankind. In this work of creation God
revealed himself to be the living God (he who has life in himself)
whose proper work is to give life. There can be no thought here of
man's assisting God in this work. Man was but a lump of
inanimate clay when God breathed into him. Yet when God
breathed into the clay, it became a living being (Gen. 2:7). Man's
life is therefore pure gift; it is not something which he has in
himself. Man has only received his life, and he lives only because
he receives it from God. When God bestows, preserves, and
renews life, therefore, he reveals himself to be the gracious God
who is God for man.

As the divine Word through whom all things were made,
Jesus is the one who gives life and who by his grace renews the
life of fallen and sinful mankind. He is the one who has life in
himself; that is, Jesus is the living God. From this perspective we
come to recognize the miracles of Jesus as demonstrations of his
true divinity. When Jesus calmed the sea (Matt. 14:22ff.), when he
healed the paralyzed (Matt. 9:1ff.; John 5:2ff.), when he gave sight
to the blind (Matt. 9:27ff.), and when he raised the dead (Matt.
9:18ff.; John 11:5ff.), he revealed himself to be the good Creator
who creates out of nothing and gives life to that which has no life.
In all these ways Jesus showed that he is *God for man* who desires
that all have life and participate in the good and gracious gifts of
God.

Similarly, when we confess that Jesus is "true man," we do
not mean only his status as human. To be sure, Jesus was truly
human and therefore was all that we humans are. He had flesh
and bones, hair and blood; he had a human will and a human
intellect; he was born of woman and was under the law of God; he
suffered anxiety, fear, and sorrow; he experienced temptation; he
suffered and died. However, Jesus was "true man" not only
because he was made of flesh and blood. He was "true man" also
in the sense that he was the perfectly sinless, obedient, and
faithful Son of God who served God in righteousness, innocence,
and blessedness. Jesus was true man in that despite temptation,
fear, weakness, suffering, and death, he yet believed God and did
God's will. The *Letter to the Hebrews* speaks of Jesus as one who in
every way shared in our flesh, in our temptations, and in our
sufferings and death. Yet he shared in these with us without sin
(Heb. 2:14–18; 4:15; see also 1 Peter 2:22ff.; 3:18).

It is important for our understanding of what it means for
Jesus to be "true man" (and for us to be truly human) to note that
Jesus was sinless not because he was God and could not sin but
because he was "true man" and did not sin. To be truly human

means to live as God's creature—that is, to live as one who thankfully receives God's good gifts and as one who trusts God as the gracious Creator who will not withhold anything that is good and beneficial to mankind. To be truly human means to live from God alone, to acknowledge him to be *my* Lord and the Giver of *my* life. To be truly human is to let God be God for us. To be truly human is to have faith.

Perhaps the creation story can be helpful also in this context. As we noted, at the creation God breathed into the lump of clay, and it became a living soul. That is simply to say, when Adam, the lump of clay, *received* God's inbreathing, Adam breathed. God's creative inbreathing became Adam's breathing. Adam's life was the life which God gave. It was no less Adam's breathing just because it was the result of God's inbreathing. Yet the creation account helps us to understand that from the biblical point of view man is always understood as God's creature, as one who receives his life and every blessing from God and from God alone. Man is never regarded as a purely self-sufficient, independent being who stands on his own and only for himself. As a creature, man is necessarily and always in relation to another—namely, to God. "True man" relates to God as one who thankfully and in trust receives from God all that God gives. Sinful man relates to God also but as one who rejects God's lordship and rebels against him.

As one who thankfully received his life and every blessing from God and who therefore freely obeyed God's will, Adam was "true man." As one who thankfully and joyfully and freely lived from God's goodness, Adam was in the image of God. He "reflected" freely and thankfully what God had given to him. However, when Adam turned away from God and believed another—namely, Satan—Adam turned from the real source of all good things and sought his life from other things. Adam became an unbeliever, one who does not trust in God as the giver of all good things, and in this unbelief Adam became a sinner and inherited death (see Rom. 5:12). Rejecting God as the source of every good gift, Adam ceased to be the creature who thankfully and in faith receives from God's hand and became the sinner who seeks after his own good. Adam became proud (he thought himself independent from God) and he became selfish (he sought his own good). Adam ceased to be "true man"; he ceased to be according to God's image.

Sinlessness therefore does not simply mean not doing anything wrong. Sin is not merely or solely disobeying God's law. Sin refers to that posture of rebellion, pride, and assumed independence which man has adopted over against God. Jesus was sinless, therefore, because he was "true man," and his sinlessness consisted in the fact that he at all times and in all circumstances trusted God and *for that reason* freely obeyed God in an active life of prayer, thanksgiving, self-sacrificing love, humility, patience, and long-suffering. The true humanity of Jesus, then, is evident in all those activities in which he is the thankful and trusting recipient of God's good gifts. We recognize his humanity in his birth in which Jesus received life by the Holy Spirit through the Virgin Mary. We recognize his true humanity in his eating and drinking, for in these he received God's gifts by which his human life is nurtured and preserved. We recognize his humanity in his sleeping, for in that he received a daily refreshment for the reinvigoration of his daily life. We recognize his true humanity in his praying, in his giving thanks, in his faith, in his works of charity and of forgiveness, and we recognize his true humanity in his refusal to yield to the temptations of the devil. When Jesus was tempted by Satan to worship him, Jesus said, "You shall worship the Lord your God and him only shall you serve!" (Matt. 4:10 RSV). Such are the words of one who is "true man." Similarly, when Jesus was in the throes of death, he prayed, "Father into thy hands I give over my life" (Luke 23:46). Such are the words of faith. Jesus is *Man for God.* As the Bible says, Jesus is the New Adam (Rom. 5:12ff.). And as the New Adam, Jesus is the image of our hope, for he is what we shall be. He is the one in whom God has again made man according to his image, the one in whom God has again made "true man," man who lives from God alone, trusts God alone, and serves God alone.

In the "true man" God's work becomes also man's work. God and man are in agreement; they are in communion with each other; they are in unity with each other. Thus in Christ, true God and true man, God's work became man's work: whereas sinful man cursed his neighbor, now the New Adam blesses his enemies: whereas sinful man is selfish and self-centered, the New Adam gives charity freely and loves his neighbor as himself. The full law of God, set in the heart of man at creation, in Jesus now receives its complete and perfect fulfillment. And this Christ did *for us* who are sinners, so that the penalty of sin—namely death—may not be our final destiny but that we may have eternal life in him who as the one "true man," the New Adam, receives life freely from God's hand. In Jesus, therefore, God renews his creation by bringing sinful man to be "true man" through the forgiveness of sins. In Jesus sinful man become "true man," the image of God, and thankfully receives life from God, reflecting the holiness and righteousness of God in a holy and righteous life (see 1 Peter 2:14–15; and especially Rom. 8:1–4).

But what about the indivisible and inseparable unity of God and man in Christ Jesus? In what way is that related to the gospel promise? When the apostle John saw the new heaven and the new earth, he saw the communion which the faithful shall have with God. But this communion with God shall be forever and ever

(Rev. 22:5). Similarly, John's Gospel promises that whoever believes in Christ shall receive eternal life (3:15–16). Our redemption in Christ shall *never* cease or come to an end. In Christ no longer, ever, will God's good purposes for the human race be subject to the work of Satan—temptation, corruption, and death. Indeed, in Christ there will be *no possibility* for human beings to once again fall into the tyranny of sin and death. The new relationship that people have with God in Christ is not exactly the same as it was between Adam and God. Although Adam was created "good" by God, yet in Adam human beings could sin and could suffer corruption because the unity of Adam and God was such that Adam could act apart from and independently of God. However, in Christ, God has put his creation on a new and more solid foundation. In Christ, God has united himself with human beings in an inseparable and indivisible way so that into all eternity people will be with God receiving thankfully all good things, especially life and immortality.

Wherein, then, lies this new solidity and permanence for the future of human being's communion with God? It lies in this: In Christ Jesus *God Himself became man.* The eternal Word of God (the Second Person of the Trinity) took to himself all that man is, and without ceasing to be true God made *in himself* the start of a new creation wherein fallen, sinful, and mortal mankind became a righteous, holy, and immortal mankind. This is the evangelical significance and justification for the notion of the "enhypostasia" of the divine Word The solidity of our redemption lies in him who became flesh.[2] Since in Christ God has become man, *in Christ* man eternally will be without sin and eternally will not be subject to death. In Christ, the New Adam, man will never again act apart from God, for in Christ, God himself is incarnate—that is, made man.

We do not usually think of christology as eschatology. Yet the doctrine of one person in two natures preserves and declares fulfilled two distinct lines of Old Testament prophecy concerning the end of time. On the one hand are those prophecies that foresee God himself in the midst of his people accomplishing new things (Isa. 2:3; 4:2ff.; 40:1ff.; 65:17ff.; Zeph. 3:14ff.). On the other hand are those prophecies that envision a new man (Deut. 18:15, 18; 2 Sam. 7). According to the New Testament, these two lines of prophecy have converged in fulfillment in the person of Jesus. The end and goal of God's purpose spoken at the beginning, that he created man in his own image, is not an event; it is a person—namely, Jesus Christ, our Lord, the Word incarnate. Nowhere is this more poetically put than in the great hymn of ascension by the Anglican divine, Christopher Wordsworth, "See, the Conqueror Mounts in Triumph":

Thou hast raised our human nature
On the clouds to God's right hand;
There we sit in heavenly places,
There with Thee in glory stand.
Jesus reigns, adored by angels;
Man with God is on the throne.
Mighty Lord, in Thine ascension
We by faith behold our own.

## ADDENDUM

For the most part my response may be understood as a
further elucidation of Professor Nicole's primary assertions, those
concerning the deity, the humanity and the unity of Christ Jesus. I
wished further to integrate the doctrine of Christ's person with
that of his work, especially as to give christological dimensions
both to the "for us" of the gospel as well as to the "to what end"
of the gospel.

With these primary purposes in mind, I have little disagreement with Professor Nicole's paper. He does, however, make
some statements along the way with which I have considerable
difficulty. I might here reply very briefly to but one of them, albeit
in my opinion the most grievous.

Professor Nicole discusses the case of infants who die in
infancy in light of the general "principle" of the centrality of
Christ in salvation. In this context he speaks of the salvation of
believers' infants who die in infancy and seems to say that they
will be saved *because* they are believers' infants. If this is what he is
saying, then it seems to be a variant of the Jews' assertion that as
the seed of Abraham they are God's people. Paul in Romans says
rather that those who are seed of Abraham are those who have
faith (Rom. 4). Similarly, the prologue of John speaks of the
redeemed as those born "not of blood, nor of the will of the flesh,
nor of the will of man, but of God" (John 1:13 KJV). It does not
suffice to speak of a "merciful provision" by God, for it would still
entail the view that faith alone and Christ alone are not constitutive factors in salvation. It must simply be asserted that the fact
that the Word who was made man is he "through whom all things
were made" and the fact that the Word incarnate is the New
Adam demand the view that in Christ both God's salvific intent
and also his salvific work envisions and includes all humanity,
and that includes also infants. While mentioning the "generic
humanity" which Christ assumed, Professor Nicole still can speak
of only "a great number of guilty sinners" whose place Christ
took. I submit that this tends to detract from the significance of
Christ's deity, which is the deity of the all-creative Word, and
from Christ's humanity, which is that of the New Adam. As the

Word incarnate and as the New Adam, Christ is "for all" and in the place of all. To speak of provisions which God makes apart from the person and work of the Word incarnate has the effect of calling into question the unity of substance and of will which exists between the Father and the eternal Word who in Christ is incarnate. Christ is not simply one provision among other possible provisions, even if he happens to be the usual one. He is God incarnate, and that implies universality.

## ENDNOTES

[1]So also Nicole: "Surely if Christ is to take our place and be our representative, as Adam once was, it is imperative that he should be a human being. . . . The reality of the connection with us of the saving work of Christ depends on the reality of his humanity."

[2]Leo, Sermon 27: "For that 'the Word became flesh' does not signify that the nature of God was changed into flesh, but that the Word took the flesh into the unity of His Person."

# A Response to
# The Savior and His Work

### Ralph D. Winter

I come to this topic with three sensitivities held consciously in mind.

First, since this is a conference on the Bible, I feel I must try to deal as much as possible directly with the Bible rather than with a theological corpus through which to view the Bible.

Second, if that will not be hard enough, I would like consciously to hold at arm's length for reexamination, if necessary, the particular point of view which we all bring along with our heritage from the roots of the Reformation and the pietistic/evangelical tradition.

Third, I carry into this discussion my own focus of thought. I must warn you that the bulk of my thinking and writing has been in the realm of mission history, theology, and strategy, and I am sure that those who invited me to participate were aware of that fact. Wanting not to disappoint such expectations, I have, in fact, concerned myself about where, if not under this topic on the Savior and his work, might there appear legitimately in this conference something about the work of our Savior on earth in its larger, global and eschatological dimension, which we usually call missions.

For example, it would surely be possible to consider the missionary expansion of the kingdom of God under the topic of the living God. Or we ought to be able to approach missions under the topic of the church and her mission. But it is equally logical that we should see or could take seriously the entire world through the prism of the topic "The Savior and His Work."

Roger Nicole has already done us all a great favor, as he has so effectively and marvelously, in the short space allotted him, gathered together a veritable floral bouquet of Scriptures which highlight many of the uniquenesses of our Lord. As for scope, he includes the entire human race in his very first sentence! He goes on to underscore the fact that the exclusivity of salvation in Jesus Christ, when offered to the whole world as Scripture has it, does not at all restrict salvation to a minority of the human race: salvation in Christ is precisely aimed at the whole world and has been from the beginning of redemptive history.

On the other hand, we do well to remember that as Evangelicals, reaching back into our pietistic and Reformation roots, we have conventionally focused our attention in the realm of christology upon the person and work of Christ as this pertains to our own salvation. Even the major creeds of Christendom do this, whether we look at the Nicene Creed or the Westminster Confession. How strange that some would take these creeds very uncritically while subjecting the Bible itself to unending criticism!

Were not the ancient creeds fashioned in semipolitical circumstances? Do they not characteristically focus more on the person of Christ than on his work, and if on his work, do they not reduce that work primarily to the Atonement and its implications for us, rather than seeing in the work of Christ his relentless concern for the largest possible audience for the Atonement?

One of the dangers to a high view of the Bible, and a danger recognized in the period of the Reformation itself, was the tendency to allow the creedal treatments of Holy Scripture a status very close to that of the Bible itself. Although the Westminster Confession was hammered out in the aftermath of the Reformation, it was not until the 1890s that Evangelicals in the Northern Presbyterian church undertook to add a chapter entitled, "Of the Love of God and Missions." This simple fact means it took almost three centuries for the pietistic/evangelical tradition (with all of its serious biblical exposition) to gain sufficient confidence for even one of its bodies to dare to alter the sacred creedal text.

By comparison, how refreshing it is to note on the front line of the missionary expansion of the kingdom the frequent reminder of how much more significant and reliable are the documents of the Bible themselves than the creeds of Christendom, as respectful as we ought to be of that institutional and quasipolitical tradition. Granted, new cultural biases arise on the mission field; not only are the old ones lost in the process as the Bible in each new group becomes freshly again the primary source of orientation. But perhaps God has intended that only in the symphony of many voices and perspectives drawn from the authentic impact of the Word of God across the globe would we be best able to reflect back upon our own cultural traditions with any objectivity and to understand the Bible with greater certainty.

It is not the Nicene Creed but the Bible which astounds us with the picture of Jesus ignoring the disciples' concern for food, claiming, "My food is to do the will of the Father and to finish his work." Is it not a bit strange that the great mass of theological writing in history, while rightly taking special interest in the work of Christ on the cross, gives so very little space to the work of Christ which we as his disciples were intended to pick up and carry forward? How easy it is, how human, to dote upon the blessing of Christ for ourselves and pass over lightly the clear call, the heavenly vision to lose ourselves for his sake and the gospel's by bending every ounce of our energy to give this great gift away to others at the very ends of the earth!

Yes, the work of Christ on the cross was unique. But so was his behavior among men. We can search the Gospel accounts in vain to discern any very great mutual understanding between Jesus and his disciples. Indeed, like us, they were interested in his person and his work as it might pertain to their own agendas. But they stumbled along quite in the dark as to the unique and unfathomably different ministry which unfolded in their presence.

We quite rightly covet the truth of the *finished* work of Christ, but humanly we are tempted to underemphasize the face of the *unfinished* work of Christ. When in the verse I have just quoted Jesus says his food is to do the will of his Father and finish his work, are we to assume he was only referring to the cross? Is that all he means to us? Are all these other little stories about Jesus meant merely to be the basis of sermons about the little things in our lives?

Surely we do well to teach our children to say that Jesus died on the cross to save us from our sins. We must not forget that Jesus also lived among us relentlessly seeking out in love the poor, the dispirited, the handicapped, the sick, the blind, the women, the Greeks, and, yes, even the Samaritans. Why? Because he died on the cross to save a lot of other peoples besides our people. Even our missionaries who go to the ends of the earth deliberately to befriend the benighted are all too often willing to spell out a traditional christology, which, as only one of many examples, allows Japanese believers to take no special interest in the one million despised and unmentionable Eta people among them or the million socially disenfranchised Koreans concentrated in Osaka. Are we more concerned about the maze of minorities in our cities?

George Eldon Ladd, whose chapel talk on the Great Commission was one of the high points of my time at Fuller Seminary, could at the very end of his teaching career come out with a huge tome on New Testament theology without a single line specifically referring to the crucial, urgent, day-to-day implications of the love of our Savior for the non-Jews and other nonentities of this day— that is to say, the global crosscultural mission which may actually be the central theme of the New Testament.

I hope Dr. Nicole will not mind if I impute to him much of my own perspective. I believe that in germ this is what he is saying when he speaks of our Lord pictured in different parts of the world in Chinese, Zulu, Navaho, and Arab clothing, and when he says that the Incarnation must lead us "all the way" to the place where we are sent as he was sent, to lead all peoples from "where they are to the loving arms of the Savior."

An inerrant Bible does no one any good if it is not accompanied by thoughtful, authentic understanding on our part. We deny our belief in the Bible if our actions do not bear out our words. The amazing, consecrated leadership in this room, giving thirty minutes a day to the concern, could terminate permanently in just five years' time, if we wanted to, the scandalous situation in which there are, for example, 723 known languages in which there are no Scriptures. What is the value of an untranslated, inerrant Bible?

Does it really matter in God's eyes what words Evangelicals parade in public about an inerrant Bible; does it matter how many times the Bible is translated into English, occasioning each time millions of dollars of new expenditures for ourselves rather than for these groups which have no Scripture at all? Surely it is possible to deny the inerrancy of the Bible by our behavior. As Paul Rees used to say, "It is easier to act our way into right thinking than think our way into right acting." That is hard for us Calvinists to take!

In conclusion let me leave with you three concepts which I believe bear significantly upon the way we deal with the topic of the Savior and his work.

## I. THE CONCEPT OF NONDISCLOSURE

We must, I believe, face the fact that the Bible is not merely God's primary instrument of *revelation*. The Bible itself clearly exposits the intended nondisclosure of God. Again and again it makes clear that it is not yet possible for us to digest all that God is and is about but that what is revealed is for our admonition in the present world and for those who are actively walking in the light they have.

For example, we must not draw too much from the fact that Jesus did not teach his disciples a course in mission strategy. The Gospel accounts reveal for them a level of understanding that would have meant total misunderstanding had they been exposed. Even late in the early ministry of our Lord in the final chapter of Luke, we see two of his followers struggling still with the obvious discrepancy between his perspective and what was their understanding of the Savior and his work. For Jesus to have explained or have tried to explain to these self-concerned disciples then or now just what was the full meaning of the Abrahamic covenant would have been like running into an accident ward of a hospital with a tennis racket, where the patients are all bundled up in splints and in traction and doped out with anesthetics, and shouting, "Tennis anyone?"

That is, to believe in the inerrancy of the Bible does not allow us to raid its treasures if we are not ready for its mandate. Jesus told the parables both to reveal and to conceal. The concept of nondisclosure is a crucial parameter in our handling of the Bible.

## II. THE CONCEPT OF THE *KAIROS*

When we speak of the Savior and his work we need to ask not only what he did and why he come but why he came when he did. We must try to see who he was and what he did in the light of God's timing in history.

When the Christ appeared, it had been two thousand years since the call of Abraham and God's crystal clear enunciation of his concern to be a blessing to Abraham and his children by faith, and through them to be a blessing to all of the other peoples of the earth.

The Bible throughout reveals God's constant concern for the other peoples of the world: when he pushes Abraham down into the very presence of the Pharaoh of Egypt; when he places Joseph there and Moses there; when he throws his people again and again into contact with many other nations, sitting in the very spot where he placed them, precisely on the land bridge connecting the continent of Africa and that of Eurasia; when he sends Jonah out to the nation of Nineveh; when he sends all the northern tribes out into a diaspora among the nations; when he sends the Judeans off to the ends of the earth (as they referred to Babylon); and, indeed, as he dispersed them throughout the Roman Empire. (We do not wonder at the fact that one of mission history's largest conquests was the Christianization of the Batak tribal peoples of Sumatra, and that, what do you know, they are now dispersed, for better or worse, throughout all of Indonesia like almost no other people.)

When Jesus appeared, what time was it? How was this nation doing with its commission to be a blessing to all the peoples of the earth? Had this nation been hiding its light in the ground? Had this nation revolted, not just against Rome but against the Land Owner who finally sent his own Son to check up on things? Were Galileans delighted that God had brought so many foreigners into their midst and that they were called Galilee of the Gentiles? (Are Evangelicals in American cities today delighted that God has brought the mission field to our doorsteps? Are we taking this as seriously as we ought?)

In this sense Jesus did not come to give the Great Commission but to take it away. We must understand the Savior and his work in the sense of God's timing. God is looking at our nation, perhaps, with the same timing in mind. Do we have infiltrated Galilees in our land today? Are we by and large quite unconcerned about giving our blessings away? Leighton Ford recently said that 85 percent of the books in our Christian bookstores focus on self-fulfillment. Is God watching his clock today?

## III. THE CONCEPT OF LITERALISM

It is an objectionable literalism which takes the Gospel accounts as they are, filled with examples of the self-seeking of the disciples, of the inability of the disciples to fathom the radical meaning of the call of Christ, and then accepts this kind of mediocrity and self-concern as normative or even adequate behavior for the disciples today. That is, in our inerrant Bibles we must admit that the real meaning of Christ's call does not show up in the bulk of the text and that it is an undesirable literalism which fails to distinguish between what happened in the Bible and what the Bible is trying to tell us ought to have happened. That is, inerrant description of errant behavior calls for more than a superficial use of the text.

We see this in regard to the real meaning of the Abrahamic covenant, which clearly and distinctly asked the chosen people to reach out with blessing to all the peoples of the earth. (It does not help when our modern translations for the most part fail to translate the Hebrew imperative in Genesis 12:2.) Despite this mandate, repeated very clearly five times in Genesis, we then read on to find that the bulk of the text of the Old and New Testaments does not portray an obedient people. It is an undesirable literalism which accepts the failures and foibles thus described so accurately as though they were to be considered normative and assumes, as so often has been the case, that there was no intention on God's part for the missionary dimension of the Abrahamic covenant to be taken seriously until two thousand years later.

Talk about distortion of the Bible. I believe that no greater single misunderstanding of Scripture exists widely among us today than the reductionism which sees the global mandate of the early chapters of Genesis as a hibernating mandate which was supposed to be held in suspense until Jesus appeared or until Jesus died or until Jesus was resurrected or until Paul was commissioned or until William Carey bestirred England, or until the preaching of the heavenly angel of Revelation 14:6–7 or . . . .

Sadly, the mandate of all Scripture implied and explained again and again, derives precisely from the scope of the work of Christ. It is thus an unwarranted literalism which accepts the common as the normal, whether in modern or Old Testament behavior. If we do not believe that the chosen people were chosen to be a blessing to all the peoples of the earth and that this mandate was in force the moment it was given, then we must believe and accept that all God was after for two thousand years was good behavior, people keeping out of trouble, and the mandate was not yet in force. We too often live within this kind of literalism. The mandate always applies to someone else, somewhere else, some other time. The sobering fact is that God does not have much use for that kind of people, no matter how highly they regard their Scriptures. How do we know this? The Bible tells us so.

# THE HOLY SPIRIT AND HIS WORK

## James I. Packer

Forty years ago when I was a student, the person and work of the Holy Spirit were neglected themes in the world church, so much so that witty folk would from time to time speak of the Spirit as the displaced person of the Godhead and the Cinderella of theology. Apart from popular evangelical exposition of what was then called holiness teaching in its two main forms, Wesleyan (entire sanctification) and Keswick (victorious life),[1] plus the Pentecostal emphasis (at that time thought eccentric) on tongues and healing as the Spirit's gifts, no sustained speaking or writing about the Paraclete went on anywhere. Potent factors operated across the Christian board to preclude any serious attention to pneumatology.

In most of the Protestant world theological initiative remained in liberal hands. But liberalism was hamstrung and hobbled in its pneumatology, as where it survives it still is, by its Unitarian or, at best, Binitarian thought-forms.[2] The liberal habit since Schleiermacher has always been to reduce the Trinity to a threefoldness in our perception of God—God above, beside, and within us; to explain or explain away the Incarnation as a special case of divine influence in a human life; and to treat the Spirit as another name either for the unipersonal God in action or for the continuing influence, however conceived, of the historical Jesus. In either case, liberals would conceive of the Spirit as the personal, relational dimension of divine life on the analogy of the human spirit as known to us by our own introspection; and this movement of thought effectively turned pneumatology into a department of natural theology. Within this frame of reference New Testament teaching about the Spirit's personhood and ministry could hardly be given proper weight and, in fact, it was not. As now, so then, liberals said little about new birth and the moral and dispositional transformation of the believer; and when they spoke of the work in the world of the divine Spirit, what they envisioned was large-scale cultural change, evolutionary or revolutionary, to be brought in by some form of political action and to be identified as the coming of God's kingdom on earth. Reflected here was liberalism's characteristic confidence in the power of latter-day Christian reason to understand Christianity better than its own founders did: this was liberalism's Pelagianism of the intellect, matching the Pelagianism of the complacent liberal certainty that the new order could be brought in by the power of education and politics. Christian interest will only ever focus on the doctrine of the Holy Spirit where the inadequacy of all human effort is acknowledged; inevitably, therefore, in the liberal world of thought pneumatology was neglected to a scandalous degree.

Moreover, traditional Trinitarianism, where it still held sway, was itself a hindrance to sustained pneumatological thought, for it fed into the main streams of both Roman Catholic and Protestant theology, with something approaching normative force, Augustine's image of the Trinity as the lover, the beloved, and the love that binds them together. But this formula fails to express, and so obscures, the Spirit's distinct personhood; and where this is played down, his ministry is bound to be played down, too. Evidence of this was the Roman Catholic habit of referring to gifts of internal grace rather than ministrations of the Spirit and the Protestant habit of calling the Spirit "it" rather than "he." To be sure, in my student days it was possible to read in English the first half-volume of Barth's *Church Dogmatics*, which rejects Augustinian analogies altogether and argues that the truth of the Trinity is to be drawn from the reality of divine revelation: *God* reveals *God* through *God*.[3] But this argumentative *tour de force* had not in those days been widely read and weighed, and its one-is-three line of analysis, coupled with its sharp rejection of liberal ways of conceiving divine personality, had brought Barth under suspicion of teaching modalism in a refined form (that is, the idea that the Trinity is fully explained by saying that one divine agent acts three roles). Also, Barth's categorical rejection of natural theology in favor of biblical revelation was at that time thought to be overdone. The truth is that, among the relatively orthodox Trinitarians, thought was languishing every way, and no part of it languished more than the doctrine of the Third Person.

At the same time, more conservative outlooks in the Roman Catholic church and older Protestant bodies were stifling reflection on the Spirit by their institutionally minded triumphalism, by which I mean their ready assumption, without evidence, that the Spirit's beneficent presence was locked into their own current practice. Then, as now, Protestants would censure Roman Catholics for assuming this in relation to the sacramental ministrations of their priesthood, as if the apostolic succession of orders that Rome claims could guarantee such a thing. But great numbers of Protestant churches, Anglican and Presbyterian in particular, were at that time contentedly running on a basis of mere moralism, divorced from any joy in worship, any zeal in witness, any incidence of conversions, or any meaningful expressions of informal Christian fellowship; and this made their censures of Roman Catholic institutionalism appear as a case of the pot calling the kettle black. For when churches trust their orthodoxy or their liturgy or their traditionalism or their up-to-dateness or anything else about themselves as guaranteeing the blessing of God, they quench the Spirit, just as they do if they regard good organization, stockpiled skills, and overall ecclesiastical expertise, as evidences of that blessing. Here, too, is a sort of Pelagian self-sufficiency, which, now as then, has the effect of damping down concern about the Holy Spirit. Serious pneumatology is only ever sparked off by recognition of spiritual need, and there was little such recognition in those days.

By a combination of circumstances that the world would call chance and I call providence and divine mercy, I stumbled during my student days on what was then literally buried treasure, namely the classic teaching on the Holy Spirit given by Calvin, the English Puritans, and Jonathan Edwards. At that time all I was competent to say about it was that this was masterful wisdom that spoke profoundly and caused Scripture to speak profoundly to both my mind and my heart. Today I would maintain in any company that as Augustine was *the* theologian of grace and Luther *the* theologian of justification, both *par excellence,* so Calvin was and remains *the* theologian of the Holy Spirit in the postapostolic Christian church, with the Puritans and Edwards in close support. No one has ever surpassed these men; few have come near them. There are amazingly pregnant declarations in Calvin's *Institutions* of knowledge of God through the Word and Spirit; of the Spirit's common grace in scholars, artists, rulers, and all architects of culture; of union with Christ through the Spirit as the principle of personal salvation and churchly identity; and of the Christian's faith and fortitude, the preacher's fruitfulness, and the efficacy of the sacraments, as flowing from the Spirit's work within us. Reading them convinced me that to call Calvin *the* theologian of the Holy Spirit, as B. B. Warfield first taught me to do,[4] was *prima facie* just. Puritan contributions, such as John Owen's massive *Pneumatologia,* along with his separate treatises on life in the Spirit (*Indwelling Sin; Mortification of Sin; Temptation; Spiritual Mindedness; The Spirit As a Comforter; Communion with God; The Reason of Faith; Spiritual Gifts, The Work of the Spirit in Prayer*), seemed to me to stand in relation to Calvin as does a massively enlarged photograph to its small but beautifully focused original. Of this body of literature on the Holy Spirit, together with Edwards's *Distinguishing Marks of a Work of the Spirit of God, Religious Affections,* and *Reflections on the Revival,* I find myself still constrained to say what David said of Goliath's sword: "There is none like it; give it to me" (1 Sam. 21:9).

In addition to this, during my student years I came under influences that formed in my mind the Trinitarian vision of the church as family of God, body of Christ, and community of the Holy Spirit that I still hold, or rather that still holds me, at this present time. The vision is of the church, both universal and local, as supernatural, Christ-animated community in which every-heart adoration of the Father and the Son through the Spirit and every-member ministry to God and men through the same Spirit, are the divine rules. The church takes the visible forms that it does, both local and connectional, in order to express and channel the life that by grace it has; its structures are secondary because its Lord and its life are primary; its organization is to be shaped by its organic life as a communion of saints in and with Christ, not vice versa. By the Spirit, Christ rules each congregation through the Scriptures, refining, reviving, and reforming as he wills according to local need, confronting his people continually as they commune with him via Word and sacrament, empowering them to be salt and light to those outside, and giving them foretastes of heaven in their worship experience. The vision remains with me, and I continue to find myself restless in congregations that do not share it and are not consciously seeking fulfillment of it.

All of this was clear to me at least fifteen years before the charismatic movement began, and none of it, of course, was new; I had simply tapped into the tradition of thought stemming from Calvin in particular which, as I now know, had sustained men like George Whitefield, Charles Simeon, and J. C. Ryle in my own Anglican fold and, outside it, men like C. H. Spurgeon and Martyn Lloyd-Jones in Britain, Murray McCheyne in Scotland, Robert Haldane in Switzerland, Jonathan Goforth in China, and Andrew Murray in South Africa. But when I was a student there was not much knowledge of this heritage nor much interest in it anywhere in the world as far as I could see, and the literature of it was not readily available as it is now.[5]

Today, however, it is a different story. Perhaps one should say that the Holy Spirit himself has stepped in and taken a hand! The pendulum has swung, and in many quarters the Spirit of God is now the subject, not of cool neglect, but of almost obsessive concentration and certainly of passionate confusion. The work of such theologians as Leonard Hodgson; the later Barth; Eberhard Jungel; Jürgen Moltmann; Thomas Torrance; Robert Jenson; and, most recently, David Brown has brought back a thorough-going

Trinitarianism with full emphasis on the personal deity of the Holy Spirit and has done much to reestablish it as normative for thought.[6] Meantime, charismatic renewal has touched and challenged the whole Christian world, and Spirit-centered literature has emerged from this movement at different levels—academic, apologetic, homiletic—in large quantities.[7] We shall not be able to discuss in the present paper all the questions relating to the Spirit's work that the charismatic movement has thrown up for debate, but some of the more interesting and weighty ones may be listed at this point.

1. *In Spirituality* (the life of fellowship with God). Is Spirit baptism, in the sense of a felt enlargement in assurance, peace, and praise, sense of Christ's love and closeness, wholeheartedness of consecration, and uninhibitedness of Christian expression, divinely prescribed for all Christian people at some point following their first believing and/or their reception of water baptism? Is it proper to direct all Christians to seek such an experience? Can it be had for the asking? Is one inevitably a deficient Christian without it?[8]

What is Pentecostal-charismatic glossolalia? Does it always accompany Spirit baptism? Does it ever occur in persons who have not been Spirit baptized in the stated sense? In what ways is it spiritually beneficial? Is it always beneficial? Is it proper to encourage all Christians to seek glossolalic ability?[9]

What expectations should Christians have with regard to the healing of body and mind through the prayers of others? What constitutes a Christian's health in this world? Is supernatural, miraculous healing ever part of the will of God in these days? Is denial of requests for supernatural, miraculous healing ever part of the will of God in these days? Will God sanctify the enduring of pain and frustration through physical and mental disability? May possibilities of supernatural healing be forfeited through prayerless unbelief? In what terms should sick Christians be counseled?[10]

By what means and how specifically will God guide believers in their decision making? How does God guide from the Bible? Does he supplement biblical guidance by direct revelations through prophecies (understood as messages given for delivery to others) or through immediate disclosures to the decision-makers? Is it proper to direct all Christians to seek and expect such messages? Are there any other modes of communication whereby the Holy Spirit gives certainty that one option should be embraced rather than another?[11]

How is faith to be exercised in prayer? What may one "name and claim" in the presence of God? In what respects must the exercise of faith exclude doubt and uncertainty as to the outcome? In what respects is the exercise of faith compatible with doubt and uncertainty as to the outcome? Does God's giving in answer to our prayers ever depend on our being subjectively certain that we shall receive exactly what we ask for? Does divine action against evil depend at all on verbal and attitudinal techniques of "binding Satan" and "taking authority" as we pray? Does faith require us to thank God for evil things, telling ourselves they are good things because they come from God?[12]

2. *In Christology.* Is it proper to see Jesus as the archetypal Charismatic and to view his water baptism as the occasion of his Spirit baptism? Does this idea reduce the incarnation of the preexistent Son of God to a special case of God indwelling a man, as liberal christology does?[13]

3. *In Ecclesiology.* Are charismatic manifestations (tongues, prophecy, claimed miracles, claimed healings, claimed interpretation of tongues) a restoring or renewing of the "sign-gifts" that authenticated the apostles?

Since gifts for ministry are given to all Christians, what is the right place for women in the church's ministering structures?

Does God give revelations today that should have canonical status for the future?

What pastoral authority structures in and over charismatic communities are appropriate? How should the relation between these and local churches be understood and managed?

Are house churches (an increasingly common charismatic structure) in any sense schismatic?

How far should the confessional differences between Roman Catholicism and Protestantism be regarded as overcome, or transcended, through sharing charismatic experience?

As was said, we cannot discuss all these questions here (in any case, I have dealt with several of them elsewhere);[14] I list them simply to indicate the range of thought about the Spirit that over a generation the charismatic movement has opened up.

Nor is the charismatic movement the only focus of contemporary Christian thought about the Holy Spirit. A small but vigorous group of evangelical speakers and writers (J. Edwin Orr, D. Martyn Lloyd-Jones, Leonard Ravenhill, Richard Lovelace, et al.) have sought to promote an Edwardian concept of revival as the outpouring of the Spirit, viewing this as involving significantly more than is found in charismatic renewal.[15] The sense of the nearness of a holy God, the intense anxiety and humbling for sin, and the violent energy of repentance, leading to rapid, deep maturing in Christ, that have characterized earlier revival movements seem to have no counterpart in the current charismatic movement, which in consequence appears to Edwardians to be somewhat shallow. The relation between renewal and revival, both conceptually and experientially, thus becomes a talking point for them.[16]

In the world of ecumenical Protestantism it is often nowadays claimed that the Holy Spirit is currently prompting (1) involvement in various forms of revolutionary violence and (2) convergence and coalescence of the world's great ethnic religions. That these are two potent trends is true, but the suggestion that the Holy Spirit of God is behind them looks in the light of Scripture too ludicrous to merit detailed treatment in this paper.

Mention of Scripture introduces the next question. What will an evangelical inerrantist bring to the discussion of the renewal-revival theme? Three things, I suggest.

First, he will bring *support for the robust supernaturalism* of these two viewpoints. The mark of an inerrantist in theology is his intense concern that everything taught in Scripture be treated with full seriousness; this is the other side of his refusal to allow that anything taught in Scripture might need to be discounted as erroneous. He knows that the effect of such discounting, when it occurs, is regularly to erode aspects of biblical supernaturalism, reducing the Trinity to some sort of Unitarianism; or the Incarnation to a case of God indwelling a man; or the penal, substitutionary sacrifice of Christ to an example of faithfulness till death; or Jesus' bodily resurrection to the continuing impact of his personality; or Jesus' miracles to honorific myths; or the Second Coming to a hope that God will triumph in the end; or the personal Holy Spirit to a pervasive uplifting influence; or the imparting of a new life by regeneration to the turning over of a new leaf by repentance; or the church from an awesome divine creation to a venerable human club. As, like a tracking dog, he sniffs out half-truths and untruths in theology, barking at them incessantly and trying to bite them to pieces lest they ruin souls, so he applauds movements of Christian thought that restore biblical supernaturalism to its rightful place, and this the viewpoints under discussion clearly do.

Second, the inerrantist will also bring *watchfulness against supersupernaturalism and subjectivism* among charismatic people. The charismatic desire, very proper in itself to maximize awareness of the supernatural in daily life, starts to go over the edge into what I call "supersupernaturalism" when the ordinary is depreciated as a field of divine action, and God is looked to to act habitually against the nature of things, producing fairy-tale miracles, cures, manifestations, and providences: The charismatic belief in revelatory prophecy constantly exposes the movement to the danger of following in good faith someone's subjective impressions which cannot in fact be from God because they run contrary to Scripture. Seeing these possibilities as occupational hazards of the charismatic movement, the inerrantist will think of himself as required when he relates to the charismatic constituency to keep a sharp lookout for them and to blow the whistle the moment he spots them.

Third, the inerrantist will in addition bring *a concept of divine communication that correlates the Spirit and the Word*. He will affirm the *coherence* of the sixty-six books of Scripture against any form of the fashionable idea that the substance of one Bible writer's teaching is inconsistent with the substance of another's (a contention, be it said, that is often declared but has never yet been demonstrated); he will affirm their God-given *sufficiency* as a guide for faith and life and a judge of any proposed supplementary guide, like *Science and Health*, or *The Book of Mormon;* and he will affirm their *clarity*, in the sense that everything essential to salvation is stated in them so fully, in so many mutually illuminating ways, that every serious reader will see it, without any need of a supposedly infallible church to interpret it to him. With this he will affirm the ministry of the Holy Spirit, the divine author of the books, who authenticates them to us as the Word of God; interprets them to us so that we see what they mean and know that the divine realities spoken of truly exist; applies to us the principles of believing and living that the Scriptures teach and illustrate; and animates us to respond to what we know in faith, worship, and obedience. He will underline again and again the incapacity of the fallen human mind to think rightly of God apart from the guidance of Scripture, and he will constantly emphasize that it is only as one who is himself the beneficiary of the Spirit's illuminating and interpreting ministry that he has any knowledge of divine things to share with others. Anything that looks to him like reliance on self-generated human speculation (going beyond Scripture) or supposed private revelation (going against Scripture) or uncriticized church tradition (overlaying and obscuring Scripture) will earn his special hostility.

When Willem Mengelberg told Arturo Toscanini that he got his way of playing Beethoven's overture *Coriolan* from the true German tradition, going back to Beethoven himself, Toscanini replied that his way of playing it came to him from Beethoven directly—through the score! ("You play it your way, and I'll play it Beethoven's way.") Toscanini would have been similarly scathing with anyone who added bars and notes to, or subtracted them from, what Beethoven had written, and for the same reason: disrespect for the composer was to Toscanini the supreme musical sin. So, too, the inerrantist, led by the Spirit himself to regard Holy Scripture as God's score for human faith and life, will insist that what is written must have full and decisive authority over everything else.

What overall view of the Holy Spirit's person and work will inerrantists deploy in their treatment of the renewal-revival theme? I now give some space to setting out one inerrantist's answer to that question.[17]

First, we glance at the Old Testament, for the New Testament builds on the Old, proclaiming the fulfillment in Christ of its principles, prophecies, types and hopes, using it as what the late Allan Stibbs called "a divine dictionary and phrase-book" for articulating the truth of Christ, and claiming it as Christian Scripture—Scripture, that is, written to instruct Christians in the knowledge and service of God and yielding up its deepest meaning only to them (Rom. 15:4; 1 Cor. 10:11; 2 Cor. 3:14–18; 2 Tim. 3:15–17; 1 Peter 1:10–12; 2 Peter 1:19–21; 3:16; cf. Heb. 10:15). To generalize, there are just under a hundred explicit references in the Old Testament to the Spirit of God. "Spirit" each time is *ruach*, a word also denoting "breath" and "wind" and signifying power let loose, or energy in exercise. Always the reference is to God himself, present and at work. Though the distinct personhood of the Spirit can and, according to the New Testament, should be read into the Old Testament, it cannot be read out of it. The eternal fact of God's triunity was not known to or expressed by the Old Testament writers. In the course of the hundred references, the Spirit of God is said to:

1. Mold *creation* into shape and animate created beings (Gen. 1:2; cf. 2:7; Ps. 33:6; Job 26:13; 33:4).

2. Control the course of *nature* and *history* (Ps. 104:29–30; Isa. 34:16; 40:7).

3. Reveal *God's truth and will* to his messengers by both direct communication and/or distilled insight (Num. 24:2; 2 Sam. 23:2; 2 Chron. 12:18; 15:1; Neh. 9:30; Job 32:8; Isa 61:1–4; Ezek. 2:2; 11:24; 37:1; Mic. 3:8; Zech. 7:12).

4. Teach God's people through these revelations *the way of faithfulness and fruitfulness* (Neh. 9:20; Ps. 143:10; Isa. 48:16; 63:10–14).

5. *Elicit personal response to God* in the form of faith, repentance, obedience, righteousness, openness to God's instruction, and fellowship with him through praise and prayer (Ps. 51:10–12; Isa. 11:2; 44:3; Ezek. 11:19; 36:25–27; 37:14; 39:29; Joel 2:28–29; Zech. 12:10).

6. Equip individuals for *leadership* (Gen. 41:38 [Joseph]; Num. 11:17 [Moses]; 11:16–29 [seventy elders]; 27:18, Deut. 34:9 [Joshua]; Judg. 3:10 [Othniel]; 6:34 [Gideon]; 11:29 [Jephthah]; 13:25, 14:19, 15:14 [Samson]; 1 Sam. 10:10, 11:6, cf. 19:20–23 [Saul]; 16:13 [David]; 2 Kings 2:9–15 [Elijah and Elisha]; Isa. 11:1–5, 42:1–4 [the Messiah]).

7. Equip individuals with *skill and strength* for creative work (Exod. 31:1–11 [Bezalel and Oholiab]; cf. 1 Kings 7:14 [Hiram]; Hag. 2:5, Zech. 4:6 [temple builders]).

In short, the Spirit of God in the Old Testament is God active as creator, controller, revealer, and enabler, making himself present to men in order that he and they might deal with each other (Ps. 139:7). But there is no clear suggestion as yet of a plurality of persons within the unity of God.

In the New Testament, however, the case is altered. All that the Old Testament says of God's Spirit is evidently taken for granted, and the Holy Spirit sent at Pentecost is identified explicitly with the Old Testament Spirit of God (Acts 2:16–21; 4:25; 28:25; Heb. 3:7–11; 10:15; 1 Peter 1:11; 2 Peter 1:19–21); but the divine Spirit is now unambiguously spoken of as a distinct person acting in defined relation to two other distinct persons, God the Father and Jesus Christ the Son. The Spirit's personhood appears from the verbs of personal action—hear, speak, witness, convince, show, lead, guide, teach, command, forbid, desire, give speech, help, intercede with groans—that are used to tell us what he does (John 14:26; 15:26; 16:7–15; Acts 2:4; 8:29; 13:2; 16:6–7; 21:11; Rom. 8:14, 16, 26, 27; Gal. 4:6; 5:17–18; Heb. 3:7; 10:15; 1 Peter 1:11; Rev. 2:7, 11, 17, 19, et al.). It appears also from the fact that he can be lied to and grieved (Acts 5:3; Eph. 4:30; cf. Isa. 63:10). It appears with supreme clarity when Jesus in John's Gospel introduces him as "the Paraclete" (14:16, 25; 15:26; 16:7); for this rich word, which means by turns counselor, helper, strengthener, supporter, adviser, advocate, ally, signifies a role which only a personal agent could fulfill. Jesus confirms this by calling the Spirit "another" Paraclete, second in line to himself and continuing his ministry after his departure (14:16); that is a way of informing us that the Spirit is as truly a person as he is himself. This point John clinches by using the masculine pronoun (*ekeinos*, "he") to render Jesus' references to the Spirit, when Greek grammar required the neuter *ekeino* ("it"), to agree with the neuter noun *pneuma* ("Spirit," the Greek equivalent of *ruach*). This masculine pronoun, which appears in 14:26; 15:26; 16:8, 13–14, is the more striking because in 14:17, where the Spirit is first introduced, John had used the grammatically correct neuter pronouns (*ho* and *auto*), thus ensuring that his subsequent shift to the masculine would be perceived not as incompetent Galilean Greek but as magisterial apostolic theology.

To understand what is said about the Spirit and the Son tritheistically, however, would be a Mormon mistake. No apostolic writer thinks of the Father, Son, and Spirit tritheistically. In the New Testament the distinct personhood of the Spirit, along with that of the Son, is only ever thought or spoken of as part of the revealed reality of the one God of Israel in action. Decisive for this way of thinking was the recognition of the risen, ascended, and enthroned Jesus as a person to be worshiped and prayed to alongside, yet in distinction from, the one whom he called Father, so that it was right to say to Jesus what Thomas said to him—"My Lord and my God!" (John 20:28)—just as it was and is right to address those words to the Father. And from this recognition of

Jesus' divinity the apostolic writers go on to link the Holy Spirit with him in what is effectively a parity relationship, one that combined solidarity in redemptive action with coequal divine dignity. This is in direct line with Jesus' declaration that in the Holy Spirit's post-Pentecostal ministry as, specifically, the Spirit of Christ, he would be the Second Paraclete, replacing Jesus permanently in order to mediate to Christians constantly the presence—not physical, but yet real and beneficent—of both the Son and the Father (John 14:16–23). Many New Testament passages speak of the Son and the Spirit side by side, correlating and coordinating them in a way that is clearly deliberate: see, for instance, Acts 9:31 (divine communion); Romans 8:9–11 (divine indwelling); 8:27, 34 (divine intercession); 15:30 (Christian motivation; cf. Phil. 2:1); 1 Corinthians 6:11 (justification); Hebrews 10:29 (apostasy); Revelation 2:1 and 7, 8 and 11; et al. (divine revelation). More striking still are the triadic passages linking Father, Son, and Spirit as collaborators in a single plan of grace: see John 14:16–16:15; Romans 8; 1 Corinthians 12:4–6; 2 Corinthians 13:14; Ephesians 1:3–13; 2:18; 3:14–19; 4:4–6; 2 Thessalonians 2:13–14; 1 Peter 1:2. These testimonies show that as in terms of role the Spirit acts as agent—colleague, we might say—of the Father and the Son, so in terms of deity he is on a par with them, and in our doxology he should be honored with them and praised alongside them.

Nor is this all. Though the Spirit is nowhere explicitly called God, the New Testament writers intimate his deity in ways clearer than any yet mentioned. Thus, "holy," like "Lord," is an Old Testament designation of God, "the Holy One"; and as the New Testament writers use "Lord" of Jesus over and over, so they call the Spirit "holy" no less than eighty-nine times. Again, "glory" in the Old Testament means deity in manifestation, Yahweh being "the God of glory" (Ps. 29:3); in the New Testament, as the Father is "the Father of glory" (Eph. 1:17) and Jesus is "the Lord of glory" (1 Cor. 2:8; James 2:1), so the Spirit is "the Spirit of glory" (1 Peter 4:14). Similarly, as the Father and the Son give "life" (a relationship of conscious response to God's grace in love, peace, and joy—spiritual *joie de vivre!*), so the Spirit gives "life" (see John 5:21, 26; 6:32–33, 63; Rom. 8:2; 2 Cor. 3:6). Ontologically and functionally, all three persons are thus identified with Yahweh in the Old Testament, the Spirit as directly as the two others.

And there is more. Lying to the Holy Spirit is diagnosed as lying "not . . . to men *but* to God" (Acts 5:3–4). Also, Jesus declares that the name of God, into which his disciples are to be baptized, is a tripersonal name: "the name of the Father and of the Son and of the Holy Spirit" (Matt. 28:19). "The name" means the designated party; "name" is singular here, for there is only one God; but God's "name"—his "Christian name," as Barth sweetly called it—is tripersonal. Again, John starts his letters to the churches by wishing them grace and peace "from him who is, and who was, and who is to come, and from the seven spirits before his throne, and from Jesus Christ" (Rev. 1:4–5). The "seven spirits" according to the number symbolism of the book signify the Holy Spirit in the perfection of his power (the NIV margin, exegeting rather than translating, actually says "the sevenfold Spirit"), and when the Spirit is set between the Father and the Son as the second of the three personal sources of divine blessing, no room remains for doubt as to his coequal deity.

Whether one finds a doctrine of the Trinity in the New Testament depends on what one means by "doctrine." As Arthur Wainwright says: "In so far as a doctrine is an answer, however fragmentary, to a problem, there is a doctrine of the Trinity in the New Testament. In so far as it is a formal statement of a position, there is no doctrine of the Trinity in the New Testament."[18] But if it is proper to give the name of "doctrine" to a position that is explicit and defined, it cannot be improper to give the same name to that which is basic and presuppositional to, and in that sense implicit in, positions that are explicit and defined; and since the Trinitarian way of thinking about God is in fact basic and presuppositional to all the New Testament's explicit soteriology, being the answer to the problem about the unity of God which the fact of Christ, the event of Pentecost, and the shape of subsequent Christian experience, had raised, it is far more accurate, profound, and enlightening to affirm that the New Testament writers teach the doctrine of the Trinity than to do as is fashionable today and deny it. Though innocent of later Trinitarian formulations, these writers do in fact think of God in the tripersonal way that the later formulations were devised to safeguard and reject other conceptions as anti-Christian (cf. 1 Tim. 3:16–4:5; 2 Tim. 3:1–9; 2 Peter 2:1; 1 John 2:18–27; 4:1–6). The true path is to affirm this and thereby negate all forms, old and new, of the idea that the Spirit is a creature of or a function of or a title for a unipersonal God. No version of this Unitarian idea can express what the New Testament writers mean when they speak of the Spirit—or of Christ and the Father, for that matter—so we shall say no more about it.

The statement that post-Pentecostal Christian experience raised a problem about the unity of God no doubt requires explanation. The problem was posed by the fact that that experience, the experience of being "in the Spirit" and "in the Lord," involved awareness of a dual relationship, to God as Father and to Jesus as Savior and Master, which relationship was seen as dependent on the personally indwelling Holy Spirit (Rom. 8:9). Thus, as James D. G. Dunn puts it: "Christians become aware that they stood at the base of *a triangular relationship*—in the Spirit, in sonship to the Father, in service to the Lord."[19] This awareness prompted the question whether God is tripersonal in himself. While knowledge of the triangular relationship would not have come without some instruction (and the gospel shows clearly who the first instructor was), it is hard to doubt that experience within the relationship shaped some of the New Testament expositions of it, Paul's in particular, and so became a means of establishing the way of thinking about God that underlies it.

Here it is appropriate to characterize the New Testament sense of God with some exactness. It is uniformly Trinitarian; more particularly, it is Christ-centered and Spirit-generated to the core. It is true to say that the Christian awareness is of God above, beside, and within, but for the New Testament that is not true enough; we need to be more precise. The authentic Christian awareness of God, as the New Testament writers exhibit it, is:

(1) a sense that God in heaven, this world's maker and judge, is our Father, who sent his Son to redeem us; who adopted us into his family; who loves us, watches over us, listens to us, cares for us, showers gifts upon us; who preserves us for the inheritance of glory that he keeps in store for us; and to whom we have access through Christ, by the Spirit (Matt. 6:1–18, 24–33; Luke 11:1–13; John 14:21; 16:27; 20:17; Rom. 8:15–17; Gal. 4:4–7; Eph. 2:18);

(2) a sense that Jesus Christ, who is now personally in heaven, nonetheless makes himself present to us by the Spirit to stand by us, to love, lead, assure, quicken, uphold, and encourage us, and to use us in his work as in weakness we trust him (Matt. 28:20; John 15:1–8; Rom. 15:18; 1 Cor. 6:17; 15:45; 2 Cor. 12:9; Eph. 3:14–19; 2 Tim. 4:17);

(3) a sense that the Holy Spirit indwells us (a) to sustain in us what nowadays is called a personal and existential understanding of gospel truth (1 Cor. 2:14–16; 12:3; 1 John 2:20–27; 5:7–8, 20); (b) to maintain in consciousness our fellowship with the Father and the Son, and to assure us that this love relationship is permanent and that glorification lies at the end of it (John 14:18–23; Rom. 8:14–25; Gal. 4:4–7; 1 John 1:3; 3:1–2, 24); (c) to reshape us in ethical correspondence to Christ (2 Cor. 3:18; Gal. 5:22–24; Eph. 5:1–2) as he induces us to accept suffering with Christ, which is the road to final glory (Rom. 8:12–17; 2 Cor. 1:5; 4:7–5:5; Phil. 3:7–10, 20–21); (d) to equip us with abilities for loving personal worship of God in praise and prayer (John 4:23–24; 1 Cor. 13:1; 14:2, 26–32; Eph. 6:18; Phil. 3:1; Jude 20) and loving personal ministry to others, expressing Christ to them (Rom. 12:4–21; 1 Cor. 12:4–13; 1 Peter 4:10–11); (e) to engender realization of our present moral weakness and inadequacy of achievement (Rom. 7:14–25; 8:22–27; Gal. 5:16–17), and to make us long for the future life of bodily resurrection and renewal, the life of which the Spirit's present ministry to us is the first fruits (Rom. 8:23) and the initial installment, guaranteeing the rest (2 Cor. 1:22; 5:5; Eph. 1:14).

This structured tripersonal sense of God is literally constitutive of New Testament Christianity, and the awareness that "the Spirit of your Father" (Matt. 10:20) in his role as "the Spirit of truth" (John 14:17, where the Greek construction is a hendiadys), the Spirit of wisdom (Acts 6:3, 10), "the Spirit of Jesus" (16:7), "the Spirit of life" (Rom. 8:2), "the Spirit of Christ" (v. 9), "the Spirit of adoption" (v. 15 KJV), "the Spirit of [God's] Son" (Gal. 4:6), and "the Spirit of grace" (Heb. 10:29), is now given to abide with all Christians is the central constituent of this sense of God. Interpreting Paul, Dunn has written:

> The risen Jesus may not be experienced independently of the Spirit, and any religious experience which is not character and effect and experience of Jesus Paul would not regard as a manifestation of the life-giving Spirit. . . . At the same time the identification of Spirit and risen Jesus in experience means that Paul can clearly mark out the limits of charismatic experience; only that experience which embodies the character of Christ is experience of Spirit. If Christ is now experienced as Spirit, Spirit is now experienced as Christ . . . the distinctive mark of the Christian is experience of the Spirit as the life of Christ.[20]

Dunn goes on to claim that on at least twenty-one occasions the phrase "in Christ" denotes religious experience (or a particular religious experience) as experience of Christ—deriving from Christ as to both its source and character, so that it "expresses . . . a consciousness of Christ."[21] In a word, the New Testament is witness that as believers know God in and through Jesus Christ, so they know Jesus Christ in and through the Holy Spirit. This makes Christian experience—that is, the Christian's affective awareness of the divine—radically and categorically different from its Jewish and Gentile counterparts.

It seems clear that the apostles' convictions and formulations concerning the Spirit are the product—the intellectual precipitate, we might say—of living in the Spirit and directly experiencing Christ in the manner described, though passion for abstract orthodoxy has sometimes betrayed Evangelicals into overlooking the fact. That the apostles' convictions are divinely revealed truths, and as such are matters of doctrine and norms of faith, is a fixed point for the present writer, as it is for all Evangelicals. But that does not necessarily mean that they popped into apostolic minds ready-made. It is more natural to suppose that they crystallized out of the experiential-ethical transformation that those who received the Spirit, the apostles among them, underwent. The insights of the New Testament writers concerning the Spirit took their rise, no doubt, from the words of Jesus but were distilled into their mature form via experiential response to experienced deity. The idea that because apostolic teaching is revealed truth it must have come to the apostles by some means other than noting, describing, and reflecting on their own experience of God appears groundless. The apostles' evident view is that experience of the Spirit comes spontaneously and directly but reveals its authenticity by creating an immediate awareness of the presence of the Christ of the gospel in love and power and by evoking a heartfelt response of confession, celebration, repentance, obedience, and praise. Those who share this experience, so they assume, will know that they have received the Spirit (cf. Acts 2:13–21; Rom. 8:23, 26–27; Gal. 3:2; Eph. 1:14; 1 John 3:24; 4:13; Rev. 1:10). The apostles recognized that some claims to be experiencing the life of the Spirit had to be challenged, for major error concerning Christ's person, place, authority, and law would show those claims to be false (see 1 Cor. 12:3; 14:37–38; 1 John 3:24–4:13), and what looked like such error was sometimes found among the supposedly Spirit-led. But the essential "unambiguity" (Alasdair Heron's word) of the Spirit's action in Christ's professed disciples is taken for granted throughout the New Testament. The apostles do not think it difficult to judge when the Spirit is at work, nor do they doubt their own participation in the Spirit's ministry. So there is no reason to doubt and every reason to suppose that their theology of the Spirit reached its mature form in and through this participation rather than being given in revelatory experiences distinct from it.

Against this background of shared conviction and experience we shall now review what is special in each of the various strands of apostolic witness to the Spirit and his work.

We start with the Gospels. Written, as P. T. Forsyth somewhere points out, for readers who had already embraced the theology of the Epistles, these are four selective accounts of Jesus' words and deeds in his public ministry, each climaxing in the Crucifixion and Resurrection, and each comprising in its totality a proclamation of the gospel (the good news about Jesus) from one particular angle. Each evangelist is an artist, writing with thought and skill in order to get his planned effect. Mark, who may have been the inventor of this new literary form, presents Jesus as the authoritative, wonder-working, disciple-gathering Son of God who became the Suffering Servant of Isaiah's prophecy. Matthew expands Mark's outline (so, at least, I think) to depict Jesus in addition as the Davidic king who is also the new Moses, reformulating God's law for the new age of the kingdom. Both evangelists leave their readers facing the fact that Jesus is now risen, alive, sovereign, and at large, Mark ending his story (so, again, I think) with the emptiness of Jesus' tomb (Mark 16:8) and Matthew ending his with the Great Commission (Matt. 28:18–20). Neither highlights the Holy Spirit; their few references to him make just two simple points.

The first point is that the Spirit was upon Jesus throughout: as a divine source of his conception and birth (Matt. 1:18–21), as the divine anointing at his baptism (Matt. 3:16; Mark 1:10), as the divine guide who led him to his temptation (Matt. 4:1; Mark 1:12), and as the divine agent of his exorcisms, which, therefore, it was blasphemous and ruinous to ascribe to Satan (Matt. 12:18, 24–32; Mark 3:22–30).

The second point is that Jesus will baptize with the Holy Spirit ("and with fire," Matthew adds) for the purging and transforming of human lives (Matt. 3:11–12; Mark 1:8). How this will happen, and what the results in experience will be, we are not told. (No doubt John himself did not know and so could not say.) Jesus later specifies one consequence: his disciples would be supplied with things to say when under pressure (Matt. 10:20; Mark 13:11). This foreshadows the realized *parrhasia* (boldness) of Acts.

The indication that the enabling Spirit with which Jesus is to baptize his followers is the same enabling Spirit with which the Father first anointed him is confirmed by the rest of the New Testament (see John 1:32–33; Acts 2:33; 10:38 with 44–48; 11:15–17; Gal. 4:4–6).

Luke's Gospel is another version of Mark's, expanded differently than Matthew's. It is the first volume of a two-part work which Michael Ramsey well describes as "the drama of the Holy Spirit." He states its plot thus:

> In the story of the conception and birth of the Messiah the work of the Holy Spirit is presented as the creation of a new era in history. . . . Filled with Holy Spirit, the Messiah teaches and heals with authority and power. . . . On the day of Pentecost the exalted Jesus pours Holy Spirit upon the Church, and the subsequent story sees the Church working in the power of the Spirit at every stage of the progress of the gospel from Jerusalem to Rome."[22]

Writing as a historian, modeling his vocabulary and style on the historical literature of both secular and Septuagintal Greek, Luke offers factual descriptions rather than theological analyses, but his interest in the Holy Spirit's ministry and his sense of its significance are plain to see.

Luke's interest in the Spirit, like that of Matthew and Mark insofar as any interest at all can be read out of what they write, is historical and eschatological rather than subjective and charismatic—it focuses, that is, on the coming of the kingdom of God rather than on the supernaturalizing of individual experience. Norms for experience are no part of Luke's concern, a fact to be remembered when we study the variety of Pentecostal happenings that he records (2:1–13; 8:14–17; 10:44–48; 19:1–6). But Luke's interest in the Spirit as leader and Lord of the church's mission is strong; indeed, the Spirit is the chief agent throughout his volume two, which might well have been called "Acts of the Holy Spirit" rather than, as in the traditional Greek title, "Acts of the Holy Apostles." So we find that Luke highlights the renewal of prophecy through the Spirit (Luke 1:15–17, 41–42, 67; 2:25–28, 36–38; Acts 2:18; 11:27–28; 13:1; 21:4, 10–11); that he speaks constantly of individuals, from John and Jesus on, as "filled with the Spirit" for faithful and fruitful service (Luke 1:15, 41, 67; 4:1, 14; Acts 2:4; 4:8, 31; 6:3, 10; 7:55; 9:17; 11:24; 13:9; et al.); and that he makes much of the Spirit as a divine gift (Luke 11:13; Acts 2:38; 5:32; 11:17) for encouragement (8:31), joy (Luke 10:21; Acts 13:52), guidance and decision-making (15:28; 16:6–10), and ability to witness to Christ with clarity and boldness (4:31). His point in all this plainly is that the Holy Spirit is the supreme resource for the church's life and mission. Only as the Spirit is poured out will there be convincing speech and convinced hearts; only so will there be power, advance, and fruit; and only through power are such outpourings effectively sought (Luke 3:21; Acts 1:14; 4:24–31).

John's Gospel, with which we may bracket his letters, has personal communion with God, for which the Johannine name is "eternal life," or "life" simply (John 17:3), as a main concern. Hence John's interest in the Spirit who rested on the incarnate Son (1:32–33; 3:34) centers on the fact that following Jesus' departure (death, resurrection, ascension) the Father and the Son would send him to the disciples to be the Second Paraclete (counselor, helper, advocate, adviser, ally, supporter, encourager, as was said earlier) in Jesus' place. His ministry as paraclete would take the form of making Jesus, and with and through him the Father, consciously present to the disciples (14:16–24), and also of making the full truth about Jesus clear to them, partly by causing them to remember and understand what he had said while he was with them, partly by additional revelation (16:13; 14:26). Thus "He will glorify me; for he will take what is mine and declare it to you" (16:14)—and the disciples will find that it was to their advantage that Jesus left them, by reason of the richness of this new relational experience (16:7). The Spirit's paraclete ministry would have an evangelistic significance, too, for he would convince the world of the truth about Jesus. In 16:8–11 Jesus speaks of this ministry in relation to Jewish unbelief in the first instance and promises that the Spirit will convince of sin, righteousness, and judgment. In 1 John 2:20–27; 4:1–6; and 5:6–10a, the apostle looks to the Spirit to attest the truth of the Incarnation against gnostic docetism, with its consequent denial of sacrificial atonement and propitiation by blood. In both cases, the Spirit acts as the Spirit of truth, vindicating the reality of the incarnate Son as our mediator, sin-bearer, and source of life against all forms of

misbelief and denial. This is his work as *witness* (John 15:26;
1 John 5:7–8).

Correlative to the Spirit's bestowal of revelation and understanding is his inward work of drawing us to Christ in faith and
keeping us in knowledge and worship of God (John 4:23–24; 17:3).
It is in this sense that the Spirit "gives life" (6:63). The life belongs
to those who see and enter the kingdom of God by putting faith in
Jesus (3:14–18), and the seeing and entering occur only through
being born again "of water and the Spirit" (3:3–7). The fact that
Jesus censures Nicodemus, "a teacher of Israel" and therefore,
presumably a biblical expert, for not knowing how new birth
could take place (3:10) indicates the interpretation: new birth is a
two-word parable of the totally new start that the prophesied
cleansing and renewing of the heart by the Spirit according to
Ezekiel 37:25–27 will effect (cf. also Ps. 51:10–12). In 1 John the
parable has become a theological doctrine in its own right: birth
from God, which makes us his children, produces true belief in
Christ, righteousness of life, and a loving disposition, and makes
habitual sin a thing of the past, since sinning is now contrary to
our renewed moral nature (2:29–3:10; 4:7; 5:1, 4, 18). Though the
epistle does not explicitly link birth from God and being "of God"
(4:6; 3 John 11) with the Spirit's inward work, clearly it is the new
birth of Jesus' speech to Nicodemus, whereby one is "born of the
Spirit" (John 3:6), that is being talked about.

The Spirit as witness to Christ, maintaining the believer's
communion with him so that "rivers of living water" (the life-
giving, health-giving influences of a transformed life) flow from
him (John 7:37–39; cf. Ezek. 47:1–12), "was not yet [Gk.] . . .
because Jesus was not yet glorified" during his earthly ministry.
Not until he had been glorified on the cross (13:31–32) and by
return to the Father's side (17:2–5) would the Spirit in his
paraclete role begin work. This had to be so, in the nature of the
case; the Spirit could not glorify Christ to the disciples by showing
them Christ's glory until Christ had entered into that glory so that
it became a reality to be shown (16:14). After the Resurrection,
Jesus breathes on the disciples and says, "Receive the Holy Spirit"
(20:22); but since at that moment Jesus had not yet ascended
(20:17) to be glorified in the full Johannine sense, it is better to
treat this as an acted promise of what would very soon happen (at
Pentecost, about which it cannot be thought that John's intended
readers were ignorant, any more than John was himself) than to
suppose that John means us to gather that the Pentecostal Spirit,
the Spirit as paraclete, was actually bestowed in that moment by
Jesus' action.

Finally, we look at Paul. As he is the widest-ranging, tautest-
reasoning, deepest-analyzing theologian in the New Testament,
so his account of the Holy Spirit is in many ways the richest, and if

we were to attempt to draw out all the implications of the great Holy Spirit statements and episodes in his letters (Rom. 7–8; 14:17; 15:7–21; 1 Cor. 2; 3:16–17; 6:9–20, 12–14; 2 Cor. 3; Gal. 3:14; 4:6, 21–6:10; Eph. 1:13–20; 2:18–22; 3:14–19; 4:1–16, 30; 5:15–33; 6:10–20; 1 Thess. 1:2–10; 5:16–20; 2 Tim. 1:6–14; Titus 3:3–7), we should be composing a book rather than concluding a paper. The outlines of Paul's thought about the Spirit, however, as distinct from its wealth and depth, can be stated in a brief and simple way.

Salvation through Christ—Christ crucified, risen, enthroned, reigning, and coming again; Christ known, loved, and adored as our path and our prize, our deliverer and our destiny—is Paul's constant theme. Salvation is the life of the new and eternal order, the life of heaven begun for us on earth through the coming of Christ and his Spirit. As Heron puts it:

> Paul regularly speaks of two realms of reality, two modes of existence. The contrast is formulated in many ways—light and darkness, faith and works, life and death, righteousness and sin, sonship and slavery, divine foolishness and human wisdom, Isaac and Ishmael, Jerusalem above and Jerusalem below, Second and First Adam, the new age and the old. All these antitheses pivot upon Jesus Christ himself. . . . in him the new age has broken in and our present life is set in the tension between it and the old. But the old is doomed, standing under the judgment of the cross, while our sharing in the new is the promise of salvation through him.[23]

As "flesh" in Paul is always some aspect of life under the old order, so "spirit"—always when used of God's Spirit and almost always when used of the human spirit, the self to which the divine Spirit ministers—points to the life of the new order. When Paul speaks of the God-sent Holy Spirit, his perspective is always eschatological, looking forward to the end of which our present experience of redemption and life in the Spirit is the beginning. The Spirit is the gift of the new age, the guarantee and foretaste pledge and first installment (*arrhabon, aparche*) of what is to come when the fullness of salvation is revealed at Christ's return (Rom. 8:23; Eph. 1:13–14).

Within this broad perspective Paul has two focal centers of interest: the individual Christian and the church, the Israel of God which is the body of Christ. In relation to the individual Christian, the Spirit's ministry is fourfold. He *enlightens*, giving understanding of the gospel so that the "spiritual" man has "the mind of Christ" (1 Cor. 2:14–16; 2 Cor. 3:14–17). He *indwells* as the seal and guarantee that henceforth the Christian belongs to God (Rom. 8:9–11; 1 Cor. 3:16–17; 6:19). He *transforms*, producing in us the ethical fruit of Christlikeness (2 Cor. 3:18; Gal. 5:22–24): love, joy, peace, patience, kindness, goodness, faithfulness, gentleness, self-control, plus (we may add, from Rom. 8:26–27; 15:13) prayerfulness and hope. And he *assures*, witnessing to our adoption by God, our eternal acceptance, and our future inheritance (Rom. 8:15–25, 31–39, which is a transcript of the Spirit's witness; Gal. 4:6).

"So the Christians are called to holiness and to sonship," writes Michael Ramsey.

> They do not, however, find sin once for all overcome, for their life is one of conflict and growth. In this conflict and growth the Spirit is their guide, and the apostle often exhorts them to yield to His promptings and to let Him complete what He has begun in them. They must be led by the Spirit, let the Spirit rule in their hearts, not quench the Spirit, not grieve the Spirit, and endeavor to guard the unity of the Spirit in the bond of peace. The conflict is variously described. It is a conflict with sin *flesh and spirit*. . . . Here is the issue. "To live according to the flesh" is to live by the world's standards, by the lower impulses (it would be clearer without the "lower") "of unredeemed human nature, as if Christ had not died and risen again and bestowed His Spirit and as if we were not living within the new order. But "to live according to the Spirit" is to live with the awareness of the new order into which we, as Christians, have been brought.[24]

Excellently said! Would that all bishops and archbishops were such good biblical theologians.

In short, as the Christian's whole life is life in Christ in terms of its meaning, center, and direction, so the Christian's whole life is life in the Spirit from the standpoint of his knowledge, disposition, and ability to love and serve. Putting off the old man and putting on the new man, which God renews (Eph. 4:20–24; Col. 3:9–10), and being new created in Christ (2 Cor. 5:17) corresponds in Paul to new birth in John, and though Paul nowhere says this explicitly, it is plain that the initial inward renewal is the Spirit's work, as is the living that expresses it. All that we ever contribute to our own Christian lives, according to Paul, is folly, inability, and need. Everything that is good, right, positive, and valuable, comes from Christ through the Spirit.

As for the church, Paul's basic idea that the community of believers, both universal and local (the latter being an outcrop and microcosm of the former) are the body of Christ (1 Cor. 12:12–31; Eph. 4:1–16) is evidently an extension of his thought that every believer is covenantally, vitally, and experientially "in Christ." That thought is extended into this metaphor in order to make the two points that Paul does make by his use of it. The first is that unity must be acknowledged and expressed by love and mutual care within the diversity of Christian individuals (1 Cor. 12:14–26; cf. Phil. 2:1–4). The second is that the diversity of *charismata*-

*diakoniai-energemata* (gifts-ministries-operations: 1 Cor. 12:4–6) in which the Spirit is manifested (v. 7) must be acknowledged and put to full use within the unity of the fellowship (vv. 4–11). To be a manifestation of the Spirit, a gift would have to be an expression of Christ in some form, and this seems to be precisely Paul's idea: a gift is an ability to express Christ by following the instincts of one's renewed nature in acts of worship and service. By this criterion gifts are to be distinguished from other sorts of performance. The Spirit creates and sustains the unity of the body (Eph. 4:3), gives the gifts, and builds up the church through their exercise (1 Cor. 14:3–4, 26; Eph. 2:22; cf. 4:16). When gifts are used, it is Christ ministering to his body through his body. The gifts themselves are diverse, some relating to speech, others to practical Samaritanship, and there is no reason to regard any of Paul's lists as exhaustive (see Rom. 12:4–13; 1 Cor. 12:8–11, 28–30; cf. Eph. 4:11, where the "gifts" are gifted functionaries; and 2 Tim. 1:6–14, where Timothy is reminded that he is a specially anointed functionary). The references to love in each gifts context (Rom. 12:9–10; 1 Cor. 13; Eph. 4:16) remind us that, whether or not love be classified as a gift of the Spirit or as a fruit of the Spirit or as both, abilities to serve cannot be exercised in a way that will edify the church and please God without it. Using four of Paul's key words, we may say that the pattern of life in the church must always be *agape* (love) expressed in *diakonia* (service, ministry) by means of *charismata* (gifts) for *oikodome* (edifying, literally the erecting of a building). Since the gifts are meant to be used for edifying, any neglect or restraint of them will quench the life of the Spirit in the church inescapably and drastically: every-member ministry in the body of Christ is meant to be the rule and is the only healthy way.

It should be said explicitly that in all this Paul is thinking in terms of relational dynamics and functions, not of organization of offices or demarcation of status. How these principles are best translated into local church order is a question which each congregation must think through for itself. First Corinthians 14 reflects one pattern, and there are others.

Our survey has now embraced all the main thoughts about the Holy Spirit that the New Testament contains, and we need not take it further. (In fact, the non-Pauline epistles and Revelation do not develop the doctrine of the Spirit very broadly at all.) If it were asked why this paper has not, as is fashionable, made much of signs and wonders (Rom. 15:19; Heb. 2:4) and tongues (Acts 2:4; 1 Cor. 14), the answer would be that these authenticating manifestations which accompanied the apostles' ministry were evidently regarded by the apostles themselves as peripheral to life in the Spirit for the Christians and churches whom their letters instruct, and it seems desirable to maintain an apostolic perspective in these matters. I repeat: in my view, all the main things have now been dealt with.

I think evangelical inerrantists in the Protestant churches will all accept the above analysis of the biblical witness, so far as it goes. (If not, tell me at once; I need to know!) But if this is so, then our range of agreement in pneumatology is revealed as impressively wide. We shall all be found as one on the fact of the Spirit's personal deity; on the fact that Jesus and the Father give the Spirit to all believers; on the fact that the Spirit within us works through our minds and wills and not apart from them (that is, he does not move us by physical force without persuasion, as one would move a stick or rock or robot); on the fact that faith and assurance, new birth and spiritual growth, spiritual gifts and ministry, holy habits and Christlike character, particularly love, humility, hope, and patience, along with boldness and usefulness in witness and Samaritanship, all flow from his work in our hearts; and on the fact that sanctification is progressive. We shall all be at one in acknowledging that faith and repentance, holiness and service, become realities through our cooperation, although not by our power, and in recognizing our obtrusive sense of present spiritual imperfection (that is, of reach exceeding grasp) as itself a reminder from the Spirit that his work in us here is no more than just—just as it is no less than—a pledge, beginning, and foretaste of glory hereafter. We shall also be at one in seeing the church as God's charismatic movement, in which every-member ministry, both Godward and manward, through the use of spiritual gifts universally given, is an abiding clause in the divine rule of life. We shall all agree that the church must see itself as the agent of God's mission, with the whole company of Christians laboring to fulfill their role as Christ's hands and feet and mouthpiece. And we shall all be as one in recognizing that as the creating of the church by regeneration is the Spirit's sovereign work, so is the renewing, reviving, and reforming of it when the fires of spiritual life have burned low. These are significant and far-reaching agreements, and the fact that they will form the framework within which continuing differences will be discussed shows at once that such differences, however passionately debated, cannot be of major importance.

The most acute tensions between inerrantists today, as have been said, concern the credentials and claims of the charismatic movement in the mainline churches. I have written about this movement in two books. In the first (*The Spirit Within You*, 1961, jointly with the late Alan Stibbs) it was maintained that Spirit baptism as Charismatics conceive it and the "sensational" manifestations which I have here referred to as "sign-gifts" are no necessary part of full Christian experience. In the second (*Keep in Step with the Spirit*, 1984) it was argued that though charismatic theology in its usual forms is not viable, charismatic experience could and should be accounted for theologically in other terms, and on that basis accepted as from God, and therefore valuable. I argued there that Spirit baptism, along with other "second-blessing" experiences (Wesley's "entire sanctification," and the "Keswick experience" of "Spirit-filling"), ought to be understood in terms of the Spirit witnessing to our adoption and mediating to us Jesus' presence and love (John 14:21–24; Rom. 5:5; 8:15–17). I am loath to repeat either argument here, and, in any case, space does not allow it. So let me simply say that I stand by the double purpose for which *Keep in Step with the Spirit* was written: first to lay a basis for mutual trust, acceptance, and cooperation between those Protestant Evangelicals who profess a charismatic experience and those who do not, and second to call both sorts to seek revival in what we may call Edwardian terms, that is, a restoration through the Spirit of the exalted quality of Christian communion with God to which most of the New Testament letters testify, and of which the charismatic renewal has given us only a small part as yet. Here, I believe, are two lines of action on which all inerrantists ought to be embarking today.

I will make two final points now, both about breadth and balance. First *just as the Word is insufficient without the Spirit, so the Spirit is insufficient without the Word.* Well may Charismatics and others censure those who seem in practice to embrace the idea that biblical orthodoxy is all that matters and biblical teaching alone produces a healthy church. The critics are right to point out that idolizing orthodoxy is not the same as worshiping God and that complacent "orthodoxism," by inflating pride, actually quenches the Spirit. But pneumatic preoccupation can slow down maturity, too. Many Charismatics appear anti-intellectual in basic attitude, impatient with biblical and theological study, insistent that their movement is about experience rather than truth, content with a tiny handful of biblical teachings and positively zany in their unwillingness to reason out guidance for life from the Scriptures. Endless possibilities of self-deception and Satanic befoolment open up the moment we lay aside the Word to follow supposedly direct instruction from the Spirit in vision, dream, prophecy, or inward impression. The history of fanaticism is gruesome; I do not want to see it rerun among my charismatic friends. But this is always a danger when the formation of the mind by the Word is in any way neglected. What is needed across the board is constant instruction in biblical truth with constant prayer that the Spirit will make it take fire in human hearts, regenerating, redirecting, and transforming into Christ's likeness at character level. Whatever agenda others have, the fulfilling of Christ's prayer that his people would be sanctified by the Spirit through God's Word of truth should be the inerrantist's first concern.

Second, *just as the Spirit must not be forgotten when we focus on the Father and the Son, so the Father and the Son must not be forgotten when we focus on the Spirit.* A full-blown, thoroughgoing Trinitarianism is the needed basis for devotion and discipleship, just as it is for theology. As some branches of Bible-believing Christendom seem clear and sound on the saving love of the Father and the Son in the covenant of grace, yet devotionally dry because of unconcern about the enlivening Spirit, so some parts of charismatic Christendom, for all their stylized exuberance, seem stunted and immature, running out of steam and stuck in their own mud because they have centered their concern on the Spirit more than on the Son and have virtually ignored the Father.[25] Exclusive concentration on the one person of the Godhead always narrows and cramps one's spiritual style. It did so in the "Jesusolatry" of older evangelical pietism, which confined its concern to the Redeemer and the redeemed life and had no adequate appreciation of creation and the created order, so that natural beauty, human creativity, the cultural mandate of Genesis 1:28, the arts, higher education, and political and social responsibilities, were neglected and the supposedly spiritual Manichean mentality, the occupational disease of pre-Reformation monasticism, was cultivated afresh in a Protestant frame.

In the same way, exclusive concentration on the Spirit and the emotional side of the Christian life (the two go together) produces its own crop of neglects, first and foremost in the realm of thought, where the primacy of the mind is forgotten and much of the revealed purpose of God is forgotten, too. To focus on the Father is to remember that this is God's world despite the demons; that its history is "his story" because the Creator is never unseated from his throne; that he is transcendently high and holy ("Our Father *in heaven*"), so that our proper passion for intimacy with him must never be allowed to banish awe and reverence for him; and that the immaturity of spiritual self-absorption must give way to an all-embracing God-centeredness ("Hallowed be *Thy name*"— "glory to God *alone*"). To remember these things is as necessary as it is to remember the Holy Spirit and to do justice to the experiential side of communion with God through Jesus Christ. As "Jesusolatry" is lopsided and deficient, so is "Spiritolatry"; comprehensive Trinitarian devotion founded on comprehensive Trinitarian doctrine is essential if today's church is to find the fullness of the renewing and reviving that it needs.

## ENDNOTES

[1] I have discussed these positions in *Keep in Step with the Spirit* (Old Tappan, N.J.: Revell, 1984), pp. 121–69.

[2] As, for instance, in G. W. H. Lampe, *God as Spirit* (Oxford: Oxford University Press, 1977) (Unitarian), or C. F. D. Moule, *The Holy Spirit* (London: Mowbrays, 1978) (Binitarian).

[3] Karl Barth, *Church Dogmatics*, 1.i., trans. G. T. Thomson (Edinburgh: T. & T. Clark, 1936).

[4] B. B. Warfield, *Calvin and Augustine* (Philadelphia: Presbyterian and Reformed, 1956), pp. 484–87.

[5] The difference is due to the reprint program undertaken by the Banner of Truth Trust, which made available the works of John Owen, Richard Sibbes, John Flavel, Jonathan Edwards, John Newton, and much more seventeenth- and eighteenth-century material.

[6] See Leonard Hodgson, *The Doctrine of the Trinity* (London: Nisbet, 1943); Colin Gunton, *Becoming and Being* (Oxford: Oxford University Press, 1978), pp. 117–85 (on Karl Barth); Eberhard Jungel, *The Doctrine of the Trinity* (Grand Rapids: Eerdmans, 1976); Jürgen Moltmann, *The Trinity and the Kingdom of God* (London: SCM, 1981); Robert W. Jenson, *The Triune Identity* (Philadelphia: Fortress, 1982); D. M. MacKinnan, "The Relation of the Doctrines of the Incarnation and the Trinity," *Creation, Christ and Culture*, ed. R. W. A. McKinney (Edinburgh: T. & T. Clark, 1976); David Brown, *The Divine Trinity* (LaSalle, Ill.: Open Court, 1985).

[7] See J. R. Williams, "Charismatic Movement," with bibliography, in *Evangelical Dictionary of Theology*, ed. W. Elwell (Grand Rapids: Baker, 1984); J. I. Packer, "Theological Reflections on the Charismatic Movement," *Churchman* 1 (1980): 7–25, especially 20ff.; F. D. Bruner, *A Theology of the Holy Spirit* (Grand Rapids: Eerdmans, 1970); ed. Kilian McDonnell, *Presence, Power, Praise: Documents on the Charismatic Renewal in the Churches*, 3 vols. (Collegeville, Minn.: Liturgical, 1980).

[8] See James D. G. Dunn, *Baptism in the Holy Spirit* (London: SCM, 1970); John R. W. Stott, *Baptism and Fulness*, rev. ed. (Downers Grove: InterVarsity, 1976); Anthony A. Hoekema, *Holy Spirit Baptism* (Grand Rapids: Eerdmans, 1972); F. D. Bruner, *Holy Spirit*.

[9] See J. I. Packer, *Keep in Step*, pp. 177–78, 206ff., 224–25, 229–30, 280–81; W. J. Samarin, *Tongues of Men and Angels* (New York: Macmillan, 1972); J. P. Kildahl, *The Psychology of Speaking in Tongues* (New York: Harper and Row, 1972).

[10] See J. I. Packer, *Keep in Step*, pp. 194–95, 214–15; "Poor Health May Be the Best Remedy," *Christianity Today* (May 21, 1982), pp. 14–16; Francis MacNutt, *Healing* (Notre Dame: Ave Maria, 1974); B. B. Warfield, *Miracles Yesterday and Today* (Grand Rapids: Eerdmans, 1953); Joni Eareckson with Steve Estes, *A Step Further* (Grand Rapids: Zondervan, 1978).

[11] See G. Friesen with J. Robin Maxson, *Decision Making and the Will of God* (Portland: Multnomah, 1980); Elisabeth Elliot, *A Slow and Certain Light* (Waco: Word, 1976); Sinclair B. Ferguson, *Discovering God's Will* (Edinburgh: Banner of Truth, 1981); M. Blaine Smith, *Knowing God's Will* (Downers Grove: InterVarsity, 1979); Dallas Willard, *In Search of Guidance* (Ventura: Regal, 1984); J. I. Packer, "Wisdom Along the Way," "Paths of Righteousness," "True Guidance," *Eternity*, April–June 1986.

[12] See Merlin Carothers, *Prison to Praise* (Plainfield: Logos, 1970); *Power in Praise* (Plainfield: Logos, n.d.); *Answers to Praise* (Plainfield: Logos, 1972).

[13] See on this the shrewd tightrope walk of Thomas A. Smail, *Reflected Glory* (London: Hodder and Stoughton, 1975), pp. 61–88.

[14] *Keep in Step*, pp. 121–69; articles in *Christianity Today* and *Eternity*, as above.

[15] The case is put in J. I. Packer, *Keep in Step*, pp. 235–62; "Steps to the Renewal of the Christian People," *Summons to Faith and Renewal*, ed. Peter S. Williamson and Kevin Perrotta (Ann Arbor: Servant, 1983), pp. 107–27. See also Richard Lovelace, *Dynamics of Spiritual Life* (Downers Grove: InterVarsity, 1979).

[16] See J. I. Packer, "Renewal and Revival," *Channels* Spring (1984), pp. 7–9.

[17] Much of what follows was originally presented at the Consultation on the Work of the Holy Spirit and Evangelization, Oslo, May 1985.

[18] Arthur Wainwright, *The Trinity in the New Testament* (London: SPCK, 1962), p. 4.

[19] James D. G. Dunn, *Jesus and the Spirit* (Philadelphia: Westminster, 1975), p. 326.

[20] Ibid., p. 323.

[21] Ibid., p. 324.

[22] Michael Ramsey, *Holy Spirit* (London: SPCK, 1977), p. 33.

[23] Alasdair Heron, *The Holy Spirit* (Philadelphia: Westminster, 1983), p. 45.

[24] Ramsey, *Holy Spirit*, pp. 67–68.

[25] This is the contention of Thomas A. Smail in *The Forgotten Father* (Grand Rapids: Eerdmans, 1981); see especially pp. 9–20. Smail was for a time secretary of the Fountain Trust, Britain's leading charismatic organization.

# A Response to
# The Holy Spirit and His Work

## James D. Brown

At the outset of this response to Dr. James I. Packer's paper "The Holy Spirit and His Work" it may be useful to state briefly the salient points of his position.

The thrust of Packer's presentation appears to be that only a full-blown Trinitarianism is capable of bringing and sustaining the spiritual renewal which the church needs so desperately. *Balance* is the key term of this approach.

In workmanlike manner, Packer develops his thesis. First, he shows how influential theological writers, such as Leonard Hodgson and others of that stripe, along with the charismatic renewal have freed the doctrine of the Holy Spirit from its dormancy in church life and doctrine. Second, the heuristic value of the doctrine is apparent in the areas of spirituality, christology, and ecclesiology where Packer asks questions which are begging for answers. Third, the biblical inerrantist's contribution to this "renewal-revival theme" is threefold: (1) He will support the "robust supernaturalism" of these two motifs; (2) the inerrantist will be a watchdog over "supersupernaturalism and subjectivism" among the Charismatics; (3) he will communicate the unity between the Spirit and the Word. Fourth, Packer gives an overall view of the work of the Holy Spirit in both the Old Testament and the New Testament in order to show how the inerrantist may treat the renewal-revival theme. Fifth, out of the generative principle of unity in the analysis of the biblical witness of the Holy Spirit, Packer avers that the credentials and claims of the charismatic movement "provide the main tensions between inerrantists," viz., the question as to whether or not sign gifts are perforce part and parcel of "full Christian experience," and the question as to the viability of the charismatic doctrine as opposed to the validity of its charismatic experience.

Sixth and finally, Packer opines that the Spirit and the Word are interdependent and that just as focusing on the Father and the Son should not be to the neglect of the Spirit, neither should focusing on the Spirit be to the neglect of the Father and the Son.

Let me state at the outset that I am a classical Pentecostal—not a Charismatic. The difference, while not essential, is real. The classical Pentecostal comes out of the revival which began at the turn of this century; the Charismatic dates his origin in the late sixties; the classical Pentecostal came out of the mainline denominations; the Charismatic in the main has stayed in these denominations; the classical Pentecostal is basically homogenous in doctrine; the Charismatic is heterogeneous. Almost without exception a classical Pentecostal could subscribe to the doctrinal stances of both Fundamentalists and Evangelicals.

The Charismatics could not do so with the same frequency. None of this is to say that either camp has greater validity than the other but only to show where I am coming from as a responder to Packer's paper.

Strangely, the seminal doctrine, at least, of the classical Pentecostal is eschatology—not pneumatology. During the latter part of the nineteenth century, following the resurgence of the doctrine of Christ's second coming, there were people who were solicitous of the logical implications of this doctrine. If the coming of Christ for the church was imminent, then it behooved the church to get people ready for this event. But to do this, divine equipment was needed. Thus, driven to the Scriptures to find the secret of power for world evangelization, those hardy believers—small in number—felt that they had found the answer in the doctrine of the baptism in the Holy Spirit. Out of that hermeneutic emerged those who are still labeled without acrimony "Pentecostal."

If ever a writer has taken his assignment seriously, Packer has done so. The subject is treated both lucidly and competently. Whether or not it is treated thoroughly is dependent upon whether or not the assignment is in the area of biblical theology or historical theology. If the former, then the assignment may be considered exhaustive; if the latter, then the paper may not be as thorough as it might be. Because if one is addressing the subject of the Holy Spirit and his work, then the matters of the charismatic renewal Edwardian revival themes need more analysis. However, the questions which Packer generates from his observation of the charismatic renewal are most incisive, and any biblical inerrantist would be well disposed to flush out their implications.

Packer has done us all a service in surfacing three things which we can bring to the "renewal-revival theme." First, he says that the renewal-revival theme goes a long way in restoring "robust" biblical supernaturalism to its proper place. It is at this juncture that Packer underscores one of the great enduring methods of evangelical hermeneutics, viz., if one can get the Scriptures on his side, the debate is over. This view pervaded Puritan preaching, and until the latter part of the nineteenth century it was also secularized into American political discourse. Witness Abraham Lincoln in his famous Cooper Union Address flogging Stephen Douglas by proving that the signers of the Constitution were against slavery.

Second, concerning Packer's neologism, "supersupernaturalism" and the dangers of its obtrusiveness, I agree that one must remember that God is indeed the God of the mundane as well as the supramundane. One of the problems with Charismatics, as well as with many Pentecostals, is that everything becomes a crisis. A demon lurks behind every bush. In a replay of the old records of neo-Platonism and docetism, reality is too often denied. To admit that one has a headache or injury is negative confession. To these people desideratum is positive confession. Shades of LaBrayere!

I must aver, though, that classical Pentecostals do not normally put credence in a prophecy which is not in accordance with the Word of God. Furthermore, even if such prophecy is adjudicated to be under the suzerainty of the Scriptures, the Pentecostals do not in the main put the gift on the same level as the Word. They have learned to "prove all things and hold fast to that which is good" (*kalon*)—that which is good in itself irrespective of the results it brings.

The third thing that Packer maintains the biblical inerrantist can bring to the discussion of the renewal-revival theme is "a concept of divine communication that correlates the Spirit and the Word." Scripture is coherent, sufficient, and clear. I could not agree more. The Scriptures are coherent in that they pit no writer against another writer. They are sufficient in that they inscripturate revelation. No extracanonical revelations are acceptable. They are clear in that the popular mind can relate to them.

There is a teaching today in some charismatic circles to the effect that although prophecy must be judged by the Word only, those who have been elevated sovereignly to prophetic status may do the judging. For the ordinary man in the pew to question them is comparable to a puppy yapping at the heels of a Doberman. Whatever happened to that Berean mentality which maintained that no man is exempted from his teaching being searched out and confirmed by the Scriptures?

The refusal to correlate the working of the Spirit with the Word leads inevitably to heteronomy. If *A* claims that his prophecies and revelations are as valid, per se, as those of the apostolic prophecies and revelation inscripturated in the Word, then what do we do when *B*'s revelations and prophecies

contradict those of *A*? Obviously, we would need some norm
outside of both *A* and *B* to judge between them. Thus, we are
right back to the Word. Let us illustrate this another way. Who
among us is not familiar with Abelard's work, *Sic et non*? In the
opus, he shows how some of the traditions of the church during
the first six centuries of Christianity contradict each other. So
much then for tradition as an alternative to the Word as the
church's ultimate authority. In 1870, however, the Church of
Rome claimed to have solved this problem by the doctrine of papal
infallibility. The pope will decide. But where did they go in their
attempt to validate the concept of papal infallibility? The Scriptures. So here we are right back to the Word again, and, indeed,
this shall always be the case when we take seriously the work of
the Spirit of God. In reminding us of this, Packer has made
debtors of us all.

Packer's paper reeks with strengths, but in my judgment the
strength of the work is the overview of the Holy Spirit's person
and work. Of such stuff is hermeneutics and, yes, even homiletics
made.

Three areas which bulk large in this section are the person of
the Spirit, the deity of the Spirit, and his relation with the other
two members of the Godhead. Argumentatively, the treatment
which Packer gives to these areas is a *tour de force*. The cogency of
his argument does not admit of easy duplication.

I would have liked, however, for Packer to have brought to
bear his expertise a little more on the questions as to what the
Spirit is doing in 1986, both in the church and society. Egregious-
ly, the New Testament writers do indeed, as Packer says, relegate
"signs and wonders" and "tongues" to the periphery of biblical
theology, but the fact remains that a spiritual upheaval—not the
ordinary—is very much a part of the contemporary church scene.
What is the Spirit saying to the churches? What, for that matter, is
he saying through the charismatic renewal?

Another area, which I regret Packer did not have enough
space to address, is the role of the Holy Spirit after the *eschaton*,
although I rather suspect that he would answer that he has no
warranty to go beyond the point where biblical revelation itself
stops.

I concur wholeheartedly with Packer when he says that "the
most acute tensions between inerrantists today, concerns the
credentials and the claims of the charismatic movement in the
mainline churches." A real theological and ethical can of worms is
opened here. How shall these "credentials" be treated, and how
shall these "claims" be handled? Where does ethics cut across the
bias? On the one hand, is it ethical to stay in a church and espouse
doctrine contrary to that of the church in question? On the other
hand, to use a threadbare cliché, should that church "throw out

the baby with the bath water?" Out of such dilemmas bishops emerge.

As a Pentecostal, I obviously disagree with Packer's assertion that "Spirit baptism, as Charismatics conceive it . . . and 'sign gifts' are no necessary part of full Christian experience." Inasmuch as he does not give his *raison d'etre* for this position, in fairness neither shall I for my view.

Packer avers that "Charismatic theology in its usual form is not viable." Here I am not certain that I know what "charismatic theology" is. If Methodists, Baptists, Roman Catholics, Lutherans, et al., have indeed transcended their own church's doctrine in uniting around a definitive corpus of charismatic theology, then unlike Paul's description of the Way, the thing *was* done in a corner.

I do know what Pentecostal theology is. If by "viable" one means "apt to live," "the potential for maturation," then Pentecostal theology is immensely viable. The Pentecostal baby has lived and, under God, has done quite well.

One of the great weaknesses, however, of Charismatics and Pentecostals alike is that a definitive Pentecostal theology remains to be written. Pentecostals, and now Charismatics as well, have been quite effective announcers—but hardly puissant as either apologists or polemicists. We have been too content to say, "A man with an experience is not at the mercy of him who has only an argument." The apostle Peter, though, talked about giving a reason, and not the mere claiming of an experience, for the hope lying within us. In goading us toward this direction, Dr. Packer has rendered Pentecostals and Charismatics of every stripe a great service.

Whatever our theology, the two concluding points Packer makes have import for us all. First of all, he says that the Word is insufficient without the Spirit, and the Spirit is insufficient without the Word, and then he assigns the biblical orthodoxist to the first category and the charismatic to the second. Being neatly compartmentalized, they can be mutually corrective. Balance is the desideratum here.

Patently, two great dangers present themselves to the charismatic and biblical orthodoxist, respectively. The Charismatic, in his propensity toward religious experience, may imperceptibly reject the Word of God as his ultimate authority. By depending on a plethora of prophecies and revelation, his sorting and discounting processes may break down. It is only a step from one seeing oneself as God's spokesman to one's perception of oneself as God himself. Pentecostals and Charismatics alike must not forget that Peter tied the events at Pentecost to the prophecy of Joel.

Biblical orthodoxists, on the other hand, must remember that Christian experience is a valid thing. Admittedly, it has a tendency to justify the status quo; it is more interested in vividness than in content, and it is essentially intersubjectively intransmissible. But Daniel Webster said before John Marshall, chief justice of the United States Supreme Court, who was hearing the famous Dartmouth College case, "There are those who love it," and I might add, need it. Someone once asked Bishop Candler of the Methodist church if he thought the holiness people would ever make it to heaven. He paused for a moment and replied, "I think they will if they don't run past it."

Packer's final point that the church needs a "full-blown, thoroughgoing Trinitarianism" is well taken. I am not so certain, however, that the Charismatic focuses his worship on the Spirit as much as he does on Jesus. Actually this is immaterial, for Packer's admonition is that no one member of the Godhead should be worshiped to the exclusion of the other two members.

One problem in attaining the Trinitarianism for which Packer justly appeals is that after the doctrine of the Holy Spirit had been neglected for centuries, it has not been easy for Pentecostals to cease and desist from talking, possibly overly so, of the Holy Spirit after the doctrine has been restored. Ideally, theology should not swing like a pendulum; realistically it does. It is to be hoped that Charismatics and non-Charismatics alike, shall shortly adjust to the swing and occupy the middle position.

In this paper Packer has performed a most difficult task. His assignment has involved hermeneutics. How do you harmonize divergent interpretations of the inerrant Word of God? Nonetheless, he has convincingly bridged "the great gulf fixed" between Charismatics and "mainliners" (whatever that may mean) and, in doing so, has more than incidently shown that the focus of biblical inerrancy is not so narrow that doctrinal issues, not immediately perceptible as indigenous to the area of biblical inerrancy, may be discussed profitably.

I suppose that the greatest benefit I have derived from attempting to respond to Dr. Packer's paper is a fresh affirmation of the big picture. We isolate ourselves much too easily. Consequently, we are too defensive in both our doctrine and our practice. Packer's paper has reminded us that the Holy Spirit is still sovereign. No segment of the church can monopolize him. We are all Trinitarians.

Packer, however, does not gloss over our theological differences. They are real. No evangelical syncretism is being called for. But the thread that keeps coming through his paper is that a balanced, biblical Trinitarianism should be our objective. To ask for less would be unthinkable; to ask for more would be superfluous.

# A Response to
# The Holy Spirit and His Work

### Richard B. Gaffin, Jr.

Within the space at his disposal, Dr. Packer has managed, in his usual balanced and magisterial fashion, to provide a wealth of historical, exegetical, and theological insights on our topic. It is difficult to list all the strong points; there are so many. Besides the lucid biblical-theological survey of the Holy Spirit's person and work that forms its heart (pp. 59–72), there are two important concerns that seem to me to tie together much of the paper: The reminder at the outset (p. 53) that essential for a proper focus on the doctrine of the Holy Spirit is a conviction of God's sovereignty, rejecting every sense of self-sufficiency, Pelagian or otherwise, that fails to acknowledge the inadequacy of all human effort; and then the concluding emphases (pp. 74–75), flowing out of such a focus, on the inseparable relationship between Word and Spirit and on the need for "comprehensive" devotion that does not slight any one person of the Trinity.

The paper's overall strategy, if I have read correctly, is to promote renewal-revival among evangelical inerrantists (pp. 58, 74). Accordingly (pp. 72–73), a major conclusion is that on the main elements of the biblical witness to the Spirit's person and work, the agreement among inerrantists is "impressively wide." Differences do remain—"the most acute tensions" concern the charismatic movement—but these differences "cannot be of major importance." A substantial, commonly held biblical basis exists, Packer maintains, for Protestant Evangelicals, Charismatics, and non-Charismatics together, to seek the level of Spirit-worked revival and communion with God documented in the New Testament. How should we assess this optimistic and challenging conclusion?

1. I want to focus my response by highlighting, somewhat

more than Packer does, the *eschatological* nature of the Spirit's work. In fact, no quality of the Spirit's activity is more basic according to the New Testament, particularly the teaching of Paul. Briefly, the Spirit, already given to the church, is the actual "down payment" or "firstfruits" of its eschatological inheritance (Rom. 8:23; 2 Cor. 1:22; 5:5; Eph. 1:14); he "seals" to believers that inheritance (2 Cor. 1:22; Eph. 1:13; 4:30), to be realized at Christ's return in their bodily resurrection and the restoration of the entire creation (Rom. 8:18–25; 1 Cor. 15:42–49; 2 Cor. 5:1–5). The Spirit is the instrumental and transforming principle in Christ's resurrection (Rom. 1:4; 1 Cor. 15:45), not merely as an isolated miracle in the past but as the actual beginning, the "firstfruits," of the future resurrection-harvest of believers (1 Cor. 15:20). All told, for Paul the Spirit is the source of a "new creation" (2 Cor. 5:17). Elsewhere, the Spirit is the "dynamic" essential to the eschatological kingdom already inaugurated by Christ's first coming (Matt. 12:28; Luke 11:20; cf. 11:13 with 12:32). The presence of the Spirit-Paraclete in the church is the function of Christ's glorification (John 7:39; cf. 14:12–26; 15:26–27; 16:7; Rev. 1:4; 5:6). The powers of the Spirit presently at work in the church are those of "the coming [eschatological] age" (Heb. 6:4–5).

Recognition of the eschatological Spirit is fairly commonplace,[1] at least on a scholarly level, but still relatively recent. That recognition is a result of the exegetical repudiation, during the early part of this century, of the older theological liberalism which tried to reinterpret or otherwise suppress eschatological elements in the New Testament in the interest of showing that Jesus and Paul especially were really exponents of a religion of self-improvement, of an idealistic religiosity of timeless moral imperatives. In reaction biblical scholars increasingly have come to see that the message of the New Testament is pervasively eschatological, including its teaching on the Holy Spirit.

Coming closer to home for many, if not for all of us, this consensus is also in tension with classical Christian theology with its undeniable tendency to keep from the present life of the church. Nowhere is this tendency to "deeschatologize" the present more true than in the way the Spirit's activity is viewed. Persistently his work in the believer is seen in a mystical or timeless sort of way; the accent tends to be on experiences that take place in the inner life of the believer, without any particular reference or connection to God's overall eschatological purposes. The results, too often, have been largely individualistic, privatized, even self-centered preoccupations with the Spirit's work. So far as the eschatological Spirit is concerned, then, we may speak of an exegetical consensus that has yet to shape the teaching of the church and, more importantly, to lay hold of and transform its life.

2. Within the eschatological perspective of its immediate context, 1 Corinthians 15:45 is pivotal for both the christology and pneumatology not only of Paul but of the entire New Testament. There, in contrast to Adam, Paul says that Christ, the last Adam, "became life-giving Spirit." In my judgment, careful exegesis shows that in this expression (1) *pneuma* refers to the person of the Holy Spirit (as in vv. 44 and 46 the correlative adjective, "spiritual," refers to the result of his work in producing the believer's resurrection body), and (2) the "becoming" in view took place at Christ's resurrection or, more broadly, his exaltation (cf. "heaven," "heavenly" in vv. 47–49). What Paul asserts, then, is an equation or oneness or unity between Christ and the Spirit (cf. 2 Cor. 3:17, "the Lord is the Spirit"), dating from Christ's resurrection (exaltation). All reflection on the work of the Spirit must remain tethered to this equation.

To discover a denial of the Trinity or a blurring of the personal distinction between Christ and the Spirit either in this exegesis or in Paul's statement itself is unnecessary. Eternal, inner-Trinitarian relationships, though certainly not foreign to Paul, are outside his purview here. He is not thinking about Christ's essential deity but in terms of his genuine humanity, as he is "the last Adam," "the second man" (v. 47). His perspective is historical; he speaks about what Christ *"became."* The oneness or equation in view is functional or eschatological, or in the language of classical theology, economic, not ontological.

Paul's point is that by virtue of Christ's resurrection (glorification) and in comparison with what was the case previously as a result of his birth and baptism, (1) Christ has come into such permanent and complete possession of the Spirit and (2) has been so thoroughly transformed by the Spirit that the two are now equated in their working; they are to be seen as one as they have become one in "life-giving" activity, the activity of giving eschatological, resurrection life, with all that that life includes. While the immediate context is directly concerned with the still future, bodily resurrection of believers, certainly in view also is who, presently, the resurrected Christ is and what his present activity in the church is.[2]

For an overall program of New Testament theology, 1 Corinthians 15:45 (cf. 2 Cor. 3:17) is, in effect, Paul's one-sentence commentary on Pentecost—clustered together as one complex of events, with the resurrection and ascension of Christ in their epochal, once-for-all significance (cf. Acts 2:32–33). The coming of the Spirit at Pentecost is not just a supplement to the finished work of Christ. Rather that coming brings to light that Christ is now present to build his church by applying the salvation he has accomplished. Pentecost is not only the outpouring of the Spirit on the church by Christ but his own coming to the church as the life-giving Spirit; the gift of the Spirit is no more and no less than the gift of the glorified Christ himself.

A similar pattern of thought is present in John 14–16. In particular at 14:12ff. the giving of the Spirit by the Father, conditioned on Jesus' own going to the Father, is at the same time the coming of Jesus (v. 18: "I will not leave you orphans, I will come to you"); the coming of the Spirit, following on Jesus' glorification (cf. 7:39), is the coming of Jesus himself. And in the Great Commission Jesus' promise, "I will be with you always, to the very end of the age," is to be understood not only in terms of his divine omnipresence but also and primarily with a view to Pentecost and the presence and activity of the Spirit.

From this perspective it can perhaps be appreciated that the remarkable experiences of those present at Pentecost are not the point. Their experience does not serve as the model for a postconversion power experience to be sought by all believers, but to attest the mode, until Christ returns, of his presence in the church in the fullness of his saving, life-giving lordship.[3] Foreign to the New Testament is the notion of a two-step distinction in Christian experience between baptism by the Spirit into Christ at conversion and baptism by Christ with or in the Spirit, usually subsequent to conversion. The thorough interchangeability of Christ and the Spirit in the experience of believers expressed in Romans 8:9–10 (you in the Spirit, v. 9a; the Spirit in you, v. 9b; belonging to Christ, i.e., you in Christ, v. 9d; Christ in you, v. 10a) does not merely describe a beginning to be followed, ideally, by a full, proper reception of the Spirit. Rather, that interchangeability structures the reality of Christian experience from beginning to end—in its ongoing ebb and flow, with virtually limitless and varied possibilities for growth; for richer, deeper, more powerful workings of the Spirit; as well as, I would remind us, for grieving and quenching the Spirit. And that convertibility, the inseparable correlation of Christ and the Spirit in our experience, holds because of what is true prior to and in back of our experience, because of who the Spirit is, "the Spirit of Christ" (v. 9c), and who Christ is, the "life-giving Spirit."

3. The question could be pressed, does the intense and widespread absorption with the work of the Spirit in recent decades not compensate for traditional neglect and shortcomings? Specifically, has the charismatic movement not seen and, in large measure, experienced, unwittingly perhaps, the eschatological nature of the Spirit's work? Besides the oblique reservations already expressed, I want here to make just one point, one on which I would hope Charismatics and non-Charismatics can agree without having to settle all remaining differences.

Within the overall working of the Spirit in the church, the New Testament distinguishes between the gift (singular) and the gifts (plural) of the Spirit. On the one hand, all believers, without exception, share in the gift of the Spirit by virtue of their union with Christ, the life-giving Spirit, and their incorporation into his Spirit-baptized body, the church (e.g., 1 Cor. 12:13); the gift of the Spirit is present in the church on the principle of "universal donation." On the other hand, the gifts are workings of the Spirit variously distributed in the church. No one gift (in this sense) is intended for every believer; the gifts of the Spirit are given on the principle of "differential distribution." This seems clear, for instance, from the force of the rhetorical questions in 1 Corinthians 12:29–30: all are not apostles or prophets . . . all do not speak in tongues or interpret them. And this is so, ultimately, by God's design (the one body with diverse parts), not because of lack of faith or the failure to seek a particular gift.

The further significance of this distinction is that the gift of the Spirit, in which all believers share, is an essential aspect of the salvation revealed in Christ and so, as such, an eschatological gift. It is bound up with "repentance unto life" (Acts 11:18) and is the "firstfruits" of resurrection (Rom. 8:23), the "down payment" on the church's final inheritance (Eph. 1:14). In contrast, the gifts of the Spirit variously distributed in the church are provisional and subeschatological. Again, this seems clear from 1 Corinthians 13:8ff. Prophecy and tongues, among other gifts, have a provisional and limited function and so are temporary, destined to pass away (vv. 8–9), while those works of the Spirit such as faith, hope, and love endure (v. 13).

It is not in the distinctives of contemporary Pentecostal and charismatic experience, however else we are to evaluate them,[4] where we find the eschatological substance of the Spirit's activity. Rather Paul is telling us that it is the fruit of the Spirit, preeminently love, that has an eschatological "reach" and effects eschatological "breakthroughs." It is faith in its modes of hoping and loving that grasps and anticipates the perfection of the order to be introduced at Christ's return.

4. Finally, some related comments on revival and sanctification. It is probably not too pretentious here to speak of an unfinished side of the Reformation. The Reformation, it is fair to say, was a (re)discovery, at least implicitly, of the eschatological heart of the gospel; the *sola gratia* principle is eschatological in essence. Justification by faith, as the Reformers came to understand and experience it, is an anticipation of final, eschatological judgment. It means that a favorable verdict at the last judgment is a present possession, the confident and stable basis of the Christian life, not, as Rome taught, an anxious, uncertain hope. Paul's ringing affirmation, for instance—"There is therefore now no condemnation for those who are in Christ Jesus" (Rom. 8:1)— is a decidedly eschatological pronouncement.

But while Protestant Christianity has grasped, at least intuitively, the eschatological thrust of justification, that is not nearly
the case for sanctification and the work of the Spirit. Undeniable is
a tendency to separate or even polarize justification and sanctification, whether in theory or practice. Justification, on the one hand,
is seen as what God does, perfectly; sanctification, on the other
hand, is what I do, imperfectly. Sanctification is viewed as the
response of the believer, an expression of gratitude from our side
for salvation defined in terms of justification and the forgiveness
of sins, usually with an emphasis on the inadequacy of the
gratitude expressed.

The intention of such an emphasis may well be to safeguard
the totally gratuitous character of justification. But church history
has made all too evident that the eventual result is the rise of
moralism, the reintroduction into Christian experience of a refined
works-principle more or less divorced from the faith that justifies
and eventually leaves no room for that faith. What is resolutely
rejected at the front door of justification comes in through the back
door of sanctification and takes over the whole house.

The solution here is not some "higher" life or perfectionism,
at least not as usually understood. Forms of "entire" sanctification
or sinless perfection, supposedly achieved by a distinct act of faith
subsequent to justification, invariably deeschatologize the gospel
by operating with domesticated, voluntaristic notions of sin and,
in their own way, give rise to moralism. Certainly we must not
forget that "in this life even the holiest have only a small
beginning" (Heidelberg Catechism, Lord's Day 44). But—and this
is the point—that beginning, however small, is an eschatological
beginning. It stands under the apostolic promise that "He who
began a good work in you will perfect it until the day of Christ
Jesus" (Phil. 1:6 ASV). In the New Testament there is no more basic
perspective on sanctification and renewal than that expressed in
Romans 6: it is the continual "living to God" of those who are
"alive from the dead" (vv. 11, 13). It is a matter of the "good
works" of the eschatological new creation for which believers have
been "created in Christ Jesus" (Eph. 2:10). The controlling
indicative of Romans 6—we have died to sin—describes not just
some but all believers, even the weakest who experience the
fiercest temptations and are the most discouraged about their sins.
"Joy unspeakable" (1 Peter 1:8) is not a sublime psychological
state granted to some believers at certain times (although it may
involve such an experience for some) but the abiding possession of
all who are "born again to a living hope through the resurrection
of Jesus Christ from the dead" (v. 3), even when they are most
distressed or their lives are in turmoil (v. 6). In their sanctification
believers begin at the top, because they begin with Christ; in him
they are those who are "perfect" (1 Cor. 2:6) and "spiritual"

(v. 15), even when they have to be admonished as "carnal" (3:1, 3).

I am not so sanguine as Packer that contemporary charismatic renewal provides a base for seeking Edwardian revival (p. 74). As one who stands closer to the concerns of the latter, it seems to me that his optimism is bound up with an assessment of the charismatic movement, particularly its distinctives, that involve a puzzling and questionable compartmentalizing of its theology (largely unsound) and its spirituality (largely sound).[5] But I do want to underline his call for greater mutual acceptance among Protestant Evangelicals in our ultimately common spiritual struggles and aspirations. It is challenging to contemplate the possibilities if we all, Charismatics and non-Charismatics alike, were more thoroughly enlivened by that eschatological root of renewal-revival expressed in Romans 6 and elsewhere. And as always, I remain optimistic about what can happen *spiritus cum verbo*—the Spirit working with the Word—when there is a common submission, no matter what differences there may be, to the final and inerrant authority of that inscripturated Word.

## ENDNOTES

[1] See, e.g., James D. G. Dunn, *Jesus and the Spirit* (Philadelphia: Westminster, 1975), pp. 41–67, 159–61, 308–18 and the literature cited there.

[2] For a more extensive discussion of 1 Corinthians 15:45, see R. B. Gaffin, Jr., *The Centrality of the Resurrection* (Grand Rapids: Baker, 1978), pp. 78–92.

[3] Chapter 1 of R. Stronstad, *The Charismatic Theology of St. Luke* (Peabody, Mass.: Hendrickson, 1984), largely misses the point. The case against the Pentecostal understanding of events described in Acts 2, 8, 9, 10, and 19 does not rest on the exclusion of those passages as doctrinally irrelevant because they are narrative in character, although admittedly the argument has been put that way. Unquestionably the narration in Luke and Acts is structured by distinctive theological concerns and emphases. At issue, however, is what that theology is, and so far as the work of the Spirit is concerned, as Packer observes (p. 00), Luke's interest is "historical and eschatological rather than subjective and charismatic."

[4] For my own evaluation, see R. B. Gaffin, Jr., *Perspectives on Pentecost* (Phillipsburg, N.J.: Presbyterian and Reformed, 1979).

[5] See the reservations expressed by J. D. MacMillan in his review of *Keep in Step with the Spirit* in *The Banner of Truth*, 257 (February 1985), pp. 21–24.

# A Response to
# The Holy Spirit and His Work

## Gordon MacDonald

A reading of J. I. Packer's paper on "The Holy Spirit and His Work" affects me deeply. It causes me to review my spiritual and theological journey over the past thirty years. Where, I ask myself, could I have found something as lucid and useful as this helpful paper in those early days when I was struggling to find my way with God?

I was raised in the tradition of dispensational Fundamentalism. There are many consequences—positive and negative—of this theological heritage. The positive consequences included a strong emphasis upon Bible knowledge and memorization and an awareness that the Bible had an intentional structure to its content and was not merely a collection of ancient religious literature. I also received a heavy dosage of Pauline teaching, especially when it came to ecclesiology and eschatology.

The negative consequences included an almost total absence of teaching on the nature of the present kingdom and the meaning of kingdom citizenship as the model for identifying with the Lord Christ. I came to see later that this tended to "dehumanize" the gospel, causing an overemphasis on what was called spiritual. Then I had little awareness of wholeness, what I sometimes later called the "earthiness" of faith.

But perhaps the most serious omission was an adequate appraisal of the person and work of the Holy Spirit. It was an omission which I have often thought originated in the tendency of early dispensationalists to err to the side of the rational for fear of appearing to be subjective. Yet while there was little subjectivism (or mysticism) in my background, it is curious that there was, in my judgment, an excess of sentimentalism which perhaps served as a compensation for that inner need for something more than mere propositions and dogma.

Perhaps there was a tendency to miss something of the Holy Spirit since the dispensationalist/Fundamentalist felt preoccupied in the areas of christology, eschatology, and biblical inspiration and its implication for revealed authority. The Holy Spirit seemed not to be an issue, at least as far as I can remember.

As a result, I first became aware of the significance of the Holy Spirit during my college days. That acquaintance came—thankfully—through the teaching of parachurch workers who taught the ministry of the Holy Spirit with fervor, emphasizing the Spirit's desire to fill the believer with power and joy. While I would later conclude that this teaching was relatively inadequate in terms of its completeness, I was and am always grateful that there were those who saw the importance of highlighting this special truth of the Third Person of the Godhead for those of us who were missing a major element of Christian truth and experience.

I now know that the simple message of the Spirit's filling was reflective of a passion for world evangelization. The objective of the collegiate ministry was to change the world. The key to that objective was a simple plan of gospel presentation and the appropriation of the indwelling power of the Spirit. It was said that if we were to achieve the objective we would need both.

At this same time (the late 1950s), the so-called charismatic movement was beginning to sweep toward prominence in other circles than just the old-line Pentecostal networks. As far as I can tell, this alternative emphasis began with *interiority* rather than the *external performance* (i.e., the visible fruits of the Spirit, power to evangelize) about which my college group was concerned. This simplistic contrast will not settle well with either of these two parties on emphasis of the Holy Spirit, but that was how I perceived their differences.

In this latter (the charismatic) view, the beginning emphasis seemed to be upon one's own spirit baptism, one's own capacity to worship, to feel whole, to find personal relief from various forms of bondage or sin. We who were threatened and put off by this seemingly competitive phenomenon found all sorts of ways and proofs to discount its validity. It is now clear to me that our counterparts were working just as hard to validate what we thought we had rationally disproved.

I have often wondered why I identified with one teaching and not the other. At first I tried to explain my choice theologically, but each time my efforts fell short, especially since there was always someone who seemed to be able to supply convincing rebuttals to my arguments. It often seemed like a theological chess game, and frankly, I usually got my "moves" from others.

Occasionally, because I felt a bit curious and not a little spiritually hungry, I tried to experiment with the alternative—the charismatic—teaching, calling out to God for any form of Spirit baptism he wished to provide. Each attempt seemed to end inconclusively with the mere assurance that I was where God wanted me; that there was no need for further quest. I began to conclude that my noncharismatic view of the Holy Spirit seemed more to be found in my temperament style than anything else. And this observation I will wish to return to later in these comments.

Later I was to learn that my understanding of the Holy Spirit and his work was actually a hybrid form of "deeper-Christian-life" Christianity, a heritage of "Keswickism," and influenced by modern Bible teachers such as Ian Thomas. At the base of this teaching was a form of passivity. I was a "glove," I was often told, and the Spirit wished to function as a "hand" taking over my tongue, my ears, my body, etc. "Let the Spirit do it through you . . ." became for me a constant and frustrating watchword. In candor this perspective rarely seemed to work for me, and while it was to be appreciated for giving me a hunger for the work and person of the Spirit, it nevertheless left me too often empty and unable to explain either my frequent failures or my strange successes in growth and service. If I noted to my spiritual mentors or directors that I was not experiencing the promised results or fruits, I was usually informed that the problem was mine and that it was probably a matter of "hidden" or unconfessed sin within. I need to remind listeners that this was more than twenty-five years ago, but while I have gone on to a broader and healthier position, I fear that some may still struggle with a view of the Holy Spirit that could be more hindrance than help.

So it is this sharp memory of earlier struggles that causes me to have such enthusiasm for J. I. Packer's presentation to us on the work of the Holy Spirit. He has provided for us a remarkable overview of the biblical teaching on the Holy Spirit that makes some of those earlier teachings on the Third Person of the Trinity seem like thin soup indeed. I do not wish to heap embarrassing or needless praise, but I feel as if I have read the work of a master, much as if I had finished listening to a Bach cantata or viewed a delicate Monet or Renoir painting. I appreciate his fine mixture of scholarship with clarity (which means I understood what he wrote) and an obvious loving worship of the God of the Bible. It is a treat to read the work of a theologian who obviously walks in intimacy with the heavenly Father spiritually as well as intellectually.

We should not fail to ponder Packer's reminder that the work of the Holy Spirit comes to prominence among those who find it possible (if not downright smart) to acknowledge the "inadequacy of all human effort. . . ." Perhaps we would find a correlation in church history between those occasional bursts of interest in the Holy Spirit and individuals or eras where it seemed clear that humankind simply did not have a prayer of going it alone without God in order to ascend above the power of evil or intimidating and crushing circumstances.

The early church's openness to the Holy Spirit seems both a joyful reveling in the prophetically promised descent of the Spirit upon all believers and a sure awareness that the dream of the kingdom was not going to be realized if there was not an inner dynamic that would come from heaven just as Jesus promised.

The emphasis upon the Spirit which Packer identifies with Calvin, Edwards, and Owen is certainly parallel with times in which men sensed great inner despair as well as the darkness of the times in which they lived.

Perhaps the present-day revival of interest in the Holy Spirit tells us much the same thing: that the common person, as well as the theologian, like poets, senses that there is little natural gift or talent in man today worth celebrating; that the twentieth century is indeed another era in which evil shows itself as more insidious than anyone would have thought or imagined. Perhaps the near global interest in the Spirit among Christians today suggests that there is an inward realization that world evangelization and a God-honoring lifestyle is absolutely impossible apart from a divinely given gift of power and resolve. Just maybe, the ordinary Christian by his/her interest is actually telling church leaders and pastors that the infinite amount of words and programs that promise fulfillment and happiness are in themselves empty, that the Holy Spirit's work is where the action really is and that when we understand that, the kingdom will once again enter a truly expansion mode.

Dr. Packer is right; as long as humankind—Christian or non-Christian—insists on an optimistic view of history without God and proposes that evil is merely a social blight to be swept away with programs, behavior modification, or a reconstruction of the genes, there will be no interest in the Spirit. But where people consciously or unconsciously sense the opposite, there the work of the Spirit will gain prominence.

One cannot read through J. I. Packer's amazing synopsis of the biblical teaching on the Holy Spirit without being newly impressed with how present the Spirit is in the works of all God's people. He offers, at least for me, a fresh new approach to the Lucan writings as he suggests that the beloved physician was actually telling us the story of the Spirit's work from conception of our Lord all the way to the incredible explosion of the church's apostolic ministry.

For those who feel the burden of underscoring the inerrantist position, Packer has been helpful in reviewing the possible contributions. It is from this inerrantist source that one is most likely to hear of the importance of affirming the "robust superna-

turalism," the miraculous work of the Spirit as recorded in
Scripture. The inerrantist will be a constant source of warning
against a mindless subjectivism in which the Spirit's ministry is
misused and often becomes exploitive and dominating. Finally,
the inerrantist, Packer says, will contribute the urgent and
frequent reminder that the present work of the indwelling and
objective truth must always be held in balance lest one appear to
militate against or eclipse the other.

Perhaps J. I. Packer had his reasons, but I would like to have
heard him speak more in his paper about the role of the Holy
Spirit first in the area of common grace. By that I mean the role of
the Spirit in the larger world than that of either the Christian or
the church.

The tradition in which I was earlier raised had—as I hinted—
an extremely inadequate view of the goodness there is in the
world. So determined were some to identify the unrighteousness
of the times that they were often led to dismiss the many
contributive and resourceful people of this world as those merely
attempting to work for their salvation. Thus a tragically negative
shade was thrown over effort and intention that frankly should
have been lauded by the Christian community. Like others I have
come to believe that all good work and innovation, whether it
comes from the hand of a follower of the Lord or an atheist, must
originate from the common (as opposed to the special) grace or
work of the Spirit. Perhaps Packer would suggest that this issue is
one of conjecture and is not adequately spoken to within
Scripture.

I am interested that he also did not make more of the Holy
Spirit in terms of his restraining activity. If it is not the Spirit of
God who holds back the total effect of evil in our world, what is it
that does? Of course, even raising this question opens doors to
other even more mysterious issues, such as why there is as much
evil as there is and by what principles might the Spirit selectively
work if he indeed functions as a restrainer.

How does the Spirit intersect with the human being in terms
of resistibility? Does Packer in his exhaustive study of the Bible on
the subject of the Holy Spirit find any sort of consistency in the
way the Spirit seems to "intrude" upon some but be "quenchable"
(Saint Paul's word) in terms of approaching others? How deeply
into personal rebellion does one sink before he/she becomes
useless to the Spirit, and why did lying to the Spirit—as did
Ananias and Sapphira—engender such a drastic consequence
then, but one that does not seem ever to be repeated as far as we
know?

Packer hints at the issue of the role of women in church
leadership when he acknowledges the indiscriminate filling and
"engifting" of all believers regardless of gender or culture. He

leaves open the interesting question of how we affirm the Spirit's call and empowerment to both men *and* women in the church if we believe in ordination for one and not the other. This has been a struggle for me and should be for many others. For the alternative view of ordination or recognition of spiritual leadership casts us toward a hierarchical or episcopal view of ordination. And I can think of one or two people who might be horrified at that notion.

If there is one issue I would like to have seen dealt with in this wonderful paper, it would have been one which has been of chief importance to me personally. I call it the issue of temperament and culture. I would like to hear Dr. Packer venture an opinion as to whether or not the Holy Spirit appears to reveal his gifts and fruits in people in terms of their personality style (temperament) or even their cultural context. Why does the Asian seem to receive the meditative and reflective gifts of the Spirit while the African gravitates toward the so-called wisdom gifts? And why does the Latin appear to be drawn to the charismatic gifts and the European/North American to the organizational? Is this merely a human phenomenon, or is the Spirit responding to a sort of contextualization?

But even more significant to me is the matter of temperament. Does the Spirit, in fact, often reveal himself to us in response to the sort of people we are in personality construct? In other words, does he *normally* speak to us and empower us in ways in which we are most likely to receive his work? Is it possible that some of us are more predisposed, for example, to a tongues experience, while others are predisposed to an inner certainty of the Spirit's work which comes through a rational or more objective experience? (The reader will appreciate that I struggle for words which explain my naïve question, while at the same time I wish to show no disrespect to those of either or other persuasions). An answer to this question, were it possible, would greatly assist, I suggest, toward greater unity between those of the charismatic and the so-called noncharismatic tradition. Knowing that the Spirit spoke to each of us both as "he wills" and as we are predisposed to receive divine ministry would dampen the intimidating clamor that often comes as people on both sides of this crucial question oppose and sadly attempt to discredit one another.

The possibility of world evangelization and great revival in the church depends to a considerable extent on both what Dr. Packer has so effectively taught us in his paper and in a resolution of some of the foregoing questions. I for one would welcome from my brothers and sisters in the inerrantist movement both a serious study of these matters and a new flexibility and tolerance that would permit the great sectors of the Holy Spirit's community, the church, to unite and to get on with the pursuit of the great task Christ gave us: to be witnesses to the nations of God's creating, redeeming, and reforming love.

# THE CHURCH AND ITS MISSION

## Edmund P. Clowney

The removal of the papal throne to Avignon in France from 1309 to 1377 was called the "Babylonish Captivity" of the church, marking almost seventy years of exile from Rome.[1] But there was a span, not of years but of centuries, when the medieval church was captive because it was a captor. Through those dark ages the church imprisoned the Bible. The Reformation removed the yoke of tradition that had subjected the Word of God to the decrees of men; it swept aside the sacerdotal magic that had perverted the gospel of grace; it turned again to the Scripture—and the Scripture alone—as the Word of God. *Scriptura sola* became the banner of liberty for faith and worship: it delivered men from ecclesiastical bondage to walk in the freedom of Christ.

The church of God lives by the Word of God. The hierarchical medieval institution became a caricature of the church of Christ by presuming to stand over rather than under the Word of God. John Calvin's diagnosis was tragically true: The church that has lost the doctrine of the Word is not just bruised or ill; its throat has been cut.[2]

In a different way the Bible has since been lost to many churches of the Reformation. The Bible has not been locked in the crypt of tradition, but it has been shredded by the scalpel of rationalistic criticism.[3] For liberalism old and new there is no such thing as revealed truth: the Bible cannot be the judge of faith and life. The consequences for the church the rejection of the authority of the Bible are still appearing. The church that turns from the written Word of God self-destructs.

Two aspects of the interrelation of the church and the Word may be considered: first, how the church is formed by the Word; second, how the church ministers the Word.

## I. THE CHURCH IS FORMED BY THE WORD

When the apostle Peter describes the church as a "chosen people, a royal priesthood, a holy nation, a people belonging to God" he applies to the church of the new covenant the most precious terms for God's nation of the old covenant.[4] The doctrine of the church as the people of God extends through all of Scripture. It centers on God himself: the church is the people of God, the body of Christ, the fellowship of the Holy Spirit. A wealth of figures is used for the people that God claims as his possession; they are the flock of the Good Shepherd, the vine of God's vineyard, the betrothed and bride of the Lord, the building and house of God.[5] One major picture of the church is more than a picture: it presents the church as God's assembly.

### A. God's Word Forms the Church As Assembly

*Ecclesia*, the New Testament word for "church," means "assembly." It may refer to any gathering, but its biblical usage recalls the assembly of Israel at Mount Sinai.[6] That was the "day of the assembly" when God called the people he had delivered from Egypt to stand before his face (Deut. 9:10; 10:4; 18:16). "Assemble the people before me to hear my words," he told Moses (Deut. 4:10). God spoke to the assembled congregation from the fire and smoke of Sinai. There he gave them the words of his covenant. God came down to Sinai as the Lord of Hosts, attended by the holy angels of his heavenly assembly (Deut. 33:2; Pss. 68:17; 82:1). At Sinai the heavenly and earthly holy ones were assembled together. Reflecting on this Old Testament picture, the sect at Qumran saw their assembly as joining with the angels.[7]

The gathering at Sinai to hear the Word of the Lord was repeated in the later history of Israel in assemblies for covenant renewal and in the three annual festival assemblies that summoned the people to Mount Zion.[8]

At the command of Jesus, the disciples were gathered together on the Feast of Pentecost for the epiphany of the Holy Spirit that inaugurated the new covenant people of God (Acts 2:1–4). When Jesus said to Peter, "On this rock I will build my *church*," he was using a familiar term for the congregation of the Lord.[9]

Israel was made to be the people of God as they stood before the Lord at Sinai; so, too, the New Testament church is constituted as God's assembly. God's appearance at Sinai was in physical fire and earthquake, with the thunder of the Lord's voice; the assembly to which we come is immeasurably more awe-inspiring. We do not come to Mount Sinai, but to Mount Zion: not to the smoking mountain in the desert, but to the mountain where

God has established his name and dwelling (Heb. 12:18–29). Yet the Mount Zion of our worship is not the earthly mountain in the land of Israel; it is the heavenly Mount Zion. The fire that we approach is not a fire that may be touched; it is the fire of God's own presence: "Our God is a consuming fire" (v. 29).

The covenant-making assembly at Sinai formed Israel as a people. The assemblies at Mount Zion distinguished Israel from the nations as the holy people of God—a kingdom of priests and a holy nation.[10] The yearning of the psalmist for the courts of the Lord expresses what was central for the life of believing Israel: to appear before the face of the Lord to hear his law. In the fulfillment heralded by the author of Hebrews, the sanctuary is the *heavenly* holy place. The feast-day assembly of the holy ones is gathered—the holy angels and the saints of God, past and present (vv. 22–23). In the midst stands Jesus, the Mediator of the new covenant, who has sprinkled the throne with his own atoning blood.

But this is not a poetic image. It is the reality that replaces all the types and shadows. Jesus has triumphed; he has entered the heavenly sanctuary for us, and it is to his assembly that we come in worship. That is not just a picture of the future; it is a description of the present. The reason that Christians are not to forsake the assembling of themselves on earth (Heb. 10:25) is because they now "draw near" to join the assembly in heaven (10:19–22; 12:22). It is the heavenly assembly that defines the church.

Because the heavenly assembly defines the church, earthly assemblies may be smaller or larger. Neither the church universal nor the local assembly can be made the definitive assembly of the church to the exclusion of the other. Indeed, house churches existed *within* city churches, and both are regarded as churches (Col. 4:15–16; Rom. 16:3–5). All who call upon the name of the Lord in a given place, whether a household, a city, or a region make up an assembly that joins with the gathering in heaven (1 Cor. 1:2).

The climax of the passage in Hebrews warns us to heed the Word of God. God assembled Israel at Sinai to hear the thunder of his voice. But the voice that we hear is not from the top of Sinai; it is from heaven. It is the voice of the Son of God. God who spoke to the fathers through the prophets has at the end of these days spoken through his Son (Heb. 1:1–2). "See to it that you do not refuse him who speaks" (Heb. 12:25).

The people of God are those who are summoned by his voice and summoned to hear his voice. Not simply the *presence* of God, but the *Word* of God is the reason that the people of God are an *ecclesia*, an assembly. The church followed the practice of the synagogue in reading and expounding the Word of God in worship; that practice was modeled on the assembly of covenant renewal in the time of Ezra and Nehemiah. The new covenant people, like the old, are "entrusted with the very words of God" (Rom. 3:2).

## B. Christ's Church Established in His Word

### 1. Promise and Fulfillment

The great time of renewal promised by the prophets can come only with the coming of God himself (Isa. 40:3). The condition of God's people is such that only God can save them. God himself will come as the true Shepherd to gather the lambs in his bosom and gently lead his sheep (Ezek. 34:11–16; Isa. 40:11). Only the Divine Warrior can liberate his people (Isa. 59:16–17). The promises of God point beyond the return of the exiles under Ezra and Nehemiah to the outpouring of all the blessings that God had promised to Abraham and through him to the nations (Gen. 12:3; Isa. 56:6–8).

The good news of the new covenant is that God has kept his promise. He has come in the person of his Son. God's covenant promise was "I will walk among you and be your God, and you will be my people" (Lev. 26:12; 2 Cor. 6:16). The Lord must come; Jesus is Lord. But the role of the servant must also be fulfilled. Israel's tragic failure cannot be remedied by another new generation emerging from the wilderness or returning from exile. Neither can the calling of God's servant be realized by another Moses or David. There must come a greater servant. To him God can say, "You are my servant, Israel, in whom I will display my splendor" (Isa. 49:3).[11] Jesus Christ is that servant. Israel was planted as God's vine: Jesus is the true Vine (Ps. 80:8–17; Isa. 5:1–7; Ezek. 19:10–14; John 15:1). He is both Son and Servant. He fulfills the ministry of the circumcision for the truth of God so that the promises of God may not fail but rather that the Gentiles may be blessed in the seed of Abraham (Rom. 15:8–9).

Christ comes on the mission of his Father. As Lord he reveals his power; he is the Creator who can command the storm and expel the demons; he is the Savior who can pronounce the peace of God upon restored lepers and open the kingdom of heaven to penitent harlots and robbers. As Lord he gathers his people, the remnant flock given him of the Father; to them he promises the kingdom (John 10:27–30; Luke 12:32). As Servant he tells them that he has come to do the Father's will, to seek and to save that which was lost, to give his life a ransom for many (Mark 10:45; Luke 19:10; John 6:38).

Jesus is not only the Promised One to whom all the Scriptures bear witness. He is also himself the true Witness. Moses, who stood on the mountain while God's voice spoke from the cloud, stood again on a mountain with Jesus. He heard the voice of God, speaking not the Ten Commandments again, but a new commandment, "This is my beloved Son: hear him" (Mark 9:7 KJV). God who spoke in many different ways to the fathers through the prophets, spoke finally and fully in his Son (Heb. 1:1–2). Jesus *speaks*, and we must hear and heed his words, for he speaks the words the Father has given him, words of Spirit and of life (John 8:26, 38, 40; 6:63). The Spirit of Christ moved the Old Testament prophets to speak the Word of the Lord (1 Peter 1:11); the New Testament apostles and prophets are also inspired by the Spirit of Christ (John 14:25–26; 16:13–14; Eph. 3:5).

## 2. *The Apostolic Confession of the Church*

Jesus spoke the words that constituted the new people of God in response to the confession of Simon Peter (Matt. 16:18). Peter's confession had been elicited by Christ himself. The most ambitious rabbi would surely have been flattered to know that people took him for a reincarnation of Elijah or Jeremiah or even John the Baptist. But Jesus was not satisfied. He is not a prophet reincarnate. He is the Son of God incarnate. "But what about you," he asked them. "Who do you say I am?" (Matt. 16:15).[12] Peter, spokesman for the Twelve, confessed: "You are the Christ, the Son of the living God" (v. 16). Peter confessed Jesus as the Messiah at a time when many had turned away from him because he would not lead revolt from the Romans. Peter knew that Jesus alone had the words of eternal life (John 6:68). Jesus is Messiah beyond the range of any prophet, any king, any man or any angel. He is the Son of the living God.

Jesus accepts and endorses Peter's confession. It has not come from flesh and blood, not even from Peter's loyal heart. It is revelation from the living God himself, Jesus' Father in heaven. To Peter's "You are the Christ," Jesus responds, "You are Peter" (Matt. 16:18). That name "Peter," given by Jesus to Simon, serves almost as a title in parallel to "Christ." Jesus is the Christ; Simon is Peter, the Rock. Peter and his confession cannot be separated. Reaction against the claims of Roman Catholic exegesis has led some Protestant expositors to exclude Peter from the reference of Jesus' words, "On this rock I will build my church." They identify the rock as the confession, not Peter. But Jesus addresses Simon Bar-Jonah (v. 17) to affirm that he is Peter (Cephas), the Rock, and adds that on *this* rock he will build his church.[13]

On the other hand, neither can the confession be excluded from the reference of Jesus. It is the *confessing* Peter who is the rock: Peter the apostle, the recipient of revelation from the Father. This is made clear by the next interchange between Jesus and

Peter in the same chapter. When Peter rebukes Jesus for speaking about going to his death, Jesus addresses Peter as Satan, tells him that he is minding the things of men rather than the things of God, and declares that he is a *skandalon* (Matt. 16:23). In Aramaic the expression would be *"stone* of stumbling," a phrase in which the name of Peter would be used.[14] Peter is called a rock by Jesus, not once, but twice. As the confessing apostle, he is a rock of foundation; as an instrument of Satan, he is a rock of stumbling. The reference to Peter's confession cannot be omitted. Apart from the confession and the revelation that was its source, Peter is no rock of foundation.

Further, Peter cannot be separated from the eleven. Jesus addresses his question to the disciples in the plural, and Peter answers as their spokesman. The power of the keys, given to Peter, is repeated by Jesus in reference to all the disciples (Matt. 18:18; John 20:23). The church is built upon the foundation of the apostles and prophets, who, like Peter, are organs of revelation (Eph. 2:20; 3:5; see Rev. 21:14).

## 3. *The Apostolicity of the Church*

Jesus is the Lord and Builder of his church. When he returned to heaven after fulfilling the mission of his Father, Jesus did not leave the task of establishing (or even inventing!) the church to the devices of those who had been more or less profoundly influenced by his ministry. To say that Jesus left no book but a fellowship is entirely misleading.[15] Jesus builds his church on the revelation given to the apostles. The Father, the Son, the Spirit are the authors of that revelation. From the beginning of his ministry Jesus makes provision for the establishment of the church in the training of the twelve. The apostles, chosen and authorized by Christ, are the divinely appointed link between the Word of Christ and the church of Christ.

Jesus chose the twelve that they might be with him (Mark 3:14), so that they might be eyewitnesses of his works and earwitnesses of his words. He gave them authority to preach, heal and cast out demons in his name (Matt. 10:1; Mark 3:14). Those who receive them, receive Christ; those who reject them, reject Christ (Matt. 10:40).[16] They are to pronounce Christ's peace on those who receive them, but shake off the dust of their feet in judicial witness against the house or town that refuses their word (v. 14). Not only will their witness prevail in the day of judgment; they themselves will sit on twelve thrones, judging the tribes of Israel (19:28). Their authority, however, is in no sense independent of the authority of the Lord. They are not made lords like the kings of the Gentiles; their calling is to serve their Lord, to minister to others in his name (20:26–28; 23:1–12). They are not the exclusive mediators of the name of the Lord (Luke 9:49–50).

The witness of the apostles, nevertheless, is formal and forensic. They form a chosen group, distinguished from the many who had seen and heard Jesus, for Jesus himself selected and prepared them (Acts 10:40–42). Their witness completes the witness of the prophets (v. 43). They are public heralds of the Lord (1 Tim. 2:7). As Jesus has been sent, so he sends them (John 17:18). They are called apostles in the context of Jesus' sending them two by two (the law requires two witnesses) to preach to the towns of Israel (Matt. 10:2; Mark 6:30).[17] To the apostles is given the charge to go and to make disciples of the nations (Matt. 28:18–20). They who saw the risen Lord bear witness in the authority of the Spirit (Acts 1:8, 22; 1 Cor. 9:1).

The witness of the apostles is foundational for the church. They are not only heralds, announcing the resurrection to the world. They are also teachers; they ground the faith of the church in the Word of Christ (Acts 2:42). Apostles can claim the obedience of the church to the Word of the Lord as they deliver it (Rom. 1:5; 2 Cor. 2:9; 1 Thess. 2:13; 2 Peter 3:2). The "tradition," the deposit of the faith as it is committed to the church by the apostles, is not tradition in the vague sense that we use the term. It is that which has been handed down with *authority* (cf. Mark 7:5). It is the teaching received from Christ, first in his earthly ministry, then in the forty days after the resurrection and finally from his throne of glory by the Spirit (John 14:26; 16:13, 15).[18] The tradition, that which has been received is received from the *Lord* and delivered to the church as the fixed deposit of authoritative teaching regarding the faith and order of the church (1 Cor. 11:2, 23; 2 Thess. 2:15; 1 Tim. 6:20; 2 Tim. 1:12, 14).

The apostles are masterbuilders, putting in place the foundation of the church in their teaching (1 Cor. 3:10). The church is a temple of God, built upon the foundation of the apostles and prophets (Eph. 2:20; Rev. 21:14). The prophets share with the apostles in receiving and communicating the Word of Christ; with the apostles they are organs of revelation (Eph. 3:5). But to charismatic prophets who might dispute his apostolic authority, Paul writes, "If anybody thinks he is a prophet or spiritually gifted, let him acknowledge that what I am writing to you is the Lord's command" (1 Cor. 14:37).

The apostolic foundation is written as well as spoken. Paul directs that his letters be read in the churches, not simply that his greetings and teaching might be conveyed, but because what he writes is the direction of the Lord, that which is ordained for the churches (1 Cor. 11:2; 7:17; Col. 4:16; 1 Thess. 5:27). In 1 Corinthians 15 we find Paul writing "in ample and deliberate scriptural form what he had first transmitted orally regarding the resurrection."[19] John, too, bears testimony in writing; what has been written leads to faith in Christ (John 20:30–31; 21:24; cf. Rev.

22:18–19). Peter includes the writings of Paul with the other Scriptures; when men twist them, they do so to their own destruction (2 Peter 3:15–16).

The claim of the apostles in the New Testament is of first importance in understanding the relation of the church to Scripture. The biblical doctrine of the church puts the church under the Bible. Herman Ridderbos has well summarized how sharply the Reformers differed from the position of the Roman Catholic church on this crucial point. "According to the Roman Catholic view, the Canon *viewed in itself (quoad se)* possesses undoubted inherent authority. But *as it concerns us (quoad nos)*, the recognition of the Canon rests upon the authority of the Church."[20] In contrast, the Reformation confessed that the Word of God is its own authority, applied to our hearts by the internal witness of the Holy Spirit. "The Church does not control the Canon, but the Canon controls the Church."[21]

Liberalism puts not the church, but religious consciousness, above Scripture. The sheer subjectivism of this enlightenment approach was modified in later dialectical theology. The Bible was distinguished from the Word of God and made to be a witness to the Word, a human and fallible response to an ineffable act of divine revelation. The Confession of 1967 of the United Presbyterian church adopted this position to undercut the Reformed doctrine of Scripture in the first chapter of the Westminster Confession of Faith. The neoorthodox position is clearly enunciated: "The church has received the books of the Old and New Testaments as prophetic and apostolic testimony in which it hears the Word of God and by which its faith and obedience are nourished and regulated."[22]

The apostles did indeed bear witness to what they had seen and heard, but their witness was inspired of the Spirit. They spoke the commandment of the Lord. The scriptural concept of witness begins with God's own witness: his Word spoken from Sinai, his inscripturated witness written with the finger of God on the tablets of witness (Exod. 31:18). Jesus Christ speaks the words given him of the Father (John 12:49–50). His witness is true. Through the apostles Jesus completes his witness to his church. That which was "spoken through the Lord was confirmed unto us by them that heard; God also bearing witness with them, both by signs and wonders, and by manifold powers and by gifts of the Holy Spirit according to his own will" (Heb. 2:3–4 ASV). The Bible is not simply a human witness where we may hear the Word of God in an existential experience. It is the Word of God, the scepter of Christ in the government of his church. When the words of the Bible are no longer normative for the life of the church, it is inevitable that whatever laws regulate the church will bind the conscience that God has set free.[23] To govern in the faith and order of Christ's church apart from the ministry of his royal Word is to impose spiritual bondage.

The apostolic foundation of the church is complete and final. Because the apostles give to the church the final revelation of God as it is in Jesus Christ, their foundational ministry is once and for all. Beyond the generation of the apostles there could not be witnesses to the words and deeds of Jesus (Acts 1:21–22). Moreover, the apostles do not elaborate new doctrines that go beyond God's revelation in Christ. Rather they are inspired to bring to the church the riches of that revelation, including many things that Jesus could not communicate to them until he had been raised and glorified (John 16:12–15). Paul, in particular, is aware of the fullness of the gospel mystery revealed to him as the last of the apostles, unworthy, to be sure, but raised up to be the Lord's servant in carrying the message to the Gentiles (1 Cor. 15:8–9; Gal. 2:7; Eph. 3:3, 8; Col. 1:25–29).[24] God's speaking through the prophets of old is now fulfilled and completed in his speaking through his Son (Heb. 1:1–2). It is that final Word of Christ that is brought to us through the apostles (Heb. 2:3–4). The apostolic foundation of the spiritual temple, the house of God, has been laid. It is not to be torn up for repaving, nor does it continue indefinitely: it is the foundation of a house, not a roadbed. The task of making disciples of all the nations continues; Jesus promised his presence in that ministry until the end of the age. Others besides the apostles are given special gifts as evangelists, missionaries to herald the gospel.[25] But the authority of the apostles transmitted the Word of the Lord to the church once for all.

### 4. Apostolicity and the Attributes of the Church

The Christian church has been confessing, "We believe . . . in one holy Catholic and Apostolic Church" since 451 A.D., when the Council of Chalcedon approved the "Nicene Creed."[26] The apostolicity of the church bears directly on its attributes of unity, catholicity, and holiness.

With respect to *unity*, the grounding of the church in the Word of Christ obviously requires acceptance of the apostolic faith for true ecumenicity. The church is called to be the "pillar and foundation of the truth" (1 Tim. 3:15). Critical biblical scholarship has promoted the view that there are diverse and conflicting theological views in the Bible and that the unity of the church demands doctrinal pluralism. Pluralism has been called a "catholic" approach, on the plea that it is embracive rather than exclusive.[27] But the fellowship of the New Testament church was found by continuing in the apostles' teaching (Acts 2:42). The one view that is intolerable to pluralism is the view that pluralism itself denies the sufficiency and perspicuity of Scripture and therefore the apostolic foundation of the church.

Yet it may fairly be asked if the ecumenical movement as represented by the World Council of Churches has not given more attention to doctrinal differences that divide the churches than has the evangelical movement.[28] Indeed, Evangelicals seem to assume that disagreements on doctrine are structural to denominational (or parachurch) institutionalism and are therefore untouchable. When divisions emerged at Corinth that were "denominational" (bearing the names of Peter, Paul, Apollos, even Christ), the apostle did not congratulate those most loyal to him, but cried "Is Christ divided? Was Paul crucified for you?" (1 Cor. 1:13). Conviction as to the apostolicity of the church must drive Evangelicals to seek a scriptural ecumenism. It will not do to plead the invincible unity of the church as God sees it (the church as invisible to us). Jesus gives the keys to the apostles for the church on earth. The unity of the Spirit must be sought in the unity of the truth, never apart from it, but what is much more, by labor together in it.

The *catholicity* of the church is grounded in the universality of the apostolic message. That message is a proclamation to be heralded to the ends of the earth and the end of time, yet catholicity is fundamentally not quantitative but spiritual. In Christ the people of God are no longer divided by social, sexual, racial, or cultural barriers (Col. 3:11). There is no difference: all have sinned and are unworthy of Christ, yet by his grace all are made children of God. Clearly no church has the right to exclude from membership in its communion one who confesses the apostolic faith. Christian missions may accommodate to the restrictions of sinful society to gain a hearing for the gospel. Yet such accommodation is always temporal and expedient. It may never baptize the very prejudices that union with Christ destroys. The danger of sectarianism appears if a church begins to define itself as something more than apostolic and therefore less than catholic.

At the heart of the apostolic message is *holiness*. The gospel as the power of God issues in new obedience, a life so distinct from the patterns of this age as to require the outpouring of the Spirit. In countless moral issues, individual and social, liberal Christianity has been conformed not only to the patterns of this age but to a rather specific and predictable "liberal" viewpoint. The danger is that Evangelicals may react by beginning with the opposing social or political tradition and amending the apostolic tradition to fit. A denatured evangelicalism, enamored of success, may select from the apostolic gospel elements congenial to its contemporary subculture and fail to grasp the meaning of gospel holiness.

## C. The Scriptural Order of the Church

Paul was forced to combat false apostles and to warn of future apostasy (2 Cor. 11:13–14; 1 Tim. 4:1–2). Over the centuries false churches have multiplied. Some are the result of apostasy: churches that once confessed the apostolic faith but turned away from it. Other groups falsely lay claim to the name Christian, though from the outset they denied basic Christian doctrine.[29]

### 1. The Marks of the Church

How are the people of God to discern the true church from the false? In the period of the Reformation, Roman Catholic polemicists externalized the attributes of the church to form marks of the church that would exclude the Protestants. Apostolicity was equated with papal authority by the claim to apostolic succession; unity was in submission to papal authority; holiness was dispensed through the priesthood as sacramental grace and therefore unavailable to schismatics; catholicity was geographical (at that time the Reformation had been confined to northern Europe, while the Roman church had been carried to all the continents by the missionary orders).[30]

In response, the Reformers insisted on the spiritual nature of the attributes of the church. Its unity is in Christ; it is not bound to the pretensions of the papacy but is manifested in the fellowship of the saints. Catholicity marks the welcome of the gospel to all races of men: it extends through time as well as space; the Roman church, by fabricating a religion of good works forsook the catholic bond with the apostolic church. The holiness of the church is the fruit of the sanctifying Spirit of Christ and cannot be dispensed by sacerdotal control.

The marks of the true church must be sought rather in the authority of the Word of Christ in which the church is founded. The Reformers defined the marks of the church as the faithful ministry of the Word, the observance of the sacraments and of discipline.[31] The standard by which the church is to be examined must begin with the orthodoxy of the apostolic foundation. Apart from the faithful preaching of the Word, the church cannot live. The Word faithfully preached is the sword of the Spirit to cut away error in doctrine or life. The sacraments are necessary as outward signs of the commitment of faith as well as means of grace appointed by the Lord. Apart from discipline the church cannot distinguish itself from the world or maintain its testimony to holiness and truth.[32]

## 2. Parachurch Organizations

The controversy of the Reformation period remains unresolved. The Roman claims for the papacy remain, as does the doctrine of the Mass as a sacrifice.[33] Evangelicalism often seems more ready to forget the issues that divide it from Rome than to understand them. But the splintering of denominationalism has raised new questions concerning the marks of the church. Renewal movements in Protestantism (pietism, the evangelical revival in Britain and America) have stimulated new concern for missions, for Bible translation and distribution, for diaconal and social service. Partly to bypass the barriers of denominational division, Christians have formed countless associations to carry forward specific aspects of the church's calling in the world.[34] How are these parachurch organizations to be viewed in terms of the marks of the church?

On the one hand, denominations often define themselves as though they were the church universal. They fail to take account of the fact that they recognize other true churches of Christ and that denominational organization is therefore broken and partial. Denominations cannot condemn parachurch organizations without also recognizing the limitations of their own structure. On the other hand, parachurch groups often acquire more inclusive ministries until they become virtually or actually denominations.[35] Gospel preaching, teaching, the observance of the sacraments, group discipline—all are carried out by organizations that do not regard themselves as churches. Indeed, it is even assumed that since the New Testament speaks only of order for the church, it is silent on the organization of associations.[36] The parachurch groups are therefore free to adopt military organization, entrepreneurial business organization, or civil organization.

## 3. Scriptural Church Order?

Of course a deeper issue needs to be raised. Granted that the apostolic deposit of sound doctrine must be maintained if the church is to be true to Jesus Christ, but are matters of church order included in that apostolic deposit? Surely the New Testament does not contain a little black book of church order nor a *Manual of Discipline* like that of the Dead Sea covenanters.[37] Why is there no Leviticus in the New Testament? Yes, the ceremonial law has been fulfilled in Christ. But Christ the Lord does more: he sends the Spirit. The presence of the Spirit transforms the obedience of the people of God to his revealed will. The demands of holiness are intensified, not relaxed, yet the working of the Spirit through the law of love *personalizes* accountability to God and to his people. Those who govern in Christ's church are shepherds, not judges.

Nevertheless, the apostolic deposit in the New Testament does provide for the ordering of the church as well as for its doctrinal establishment. Indeed, some of the strongest claims for apostolic authority are made as the apostle orders the life of the church (1 Cor. 7:17; 14:33–38; 1 Tim. 3:14). The biblical instructions for the order of the church are given in the same way as the apostolic instructions for the faith of the church. For neither faith nor order is there a compendium in the New Testament. The doctrines of the faith are recorded in missionary letters and in Gospel narratives. The rich *form* of New Testament revelation rewards and renews understanding. Dogmatic theology cannot once for all digest the full apostolic teaching; it must interpret the New Testament message in new cultures and new times and gain the fuller understanding into which the Spirit leads the church. So, too, principles of church order need to be interpreted in their context and applied to the situations in which they are now to be observed.

The fact that we may trace a gradual revelation of the order of the church during the New Testament period in no way limits our acceptance of the principles and ordinances the Lord has revealed. We must, indeed, translate the cultural forms: we may want to translate "holy kiss" as "hearty handshake." Yet the ability to make such translations depends upon the accuracy of our understanding of the meaning of the text.

## 4. Women in the Church

The place of women in the church has become a crux for the interpretation and application of the teaching of Scripture regarding the order of the church.[38] The continuing debate has advanced understanding of some controverted passages. It has been well argued, for example, that the silent behavior that the apostle requires of women in 1 Corinthians 14:34–35 is in the context of the discerning of prophecy and that this statement therefore does not contradict the recognition of women's praying or prophesying in 1 Corinthians 11:5.[39]

There is the danger, of course, that we will read into the New Testament our own prejudices for male chauvinism or women's liberation. If hermeneutics is to maintain a grasp on meaning, we must hear what Paul is saying, not engage in ventriloquism. The deeper issue is whether, having heard Paul's words, we will heed them.

Heeding the words of the apostle requires us to take account of his full teaching. We must begin where Paul begins all his teaching regarding the faith and order of the church: in Jesus Christ the Savior. All government in the church is subordinate to the mediatorial lordship of Jesus Christ; union with Christ transforms the life of the church. Paul teaches, as Jesus taught his disciples, that office in the church is ministry. Paul equates the role to be fulfilled in any ministry with the gift of grace that enables it. When he writes, "I say by the grace given me," he means, "I say as an apostle" (Rom. 12:3; 15:15; Gal. 2:7–9). Some gifts require public recognition for their proper exercise, among them the gift for government in the church. An office is a publicly recognized function of ministry.

Paul resisted the Corinthian fascination with spectacular gifts. He wrote about love as the greatest gift of the Spirit; the saints at Corinth should not seek glory but should find their joy in advancing the things of others. The principle of self-sacrificing love orders the life of the church. Submissiveness for Christ's sake becomes the theme of the apostolic order.[40]

This instruction includes two poles. On the one hand is the service theme: The one who is first in the kingdom is the servant of all. True greatness consists in humbling oneself to serve (Matt. 20:25–28; John 13:13–17). On the other hand is the recognition of distinct roles to be filled in the community of God's people. In the family, husbands and wives fulfill role relationships as do parents and children. In the extended household the relationship of masters and servants is also taken account of. In the broader social context there are the roles of magistrates and citizens, governors and governed. So, too, there are roles in the church, the family of God.[41]

Paul finds in the relation of husbands and wives an analogy for the relation of Christ and the church; or rather the analogy operates in the other direction. Christ's relation to the church becomes the model for the relation of husbands and wives. The role relationship includes an authority structure; the primacy of the man in that relation is traced back to God's ordinance in creation (1 Cor. 11:7–9; 1 Tim. 2:13). The headship of Christ as the Second Adam applies to the church. On the other hand, the relation requires interdependence and communion (1 Cor. 11:11). While Christ is not dependent upon the church, he is nevertheless united to the church, which is "bone of his bone, and flesh of his flesh" (Gen. 2:23–24; Eph. 5:29–32).

The order of the church and the structure of authority in the church flow from the present existence of the church in the time between the first coming of Christ and his return. In the church the life of the Spirit is already given, the powers of the age to come already operate (2 Cor. 3:17–18; Heb. 6:5). All who are united to Christ already share the glory of his risen life. In Christ, therefore, "there is neither Jew nor Greek, slave nor free, male nor female, for you are all one in Christ Jesus" (Gal. 3:28). Yet the church continues an earthly existence. It lives in a world under the curse, and the ordinances that govern a fallen world still apply to the life of the church. The transformation wrought by the Spirit of Christ does not take us out of the world; the discipline of the church operates on earth even though its sanction is in heaven. In heaven there will be no marriage; the male/female distinction will be transcended. But marriage continues as God's institution on earth. In the church of Christ it is sanctified by the model of Christ's relation to the church. The representative and vital union that exists between Christ and the church becomes the paradigm for the relation between husband and wife.

God's appointment of a role relationship between man and woman is not removed in this age by the redemption of Christ. Rather it is deepened, even as it is transformed. The Christian woman will not resent the submission that her role demands, for all Christian living requires submission to others. The Christian man, on the other hand, will understand that his authority is given for service, not dominion, and that the measure of his submission to Christ is his humility in seeking the honor and blessing of his wife.

The roles appointed by God to order the relation of man and wife are respected and not set aside in the church.[42] Not only does the church incorporate families; the church is a family, the family of God (Eph. 3:15).[43] Paul, with inspired authority, forbids to women the office of authoritative teaching and ruling in the church (1 Tim. 2:12). The restriction on women's participation in the judgment of prophecy has this same purpose (1 Cor. 14:34-35).

The question of the exercise of diaconal office by women remains distinct because of the serving function of the diaconate. It is possible that two passages directly recognize women as deacons. In 1 Timothy 3:11 the parallelism in form and content with verse 8 would seem to indicate a parallel function and recognition. In Romans 16:1-2 Paul writes to endorse the ministry of Phoebe and to ask recognition and support for her ministry in Rome. In that context her designation as *diakonos* would seem to imply office as publicly recognized function.[44] On the other hand, Paul's description of the ministry of older widows who are to be enrolled and supported also implies a form of office that may be in addition to the office of deacon rather than part of it (1 Tim. 5:4-10).

In any case, even if women are not regarded as deacons in the technical sense in the New Testament, their ministry is widely recognized. Women are to learn and share their understanding of the Word of God. Some ancient rabbis scorned the ability of women to learn the Scriptures. In contrast, Jesus defends Mary's zeal for hearing his words; he refuses to send her to the kitchen (Luke 10:42). Women are to teach other women (Titus 2:3-4), and we find Priscilla joining her husband Aquila in instructing Apollos in a fuller understanding of the way of God (Acts 18:26). Paul does not hesitate to speak of women as fellow-laborers in the gospel (Phil. 4:2). The honor given by Jesus to women continues in the apostolic church.

## II. THE CHURCH MINISTERS THE WORD

Christ forms his church by his Word and Spirit; he calls his church to minister his Word in the Spirit. The church ministers to God in worship, to the saints in nurture, and to the world in witness.

### A. Worship: The Church Ministers to God

As we have seen, the church is called into assembly to hear the Word of the Lord. Further, the church is a *festival* assembly, gathered not only to hear the Word but also to respond in worship. That response is evoked by the glory of God's presence in the midst of his people. In worship we praise God for what he has done: his works of creation, providence, and salvation. From that joyful tribute we are drawn to bless God for who he is, for "from him and through him and to him are all things. To him be the glory forever!" (Rom. 11:36). No human relation or activity can compare with the worship of God. We do not relate to God with a part of our being; before him we do not play a role. The psalmist cries:

My soul thirsts for God, for the living God.
When can I go and meet with God? (Ps. 42:2)

What the psalmist desires is the supreme fulfillment of the creature made in God's image and remade in the image of Christ. Worship can hold nothing back; it is always extravagant (Deut. 6:4–9; John 12:1–8). That offering of praise is to be shared. Worship is corporate as well as private. The assembled congregation lifts up the name of the Lord.

Our worship is determined by the Word of the Lord. We worship for his pleasure, not our own. The form and the content of our worship must therefore be pleasing to him. We must worship as he commanded in his Word (Deut. 12:30–32). He will not tolerate worship through idols; worship is defiled if we do not worship God alone (Exod. 20:5; 34:13). It is the richly indwelling Word of Christ that comes to expression in the psalms, hymns, and spiritual songs by which the saints praise God and encourage one another (Eph. 5:19–20; Col. 3:16).

Jesus Christ himself sings in the midst of his assembled congregation; he is the sweet psalmist of Israel, leading his brethren in his Father's praise (2 Sam. 23:1; Ps. 22:22; Heb. 2:12).

The song of the church bears witness before the nations; Jesus, who fulfills the ministry of the circumcision, sings also among the Gentiles to the Father's name (Rom. 15:8–9). The witness of the church to the nations is doxological. We sing in harmony with the Psalms, calling all people to join with us in praising the God of salvation (Ps. 96; Isa. 43:21; 1 Peter 2:9).

## B. Nurture: The Church Ministers to the Saints

The pure milk of the Word nourishes our spiritual growth (1 Peter 2:2). It does so as we gain insight into the Word and as we apply it in the testings of our lives. The scriptural ideal of wisdom begins with meditation on the Word of God (2 Tim. 3:15). As the will of God expressed in his revelation is brought to the issues and decisions of our daily lives, we prove what is the good and acceptable will of God (Rom. 12:2; Phil. 1:10; Col. 1:9–10). By the preaching of the Word, the church grows (Acts 6:7; 12:24; 19:20); the Word is the means for the encouragement and correction of the church (2 Tim. 3:16). In a magnificent passage Paul describes how the church grows into maturity in Christ through the proper functioning of every member. He begins, however, with the function of those who are ministers of the Word (Eph. 4:11–12). The gift of teaching and the authority of the teaching office is essential to the nature of the church as well as to its worship and the witness. The Word is the sword of the Spirit in our struggle against the hosts of evil (Eph. 6:17), and it is a sharp sword to discern our own thoughts (Heb. 4:12).

For this reason, the people of God are to bring up their children in the nurture and admonition of the Lord (Eph. 6:4). That means an atmosphere in which the Word of God is spoken of early and late, at home, at work, at play. God's Word must be written on our forehead, our hands, and the doorposts of our homes (Deut. 6:4–9). We may regret the literalism that put this bit of Scripture (the "Shema") in phylacteries bound to one's head or in capsules screwed to a doorframe, but what have we done to obey it in the education of our children? Do we imagine that a religiously pluralistic state can provide the nurture to which Christian children are entitled? Or do we think God's requirement can be met by one hour of Sunday school a week? Have we seized the great opportunity offered by America's freedom for Christian schools? Have we saturated our home life with the Word of God?[45]

## C. Witness: The Church Ministers to the World

*1. The Word of the Gospel Is Central in the Mission of the Church*

The mission of the church is not an addendum; it is identified with the nature of the church and with the gospel that brings the church into existence. Jesus announces in the synagogue of Nazareth, "Today this Scripture is fulfilled in your hearing" (Luke 4:20). The gospel is proclamation, announcing the coming of God's salvation in Jesus Christ. Because Jesus is the Son of God, because his salvation is the final and only salvation for the children of Adam, the message must be announced to all the world. Paul, the apostle to the Gentiles, joins the finality of Christ's work with the imperative to proclaim it to the ends of the earth. There was a time when God overlooked, as it were, the sins of the Gentiles, but now the day of reckoning is at hand, for God has appointed a day and a Man for the judgment of the nations (Acts 17:30–31). In his Epistle to the Romans Paul expounds his gospel; the epistle is in every sense a missionary document: "Faith comes from hearing the message and the message is heard through the Word of Christ. . . . 'Their voice has gone out into all the earth, their words to the ends of the world' " (Rom. 10:17–18).

The gospel breaks down the wall that had divided Israel from the nations: all have sinned, Jew and Gentile alike, and there is but one Savior, a Jew according to the flesh, but the Son of God and only Savior of the world. God's salvation is the gift of his free grace; it cannot be merited or earned by anything that we are or do. God himself, in infinite love, has paid the price of our redemption. The ineffable love of God wrought our salvation; that love is the heart of our proclamation (John 3:16). Those who are claimed by God's electing love know the meaning of undeserved compassion. Jesus has found them by the roadside, has lifted them up and poured in the oil and wine of his saving love. If they truly know this love, they cannot but show compassion to other lost sinners; they cannot but share the gospel of grace in the Savior's name. Jesus, the Good Shepherd, the true Older Brother, has found us in the far country and brought us home to his Father's feast of welcome. He knows his Father's heart of love, and if we know him, we, too, know that love. Mission and gospel are not even two sides of the same coin: they are the same side.

For this reason the mission of this church is both drawing in and going out. In the Old Testament the nations were to be drawn to the dwelling of God on Mount Zion. The Psalms called on all the peoples to join in the praise of the only living God. In the fulfillment in Christ, the Mount Zion to which we are called is no longer on earth but in heaven. The movement to the center is now to the heavenly center. There is no longer a sanctuary on earth;

mission reaches to all the earth to call the Gentiles to join in heaven's praise (Rom. 15).

With the spread of the Word, the church spreads (Acts 6:7; 12:24; 19:20). The apostles refused to be silenced in their daily preaching in the temple; when threatened with prison or worse, they prayed to speak the Word with boldness, a prayer that Paul sought on his behalf to the end of his ministry (Acts 4:29; Eph. 6:19–20; cf. 2 Tim. 4:17).

### 2. Mission Proclaims the Word in Context

Since the gospel proclaims what God has done in Jesus Christ, it is a fixed and objective message. God spoke from heaven, "This is my Son, whom I have chosen; listen to him" (Luke 9:35). Jesus spoke the words given him of the Father and attested the words of the Old Testament as God-given. God's Word is his own witness. God is not handicapped in addressing himself in human language to creatures that bear his image. Yet to understand what God has revealed, we must understand the language that he used. We must respect the time in which the revelation was given, taking account of the experience of the human author, the situation of those who were originally addressed, and the forms of the language used. We are encouraged by the conviction that understanding is possible. We have much more than our humanity in common with the human authors of Scripture: we have been given the Spirit of the divine Author, whose work it is to lead us into the truth he has revealed.

If Scripture is to be preached, it must also be related to the context of those who hear it. Obviously there is a third context to be considered: our own context as we seek to understand and declare the Word of God. Again, what the Bible teaches about itself is essential to the mission of the church. If the Bible presents only a fallible human witness to the inexpressible event of revelation, we can have no assurance of truth in words. We may then despair of gaining the meaning of a text written in an alien culture, despair of the inescapable bias of our own culture, and despair of any real penetration into the context of the "receptor" culture. That despair is removed by the sovereign work of the Spirit. The power of the Spirit inspired the apostles and prophets to write his Word for the church and the world. The power of the Spirit uses the Word as his sword in the minds and hearts of men. We study the Word with the illumination of the Spirit. In the Spirit we seek to understand it. We do not manipulate it; we serve it. The Word of God creates its own context. It is not untranslatable, as the Quran claims to be. When it is translated into another language it transforms the tongue that expresses it, giving words a new meaning in their biblical context. J. H. Bavinck, a missionary theologian, used the Latin word *possessio* to describe the transformation of culture by the gospel.[46] Scripture itself has that power. It engages the language of the culture and speaks as the Word of God.

The task of crossing cultures with the gospel remains; it continues to claim the lives of God's messengers. But because of the work of the Spirit it is not a hopeless task, as the history of missions shows. True, there remains the danger that unthinking ambassadors of Christ will confuse their cultural prejudices with the gospel message or will fail to understand that the gospel works within a culture and that the culture must be transformed by those who know it from within. But there is another danger that can be even more insidious: that the gospel itself will be lost in the fragmentation of cultural relativism where the medium becomes the message.

The preaching of the Word must take seriously the concerns of the hearers. Direct proclamation that ignores differences in the situation is not the biblical approach. (Contrast Paul in the synagogue with Paul before the Aeropagus: Acts 13:16–41; 17:22–31.) Contextualization that takes account of the situation does not remove the offense of the gospel. Indeed, it sharpens the confrontation and makes the challenge of the gospel more meaningful. It also shows respect as well as love for those who have been created in God's image. The richness of form and approach in Scripture itself reminds us of the flexibility of form that presenting the gospel requires. Yet our ultimate trust must be in the power of the Spirit using the Word. Apart from God's work no amount of cultural affinity, social identity, or physical consanguinity can open a sinner's heart to the truth.

### 3. Mission Proclaims the Word in the Spirit

The Spirit who inspired the Word and gives it power to transform the hearts and lives of men also fills those who proclaim the Word. As we have seen, the apostles were called to mission as well as to ground the church in their teaching. The Holy Spiritual gifts of evangelism, preaching, teaching, witnessing, and caring continue to equip the church. Not all Christians have these gifts to the degree that constitutes a call to full-time ministry. Yet every Christian must confess Christ's name before men with boldness and must, with unselfish love, minister to others in Christ's name. Further, every Christian must model the nature of the kingdom in his family life and in the roles that he fulfills in the world. Management and labor, governors and citizens all receive their charge in the New Testament (Rom. 13:1–10; Eph. 5:22–6:9; Col. 3:18–4:1; 1 Peter 2:11–3:12).

Christian witness is not simply individual; it is also corporate.

That corporate testimony is given in the fellowship of the church. The church is the people of God in the world. Paul insisted that the church was the true circumcision, that those who were once Gentiles, aliens from the commonwealth of Israel are no longer outside but inside: fellow citizens with the saints of all ages. The concept of the "peoplehood" of the church has been lost from view. With that loss has come a loss of witness as well. If the church is composed only of those who meet once a week to sing and listen to a preacher, it can well be thought of as irrelevant in the crises of contemporary society, whether in the first world or the third. But if the church will model before the world a community of love and service, it will point to the heavenly reality that is its true nature. Only as the Word is taken seriously can the relation of the church to the world be understood and sustained. Scripture makes it plain that the church is called in the time between the first and second coming of Christ. The gospel of God's saving rule is seen in the church where that rule is acknowledged and obeyed. Yet the consummation of God's rule has not yet come. The Day of Judgment is postponed in the mercy of God so that men might hear the gospel, repent, and be saved from the wrath to come. The church participates already in Christ's glory; its earthly discipline has heavenly sanction. But for that very reason, the church is restrained from using the sword. The church is not called to implement the last judgment; its government is spiritual. Since the kingdom of Christ is not now to be enforced by the sword, the church is not called to govern the nations. Rather the people of God are in a situation similar to that of Israel in dispersion (1 Peter 1:1). They must prepare to live under the rule of secular states and to pray for the peace of the state in which they live as aliens-in-residence (Jer. 29:7; 1 Peter 1:1, 17; 2:11; Heb. 11:9). The weapons of the church's warfare are spiritual and, for that reason, have a power that material armaments cannot boast (2 Cor. 10:3–6). Armed crusades cripple and destroy the mission of the church; preaching, praying, and caring advance it.

## 4. Mission Joins Word and Deed

The compassion of God's grace that is preached in the gospel must be shown in deeds of compassion. Jesus accompanied the preaching of the kingdom with signs of mercy. Providing funds and comfort for those in distress are ministries of the Spirit. To bind Christian Jews and Gentiles together, Paul collected money in the Gentile churches for the needs of the saints in Judea. Diaconal ministry flows from the love of Christ. Secular nations, jealous of the influence of Christian benevolence, have expropriated mission hospitals and relief ministries. To the growth of governmental social services has led the church to demit its responsibility. Far beyond what any state can provide is the love and caring for those in distress that marks the gospel.

Deed must be joined to word not only in the church's mission but in the whole life of the church in the midst of the world. Those who are most zealous for the authority of the Word should pray for equal zeal in obeying the word in their occupations and in their communities where, as lights in the world, they hold forth the Word of Life (Phil. 2:15–16).

## ENDNOTES

[1] Williston Walker, *A History of the Christian Church*, rev. and ed. Cyril C. Richardson, Wilhelm Pauck, Robert T. Handy (New York: Scribner, 1959), p. 262.

[2] John Calvin, *Institutes of the Christian Religion*, trans. John Allen, 2 vols. (Philadelphia: Presbyterian Board of Christian Education, 1936), 2:302, 308 (IV.2.i.iv).

[3] Underlying the theologies of revelation advanced since the Enlightenment is the conviction that God can neither speak nor inspire men to write revealed sentences. As John Baillie put it, "We are not so naïve as to suppose that God speaks to us with a physical voice—with what Addison called, not very happily, 'a real voice or sound.'" *The Idea of Revelation in Recent Thought* (New York: Columbia University Press, 1956), p. 142; see also pp. 33ff.

[4] First Peter 2:9. For bibliography see John Hall Elliott, *The Elect and the Holy: an Exegetical Examination of 1 Peter 2:4–10* (Leiden: Brill, 1966).

[5] Paul S. Minear, *Images of the Church in the New Testament* (Philadelphia: Westminster, 1960). Avery Dulles, *Models of the Church* (Garden City: Doubleday, 1974).

[6] Like *qahal*, its nearest equivalent in the Hebrew Old Testament, *ecclesia* usually describes a group actually gathered rather than the members of a group that may gather. (Contrast the use of "congregation" in current English.) Since an unruly civic assembly in Ephesus may be called an *ecclesia* (Acts 19:41), scholars once concluded that the church was called an *ecclesia* simply as a gathering. See J. Y. Campbell, "The Origin and Meaning of the Christian Use of the Word ΕΚΚΛΗΣΙΑ," *The Journal of Theological Studies* 49 (1948): 130–42. James Barr, *The Semantics of Biblical Language* (London: Oxford University Press, 1961), pp. 119–29. But this ignores the meaning that this term had in application to Israel, the assembly of the Lord. See my discussion, *The Doctrine of the Church* (Philadelphia: Presbyterian and Reformed, 1974), pp. 11–13.

[7] "Those whom God has chosen He has established as an eternal possession. He has bestowed upon them a share in the lot of the holy ones. With the sons of heaven He has united their assembly for a council of community." 1 QS 11:7–9 (P. Wernberg-Moller translation in *The Manual of Discipline [Studies on the Texts of the Desert of Judah]*, ed. J. van der Ploeg [Grand Rapids: Eerdmans, 1957], 1:38f). See also 1 QS2:25; 1 QH 3:21; 11:11–12.

[8] Assemblies of covenant renewal were stipulated in the Law (Deut. 31:11–12). They are described in the history of Israel (Josh. 8:35; 1 Chron. 28:28; 29:10; 2 Chron. 20:5, 14; 23:3; 29:23–32; 30:2–25; Neh. 5:13). The festival assemblies (Lev. 23) were the Passover (Exod. 12:3–20; Deut. 16:1–8), Pentecost (Exod. 23:16; 34:22; Num. 28:26), and Tabernacles (Exod. 23:16; 34:22; Num. 29:12–38; Deut. 16:13).

[9]Assuming that Jesus spoke in Aramaic, he may have used the word k<sup>e</sup>nishta' or q<sup>e</sup>hala' (a loan word from Hebrew). In any case, Aramaic usage reflected the Old Testament understanding of the congregation. See K. L. Schmidt, "Ecclesia," in *Theological Dictionary of the New Testament*, ed. Gerhard Kittel, trans. Geoffrey W. Bromiley (Grand Rapids: Eerdmans, 1965), 3:524–25.

[10]Exodus 19:6; 1 Peter 2:5, 9.

[11]On the application of this passage to the individual servant, see Henri Blocher, *Songs of the Servant* (London: InterVarsity, 1975), pp. 39–42.

[12]I have added the third-person-plural pronoun to the New International Version translation. It is in the Greek and helps to indicate in English that the second-person pronouns are plural.

[13]The fact that the name of Peter (*Petros*) is masculine and the word for "rock" is feminine (*petra*) cannot break the connection of the two. There was some distinction in meaning between the two genders in classical and Hellenistic Greek. *Petra* referred to rock lying in strata, while *petros* designated a free-standing boulder. See H. G. Liddell and R. Scott, *A Greek-English Lexicon*, new ed. (Oxford: Clarendon, 1957), 2:1397; J. H. Moulton, G. Milligan, *The Vocabulary of the Greek New Testament* (London: Hodder and Stoughton, 1930), p. 511. *Petros* of course is necessarily masculine as a proper name, and it would have been awkward to use the masculine to describe the rock of foundation, since that is obviously bedrock, not a boulder (Matt. 7:24). For discussion and literature on this passage, see Oscar Cullman, *Peter: Disciple—Apostle—Martyr*, trans. Floyd V. Filson (Philadelphia: Westminster, 1953); R. Newton Flew, *Jesus and His Church* (London: Epworth, 1943); E. P. Clowney, *The Biblical Doctrine of the Church*, vol. 1 (Nutley, N.J.: Presbyterian and Reformed, 1979).

[14]A *skandalon* is something that one trips over. In the rocky terrain of Israel this is most usually an outcropping of rock. The well-known passage Isaiah 8:14 speaks of a "stone of stumbling and a rock of offense." The Aramaic Targum of that passage uses the word that is found in the name "Cephas" (*Ceph*). See J. F. Stenning, ed., *The Targum of Isaiah* (Oxford: Clarendon, 1949). Peter himself speaks of a *skandalon* as a stone of stumbling when he contrasts it with the cornerstone (1 Peter 2:4–8).

[15]William Temple, "It is of supreme importance that He wrote no book." Quoted in John Baillie, *Revelation in Recent Thought*, p. 114.

[16]The *schaliach*, a legally commissioned agent of another has been thought to be the background in Judaism for the office of the apostle. The arguments are considered and rejected in Walter Schmithals, *The Office of the Apostle in the Early Church* (Nashville: Abingdon, 1969), pp. 98–110. Schmithals stresses the eschatological orientation of the apostleship and the mission of the apostles. It should be noted that the apostles were bound by the message and teaching they received from Christ and were not agents who were free to negotiate with power of attorney.

[17]The thesis of Schmithals that the circle of the Twelve did not exist before the Resurrection and that the Twelve were not apostles and did not have a mission rests upon reconstruction of the Gospels and arguments from silence. Herman Ridderbos presents a clear account of the apostleship while acknowledging difficulties in interpreting certain passages: *Heils-Geschiedenis en Heilige Schrift* (Kampen: Kok, 1955), pp. 34–40; "The Canon of the New Testament" in Carl F. H. Henry, ed., *Revelation and the Bible* (Grand Rapids: Baker, 1958), pp. 192–95; *Paul, An Outline of His Theology*, John R. De Witt, trans. (Grand Rapids: Eerdmans), pp. 448–50. For the literature on this question see Schmithals, *Office of the Apostle*, pp. 11–15.

[18]Ridderbos observes that the message Paul has received from the original witnesses he has received from the ascended Lord: "The testimony of the eye-witnesses is for him as apostle the delivered word of the glorified Lord" ("Canon," p. 194).

[19]Ibid.

[20]Ibid., p. 190.

[21]Ibid., p. 196.

[22]The Confession of 1967, 9.27. See Edward A. Dowey, Jr., *A Commentary on the Confession of 1967 and an Introduction to "The Book of Confessions"* (Philadelphia: Westminster, 1968), p. 18. Pressure from conservatives in the denomination led to the inclusion in the Confession of the phrase, "the Word of God written." But as Dr. Dowey says, this phrase "cannot be construed in this context after the manner of the same phrase as it appears in the Westminster Confession. Here, Scripture derives its name from its role as witness to Christ; there, it 'is' the word written by virtue of its author, God" (p. 103). As Dowey also points out, "The Confession [of 1967] carefully avoids saying either that Scripture 'is' God's Word or that Scripture 'is' unique and authoritative as such or in its own right" (p. 100). The character of apostolic testimony has been fundamentally altered.

[23]The Westminster Confession, 22.2: "God alone is Lord of the conscience and hath left it free from the doctrines and commandments of men which are in anything contrary to his word, or beside it, in matters of faith or worship."

[24]See Peter Jones, "1 Cor. 15:8: Paul the Last Apostle," *Tyndale Bulletin* 36 (1985): 1–34.

[25]William Carey rightly argued from the Great Commission that, if Jesus promised his presence in its accomplishment to the end of the age, the imperative of the commission must continue. He therefore corrected a wrong conclusion from the finality of the office of the apostle—namely, that the mission of the church was also completed in the apostolic age. Carey's argument is contained in his treatise *An Enquiry into the Obligation of Christians to Use Means for the Conversion of the Heathen* (1792), facsimile ed. (London: Baptist Missionary Society, 1942). See Stephen Neill, *A History of Christian Missions*, Pelican History of the Church (Harmondsworth, Middlesex: Penguin, 1964), 6:261.

[26]*Documents of the Christian Church*, The World's Classics, no. 495, ed. Henry Bettenson (London: Oxford University Press, 1943), pp. 36–37.

[27]This is done, despite disclaimers, in *The Report of the Theological Commission on Christ and the Church* (to the Fourth World Conference on Faith and Order, Montreal, 1963), Faith and Order Paper No. 38, ed. Paul Minear (Geneva: World Council of Churches, Commission on Faith and Order, 1963), pp. 11–15; reprinted in *Faith and Order Findings*, ed. Paul Minear (Minneapolis: Augsburg, 1963). The Bible is rejected as a "verbal court of last appeal." Instead the Bible is said to reflect "the endless pluralism in the Spirit's activity and in the conscious responses which have been made to that activity" (p. 12).

[28]The long series of papers issued by the Faith and Order Commission are evidence of the continuing discussion of doctrinal issues that divide the churches. This interest has been heightened in the recent discussions of baptism, Eucharist, and ministry, vitiated as they are by an erroneous doctrine of Scripture. See *Baptism, Eucharist and Ministry*, Faith and Order Paper No. 111 (Geneva: World Council of Churches, 1982). Evangelical conferences and congresses have issued statements like the Lausanne Covenant affirming agreed doctrines, but such statements have been phrased to avoid areas of denominational disagreement.

[29]New England Congregational churches became apostate when they became Unitarian. The Church of Jesus Christ of Latter-Day Saints falsely claims to be Christian, for it sets aside scriptural teaching by the alleged revelations claimed by Joseph Smith.

[30]See the summary of this controversy in Herman Bavinck, *Gereformeerde Dogmatiek*, 2d ed., rev. and enlarged, 4 vols. (Kampen: Kok, 1911), 4:333–43.

[31]John Calvin, *Institutes*, 4.2.1. The Reformers sometimes spoke only of the profession of the true faith as the mark of the church. At other times, as in the passage cited, the ministry of the Word and the sacraments are mentioned. The addition of church discipline does not represent a different opinion, since discipline was included in the ministry of the Word and the sacraments.

[32] For a brief summary of the scriptural requirements for discipline, see Daniel E. Wray, *Biblical Church Discipline* (Edinburgh: Banner of Truth Trust, 1978). A recent treatment is by John White and Ken Blue, *Healing the Wounded* (Downers Grove: InterVarsity, 1985).

[33] "For the Roman Pontiff, by reason of his office as Vicar of Christ, namely, and as pastor of the entire church, has full, supreme and universal power over the whole church, a power which he can always exercise unhindered" (*Dogmatic Constitution on the Church*, Vatican II [*Lumen Gentium*]). *Vatican Council II: the Conciliar and Post Conciliar Documents*, ed. Austin Flannery, O.P. (Northport: Costello, 1975), p. 375.

"Our Savior at the Last Supper on the night He was betrayed instituted the eucharistic sacrifice of His Body and Blood so that He might perpetuate the sacrifice of the cross throughout the centuries till His coming . . ." (*Constitution on the Liturgy*, 2:47 [ibid., p. 16]). "Hence the Mass, the Lord's Supper, is at the same time and inseparably: a sacrifice in which sacrifice the cross is perpetuated; a memorial . . . ; a sacred banquet . . ." (*Instruction on the Worship of the Eucharistic Mystery*, C:1 [ibid., p. 102]).

> The celebration of the Eucharist which takes place at Mass is the action not only of Christ, but also of the church. For in it Christ perpetuates in an unbloody manner the sacrifice offered on the cross, offering Himself to the Father for the world's salvation through the ministry of priests. The Church, the spouse and minister of Christ, performs together with Him the role of priest and victim, offers Him to the Father and at the same time makes a total offering of herself together with Him (ibid., p. 103.

[34] German Pietism and the evangelical revival in Britain led to the establishment of many societies for mission, Bible study, and charitable purposes. The last decade of the eighteenth century and the first of the nineteenth saw an explosion of such organizations. See James H. Nichols, *History of Christianity, 1650–1950* (New York: Ronald Press, 1956), pp. 306–10.

[35] For example, the Christian and Missionary Alliance. See Kenneth Scott Latourette, *A History of Christianity* (New York: Harper, 1953), p. 1260.

[36] An opinion that was emphatically expressed at Green Lake '71, a missions consultation of the EFMA and the IFMA.

[37] See G. Vermes, *The Dead Sea Scrolls in English*, Pelican Books A551 (Baltimore: Penguin, 1965), pp. 71–94.

[38] See the bibliography in James B. Hurley, *Man and Woman in Biblical Perspective* (Leicester: InterVarsity, 1981; reprint, Grand Rapids: Zondervan, 1982), pp. 272–80.

[39] Ibid., pp. 185–94; N. J. Hommes, *DeVrouw in de Kerk* (Franeker: T. Wever, 1951), pp. 52ff.

[40] Note the emphasis on the theme of submissiveness as the key to Christian behavior in 1 Peter 2:11–3:12. See David L. Balch, *Let Wives Be Submissive: The Domestic Code in 1 Peter* (Chico: Scholars Press, 1981).

[41] As Balch points out, an orderly lifestyle such as Peter describes would have apologetic value by commending Christianity to Hellenistic society. But social acceptability is not the basic rationale for such living. Rather, it is the appointment of the Lord, who has set us in families and established government in his church.

[42] The issue is not simply the preservation of the husband-wife roles in the family of God. There is deeper mystery in the male/female roles that we discharge this side of glory. The Son of God became incarnate as a man, not as a neuter being. Christianity would not be the same religion if a mother goddess were substituted for our Father in heaven. See C. S. Lewis, "Priestesses in the Church?" in Louis Bouyer, *Woman in the Church*, trans. Marilyn Teichert (San Francisco: Ignatius Press, 1979), pp. 123–32; Donald G. Bloesch, *The Battle for the Trinity: The Debate over Inclusive God-Language* (Ann Arbor: Servant, 1985).

[43] In Ephesians 3:15, as in 2:21, *pasa* may best be translated with the New International Version "the whole" rather than "every," in spite of the usual meaning of *pas* before an anarthrous noun.

[44] *Diakonos* is used in the New Testament in a variety of meanings, technical and nontechnical. Even when it is used technically to describe officers of the church (Phil. 1:1), it describes a variety of functions (including both financial support and care for the distressed, Rom. 12:8; 1 Cor. 12:28). Ordination, too, is more broadly conceived in the New Testament than in current ecclesiastical practice. It is an act of blessing, committing the one blessed to a particular ministry (Acts 6:6; 13:2–3; note that Barnabas and Saul were already teachers of the church when they were set apart for a new task). All the people of God are blessed by him (the "general office" of believers): the benediction in worship service blesses the people of God (Num. 6:22–27; 2 Cor. 13:14).

[45] Lawrence O. Richards emphasizes the life setting of Christian nurture in opposition to an intellectualistic view of Christian education. He stresses "life" as a theme of the Gospel of John, taking for granted the theme of "truth" in the same Gospel. His book is written for the Sunday school, however, where the possibilities of a life-modeling setting are severely limited. *A Theology of Christian Education* (Grand Rapids: Zondervan, 1975).

[46] J. H. Bavinck, *An Introduction to the Science of Missions*, trans. David H. Freeman (Philadelphia: Presbyterian and Reformed, 1960), pp. 178–90.

# A RESPONSE TO
# THE CHURCH AND ITS MISSION

## Eugene W. Bunkowske

Dr. Edmund P. Clowney has done a masterful job of opening up this subject for those of us who are participants in ICBI's Summit III. His two-part analysis under the topics "The Church Is Formed By the Word" and "The Church Ministers the Word" is totally appropriate to our overall concern for biblical inerrancy. His introductory remarks under the metaphor of the Babylonian captivity of the Word immediately caught my attention, and I believe need to be highlighted and further unpacked as a major concern for any serious consideration of the application of the inerrant, revealed Word of God, especially as it applies in the Western world and the parts of the non-Western world that are increasingly falling under the intellectual sway of the West. I will be coming back to this point in the latter part of this response.

## I. THE BROAD BRUSH STROKES

Let me begin by expressing my delight at the way that Dr. Clowney develops his thesis on "The Church Is Formed by the Word," especially his development of church as assembly, his integrative understanding of "heavenly assembly" and "earthly assemblies," his utilization of the building and house-of-God figure, and his focus on the prophets and apostles as Spirit-of-God inspired open channels between the oral and written Word of God.

Basic to what Clowney shares on these topics is the covenantal concept of interpersonal and interactional communication. Clowney puts forward Deuteronomy 4:10, "Assemble the people before me to hear my words," as his basic text. It may also be appropriate to add the following texts: Genesis 9:15–16; 12:2–3;

15:1–21; 17:2–27; Exodus 6:4–8; and 24:7. These texts point us even further back to the very beginnings of God's relationship with man as they walked and talked together in the Garden (Gen. 1:28–30; 2:16–23; 3:8–21). Certainly assembly or community of any kind cannot be conceived of as existing or staying in place for any extended period of time without communication—without words.

Clowney sees the oral and written Word of God as the same word in different media. Although he speaks mainly in New Testament terms by implication, I believe we can and need to say that for Clowney the prophets and apostles, chosen and authorized by God, are the divinely appointed and Spirit-of-God-inspired link—between the Word of God and the church of God; between, in strictly New Testament terms, the Word of Christ and the church of Christ; between the oral Word of God (Old Testament) and Christ (New Testament) and the written Word of God throughout the Bible; and between the "heavenly assembly" and the "earthly assemblies."

Clowney places it all into the bigger picture by speaking of the "heavenly holy place" or "heavenly assembly" which not only gives form and substance to the "earthly assemblies" but which is by definition an essential and integrated part of the "earthly assemblies." For him the church can only be *ecclesia* in the New Testament sense of the term if it is an assembly in which the communication between God and man is absolutely basic. Without the Word of God, whether that be the original Word of Christ or the same Word in written form given by the Spirit of God through the prophets and apostles, there is no true *ecclesia*—no true church. Where the inerrant Word of God is in question, the *ecclesia* is in question. Where the inerrant, revealed Word of God is scattered, the *ecclesia* is scattered. Where the inerrant, revealed Word of God is set aside, the *ecclesia* is set aside.

For Dr. Clowney the church as *ecclesia* is not just "formed by the Word," but it also "ministers the Word." That is, for Clowney, Word and ministry are framed together in a fitting way by *ecclesia* especially, as *ecclesia* is illuminated and enunciated by the figure, church as building. In this figure we see church as the temple of God (Eph. 2:21). The foundation of this building, put in place by the activity of the Spirit of God through the prophets and apostles, is the Word of God (Eph. 2:20); and the work of building the *ecclesia* through Christian worship, nurture, and witness is ongoing (1 Cor. 3:9–13) through worldwide Christian outreach, proclamation, sacramental acts, and teaching (Matt. 28:16–20; Mark 16:15–16; Luke 24:45–49; John 20:21; Acts 1:8; 1 Cor. 11:26).

## II. THE HEART OF THE APOSTOLIC MESSAGE

I find myself feeling very comfortable with Dr. Clowney's position on the foundational nature of the apostolic message, but I would like to examine his contention that "at the heart of the apostolic message is *holiness*." It would rather appear to me that the heart of the apostolic message is repentance, baptism, the forgiveness of sins, and God's gift of the Holy Spirit and salvation, received by faith in the crucified and resurrected Christ (Acts 2:36–38; 3:18–19; 4:12; 5:31–32; 8:21–23; 13:38–39; 16:29–34; 20:20–21; 26:18–23). Already in the Acts of the Apostles the apostolic message is referred to in abbreviated terms by calling it the gospel, or Good News (Acts 15:7; 20:24). This became a common practice throughout the rest of the New Testament (Rom. 1:1; 1 Cor. 4:15; 2 Cor. 2:12; Gal. 1:11; Eph. 1:13; Phil. 1:7; et al.).

The Christ himself signaled what the heart of God's message was when he shattered the holiness-oriented Pharisee with the news that even as good a man as Nicodemus would not see the kingdom of God unless he was born again (John 3:3–5). This well-known chapter comes to a climax in John 3:16–18 which Protestant Christians often quote as the heart of the Christian message in capsule form.

Having made this point, I want to immediately make clear that *gospel holiness* and *new obedience* are important parts of the apostolic message even though they are not the heart of that message. What then is the relationship between the heart of the apostolic message which is repentance, baptism, the forgiveness of sins, and God's gift of the Holy Spirit and salvation received by faith in the crucified and resurrected Christ and gospel holiness and new obedience? Romans 12:1–2 signals that holiness and a life of obedience are a natural, positive response to the heart of the apostolic message when it says, "So then, my brothers, *because of God's great mercy to us* I appeal to you: offer yourselves as a living sacrifice to God dedicated to his service and pleasing to him. This is the true worship that you should offer. Do not conform yourself to the standards of this world, but let God transform you inwardly by a complete change of your mind." This relationship of God's gift of spiritual life in union with Christ and the resultant life of holiness is further explained in Colossians 2:11–4:6.

## III. LAW AND GOSPEL

Reading a paper like "The Church and Its Mission" reminds me again that human beings, including Dr. Clowney and myself, by definition perceive communication through our own personal act of mental filters. We also use our own personal perceptional grid when we prepare a paper, or for that matter, a response to a paper.

Dr. Clowney did exactly that when in addition to speaking about the heart of the apostolic message, he attempted to further define the apostolic message by developing a taxonomic list of subjects such as: "the attributes of the church," "the scriptural order of the church," "the marks of the church," "parachurch organizations," "scriptural church order," and "women in the church." Rather than to suggest an expansion of that list or comment on each of the topics listed, I would prefer to deal with a binary issue which my personal, perceptional grid signals as absolutely basic—that is, to take a deeper look at the heart or basic nature of the apostolic message from the viewpoint of law and gospel.

This seems particularly important in our times when the idea of sin has been almost completely overlooked, and so there appears to be no need for the message of forgiveness of sins, life, and salvation.

In contrast to our times, the climate and context in which the apostolic message communicated was one in which the unspoken assumption was that man was sinful and in need of salvation. The Old Testament prepared the Jew for a Messiah who would be God's answer to the sin problem which dated back to the time of Adam and Eve (Gen. 3). The message of John the Baptist was, "Turn away from your sins and be baptized" (Mark 1:4). Jesus not only healed people, but he forgave their sins (Matt. 9:2; Mark 2:5; Luke 7:48; 23:34). In 1 Timothy 1:15 the great apostle Paul underlines the situation by saying, "This is a faithful saying and worthy of all acceptation, that Christ Jesus came into the world to *save sinners; of whom I am chief*" (KJV, italics mine).

Sin is recognized as a reality because of law which defines and determines what is and what is not sin, not only the Levitical law and the law of Moses, but also the natural law written in men's hearts (Rom. 2:14–15). If the law is dormant or hidden, covered and denied, sin is covered and denied, and there seems to be no need for the good news of salvation in Christ.

The point that I am making here is that in order for the "heavenly assembly" to effectively tabernacle with the "earthly assemblies" and to communicate an inspired, inerrant, revealed message from God that cuts through to where bone and marrow meet, it must reflect at its very heart and center the full apostolic message. That is, it must proclaim the law of God in all its severity so that man will see himself as a sinner who is hopelessly guilty and without human alternatives for restitution before the bar of God's justice. At that point the law must still be pressed home until man is brought to repentance in readiness for the news of salvation in Christ. Then at that very moment the apostolic message requires the pouring forth of the good news of the gospel which offers the free gift of salvation, freedom from guilt, and the accompanying spiritual power to live a holy and obedient life of witness for Christ.

Only if we properly recognize the apostolic message for what it is at its heart and center, and fully utilize it, will it really function to form a New Testament *ecclesia* and empower that *ecclesia* for ministry and witness. Without the complete apostolic message we will have form without God-directed function and passive structure without Spirit-endowed content.

## IV. SOCIAL AND POLITICAL CONCERNS

Dr. Clowney points out that "In countless moral issues, individual and social, liberal Christianity has been conformed not only to the patterns of this age but to a rather specific and predictable 'liberal' viewpoint." He sees the danger that Evangelicals may react by beginning with these culturally conditioned patterns and amend the apostolic tradition to fit the cultural model.

There is no doubt that this is a great danger in our times and that it regularly occurs. Here I believe that the best defense is a good offense. That is, as we emphasize the heart of the apostolic message as it concerns itself with law and gospel and with repentance, baptism, forgiveness of sins, and God's gift of his Spirit and salvation by faith in Christ, we will find ourselves marching to a different drummer than the world or worldly oriented Christianity.

Not that we will avoid or reject as unimportant social and political issues but that we, like the early *ecclesia*, will be known by the world for our actions of love, generosity, and hospitality. This Good News in action will be an integrated and important part of our compassion, pity, and concern (Matt. 9:35–38) for all others for whom our Savior gave his life and to whom we witness in word and deed so that they too may see, hear, believe, be saved, and confess Christ as Savior and Lord before the world.

This really does mean taking the apostolic message and tradition seriously and, above all, opening the doors of our heart so that the Spirit of God can transform us through the Word of God which is the power of God unto salvation (Rom. 1:16) and unto Spirit-directed living (Eph. 6:17).

## V. THE WORD AND "EARTHLY ASSEMBLIES"

While the apostolic foundation of the *ecclesia* is one and unchangeable, the "living stones" (1 Peter 2:5) that are built together on this apostolic foundation through the worship, nurture, and witness of the church are many. Not only are they many in number but also diverse in language, ethnicity, tradition, geographic location, race, and nationality. This means that the one and ever-relevant apostolic message centered in the chief cornerstone (Eph. 2:20; 1 Peter 2:5–8; Acts 4:11–12), the Christ, is continually on the move from person to person, from language to language, from ethnic group to ethnic group, from tradition to tradition, from geographic location to geographic location, as it brings the forgiveness of sins, life, salvation, and new obedience to people in all kinds of earthly situations.

This movement of the message was already evident two hundred years before the coming of the Christ when the Old Testament in Hebrew was translated into the Greek language so that Jews, who no longer grew up knowing Hebrew or Aramaic, could have the message of life in a language that they could easily understand and regularly use for normal oral communication. In the medium of language this process has gone on until over 1,800 of the 7,011 languages of the world have some part of the Scripture written in their system of communication. At the end of 1984, 286 languages had full Bibles, and an additional 594 had New Testaments, and an additional 928 had some portion of the Scripture.

It is easy to say that the church ministers the Word in a diverse world. It is much more difficult to actually do that without losing the apostolic message in the process or, on the other hand, damaging the "living stones" in the process of attempting to fit or at times jam them into the house of God. The key, I believe, using the metaphor of Clowney, is in understanding that while the "heavenly assembly" is one, the "earthly assemblies" are many.

The point here is that the various earthly assemblies are not required to look or sound alike. Their superstructure may, in fact, be very different, especially when it comes to the physical, material, structural, organizational, and even many of the social components. The only universal requirement is that each "earthly assembly," yes, each "living stone," is solidly built on the apostolic foundation and directly fitted into the chief cornerstone (the Christ) through trusting faith.

As an integral part of the body of Christ, each "living stone" is then empowered to enjoy the forgiveness and love of God and to participate with Christ in building the *ecclesia* (God's church) through an ongoing life of holiness, witness, and sharing. This is not only possible but natural no matter what the socioeconomic condition, the education, the literacy or illiteracy, the style of eating and dressing, or the language, race, tribe, or nation. In Christ we are all one even if we are very different in other matters and things.

## VI. THE PRESENT BABYLONIAN CAPTIVITY

In his introduction Dr. Clowney used the metaphor of the Babylonian captivity to suggest various ways in which the Word of God has been taken captive over the centuries. He speaks of the captivity of the doctrine of the Word as the "hierarchical medieval institution became a caricature of the church of Christ by presuming to stand over rather than under the Word of God." In reference to our present-day situation, Clowney speaks of captivity under the hand of "rationalistic criticism" and under a "turning away from the written Word of God as revealed truth."

It is my opinion that the present-day captors of the Word of God mentioned by Clowney are really only surface manifestations of a far more difficult and pervasive underlying entrapment that at the present time is being projected around the world as an angel of light under the guise of so-called enlightened, Western thinking and logic. In order to expose or unpack the present situation a bit more completely, we need to think in terms of the underlying metaphor (conceptual framework) that directs people's living and thinking.

Man by nature looks at the world in terms of cause and effect. The mathematician at M.I.T. does this and so does the concerned mother of eight in a tribal village setting. Until the end of the Middle Ages, the unmarked or primary world view of humankind all over the world was one that understood spiritual power (God of gods, etc.) as the basic, causal factor behind all effects in the world. This was true for the followers of traditional religion as well as for the Muslim, Hindu, Christian, Taoist, Buddhist, and the many others who may not have been able to identify themselves with any specific set of religious propositions.

To be sure, even in earlier times, there have been secondary or marked views of the world that proposed a different, basic causal component than spiritual power or powers. A good example of this was atomistic Epicureanism. However, in earlier days these alternative world views did not provide the normal conceptual framework in which the great majority of people uncritically did their thinking.

Since the end of the Middle Ages and especially in our times, this situation is changing dramatically. Today in the West the unmarked, normative conceptual framework for thinking about cause and effect is one that searches for basic causal reality in the realm of the physical and by definition rules out spiritual power or powers as candidates for basic causality. The normal conceptual framework is one in which the average person in the West proceeds uncritically through life looking for answers to basic causality in the limited realm of what can be measured or tested, felt or seen. In this limited channel, there is no need for knowledge of God or spiritual matters. In this life situation, a discussion about whether the Bible is the inerrant, revealed Word of God or a developed word of man is really only academic and of little interest or relevance. After all, what does it matter what God said if, in fact, he is only a figment of man's creative imagination, a myth at best, and by definition not at all related to basic causal reality in our universe.

Here, as I see it, is the "Babylonish Captivity" for the Word of God in our time. It is not just a matter of competitive philosophies or theologies—not just a different method of doing biblical exegesis but a pervasive structural view of reality and a model of thinking about reality which make it unpopular, yes, almost subhuman and in some quarters very costly to even consider the possibility of a revelation from outside of the human mind as a legitimate or potentially relevant element in the search for ultimate answers about basic causality in our universe.

This is the "Babylonish captivity" that provides the normal conceptual framework, the accepted logical basis, and the unconsciously agreed upon "ultimate truth" that pervades and undergirds the vast majority of our teaching in Western education. Unfortunately, it is also being uncritically exported by the West to the ends of the earth under the rubric of development, progress, and educational advancement.

It becomes transparent as well that this spreading conceptual framework for thought and life has major implications not only for the Word of God as recorded in the Bible but also for the church and its mission, if its mission is to remain centered on the God of the Bible—that is, if its mission is primarily to worship that God, nurture those who believe in that God, and witness the message of that God to the world.

# A Response to
# The Church and Its Mission

Earl D. Radmacher

The wording of the title to Edmund Clowney's paper is significant. It is not simply "The Mission of the Church" but rather "The Church and Its Mission." The former would simply emphasize what the church is supposed to do, whereas the latter must deal with what it is as well as what it is to do. Many contemporary volumes on the church launch into a discussion of the church's mission before defining its nature. This leads to confusion. The late Francis Schaeffer put it right when he said, "Form must precede function. Being must precede doing. Nature must control mission."[1]

Clowney shows appreciation for this order of things in the twofold division of his paper as follows: "first, how the church is formed by the Word; second, how the church ministers the Word." Furthermore, he is right on target in making the Word central to both. Too many job descriptions for the church today grow out of tradition or the contemporary culture rather than out of the Word. We do well to deliver the doctrine of the church from the enslavement to tradition or the relativizing of culture. Founded on the Word and focused on the world should be the controlling factors.

As Clowney begins to give definition to the church from the Word, there seems to be need for clarification. Is the church to be identified as the people of God throughout all of Scripture, or does it have a specific beginning and uniqueness in the New Testament? On the one hand, he states, "The doctrine of the church as the people of God extends through all of Scripture" (p. 98). On the other hand, he states, "Israel was made to be the people of God as they stood before the Lord at Sinai; so, too, the New Testament church is constituted as God's assembly" (p. 98). And,

131

again, "Scripture makes it plain that the church is called in the time between the first and second coming of Christ" (p. 117).

Without a doubt there is a continuity to be seen in "the people of God" throughout the Scripture, especially as we think soteriologically. But a failure to see the uniqueness of the church in this interadvent time and its discontinuity with Israel is to confuse the purposes and missions of both Israel and the church. If clarity of mission for the church is to be found, there must be clarity of definition of the church. Failure to achieve this has led to unfortunate spiritualization of Scripture. The long-time professor of dogmatic theology of the University of Utrecht, Arnold A. van Ruler, cogently observed:

> To the very depths of Old Testament expectation, the people of Israel as a people, the land, the posterity, and theocracy play a role that cannot possibly be eliminated. This role cannot be altered by regarding Christ and His Church as the fulfillment, in other words, by spiritualizing. There is a surplus in the Old Testament, a remnant that cannot be fitted into the New Testament fulfillment.[2]

Again, van Ruler cautions:

> A renewal of allegorizing may seem to offer a way of assigning an authentic function to the Old Testament in the Christian situation. . . . I believe we must resist to the last the temptation lurking in this idea. The idea is in fact a temptation, for it seems that allegorizing can solve all the problems of the Christian Church in relation to the Old Testament. . . . Allegorizing gives the appearance of making it perfectly plain that the Old Testament is wholly and exclusively the book of the Christian Church, which can be exploited fully by it alone.[3]

After carefully noting the uniqueness of emphasis on the kingdom and the earth in the Old Testament and the "surplus" that cannot be assimilated in the mission of the church, van Ruler concludes with these questions:

> Does everything end in the Church? Does everything, not only Israel, but history and creation, exist for the sake of the Church? Or is the Church only one among many forms of the kingdom of God, and does its catholicity consist precisely in the fact that it respects, acknowledges and holds dear all forms of the kingdom, for example, even the people of Israel?[4]

These remarks from van Ruler are insightful. And if we are going to understand the mission of the church, then we must understand its distinction from Israel and other entities within the multiformity of the kingdom program of God. The church and the kingdom are not the same although one can never be thought of without the other. Some have thought it strange, indeed, that the Gospel writers, who regularly address the subject of the kingdom (βασιλεια, 128 times) interrupt the kingdom message with the announcement by Jesus of the church (εκκλεσια, 3 times) upon the confession of Peter, "You are the Christ, the Son of the living God." It would be for the apostle Paul to later explain this mystery "that has been kept hidden for ages and generations, but is now disclosed to the saints" (Col. 1:26). Most of Ephesians and Colossians is given over to an explanation of this mystery, the church, which is most often, though not exclusively, designated as the body of Christ. This close identification of the church with Christ is seen in germinal form in Christ's declaration: "I will build my church [εκκλεσια]." *Ecclesia* was certainly not a new word to the apostles, for it had a rich history in both Greek and Jewish traditions. But Jesus infused it with a personal and permanent element that would lift it forever out of the common discourse. This was his personal project that would be founded on his resurrection, and the gates of Hades would never prevail against it.

Clowney has spoken excellently concerning the apostolicity of the church. He sees Jesus as personally shaping the foundation stones that were to be the link between the Word of Christ and the church of Christ. He carefully guards this foundation as complete and final. Especially vivid is his statement: "The apostolic foundation of the spiritual temple, the house of God, has been laid. It is not to be torn up for repaving, nor does it continue indefinitely: it is the foundation of a house, not a roadbed." Amen! Nor may the foundation get confused with the roof line which seems to be the case for those who claim to have the apostles today.

But Clowney is less clear when he discusses the visible organization of the church into churches. Part of the problem is seen in that, whereas he strongly affirms that the revelation in Scripture includes elements of order as well as faith, he leaves one wanting with respect to specifics. For example, one could wish for some discussion about what is prescriptive and what is descriptive in New Testament church order and organization. Early in his paper, Clowney states that ". . . the heavenly assembly defines the church" (p. 99) and that "All who call upon the name of the Lord in a given place, whether a household, a city, or a region make up an assembly that joins with the gathering in heaven" (p. 99). Is Clowney thereby saying that the only prescriptive element for a local assembly is a gathering of believers? Later discussion on "The Marks of the Church" would leave the impression that he sees more prescriptive elements, but this is never clearly delineated. Granted, time and space constraints are a factor, and that is understandable. In the light of these constraints, therefore, one might question the inclusion under the scriptural order of the church of the discussion of "Parachurch Organizations" and "Women in the Church."

The first is too brief to be helpful. The problem of parachurch organizations and their relation to the churches is mammoth, and it is, for the most part, unique to this generation. Various estimates of the proliferation of parachurch agencies range from two thousand to eight thousand. This would have been unheard of thirty to fifty years ago. If one wants to get immersed in the subject, he should begin by reading Jerry White's *The Church and the Parachurch*, the only full-length book treatment in print to my knowledge.

The discussion of "Women and the Church" seems too cut and dried and quite one-sided, especially in the light of much fine material being worked through today on issues he raised, such as "the recognition of distinct roles" and "the primacy of man." Much more needs to be said about the implications of mutual submission in a macho culture that has been deeply infected by "chain of command" in both the family and the church.

Whereas the first two-thirds of the paper deal with the nature or being or form of the church, the last third deals with its purpose or function or mission. Inasmuch as Summit III, for which this paper was prepared, has the purpose of emphasizing the practical application of scriptural truth that has been discerned through proper interpretation of the inspired text, this is the point of the paper where creative insight is needed if the churches are going to rise to the challenge of this generation and the next.

Clowney's development of the ministry of the church is divided between worship, nurture, and witness, with three-fourths of the space given to the last section on witness, which he totally identifies with the mission of the church. "Mission and gospel are not even two sides of the same coin," says Clowney; "they are the same side." One wonders if such a view of the mission of the church does not betray an overemphasis on soteriology as opposed to theology proper and, more particularly, christology. In any event it seems that the areas of worship and nurture (or edification) are ripe for a more balanced emphasis today.

Great strides have been made in this generation in the matter of worship. A typical article written a generation ago on the mission of the church would have been divided between edification and evangelism. In fact, in practice, the mission would likely be exhausted in evangelism. The so-called Great Commission of Matthew 28:19–20 was narrowed down to a "Go ye," broader mission—namely, "Make disciples"; thus edification of the saints was seen as basic to evangelization of the sinners. Those who were set apart by God as evangelists, pastors, and teachers began to see that their task was not basically saint begetting but saint building. Sheep beget sheep, especially if they are healthy.

Even more recently another step has been taken. Earlier than most, A. W. Tozer raised the question of the missing jewel: worship. Ronald Allen and Gordon Borror picked up on that in their excellent volume, *Worship: Rediscovering the Missing Jewel.* Several others have addressed this great theme in our day.

Another line of study that has encouraged worship is a renewed interest in the study of God. Little did James Packer realize when he wrote his series of articles on the attributes of God for periodical publication that they would become the first "best seller" on the person of God in American history.

Growth in worship is even seen in the singing of the youth. What a pleasure it is to hear them sing the Psalms instead of so many of the trite and silly ditties that were sung in the youth groups of a generation ago.

Both in form and in content, great progress has been made in worship, but there is still a long way to go, especially as it relates to prayer—corporate prayer (Acts 2:42). What a contrast to today is seen in the priority of prayer in the first church where the leaders said, "We will give ourselves continually to prayer and to the ministry of the Word." At best, we tend to reverse those or, at worst, leave prayer out altogether.

One further thought must be mentioned with respect to worship. When the writer to the Hebrews draws attention to our worship, he does not stop with "the sacrifice of praise" but concludes with "to do good and to share . . . , for with such sacrifices God is pleased" (Heb. 13:15). The lack of sacrifice as evidenced in the giving patterns of American Christians is a disgrace. This must be seen as an act of worship, and much more creative thinking needs to be invested in lifting the level of the sacrifice of our possessions along with our praise.

There is one area of the mission of the church that is characteristically overlooked, and yet it is extremely important to the eternal purposes of God. C. S. Lewis's *Weight of Glory*, speaks of it from Paul's words: "For our light affliction, which is but for a moment, is working [producing] for us a far more exceeding and eternal weight of glory" (2 Cor. 4:17). To the Romans, Paul explained that we are "joint heirs with Christ, if indeed we suffer with him, that we may be glorified together" (Rom. 8:17). Paul encouraged young Pastor Timothy, "For if we died with him, we shall also live with him, if we endure, we shall also reign with him" (2 Tim. 2:11–12).

There is abundant evidence in Scripture that one of the major programs God is carrying out in the church today is that of determining the position or level of service that the sons of God will have with Christ in the life to come. God is doing more than redeeming the lost through the church. In Anthony Hoekema's book on eschatology, *The Bible and the Future*, he briefly touches upon this:

The relationship between the already and the not yet is not the one of absolute antithesis but rather one of continuity. The former is the foretaste of the latter. The New Testament teaches that there is a close connection between the quality of our present life and the quality of life beyond the grave. To indicate the way in which the present life is related to the life to come the New Testament uses such figures as that of the prize, the crown, the fruit, the harvest, the grain, and the ear, sowing and reaping . . . what believers do in this life will have consequences for the life to come.[5]

Unfortunately, the typical believer does not understand that this is a training period for him, that he is becoming today what he will be in the life to come. Instead he lives with the mistaken belief of equality of position of service with all other believers in the future reign with Christ. But not so! Members of Christ's family are today developing their future capacity of glory by what they do with what they have.

This brings to the fore one last item for consideration. What is it that every member of the body of Christ, without exception, has? Several major passages of Scripture address it, but 1 Peter 4:10 puts it succinctly and comprehensively:

As each one has received a gift, minister it to one another, as good stewards of the manifold grace of God.

Every believer has a gift or gifts.

He/she is responsible to manage that gift/gifts for God's benefit and glory.

He/she will receive a position of service with Christ in the life to come in direct proportion to his/her stewardship of that gift/gifts in this life.

In the light of the foregoing, it is most difficult to understand how the churches can be so nonchalant and dilatory about discovering and developing the gifts of their members.

Before 1960 it was impossible to find one book on the doctrine of spiritual gifts in *Books in Print*. The area was a virtual vacuum. For example, thousands of sermons have been preached over the years on those favorite verses, Romans 12:1–2, without ever relating them to verses 3–8, in spite of the obvious grammatical connection in the text.

Twenty-five years later there are dozens of books on the doctrine of spiritual gifts. Some are very good, but there are still very few churches that have taken seriously the task of mobilizing the membership of their church according to the gifting of the people. Would that we had a flood of people like Joses in the first church who discovered and developed his gift so well that people began to forget his name and address him by his gift—Barnabas, which is translated Son of Encouragement.

# ENDNOTES

[1] Francis Schaeffer, *The Church at the End of the Twentieth Century* (Downers Grove: InterVarsity), p. 153.

[2] Arnold A. van Ruler, *The Christian Church and the Old Testament* (Grand Rapids: Eerdmans, 1971), p. 45.

[3] Ibid., p. 57.

[4] Ibid., p. 98.

[5] Anthony A. Hoekema, *The Bible and the Future* (Grand Rapids: Eerdmans, 1979), p. 343.

# SANCTITY OF HUMAN LIFE

## Norman L. Geisler

## I. WORLDS IN COLLISION

Two great value systems are in headlong conflict in today's society. Popularly they are called "secular humanism" and "Judeo-Christian values." These two systems are diametrically opposed on the basic issues.

### A. The Ultimate Source: God Versus Nature

Every system has an ultimate. The secular humanist explains the world without God. *Humanist Manifesto I* declared: "We are now convinced that the time has passed for theism, deism, modernism and several varieties of 'new thought.'" Therefore, "as non-theist[s], we begin with humans not God, nature not deity."[1] Nature is ultimate and impersonal, operating by nonrational laws.

Life arose spontaneously against overwhelming odds. The Nobel-prize-winning biologist George Wald declared that the spontaneous generation of life is statistically zero. He confessed that "One has only to contemplate the magnitude of this task to concede that the spontaneous generation of a living organism is impossible." He goes on, however, to triumphantly declare his belief in purposeless chance:

> However improbable we regard this event, . . . given enough time it will almost certainly happen at least once. . . . Time is in fact the hero of the plot. . . . Given so much time, the "impossible" becomes possible, the possible probable, and the probable virtually certain. One has only to wait: time itself performs miracles.[2]

In stark contrast to this faith in blind force of nature is the Judeo-Christian view expressed in the Scriptures: "In the beginning God created the heavens and the earth" (Gen. 1:1). "By Him all things were created, both in the heavens and on earth . . ." (Col. 1:16 NASB).

This view of the ultimate source of human life was indelibly inscribed in the founding documents of our country. Although Jefferson was a deist who denied the reality of biblical miracles, nonetheless he was firmly committed to a belief in the Creator and the dignity of man who was created in God's image. The Declaration of Independence (1776) speaks of "Nature's God" and that it is "self evident that all men are created equal, that they are endowed by their Creator with certain inalienable rights. . . ." So ingrained were Judeo-Christian beliefs among the colonists that some states insisted on belief in God as a condition for holding public office. Gradually, however, there was a shift in value base from a Judeo-Christian one to a secular humanist one.

This contrast between the two systems can be summarized as follows:

| Declaration of Independence | Secular Humanist Manifestoes |
|---|---|
| Creator | No creator |
| Creation of man | No creation of man (rather evolution) |
| God-given moral absolutes | No God-given moral absolutes |

The Declaration of Independence declared that it is self-evident that there was a creator, that man was created by God and hence had certain "inalienable rights" based on "Nature's Laws" which came from "Nature's God." And that among these moral rights which governments cannot give or take away are "life, liberty and the pursuit of happiness." Secular humanists' beliefs are diametrically opposed to all three of these Judeo-Christian tenets embodied in the founding document of our country. In their own words they "reject theism" and even "deism."[3] Further, secular humanists reject the creation of man for evolution. For secular "humanists regard the universe as self-existing and not created." And secular "humanism believes man is a part of nature and that he has emerged as a result of a continuous [evolutionary] process."[4] Finally, secular humanists deny all God-given, absolute values, insisting instead that "Humanism asserts that the nature of the universe depicted by modern science makes unacceptable any supernatural or cosmic guarantees of human values."[5]

## B. Man's Origin: Creation Versus Evolution

Biblical Christianity in contrast to secular humanism believes in the special creation of man, not evolution.[6] For either man was directly created by God or else he "emerged as the result of continuous process." That is, either there was a direct supernatural act of creation, whatever material (e.g., "dust") was utilized, or else man resulted from purely natural causes. And it makes no difference whether or not a creator set up these natural laws as theistic evolutionists believe.[7] The question is whether man resulted from purely natural processes (created or eternal) or from a direct supernatural act of the Creator. The two views are incompatible.

Second, it is a mistaken notion to assume that the Darwinian doctrine of evolution is not opposed to the Judeo-Christian teaching about creation but is simply a biological means God may have used. Both Darwin and his immediate contemporaries saw evolution as replacing a Creator. It is not well known that Darwin made no reference to a "creator" in the first edition of his famous *On the Origin of Species.* A reference to a possible "creator" was added to the last paragraph of the second edition because of religious opposition, and it has appeared in editions since then. It is even less known that Darwin referred to evolution as "My deity 'Natural Selection.' "[8] He believed that the role of the Deity in creating man was replaced by his deity "Natural Selection." In the *Descent of Man* (1871) Darwin concluded that "there is absolutely no evidence that man was aboriginally endowed with the ennobling belief in the existence of an Omnipotent God."[9] Indeed, Darwin eventually became agnostic, concluding "that the whole subject is beyond the scope of man's intellect. . . . The mystery of the beginning of all things is insoluble by us; and I for one must be content to remain as Agnostic."[10] Thus in Darwin's mind evolution had replaced the need for a creator.[11]

Another contemporary of Darwin, Friedrich Nietzsche, left absolutely no doubt what this all meant.

> "Whither is God" he cried. "I shall tell you. *We have killed him*—you and I. All of us are his murderers. . . . Do we not hear anything yet of the noise of the gravediggers who are burying God? Do we not smell anything yet of God's decomposition? Gods too decompose. God is dead. God remains dead. And we have killed him."[12]

So in spite of pious protest to the contrary, evolution and creation are opposites. This is so both biblically and historically. Indeed, it is true logically as well. The old Princetonian Charles Hodge wrote a penetrating critique of Darwinism entitled *What is Darwinism?* (1878). In it he forcefully reasoned as follows:

What is Darwinism? It is atheism. This does not mean, as before said, that Mr. Darwin himself and all who adopt his views are atheists; but it means that his theory is atheistic; that the exclusion of design from nature is, as Dr. Gray says, tantamount to atheism.[13]

In other words, evolution declares that there is no real design in nature, only adaptation by natural selection and other forces. But if there is no design in nature, then logically there is no designer of nature. And if there is no creation of different living things (but only evolution), then logically there was no creator. Thus evolution is opposed to the Judeo-Christian belief in a creator. For either man was specially created by God, as Christians believe, or else man evolved, as Darwin believed. And from these radically opposed beliefs there are crucial moral differences which follow naturally.

## C. Man's Moral Obligation: Duty to God Versus Duty to Man (or Nature)

Many non-Christians have seen the clear connection between the denial of the Creator and man's moral obligation. Nietzsche believed that when God died all absolute values died with him. As Ian Barbour put it, "Nietzsche maintained that if evolution is taken seriously as a norm for man, our traditional values will have to be turned upside down."[14] In fact, Nietzsche said "morality must be shot at."[15] As to Christian morality, Nietzsche saw even in the Sermon on the Mount an "acute form of stupidity." He even called Christ an "idiot."[16] He said, "I condemn Christianity. I raise against the Christian Church the most terrible of all accusations that any accuser ever uttered. It is to me the highest of all conceivable corruptions."[17]

The French existentialist, Jean Paul Sartre, saw a direct connection between the denial of a Creator and the loss of absolute values. He explains, "If God does not exist, [we are not] provided with any values or commands that could legitimate our behavior. . . . We are left alone, without excuse."[18]

Of course not all nontheists negate objective, God-given values the way Nietzsche or Sartre did. In fact, most take seriously Nietzsche's suggestion to "create values." Most often these values are consistent with their denial of a creator and/or their belief in evolution. Adolf Hitler, for example, built his anti-Semitic genocide doctrine on Darwin's principle of natural selection.[19] Others like Julian Huxley have developed an evolutionary ethic, declaring that "In the light of evolutionary biology man can now see himself as the sole agent of further evolutionary advance on this planet, and one of the few possible instruments of progress in the universe at large."[20]

But if man is not a special creation of God but only a higher animal, then there are radical ethical differences in what his moral obligation is and to whom it is owed. Carl Sagan, for example, suggests that since the cosmos is all there is, that man has a moral obligation to it. He declares that "Our obligation to survive is owed not just to ourselves but also to that Cosmos, ancient and vast, from which we spring."[21]

One thing is clear: Sagan has the logic right. Man does have a moral obligation to his Creator. However, the cosmos is not our creator, but the Creator of the cosmos is. In fact, Sagan is worshiping "the creature rather than the Creator" (Rom. 1:25 NASB). For as John tells us "the world [Greek *cosmos*] was made by him . . ." (John 1:10 KJV). Indeed, "all things came into being by Him, and apart from Him nothing came into being that has come into being" (v. 3 NASB).

But if man is created in God's image, his life is sacred and a whole different set of ethical principles follows. Indeed, the Scriptures literally abound with such inferences. Because man is created by and like God, he is responsible to God (Gen. 2:16–17) and for the life of other humans (4:9–15). In fact, the Bible explicitly declares that it is wrong to kill innocent human beings, because they are made in God's image (Gen. 9:6). It is even wrong to curse them for this same reason (James 3:9).

## II. VALUE SYSTEMS IN CONFLICT ON LIFE AND DEATH ISSUES

There are two basic affirmations in Scripture about the nature of human life. First, God is sovereign over it because he created it. Second, because God created human life in his image, it is sacred and should be preserved and protected by man.

### A. WHO IS SOVEREIGN?

#### 1. Secular Humanism: Man Is Sovereign

It is clear from the statements of those influenced by a secular humanist ethic that they believe that man is sovereign over life and death. This, for example, is behind the very concept of the so-called pro-choice movement. Of course, once God is eliminated then man is free to install himself as sovereign. The very title *pro-choice* implies that a woman has a sovereign right over the life of another life nested within her womb. *Humanist Manifesto II* explicitly states that one has "the right to . . . abortion," "the right to . . . euthanasia and the right to suicide."[22]

This same humanistic assumption that man is sovereign is reflected in many of the public statements in justification of abortion and euthanasia. In 1973, just six months after the Supreme Court ruled that an unborn human is not a human person protected by the Constitution (*Roe v. Wade*), Dr. Peter A. J. Adam experimented on twelve babies who were born alive by hysterotomy abortion. He cut off their heads and kept the heads alive by placing a tube in the main artery, feeding the brain much as the Russians had done with dog's heads in the 1950s. His justification for this barbaric act reveals that he, too, believes man is sovereign over human life. In response to criticism he said, "Once *society's declared* the fetus dead and abrogated its rights, I don't see any ethical problem. . . . Whose rights are we going to protect, once *we've decided* the fetus won't live?"[23] Notice that the implication is that "society" decides who is "dead," even if they are alive. Further, the phrase "once *society's* declared" which fetus should live shows man has assumed sovereignty over the life and death of the fetus.

Dr. Martti Kekomaki, who conducted experiments of slicing open the stomachs and cutting off heads of live aborted babies, went so far as to say "an aborted baby is just garbage and that's where it ends up."[24] It is one thing for evolution to declare humans to be animals; it is another to treat unborn humans like garbage. But once it is denied that man is the special creation of a sovereign God and there are no moral absolutes, then what hinders such conclusions?

The same indication that in the absence of God man assumes sovereignty over life extends to the postnatal state as well. In other words, to borrow phrases from the secular humanist and situation ethicist Joseph Fletcher, abortion is really "prenatal euthanasia," and euthanasia is actually "postnatal abortion." Several recent cases bear out this connection. In the famous *Baby Doe* case the Indiana Supreme Court gave permission to allow the baby to starve to death (April 1982). This was done, to quote one report, "After his parents and doctor decided his life was not worth sustaining."[25] Again it was humans who "decided" whether the baby should live.

Some of the most famous scientists in the world are now recommending infanticide for the genetically imperfect. Nobel prize winner Francis Crick said, "No newborn infant should be declared human until it has passed certain tests regarding its genetic endowment and . . . if it fails these tests, it forfeits the right to live."[26]

His colleague, James Watson, recommended that

> If a child were not declared alive until three days after birth, then all parents could be allowed the choice only a few are given under the present system. The doctor could allow the child to die if the parents so chose and save a lot of misery and

suffering. I believe this view is the only rational, compassionate attitude to have.[27]

The word "choice" here is one where humans (parents) are exercising sovereign right over whether a baby lives after birth. This is infanticide.[28]

In point of fact, the sovereignty of man over life has been extended by secular humanists to suicide and euthanasia, as *Humanist Manifesto II* declared. Indeed, there are organized groups that encourage suicide and euthanasia. In England the group is called Exit,[29] and in the United States a parallel group called the Hemlock Society[30] has thousands of members. Thus the sovereignty secular humanists have assumed over life extends from before birth to death.

### 2. Judeo-Christian View: God Is Sovereign

In stark contrast to the secular humanist view of man's sovereignty over life, God's infallible, unerring Word declares that God alone is sovereign over the life and death of innocent human beings. This is so because God alone created human life in his image (Gen. 1:27), and he alone has the right to take it. Many passages of Scripture bear this out. In the face of the death of his family, Job declared:

"The LORD gave and the LORD has taken away;
Blessed be the name of the LORD" (Job 1:21 NASB).

The Lord, speaking to Moses, said:

"See now that I, I am He,
And there is no god besides Me;
It is I who put to death and give life . . ."

(Deut. 32:39 NASB).[31]

From beginning to end the Scriptures reveal that God is sovereign over all life (cf. Ps. 135:6; Rev. 4:11). It is God who opens and closes the womb (Gen. 20:18). It is God who creates life in the womb (Ps. 139). And it is God who appoints the day of one's death (Heb. 9:27). God is the sovereign Creator of human life, and he alone has the right to call it back to himself (Eccl. 12:7).

### B. Human Beings: Animals Versus God's Image

The difference between the secular humanist and Christian points of view are vividly contrasted in the painful death situations. The moral relativist suggests that if in mercy we shoot a horse trapped in a burning barn, then we should show the same kindness to a human being. But this implies that humans are animals and should be so treated. For the Christian, the precise reason he does *not* kill the man along with the horse is *because he is a human, not a horse!* Man has been given the right by God to kill animals for food, clothes, and (in the Old Testament) for sacrifices. But God has retained for himself the sovereign right over innocent human life and has explicitly commanded man: "You shall not murder" (Exod. 20:13). We must not deviate from this principle simply because the circumstances are adverse.[32]

Another example of degrading man who is created in God's image is in the contemporary secular humanist's commendation of infanticide. *Newsweek* magazine carried this caption:

BIOLOGISTS SAY INFANTICIDE IS AS NORMAL AS THE SEX DRIVE—AND THAT MOST ANIMALS, INCLUDING MAN, PRACTICE IT.[33]

Above this quote was a picture of a baboon presumably killing one of its young. The implication of the article is: "Baboons do it; why shouldn't humans?" Well, it is precisely *because we are not baboons* that we do not commit infanticide. Since when does animal behavior become normative for humans? The secular humanist could very well answer: "Since Darwin!" For once evolution affirms no creator is needed and man is merely a higher animal genetically connected with baboons, monkeys, and apes, then there is no sufficient reason why he should not be treated like an animal.

This lack of regard for human life is a dramatic illustration of the fact that when the dignity of man in the image of God is reduced to the level of animals, then the immoral becomes "moral," neglect becomes "caring," destruction becomes "compassion," and the irrational becomes "rational."

This same point is vividly manifest in the rationale given for infanticide in the Indiana *Baby Doe* case. The attorney praised the parents' "courage," insisting that "It was caring so much about the child that prompted them to make this decision. . . ."[34]

The famous scientist Dr. James Watson called the starving to death of deformed infants "the only *rational, compassionate* attitude to have."[35] Of course, the reason these terms have such a different meaning for a secular humanist is that he has an entirely different basis for his ethic. In the Judeo-Christian context human life is sacred. It has dignity because it was created Godlike. Man has no right to take it because he did not make it. God alone is sovereign over it.

## III. LIFE AND DEATH ISSUES: A BIBLICAL VIEW

Several life-and-death issues call for special attention in view of the clash of value systems in today's society. Suicide, abortion, euthanasia, and capital punishment all involve taking a human life. The Bible speaks authoritatively on all these issues, and believers must heed its commands.

## A. Suicide: Killing Oneself

### 1. Taking One's Own Life Is Wrong[36]

The command "you shall not murder" (Exod. 20:13; Rom. 13:9) applies to oneself as well as to others. Murder is an act of anger or hatred (Matt. 5:22), and we are not to hate our own life but to nourish and cherish it (Eph. 5:29). We must respect the image of God in ourselves as well as in others. And killing a human, whether oneself or another, is an attack on the image of God.

Furthermore, suicide is a denial of God's sovereignty over life. It fails to respect the fact that "the LORD gave and the LORD has taken away" (Job 1:21). Suicide is also a selfish act. It is usually an attempt to relieve oneself of misery or to avoid some difficult or embarrassing circumstance.[37] First Corinthians 13:2 makes it clear that one can give his "body to be burned" and still "not have love" (NASB). Saul's suicide was out of vain motives. He asked his armorbearer to kill him "lest these uncircumcised come and pierce me through and make sport of me" (1 Sam. 31:4 NASB). Even one who pours gas on his body and lights a match or who starves himself to death can be doing it out of the desire for vainglory or the obstinate commitment to a self-centered cause. But whatever the motive, suicide is wrong because God alone is sovereign over human life, and he has commanded us to respect his authority over us and his image within us.

### 2. Sacrificing One's Life Can Be Right

While it is always wrong as such to *take* an innocent human life (even one's own), it is not wrong to *give* one's life for others. Samson sacrificed his life to avenge the Philistines (Judg. 16:28). The apostle Paul was willing even to be "accursed, separated from Christ" for the salvation of his Jewish brethren (Rom. 9:3). John exhorted Christians to follow Jesus' example in that "He laid down His life for us; and we ought to lay down our lives for the brethren" (1 John 3:16 NASB). Thus Caiaphas, the high priest, unwittingly expressed a truth when he said that "it was expedient for one man to die on behalf of the people" (John 18:14 NASB). The apostle recognized the fact that occasionally "for the good man someone would dare even to die" (Rom. 5:7 NASB). The soldier who falls on a hand grenade to save his buddies from death exemplifies this principle. Of course, the greatest example of all is Christ who "died for the ungodly" (v. 6). He sacrificed his life for sinners who nonetheless had great value as creatures in God's image.

But in each of these cases it is not suicide—the *taking* of one's life. Rather it is a loving *sacrifice* of one's life. And "greater love has no one than this, that one lay down his life for his friends."

## B. Abortion: Taking the Life of the Unborn

### 1. The Biblical Basis Against Abortion

From a Christian perspective abortion is the number-one ethical problem in America. Some 1.5 million unborn are killed each year. This is 4000 per day, or one about every twenty seconds. The sum total of unborn humans sacrificed on abortion altars since the Supreme Court sanctioned abortion on demand (*Roe v. Wade,* 1973) is now 18 million.[38]

Of course, the horror of this situation depends on the premise that the unborn is truly human, a truth well supported by Scripture and science. Medically when a human sperm unites with a human ovum, conception occurs and the result is a separate, tiny human being. This is a biological fact. Despite talk to the contrary about it not being a human "person," it is a genetic and biological fact that it is a separate, individual human being all of its own.[39]

The Bible supports this view of the unborn, treating it as a human being created in God's image. David said, "In sin did my mother conceive me."[40] Thus not only does human life begin at conception but sinful human life begins at that point. The psalmist wrote, "The wicked are estranged from the womb" (Ps. 58:3 NASB).

Jeremiah was known of God and called by him while yet in his mother's womb (Jer. 1:5). John the Baptist "leaped for joy" (Luke 1:44) and was "filled with the Holy Spirit" in his mother's womb (v. 15). Indeed, Jesus was "conceived" of the Holy Spirit (Matt. 1:20) in Mary's womb, and the Scriptures point to that as the beginning of his human nature.

Psalm 139 gives a specific account of the human embryo as a substance being formed by God. In beautiful figures it describes the embryo as being "woven together" (v. 15) and "fashioned" (v. 16 KJV) by God. According to the psalm, God has even written down the embryo's name in his book in heaven (v. 16). The Bible leaves no doubt that the God who makes man in his image and likeness (Gen. 1:27) does this in the womb before birth.[41]

Once it is understood that the unborn from conception on is fully human, then the prohibition against murder applies (Exod. 20:13). "You shall not murder" applies to all human beings, because murder is the intentional taking of an innocent human life.

Accidental killing is not a capital crime.[42] But intentionally killing innocent human life is murder. And the unborn is also a human being, made in God's image. Hence, killing the unborn is murder, whether it is done maliciously or with good motives, for good motives do not justify murder (Prov. 16:25). The end does not justify an evil means.

Of course, not all killing is murder. For example, the Bible is not opposed to protecting one's own life, even if it is necessary to take the life of someone who is threatening it. Exodus 22:2 says, "If the thief is caught while breaking in, and is struck so that he dies, there will be no bloodguiltiness on his account" (NASB).

Accidental killing is not a capital crime (Num. 35:11–12), but intentionally killing an innocent human life is murder. The Authorized Version of the Bible translates the commandment: "You shall not kill" (Exod. 20:13), but the Hebrew word used in this prohibition is not the term which simply means to kill (*shachat*, cf. Exod. 12:6). Rather it is the word which means to murder (*ratsach*). So while the Bible does not condemn all killing, it does condemn *intentional* killing of *innocent* human lives, whether of young or old, born or unborn. Exodus 1 is a prime example. The king of Egypt commanded the killing of all male babies born. But the midwives refused to obey the royal edict, and God blessed them for their compassion and courage (v. 21).

Murder of a human being made in God's image is a serious crime. Since man is made in God's image, murder is an attack upon God. This is a very serious matter. God does not treat it lightly (Rev. 21:8), and neither should we.

### 2. Some Special Problems

Several special problems call for attention. First, what about abortion for severely deformed babies? The answer should be clear in the light of the foregoing discussion. Severely deformed humans are still *human*. Human life must be protected and preserved no matter how devastating the effects of physical depravity may be. If it is murder to kill deformed children and adults, then it is also murder to take the lives of unborn deformed humans.

Second, what about those conceived of rape and/or incest, which is a special kind of rape? Rape is one of the worst indignities a person can suffer. One must have great compassion for rape victims. However, several things must be kept in mind. First, there is no way to become unraped. Becoming unpregnant (via abortion) does not make one unraped. Second, justice is not served to the rape victim by punishing the unborn baby resulting from the rape. Two wrongs do not make a right. The guilt of a murder on top of the indignity of the rape will not help the mother. Rape is not a crime for the victim. But killing an innocent life of the unborn is a crime. Why should we punish the innocent product of a rape? Let's punish the guilty producer of the rape—the rapist! Although conception seldom occurs from rape, the few babies who are conceived by rape also have the right to live. They, too, are made in God's image (Ps. 139:13–16).

But should not a woman have the right to control her own body? First of all, the baby is not part of the mother's body. It is an individual human being with its own separate body. To be sure, the mother is "feeding" the unborn baby, but does a mother have the right to stop feeding her baby after it is born? This would be murder by starvation. Likewise, to cut off the source of life for an unborn baby is also wrong. Even if the unborn baby were part of the mother's body, she would not have the right to do anything she wants to her body. For example, she does not have the moral right to mutilate her own body by cutting off a hand or a foot. Nor does she have the right to kill her own body by committing suicide.

Finally, what if the baby's presence is threatening the life of the mother? Here Christians differ. The traditional Roman Catholic view is to save the baby because one should not *take* a life (the baby's) but only *allow* a death (the mother's) in such conflicts. Many Protestants have argued to the contrary on a self-defense basis, insisting that the mother has the right to protect her life against anything which threatens it, even if it is another human being (Exod. 22:2). Technically, such a defensive action should not be considered an abortion but a surgical procedure necessary to save the mother's life, which also leads to the death of the embryo. Some comfort can be taken in light of the fact that seldom does such a dilemma ever eventuate. Usually it is not necessary to kill either.

What makes these situations difficult is that two human lives are at stake. Thus there is a clash of ethical obligations to preserve both lives. In such cases one must try to discover which norm is the highest obligation. Then in following the "weightier matter of the law" he is exempt from the lower moral duty.[43] In similar ethical dilemmas the believer is exempt from obedience to God's command to obey government in view of his obedience to the higher moral command to be faithful to God (cf. Exod. 1; 1 Kings 18). Likewise, in the case of saving the mother over the baby in the pregnancy threatening her life, one is exempt from the moral duty to save the baby's life in view of the presumed overriding duty to save the mother's life.

### C. Euthanasia: Taking the Life of the Unfortunate

Euthanasia comes from two Greek words meaning literally "easy death." It is usually thought of as a mercy killing or taking the life of the unfortunate. We will use it here to include infanticide, which is taking the lives of infants (usually deformed ones).

### 1. The Principles

#### A. IT IS WRONG TO INTENTIONALLY *TAKE* AN INNOCENT HUMAN LIFE.

The principle is clear: Intentionally taking the life of an innocent human is always wrong as such. It is murder (Exod. 20:13; Rom. 13:9). God alone is sovereign over human life. Man should not *play* God by taking life but *serve* God by protecting it. God alone gives human life, and he has reserved to himself alone the right to take it. Man, even fallen man (Gen. 9:6; James 3:9), is in the image of God no matter how marred it is by depravity. A fallen human being is still a *human being*. There is a divine dignity about life which must be respected, even under the most desperate of circumstances.

#### B. IT IS NOT INTRINSICALLY WRONG TO *ALLOW* NATURAL DEATH.

The other side of the moral principle which forbids *taking* innocent human life is the one which *allows* natural human death. Since God is sovereign over both, interference with either is wrong. For while we have the moral obligation to *perpetuate human life*, we do not have an ethical duty to *prolong human death*. Thus while *mercy killing* is always wrong as such, *mercy dying* is not. Indeed, the Scriptures speak directly to this issue when they encourage giving strong drugs to those who are dying (Prov. 31:6). We have a moral obligation for the alleviation of their pain but none for the prolongation of their death.[44]

### 2. The Practice

It is always easier to *state* a principle (law, norm) than to *apply* it. However, it is immeasurably easier to apply a principle one understands clearly than to make valid moral decisions without moral laws, simply on what some relativists call the "existential particularity" of the situation. Being in the fog is one thing, but having no road signs or traffic signals to designate the correct way is quite another.

Two important issues emerge in the practice of the above principle that natural mercy dying is permissible. First, *when* is someone "dying"; and, second, who should "pull the plug"? As to the first question, the biblical principle of using "two or three witnesses" (Num. 35:30; Matt. 18:16) in life-and-death situations could be applied. This would mean that at least two medical opinions should be sought as to the irreversibility of the dying process. As to the second question, it seems that wisdom is in the multitude of counselors (Prov. 11:14). There ought to be unanimity between legal, medical, spiritual, and family members as to the decision. Of course, if the patient is conscious, he or she should have veto power.

Before any of this, however, God should be repeatedly (2 Cor. 12:8) and collectively (James 5:15) invoked for a divine healing. But when neither God is willing nor medical science able to perform a wonder, then a unanimous decision to allow death to occur naturally (though as painlessly as possible) should be made to "pull the plug." But only mechanical life support systems should be removed, not natural ones such as food, water, and air. Heroic means should be used to preserve a life, not to prolong death. This respects both man's dignity in life and God's sovereignty over death (Heb. 9:27).

## D. Capital Punishment: Taking the Life of the Guilty

While the Bible is clear that one should never intentionally take the life of an innocent human being, this does not apply to taking the life of those guilty of capital crimes. There are at least two contexts in which this is true. First, on the *individual* level, killing in self-defense is justified (Exod. 22:2). Second, on a *national* level, the state is given the sword to use on capital criminals. This was true long before the law of Moses when God said to Noah,

"Whoever sheds man's blood,
By man his blood shall be shed,
For in the image of God
He made man" (Gen. 9:6 NASB).

The right of the state to wield the sword is restated in the New Testament when Paul wrote, "Let every person be in subjection to the governing authorities. For there is no authority except from God. . . . for it does not bear the sword for nothing" (Rom. 13:1, 4 NASB).

### 1. The Principle: Penal Versus Reformatory View of Justice

Behind capital punishment lies the penal view of justice. Without it capital punishment makes no sense. Thus a comparison and contrast between the Judeo-Christian concept of punishment and the secular humanist concept of reformation is necessary background for the discussion. The two views are contrasted in the following chart.

| JUSTICE: | REFORMATORY VIEW | PENAL VIEW |
|---|---|---|
| Nature | Reformative (Remedial) | Retributive (Penal) |
| Offense | Pathological (Sickness) | Moral (Sin) |
| Individual | A Patient (an object) | A Person (a subject) |
| Purpose | To cure | To punish |
| Capital Punishment | No | Yes |
| Pardon Possible | No | Yes |
| World View | Secular Humanism | Judeo-Christian |

There are numerous objections to the reformatory view of justice though there is nothing wrong with attempting to get people to reform. C. S. Lewis summarized them well in his article on the topic.[45] Lewis strikes at the heart of the issue in this statement:

> To be "cured" against one's will and cured of states which we may not regard as disease is to be put on a level with those who have not yet reached the age of reason or those who never will; to be classed with infants, imbeciles, and domestic animals. But to be punished, however severely, because we have deserved it, because we "ought to have known better," is to be treated as a human person in God's image.[46]

Contrary to "popular" (humanistic) opinion, punishment is more humane than the reformatory view of justice, because punishment respects the image of God, the dignity and responsibility of man, whereas the alternate view treats man like an animal or less.

Now it is in this context that capital punishment makes sense. For the punishment should fit the crime. But the only punishment that fits a capital crime is a capital punishment, life for life. Indeed, it is the very principle behind the substitutionary Atonement (2 Cor. 5:21; 1 Peter 2:24; 3:18). For if God could have saved us from the death we deserve (Rom. 6:23) in any other way than through the substitutionary death of his Son (5:6–8), then surely he would have done so. "But the LORD was pleased to crush Him [Christ]" (Isa. 53:10 NASB) that we might have life (John 10:10).

Capital punishment of capital crimes was instituted before the law (Gen. 9:6), was later incorporated in the law of Moses (Exod. 21:12, 23), but is also reaffirmed in the New Testament (Rom.

13:4). In fact, Jesus recognized the God-given capital authority of Rome when he said to Pilate (who claimed the right to kill him), "You would have no authority over Me, unless it had been given you from above" (John 19:11 NASB). The apostle Paul recognized the same when he said, "If then I am a wrongdoer, and have committed anything worthy of death, I do not refuse to die; but if none of those things is true of which these men accuse me, no one can hand me over to them" (Acts 25:11 NASB).

## 2. The Practice

Here, too, the practice is harder to get at than the principle. A few comments are in order.

First, capital punishment was instituted by God for capital crimes. It is for those "who shed man's blood . . ." (Gen. 9:6 NASB). It is true that the law which was given in Israel (a theocracy) included capital punishment for many things other than murder, such as kidnapping (Exod. 21:16), causing a miscarriage (vv. 22–23), sorcery (22:18), sodomy (v. 19), idolatry (v. 20), owning a killer ox (v. 28), cursing parents (Deut. 5:16), being a rebellious son (Deut. 21:20–21), being a drunkard (vv. 20–21), rape (22:25), and adultery (Lev. 20:10). However, there is no evidence in the Old Testament that God intended these penalties to be applied to the unbelievers, and the New Testament does not even apply them to believers (e.g., 1 Cor. 5:1–5). But the New Testament does reaffirm that the "sword" should be used by Gentiles, because it was instituted by God for all men (Rom. 13:4).

Second, for capital crimes there must be "two or three witnesses" (Num. 35:30; Matt. 18:16). This would translate into "beyond doubt" in today's legal parlance. It is interesting to note that in the Old Testament the witness was required to throw the first stones (Deut. 17:7). This would certainly test his sincerity.

## 3. A Problem

Does capital punishment violate the prohibition against murder? Obviously not, since God commanded both in the same Law. In fact, capital punishment is right because murder is wrong. There are two major differences. First, murder is the killing of an *innocent* person. Capital punishment is the killing of a *guilty* person. Second, murder is killing by an *individual*, whereas capital punishment is execution by the *state*. There is a vast difference between these two.

It is worthy of noting that in both the prohibition against murder and the command to execute capital punishment there is a common denominator: both imply a high view of man. It is wrong to murder because "For in the image of God He made man" (Gen.

9:6 NASB). Likewise, it is right to exercise capital punishment because "to be punished, however severely . . . is to be treated as a human person made in God's image."[47]

## E. War: Taking the Lives of Aggressors

Space does not permit a detailed discussion of the topic of war.[48] Several things need to be noted here.

First, a just war can be seen as a broader application of the biblically based principle of self-defense (Exod. 22:2). Jesus even commanded his disciples to buy a sword (Luke 22:36), apparently for their own defense. And Paul did not hesitate to use the protection of the Roman army when his life was in danger (Acts 22–23).

Second, a just war is not murder. Murder is the intentional taking of an *innocent* life. An aggressor is hardly innocent. Abraham engaged in war for the purpose of rescuing Lot from those who aggressed on him (Gen. 14). This was long before God established the theocracy under Moses (Exod. 19f.).

Third, the use of force to the point of life-taking is well established in Scripture by capital punishment. In both capital punishment and war there is God-given authority (cf. Gen. 9:6; Rom. 13:4) to execute justice on the guilty. Just war is simply an intentional application of the principle of which capital punishment is a national use.

Fourth, not all wars are automatically justified. Logic demands that if it is just to defend against the aggressor, then it is unjust to be the aggressor. Blind obedience to government is not commended in Scripture, as is clearly illustrated by the cases of the Hebrew midwives (Exod. 1), the three Hebrew children (Dan. 3), and others.[49] "My country, right or wrong" is patriolatry, not patriotism.

Fifth, the criteria of a just war include a war which is:

1. Declared and engaged in by proper (governmental) authority. God gave the sword to the government (Rom. 13:4) to use on its citizens, not citizens to use on its government nor in vigilante activity to execute justice.

2. Engaged in for the protection of the innocent (against aggressors). A just war is basically defensive not aggressive, though it may involve action on enemy territory (Gen. 14).

3. Fought only if all peaceful negotiation fails to attain justice. "If it be possible . . . live peaceably with all" (Rom. 12:18 KJV). The children of Israel were told to offer peace to an enemy city. They were also told, however, "If they refuse to make peace with you and they engage you in battle, lay siege to that city" (Deut. 20:12).

4. Fought with realistic expectation of success (Luke 14:31–32). For without the calculated odds for success, there is a

merciless slaughter of innocent lives. Mass suicide is morally wrong, too.

5. A justly waged war, even a righteous cause can be invalidated by unrighteous means of accomplishing it. The Scriptures, for example, forbid unnecessary destruction of life supporting environment. Killing babies in mothers' arms is certainly an unjust act of war. Most agree that germ warfare is immoral. And macronuclear attacks on population centers would be difficult to justify as well, though weapons directed at military targets which "spill over" on civilians cannot always be avoided.

War is an ugly spectrum. But as Francis Schaeffer correctly noted, "in a fallen world, force in some form will always be necessary."[50] The force used must be to protect innocent life and punish the guilty. God has so ordained. In both cases it is in accord with God's sovereignty and man's dignity which must be preserved in the face of human depravity. In no case has God given today the authority to the state or to the individual to kill intentionally the lives of innocent human beings.

## IV. CONCLUSION

A biblical view on the life-and-death issues stresses two things. On the "upper" side it is God's sovereignty over human life. On the "lower" side it is human dignity and responsibility. A secularist society has denied God's sovereignty by its a-theism and has debased man's dignity by evolutionism. Only the reaffirmation of man's moral dignity and responsibility as a creature made in God's image can correct this social ill. Both of these God has revealed to all men in his general revelation (Rom. 1:18–20; 2:12–14)[51] and detailed to believers in special revelation (in his inspired Word). While the inerrant Word of God is not *normative* for civil law,[52] it can be *informative* for it, and it is certainly not contradictory to good civil law. Hence, it is our duty as citizens to promote a civil order in line with God's moral law. For without God's law there is no liberty. Can the liberties of a nation be secure when we have removed a conviction that these liberties are the gift of God?"[53]

## ENDNOTES

[1] Paul Kurtz, *Humanist Manifestos I & II* (Buffalo: Prometheus), 1:6; 2:1.
[2] George Wald, "The Origin of Life," *Scientific American*, August 1954, p. 12.
[3] Kurtz, *Humanist Manifestoes*, 2.15; 1.6.
[4] Ibid., 1.8.
[5] Ibid.

[6]Some Christians, particularly those favoring theistic evolution views, object to stating the second crucial difference between Judeo-Christian beliefs and secular humanism in terms of a creation-versus-evolution disjunction. They insist that the Creator created man (at least in part) through the process of evolution. It is true that nearly all creationists recognize the legitimacy of "microevolution," or small changes in species (also called "horizontal evolution"). However, many prefer to call this "variation" rather than "microevolution." Be that as it may, there is still a clear disjunction between "microevolution" (commonly called "evolution") and creation.

[7]Some theists (even Christians) insist that evolution is to be understood as a mere biological process which God used to create, not as anything necessarily in opposition to man's creation in God's image (and consequent dignity). In so doing they overlook several important factors. First, this is not the biblical picture of man's origin which presents man: (1) as being directly "created" by God (Gen. 1:27) who used the "dust of the earth" (2:7) not lower animals, and (2) who created woman out of a rib from man (v. 21), not from lower animals. (3) The whole context of this text is literal, including the conclusion, "for this cause a man shall leave his [literal] father and mother and cleave to his wife" (v. 24). Indeed, (4) Jesus understood this passage literally and used it as the basis for his teaching about the permanence of marriage (Matt. 19:4–5).

In fact, the New Testament uses a literal understanding of Adam and his creation as a basis for its divinely authoritative teaching about (1) marriage (Matt. 19:4–5), (2) the fall of man (Rom. 5:12), (3) the resurrection of Christ (1 Cor.15:22), (4) the headship of the man over woman (1 Cor. 11:3, 9), and the authority of teaching elders (1 Tim. 2:12–14) in the church. In addition, (5) Adam is listed as a literal human being created by God in the genealogy of other literal human descendants who came from him, including Christ (Luke 3:23–38). It is no exaggeration to say, then, that the whole fabric of New Testament teaching on man's fallen nature, his salvation (and resurrection), his dignity, and his authority in the home and church is inseparably intertwined with the doctrine of the literal creation of man in God's image and likeness.

[8]Charles Darwin, *Letter to Lyell*, October 20, 1859.

[9]Charles Darwin, *The Descent of Man* in *Great Books of the Western World*, ed. Robert M. Hutchins (Chicago: Encyclopedia Britannica, 1952), 49:302.

[10]Cited by Paul Edwards, *Encyclopedia of Philosophy* (New York: Macmillan, 1967), 4:295.

[11]The cofounder of the principle of natural selection, Alfred Wallace, said "Natural selection is supreme" (Edwards, *Encyclopedia*, 8:276). Evolution is more than a biological mechanism for Wallace. It is the outworking of a cosmic force that is "not only adequate to direct and regulate all the forces at work in living organisms, but also the more fundamental forces of the whole material universe" (ibid.).

T. H. Huxley, called "Darwin's bulldog," also saw evolution as replacing the need for a creator. He wrote, "I can see no reason for doubting that all are coordinate terms of nature's great progression, from formless to formed, from the inorganic to the organic, from blind force to conscious intellect and will" (Huxley, *Evidence*, p. 107).

Another contemporary, Herbert Spencer, whom Darwin referred to as "our great philosopher," saw evolution as a universal cosmic force. He wrote, "We think of evolution as divided into astronomic, geologic, biologic, psychologic, socio-logic, etc. . . ." And

> The recognition of a persistent force, ever changing its manifestations but unchanged in quantity throughout all past time and all future time, is that which we find alone makes possible each concrete interpretation and at last unifies all concrete interpretations. (Spencer, *First*, ch. 24)

In Germany the famous evolutionist Ernest Haeckel triumphantly proclaimed that evolution had annulled God, arguing that with "this single argument [of evolution] the mystery of the universe is explained, the deity annulled, and a new era of infinite knowledge ushered in" (Haeckel, *Riddle,* p. 337).

Karl Marx, to whom Darwin wanted to dedicate *On the Origin of Species* (but didn't) rejoiced at the victory of Darwin's view of evolution, saying, "But nowadays, in our evolutionary conception of the universe, there is absolutely no room for either a Creator or a ruler" (Niebuhr (ed.) Marx and Engels, *On Religion,* p. 295). Like the others, Marx leaves little doubt that he believed that Darwin's evolution and the Judeo-Christian concept of creation are diametrically opposed.

[12] Walter Kaufmann, *The Portable Nietzsche* (New York: Viking, 1968), p. 95.

[13] Charles Hodge, *What is Darwinism?* (New York: Scribner, Armstrong and Company, 1874), p. 177.

[14] Ian Barbour, *Myths, Models, and Paradigms* (New York: Harper and Row, 1976), p. 110.

[15] Kaufmann, *Nietzsche,* p. 472.

[16] Ibid., pp. 487, 601.

[17] Ibid., p. 655.

[18] Jean Paul Sartre, *Existentialism and Humanism* (London: Methuen, 1948), p. 34.

[19] Adolf Hitler, *Mein Kampf* (London: Hurst and Blackett, 1939), p. 242.

[20] Julian Huxley, *Evolution in Action* (London: Chatto and Windus, 1953), p. 132.

[21] Carl Sagan, *Cosmos* (New York: Random House, 1980), p. 345.

[22] Kurtz, *Humanist Manifestos,* pp. 6–7.

[23] John Whitehead, *The Stealing of America* (Westchester, Ill.: Crossway, 1983), pp. 52–53, italics mine.

[24] William Brennen, *The Abortion Holocaust* (St. Louis: Landmark, n.d.), p. 62.

[25] Quoted in *Christianity Today,* May 20, 1983, p. 41.

[26] Cited in *Bible-Science Newsletter,* June 1983, p. 3.

[27] Ibid.

[28] One noted Stanford philosopher, Dr. Michael Tooley, recommends that one is human with a right to live only if he is self-conscious, saying, "An organism possesses a right to life only if it possesses the concept of a self as a continuing subject of experience and other mental states and believes that it is itself such a continuing entity" (cited in Brennen, *Abortion,* p. 82). Since a young child does not gain self-consciousness until the age of one and a half, this would permit infanticide on those who are approaching two years after birth, to say nothing of permitting euthanasia for those in comas.

[29] One famous member of this group, the author of *Darkness at Noon,* Arthur Koestler, committed suicide with his wife by taking an overdose of barbituates (see *U.S. News,* July 11, 1983).

[30] Their book, *Let Me Die Before I Wake,* includes case studies of those who have committed suicide as well as the means to do it. Derek Humphrey, the group's founder says, "We have made it respectable to debate and discuss euthanasia. We've also helped a lot of people die well" (Humphrey, *Reader,* June 29, 1983).

[31] Even the most desperate of believers in Scripture, who would be candidates for suicide by today's humanistic standards, did not entertain the idea. As Jonah said in his moment of despair, "O LORD, please take my life from me . . ." (Jonah 4:3 NASB). It is noteworthy that he assumed that only God has the right to do this. Likewise, in the midst of his misery Job did not contemplate suicide, though he did wish that he had been stillborn or miscarried (Job 3:11, 16). When the unbelieving do commit suicide in the Bible, there is an implied (or stated) condemnation in the passage. Even then they do not literally take their own life but ask someone to do it for them. Such is the case with Saul's fateful death (1 Sam. 31) and Abimelech's (Judg. 9).

[32] The important phrase here is "simply because." There are times when the issue is more than mere circumstance. It involves the genuine conflict of moral laws, such as killing in self-defense (Exod. 22:2). In such cases there is a divinely appointed higher law (or right) which is to be followed (see Geisler, *Options*, ch. 5).

[33] *Newsweek*, September 6, 1982, p. 78.

[34] Cited in *Bible-Science Newsletter*, June 1983, p. 3.

[35] Ibid.

[36] This discussion follows that presented earlier in my *Christian Ethic of Love* (1973), pp. 100–103.

[37] The wounded Abimelech's request for aid in committing suicide is a case in point: "Draw your sword and kill me, lest it be said of me, 'A woman slew him' " (Judg. 9:54 NASB).

[38] Hitler only killed six million Jews, and this is called a holocaust. In fact, all the United States military personnel killed in all the wars in two hundred plus years of United States history total less than a million and a half. Abortion takes that many lives each year.

[39] The following is a change of my previously published view (*Ethics: Alternatives and Issues* [Grand Rapids: Zondervan, 1971]), where nonviable unborn were considered only "potential persons." See the updated view in my article in "The Bible, Abortion, and Common Sense," *The Fundamentalist Journal*, pp. 24–27.

[40] There is a remarkable unanimity between the Bible and medical science as to when an individual life begins. A human zygote is comprised of a human sperm and a human ovum. Less than a month after conception the unborn has its own heart. And by a month and a half it has its own lifelong brain wave. Before it is two months old it has all the internal organs of an adult. And within another week it has all the external organs as well. At no time is it anything but a tiny, growing human being.

[41] Some have argued that an unborn is less than human because Exodus 21:22–23 did not exact capital punishment—only a fine—for the death of a fetus. But this passage refers to unintentional death where no capital punishment was used even for an adult. In addition, the word used means "young child" (*yeled*), not fetus. Also, the word used for the baby coming out (*yahtzah*) never means miscarriage in the Old Testament but always a birth. Hence, the judgment of "life for life" in verse 23 would apply to the death of either the mother or the baby, treating them both as equals.

[42] Moses wrote, "Then ye shall appoint you cities to be cities of refuge for you; that the slayer may flee thither, which killeth any person at unawares. And they shall be unto you cities of refuge from the avenger; that the manslayer die not, until he stand before the congregation in judgment" (Num. 35:11–12 KJV).

[43] For even though there is a divine command to obey government (Rom. 13:1; Titus 3:1; 1 Peter 2:13), nonetheless there are seven instances in Scripture where there is explicit (or implicit) divine approval of disobeying human government. For example, disobedience is commended when the government takes the place *of* God, rather than taking its place *under* God. The Bible lists several instances of divinely approved disobedience to authorities:

1. When it does not allow worship of God (Exod. 5:1).
2. When it commands believers to kill innocent lives (Exod. 1:15–21).
3. When it commands that God's servants be killed (1 Kings 18:1–4).
4. When it commands believers to worship idols (Dan. 3).
5. When it commands believers to pray only to a man (Dan. 6).
6. When it forbids believers to propagate the gospel (Acts 4:17–19). (The "authority" here is religious, not civil.)
7. When it commands believers to worship a man (Rev. 13).

[44] Geisler, *Ethics: Alternatives and Issues*, ch. 13.

[45] C. S. Lewis, "The Humanitarian Theory of Punishment" in *God in the Dock* (Grand Rapids: Eerdmans, 1970), pp. 287–94. The "as such" is important because it presumes no real moral conflict. When there is a moral conflict, such as killing in

self-defense, the believer's duty is to follow the higher moral law (see Geisler, *Options*, ch. 5). Lewis gives at least eight arguments against the reformatory view of justice.

1. It is tyrannical to submit a man to a compulsory cure unless he deserves it.
2. It is an illusory humanitarianism which disguises possible cruelty and injustice.
3. It is based on the false premise that crime is pathological and not moral.
4. It dehumanizes the individual from the moment he commits the crime on, making a "case" or "patient" of him.
5. It takes the criminal out of the hands of the jurist and justice and places him in the hands of the psychotherapist who has social, not moral, norms.
6. The process of psychotherapy is often a worse form of punishment—longer and more shameful, etc.
7. It has sinister political implications in the hands of the state (anything the state pronounces a "disease" will rob a man of his freedom, even religion).
8. It eliminates the concept of pardon which is the mercy with which justice is tempered (you cannot pardon a man of a sickness).

46 Ibid., p. 292.
47 Ibid.
48 See Geisler, *Ethics: Alternatives and Issues*, ch. 9; and *The Christian Ethic of Love* (Grand Rapids: Zondervan, 1973), ch. 11.
49 See note 43 above.
50 Francis Schaeffer, *A Christian Manifesto* (Westchester Ill.: Crossway, 1981), pp. 103–4.
51 To argue, as some, that general revelation has no content and/or that it is so distorted by fallen man that it is ineffective, is wrongheaded for several reasons: First, the Bible says general revelation is "clear" and "evident" to fallen man (Rom. 1:19). Second, the law "written on the hearts" is clear enough that God condemns people to eternal hell for not believing it (Rom. 1:20; 2:12). Third, depraved man's distortions of general revelation are no greater than his distortions of special revelation. So if depravity invalidates one, it would also invalidate the other. Fourth, there is more agreement on the content of the general moral law than is sometimes supposed, as C. S. Lewis showed in the appendix to *The Abolition of Man*. Finally, the content of the moral law should be read, not from what men *do*, but what they believe *ought* to be done. It is understood not from men's *actions* but from their *reactions* to what others do to them.
52 See N. L. Geisler, "A Premillennial View of Law and Government" *Bibliotheca Sacra* 142:567 (July–September 1985): 250–66.
53 Inscribed on the Jefferson Memorial, Washington, D.C.

# A Response to
# Sanctity of Human Life

## Robert T. Jensen

I have enjoyed Dr. Geisler's friendship and scholarship for a
number of years, and I now count it a real privilege and an honor
to be a responder to his paper on "Sanctity of Human Life."

My concerns with this subject are more practical than
theoretical. As a Christian who believes the Bible to be true and
authoritative, I agree with Dr. Geisler's central thesis which
contrasts the terms "sanctity of life" and "quality of life" as
representative of different world views concerning the origin,
nature, and purpose of the human race. Dr. Geisler has correctly
stated the Judeo-Christian position that mercy killing is always
wrong while mercy dying is not necessarily wrong, and he wisely
urges the use of two or three witnesses in the determination of
when to cease death-delaying medical measures. However, as a
practicing physician and teacher of geriatric medicine and as a
member of the bioethics committee of a major hospital, I have not
always found it easy to distinguish between prolonging life and
delaying death. Moreover, there are now so many factors involved
in bioethical decisions that philosophical differences on the
inherent value of biologic human life may be lost amid contending
interests. In order to sharpen our focus and hopefully offer a few
practical suggestions I will comment on three areas of concern
which complicate the application of the sanctity-of-life principle.

## TERMINOLOGY

The term *sanctity* is a religious term which presupposes that
there is a God and that some things are sacred. When believers
come together, religious terms are used freely and with common
appreciation. However, if I were to use the term *sanctity of life* in a

hospital bioethics committee discussion, it would probably be viewed as an introduction of an inappropriate and undefinable religious concept, this not withstanding the presence of a pastor and a priest on the committee. Indeed, Dr. Clouser, in 1973, wrote as follows:

> The sanctity of life concept as it is generally used—not in its original religious sense—is only a slogan. It not only gives no clear guidance, but it can be positively misleading. There is no place for it in the formal structures of ethics, and what good emphases we can find within the concept are already taken care of by clearer, more defensible rules within ethics. Its best use as a slogan would be as a rhetorical reminder, urging us to weigh life heavily when it is balanced against other goods.[1]

Please note the point that life is to be balanced against other goods! There are no absolutes, only a balance of goods.

It is not my intention to defend the views of Dr. Clouser or others involved in the issues of medical ethics; however, such views represent the secular majority today, and little is gained by ignoring this reality. In an editorial in a medical journal in December 1985, Sidler and Clements noted that "the new ethics splits facts from values" and that "medical ethicists, unlike physicians, have no tradition of accountability to patients for consequences of their interventions."[2]

Fletcher has proposed a case-centered approach to medical ethics compatible with the clinical decision-making process.[3] Indeed, that is how most of these life-and-death issues are being decided now—that is, as a joint effort by a representative of a hospital ethics committee, the physician, the patient, and the family—and not by an individual physician or by the courts. If a judge's authority is required, every effort is made by the ethics committee to steer the matter to a judge who would be most likely to give the desired opinion rather than to a judge who has a reputation for complicating matters. It is important for Christians to realize that their witness has been compromised by their acceptance of the world's terminology. Currently the world will not listen, and one would not long remain on an ethics committee if one spoke with authority from Scripture—"thus says the Lord." This is a matter that requires repentance and prayers for revival so that the Spirit of God might go before to convict the world with fear and trembling. As it is, the Christian can only be modestly effective in defending the sanctity of life by being on bioethics committees, by being available, and by using acceptable terminology such as "respect for life," "importance of life," "value of life," or "right of life" as life-and-death decisions are being made on a case-by-case basis.

## TECHNOLOGY

Another reason that medical ethics has become such an issue today is that modern scientific technology has blurred the dividing line between living and dying. Fifty years ago, before the antibiotic era, pneumonia was feared, but it was also called the old man's friend. As the elderly became feeble and usually before they became demented, they would be quietly claimed by death through the aegis of pneumonia. Now most cases of pneumonia can be cured, thus allowing the person with end-stage chronic obstructive lung disease or emphysema to continue to painfully gasp for air. It also presents the patient and physician with the difficult decision of whether to place such a person on a respirator to live a few more weeks or months with the prospect of dying an even more miserable death connected to a machine. There also is the demented person who gets pneumonia after choking on food, drink, or secretions. Now the aspiration pneumonia can be treated, but the result may be months or years of tube feeding with the patient crying, resisting, and babbling incoherent objections. Who is to say whether this is prolonging life or delaying death? And we also now have the medical legal jungle where a physician may be sued for a wrongful life (failure to do an amniocentesis so that the mother might have had the option of having an abortion of a Down's syndrome child) and for a wrongful death (failure to use maximum medical intervention to save a life).

But what of the future, with organ transplants, genetic engineering, and possibly permanent replacement of major portions of the human anatomy and organ systems with sophisticated machinery? In the future it might be technically feasible, given enough resources and time, to dispense with a disease- or injury-wrecked lower body and mount a living head with shoulders and arms on a mobile heart, lung, kidney, artificial feeding machine console that could be controlled by the remnant of the person involved. At the present time we cringe at such a grotesque thought, but people can be educated or conditioned to accept almost anything. Today research work is underway in different places on various parts of such biotechnical apparatus, and it is only a matter of time until someone starts putting the pieces together for some type of multisystem replacement job.

At the time of the Tower of Babel,

> the LORD came down to see the city and the tower, which the sons of men had built. And the LORD said, "Behold, they are one people, and they have one language; and this is only the beginning of what they will do; and nothing that they propose to do will now be impossible for them. Come, let us go down, and there confuse their language, that they may not understand one another's speech."[4]

In looking toward the future through Daniel's eyes we know that "many shall run to and fro, and knowledge shall increase."[5] Today computers have solved the language and knowledge manipulation problem, but they have not provided wisdom. Once again, nothing is impossible for man except for the gift of life, the consequences of sin, and the inevitability of death. With pride, dedication, and great technological skill, humans continue to assault the life-and-death barriers. However, with millions of hungry, frustrated, redundant, poorly prepared, and poorly endowed people on earth, those who value the sanctity of life cannot avoid questions concerning priorities for research in life-extending technology and priorities on whose life and what type of life is to be extended. If a means of medical intervention is available, it will be used; and, indeed, medical ethics will demand its use unless "other goods" have greater priority. Often there are no good answers because humankind continues to behave badly. So once again the Christian has no choice but to be involved in the world's struggle over values.

## ECONOMICS

Today over 11 percent of the gross national product of the United States is devoted to health care,[6] and there is no limit in sight. There is, however, a limit to the cost reductions that can be achieved by freezing fees and hospital reimbursements without causing a reduction in the quality and/or quantity of services provided. In the United Kingdom the socialized health service does not provide coronary artery bypass surgery for people over age sixty-five. If that rule was applied in this country, many people who have received real benefit from that procedure would have died. However, there are now trends in health care financing in this country that may reduce the quality of health care for the elderly. There is also now a bill before Congress to have the federal government pay for the cost of heart, bone marrow, and liver transplants as well as for kidney transplants. The cost will be multiple billions. It is easy for an uninvolved person to vote no, but it is quite another thing to vote no if one of your children needs the transplant to survive.

Today in China, as well as in other parts of the world, infants with birth defects are aborted or allowed to die after being born.[7] With great social pressure to limit the size of families few parents in China wish to sustain the life of a defective child. With families restricted in the number of children permitted, there is coercive pressure on pregnant single girls to have abortions. The result of such social policies is to reduce health costs by providing priority in health services to healthy children and workers. These policies also reduce delinquency and force the youth to continue in education or training programs until they have matured and mastered skills required for employment. These are some of the reasons that it has been predicted that Asia will surpass the West in the next century; "powered by a combination of high technology, high productivity, high savings, low taxes, free trade fervor and the spirit of free enterprise. . . . What will enhance Asian life above all else is a swift and joyful acceptance of new technology."[8]

Those who believe in the sanctity of life should not ignore these trends in the world. For if prosperity flounders in America under the load of unskilled, functionally illiterate, and unwanted welfare populations; under the high cost of health care for a rapidly expanding elderly population; under the profits without social responsibility attitude of many in both labor and management; and with family life disintegrating with the sexual revolution and self-centered lifestyles, it may be difficult to prevent a reactionary swing of public policies toward euthanasia and against not only the Right-to-Life movement but also against the free choice that exists today.

## CONCLUSION

Dr. Geisler has rightly questioned whether the liberties of a nation can be secured when we have removed the conviction that these liberties are a gift of God. We are now in the process of losing liberties as a consequence of our abandonment of God's moral standards. Sad as it may seem, there are many countries in this chaotic world today where people would willingly trade their liberty for security and prosperity, and America in decline will be no exception. If war or revolution can be avoided, a reasonable level of prosperity can usually be achieved without liberty by the simple expedient of killing off the nonproductive, by making slaves of reluctant or liberty-minded workers, and by educating and rewarding the conforming masses. Obviously, the sanctity of life is not a concern in such a society. Currently our country has rejected sacred terminology, has rejected God's standards of morality, has made idols of modern technology and sex, and has squandered our grandchildren's resources on opulence, war, and debauchery. If we are to be truly effective in advancing the concept of the sanctity of life, it must be as a part of a spiritual awakening throughout the land. When that occurs, we will not be so concerned with balancing life with other goods, for the people themselves will be good. We need both prayer and action now as we await the Lord's revival or his return.

# ENDNOTES

[1] K. Danner Clouser, Ph.D., "The Sanctity of Life," *An Analysis of a Concept; Annals of Internal Medicine* 78 (1973): 119–25.

[2] Roger C. Sidler, and Colleen D. Clements, *The New Medical Ethics, Archives of Internal Medicine* 145 (1985): 2169–71.

[3] J. Fletcher, *Situation Ethics: The New Morality* (Philadelphia: Westminster, 1966). Quoted by Sidler and Clements in (2).

[4] Genesis 11:5–7 RSV.

[5] Daniel 12:4.

[6] National Center for Health Statistics.

[7] Personal communication with Chinese physicians and travelers.

[8] *World Development Forum*, vol. 4, no. 5 (March 15, 1986).

# A Response to
# Sanctity of Human Life

## C. Everett Koop

Dr. Norman Geisler has written a generally fine paper on "Sanctity of Human Life." He has chosen to place the argument on whether or not life is precious to God in the context of the antithesis of two opposing world views—secular humanism and Judeo-Christian values.

Geisler very nicely points out that his two opposing views in modern society lean heavily on their belief either in the random process of selection called evolution or in the biblically based supernatural process of creation with its major tenet that man was created in the image of God. He leaves no room for doubt that evolution and creation can be married in any way; they are biblically, historically, and logically opposites.

Secular humanism, where man is at the center of all things, clearly leads to man's sovereignty in the decision-making process of such life issues as abortion, infanticide, euthanasia, and suicide. Documentation of the secular humanist position is ample with quotations of a broad order, from Darwin through the *Humanist Manifestoes I* and *II*, to quotations from recent Nobel laureates whose attitudes toward the sanctity of human life reflect humanist philosophy.

On the other hand, the author documents the Christian position on the sanctity of human life and the creation of man in the image of God on innumerable and appropriate biblical references which he obviously believes to be inerrant.

In the third section of Dr. Geisler's treatise, he discusses life-and-death issues from a biblical view and specifically mentions suicide, abortion, euthanasia, capital punishment, and war. He never again mentions war, which is all to the good. But on capital punishment he develops strong arguments biblically based on the one hand and strongly supported by arguments concerning justice from the reformatory view versus the penal view on the other. This rather long excursion into capital punishment fragments the thrust of his otherwise excellent presentation, for it would have sufficed to say, "From a Christian perspective all of the life issues affect *innocent life*, whereas any discussion of capital punishment presumes guilt."

In emphasizing several portions of Geisler's work that are outstanding, it is not my intent to indicate that the remainder of the work is deficient, rather only that there are several strong points worth mentioning.

For example, in the summary paragraph just before the beginning of the section on value systems in conflicts on life-and-death issues, the whole argument seems beautifully connected: Man, created in the image of God, is responsible to God. In my own life, as a Christian and as a surgeon, I have reduced this to the understanding that we hold our own lives and those lives entrusted to us in stewardship and are ultimately accountable to God for the manner in which we handle that responsibility.

Shortly after the section referred to above, the interdependence of the life issues becomes very apparent. Illustrations abound on the humanist philosophy which permits semantic confusion to obscure truth, such as Joseph Fletcher's "prenatal euthanasia" being the equivalent of abortion and "postnatal abortion" being the equivalent of euthanasia. I have always likened the three main issues of abortion, infanticide, and euthanasia to the falling dominoes that children stood on end to see topple one after the other. The first domino that fell was abortion, and it fell with a very loud thud and is known by everyone. Infanticide was the silent domino because it was practiced behind the protective façade of a hospital and was usually part of a tightly held conspiracy involving parents and a physician and sometimes a nurse and a few others. Unfortunately the third domino has been struck and is falling, and that is euthanasia. The manner in which historians of the next century will portray the next several decades will depend upon the response of Christians to meeting the challenge of euthanasia with adequate and appropriate alternatives.

The number of biblical supporting references to the sanctity-of-life position is impressive. One which is not usually quoted is Exodus 1:21, where the midwives in Egypt refused to obey the royal edict to kill all male children, and God blessed them for their compassion and courage.

Another excellent section is that on the discussion of human beings in reference to being animals versus creatures in God's image. After a discussion of the secular humanist view on infanticide, Geisler asks the very pertinent question: "Since when is animal behavior normative for humans?" Infanticide as practiced in the animal kingdom other than man has no connection with the practice of infanticide as practiced by human beings. Although there are multiple reasons for animal infanticide, infanticide in human beings, although ostensibly offered for the betterment of the victim, is often very patently for the convenience and comfort of surviving family members. When I graduated from medical school it was with the understanding that I was called to save lives and alleviate suffering. The lives I was to save were the lives of my patients, and the suffering I was to alleviate was the suffering of my patients. Now, in the twisted logic of the secular humanist, I save lives when I can, but it is quite acceptable in the eyes of the secular humanist, when I am responsible for a less than perfect baby, to alleviate the suffering of the parents by terminating the life of the child. Geisler says that when the dignity of man and the image of God is reduced to the level of animals, then the immoral becomes "moral," neglect becomes "caring," destruction becomes "compassion," and the irrational becomes "rational." Or, as I might say it, if human beings treat other human beings as animals, animals they will become.

For all of my professional life I dealt constantly with less than perfect newborns who required life-saving surgery, the result of which was not always a perfect child. I took great comfort from the statement God made to Moses at the burning bush when he said in Exodus 4:11: "Who gave man his mouth? Who makes him deaf or mute? Who gives him sight or makes him blind? Is it not I, the LORD?" Instead of referring to the deaf and the blind, God could have told Moses about atresia of the esophagus, spina bifida, and imperforate anus, but Moses would not have understood him.

One of the great medical arguments today is the difference between giving the patient all the life to which he or she is entitled as opposed to prolonging the act of dying. Geisler puts this in very human terms that cannot be misunderstood. He enunciates well the moral principle which forbids taking human life but allows natural human death. Very correctly he says, "Thus while mercy killing is always wrong as such, mercy dying is not."

There are three issues where I would register mild to strong disagreement with Dr. Geisler's presentation. The first of these, tubal pregnancy, is not a subject well understood by nonmedical people but which unfortunately has produced a lot of misconceptions in those concerned with the issues involving the sanctity of life.

Second, I am not certain that the biblical principle of using "two or three witnesses" (Num. 35:30; Matt. 18:16) pertains to medical opinions on "pulling the plug," although more than three witnesses is ideal.

Third, I would have some minor objections to the manner in which the author suggests that God should be repeatedly and collectively called upon for a divine healing.

## I. TUBAL PREGNANCY

Under ordinary circumstances when conception takes place, the egg, descending the fallopian tube toward the uterus after it has been extruded from the ovary, encounters one of a large number of sperm which accomplishes the act of fertilization. After the moment of fertilization twenty-three chromosomes from the egg and twenty-three chromosomes from the sperm are united in one cell called the zygote, which contains all of the DNA and the whole genetic code for the next generation. The fertilized egg then descends further in the fallopian tube into the uterus where it implants on the wall of the uterus and the development of pregnancy as we know it continues apace.

Every so often a fertilized egg (zygote) does not descend further into the uterus but instead implants on the wall of the fallopian tube. This is one of several varieties of ectopic pregnancies (i.e., where the implantation takes place at a site other than the usual intrauterine site). It is not possible for the fallopian tube to provide the necessary environment for the growth of a placenta, umbilical cord, and sufficient room for the domicile of the developing embryo and fetus. The most common course of events is that eventually in the implantation process a perforation is made in the wall of the fallopian tube and bleeding ensues; indeed, the bleeding is frequently a hemorrhage and not uncommonly is life threatening.

Under these described circumstances, the developing embryo, deprived of blood supply, is either already deprived of life, or in the course of ensuing events with the continued bleeding, will be deprived of life. Therefore the whole medical decision-making process shifts from whether or not to save the life of the mother or the child to a situation where the child's life has already been forfeited and now the physician's only responsibility is to operate, stop the bleeding, remove the products of conception and the associated ruptured fallopian tube, and save the mother's life.

This is a far cry from any discussion over whether the life of the unborn baby takes precedence over the life of the mother; in modern-day obstetrics it is an almost unknown situation. I, personally, have never known of a situation where an abortion would save the life of a mother at the expense of destroying the baby. Even in most unusual situations, where in pregnancy the mother develops a malignant tumor and the question of abortion arises, the destruction of the unborn child will not affect the eventual outcome of the life of the mother.

Therefore I believe that tubal pregnancy should never be discussed in reference to the indications for abortion if one is considering the moral and ethical question of the life of the mother versus the life of the baby, because the life of the baby is gone and the life of the mother is absolutely necessary to save.

## II. TWO OR THREE WITNESSES

Although to my way of thinking, this biblical principle may not be applicable to situations where decisions are being made toward the end of life, the logical principle is very appropriate. Not only is the second opinion in medicine a justifiable means of checking on the skill and integrity of the first opinion, but as Dr. Geisler suggests, there is wisdom in the multitude of counselors (Prov. 11:14). The government's efforts in reference to the Baby Doe situation resulted in voluntary guidelines for hospitals dealing with handicapped newborns, suggesting the formation of patient care review committees where it was not the numbers that were important but the disciplines concerned. It was suggested that when there were discussions about the life of a handicapped child, the minimum representation should be a physician and, if necessary, a surgeon, a nurse, a hospital administrator, a legal counsel, a member of the handicapped community, and an individual appointed as a child advocate. The latter two are most important. A member of the handicapped community understands better than others how differently the handicapped individual looks upon barriers that would seem insurmountable to the nonhandicapped but which are taken somewhat in stride by the handicapped. The child advocate on such a committee guarantees that someone will represent the rights and the needs and the potential of the child in spite of all else. Experience with such patient care review committees has indicated that they not only function well but go beyond their intended purpose, which is to serve parents in difficult decisions which may not even be absolute in reference to life or death but be relative in reference to quality of life in the future.

## III. DIVINE HEALING

Arguments concerning divine healing usually generate more heat than they do light. I have always maintained that someone in my position had a message for those who were concerned about divine healing. I am a Christian, I am a physician, I believe in miracles, I know that all healing comes from God, I believe that healing takes place according to God's natural laws; and yet I have never seen what a "professional divine healer" would call a "divine healing." Time does not permit a full discussion of this subject.[1] If, as the author contends and I firmly believe, God is sovereign and the life of an individual patient is securely in his hands, how does the suggestion that "before any of this, however [referring to "pulling the plug"], God should be *repeatedly* and *collectively* invoked for a divine healing" (italics mine) fit into the picture? In almost a half century as a surgeon I have always felt—indeed, knew—that God was the Healer and that I was the instrument. The patient was in his hands, and I did what I was able to do with medical and personal skills, mindful of the stewardship of life entrusted to me; and therefore I never felt obligated to repeatedly, and especially collectively, implore God for divine healing before making a decision that I felt was already in his hands.

"Pulling the plug" has come to be a popular euphemism for making a decision to withhold further "extraordinary" or "heroic" care of the patient whose death is imminent. In the bygone era when patients were not as mobile as they are today, and when most patients faced their terminal illness in the hands of a physician they had known all of their lives, this decision-making process at the end of life was in the realm of trust between the physician and his patient. Today, with a much more mobile society and with many deaths being of accidental etiology with a terminal situation in the hands of physicians who never knew the patient, the luxury of this trust has somewhat disappeared. Most physicians have worked out a method of handling the decision-making process at the end of life, although they may not articulate it in the same way that I do. Even though I believe in this strong difference of giving the patient all the life to which he or she is entitled and prolonging the act of dying, I do not believe that the living will or a euphemism such as "death with dignity," serves the need of the patient and his surviving relatives nearly as often as advertised.

Over and above all that individuals may desire about the ends of their own lives and above all that their relatives would wish for them hovers the specter of litigation against the decision makers and the medical profession. Therefore it is important that individuals discuss with their younger relatives their desires about the manner in which they would like to see their lives end so that the unnecessary and highly emotional argumentation that can take place around the decision-making process at the end of life can be avoided.

If I were able to add anything to Dr. Geisler's paper to make it "complete," it would be a discussion of four things: motivation; the test-tube baby; the demographics of the elderly; and alternatives to abortion, infanticide, and euthanasia.

## A. Motivation

With the understanding that life should be preserved in general but never terminated deliberately, motivation has a tremendous amount to do with the decision-making process at the end of life. One example will make it' clear. If a patient is in a terminal illness and having intractable pain, the saving of a life becomes secondary to the alleviation of suffering. The suffering, let us say, can be alleviated only by giving increasing doses of a drug such as morphine at shorter and shorter intervals with the knowledge that such a course of action will shorten the patient's life. Ethically and morally that is certainly permissible, because the motivation is to alleviate suffering and not to terminate life.

## B. Test-Tube Babies

In vitro fertilization and embryo transfer, as it is scientifically called, proves beyond any doubt that life begins at conception. After the junction of sperm and egg in a test tube or petri dish, and once the zygote is formed and transferred to the uterus of the mother-to-be, nothing is added to that zygote except nutrition provided through the umbilical cord from the mother. Her only other contribution is to provide a place of domicile for the baby.

In *Roe v. Wade* the Supreme Court said that it did not know when life began. Two years later, in 1975, in a case known as *Danforth*, the Supreme Court said they did not know when life began on the basis of present knowledge. In 1984 they had a marvelous opportunity to back away from their hard-nosed position on abortion and say that they did know, on the basis of the test-tube baby, that life begins at conception. Of course, they did not take this opportunity.

## C. Demographics of the Elderly

Even now when euthanasia forces are abroad in our land, hiding behind euphemisms such as "concern for dying," the elderly are caught in the cross fire between cost containment for health on the one hand and the rising chorus for euthanasia (by whatever name) on the other. Economics will be the telling factor, I believe, in the argument for euthanasia.

In forty years the population in America of people over sixty-five will double. In that same forty years, the number of tax-paying wage earners will only increase by 30 percent. Another way of saying it is that while there are now five tax-paying wage earners for every person over sixty-five, in forty years there will be only three, and that estimate is based on an optimistic view of an increase in the birth rate. One does not have to be much of a prophet to predict the future.

## D.  Alternatives

It is not sufficient to be against abortion, infanticide, and euthanasia. The Christian church has to provide alternatives, and the opportunities for doing this in reference to all three of the aforementioned life issues are almost legion. Time does not permit a full discussion of this subject, but it is up to the Christian church, if it is interested in doing away with the threat to the sanctity of life, to provide alternatives that make the choice easy for those who are involved.

Finally, I would have hoped that Dr. Geisler would have used a closing quotation, either from a Christian or from the Bible rather than from Thomas Jefferson. Given the opportunity to do so, I would use the dedication that Francis Schaeffer and I used in *Whatever Happened to the Human Race?*

> To those who are robbed of life, the unborn, the weak, the sick, the old, during the dark ages of madness, selfishness, lust and greed for which the last decades of the 20th Century are remembered.

## ENDNOTES

[1]C. Everett Koop, *Faith Healing and the Sovereignty of God*, Philadelphia: Conference on Reformed Theology, April 23–25, 1976.

# A Response to
# Sanctity of Human Life

## Curtis J. Young

In his article, "Sanctity of Human Life," Dr. Norman Geisler has provided the church with a concise and helpful treatment of the subject. For the Christian studying the biblical view of man and its implications for issues of suicide, abortion, euthanasia, capital punishment, and war, the paper is a worthwhile introduction.

This is particularly the case because of the manner in which Dr. Geisler frames the arguments. The biblical message concerning the nature and value of human life is contested and denied by the major institutions of our society. This rejection of biblical authority has led directly to the removal of legal protection for defenseless human beings deemed unwanted or burdensome.

The practice of abortion is now commonplace. While the society remains ambivalent over euthanasia, this practice, which includes infanticide, is becoming more frequent. In incremental fashion our courts accord euthanasia increasing legal support.

Under these circumstances of escalating violence against the helpless, any treatment of the sanctity of human life should be rigorous and precise so the teaching and requirements of Scripture are clearly distinguished from the antagonistic views of secularism. Otherwise, the church will be left in a state of perpetual ambivalence or, even worse, toleration for practices that are intolerable to God. In this regard Dr. Geisler's paper is good tonic.

By contrasting the views of secular humanism with those of biblical Christianity, an unmistakable theme emerges, although it is not explicitly stated: Toleration within the church for practices like abortion, which are rooted in a low view of human life, reflects a low view of Scripture. The authority of the Bible is challenged, not because its injunctions are rejected as false but because they are ignored.

175

Dr. Geisler indicts evolutionary theory as the great threat to the sanctity of human life since it denies that God created man in his image. Although his observation does not explain the immediate reason many discount the value of human life, it is an important insight. Ethicists who expound the "new" view of man and human obligation are keenly aware that evolutionary theory has shaped their thinking.

This was well illustrated during the intense debate over infanticide in 1983 when the American Academy of Pediatrics published an astounding commentary justifying the practice in *Pediatrics*. Written by Australian "bioethicist" Peter Singer, the lead editorial postulated:

> We can no longer base our ethics on the idea that human beings are a special form of creation, made in the image of God, singled out from all other animals, and alone possessing an immortal soul. . . .

> If we compare a severely defective human infant with a nonhuman animal, a dog or a pig, for example, we will often find the nonhuman to have superior capacities, both actual and potential, for rationality, self-consciousness, communication, and anything else that can plausibly be considered morally significant. Only the fact that the defective infant is a member of the species *Homo sapiens* leads it to be treated differently from the dog or pig. Species membership alone, however, is not morally relevant.[1]

On May 29, 1984, a Congressional reception was held in honor of Dr. Singer as a founder of the animal rights movement! His 1975 book, *Animal Liberation*, has become the bible of that effort to end animal abuse on factory farms and in laboratories.

Ultimately, the theory of evolution is not the culprit behind the utilitarian view of human life so prevalent in our day, but sin, that twist in our nature that leads us to exalt ourselves and destroy our neighbor. This observation is not made as a mindless reduction of the conflict over human life but as a reminder that fundamentally the issue at hand is not philosophical but spiritual. If men did not have evolution as a rationalization for violent practices that extend from antiquity, they would invent some other. After all, men behaved like "unreasoning animals" long before *The Origin of Species* was written.

Sin blinds men to the fact that others are made in God's image, uniquely created to know and even to resemble him as, "Father, who art in heaven." Moreover, sin can so affect the circumstances, appearance, behavior, or human capacities of men that their native majesty is not readily apparent, not even to those who confess the sanctity of human life. As a result, sin may at once lead to violence against the innocent or to toleration of the same when the victims seem insignificant or burdensome. The people of God have, on occasion, fallen prey to the latter vice, with disastrous results.[2]

After the Fall men denied the sanctity of their lives, but this denial did not negate the fact. This is evidenced by God's judgment on sin, by his role in vindicating the oppressed and commanding that men do likewise, and most important, by his promise that the glorious purpose for which he created men would be brought to completion through the Messiah.[3] Regardless of how they looked or what they did, men were still valuable in his sight. Transgressions against the creature were transgressions against the Creator. The corruption that did exist would be removed through "the seed of the woman."[4]

Christians, of all people, should be persuaded of the sanctity of human life. In creation God made man in his image. In redemption God identified with man to the point of becoming a man and suffering for men. Both in creation and redemption, then, God has shown how valuable we are in his sight.

Jesus taught his disciples to regard men accordingly. Their duty extends to caring for weak, defenseless people whom the world rejects as worthless and burdensome. The analogy Jesus used is arresting. Christians are to care for them as though they are caring for him. Mother Teresa has captured this point beautifully in observing that among the oppressed and outcast members of humanity, we find "Christ in distressing disguise."[5] Our regard for them is a measure of our regard for him.[6]

Serving those on the raw edges of life teaches more dearly than words the sanctity of all human life. This is indispensable for the church if its message is to be understood and obeyed. Mercy missions, such as ministries in alternatives to abortion and care for the elderly ill and dying, are needed. So are prophetic works of standing for righteousness. These may take many forms, from standing publicly in protest against abortion, to admonishing civil authorities to fulfill their divine obligation to protect the innocent.

This standard of regard for the weak, though personalized by Jesus, is not foreign to the Old Testament as a requirement of the law. Repeatedly, the triad of "the widow, the fatherless, and the alien" was used to designate vulnerable, defenseless people. Israel had a particular duty to protect and to care for them.[7]

These paradigms are valuable, for they frame reality from the divine perspective. Particularly on the issue of abortion false paradigms are used to justify the murder of innocent human beings. By countering with true perspective, both the Christian community and the public at large can be moved to action.

The arguments for abortion are many, but all are rooted in an evaluation of the unborn human being as something other than we, less than we, worth less than we who are born, who reason, who achieve.

Different terms have been invented or redefined to make the distinction between us and them. They are called "potential life" whereas we are human lives. They are called "nonpersons" whereas we are persons.

Arguments that discount the unborn in this manner reflect the depravity of human nature—they reflect arrogance and ignorance on the part of men.

Men are arrogant to assume that somehow they are better, more worthy of protection and the gifts of God; that the unborn have not achieved, earned, or experienced those distinguishing characteristics that make the rest valuable. They are oblivious to the fact that their long-standing alliance with sin makes them more wretched in God's sight and more deserving of eternal destruction. The humility and perspective of the psalmist has been lost: "What is man, that thou art mindful of him? and the son of man, that thou visitest him?"[8]

In their ignorance men discount the unborn, for they ignore the fact that they also were once "unborn." In moving personhood (whatever that means) beyond the grasp of fetal life, they make their own grasp of personhood tenuous at best. For there was a time when they did not have it. If the all-important personhood is something one acquires or grows into, then it is something one may lose or grow out of.

Within the Christian church the discounting of the unborn works a disservice to the gospel and to the kingdom of God. The following three statements come from women who have had abortions and have sent letters to the Christian Action Council, the evangelical organization that has pioneered Crisis Pregnancy Center ministries, providing alternatives to abortion. They will lend perspective.

> You get to thinking how your mate let you down, and it really hurts. It just doesn't seem fair to you at all because you know you didn't get pregnant all by yourself. But yet he leaves you all alone. . . . You feel as if you have paid someone to kill your baby.

> My abortion is something that I wish I never had done. I can remember looking at the doctor when it was done and saw him putting my baby in a plastic bag and throwing it away in a garbage bag. Do you know how bad that feels?

> The miracle of life is so incredible. The guilt I feel is so breathtaking. My baby no longer exists. My heart aches to know of my mistake which has destroyed both of us. I want you inside my womb where you belong. Baby, I'm so sorry I was so weak and didn't do the right![9]

Who is right? Are these women right who say they destroyed their babies in abortion—sons and daughters, human beings entitled not only to protection but to a mother's love?

Or do the ethicists and jurists correctly perceive reality with their new words and concepts, like potential life and personhood? For if they do, we have nothing to offer these women except to persuade them that the guilt they feel is exaggerated; it must be put in perspective, for, after all, this was only potential life, not really a son or daughter.

After years of counseling and interviews, I must report that the grief and sorrow experienced by the woman who has aborted cannot be so easily reduced. If we minimize what she has done, as the discounting of the unborn child requires, we rob her of the opportunity to know the power of the gospel of Jesus Christ and to be healed. In this we deny Christ himself.

The concepts of personhood and potential life are abstractions. They do not correspond to reality or to the Word of God which calls forth reality. To root these concepts in ancient history, one must go back to Aristotle, not to Moses, not to Isaiah, not to Paul. They did not think in these terms; they did not teach in these terms; and most important, they were not inspired to present reality and our human obligation in these terms.

To the Supreme Court a potential life has very little value. It may be destroyed at any point prior to birth if this is the mother's choice. Some evangelical scholars teach that a potential life has more value than that and deserves protection unless it is conceived as a result of rape or incest, or unless it has passed an undefined point of defectiveness. Still others argue that potential lives have value, but it is wrong to secure any legal protection as though they were born individuals.

Not only do such paradigms mean different things to different people, they can mean different things to the same person. In 1970 Joseph Fletcher taught that a life may be destroyed unless it has met most of fifteen positive criteria and avoided most of four negative criteria.[10] By 1974 he had economized his position so that life may be destroyed unless it has passed four "indicators of humanhood."[11]

If Christians build their ethic around the abstractions of "potential life" and "personhood," no matter how loudly they insist on their "baptized" definitions of the terms, they will not determine their definition. The concepts already are used broadly in justifying abortion, and even if they do not intend to do this, those they teach, faced with input from many sources, are bound to be confused, if not worse. Confusion and ambivalence on the issue of abortion breeds apathy and the toleration of violence against the fatherless.

The "fatherless" are a real group of human beings. In the Old Testament the term connotes those defenseless sons and daughters of every generation who have no father protector. As a result they face exploitation, abuse, and destruction. The term fundamentally connotes helplessness and recalls the duty of others to provide protection and care, much like "the hungry" recalls the duty of others to provide food. The condition of the one and the obligation of the many are inseparable.[12]

The fatherless suffer in every generation. They have been abandoned, enslaved, worked to death in mines and factories, and abused in unspeakable ways. The cruel mistreatment has come not only at the hands of seedy persons but at the hands of the respected and powerful who enact laws "that they may plunder the fatherless."[13]

Can anyone seriously doubt that the unborn are the fatherless of our day? Our courts have denied fathers any right to protect their sons or daughters from abortion.[14] Very often the unborn and their mothers are actively abandoned by the fathers, and this leads women to seek abortion.

Today sophisticated technology permits men to snatch the fatherless from their mother's womb rather than "from the breast," as in Job's day, in order to destroy them. The grisly techniques of abortion take advantage of their greater vulnerability before birth and accomplish the killing in a dark and hidden place. Let not the subtlety of the violence deceive anyone into thinking it is acceptable, that the duty to "defend the fatherless" does not apply.

> Destruction of the embryo in the mother's womb is a violation of the right to live which God has bestowed upon this nascent life. To raise the question of whether we are here concerned already with a human being or not is merely to confuse the issue. The simple fact is that God certainly intended to create a human being and that this nascent life has been deliberately deprived of his life. And that is nothing but murder.[15]

Just as false paradigms of personhood are used to justify the violence of abortion, they also are used to justify the violence of euthanasia, whereby burdensome people are killed either through deliberate neglect or some direct action. Regardless of the means, euthanasia is a form of abandonment and has been throughout the centuries.

This issue is more difficult to deal with than abortion. Coupled with the euthanasia movement and its semantic non-sense which is being enshrined in a growing number of court cases, a pervasive concern for economics fuels the current debate. The susceptibility of persons to fears concerning medical costs and technology in the face of death has preempted needed analysis; and, as a result, the drive for euthanasia faces little articulate opposition.

The euthanasia movement in the United States is not a recent phenomenon, but it did gather tremendous momentum as a result of the fearful questions surrounding the Karen Ann Quinlan case in 1975. The movement seized on the opportunity to redefine its message and its image. In particular, two concepts emerged which, taken together, established the euphemistic framework necessary for the promotion of euthanasia.

The first of these was the romanticized ideal of the "natural death" or "death with dignity." In this construction death is not the enemy, but attempts to arrest the process are, for these rather than the dying process are principally responsible for the loneliness and suffering that precede death. With this ideal, death has become the desired end since it signals the end of suffering.[16]

The second concept to emerge was that of "the right to die." This is not a legal concept, but it has become part of the public consciousness. It presumes that people have the right to determine the time and circumstances of their death. Implicit in the "right to die" is a new duty for medical personnel to hasten the deaths of their patients.[17]

The Euthanasia Society of America, formed in 1938 to work for "lawful termination of human life for the purpose of avoiding unnecessary suffering," renamed itself the Society for the Right to Die in 1975. More recently, in 1979, it replaced its embarrassing purpose statement to read, "to work for recognition of the individual's right to die with dignity."[18]

The goals of the euthanasia movement are clear from shifts in the legislation and litigation it has supported. In a 1973 version of the Living Will, a patient could request only that "artificial means or heroic measures" not be used in the event that he or she was dying. In January 1976 the advisory committee of Concern for Dying introduced a Living Will bill (S. 487) in the Massachusetts Senate that would require physicians to withhold "non artificial oral feeding" (i.e., a cup of water, a spoonful of food) from patients who "request" it.

Litigation has traveled a similar course. In 1975 the New Jersey State Supreme Court ruled *In re Quinlan* that the law should permit a respirator to be removed from a patient in a permanent coma, even though she would die as a result. In January 1985 the same court ruled *In re Conroy* that food and water administered via a tube could be withdrawn from a senile nursing home resident to hasten her death if the guardian makes the case that the benefits of the patient's life are outweighed by the burdens for the patient.

Although the euthanasia movement emphasizes that such lethal actions would only be taken when this is the "patient's choice," this promise of control offers no comfort when the courts interpret a patient's "right of self-determination" so broadly that, in the case of an incompetent person, someone else may "exercise this right for him" and, with no prior indication of the patient's wishes, order the withdrawal of water and food.

The euthanasia movement in the United States is following the template of its sister movement in Holland where Living Wills today order doctors to end their patients' lives and where an estimated one-sixth of persons who die are put to death by doctors, principally by lethal injection or a combination of medications.[19] In the United States the Hemlock Society denounces death by starvation only to argue that medically supervised "suicide" by means of lethal injection or medication is more humane. This view has gained some judicial support.

On April 16, 1986, a three-judge panel in a California appeals court ordered High Desert Hospital to withdraw food and water from twenty-eight-year-old Elizabeth Bouvia, a quadriplegic suffering from cerebral palsy. Repeatedly she expressed the desire to have the feeding tube removed so she could starve to death under medical supervision that would include pain-killing medicines. In concurring with the opinion, Judge Compton wrote:

> I have no doubt that Elizabeth Bouvia wants to die; and if she had the full use of even one hand, could probably find a way to end her life—in a word—to commit suicide. . . . I believe she has an absolute right to effectuate that decision. This state and the medical profession instead of frustrating her desire, should be attempting to relieve her suffering by permitting and in fact assisting her to die with ease and dignity.[20]

The final argument employed by Compton is an appeal to the willingness of the medical profession to practice abortion. If one "deviation" from the Hippocratic Oath is permissible, he reasoned, why not another?

Whereas the sixth commandment applies to euthanasia as well as to abortion, the fifth commandment, "Honor your father and mother," also applies to euthanasia since the elderly are the class of persons most directly threatened with it and since the command applies with equal force to sons and daughters throughout the course of their lives. While obedience[21] and heartfelt respect[22] are enumerated as duties under the command, the duty to protect and support elderly parents also is in view.[23] Thus euthanasia or any lesser form of abandonment is out of the question.

In the New Testament Jesus underscored the obligation to provide material support for elderly parents when he quoted Isaiah's frightening denunciation of Judah: "This people honors me with their lips, but their heart is far away from me," after noting that the Pharisees taught that the people could withhold material assistance from their parents when instead it was given to pay for religious services.[24]

Similarly, Jesus' last act of ministry before expiring on the cross was to provide for his mother's care and protection. The only words he need utter to John to assure that he would take her into his home were, "Behold, your mother!"[25]

Paul taught the same obligation to the church when he wrote to Timothy regarding the care of widows: "But if any widow has children or grandchildren, let them first learn to practice piety in regard to their own family and to make some return to their parents; for this is acceptable in the sight of God." Paul went on to tell his disciple that failure "to provide for his own" makes a believer "worse than an unbeliever."[26]

In our day this standard of personal commitment to parents and, more generally, to the elderly, has been lost. Responsibility has shifted to the government with its health and welfare "safety nets." Given excessive medical inflation in recent years, the aging of the American population, and the erosion of medical ethics, it has become frighteningly clear that elderly persons in the future will not enjoy the same guarantees of health care and even humane care that they have enjoyed in the past.[27]

The biblical standard of familial care and supervision for the elderly must again be taught as part of the church's commitment to the sanctity of human life. Just as important, ministries must be developed to support the frail and ill elderly and the families who care for them. With God's help, "home care," "adult day care," "hospice," and "support groups for caregivers" will become common parlance in the description of church ministries in the coming years. Otherwise, the "great concern" of our surgeon general, C. Everett Koop, will certainly occur, "that there will be 10,000 Grandma Does for every Baby Doe."[28] May the confession and prayer of the psalmist be answered:

> By Thee I have been sustained from my birth; Thou art he who took me from my mother's womb; My praise is continually of Thee. . . .

> Do not cast me off in the time of old age; Do not forsake me when my strength fails.[29]

## ENDNOTES

[1]Peter Singer, "Sanctity of Life or Quality of Life," *Pediatrics* 72:129.

[2]In Isaiah 1:10–20 the prophet's announcement of judgment on Judah was occasioned by the people's toleration of violence against the "fatherless" and the "widow." The gravity of their sin was indistinguishable from that of the murderer, as evidenced by God's indictment in verse 15, "Your hands are full of bloodshed."

[3]Genesis 4:10–11; Psalms 10, 68, 82; Genesis 3:15.

[4]The Messiah was God incarnate. From conception, Jesus identified completely with us only to be rejected and to suffer for our sin. He did not execute judgment but suffered in order to forgive as many as believe in him. After suffering to the point of death, he rose from the dead and ascended on high, the Lord of

Lords. He continues to deliver those who believe in him through his ministry of intercession and the outpouring of the Holy Spirit. Through the sacrifice of himself Jesus conquered sin and broke the bonds of death both for himself and for a people he would create. This people who once lived in bondage to sin and the fear of death now "walk in newness of life." They know God as their Father and reflect his character. They have been recreated according to his image (Eph. 4:24; Col. 3:10).

[5] Mother Teresa, *Words to Love By* (Notre Dame: Ave Maria, 1983), p. 80.

[6] Matthew 25:31–46.

[7] Deuteronomy 10:17–18; 14:29; 24:17–18; 27:19.

[8] Psalm 8:4 KJV.

[9] The entire text of these and other letters of testimony are on file at the Christian Action Council.

[10] Joseph Fletcher, *Humanhood: Essays in Biomedical Ethics* (Buffalo, N.Y.: Prometheus, 1979), pp. 12–18.

[11] Joseph Fletcher, "Four Indicators of Humanhood—The Enquiry Matures," *The Hastings Center Report* 4, no. 6 (December 1974): 4–7.

[12] With one exception, Psalm 109:12, all references to the fatherless in the Old Testament are accompanied, whether in negative or positive terms, by an injunction to protect and provide for them. Men who do violence to the fatherless are judged. See Deuteronomy 27:19; Psalm 94:6; Proverbs 23:10–11; Ezekiel 22:11; Malachi 3:5. Those who defend the fatherless obey God and follow his example. See Deuteronomy 10:17–18; Isaiah 1:17; Psalm 10:14, 18; 68:5; 82:3; Jeremiah 22:3. "Orphan" is a poor translation of יָתוֹם because it misses the emphasis of the Hebrew. "Orphan" connotes only the young whose parents are dead. In keeping with the connotation discussed above, יָתוֹם is used more broadly to include the unprotected child in the company of his mother, even at her breast. See Job 24:9.

[13] Isaiah 10:1–2.

[14] *Planned Parenthood of Central Missouri v. Danforth*, 428 U.S. 52 (1976).

[15] Dietrich Bonhoeffer, *Ethics* (New York: Macmillan, 1965), pp. 175–76.

[16] Dr. Geisler's use of the "natural death" paradigm to articulate the biblical position on euthanasia is subject to objection. In uncritical fashion he uses the established language of the euthanasia movement to articulate a position which is supposed to be antagonistic to euthanasia. The result is confusing. A similar problem has occurred in the past with Dr. Geisler's use of the "potential life" paradigm to articulate a position opposing abortion. With respect to his other paradigms, such as "mercy dying," a problem exists because the rhetoric lacks sufficient definition. On an issue such as euthanasia where linguistic distortion is common, greater precision is needed. In particular the duty to care for the dying person should be framed in terms of the purposes of care rather than in terms of the terminal condition. To heal, to cure, to relieve pain and suffering are traditional yet relevant purposes of care. The latter may always be served even in cases where patients are dying. These underscore that the proper orientation of medical intervention is toward life rather than toward death. In current discussions of biomedical ethics, however, this orientation is surrendered *a priori* as a rejection of vitalism, which holds that all steps should be taken to prolong life regardless of the patient's condition or prognosis. No one holds this extreme view. It is a straw man supposedly embodying the sanctity of life ethic. Once it is dismissed, quality-of-life ethics immediately determines the course of a debate that is now oriented toward the patient's death. Developed around the pleasure/pain principle, quality-of-life ethics holds that the person who is dying is literally better off dead. The duties of care are redefined accordingly.

[17] Under common law and in conformity with Christian ethics, a long-standing right exists for any patient to *refuse* medical treatment. This is based neither on an idealized view of death nor on a view of the individual as absolutely autonomous. Rather, the right to refuse medical treatment rests on the notion that involuntary subjection to physical constraint is a form of assault, except where

constraint is necessary to prevent the destruction of self or others. The euthanasia movement exploits citizens' ignorance of their fundamental right and the fear generated by horror stories of "overtreatment" by physicians who fear medical malpractice.

[18] Its companion corporation, the Euthanasia Educational Fund, founded in 1967 to work for the passage of Living.Will laws, renamed itself in 1978 to Concern for Dying—An Educational Council.

[19] "The Last Right," *Sixty Minutes* (January 5, 1986): vol. 18, no. 17.

[20] *Elizabeth Bouvia v. Superior Court of the State of California for the Court of Los Angeles*. In the Court of Appeal of the State of California, Second Appellate District, Division Two, filed April 16, 1986.

[21] Deuteronomy 21:18–21; Proverbs 23:22; Ephesians 6:2–3; Colossians 3:20.

[22] Exodus 21:17; Leviticus 20:9; Proverbs 20:20; 30:11, 17.

[23] Both Jewish and Christian commentaries on the Old Testament have generally regarded verses about children robbing their parents as referring to the usurpation of parental wealth and the failure to provide them with the care and support that is due. See Proverbs 19:26; 28:24.

[24] Matthew 15:1–9.

[25] John 19:26–27.

[26] 1 Timothy 5:3–8.

[27] According to the Bureau of the Census, in 1940 there were 9 million elderly persons (age sixty-five or older) accounting for 6.8 percent of the population. By 1980 this number increased to 25 million, or 11 percent of the population. By 2020 the figure will reach 51,000,000, or 17 percent. The fastest-growing segment of our population by far is the "very elderly" (age eighty-five or older). According to the Health Care Financing Administration, the United States spent $12.7 billion, or 4.4 percent of the GNP, on health care in 1950. By 1984 the figure had climbed to $420 billion, or 10.5 percent of the GNP. By 1990 projections are that $660 billion will be spent for a total of 11.3 percent of the GNP.

[28] "Dr. Koop on Euthanasia," *Action Line* 4 (July 12, 1985): 3.

[29] Psalm 71:6, 9.

# MARRIAGE AND THE FAMILY

## William and Mary Pride

## I. INTRODUCTION

God created the family. All who believe in the divinely inspired creation account know this. But did God merely establish marriage and the family and leave it at that? Are we left adrift to struggle with our roles and relationships in a changing world without benefit of divine guidance? Is the family nothing more than a convenient social form, a bit outdated perhaps, that we can mold to our fancies or even reject? These are the questions the world is now asking and which this paper will address.

## II. INERRANCY AND THE BIBLE'S VIEW OF THE FAMILY

Before we go any further it should be noted that an effort is now being made to discredit what the Scriptures have to say about the family. It is being claimed that most of the Bible's teachings on the subject are "culture-bound," that is, tied so narrowly to the culture in which they were written that they are irrelevant for us today. The standard becomes not what the Scripture says but what some writers consider possible or desirable.

This type of "exegesis" makes shipwreck of *any* Bible teaching that is not currently in vogue in our culture. If Scripture becomes irrelevant merely by virtue of commanding a different lifestyle than the current worldly fad, how can we ever be rebuked for sin? The Ten Commandments become the Ten Suggestions, or even the Ten Irrelevancies, in this view, and the Bible's teaching is reduced to the Marquis de Sade's dictum, "Whatever is, is right."

We do not have space here to exhaustively refute this method of interpretation. We do want to mention, however, that the entire "biblical feminist" wing has embraced this approach in order to justify its views, and it has thereby abandoned inerrancy and the inerrancy hermeneutic, as Susan Foh points out so cogently in her book *Women and the Word of God*[1] and as one of the authors of this paper showed at some length in her book *The Way Home: Beyond Feminism, Back to Reality*.[2] She recently had personal confirmation of this when she guested on a radio talk show in Boston. Her fellow guest, Susan Horner, was representing the "Christian feminist" position. Not too far into the program, Ms. Horner turned to her and said, "The difference is the way we look at Scripture. You take it literally, and I don't."[3]

## III. DEFINITIONS

### A. Marriage

Marriage is a physical and economic covenant (Gen. 2:24; Exod. 21:10; Mal. 2:14) upheld spiritually by God, who joins the two covenanting parties together (Mal. 2:14; Matt. 19:6; Mark 10:9); and it should not be broken by human beings (Matt. 19:6; Mark 10:9). A covenant is, in the words of *The American Heritage Dictionary*, "a binding agreement made by two or more persons or parties; a compact; contract." This definition agrees with the way the word is used throughout the Bible.

Our understanding of marriage as a binding contract has almost totally been lost today. What is the force of a marriage vow if no sanctions are exerted against one who breaks it? What does it mean for a man to solemnly pledge that he will "nourish and protect" his wife and "forsaking all others, cleave unto her," in the words of the liturgy, if he may with impunity divorce her? And the question applies equally well to the woman's marriage vows.

If two parties agree to a *business* contract and one defaults, that one legally forfeits whatever property is required to make up the partner's losses. How is it, then, that a man or woman who promises to be faithful is allowed by our laws to commit adultery and yet retain his or her claim on the mutual property and mutual children? How is it that so many churches willingly accept into full membership those who have broken their vow to remain with their partner "until death do us part"? Would it not be more honest for the minister to *refuse* to allow the couple to exchange vows if he knows his church will not hold them to these vows? Should not the marriage vows take a form something like this:

> I, John Doe, do solemnly promise nothing at all to my future wife. She can expect no share in my income, no protection from my presence, no guarantee of my continued presence, and no

commitment to sexual fidelity. When I decide I am tired of her I will feel free to leave, taking as much property with me as I can manage, and possibly our children as well, and refuse to support her thereafter. I expect the church and state to uphold me in my decision.

Jane's vows would be similar.

We suggest that the only consistent courses open to the church are to (1) embrace a marriage service like the one outlined above or (2) work toward reinstituting marriage as a contract with penalties for those who break it. Adulterers and perverts should not be allowed to maintain custody of children. Men and women who deliberately break up a marriage, ignoring the wishes of their spouses and the needs of their children, should not be rewarded with property and custody. Men who promise to provide for their wives should not be able to unilaterally plunge their wives into welfare and their children into day care, as our obscene "no-fault" divorce laws allow. There *is* fault in breaking up what God has joined together, and the victim should not bear the penalty.

If the church is going to take the responsibility of marrying couples, she should go further and require them to sign a contract outlining their marriage promises, with penalties agreed to in advance. (In biblical times the presence of witnesses, without which no wedding took place, accomplished the same thing.) We are not clear as to whether such a contract would hold up in court; however, the church should at least *spiritually* enforce its members' marriage vows, and this is easier if they are agreed to in advance, in writing. At the most basic level, that of simple honesty, God has never said that he allows his children to break their vows. Blessed is the man "who keeps his oath even when it hurts" (Ps. 15:4).

## B. Family

The biblical writers referred to the family in two basic ways: as a group of individuals related by blood and as a household. The first concept is contained in the Hebrew word *mispahah*. This word refers to the immediate family but can also refer to the clan (Gen. 10:31), the tribe (Judg. 13:2), and even the nation (Jer. 8:3; Zech. 14:8). A person does not choose his *mispahah;* he is born into it. The members of a family are all related by blood, with the exception of someone who is adopted or of a woman who marries into the clan.

This idea of family is static. It views a person in his blood relationship to some ancestor, either his father or one of his paternal ancestors—for example, the family (nation) of Israel, or the family (tribe) of Dan. The Greek word *genos* captures this same meaning in the New Testament (Acts 4:6; 13:26).

Never is "family" used in Scripture for a mere grouping of people with common interest or cause as we loosely use it (e.g., the literature from a hospital referring to its employees as the "hospital family"). Neither does the Bible use family to denote merely a collection of individuals living under the same roof. The word always refers to what we call the nuclear family—husband, wife, and children by blood or adoption—or to the extended family. The campaign to broaden the word *family* to refer to almost any group living under the same roof—roommates, communes, unmarried sexual partners, or homosexuals—is grossly unbiblical.[4]

## C. Extended Family Versus Nuclear Family

At this point we would like to mention a dispute that is currently going on between those who are trying to revive the extended family and those who say the nuclear family should be the ideal.

The Bible makes no distinction in its usage between nuclear family and extended family. The same word is used for both. It is difficult to tell in many instances which kind of family a passage is referring to.

A more appropriate term for a biblical family is "modular family." A modular bookcase is made up of pieces, each of which by itself is a bookcase, yet when the modules are put together, the result is still called a bookcase. In the same way, each nuclear family is a biblical family, and the clan, which consists of a group of related families, is also a biblical family.

Those who argue against the extended family do so for two reasons, one economic and the other scriptural. Some Christian and secular economists argue that living in an extended family kills the entrepreneurial spirit of the younger generation. If a man has his family to rely on for his support, the argument goes, then he will not have the incentive or the ability to produce on his own.[5]

This is the identical argument used against justification by faith, viz., that people who know they are justified will have no incentive to do good works, and it is just as false. Christians who have the Spirit and consequently desire to please God will work hard whether or not their survival depends on it. Even non-Christians, desiring to increase the glory and wealth of their families, continue to work, even though they may be already well off. This is seen quite clearly in the mercantile families of the expatriate Chinese, for example.

To use another analogy, no one says that the work done by the second stage of a rocket is insignificant merely because it builds on the achievement of the first stage. If each generation must start from scratch, progress from generation to generation will be small. Each generation should be allowed to build on the foundation laid by the one before. With the work ethic preached in the Bible, the man who has the support and the experience of his parents to build on will be able to accomplish much more than someone who is forced to make his own way from ground zero.

The scriptural objection to the extended family is based on Genesis 2:24, "For this reason a man will leave his father and mother and be united to his wife, and they will become one flesh." Those who claim that the isolated nuclear family is the scriptural norm stress the importance of a man leaving his former family to establish his own household. But what kind of "leaving" is the Bible talking about here? Is it physical—moving to a different location or moving out of the parental home? Is it isolationist—the new family cutting off ties with the old? Is the nuclear family supposed to exist totally apart from the influence, aid, and proximity of the parents?

Calls for the nuclear family to cut itself off from the parent family are unscriptural. *Leaving* one's parents is contrasted with *cleaving* to one's wife. The point is that parents may not come *between* a man and his wife, not that the new household should be established totally independently. God himself both authorized and honored the extended family (clan, tribe) structure. In all his dealings with Israel, each tribe had its own leaders and its own land. God even stretched relatedness to the point of insisting that the Israelites, who had not intermarried with the Edomites for generations, not abhor an Edomite "for he is your brother" (Deut. 23:7). The Scriptures are full of similar examples, making it clear that God considers a man's family not just to be his immediate household. In circumstances that call for common (familial) action, a man's family may extend to all his known patrilineal relatives.[6]

The caricature Victorian patriarch, ruling over his sons and their wives and children by fear and terror, perhaps all living in the same home, is definitely not a scriptural figure; and in rejecting this cartoon figure the opposers of extended families are correct. But God does not intend families to be isolated—either financially, spiritually, emotionally, or physically. Even we Westerners recognize the need for extended family bonds when a family member dies. It is still considered a gross breach of etiquette to fail to attend the funeral of a near relative, and at such occasions often even distant branches of the families are represented.

Scripturally speaking, family bonds, especially between generations, are based on influence and aid rather than on coercion. Grandparents can and should have influence over their children's families, influence based on their personal uprightness and wisdom and helpfulness. Relatives should be able to depend on each other in time of need (Prov. 17:17). The modular family's links are based on common needs (such as a clan banding together against its enemies) and common goals. For Christians, the common goal is that of advancing God's kingdom in this world.

## D. Singles and the Family

God "setteth the solitary in families" (the word here is "houses"; Ps. 68:6 KJV). God did not intend that a single person be isolated or autonomous in the church. In the Old Testament a woman remained in her father's house until she was married, and she sometimes returned to it if something happened to her husband (Gen. 38:11; Lev. 22:13; Deut. 22:21; Ruth 1:8). Paul lived with Priscilla and Aquila in Corinth, and he and Silas stayed with Lydia's household in Philippi. When Jesus sent out the apostles, he told them to stay in the house of a worthy family rather than to take a room in the local inn.

We need a revival of hospitality and sharing in the church. The modern fetish for privacy on the part of both singles and families is a great barrier to biblical hospitality. It is also sinful and selfish. We should become willing to "adopt" people who are alone into the life of our families. Our churches should work toward setting the solitary in families, not toward further isolating them in "college/career" and "single" groups.

## E. Household

The Bible also looks at the family as a "house." The Hebrew word for house is *bayith;* the Greek word is *oikos.* Both these words mean house, the literal building in which a family lives. Both words also refer more abstractly to a household, i.e., to the family and all that belongs to it, including servants.

The word "family" only classifies a man by his descent, but the word "house" is more dynamic than that. A man or woman can build a house (Deut. 25:9; Prov. 14:1) or tear it down (Prov. 14:1). Even after a man dies his house may carry on and grow mightier through his descendants. One of the greatest blessings God can bestow on a man is to establish his house (2 Sam. 7:25–29).

We have completely lost the idea of a house in modern Western lands. Each generation is taught to begin building from scratch and to let its children do the same. Although Americans have a ruling elite who have established houses (the Rockefellers and the Kennedys, for example), and the European aristocracy definitely think in terms of preserving their houses, the masses are discouraged from this kind of ambition for their children.

A study of the word *house* is more important than a study of the word *family* when discussing the application of the Bible's teaching on the family.

## III. THE PURPOSE OF THE FAMILY

In the beginning God instituted the family with the charge: "Be fruitful and increase in number; fill the earth and subdue it. Rule over the fish of the sea and the birds of the air and over every living creature that moves on the ground" (Gen. 1:28). Adam's house was to increase in size and in influence and to have dominion over the whole earth.

Christians are still bound by the dominion mandate, enriched in the light of Jesus' commission to the church (Matt. 28:19–20). God still wants Christians to be fruitful, physically as well as spiritually, raising godly children who will carry his kingdom to the ends of the earth.

The Christian family's goal, therefore, is to establish an enduring and ever-increasing house to aid in the expansion of God's kingdom. A non-Christian might establish a house for his own glory and the increasing power of his family, but a Christian builds his house to the glory of God and for the increasing influence of God's church.

## IV. FAMILY STRUCTURE

God has designed the family as follows: the husband is the head (Eph. 5:23), the wife is his helper (Gen. 2:18), children are trainees to carry on the parents' spiritual work (Ps. 78:6), and grandparents are the storytellers, the guardians of heritage (Deut. 4:9; Ps. 78:4–6). The Christian family is a "house" of warriors waging spiritual warfare (Ps. 127:4–5). Each married Christian is called to build an enduring physical dynasty as far as he is able. Single Christians have a "house" also, but theirs consists solely of spiritual children—those they have led to the Lord and discipled (Isa. 56:3–5). In no other way does the command to "be fruitful and multiply" make sense (Gen. 1:27). The children of God's people are called a "reward," a "heritage," and "arrows in the hand of a warrior" (Ps. 127:3–4).

Throughout history godly men and women have desired children (Gen. 15:2; 15:21; 16:1–2; 21:6–7; 29:31–30:24; 33:5; 48:8–9; 1 Sam. 1:11; 2:20–21; Job 42:12–13; Ps. 128:3; Luke 1:24–25; et al.). One of the great blessings God promised his covenant people if they obeyed him is that they would have many children (Deut. 28:4, 11). That so many professing Christians in our day dislike children and employ means to reduce their fertility or to make themselves infertile, is a great evil. It reduces the numerical strength of the church and strangles her witness against the antichild spirit of this age.[7]

Since children are our inheritance and the kingdom of God is meant to prosper not only through the preaching of the gospel but also through the multiplying of covenant families, the need for marital commitment is obvious. Who can build a house by continually tearing down what he has built, casting his materials to the winds and starting anew? This is why God hates divorce among his people: "Has not the LORD made them one? In flesh and spirit they are his. And why one? Because he was seeking godly offspring. So guard yourself in your spirit, and do not break faith with the wife of your youth" (Mal. 2:15).

Marriage itself only makes sense as two people contracting to build a "house" together. Without this understanding, the Bible's prohibitions against homosexual unions and adultery lose their force. If marriage is merely legalized sex, why would homosexuals not be allowed to marry? If sex is merely for personal pleasure, why confine oneself to one partner? The church *must* recover her understanding that marriage is for building a "house" in order to speak credibly to the world of these matters.

God does not put us into families for our own self-fulfillment. Although selfishness is now peddled as a virtue under the brand names Self-Esteem, Self-Actualization, Meeting My Needs, and Fulfilling My Potential, the Bible everywhere condemns it. Jesus emphasized that whoever wanted to follow him would have to deny himself, putting God's kingdom first (Matt. 6:33; 16:24; Mark 8:34; Luke 9:23). This does not mean that we "scorn delights and live laborious days" but that we get more excited about God's glory than our immediate pleasure. Jesus also said that those who pursue their own fulfillment will lose it; and in a very real sense anyone who would break up a God-sanctioned marriage for the sake of an illusory happiness can expect to be cheated even in this world and certainly in the next. Without the vision (for a carnal man) of a house descended from him, making his name powerful in future generations, or (for a spiritual man) of a house of physical and spiritual descendants[8] carrying on his life's work and building God's city on his foundation, the incentive to maintain a marriage despite obstacles simply is not there. If we sow the wind of personal fulfillment, we shall reap the whirlwind. Indeed, we are reaping it now.

## V. FAMILY AS THE CHURCH'S TRAINING GROUND

Immediately after God gave the Law to Israel, he commanded the Israelites to teach it to their own children (Deut. 6:7). God did not set up an institution to train Israelitish children in his commandments, such as a Sunday school or daily academy. The precepts, which are repeated for force in both Deuteronomy 6:7 and 11:19, require the Israelites to teach their *own* children in a *home* situation: when they sit at home, when they walk along the road, when they lie down, and when they get up. This theme is repeated throughout the Scriptures. The home is a spiritual training ground for God's children.

The home is also where *adults* are trained for leadership in the church. In both places where the requirements for elders are listed, great prominence is given to the requirement that the elder's children be obedient and well-managed (1 Tim. 3:4–5; Titus 1:6). In fact, the apostle goes so far as to suggest that a man who cannot control his children is not able to manage the church (1 Tim. 3:5)! Deacons, too, must have learned to control their children before they can serve (1 Tim. 3:12). Elders are also required to have shown themselves hospitable, a skill they could hardly have learned anywhere but in their homes (1 Tim. 3:2; Titus 1:8). Likewise, the older women are expected to be able to train the younger ones in how to handle their children and how to work at home (Titus 2:4), and the first qualification that a widow must possess before being considered for enrollment on the church relief list is "bringing up children" (1 Tim. 5:10).

In the bringing up of children every character trait that the older man and older woman are supposed to possess has an opportunity to bloom. Self-control? Who has more chance to practice this than the mother or father of preschoolers? Gentleness? Who needs it more than a father? "Apt to teach?" Where can a potential elder learn this better than by instructing his own little flock as they congregate around God's Word in their family worship? Godly children even provide "a good reputation with outsiders" (1 Tim. 3:7) as Psalm 127 reminds us (cf. Prov. 27:11).

Hospitality *begins* with welcoming God's children into your home. If a man will not welcome his own son, how can he welcome others? As Jesus said, "Whoever welcomes a little child like this in my name welcomes me" (Matt. 18:5; Mark 9:7; Luke 9:48). Hospitality continues on to sharing the family's love and resources with singles and younger couples. In this way elders disciple the rising generation of first their own children and then their spiritual children.

We now have the debilitating situation wherein the elders and deacons see their function as "ruling" rather than serving. A man can become a ruler in our churches without any inquiry into his family life. The home is despised and church leaders are expected to attend meetings, spending most of their nights away from their families. This has led to women demanding institutional leadership positions, since their positions at home are considered of no value. It has also led to lowered standards for Christian children. We are no longer even surprised when the child of Christian parents is caught up in worldliness or overt sin. This need not be. Rather than searching for yet another institutional answer (perhaps a seminar on family life or a class on how to have a happy home), we need to restore the household to its rightful position, in partnership with the church, working together in the ministry of the Lord.

## VI. THE STATE VERSUS THE FAMILY—THE CHALLENGE

Historian Paul Johnson has said that the most important movement of modern times is the move toward political totalitarianism.[9] The modern state is not founded on the absolute of God's kingship and law, and consequently its only restraint is the free-spiritedness of its people. If the people are willing to let the state enslave them, then the state is all too ready to comply.

Today, as never before in the West, the state is claiming total dominion over the household, slowly but surely taking over for itself responsibilities that traditionally belonged to the family. Christian families must not let the state steal their God-given responsibilities from them. Christians are Christ's freedmen and not the slaves of bureaucrats.

These are the areas in which the state is unbiblically challenging the family:

### 1. Care of Aged Relatives

In the United States, social security with its health insurance programs is second in the budget only to the interest on the national debt. The current work force is being forced to support to some extent every retired person in the country. The tax burden for social security exceeds a tithe for self-employed people and is approaching a tithe and a half in combined employer and employee contributions for the rest. This should not be.

The Bible teaches that a man should support himself, not retire and be supported by others (2 Thess. 3:10). If a family member is unable to support himself, his family is responsible to support him (1 Tim. 5:8). A widow is the responsibility of her children, grandchildren, or female relatives (vv. 4, 16). Christian widows with no relatives should be cared for by the church (vv. 3–4).

It is totally unfair that everyone should be forced to pay for the support of retired people who are not related to them. Children should be willing to return their debt to their parents when their parents become too old to work (1 Tim. 5:4). Old people should be willing to risk "being a burden" on their own children rather than to actually be a burden to everyone else's children. A Christian grandmother who performs her function in the clan should be a blessing to her family, not a burden.

## 2. Having Children

Some world governments are currently limiting the size of their citizens' families. In China, for example, a couple is highly commended for only having one child, and an abortion is forced on anyone who dares to conceive a third child. There are people even in the United States who want to sterilize families who have too many children and to sterilize the baby if the parents will not comply.[10]

The Bible says,

Sons are a heritage from the LORD,
children a reward from him (Ps. 127:3).

It is no one's business to try to usurp God's prerogative in handing out his rewards. Neither the state nor anyone else has the right to limit God's bounty.

## 3. Children's Education

The Bible gives the responsibility for children's education to parents (Ps. 78:4–6; Deut. 6:6–9, 11–19). It is conceivable biblically that parents may delegate the teaching of skills such as reading or carpentry, but teaching spiritual truth and impressing God's law on the children may not be delegated. When a school refuses to teach only skills and insists on influencing students' values, even to the neglect of teaching skills, that school is not the place for a Christian child.

Some Christians teach that we should send our children to public school so they can witness to their schoolmates and teachers. On the same philosophy, we should send our ministerial students to Mr. Sun Nyung Moon's academies for their training. We do not, because we are aware of the danger and because the seminarians would not get a proper training there. How much more should we disciple our own children when the future of our children and our houses is at stake!

The Supreme Court of the United States has ruled that the states do have an interest in ensuring that the children in them are educated. It has not yet decided to what extent states can regulate *how* they are educated. Even if the *court* rules that the states have the right to forbid all but public education, the *Bible* gives parents the responsibility to make sure that their children are educated God's way. We must resist all state interference with our responsibility.

## 4. Raising Our Children

Just as it is not the state's province to teach values to children, it is not the state's province to enforce them. As long as the children of a family are not breaking any of God's civil laws, the state has no part in disciplining them. The Bible recognizes the possibility that the master of a household may exceed his God-given authority in the area of discipline, permanently injuring his children. In such cases, the offender should be punished, eye for eye and tooth for tooth (Lev. 24:19–20). The victim should not be punished by removing him from his family.

The current trend to replace criminal justice with psychological law is the greatest danger the church has faced since the Inquisition. The state could decide tomorrow that conservative Christianity is an antisocial force and needs to be eliminated. The first attack has come in this area of "child abuse prevention" and needs to be met head-on.

## VII. THE FAMILY AS A CENTER OF PRODUCTIVITY— THE SOLUTION

The family can drive back the totalitarian state. Christian families can be physically eliminated, as Hitler did to the Jewish populace, "but [the family] could not be corrupted and pervert-ed," as Paul Johnson states from his research concerning totalitar-ianism.[11] "A society in which the family, as opposed to the political party and the ideological programme, was the starting-point for reconstruction, was the answer to the totalitarian evil."[12] The difference between economic free enterprise and socialist tyranny is the independent household, as many writers have pointed out. God has graciously given us this means for securing his economic blessings to our countries—now what are we doing about it?

God commands Christian wives to be "homeworking" (an exact translation of the word *oikourgous* in Titus 2:5). The household cannot maintain its independence if all its functions are swallowed up by the state. The homeworking wife is God's agent for political independence. This being so, the church should encourage wives to stay home and be *productive* there.

All of Scripture makes it plain that the household is not just an organized group of consumers but a *center of productivity*. Young wives are supposed to be home*working*, not just home. *All* Christians are called to be fruitful in all their occupations, doing *everything* "with all your heart, as working for the Lord, not for men" (Col. 3:23).

The reason Western countries are falling apart is not so much that Christians have actively pursued evil as that we have failed to do good. "One who is slack in his work is brother to one who destroys" (Prov. 18:9). And what does God say will happen if we do not "serve the Lord [our] God joyfully and gladly in the time of prosperity" (Deut. 28:47)? The non-Christians among us will rise higher and higher, and we will sink lower and lower (v. 43). Crime will increase (vv. 29–31). Our sons and daughters will be taken from us (v. 32). This judgment is beginning to come upon us, but *it can be averted* if we return to the Lord and *actively* serve him.

We have been content to be "against abortion." We must do more and *actively* seek God's blessing of children (Ps. 127).

We have fought for "clean television entertainment." We should *actively* spend our time serving God and our families.

We have allowed our families and churches to go into debt. The Bible says we should not only get out of debt but leave our children an inheritance (Prov. 13:22).

We have crusaded for better values in the public school. We must go further and take up our responsibility for training our children ourselves (Deut. 6:7; 11:19).

We must stop turning all our family functions over to institutions—the state, the charitable society, the church, the school. We must stop turning women out of their homes and encouraging them to seek "fulfilling careers" in place of their domestic responsibilities. Fathers especially should plead with God for greater love for their children and make it their solemn aim, before all else, to bring up their children as Christians. When the hearts of the fathers are turned to the children, we may have some reason to expect revival (Mal. 4:6).

## VIII. CONCLUSION

The most crucial issue before us as Christians today is the restoration of our houses. God's city cannot be built without houses. If we refuse to have children or to raise our children according to God's way, or if we let others take them away, we have lost our saltiness and deserve to be trodden under foot by men.

The only reason totalitarianism has succeeded as far as it has in an originally free country like America is that men have stopped defending their houses. When career or money or pleasure becomes more important than leaving a godly inheritance to one's children, then the house is left unguarded, and it is no wonder that it is attacked.

God has called Christian men to defend and nourish their families. He has called them to provide economically for their families and not to enslave their wives for the sake of a few more dollars. God has called Christian wives to be homeworkers, concentrating on the ministry of raising up a physical and spiritual house for the Lord. God has called Christian children to obey their parents and to learn from them, preparing to fight the Lord's battles rather than waiting for a "fulfilling career" and frittering away their youth in irresponsibility. God has called grandparents not to retirement but to serving the young families descended from them and others like them, helping their physical and spiritual children of even the third generation find the way. God has called single people, men and women, to either marry and start raising a family or to devote themselves to the service of the saints. Men, women, and children should strive to make their homes productive economically, artistically, and spiritually. Each of us should be building his or her "house" in the humble expectation that it will stand the test of history and leave us with a memorial in this world and in heaven as well.

# ENDNOTES

[1] (Phillipsburg, N.J.: Presbyterian and Reformed, 1979), *passim.*

[2] Mary Pride, *The Way Home: Beyond Feminism, Back to Reality* (Westchester, Ill.: Crossway, 1985), pp. 4–13.

[3] WEZE Boston. Call-in show with hostess Jeanine Graf, August 7, 1985.

[4] This campaign was kicked off by the White House Conference on Families, whose very title was chosen as an affront to *the* family, i.e., the biblical family.

[5] Possibly the most influential work espousing this viewpoint: George Gilder, *Wealth and Poverty* (New York: Basic Books, 1981), pp. 71–72.

[6] Both man and wife count the man's parents as their family line. "Forget your people and your father's house," is the Bible's admonition to brides: your husband's house is yours, and "your sons will take the place of your fathers" (the plural is significant) (Ps. 45:10, 16).

[7] For further discussion of this very important point, including refutations of the usual arguments against trusting God with our fertility, see Pride, *The Way Home,* chs. 2–6.

[8] Even spiritual children need a godly, stable family environment for their Christian growth. Anyone who thinks he or she can have a great Christian ministry after willfully and unjustly divorcing a spouse will be bitterly disappointed. Remember Anita Bryant.

[9] *Modern Times* (New York: Harper and Row, 1983), p. 729.

[10] Among Planned Parenthood International's "examples of other proposed measures to reduce U.S. fertility" are:

. . . compulsory abortion for out-of-wedlock pregnancies; compulsory sterilization of all who have two children—except for a few who would be allowed to have three; confining childbearing to only a limited number of adults; and stock-certificate type permits for children.

From *U.S. Population Growth and Family Planning: A Review of the Literature* (New York: Planned Parenthood-World Population), p. viii. Cited by James Weber, *Grow or Die!* (New Rochelle, N.Y.: Arlington House, 1977), p. 180. Weber's book is well worth reading.

[11] *Modern Times,* p. 581.

[12] Ibid.

# A Response to
# Marriage and the Family

**Paul E. Steele**

There is no question that our age has bought "the lie"[1] concerning God's formula for the successful home and is reaping the consequences of the "new morality," which, as someone said, "is neither 'new' nor 'morality.'" Since the early 1960s there has been a blatant attempt to disrupt family life in Western culture. The so-called women's liberation movement, the sexual revolution, the gradual and insidious acceptance of sodomy as "normal," the increase of pornography, and the legalization of abortion, each has contributed to the breakdown of relationships and brought with it broken homes, broken hearts, and shattered ideals. The fundamental problem is a rejection of the idea that an inerrant Scripture, which is "God breathed," speaks relevantly today to this modern world.

If one accepts the evolutionary model instead of the Genesis account of the origin of man, it is an easy step to the speculation espoused by Kathleen Gaugh in a 1971 article:[2]

> It is not known when the family originated, although it was probably between two million and a hundred thousand years ago. It is not known whether some kind of embryonic family came forth, with, or after the origin of language . . . the chances are that language and the family developed together over a long period, but the evidence is "sketchy."

With no understanding of where the family originated, one is left to open speculation as to the "ground rules" for operating this most important social unit. This is graphically illustrated by an incident which was reported by Paul Harvey on his newscast of June 28, 1979. He related a story of a man who assaulted and raped a girl in a bus depot. In his own defense the man pled that what he did was a ritual of courtship. He said society calls it rape, but his standard is different than society's and, therefore, he should be released. The judge then sentenced him to five years and told him that, under the rules of *this* society, he was guilty of rape; but then the judge encouraged the man to keep on campaigning to change the standards of society.

The result of this "liberated" outlook has been "open season" on traditional values and the conclusion that man is autonomous in determining what is "best" for him. This has led to communal living, open adultery, premarital promiscuity, easy divorce, and "living together" arrangements that would have been taboo a quarter of a century ago. With it has come an epidemic of teenage pregnancies, increased social disease, "latch-key kids," child molestation, incest, and rape.

It is time that Evangelicals who have a high view of Scripture speak out and let the world know that God created marriage and the home and the family, and he has the right to tell us the best way to conduct ourselves.

As Carl Wilson says so clearly:

> . . . the family, with traditional religious roles for men and women in a life-long monogamous marriage relationship is the abiding natural foundation for social order, happiness and stability. When that view is abandoned for selfish individualism, the society will collapse and die. . . .[3]

It is gratifying to me, in reviewing the paper on "Marriage and the Family"[4] to note the authors' respect for an inerrant Scripture, their obvious commitment to the family and a strong stand on the permanence of marriage. I appreciate the definition of marriage as a covenant but feel that a biblical definition of a covenant would have been stronger than a dictionary definition. In such a definition we might have the following elements:

1. A solemn compact or agreement between individuals[5] by which each party bound himself to fulfill certain conditions.
2. The solemn invoking of God as a witness.[6]
3. The swearing of an oath.[7]
4. The regarding of a breach of the covenant as a very heinous sin.[8]

A further elaboration on the sacredness of the vow might have been helpful.[9] I certainly would agree that stronger marriage vows for our churches and penalties for those who break them would be appropriate but would be unenforceable until we, as Evangelicals, reach a consensus on the divorce question. The traditional Protestant view of divorce and remarriage is simply not adequate and is subject to the whims of man. An authoritative "Thus saith the Lord" is needed today as never before.

While I agree that we must not explain away Scripture on the basis of a passage being "culture bound," I would suggest that a proper hermeneutic includes addressing the transcultural problem. Lacking a clear mandate from God and especially New Testament confirmation, one cannot, in a wholesome manner, transfer the customs of the New Testament Israel into our modern culture.[10]

This problem is evident as they discussed the "modular family."[11] Frankly, the argument was difficult for me to follow—I am not sure exactly what is being proposed here. If the suggestion is only that there should be closer and more intimate social ties between family members (i.e., grandparents with grandchildren), I would wholeheartedly agree.[12]

But if the authors are proposing reverting to family communal living following the pattern of the Old Testament patriarchal lifestyle, I would suggest that such an idea lacks a clear biblical mandate. The most clear commands we have in Scripture in establishing a home are Genesis 2:24 and Exodus 20:12.[13] The Genesis text would seem to establish the new home as a separate and autonomous unit, while the Exodus passage commands that a continuing parental respect and honor be maintained. These balancing truths still allow for a great variety of family models.

While I would be in agreement on most of the points made on God's design for the family structure (pp. 193–94), I would take issue with the idea that all attempts to limit the size of one's family are evil or that we are mandated to have large families. It is interesting to note that the New Testament is virtually silent on the subject of family size, and the Old Testament matter of the importance of fruitfulness in a physical sense was largely linked to the promises exclusively given to Israel concerning the land (Palestinian covenant), the seed (Abrahamic covenant), and the throne (Davidic covenant). One would be hard pressed to prove from Scripture that birth control is, in and of itself, evil.

Nor is fear of overpopulating the earth or fear of raising a child in today's society a proper motivation. Consideration of the health of the mother or of dangers in certain cases involved in childbirth might be acceptable reasons for having no children. To suggest long-term abstinence in such cases would be to defraud one's partner.[14]

I wholeheartedly agree with Mr. and Mrs. Pride that the home is the training ground for children and that the church and home should be in partnership in that ministry. Spiritual and moral training are functions of the church and the home, and we must take our stand against allowing a humanistic system to take over that responsibility. I do not believe, however, that we can abandon our responsibility to be salt and light[15] in all social structures, including the school system, since we are to be "in" this cosmos and not "of" it.[16]

It would make sense for parents to seek to impact the school system and channel the efforts of the child toward an effective witness while at the same time combating the error the child might encounter with a solid foundation of truth.

There are some additional factors that must be added to the whole issue of marriage and the family.

## I. PREDATING, PREENGAGEMENT, AND PREMARITAL COUNSEL

It should be the responsibility of the home, assisted by the church, to teach young people what the Scripture has to say concerning relationships. They need to learn what to look for in friendships[17] and then, as they mature, what qualities to look for in a mate.[18]

They need to prepare themselves to be godly husbands and wives by seeing now the importance of the filling of the Holy Spirit[19] and allowing him to produce the fruit of the Spirit.[20] They need to be taught practical things, such as communication,[21] wisdom,[22] kindness and supernatural forgiveness,[23] a Christian walk,[24] the meaning of unity[25] in diversity,[26] financial principles,[27] marriage roles,[28] and the various facets of love.[29]

## II. THE ROLES IN MARRIAGE

A large part of the battle being waged today between the one committed to biblical truth for the family and those who would operate the family without the absolutes Scripture provides is in the area of male/female roles. This is nothing new. The church father John Chrysostom, presbyter at Antioch in the late fourth century and later bishop of Constantinople, addresses the Christian husband who is struggling with a wife who will not submit and says:

> "But what," one may say, "if a wife fear me not?" Never mind, you are to love, fulfill your own duty. For though that which is due from others may not follow, we ought of course to do our duty. This is an example of what I mean. He [Paul] says, "Submitting yourselves one to another in the fear of Christ." And what if another submit not himself? Still you should obey the law of God. Just so, I say, is it also here. Let the wife at least, though she be not loved, still fear notwithstanding, that nothing may lie at her door; and let the husband, though his wife fear him not, still show her love notwithstanding, that he himself be not wanting in any point. For each has received his own.[30]

Ambrose, bishop of Milan and a contemporary of Chrysostom, dealt with this same issue and sought, like him, to bring the roles into harmony and balance. He wrote:

Woman must respect her husband, not be a slave to him; she consents to be ruled, not to be forced. The one whom a yoke would fit is not fit for the yoke of marriage. As to man, he should guide his wife like a pilot, honor her as a partner in life, share with her as a co-heir of grace.[31]

The households of today share in common what the households of the New Testament era and the early Christian church faced: a tension in the roles for husband and wife. Their solution is the only possible solution today—a commitment to obey Scripture, no matter what society did. This means that passages such as Ephesians 5:22–35 and 1 Peter 3:1–7 are to be seen as normative for the Christian home today. God expects the husband to be a loving leader who serves his wife tenderly and in an understanding way, while, at the same time, the wife is to quietly and in an attitude of trusting God submit to the authority of her husband. Husbands and wives are not to abdicate their responsibility because it is hard or because of social pressure. They are to take these commands seriously as a matter of obedience to their Lord Jesus Christ.

To quote Chrysostom again:

> For there is nothing which so welds our life together as the love of man and wife. For this many will lay aside even their arms, for this they will give up life itself, and Paul would never without a reason and without an object have spent so much pains on this subject, as when he says here, "Wives, be in subjection to your own husbands, as to the Lord." And why so? Because when they are in harmony, the children are well brought up, and the domestics are in good order, and neighbors, and friends, and relatives enjoy the fragrance. But if it be otherwise, all is turned upside down, and thrown into confusion. And just as when the generals of an army are at peace, one with another, all things are in due subordination, whereas on the other hand, if they are at variance, everything is turned upside down; so I say, it also is here. Therefore he says, "Wives, be in subjection to your own husbands, as unto the Lord."[32]

A modern writer says it succinctly: "God has made the well-being and happiness of the family absolutely dependent upon the observance of His divinely appointed order."[33]

## III. DISCIPLINE OF CHILDREN

God's commendation of Abraham was, "For I know him, that he will command his children and his household after him, and they shall keep the ways of the LORD. . . ."[34]

In our homes today there is a desperate need. Teenage suicide is pandemic.[35] Teenage runaways are on the increase.[36] Armand

Nicholi, a psychiatrist at Massachusetts General Hospital and a faculty member of Harvard Medical School said, "If any one factor influences the character development and emotional stability of an individual, it is the quality of the relationship he or she experiences as a child with *both* parents."[37]

With absentee parents, and the number of working mothers now estimated at almost 75 percent of all mothers, and fathers caught up in the materialistic "rat race," our future generations are in serious peril. As never before, the evangelical church needs to review its calls to "bring [our children] up in the training and instruction of the Lord."[38]

In an article in *Moody Monthly* Kenneth Taylor said, "Teaching the Bible to our children is dangerous unless we also teach them what the Scriptures call the fear of God."[39] What he said then is still true today. "The fear of the LORD is the beginning of knowledge."[40] This training must begin in the home. It requires parents who have a commitment to a Christian lifestyle, personal example, consistent training and discipline, the wisdom of God, and a lot of love. Each parent must draw on the grace of God "that brings for us the discipline of renunciation of impiety and earthly passions, the discipline of living lives of self-control."[41] G. Campbell Morgan once said, "What God is to the adult, parents are to the child—lawgiver and lover, provider and controller." The fear of the Lord is taught by parents personifying God by exercising caring authority. This is costly in terms of time commitment, but it is worth it. Studies have been made that indicate that fathers spend less than thirty-seven seconds per day on the average with their children. The man who is tempted to use the excuse that he is too busy should heed the words of Socrates from 450 B.C.:

> If I could get to the highest place in Athens, I would lift up my voice and say, "What mean ye fellow citizens that ye turn every stone to scrape wealth together and take so little care of your children to whom ye must one day relinquish all."

And we must pray the prayer that Catherine Booth desperately prayed: "Lord, I will not have a godless child."

## IV. INCREASED COMMUNICATION, INTERDEPENDENCE, AND INTIMACY

I agree with J. Allen Peterson when he wrote:

> There is one primary problem in marriage, most of the other problems—difficulties involving money, sex, in-laws, communication, are usually symptoms of this underlying and universal cause: a selfish independence.[42]

There is a need for an increasing ministry of interdependence to offset the selfish independence that is so prevalent today. Someone said:

> Don't ask me to walk in front of you because I may not be a leader and don't ask me to walk behind you because I may not be a very good follower; but invite me to walk alongside of you so we can learn together.

It is this kind of interdependence that God intended from the beginning,[43] and it finds its fulfillment in the Christian marriage.[44] The Christian home should lead the way in the highest form of transparent communication[45] and the deepest form of intimacy.[46]

## V. A FINAL WORD

In 1975 a Continental Congress on the Family was held in which a ten-part affirmation on the family was adopted. It is a shame that this document has not been adopted as a standard for all Evangelicals and given wide circulation among our churches. There is desperate need for us who hold a high view of Scripture to adopt a statement such as this and show solidarity in our stand on home and family values. Lacking such a consensus sets us adrift among the speculative and uncertain values of a relativistic society.

We should take the lead in what Ted Ward calls "Distinctive Values in the Christian Family":[47]

1. The sanctity of and commitment to the marriage relationship.
2. The home as a place of warmth, nurture, acceptance, and healthy stimulation.
3. Growth in grace and the knowledge of God as a family and as individuals through the Bible and its implementation in just, merciful, and loving lifestyle.
4. Involvement in outreach, through the church, participating in God's redeeming work in society.

It is important for us, like the sons of Issachar, to be individuals who "know the times and know what to do."[48] Let us stand up and be counted to reestablish the values given to us by God concerning the home and the family.

## ENDNOTES

[1] Second Thessalonians 2:10–12.

[2] Kathleen Gaugh, "The Origin of the Family," *Journal of Marriage and the Family,* November 1971, p. 760.

[3] Carl W. Wilson, "Our Dance Has Turned to Death," *Renewal* (Atlanta, 1979).

[4] Submitted to the International Council on Biblical Inerrancy by Bill and Mary Pride.

[5] Genesis 31:44.

[6] Genesis 31:50.

[7] Genesis 21:31.

[8] Ezekiel 17:12–20.

[9] It would certainly be appropriate to treat a number of texts (e.g., Num. 30:2; Deut. 23:21; Job 22:27; Ps. 15:4; 50:14; 76:11; Eccl. 5:4) in dealing with marriage vows.

[10] Henry A. Virkler, *Hermeneutics, Principles and Processes of Biblical Interpretation* (Grand Rapids: Baker, 1981), pp. 211–29.

[11] Bill and Mary Pride, "Marriage and the Family," pp.189–95

[12] I could only wish that more Scripture had been offered to solidify that point—i.e., influence of grandparents (Exod. 10:2; Deut. 4:9; Prov. 17:6; 1 Tim. 1:5), the wisdom of old men (Lev. 19:32), and care for relatives (1 Tim. 5:4, 8).

[13] Genesis 2:24: "Therefore shall a man leave his father and his mother, and shall cleave unto his wife: and they shall be one flesh" (KJV).

Ephesians 5:31: "For this cause shall a man leave his father and mother, and shall be joined unto his wife, and they two shall be one flesh" (KJV).

Exodus 20:12: "Honour thy father and thy mother: that thy days may be long upon the land which the LORD thy God giveth thee" (KJV).

Ephesians 6:2–3: "Honour thy father and mother; which is the first commandment with promise; that it may be well with thee, and thou mayest live long on the earth" (KJV).

[14] First Corinthians 7:2–5.

[15] Matthew 5:13–16.

[16] John 17:11, 14, 18.

[17] Proverbs 28:7; First Corinthians 5:9; 15:33; 2 Thessalonians 3:14.

[18] Psalm 15; Proverbs 31:10–31; Titus 2:2–8.

[19] Ephesians 5:18.

[20] Galatians 5:22–24.

[21] Proverbs 17:27; Matthew 5:37; Colossians 4:6; James 3:1–12.

[22] James 3:13–18.

[23] Ephesians 4:31–32.

[24] Ephesians 4:1–2.

[25] Ephesians 4:3.

[26] First Corinthians 12:4–26.

[27] Matthew 6:19–33.

[28] Ephesians 5:18–33.

[29] Αγαπη (*agape* = unconditional love); φιλος (*philos* = friendship love); ερος (*eros* = sexual love).

[30] Chrysostom, *Homily XX on Ephesians*, p. 62.

[31] Ambrose, *Ephesians LXIII, 79*.

[32] Chrysostom, *Homily XX on Ephesians*, p. 62.

[33] Larry Richardson, *The Christian Family* (Minneapolis: Bethany, 1970).

[34] Genesis 18:19 (KJV).

[35] Having risen by 250 percent in the past twenty years and up 800 percent in one generation among preteens.

[36] Total 600,000 each year.

[37] Armand Nicholi, *Evangelical Agenda: 1984 and Beyond* (Pasadena: William Carey Library, 1979).

[38] Ephesians 6:4.

[39] *Moody Monthly*, March 1953.

[40] Proverbs 1:7.

[41] Titus 2:11–12 (Arthur Way Translation).

[42] J. Allen Peterson, "The Biggest Problem," *The Alliance Witness*, April 1, 1981, p. 6.

[43]Note Genesis 2:20–24.
[44]First Peter 3:7–8.
[45]Ephesians 4:29; Colossians 3:8–14.
[46]Romans 12:9; 1 Corinthians 13; 1 Thessalonians 3:12; 1 Peter 1:22.
[47]Dr. Ward is professor of Christian Education and director of the Ed.D. program at Trinity Evangelical Divinity School. Quoted from an article entitled, "The Church and the Christian Family" (publisher unknown).
[48]First Chronicles 12:32.

# A Response to Marriage and the Family

## Michael D. Warner

This paper is a response to Bill and Mary Pride's document entitled "Marriage and the Family." The Prides are to be complimented on the seriousness with which they undertook their task, their commitment to the literal truth of God's special revelation, and their willingness to attempt to explore so many of the areas and issues legitimately included in such a broad topic as marriage and family living. I suspect that the Prides have much more to say about many of the issues upon which they could only barely comment because of space limitations. Although one may not agree entirely with their views on current practices, such as present-day care of aged relatives, the role of the state in educating children, and certain legislation that affects marital and family life, they are to be commended for their forthrightness and candor in delineating some of the practical implications of their ideas.

This response will not attempt to speak to the Prides' paper point for point. Rather it will serve as a continuation of their document by attempting to fill a theological gap created at the outset of their paper in the section in which they present their theological understanding of marriage. The weakness of their presentation is not so much in what they said but rather in what was left unsaid and which, therefore, necessarily affected the flavor of the rest of their presentation.

Marriage is at its heart a theological institution. The same can be said for the family, regardless of whether one thinks of the nuclear family or the extended family. From the broader view the family is the basic unit of society. From the narrower view marriage must be defined as the basic unit. As the Scriptures affirm and as social scientists have observed, as the marriage goes, so goes the family. I would suggest that contrary to the Prides' implication that the state is wreaking havoc on the family, one might more appropriately look to the marital partners whose sinful inability to negotiate God-pleasing marital unions filters its way down through the familial subsystems so that the sins of the fathers come to rest on the sons and on the sons' sons. One need only look at the poor marriages recorded in the inspired Scriptures to see the consequences of inappropriate parent-child coalitions where a parent and child coalesce against the other parent, where parents are unable to unite themselves over against rebellious children, and where sins committed in the marriage have their devastating effects on the spiritual, emotional, and physical lives of the children.

Yet in spite of all this, I suggest that God's original intent in establishing marriage and, subsequently, the family was that he intended Adam and Eve to *reflect his image* dynamically in their marital union. Orthodox theologians have had a great deal to say about the image of God as a theological concept. They have spoken of its qualities as it resided in Adam and in Eve until they ate the forbidden fruit. Traditionally, God's image has been presented as a rather static concept describing a perfect moral and spiritual condition residing in two individuals. Thus Adam possessed God's image, and so did Eve. All this is true; the Scriptures cannot be broken.

However, this understanding is rather short-sighted and incomplete. Consider God's original intention. He intended that Adam and Eve relate to each other in *dynamic*—not static—harmony with him and with each other. Thus their marriage *relationship* also was to be a reflection of the image of God, with Adam and Eve working side by side as head and helpmeet in subduing and filling the earth. Each was to *experience* in each other a reflection of his/her oneness with God so that each could think, "If this is the love and faithfulness with which my mate treats me, then how much more loving and faithful must my heavenly Father be, who gave me my mate." In this view, the first couple on earth were to live out and experience in their marriage what *marriage in God's image* was meant to be. Their marriage was to be a mirror, a copy, a reflection of the oneness between themselves as individuals and as a couple on the one hand and with God on the other hand.

When sin entered the marriage, God's relationship to Adam and Eve was broken. Not coincidentally, so was the marital bond of oneness and fidelity, as Eve seduced Adam away from obedience to God and as Adam later attempted to make Eve the scapegoat for his sin. Thus we see that immediately after the Fall the husband-wife relationship once again mirrored the God-human relationship, this time in its brokenness. The brokenness that occurred between Adam and his wife was a fitting metaphor for the brokenness between Adam and his God.

This brokenness was repaired only by grace as it applied both to the relationship between God and human beings and also to the marital pair. That Eve understood the promise of Genesis 3:15 to be messianic is without doubt. So excited, hopeful, and expectant was she that God would keep his promise that she mistakenly thought her first-born to be the fulfillment of the promise; thus, she named him, literally, "Got." It was God's forgiveness—based on the death of the Savior who would come—that restored the first husband and wife in their relationship with God and in which we say the image of God was partially restored. It was willingness to appropriate this same grace to each other that allowed Adam and Eve to continue as husband and wife in a marriage that also dynamically reflected the broken-but-restored nature of their spirits. To date, each had learned experientially, in the context of the marriage, something of the security and harmony of perfect, God-authored love; each experienced in marriage the partially restored image of God and the necessity of applying grace to sin if the relationship was to continue.

Whereas Adam formerly had been perfect, he now was spirit and flesh. These spirit-and-flesh people related to each other in such a way that sometimes Adam's spirit was in communion with Eve's spirit and their marriage was a foretaste of heaven; or, at least, it was a somewhat smeared reflection of the perfect way things used to be between them. At other times Adam's sinful flesh snared Eve's sinful flesh, no doubt, as arguments and temporary marital division erupted. Thus it is possible to speak, again in dynamic rather than static terms, also of a *marital* spirit and a *marital* flesh in their union, so that at times they experienced the sin and stress of flesh-level marital relating. Though born with concupiscence, Cain also learned how to sin by observing his parents when their sinful flesh was in collusion. He also learned through the Word spoken by his parents how to apply and to receive grace, to forgive and to be forgiven by grace. Since this first couple and first family were so intimately bound together, there can be no question that each knew how to please each other and that each knew what it would take to "snag" the flesh of the other. In large part each family member's behavior was in some way a response to some other family member's behavior, so that the whole spirit-level and flesh-level interactional patterns developed in this first family.

In the meantime, God's original intent had never changed. Husband and wife still were to form the spiritual, emotional, and physical bond necessary to subdue and replenish the earth and, at the same time, to set a godly example for the children of the marriage. They were to train up their children as two parents in godly alliance with each other. The children were to experience peership with each until they, too, took their place as godly procreators who nevertheless continued to honor both father and mother. Sin had made all that utterly impossible. Grace had restored the divine mission of the family, but sin would always be a force with which to reckon.

Yet the mission continues today. The marriage, and subsequently the family, is the application-site of both God's law and his redeeming gospel in Jesus Christ. The purpose of Christian marriage is to be a reflection of the grace of God in Jesus Christ so that each spouse reflects Christ and the fruits of his Spirit (Gal. 5:22–23) to the mate in a way that enables the spouses, as individuals and as a married couple, to attempt to live out dynamically the image of God in the context of their marriage. The Christian family is to be a nursery in which this restored-by-grace image is taught and lived so that the Christian family becomes the launching ground for fighting the devil, the sinful world, and the flesh, and to evangelize the world through the gospel of Christ.

If this all has seemed to be a rather lengthy excursis into already-known and therefore mundane theological ground, it has been for one reason only. *Any* theological understanding of marriage and family life that emphasizes what *ought* to be the case in marriage and family life and that ignores the need for grace and a specifically christocentric understanding of marriage and family is doomed to degenerate into Pharisaic, law-filled prescriptions guaranteed to produce only guilt, hopelessness, and even outright rejection of a truly biblical understanding of God's plan for marriage and the family.

Paul, speaking by inspiration of the Holy Spirit, was right on target in focusing on Christ's relationship to the church as the example for which Christian marriage should be the metaphor. Husbands, love your wives! How? Even as Christ loved the church. How did Christ love the church? He "gave himself for it." Wives, be subject to your own husbands! How? "As to the Lord," that is how. In what sense is husband the head? As bossy tyrant? No, "as Christ also is the Head of the church, he himself being the Savior of the body."

It is no secret today that marriages are in trouble. It is also not surprising that family therapy is a flourishing enterprise. Marriages have always been in trouble. Families have always been in trouble. The problem is not simply "society," capitalism, communism, television, the liberation movement, the legal system, the public schools, the Moonies, or even liberalism in the church, though these all provide ample reflections of evil in our day. The tendency of the church has been to condemn sin, to shun those who fail in marriage, and to issue prescriptions. We must condemn sin. Failure to do so results in our own spiritual damnation, according to Scripture. Issuing prescriptions, also, is properly a function of proclaiming God's holy law.

However, where we as the body of Christ on earth are woefully weak is our inability—even our corporate unwillingness—to speak the word of grace to those whose marital and family lives are filled with pain and failure and to disciple those who by reason of sin have failed at putting together marriages and families in the image of God. We have failed our children because our pastors have not known how to speak to the children of divorce, much less to the spouses who divorce. We shout, "Put your marriage back together!" but we do not show how. We shout, "Get some counseling!" but then decry humanistic psychology from the pulpit and sabotage the efforts of even the best Christian counselors and psychotherapists. We preach on the inspired words, "There is not a righteous man that doeth good and sinneth not," but then speak of "guilty" parties and "innocent" parties. And what do our children learn? Some conclude it is better to live in an uncommitted cohabitational relationship like the woman Christ met at the well. Others are so emotionally devastated that they are doomed to repeat the sins of their fathers—and mothers—in their own eventual marriages. Is marriage enrichment, the kind in which Christians employ legitimate relationship skills for teaching one another, for the church? Should the church require premarital counseling? (It is harder to obtain a driver's license than to get married!) Should the church be in the business of Christian sex education? Should the church form support groups for divorced people? The answer to all these questions—and a host of others—is an unreserved, "Yes!"

Unfortunately, it appears that it is now safe everywhere *except* in the church to talk about our personal difficulties, our failures, and our guilts. Today's psychologists rapidly are becoming the secular "pastors" who form secular support groups because the church is not the place where we "bear one another's burdens." We in the church must stop acting as though to talk about sin is to commit it and as though to discuss infidelity—not simply preach against it—is to encourage it or to teach Christian sex education is to promote premarital sex. The church is the one place on earth where we legitimately can take our hopes, our fears, our guilts, and our failures, and have them all transformed and redeemed by the blood of Jesus Christ. Nor is this notion a suggestion that the church replace the legitimate function of the Christian family. Christian families make up the church and enable the church as institution to marshal the resources and expertise competently and pastorally to teach, guide, sustain, and communicate God's will and his grace in Christ in both preventive and remedial ways.

Believers do fail in their personal lives. They know it when it happens, and they experience a profound sense of guilt as well as alienation from God and his people in the church. The adulterer, the divorced person, the child molester, the abusive drinker, the rebellious teenager, the middle-aged spouse who for years has been experiencing a running battle with the in-laws, the wife- or husband-beater—these all are people who claim the name of Christ in their hearts and who sit in our pews Sunday after Sunday, spiritually immobilized by guilt and feeling trapped in sinful situations they feel powerless to overcome. They know God's will for the family; they hear it every Sunday. What they need is the compassionate Christ who competently offers them both pardon from guilt and release from their bondage to sin.

I presently am a family therapist in a Christian counseling center. I am amazed time and again at the kinds of failures people bring to me for help, people who call themselves Christians and who are active members of Christian congregations. If their pastors only knew what they were telling me about their lives! One wonders whether they might be excommunicated. Not once in all the years when I was a parish pastor did my parishioners bring to me the kinds of problems I see daily in my office at the counseling center where I minister. My parishioners knew my credentials. My academic regalia had been printed in the community newspaper and on the back of the service bulletin on the Sunday I was installed as pastor. Why, in spite of my training, did my parishioners elect not to come to me with the same kinds of problems I now regularly see? Why did parishioners from neighboring congregations come to me confessing their sins and seeking my pastoral help? I doubt that it was simply because their pastors did not possess the degree of counseling training I had received. I believe it was because the church has become a place mainly to confess sin in the past tense rather than receive compassionate mind-of-Christ help in overcoming sin and its feelings of alienation in the present tense.

If it is true that sin is more prevalent these days and that people are given more license openly to sin than previously, then the task is not merely to thunder God's law louder and more angrily than before. This will never motivate sanctified living in itself. We must show people the Christ whose gospel of grace, mercy, and forgiveness motivated the woman at the well, whose gentle absolution inspired the woman taken in adultery, whose forbearance allowed Abraham to continue on his mission even after he gave his wife to the Egyptian Pharaoh, whose compassion restored Peter's apostleship after he had denied him, and whose love for David allowed him to continue as God's servant even after his scandalous sin.

God-fearing spouses scratch their heads and wonder why they cannot get along with their mates in spite of the fact that they both are Christians who want nothing more than to get along with each other in the way their pastor describes a Christian marriage. Christian parents and their children cannot understand why they seem to be always bickering in spite of the fact they would like nothing more than to get along with each other the way they learn it should be from their Sunday school lesson. Christian couples attend Bible studies on Christian marriage, agree with everything the printed material presents, go home afterward with the best of intentions, and then wonder what went wrong when it does not "work." Each spouse concludes there must be something wrong with him/herself, but cannot seem to find the key to the solution of the marital discord.

We have failed in teaching single people Christian relationship skills, we have failed in making the church a place where married couples can share feelings and frustrations and learn skills in relationship building, and we have largely concluded that when a child acts rebelliously the simple answer is to be more strict and less permissive with him. Let us learn how to get our hands dirty by learning how to deal with marriages whose partners feel "stuck" and powerless. Let us stop talking about how the church can coalesce to punish the "guilty" party who obtains a divorce and learn how to minister both law and gospel to his/her pain, guilt, and sense of failure. Let us stop isolating the so-called "innocent" party of divorce who intuitively knows that he/she in some way contributed to the marital failure and help that hurting soul explore how things came to be the way they turned out. Let us stop dragging the errant child into the pastor's or principal's office to lecture him/her and start learning something about how that child's behavior might be connected to pain somewhere else in the family. Let us end our corporate naïveté about widows and recognize their need for intimacy—not only sexual—in their lives. Let us stop organizing singles' groups long enough to listen to them tell us how they perceive the church to be an institution that brands singles as outcasts and incomplete until they marry. Let us pause long enough in our condemnation of homosexuality to learn how to minister to the "gay" who already knows his/her attraction to the same sex is a sinful condition but who wants to learn *how to deal with it*. Let us spend a bit less time reiterating the obvious ideal situations we would like to see obtained in marriages and families and spend more time learning to listen with the mind of Christ! Instead of talking about the way things should be and complaining when they are not, let us look at the way things really are and make the church a place where people feel safe to talk about their less-than-perfect situations and learn how to apply God's grace to their lives as they attempt to grow as Spirit-filled people.

The only major weakness in the Prides' document is that,

from my viewpoint, I did not see Jesus. I went away thinking, "But what about those situations that do not measure up to this ideal? What do we do for them, from a theological and pastoral perspective?" Any model of marriage or family that omits Christ and grace from its theological stance necessarily leaves no room for failure and forgiveness. This is unrealistic.

# DIVORCE AND REMARRIAGE

## William A. Heth

### I. INTRODUCTION

Today evangelical writers are giving a number of different answers to the questions: When may a Christian separate from his or her spouse? and When may a Christian remarry after divorce? Behind the answer to the latter question is an even more fundamental one: "How enduring or permanent is the marriage relationship that comes into being when male and female become 'one flesh'" (Gen. 1:27; 2:24)? In other words, except for the dissolution of marriage through the death of one of the partners (cf. Rom. 7:2–3; 1 Cor. 7:39), are there any sins that so fundamentally strike at what has been witnessed (Mal. 2:14) and joined by God (Matt. 19:6; Mark 10:8b–9) that we can pronounce the one-flesh union ended and nonexistent? In such cases remarriage to another would not be considered adultery. If the bond between the spouses has been dissolved or obliterated in some way, then remarriage is not adultery, for there remains no tie to the former spouse against whom one would commit this offense.

The question of the nature and permanency of the marriage relationship deserves careful consideration, for no disciple of Christ would wish to counsel divorcées to remain single if their Lord permitted them to remarry; nor would we want to encourage divorcées to remarry if Jesus calls remarriage adultery. Whatever convictions Christians may have about this or any other emotionally charged issue, we must keep in mind Geoffrey Bromiley's statement that happiness "cannot be attained, nor can human life be fulfilled, where there is conflict with God's stated will or a defiant refusal to see that true happiness and fulfillment lie only in a primary commitment to God's kingdom and righteousness."[1]

The issue of what, in the eyes of God, makes a marriage and how permanent that marriage relationship is, is a matter of confusion within evangelical circles today. Though all would declare that marriage is to be a permanent, lifelong relationship, there are great differences of opinion over the extent to which the ideal should be maintained in the face of human hard-heartedness. The different answers given to the question, When may a Christian remarry after divorce without committing adultery? reveal different conceptions about the nature and permanence of the marriage union. These different conceptions of the marriage relationship result in turn in the conflicting counsel Christians so often receive when they turn to their leaders for guidance when marital breakdown occurs.

For example, many Evangelicals agree with the classic Protestant answer given to this question by John Murray in his book *Divorce* (1953).[2] Murray and those who defend this view today believe that in Matthew 19:9 Jesus does not only permit a Christian to divorce a spouse guilty of serious sexual sin(s); he further permits the innocent spouse to remarry another without committing adultery. Forgiveness (cf. Matt. 18:21–35) and reconciliation, however, are encouraged above anything else in this situation. This view also holds that in 1 Corinthians 7:15 Paul adds another ground for divorce and remarriage—namely, when a believer is deserted or abandoned by an unbeliever. Other writers believe that the only ground for divorce and remarriage is the sin of adultery; desertion of a believer by an unbeliever does not constitute grounds for remarriage.[3] On the other hand, Bromiley believes that divorce with the right to remarry is *not* envisaged by Jesus in Matthew 19:9, but he *does* understand Paul to permit remarriage to the believer deserted by the unbeliever in 1 Corinthians 7:15.[4] Still others believe that *neither* the innocent *nor* the guilty party in Matthew 19:9 and 1 Corinthians 7:15 may remarry without being guilty of the sin of adultery (whether his or her previous partner has remarried or not).[5] And though these are the major evangelical positions on what the Bible teaches about divorce and remarriage, even the preceding summary does not exhaust the situations in which some Christian counselors would allow for divorce and remarriage.[6]

None of these views should be labeled as "loose" or "strict." These types of designations only muddle the emotional waters in an already disquieted pool. What *is* important is how each position handles all of the biblical data it appeals to for support. Whether the biblical view is "loose" or "strict" in one's opinion, Christians must be faithful to what their Lord taught and must seek to honor him both in what they teach and in how they live.

Does Jesus, in Matthew 19:9, say that certain sexual sins are grounds for divorce *and* remarriage? Does Paul, in 1 Corinthians

7:15, teach that the Christian spouse deserted by an unbeliever is free from those marriage ties for remarriage to another? We have already noted that intelligent and sincere Christian leaders are divided in their answers to these questions. And it is highly unlikely that further discussions of these controversial sayings from the ministries of Jesus and Paul will resolve the debate over the actual "indissolubility" of the marriage union. Therefore, I would like to submit that another approach is needed. This approach would focus on a portion of the Scriptures that popular treatments of the subject of divorce and remarriage have hurried over or mishandled in their eagerness to get to the debated New Testament texts: the Old Testament, and in particular, the meaning of "one flesh" in Genesis 2:24.

In Matthew 19:4–6 our Lord reached back to the first two chapters of the Bible to validate his understanding of the permanence of marriage over against what the religious teachers of that day were sanctioning. He grounded all that he taught about the indissolubility[7] of marriage in the created nature of mankind as "male and female" (Gen. 1:27)—a phrase that Jesus linked with the specific man and woman who "leave," "cleave," and become "one flesh" in Genesis 2:24. Whereas Genesis 2:24 in and of itself may not give us any indication of what sins, if any, so strike at this one-flesh union so as to dissolve or break it, two other pieces of Old Testament legislation (Lev. 18:6–18; Deut. 24:4) that are based on the one-flesh concept of Genesis 2:24 do address this issue.[8] Neither of them lends any support to the contention that extramarital sexual sins dissolve or obliterate the original one-flesh union. Rather they suggest that even though someone may choose to divorce and separate from a spouse, the one-flesh union still continues and affects subsequent behavior.

One searches popular evangelical works on divorce and remarriage in vain for an accurate discussion of the meaning of "one flesh" in its Old Testament context.[9] Yet this is the very concept on which our Lord grounded his teaching on divorce and remarriage.

## II. OLD TESTAMENT TEACHING[10]

### A. Introduction

We begin our study of the biblical teaching on divorce and remarriage at the beginning of the Old Testament. From the standpoint of method, it is only proper that we approach our subject chronologically, beginning with the creation ordinances of Genesis 1–2, and then following the historically conditioned progress of God's revelation on this subject through the Bible.[11] The polygamy and divorce that was practiced in the Old Testa-

ment will meet with "the severest reproof and condemnation in
the New Testament; . . ."[12] It must be recognized, therefore, that
although God's righteous standards for the marriage relationship
have always been and always will be the same, there was a period
of salvation history in which the Mosaic law conceded (or did not
prohibit) the practice of various marital customs that Israel shared
with her ancient Near Eastern neighbors. Nevertheless, numerous
sexual regulations in the Pentateuch teach us about God's
perspective of the marital relationship and how seriously he views
any attempt to violate the sanctity of it.

## B. Genesis 1–2[13]

In going back to "the beginning" for the basis of his
prohibition of divorce and remarriage, Jesus understood that God
revealed his will for marriage "not in a biblical commandment but
in the nature of created human life in maleness and femaleness
and in the marriage relationship."[14] All the commentators agree
that Genesis 2:18–25 covers the same ground as 1:26–28, but in a
significantly different way. Genesis 2:18–25 points out that
without the woman there can be no society, no realization of the
creation directives (Gen. 1:28), and, in short, no human race.
There seems to be little doubt that the "male" and the "female" of
Genesis 1:27 are the specific male and the specific female whose
marriage relationship is related in detail in Genesis 2:24. The
marriage of Adam and Eve is the pattern for all marriages within
the human race. To understand the concepts found in Genesis
2:24 is to understand the nature of the marriage relationship itself.
To understand this is to understand the basis for Jesus' teaching
on divorce and remarriage.

We read in Genesis 2:24: "For this cause a man shall *leave* his
father and his mother, and shall *cleave* to his wife; and they shall
become *one flesh*" (NASB; italics mine). Two important concepts
about marriage are taught in this verse. The first one concerns the
words "leave" and "cleave," and the second one concerns the
nature of the new one-flesh unit that is predicated upon the
consummation of the marriage through sexual union.[15] A careful
understanding of both of these concepts will lead us to an
appreciation of the nature and permanence of the marriage
relationship.

The first thing that must be noticed is that the words "leave"
and "cleave" embody covenant terminology. When they are used
of interpersonal relationships—either between human beings or
between God and humans—they are clearly covenant terms.[16] An
excellent example of the use of both "leave" and "cleave" with
this significance is found in the Book of Ruth. Ruth questions Boaz
in Ruth 2:10–11 about why she had gained such favor in his eyes

even though she was a foreigner. Boaz answers: "All that you have done for your mother-in-law after the death of your husband has been fully reported to me, and how you *left* your father and mother and the land of your birth, and came to a people that you did not previously know" (v. 11 NASB; italics mine). Here and in many other places in the Old Testament (cf. Deut. 28:20; 31:16; Jer. 1:16; Hos. 4:10) the term "leave" refers to abandoning one covenant commitment for the sake of another. The word "cleave" is used in Ruth 1:14 after Ruth and her sister-in-law Orpah had persistently said no to Naomi's wishes (vv. 8–9, 11–13) that they return to their mother's house. Finally, we read that Orpah kissed Naomi and returned to her mother's house, "but Ruth *clung* to her." Then Ruth says, "Do not urge me to leave you or turn back from following you; for where you go, I will go, and where you lodge, I will lodge. Your people shall be my people, and your God, my God" (1:16 NASB). This was the point of Ruth's conversion *from* the gods of her Moabite heritage *to* the God of Israel. The words that Ruth utters in verse 16 are very significant. They are known as solemn words (*verba solemnia*). These consisted of an unwritten agreement, which, by themselves or along with other symbolic rites, were employed in ancient Near Eastern legal systems to explicitly fix the moment of legal change.[17] Thus Ruth knows and uses the terminology of covenant relationships.

The word "cleave" is especially prominent as a technical term in the covenant terminology of Deuteronomy (10:20; 11:22; 13:4; 30:20; cf. Josh. 22:5; 23:8). Earl Kalland notes that in these verses where the Israelites are to cleave to the Lord in affection and loyalty, "parallel words and phrases that describe this proper attitude to the Lord are: fear, serve, love, obey, swear by His name, walk in His ways, and keep His commandments."[18] In short, the use of "cleave" in Genesis 2:24 has no specific sexual significance[19] but points to a covenant relationship modeled after God's covenant with Israel in the Old Testament (cf. Ezek. 16:8, 60; Mal. 2:10–16). It refers to "a situation of very personal concern, fidelity and involvement."[20]

What does the institution of marriage as a covenant teach us about its duration? Do violations of the covenant annul or break the covenant resulting in a dissolution of the relationship? Or does human sin only violate the covenant stipulations while the covenant still remains in effect? In the Old Testament when there was disobedience and unfaithfulness to God's covenant with Israel, punishment ensued in the form of the covenant curses (Lev. 26; Deut. 28) in order to enforce the covenant and maintain it. Israel's later history records the numerous and flagrant violations of the covenant (under the imagery of a wife unfaithful to her husband) that seemingly break the covenant and bring the relationship between God and his people to the point of potential permanent dissolution. Nevertheless, God says that he will not cast off his people completely but will call his unfaithful people back (cf. Lev. 26:44–45; Judg. 2:1–3; Isa. 50:1; Jer. 3:8, 12).[21] The maintenance of the covenant in the face of flagrant violations is fleshed out in Hosea's marriage to and broken relationship with Gomer (Hos. 1–3). Hosea 2:2b is not a divorce formula but in this context (cf. 2:5 with 2:13) means "We are no longer living together as husband and wife."[22] F. I. Andersen and D. N. Freedman further note that Hosea 1:9 is *not* an announcement of God of the dissolution of the covenant comparable to divorce. They write:

> The covenant nowhere makes provision for such an eventuality. Covenant-breaking on the part of Israel (unilateral withdrawal) calls for severe punishment. Israel cannot opt out by no longer acknowledging Yahweh. The punishment is not an expression of a broken relationship. On the contrary, it is enforced within the relationship; punishment maintains the covenant.[23]

"Can covenant bond be broken—and at the same time persist? Can God sever a relationship as a result of covenant violations—and nevertheless maintain it in perpetuity? The Bible seems to answer in the affirmative."[24] So much more study is needed in this comparison of God's covenants with Israel and the nature of commitment in the marriage covenant;[25] but at this point we must be cautious of how far such analogies should be pushed. One thing seems certain: The love, commitment, and loyalty that are part and parcel of the marriage covenant can no doubt be violated by human sin. Human sin and unfaithfulness may well result in a permanent breaking of the love relationship in a marriage. Yet the terms "leave" and "cleave" in Genesis 2:24 teach us that the essence of the marriage covenant is commitment to the covenant partner. Any legal action like that which God took against Israel and which Hosea threatened to take against Gomer should be aimed at bringing about the restoration of the faithless mate.

> The question that should be asked is not whether the actions of the faithless mate are bad enough to relieve one of his commitment but whether legal action is the only recourse to remind the unfaithful [partner] of their commitment to the covenant. The question is not whether divorce is legal. The question is, "Do I feel the same way about divorce that God does?" To answer this question in the affirmative is to abhor divorce as a breach of covenant and to revert to its use only when all other attempts to restore the relationship have failed. But then, even in divorce, to use the action as a means of restoration and not as a license to withdraw one's commitment from the marriage partner.[26]

Genesis 2:24, however, does not end with its comments about "leaving" and "cleaving." The biblical description of the marriage relationship goes beyond the discussion of marriage as a covenant. Genesis 2:24c goes on to describe marriage as a kinship, or "blood relationship," as denoted by the concept of "one flesh."[27]

We are able to appreciate even more Jesus' teaching about divorce and remarriage when we grasp the meaning of a second and equally important point about the *nature* of the marital union. This is indicated by the final words in Genesis 2:24: "they shall become one flesh." Technically this statement does not refer to the sexual union of the man and his wife, nor does it refer to the child who would come from the fruit of their relationship. The word "flesh" (בָּשָׂר) is capable of carrying a number of different nuances, and so it must always be considered in each individual context in order to appreciate its significance. The meaning of "flesh" in Genesis 2:24 carries the same nuance as it does in the more concrete statement in which it occurs in Genesis 2:23: "And the man said,

> This is now bone of my bones,
>   And flesh of my flesh;
> She shall be called Woman,
>   Because she was taken out of Man' " (NASB).

But what does it mean for someone to be "bone of my bones and flesh of my flesh"?

Adam's statement,

> "This is now bone of my bones,
>   And flesh of my flesh,"

is more than just a joyous statement arising out of his recognition that Eve was a creature with whom he could form a true partnership. We find in Genesis 2:23a not primarily a declaration of love but "the formula of relationship."[28] This same formula is used elsewhere—Genesis 29:14; Judges 9:1–2 (cf. vv. 3, 18); 2 Samuel 5:1; and 19:12–13 (cf. 1 Chron. 2:13–17)—and in each case it indicates a permanent relationship, namely a kinship relationship. This is what the abbreviated "one flesh" signifies in Genesis 2:24 (cf. Gen. 37:27).

Some studies have implied that the statement "they shall become one flesh" indicates a relationship that is to be realized and developed over a period of time. While it is true that every marriage relationship takes time to develop and grow, there is also that aspect of the marital relationship which involves its coming into being at a point in time. The latter appears to be the emphasis in Genesis 2:24.[29] A man and woman become married when they pledge their loyalty to one another (covenant)[30] *and* consummate their marriage. The biblical picture of marriage appears to indicate

that both elements—covenant and consummation—are necessary
to form a genuine marriage. One without the other (cf. 1 Cor.
6:16) is no marriage.[31]

Something unique and "creational" takes place when husband and wife consummate their marriage: they become closely
related ("one flesh"). Marriage is more than a covenant between a
man and a woman to belong to each other in mutual commitment.
Jesus' interpretation of Genesis 1:27 and 2:24 in Matthew 19:6 and
Mark 10:9 implies that God himself is involved in—may I say—
creating this new relationship, which is also the beginning of a
new family unit. Thus we learn from Jesus that marriage involves
three persons: a man and a woman and the One who, in the
beginning, created mankind as male and female.

But what about the permanency of this marital union? If the
"one flesh" in Genesis 2:24 is not to be equated with sexual union
but denotes a kinship relationship that is predicated on the
consummation of the marriage through sexual union, is it not
possible that sexual sin is a *de facto* violation of the marriage bond
which, in effect, dissolves it?[32] If the relationship, or kinship,
formula has not already suggested the permanent nature of the
marriage relationship, a study of two other passages in the Old
Testament *will* suggest just how enduring the marriage relationship is—even in the face of sexual violations of it.

## C. Leviticus 18:6–18

The biblical legislation concerning certain forbidden marital
and sexual unions (Lev. 18:6–18; 20:11–12, 14, 17, 19–21; Deut.
22:30; 27:20, 22–23) further illustrates the fact that the one-flesh
relation in Genesis 2:24 denotes the establishment of a new
kinship, a new family unit. The various prohibitions in Leviticus
18 and elsewhere are not only predicated on literal blood lines
(i.e., between parents and children) but also on "blood," or
kinship, relationships created through marriage (cf. Lev.
18:7–8).[33] The opening refrain in Leviticus 18:6–18 directs:
" 'None of you shall approach any blood relative of his to uncover
nakedness; I am the LORD' " (v. 6 NASB). "Uncover nakedness" is a
euphemism for sexual intercourse, and "blood relative" is literally
"flesh of his flesh" (cf. Gen. 2:23).[34] These regulations interpret
relationships of affinity (connection by marriage) in terms of the
principle that man and wife are "one flesh"—that is, kin or blood
relations.[35]

These regulations thus define the limits within which a man
may seek a wife. The moment a man married a woman she
became an integral part of his family in the same way in which
children born into that family do. Similarly he became related to
her close female relatives, and should his wife die or should he

divorce her, he could not marry them, for that would be a form of incest. From this we observe that already the Old Testament law places restrictions on the right of a man to remarry whomever he pleases. (In two other situations the Mosaic law removes the right of the man to divorce his wife "all his days" [Deut. 22:13–19, 28–29].) "The prohibitions, with one exception, are unqualified as to their duration, and hence one can only assume that they are permanent and are not terminated by the death of a person who forms a link in a chain of relationship by marriage."[36] These regulations are not concerned with prohibiting sexual liaisons with another party when that person is formally married, for this is covered by the prohibition of adultery (Exod. 20:14; Lev. 18:20). Marriage to a spouse's close relatives after her death or after she has been divorced is governed here.

The Mosaic legislation in Leviticus 18—still binding today[37]— makes it clear that legal divorce does not dissolve "one flesh," nor the extended relationships that arise through a covenanted and consummated marriage. A second passage, sharing a number of points in common with the Leviticus 18 incest legislation, goes even further in suggesting that neither legal divorce nor extramarital relations with a third party are capable of dissolving or annulling a covenanted and consummated marital relationship.

## D. Deuteronomy 24:1–4

A considerable number of Evangelicals who believe that Jesus permitted remarriage after divorce for immorality (Matt. 5:32; 19:9) find support for this in their understanding of how the bill of divorce operates in Deuteronomy 24:1–4. Murray, for example, teaches his readers that "the dissolution permitted or tolerated under the Mosaic economy had the effect of dissolving the marriage bond."[38] From this he concludes that remarriage after a proper divorce in Matthew 5:32 and 19:9 does not constitute adultery. Today, no one who is familiar with the scholarly literature on Deuteronomy 24:1–4 would ever seek to argue that the Mosaic bill of divorce dissolves the marriage bond. As a matter of fact, the only piece of legislation found in Deuteronomy 24:1–4—namely, verse 4—is itself based upon the continuing existence of the one-flesh relation established via the first marriage.

An extensive discussion of the five different interpretations that have been offered for the legislation found in Deuteronomy 24:1–4 cannot be undertaken here.[39] We have already noted above that the Leviticus 18:6–18 legislation is concerned with prohibiting certain marital unions with near relatives after the death of or divorce by a spouse. Deuteronomy 24:4, however, is concerned with prohibiting *the restoration of a previous marriage* after a woman has been divorced by her second husband or he has died. By far the most satisfactory explanation for the legislation found in verse 4 is that the restoration of the first marriage, after the intervening marriage with its concomitant "defiling" relations, is regarded as a type of incest.

> Through her first marriage the women entered into the closest form of relationship with her husband. . . . divorce did not terminate this relationship; she still counted as a very close relative. If a divorced couple want to come together again [after she has become closely related to a second husband], it would be as bad as a man marrying his sister. That is why it is described as "an abomination before the Lord" that "causes the land to sin."[40]

The result is paradoxical. A man may not remarry his wife because his first marriage to her made her into one of his closest relatives. Upon consummating (cf. "defiled") her marriage with a second husband she in turn becomes closely related to him and, in effect, now forms a link in the close relationship between the two men. To reunite with one's former husband after the death of or divorce by the second would be as bad as a man marrying his sister.

Deuteronomy 24:4 has taken the theological logic of Leviticus to its limit.[41] It illustrates once again the notion that underlies the incest laws: a covenanted and consummated marriage results in "one flesh." Marital intercourse not only creates vertical blood relationships through the procreation of children but horizontal ones as well: the partners to a marriage become "one flesh." These horizontal relationships are just as enduring as the vertical ones. Deuteronomy 24 does not teach that legal divorce and subsequent marriage (which "defiles" the wife) dissolves "one flesh." On the contrary, the passage seems to imply that to seek a divorce in order to remarry is to try to break a relationship with one's wife that in reality cannot be broken save by death. Just as we cannot "divorce" our children from being our own flesh and blood no matter how disreputable or immoral they may be, so a man cannot "divorce" his wife who is his own flesh and blood (cf. Lev. 18:7–8) through the covenant and consummation of marriage.[42]

Thus Deuteronomy 24:1–4 understands the "one-flesh union" to survive legal or customary divorce as well as sexual relations with a third party. Indeed, the permanent nature of "one flesh" is the very basis for the legislation found in Deuteronomy 24:4.

## E. Divorce in the Old Testament

Before moving on to our brief survey of the New Testament teaching on divorce and remarriage, we ought to make a few more comments about divorce in the Old Testament and Deuteronomy 24:1–4. In the Old Testament, divorce, like polygamy, was an ancient Near Eastern legal practice that Israel shared with surrounding nations. The Mosaic Law presupposes the exercise of *an already existing divorce procedure* (Deut. 24:1–3) but says little about its operation. There is, in fact, no law in the Old Testament which *legislates* grounds for divorce; but as we have just seen, one Mosaic regulation does forbid a man to take back the wife he divorces if her marriage to another man has been consummated (v. 4). This regulation, rooted in the concepts taught in Genesis 2:24, is still applicable today.

One of two errors is commonly made in both popular and scholarly treatments of Deuteronomy 24:1–4. The first one is made when interpreters fall into the mistaken notion that the giving of the bill of divorce was a practice instituted by Moses and thereby became a part of the Old Testament law.[43] This interpretation fails to notice that Deuteronomy 24:1–4 is laid out in the straightforward *"If . . . then . . ."* structure common to all of the case laws in the Mosaic legislation. The "if" portion notes the relevant facts of the case that is being decided upon in the "then" portion. We read, for example, in Deuteronomy 24:7: "*If* a man is caught kidnapping any of his countrymen of the sons of Israel, and he deals with him violently, or sells him, *then* that thief shall die; . . ." (NASB; italics mine). No one would suggest from the "if" portion of this case that Moses is legislating the way in which a fellow Israelite should be kidnapped if a kidnapping takes place! Nor should one suggest from the "if" portion of Deuteronomy 24:1–4 (i.e., vv. 1–3) that Moses is setting forth the proper procedure for divorce should a divorce take place. What makes Deuteronomy 24:1–4 less clear than the case ruled upon in verse 7 is that Deuteronomy 24:1–3 records an already existing divorce procedure that Israel followed in accordance with the customs of the non-Israelite peoples.[44] Verses 1–3 only provide the relevant facts of the case ruled upon in verse 4. They do not institute or sanction the customary divorce procedures that Israel shared with neighboring nations.

The second error commonly made in popular discussions of Deuteronomy 24 concerns its bearing on Jesus' teaching on divorce and remarriage in the New Testament. These writers usually recognize that Deuteronomy 24 neither authorizes nor condones the practice of divorce, but when they come to Matthew 5:31–32 and 19:3–9 they feel constrained to explain how Jesus' teaching—exception clause and all—relates to Moses' teaching in

Deuteronomy 24. This approach to the New Testament divorce texts goes astray on two accounts: (1) it seems to slip back into the mistaken notion that Deuteronomy 24:1–3 stems from the "mind of Moses"; and (2) it is guilty of reading New Testament teaching back into the Old: it finds in the "defiled" of Deuteronomy 24:4 a reference to the adultery that is committed when someone divorces for reasons "*other* than the divine provision." Thus MacArthur writes: "Consistent with His claim in Matthew 5:17–18, Jesus affirms in verses 27–32 exactly what Moses is saying in Deuteronomy 24."[45]

In response to this line of reasoning, it is by no means certain that "defiled" in Deuteronomy 24:4 hints at the New Testament teaching that remarriage after an improper (or any) divorce amounts to adultery.[46] The phrase "after she has been defiled" may only mean "after she has consummated her marriage." This would mean that if a woman legally married a second husband after being sent away by the first but did not consummate the second marriage, she could still return to her original husband. Furthermore, once it is understood that Deuteronomy 24:1–4 is not concerned with divorce legislation nor with the impropriety of remarriage after divorce, but *is* concerned with a particular case of the restoration of a marriage, all attempts to make Jesus' teaching on divorce and remarriage agree with what Moses taught in Deuteronomy 24:1–4 are totally misdirected.

## F. Conclusion

One of the most serious shortcomings of popular evangelical approaches to the divorce question is the failure to see the relationship between the meaning of "one flesh" in Genesis 2:24, the Leviticus 18 legislation concerning forbidden unions, and the remarriage legislation of Deuteronomy 24:1–4. The preceding discussion has attempted to bring to the forefront of the biblical teaching on divorce and remarriage the importance of knowing exactly what the nature of the marriage relationship is. We found that Genesis 2:24 conveys two equally important concepts about marriage. Not only does marriage consist of a covenant; it also consists of a consummation, which results in husband and wife becoming "one flesh." The biblical kinship view of marriage was further illuminated by two other pieces of Old Testament legislation that, like Genesis 2:24, stems from the hand of Moses. We saw in Leviticus 18 that the relationships that come into being through marital relations with one's partner are not dissolved by his divorcing her or by her death. Finally, we found in Deuteronomy 24:1–4 that the kinship ("one flesh") aspect of marriage survives both legal divorce as well as subsequent sexual relations with a third party. That some kind of relationship still exists between the original couple is the very basis for the legislation found in Deuteronomy 24:4.

## III. NEW TESTAMENT TEACHING[47]

When it comes to the biblical teaching on divorce and remarriage, it is not an exaggeration to say that apart from a clear understanding of the Old Testament passages we will have little hope of resolving our differences over the debated New Testament texts (Matt. 19:9; 1 Cor. 7:15). But if we have properly understood the biblical kinship view of marriage as it is portrayed in the Old Testament—especially the texts from Genesis upon which Jesus based his own pronouncements on divorce and remarriage—then one will find it more difficult to interpret the debated New Testament texts in a way that allows remarriage after divorce than if we had not clarified the Old Testament teaching.

The teaching of the New Testament on divorce and remarriage may be summarized in the following statements.

1. God intends that marriage be a lifelong relationship. "What . . . God has joined together, let no man separate" (Matt. 19:6 NASB; see vv. 3–8; Mark 10:2–9).
2. Divorce followed by remarriage constitutes adultery (Matt. 5:32b; 10:11–12; Luke 16:18).
3. Married couples should not separate or divorce (1 Cor. 7:10).
4. In cases of separation or divorce, those involved must remain single or be reconciled (1 Cor. 7:11).
5. Divorce is a kind of adultery and leads the woman to commit adultery, except in the case of unchastity (Matt. 5:32a in the context of vv. 27–32: violations of the seventh commandment).
6. "Whoever divorces his wife, except for immorality, and marries another woman commits adultery" (Matt. 19:9 NASB).
7. The Christian spouse who is deserted by an unbeliever is "not under bondage" (1 Cor. 7:15 NASB).

Statements 1–4 present a unified picture of the permanence of the marriage union. Nowhere in the Gospels and in Paul do we find a clear and unambiguous mandate for remarriage after divorce, though statements 6 and 7 may come closest. Two other relatively clear passages from Paul not listed above agree particularly well with statement 2. These are the passages in which Paul plainly states that remarriage before the death of one's spouse is adultery (Rom. 7:2–3) and the passage in 1 Corinthians 7:39 where he specifically states that a Christian may remarry when his or her spouse has died (cf. vv. 8–9).

Only statements 5–7 appear to conflict with statements 1–4.

However, further consideration of statement 5 should reveal that
there is really no conflict between it and sayings 1–4. If lust is seen
as a breach of the seventh commandment, "adultery in the heart"
(Matt. 5:27–30), it is not surprising to find divorce condemned in
similar terms (vv. 31–32). The way that these two antitheses are
arranged under the topic of the seventh commandment indicates
that both "lust" and "divorce," when the divorce is not for
unchastity, violates the spirit of the seventh commandment, "You
shall not commit adultery" (v. 27). Remember that in the Jewish
marriage customs of Jesus' day the bill of divorce, once delivered,
guaranteed the freedom of the woman to remarry (v. 31). So
when Jesus says that the man who divorces his wife makes her
commit adultery, he is saying two things. First, Jesus is saying
that the bill of divorce does not do what the Jews thought it did: it
does not dissolve the marriage union. This is why remarriage is
adultery. Secondly—and there is complete consensus on this
point—Jesus' statement ("makes her commit adultery") points a
finger at the divorcing husband and makes him morally responsible for making his wife and her second husband commit adultery
against him.

But what is the meaning of the "except for unchastity" clause
in this context of sins that violate the spirit of the seventh
commandment? The answer to this question is not nearly as
complicated as some of the popular works on divorce and
remarriage have made it. The "except for unchastity" clause does
not need to mean any more than the fact that divorcing an
unchaste wife would not *make* her an adulteress, for she has *made
herself* an adulteress, adultery being the most common type of
sexual offense covered by the term "unchastity." The exception
clause here is simply a matter-of-fact recognition that if the wife
has already committed adultery, her husband cannot be held
guilty of driving her into it by divorcing her. *She* is the one who
will be held guilty of violating the seventh commandment in this
situation, not he.

This leaves only statements 6 and 7: Matthew 19:9 and
1 Corinthians 7:15. At the beginning of this paper I called
attention to the fact that Evangelicals cannot agree on the
interpretation of these passages. Does remarriage after divorce in
these situations amount to adultery or not? I suggested that
further discussion of these New Testament problem passages
would take us no further than we have already come in our
differences over them. So I proposed that a new approach was
needed, one that focused on that portion of the Scriptures Jesus
went to for his own understanding of the marriage relationship.
From my own study of the subject of divorce and remarriage it
appeared to me that virtually every existing evangelical work on
this subject had overlooked or was unaware of the two-pronged

nature of the marriage relationship as taught by Genesis 2:24 *and* elucidated by Leviticus 18 and Deuteronomy 24. This paper is a brief attempt aimed at clarifying how these Old Testament passages bear upon one another and help define in what way marriage is indissoluble.

Some have proposed that we should interpret the ideal (Gen. 2:24) in light of the exceptions (Matt. 19:9; 1 Cor. 7:15) and thereby permit divorce and remarriage in certain cases.[48] But this is a dangerous path to take if the ideal is not defined. For if the marriage bond is not dissolved by sexual sin nor by some ethical consideration ("What ought to be not always can be"), then in remarriage one commits adultery against his original spouse and in the sight of God. If, however, our interpretation of the biblical kinship view of marriage is correct, then we ought to be reluctant to interpret Matthew 19:9 in a sense that permits remarriage—a sense that is nowhere hinted at in the divorce sayings in the other Gospels. My preference is to interpret the debated exceptions[49] in light of the teaching of the Old Testament, which defines quite clearly what is meant by the ideal.

## IV. THE ISSUE OF REMARRIAGE AFTER DIVORCE

My own understanding of Matthew's exception clause is one that neither sanctions divorce for immorality nor permits remarriage should separation for marital unfaithfulness occur. The words of the exception clause were uttered in the context of Jewish marital laws, which looked upon a wife's unfaithfulness as making the continuation of marriage as quite impossible (cf. Matt. 1:18–19). In my understanding of the exception clause Jesus is not saying that "unchastity" ($\pi o\rho\nu\varepsilon\iota\alpha$) is the only ground for separating from a spouse. He is simply taking note of a situation that his disciples would encounter in the face of Jewish marriage customs that did not permit but *demanded* the divorce of an unfaithful adulterous wife. It is utterly arbitrary to define "unchastity" as denoting a lifestyle of immoral sexual behavior and then to permit divorce *and* remarriage in this situation.[50] It is one thing to advise separation or legal divorce when one's partner is involved in numerous immoral relationships (cf. 1 Cor. 5:11) or when the lives of the wife or the children are endangered; but there is a large gap that must be jumped between the idea that marital unfaithfulness results in a disruption of the love relationship (which may or may not be possible to forgive *and* resume) and the further idea that the offended partner is now free to enter into another marital union. If our understanding of the roots of Jesus' teaching in the Old Testament is correct, Jesus recognized that human hard-heartedness may well destroy the love relationship, but, in view of the indissolubility of the kinship relationship, he absolutely prohibited remarriage.

If Jesus called remarriage adultery, then the believer's highest blessing lies in another direction. Where reconciliation with a mate is impossible, a believer must trust in the infinitely good God who knows his or her situation and yet points to a life of singleness (cf. Matt. 19:9–12; 1 Cor. 7:11a, 32–35) as the path of greatest fulfillment and highest blessing. Fellow believers must be ready to help and financially support in whatever ways possible the divorced person who seeks to honor his or her Lord by being obedient to Jesus' teaching that his disciples do not remarry after divorce (Matt. 19:9–12).

What about those who have already remarried after divorce? I believe that you should view your present marriage as God's will for you. Deuteronomy 24:4 actually says that it would be an abomination for you to return to your previous spouse now that you have consummated your marriage to another. Seek to be the best husband or wife you can be, rendering to each other your full marital duty. If you come to the realization that Jesus calls remarriage after divorce adultery, then call sin "sin" rather than seek to justify what you have done. I believe this will bring about great freedom in your own marriage and that it will break down barriers to ministry you may have encountered before. Those who remarry after divorce and have repented of their sin can count on God's forgiveness (cf. 1 Cor. 6:9–11) and his grace and his mercy. They cannot, however, claim his highest blessing even though he may still bestow it upon them.

While there are some Christians who will live their lives and do as they please in the matter of divorce and remarriage, many Christians sincerely desire to know God's will for them—whether they are happily or unhappily married, separated or legally divorced, or remarried. This paper has been written for those who wrestle with the biblical teaching on divorce and remarriage and who seek to be obedient to what their Lord taught, no matter what it may cost them in terms of the "happiness" the world offers. They can be confident that God's ways are good and perfect for them (cf. Ps. 19:7–14). Part of the problem behind divorce and remarriage among Christians today is the confusion that exists over the nature and permanence of the marriage union and the degree to which human hard-heartedness disrupts this ideal. By examining the Old Testament roots of Jesus' teaching, I have sought to clarify the way in which he viewed marriage as indissoluble. The biblical evidence leads me to the conclusion that human sin may disrupt or violate or even permanently cut off restoration of the marital *love* relationship; but human sin does not destroy the covenanted and consummated marital *kinship* relationship, which has been joined by God. This is why Jesus calls all remarriage adultery. The scandal of divorce and remarriage among Christians affects far more than the individuals and the families involved. Obedience to Christ's teaching on this matter affects the purity, power, and witness of the Christian church (cf. 1 Cor. 5:1–8) in our world, which is badly in need of the Savior.

# ENDNOTES

[1] G. Bromiley, *God and Marriage* (Grand Rapids: Eerdmans, 1980), p. 41.

[2] Murray's conclusions were first given to the public in six issues of *The Westminster Theological Journal* (1946–49). Many of Murray's arguments, however, are already found in R. H. Charles, *The Teaching of the New Testament on Divorce* (London: Wms. & Norgate, 1921). Those who follow Murray's reasoning today understand πορνεία in Matthew 5:32 and 19:9 to include a wider range of sexual sins than just adultery. Cf. G. Duty, *Divorce and Remarriage* (Minneapolis: Bethany, 1967), pp. 52–62; J. R. W. Stott, "The Biblical Teaching on Divorce," *Churchman* 85 (1971): 165–74; C. Brown, s.v. "χωρίζω: Divorce, Separation and Remarriage," *The New International Dictionary of the New Testament Theology*, ed. C. Brown, 3 vols. (Grand Rapids: Zondervan, 1975–78), 3:534–43, esp. p. 538; D. Atkinson, *To Have and To Hold* (Grand Rapids: Eerdmans, 1981), p. 118; and J. Adams, *Marriage, Divorce and Remarriage in the Bible* (Phillipsburg, N.J.: Presbyterian and Reformed, 1980), pp. 6, 51–55. Both J. MacArthur, Jr. (*The Family* [Chicago: Moody, 1982], pp. 107–28) and C. Swindoll (*Divorce* [Portland, Ore.: Multnomah, 1981]) would tend to see in πορνεία a sustained form of adulterous behavior.

[3] S. A. Ellisen, *Divorce and Remarriage in the Church* (Grand Rapids: Zondervan, 1977), pp. 49–59; and G. L. Archer, *Encyclopedia of Bible Difficulties* (Grand Rapids: Zondervan, 1982), pp. 399–400.

[4] Bromiley, *God and Marriage*, pp. 38–46, 66–68.

[5] J. C. Laney, *The Divorce Myth* (Minneapolis: Bethany, 1981); P. E. Steele and C. C. Ryrie, *Meant to Last* (Wheaton, Ill.: Victor Books, 1983); and W. A. Heth and G. J. Wenham, *Jesus and Divorce* (Nashville: Thomas Nelson, 1985).

[6] Adams (*Divorce and Remarriage*, pp. 88–91), for example, permits an innocent Christian wife to remarry if her Christian husband divorces her for reasons of incompatibility and refuses to be reconciled to her when the church discipline steps of Matthew 15:15–17 are fully carried out; the excommunicated, unrepentant husband falls under the 1 Corinthians 7:15 situation: faithful Christians who are deserted may marry.

[7] Evangelical writers who allow one or more grounds for divorce and remarriage continue to use this term, yet never do they discuss in what sense marriage is supposed to be indissoluble. Ellisen, for example, repeatedly states that the sin of adultery "breaks" or "dissolves" the one-flesh union of husband and wife (*Divorce and Remarriage*, pp. 52–53, 58, 68, 72, 97–99). Ellisen mentions "one flesh" at least five times but never once tells us the nature of it and in what sense it is dissolved!

[8] I discussed this point earlier in "The Meaning of Divorce in Matt. 19:3–9," *Churchman* 98 (1984): 136–52. Cf. also Heth and Wenham *Jesus and Divorce*, pp. 100–113. In the present study the discussion of Genesis 2:24 is developed in far greater detail, and some new points are added to the discussion of Deuteronomy 24:1–4.

[9] MacArthur (*Family*, pp. 109–10), for example, says that Genesis 2:24c "means the man and woman are indivisibly joined: one is the indivisible number! They are one—spiritually, socially and sexually." Explanations like these miss the crucial concept about the nature of marriage, a concept that other pieces of Old Testament legislation actually take up and build upon. See note 7 also.

10I have found two writers especially enlightening on the Old Testament teaching: from a theological perspective, Bromiley (*God and Marriage*, pp. 1–34); and from the legal/exegetical perspective, G. J. Wenham, "The Biblical View of Marriage and Divorce 1—Cultural Background," *Third Way*, October 20, 1977, pp. 3–5; and "2—Old Testament Teaching," *Third Way*, November 3, 1977, pp. 7–9.

11Although space will not permit, ideally I would like to have covered the following passages in the following order: Genesis 1:26–28; 2:18–25; Exodus 20:14, 17 (cf. Prov. 2:16–17); Leviticus 18, 20; 21:4–15 (cf. 1 Tim. 3:2, 12; Titus 1:6); Numbers 5:11–31; Deuteronomy 22:13–29 (cf. vv. 28–29 with Exod. 22:16–17); 24:1–4; Hosea 1–3; Ezra 9–10; Malachi 2:10–16; Mark 10:1–12; Luke 16:18; Matthew 5:32; 19:3–12; Romans 7:1–3 (cf. 1 Cor. 7:39); 1 Corinthians 6:12–20; 7:8–16, 25–38 (esp. vv. 25–28). I have been told by a number of people that sitting down with pen and paper to read and make observations on all of these passages has done the most to clarify in their minds what the Scriptures teach about divorce and remarriage.

12J. Murray, *Principles of Conduct* (Grand Rapids: Eerdmans, 1957), p. 15. "Progressive revelation, progressive realization of redemption, and progressive disclosure of the grace of the Spirit have been the method by which God's redemptive purpose in the world has been fulfilled" (ibid., pp. 18–19).

13In addition to the major commentaries on Genesis 1–2, see the excellent treatment by S. B. Clark, *Man and Woman in Christ* (Ann Arbor: Servant, 1980), pp. 9–23. Clark is especially helpful in correcting the mistaken idea that man's "aloneness" in Genesis 2:18 refers to his "loneliness" (so Ellisen, *Divorce and Remarriage*, pp. 28, 69–70; MacArthur, *Family*, p. 54). Adams, in fact, goes straight to Genesis 2:18 for his definition of marriage. He says "*Companionship*, . . . is the essence of marriage," and from this he defines divorce as "the repudiation and breaking of that covenant (or agreement) in which both parties promised to provide companionship (in all its ramifications) for one another. A divorce is, in effect, a declaration that these promises are no longer expected, required or permitted" (*Divorce and Remarriage*, pp. 8, 32; cf. E. Dobson, "What Is Marriage?" *Fundamentalist Journal*, September 1985, pp. 40–41). Adams is reading Genesis 2:18 with modern-day psychologically tinted glasses. Man's "aloneness" here is not his "loneliness" but his "helplessness," his inability, apart from the woman, to carry out God's creation directives (Gen. 1:28) to perpetuate and multiply the race and to cultivate and govern the earth.

14A. F. Johnson, "Is There a Biblical Warrant for Natural-Law Theories?" *Journal of the Evangelical Theological Society* 25 (1982): 191.

15Both concepts correspond for the most part to the essentials of marriage in its simplest form; these involve "(*a*) an intention of the parties to enter into a binding marital union and (*b*) actual consummation. Neither the mere intention nor the sexual act was in itself sufficient. Intention would be indicated by conduct such as courtship or by promises or other expressions aiming at an immediate union" (E. Neufeld, *Ancient Hebrew Marriage Laws* [London: Longman's, Green & Co., 1944], p. 89).

16Cf. G. Wallis, s.v. "דָּבַק," *TDOT* 3 (1978): 80–81, and W. Brueggemann, "Of the Same Flesh and Bone (Gen. 2:23a)," *Catholic Biblical Quarterly* 32 (1970): 532–42, esp. 540.

17Cf. S. Greengus, "The Old Babylonian Marriage Contract," *Journal of the American Oriental Society* 89 (1969): 515. The fact that Ruth's words in Ruth 1:16b–17 closely resemble ancient Near Eastern marriage contracts and adoption documents further suggests that "cleave" here is the language of covenant (cf. M. Weinfeld, "The Covenant of Grant in the Old Testament and in the Ancient Near East," *Journal of American Oriental Society* 90 [1970]: 194, and Greengus, pp. 515–21, esp. p. 521).

18E. S. Kalland, s.v. "דָּבַק," in *Theological Wordbook of the Old Testament*, ed. R. L. Harris, 2 vols. (Chicago: Moody, 1980), 1:178.

19 R. E. Showers (*Lawfully Wedded* [Philadelphia College of the Bible Publication, 1983], p. 8), following K. L. Schmidt (s.v. "κολλάω προσκολλάω," *TDNT* 3 [1965] pp. 822–23), believes (προσ) κολλάω refers to sexual union in Matthew 19:5 and Mark 10:7 (longer reading preferred). Both Wallis (*TDOT* 3, p. 81) and Schmidt (*TDNT* 3, p. 822) agree that דָּבַק never has a sexual sense in the Old Testament, yet both go on to say that κολλάω and προσκολλάω acquire this sense in the New Testament (Matt. 19:5, Mark 10:7; 1 Cor. 6:16; Eph. 5:31). There is virtually no basis for such an assertion. Only in 1 Corinthians 6:16 might κολλάω have a sexual sense, but even this is doubtful. Note the parallel use of κολλάω in verse 17, and see Heth and Wenham, *Jesus and Divorce*, p. 240, n. 104.

20 C. Westermann, *Genesis 1–11*, trans. J. J. Scullion (Minneapolis: Augsburg, 1984), p. 234.

21 In arriving at a biblical theology of divorce and remarriage it is totally inappropriate to appeal to passages like Isaiah 50:1 and Jeremiah 3:8 (cf. T. Crater, "Bill Gothard's View of the Exception Clause," *Journal of Pastoral Practice* 4/3 [1980]: 9–10) to justify the propriety of certain views of divorce *and* remarriage arrived at in the New Testament. Though polygamy and divorce were concessions to hard-heartedness in the Old Testament, they were nevertheless relational customs that carried meaning for the people of that day. Thus God can and does use these familiar social customs to represent his relationship with Israel (Jer. 3:1, 6–10). But Jesus' saying on divorce and remarriage utterly altered this Old Testament stance.

22 F. I. Andersen and D. N. Freedman, *Hosea*, Anchor Bible (Garden City: Doubleday, 1980), p. 220. D. H. Small ("The Prophet Hosea: God's Alternative to Divorce for the Reason of Infidelity," *Journal of Psychology and Theology* 7 [1979]: 133–40) lists ten reasons why it cannot be said that Hosea "divorced" Gomer.

23 Andersen and Freedman, *Hosea*, p. 221.

24 D. N. Freedman, "Divine Commitment and Human Obligation," *Interpretation* 18 (1964): 429.

25 A valuable unpublished study on this subject is R. S. Westcott, "The Concept of *berit* with Regard to Marriage in the Old Testament" (Th.M. thesis, Dallas Theological Seminary, 1985).

26 "The Concept of *berit*," pp. 83–84. First Corinthians 7:15 would suggest that such legal action is not appropriate for marriages where the husband or wife is not a Christian.

27 Cf. BDB, s.v. "בָּשָׂר," 4, p. 142; F. Baumgärtel, s.v. "σάρξ," *TDNT* 7 (1971): p. 106; and N. P. Bratsiotis, s.v. "בָּשָׂר," *TDOT* 2 (1977): pp. 327–28.

28 Cf. W. Reiser, "Die Verwandtschaftsformel in Genesis 2:23," *Theologische Zeitschrift* 16 (1960): 1–4.

29 Cf. Heth, "Meaning of Divorce," p. 151, n. 30; and Heth and Wenham, *Jesus and Divorce*, p. 229, n. 8.

30 Marriage agreements in the ancient Near East consisted of two parts: oaths/vows and witnesses. I would like to suggest that a marriage covenant with no witnesses to it (i.e., a secret marriage) is no covenant. On the other hand, I tend to believe that common-law marriages in states that recognize them are genuine marriages if the couple give every indication they view themselves as married and are living together as husband and wife and it is obvious to others.

31 I agree with the view that "if a physical union does not . . . take place, then the marriage is not a true marriage and it can rightly be annulled" (J. M. Boice, *Genesis*, 3 vols. [Grand Rapids: Zondervan, 1982], 1:111). In those few cases where consummation is not possible (due to war injuries, certain forms of paralysis, and other circumstances beyond one's control), however, the marriage, in God's sight, would seem to be nothing less than a genuine marriage.

32 S. A. Ellisen, *Divorce and Remarriage*, p. 58; and D. A. Carson, "Matthew," in *The Expositor's Bible Commentary*, 12 vols., ed. F. E. Gaebelein (Grand Rapids: Zondervan, 1984), 8:417.

33 Cf. G. J. Wenham, *The Book of Leviticus*, New International Commentary on the Old Testament (Grand Rapids: Eerdmans, 1979), p. 255; and R. K. Harrison,

*Leviticus: An Introduction and Commentary*, Tyndale Old Testament Commentaries (Downers Grove: InterVarsity, 1980), p. 186. Philo leads into his exposition of the Mosaic incest laws after making the statement: "For intermarriages with outsiders create new kinships not a wit inferior to blood-relationships" (*Special Laws*, 3.25).

[34]See note 27 above.

[35]Cf. Wenham, *Leviticus*, p. 253; and Neufeld, *Marriage Laws*, pp. 191–93.

[36]Neufeld, *Marriage Laws*, pp. 193–94.

[37]Cf. Murray, *Principles*, pp. 49–54. Murray, however, was not aware of the connection between the "one flesh" of Genesis 2:24 and the forbidden degrees of kinship.

[38]Murray, *Divorce*, p. 41. Cf. Duty, *Divorce and Remarriage*, pp. 32–44; and R. L. Saucy, "The Husband of One Wife," *Bibliotheca Sacra* 131 (1974): 232–33.

[39]For this, see the discussion and literature cited in Heth and Wenham, *Jesus and Divorce*, pp. 89–90, 106–10.

[40]G. J. Wenham, "The Restoration of Marriage Reconsidered," *Journal of Jewish Studies* 30 (1979): 40. Wenham's interpretation has been both quoted with approval (A. Phillips, "Another Look at Adultery," *Journal for the Study of the Old Testament* 20 [1981]: 14; and C. D. Stoll, *Ehe und Ehescheidung: Die Weisungen Jesu* [Giessen: Brunnen, 1983], pp. 15, 44) and essentially adopted (W. C. Kaiser, Jr., *Toward Old Testament Ethics* [Grand Rapids: Zondervan, 1983], pp. 202–3).

[41]For a discussion of the more periphrastic sexual terminology found in Deuteronomy's corresponding portions to Leviticus, see A. Isaksson, *Marriage and Ministry in the New Temple*, trans. N. Tomkinson with J. Gray, ASNU 24 (Lund: Gleerup, 1965), p. 26.

[42]Did the Pharisees who debated with Jesus in Matthew 19/Mark 10 understand the one-flesh concept that we have been discussing? Philo (about 20 B.C.–A.D. 45) seems to know that marriage results in kinship relationships (see note 33), but elsewhere he argues that it is the legal documents that make a betrothal or a marriage (*Special Laws* 3.72). L. M. Epstein's (*Marriage Laws in the Bible and the Talmud*, HSS 12 [Cambridge: Harvard University Press, 1942], p. 294–95) discussion of rabbinic *halakah* surrounding the prohibition of Deuteronomy 24:4 also evidences the rabbis' preoccupation with legal documents almost to the exclusion of the importance of the physical union. Thus it seems that "most of the rabbis did not share the OT idea that sexual intercourse is what creates the relationship" (Wenham, "Cultural Background," p. 5).

[43]Cf. L. Richards, *Remarriage: A Healing Gift from God* (Waco: Word, 1981), pp. 19, 21–22. Scholars who hastily interpret Deuteronomy 24 in this way then find that Jesus is abrogating this "Mosaic" legislation in both Matthew 5:31–32 and in the Matthew 19/Mark 10 passages (cf. S. F. Wilson, *Luke and the Law*, SNTSMS 50 [Cambridge: University Press, 1984], p. 30; and D. O. Via, Jr., *The Ethics of Mark's Gospel—In the Middle of Time* [Philadelphia: Fortress, 1985], p. 101). Moses, of course, never gave any legislation regarding divorce procedures. Thus Jesus could not have revoked something that Moses never provided.

[44]The certificate of divorce almost certainly did not arise within biblical law. This is suggested by the observation that כְּרִיתֻת in סֵפֶר כְּרִיתֻת (lit., "document of cutting") has been traced back to a formula of divorce in early Babylonian law (J. J. Rabinowitz, *Jewish Law* [New York: Bloch, 1956], pp. 6–7). The verb כָּרַת (BDB, pp. 503–4) is never used in the Bible in connection with divorce. "The occurrence of the abstract noun, not derived from a verb connected with divorce, in the expression 'bill of divorce' suggests that the bill of divorce did not develop within Biblical law, but was imported from abroad. An indigenous term, based upon biblical usage, would have been *sepher šillihim*, or *gerušim*, or better *sepher śinah*" (R. Yaron, "On Divorce in Old Testament Times," *Revue Internationale des Droits de l'Antiquité* 3 [1957]: 127).

[45]MacArthur, *Family*, p. 118. Cf. Charles, *Teaching*, pp. 16–17; and Adams, *Divorce and Remarriage*, pp. 62–68.

[46] In contrast to MacArthur's approach, Murray (*Divorce*, pp. 14–15, 41–42) is careful *not* to characterize the wife's second marriage in Deuteronomy 24:1–4 as adulterous.

[47] More complete discussions of all the points made in the New Testament section of this paper can be found in the relevant sections of Heth and Wenham, *Jesus and Divorce*.

[48] Cf. "Requests to Remarry: The Pastor's Catch-22," *Leadership* 4/3 (1983): 111–21. The position of Robert Wise in this forum is, in my opinion, confusing and dangerously free from any biblical boundaries. Jesus does give believers moral standards that, by God's grace, he expects them to fulfill. I am most comfortable with the advice of J. Hardin Boyer and find many valuable points in Harold Ivan Smith's responses.

[49] The interpretation of 1 Corinthians 7:15 is really dependent upon what we decide about Matthew 19:9. From 1 Corinthians 7:10–11 it appears that Paul shared Jesus' interpretation of the marriage relationship. Furthermore, Genesis 2:24 refers to the binding nature of the marriage relationship irrespective of one's faith or the lack thereof. Marriage is a creation ordinance binding on Christians and non-Christians alike.

[50] In my understanding of the exception clause it is also unnecessary to justify grounds for separation in cases of wife beating by trying to find out if the interpersonal violations by wife battering are comparable to those brought on by adultery (cf. G. P. Liaboe, "The Place of Wife Battering in Considering Divorce," *Journal of Psychology and Theology* 13 [1985]: 129–38). It is hard to imagine someone teaching that Jesus forbids separation even when the wife's life is in danger. This further shows the improbability that by the exception clause Jesus intended to mark off specific grounds for separating from a spouse.

# A Response to
# Divorce and Remarriage

## Harold W. Hoehner

This is not the first work Dr. Heth has done on the subject of divorce and remarriage. He researches his topic well by reading the various sources which present several perspectives. He is fair both with those who agree and with those who disagree with him.

This particular paper is no exception. One can see that he is aware of the current literature, not only on the topic, but also on areas that relate to it. He interacts with the literature fairly. He wants most of all to see what the biblical text has to say on this subject. He does not like to have any views be labeled "loose" or "strict" because of the danger of emotional overtones. He is gentle with those who hold and have practiced that which is in opposition to his view. Specifically, since he has no place for remarriage after divorce, he feels that those who have already remarried are to confess their wrong and continue, rather than undo, their marriage.

Heth thinks that no one has really dealt adequately with the concept of "one flesh" and its implications for the marriage bond. It is good that he did take the time to look in passages that so often are assumed and as a result may have been passed over.

However, there is a need to take a second look at the three major passages Heth discusses. The first major passage is Genesis 2:24, which states that when one marries he shall *leave* his father and his mother, and shall *cleave* to his wife and the two shall become *one flesh*. In dealing with the *leave* and *cleave* language, Heth suggests that it embodies covenant terminology. His illustration of this is Ruth, who left her country Moab and cleaved to Naomi. Ruth promised never to leave her new partner, Naomi (Ruth 1:16–17), yet she left Naomi for Boaz. Does this mean she broke her covenant relationship with Naomi? On the contrary, this is a clear indication that there are different types of covenants, and each must be considered on its own merit.

Heth goes on to illustrate that God's covenant relationship with Israel was never broken, regardless of how wicked the people were. There is no reason to believe that what is true for a governmental covenant between God and Israel is completely analogous to a covenant between two people. Heth states that marriage between two people is a covenant and also consummation through sexual union. Heth seems to want it both ways, for he states earlier that the "one-flesh" concept in Genesis 2:24 has no sexual significance, and then later he states that there is no "one flesh" unless there is both the covenant and the consummation through sexual union. On the one hand, his analysis of Genesis 2:24 having no sexual significance is unwarranted, for the whole context is about the woman being created out of man, man leaving father and mother and cleaving to his wife, and both being unashamed of their nakedness. To suggest that there is no sexual significance in the term "cleave" seems to ignore this context. On the other hand, it is incorrect to insist that a one-flesh concept is not feasible unless there is both a covenant and consummation through sexual union. Paul quotes Genesis 2:24 as a proof text to show that merely a sexual encounter with a harlot is considered a one-flesh union (1 Cor. 6:16). In this case, there is no marriage covenant at all, yet the two are considered one flesh. Therefore, "one flesh" evidently involves sexual relationship in Genesis 2:24 as Paul's quotation of that text in 1 Corinthians 6:16 demonstrates.

The next thing Heth attempts to establish is that the one-flesh relationship in the marriage corresponds to Adam's declaration, at the creation of his wife, Eve, "bone of my bones, and flesh of my flesh" (Gen. 2:23). However, it must be realized that Eve was created out of Adam, whereas every other wife is not created out of her husband. Heth cites several passages where this formula is used in the Old Testament to indicate a kinship relationship. The proof texts cited (Gen. 29:14; Judg. 9:1–2; 2 Sam. 5:1; 19:12–13) do not apply to the husband and wife relationship, because each of these speaks of blood relatives, whereas the husband and wife are not blood relatives. Hence, the idea of one flesh indicating kinship is plausible with respect to blood relatives. The one-flesh idea is to denote a solidarity between husband and wife such as there is between blood relatives, but without actually being blood relatives. When interpreting any given passage, one must allow a metaphor to remain as a metaphor.

The second major passage is Leviticus 18:6–18 (cf. also 20:11–12, 14, 17, 19–21; Deut. 22:30; 27:20, 22–23) where he tries to show that exposing nakedness in the family is not only on literal blood lines but also on kinship relationships created through marriage. Although this is true, it does not prove that husband and wife have become brother and sister, and the Old Testament never speaks of them as such. Thus the family relationships are indeed enlarged through marriage, but it is by marriage not adoption that they become brother and sister.

Heth also makes a point that because one has a kinship relationship due to the marriage, one cannot marry relatives of the spouse for it would be counted as incest. What about the levirate marriage? If a married man died without a son, his brother was to go into the widow to raise up seed for him (Deut. 25:5–10; cf. Gen. 38:8–10). This would, according to Heth's view, be an incestuous relationship. Of course, one may reply that the brother had died. However, if as Heth suggests, this brother is a blood relative, how can he marry his sister? Since God would not command an incestuous relationship, the blood relationship theory cannot be valid. Heth specifically states: "he became related to her close female relatives, and should his wife die or should he divorce her, he could not marry them, for that would be a form of incest." But when one reads Leviticus 18:18, it states that he cannot marry the wife's sister "while the wife is alive," which implies that it is all right to marry the sister-in-law after the wife's death. Heth appears to be reading into the Scriptures more than is actually intended.

Finally, a small but important point: Heth wants to make the Mosaic legislation in Leviticus 18 binding today. What about the Mosaic legislation in the near context, such as Leviticus 16 (Day of Atonement) or in the other chapters he cited: Leviticus 20 (clean and unclean foods), Deuteronomy 22 (laws in building houses and not mixing crops), and Deuteronomy 27 (building an altar on Mount Ebal)? It is not possible to use one part of the Mosaic legislation as a proof text unless there is a willingness to accept the other parts as binding for today. Otherwise this becomes subjective and dangerous as each person selects as he wishes.

The third major passage is Deuteronomy 24:1–4. His main point here is that a wife cannot come back to her first husband after she has been married to another man because she would be marrying back into the family, creating an incestuous relationship. The text does not indicate this, and Heth has not established that any terms in the text imply this. The text merely states that such an action is an abomination before the Lord. It may well be that a woman who was divorced from her first husband, possibly because of some indecency, and marries another is not to be trusted, and thus God forbids it for the first husband's protection and purity. Another explanation is that it may be for her protection so that she not be passed back and forth like a piece of property. Or possibly it may be given as a restraint on breaking up the first marriage by remarrying, so that the parties would realize that they could never get back together if a new marriage union was formed. Perhaps this principle influenced Paul in his instructions that one should remain unmarried or be reconciled (1 Cor. 7:11). If he or she remarries, then he or she can never be reconciled in marriage to the first spouse. Regardless, if Heth's view that the first marriage is never dissolved is correct, it seems strange that the original marriage partners are forbidden to remarry even after the death of the second spouse.

Furthermore, Heth makes an unwarranted leap in dealing with this passage by stating that marriage creates not only a vertical blood relationship (through the procreation of children) but also a horizontal one (partners become one flesh), which means that the husband and wife are related to each other in flesh and blood. When would they become related to each other in flesh and blood? Is it at the time of their divorce? If it is at the time of their marriage, then would it not be an incestuous marriage? A couple is one flesh but not one flesh and blood. Hence, a marriage is a "one-flesh" relationship, but that is not the same as a "flesh-and-blood" relationship.

Does not the episode of Hosea and his wife bear this out? She played the harlot with other men, yet God told Hosea to bring her back. It is true that she did not officially divorce Hosea, but she had a relationship with others, and yet she was to go back to Hosea. God was not commanding Hosea to commit incest, was he?

Heth then proceeds to discuss briefly divorce in the Old Testament. He says that there are two common errors made among interpreters. The first error is to deduce from Deuteronomy 24:1–4 that the bill of divorce was instituted by Moses. Heth's point has some validity; nevertheless, apparently there was the bill of divorce, and hence it was practiced, and Moses cites legislation relating to the existing conditions. Legislation such as given in Deuteronomy 24:1–4 was built on concrete cases. He does not condemn the bill of divorce as something that is not allowed in Israel. Yes, divorce is not God's ideal, but still the bill of divorce was not condemned even though it was not the ideal. The practice of the bill of divorce was used in later Old Testament history (Isa. 50:1; Jer. 3:8) and in New Testament times (Matt. 5:31; 19:7).

Second, Heth thinks it is wrong to assume from Deuteronomy 24:1–4 that the "some indecency" (עֶרְוַה דָּבָר, 'erwah dābār) is the same thing as "fornication" in Matthew 5:31–32 and 19:9. Certainly the fornication mentioned in the two passages in Matthew would fit within the rubric of "some indecency" in the case study in Deuteronomy. This is not saying that Moses created the law for divorce in Deuteronomy 24:1–3, but it is also true that the religious leaders in questioning Jesus were thinking of this Old

Testament passage and were setting up the same scenario. Jesus and the religious teachers were working with a passage that was familiar to all. This being the case, it does not seem unreasonable to think that "fornication" fits easily within the category of "indecency" in Deuteronomy.

In the revival mentioned in Ezra (10:3–5, 10–19) the men put away their foreign wives. Does this mean that they did not remarry within the nation? The text does not explicitly state whether or not they did remarry. However, it seems strange that there were no explicit instructions for them not to marry Israelite women, thus raising children to keep the nation pure. In the Semitic world it was a shame not to be married. Their not marrying again would not help in keeping the race pure but would actually thwart the purpose of raising up seed from a pure stock.

In conclusion, I do not believe that it has been established from the Old Testament passages that the concept of "one flesh" with respect to husband and wife is the same as the flesh and blood of relatives. Whereas the flesh-and-blood relationship can be dissolved, the fact that there is a bill of divorcement that is mentioned in the case study in Deuteronomy 24 indicates that there was a dissolving of marriage relationships of such significance that Moses decreed that the first marriage could not be reconsummated—that is, that it was permanently dissolved.

Contrary to Heth's conclusion, there was still an allowance for divorce and remarriage; and under certain circumstances, nothing was specifically commanded against this. The only person who was commanded not to marry a divorced woman was a priest (Lev. 21:7, 14), which certainly implies that other men could marry divorced women. Certainly divorce and remarriage are due to the hardness of men's hearts, and even though God said that he hates divorce (Mal. 2:16), yet he did not condemn them as he did, for example, homosexual relationships. It might be argued that homosexuality was due to the hardness of the heart, but God commanded that such partners were to be put to death (Lev. 18:22; 20:13), a sanction never applied to divorce and remarriage.

Much more emphasis should be placed on the New Testament teaching of the subject. Clearly one needs to turn to Matthew 5:32 and especially 19:9. When one reads Matthew 19:9 without the exception clause it is no different than what is given in Mark 10:11 and Luke 16:18—namely, that whoever divorces his wife and marries another commits adultery. Mark adds that the reverse is true as well, and Matthew 5:32 and Luke add that whoever marries a divorced woman commits adultery.

Since both passages in Matthew have the exception clause, the situation is altered when that exception occurs. There is much debate as to the nature of the exception clause and what is meant by πορνεία (porneia). A word study of πορνεία, reveals that it is not the same as μοιχεία (moicheia), adultery. Certainly, one who commits μοιχεία commits πορνεία, but the reverse is not necessarily true, for πορνεία is used of an incestuous relationship in 1 Corinthians 5:1; this is not regarded as μοιχεία on the part of the unmarried man. The term πορνεία means an illicit physical sexual act; that would include illicit sexual relationships involving a married person with an unmarried person (Gen. 38:24; Hos. 2:4–5), an incestuous relationship (1 Cor. 5:1), or (its most frequent use) sexual indecency without specifying the marital status (e.g., Num. 14:33; Matt. 15:19; Mark 7:21; 1 Cor. 6:18; 7:2; Gal. 5:19; 1 Thess. 4:3; Rev. 9:21; 17:2, 4). The simple fact stated in Matthew 5:32 and 19:9 is that when one divorces and marries another there is an adulterous situation, with the exception of a divorce and remarriage where there was the occurrence of πορνεία. To say that Matthew has the exception clause because of Matthew's Jewish audience is begging the question. Matthew is reporting what Jesus said. If Jesus said it, it does not matter in which Gospel it appears. Regardless of which Gospel it appears in, if Jesus said it, he said it to a Jewish audience. Why the other Gospels omit it and Matthew includes it has not been indicated. However, what is clear is that Jesus is prohibiting indiscriminate divorce and remarriage in all the Gospel accounts, and this is common to them all. The exception clause does not take away this commonality or change this emphasis. It simply makes an exception. Heth's statement that Jesus "absolutely prohibited remarriage in the view of the indissolubility of the kinship relationship" is misleading, for Jesus, in discussing the Deuteronomy 24 passage with the Jewish leaders, appears to have assumed with them that there was remarriage after divorce; and he stated that it was considered adultery unless there was fornication by the unfaithful partner. Essentially Heth ignores the exception clause. If Jesus had not stated the exception clause, then Heth would have a clear case. But Jesus stated the exception clause, and it must be heeded. Furthermore, the exception is relating to the remarriage as much as to the divorce. It is Jesus' own exception to his otherwise absolute prohibition of divorce and remarriage.

The other New Testament passage that needs to be considered is 1 Corinthians 7:12–16. If the unbelieving partner wants to stay with the believing spouse, the Christian is not to break up the marriage. However, if the unbelieving partner wants to separate, the believing spouse is to allow it and is not bound. There is debate regarding the meaning "to be bound," but the most natural sense is that the believing partner is not bound to the marriage covenant and is free to remarry (cf. the analogous language in 7:39). This applies only in the case of an unbelieving partner wanting a divorce. In the case of the two believers, the only options are separation (and possibly not divorce) or reunion with one another but not remarriage to another person (1 Cor. 7:10–11). Hence, divorce and remarriage are restricted in this context to couples in which one of the partners is not a Christian and in which the unbelieving partner breaks up the marriage.

In conclusion, it seems that Heth has overstated the case of the one-flesh relationship as being irrevocably permanent. It is true that God's standard is that the married couple who are one flesh should remain together until the death of one of them. This is what every Christian couple should attempt to achieve in their own marriage and should encourage others to do also. When looking at the Old Testament and New Testament passages, it seems that the plain assumption and teaching allows for divorce and remarriage without the idea that those involved are living in adultery, if due to fornication or desertion on the part of the unbelieving partner. This does not mean that if one's partner has committed fornication that the other partner should immediately sue for divorce. The whole tone of the Bible is one of forgiveness. However, if there is no desire on the part of the erring partner to change his or her ways, then the "innocent" partner can divorce and remarry without being considered adulterous. Surely that partner can choose to remain unmarried but also has the option to remarry without being stigmatized as living in adultery.[1]

## ENDNOTES

[1] I want to thank Darrell Bock and David Lowery of the New Testament Department at Dallas Theological Seminary, George Knight of the New Testament Department at Covenant Theological Seminary, and Philip Jensen and Timothy Savage, candidates for the Ph.D. at Cambridge University, for their helpful insights and comments after reading the early stages of the response. I am also indebted to the many commentators and authors of articles written on this subject, but I did not specifically mention them because this is a response to an article rather than the proposal of a thesis and because of the length allowed for a response.

# A Response to
# Divorce and Remarriage

### Ray C. Stedman

The paper entitled "Divorce and Remarriage" by William A. Heth is clearly intended to pursue a hither untrodden path in defending the position that the Bible does not permit remarriage after divorce no matter what the ground of the divorce. He seeks to establish the position from the Old Testament, rather than from the New, arguing from Genesis 2:24; Leviticus 18:6–18; and Deuteronomy 24:1–4. The author pursues his argument with commendable grace, recognizing from the beginning the heated debates that have raged over this issue, and invites dissent ("Correctives would be greatly appreciated").

From Genesis 2:24 the author properly establishes marriage as constituting both a covenant (leave and cleave) and a consummation (one flesh). He sees the covenant as unbreakable (using God's covenant with Israel as an example), and the consummation as establishing a permanent bond. Thus, he argues, marriage was clearly intended to be permanent, and in the eyes of God, nothing breaks it, even sexual infidelity or divorce.

But let us examine these claims. No one, of course, argues the point that God's intent in marriage was to form a permanent bond. This is as clear as the biblical statement: "God is not willing that any should perish." But like that statement it leaves unexplained the fact that humans do perish and marriages do end in divorce, each occurring within the limits of God's permissive will.

The argument that God's covenant with Israel is an example of the unbreakable nature of a covenant is not well taken, for it ignores the fact that Israel's restoration to God's favor rests, not on the original covenant made through Moses, but on the new covenant of which Jeremiah speaks so eloquently in Jeremiah 31,

247

and which the writer of Hebrews refers to in Hebrews 8. Israel did break God's original covenant with them, and God did cast them off as a chosen people (cf. "not my people" in Hosea), using the symbol of divorce. Their restoration rests wholly on the new covenant.

Likewise, Scripture's statement concerning the one-flesh relationship established by a sexual consummation need not necessarily envision a permanent tie. This is made clear by the use of this phrase in other places. Consider, for instance, Paul's quotation of Genesis 2:24 in 1 Corinthians 6:15–17 concerning the case of a Christian becoming sexually involved with a prostitute. Heth cites this reference once but does not comment on the clear statement that this also constitutes a one-flesh tie. Granted, it is not a marriage, for that would require a "covenant" relationship as well. But it is beyond argument that it is a one-flesh relationship, for the apostle argues that the man is thus taking the "members of Christ" and making them "members of a prostitute," and he cites Genesis 2:24 in support. But if one-flesh relationships are permanent, how many can be valid at one time? What if it is an already married man who thus dallies with a prostitute; is his one-flesh time with his wife the valid one, or is it the new one-flesh time with the prostitute? And what about the polygamy of the Old Testament patriarchs? Jacob had two wives, Leah and Rachel. Was only one of these valid in the eyes of God? David had several wives. Which were unbreakable unions in the eyes of God, and which were not? These questions Heth does not face in his paper.

To support his claim that a one-flesh tie is always considered unbreakable in the Bible, Heth turns to Leviticus 18:6–18. These are the well-known "laws of consanguinity" which seek to regulate sexual unions within family groups. The author properly points out that "uncover nakedness" is a euphemism for sexual intercourse, and "blood relative" (RSV "near of kin") is literally "flesh of his flesh." He states, "These regulations thus define the limits within which a man may seek a wife." But that cannot be, for it is his marriage to a wife which creates the "nearness of kin" which is under regulation. He is not seeking a wife; he already has one, or the passage is meaningless.

Further, the author states, "Similarly he became related to her close female relatives, and should his wife die or should he divorce her, he could not marry them for that would be a form of incest." But there is no hint in the passage that these prohibitions envision a death or a divorce! This seems to be an arbitrary interpretation which the author brings in without warrant. They are simply prohibitions against incest within family groups and do not touch the question of whom a man may marry after the death or even after the divorce of his wife.

It is somewhat strange that Heth does not quote verse 18 of this same chapter which states, "And you shall not take a woman as a rival wife to her sister, uncovering her nakedness, while her sister is yet alive." The prohibition is not against taking a rival wife but against taking the wife's sister while the wife still lives. This would seem clearly to imply that the man is free to marry the sister if his wife has died. Further, Heth's understanding of this passage would contradict the regulation of Deuteronomy 25:5–10, the law of levirate marriage, which *requires* a man to marry his dead brother's wife if she has no son to sustain her inheritance in the land and to raise up a son or sons to his name.

All the above highlights the danger of taking these Mosaic regulations as applying directly to believers today. Heth states several times that they are "still binding today" but does not deal with the requirements to stone adulterers, make loans to relatives without interest, allow the newly married to be exempt from war service for a year, and avoid putting tassels on our clothes, etc. In view of all this, we must consider this passage in Leviticus 18 as having no bearing on the question of remarriage after divorce whatsoever.

Well, then, what about Deuteronomy 24:1–4? This is the very passage which the Pharisees quote to Jesus when they ask him about divorce, and it is one which author Heth feels strongly supports his position. He states, "No one who is familiar with the scholarly literature on Deuteronomy 24:1–4 would ever seek to argue that the Mosaic bill of divorce dissolves the marriage bond." This would seem to make that body of literature an extremely important matter to consider here, but the author makes no further statement about it.

He does, however, clearly point out that those interpreters who take the position that this passage proves that Moses instituted the practice of divorce are badly mistaken. Moses does no more than sanction and regulate a practice already followed in Israel, perhaps derived from neighboring nations. Heth would question the word "sanction," but here we must hear Jesus' statement, "For your hardness of heart Moses allowed (*epetrepsen*) you to divorce your wives. . . ." The Greek word means "to permit or give leave." It is clear that Moses did sanction a practice which arose out of the sinful hardness of men's hearts. Since Moses always speaks with God's authority, we have here another example of divine permissiveness which falls short of God's desire.

Deuteronomy 24:1–4 actually only prohibits the remarriage of a woman to her first husband after he has divorced her and she has married another who either dies or divorces her in turn. The passage hangs upon the sentence, "her former husband, who sent her away, may not take her again to be his wife, *after she has been defiled;* for that is an abomination before the LORD. . ." (v. 4 RSV, italics mine). The emphasized words are crucial to the understanding of this passage. Heth takes the defilement to refer to the woman's second marriage. He states that there are five different interpretations of this sentence, though he does not list them. Of the five he rather arbitrarily chooses the one that fits his thesis best. But it is far more likely that the defilement is the first divorce, for that is what evidences "hardness of heart." This is supported by the reproaching words, "who sent her away," placing the blame not on the woman but on the first husband. The argument then is that since he "defiled" his wife by putting her away, he cannot then take her again (thus treating her as baggage, to be taken at will), for this is an abomination to the Lord.

Taken in this sense the passage says nothing about a one-flesh union surviving divorce or sexual relations with a third party. If that were the case, then the woman would still be considered married to her first husband, and their reunion would seem to be virtually mandatory. But this is the very thing the passage prohibits. It does establish the fact that divorce was practiced in Israel, that Moses (God) sanctions it for humanitarian reasons (to protect the divorced wife), and it says nothing at all as to the right to remarry after a divorce on the grounds of unchastity.

The author devotes the latter part of his paper to a brief survey of New Testament teaching on divorce and remarriage. He gives a helpful summary of seven points which skillfully gathers up the several passages that deal with this subject. His statement about the famous "exception clause," however, leaves much to be desired. His view is: "[It] is simply a matter-of-fact recognition that if the wife has already committed adultery, her husband cannot be held guilty of driving her into it by divorcing her." But this ignores the fact that it is the man's possible adultery that the Lord's statement seeks to prevent. If he divorces his wife for any other reason than her adultery, *and he marries another,* he commits adultery. Remarriage after divorce is adulterous unless the divorce was for sexual infidelity. That is the clear statement of the New Testament.

Heth states at the beginning that he does not feel it helpful to reexamine at length the New Testament battlefield on this question. He therefore contents himself with a very brief review. His own interpretation is, of course, colored by what he feels he has proven from the Old Testament based on Genesis 2:24; Leviticus 18:6–18; and Deuteronomy 24:1–4. We have demonstrated that these passages do not contribute anything helpful to the divorce/remarriage debate. Therefore we must reluctantly conclude that, despite a sincere attempt to plow new ground, the present paper does not seem to add anything of substance to the debate and leaves the question of remarriage after divorce unresolved.

# SEXUAL DEVIATIONS

## John White

## I. INTRODUCTION

When Christians talk about sexual *deviations* they refer to deviations from scriptural norms. Deviations from God's norms are *sinful* deviations. God's norms for sexual behavior find their roots in his creation of mankind. Sex had then and still has the purpose he originally planned.

Deviations are of course always deviations *from* something. The human sciences do not accept God's norm and so differ in their view of deviation. But they face a difficulty in discovering norms of their own. Behavioral norms vary, too, from one culture to another and from one period of history to another. So for the human sciences there can be no firm lines from which to deviate. Deviancy to the human sciences has become a sort of mixture of the *unusual* and the *socially unacceptable*.

Until a few years ago, for instance, the American Psychiatric Association regarded homosexual behavior as deviant behavior. In 1973 I was in Anaheim at the annual convention of the American Psychiatric Association listening to papers on homosexuality when the meeting was interrupted by invading, banner-carrying protesters from the Gay Liberation Front and the Women's Liberation Movement. (The campaign against conventional psychiatry had begun in 1970.) The protests and disturbances led to "dialogues," following which the APA removed the objectionable terms "deviant" and "pathological" from their descriptions of homosexual behavior.

## II. THE BIBLICAL BASIS FOR NORMAL SEXUAL BEHAVIOR

In answering questions about divorce in Matthew 19:3–12, Jesus bases his teaching about divorce on Creation, on the Creator's original purposes *in, at,* and *from* the beginning. From what Jesus says here, two important principles may be inferred not only about divorce but about all sexual relationships.

First, God's standards for normalcy and, therefore, for deviancy are to be found in the Genesis account of our creation. As Heth expresses it, "To understand the concepts found in Genesis 2:24 is to understand the marriage relationship itself."[1] Indeed we must expand his statement and declare that the concepts found in Genesis 2:18–3:21 form the foundation for all our understanding of sexual normalcy and enlighten us as to the effect of the Fall on human sexual behavior.

Second, Christ's teaching reminds us that both sinners and their victims must be viewed through merciful eyes. Rightly understood, this is what his comment about the hardness of men's hearts implies. This does not mean that God has ever lowered or will ever lower his standards. They remain inviolate. His wrath burns against all forms of sin.

But in wrath he has remembered mercy, and so must we. This is important in a day when Christian opinion is polarized. On the one hand, there are those who battle in the political arena against sexual deviancy but who show little interest in seeking out and delivering enslaved sexual sinners; and on the other, those who treat sinners kindly but who seem to equate mercy with a lowering of divine standards.

In his mercy God takes into account the effects of the Fall on our behavior. Moses had permitted divorce because of the sinful hardness of human hearts which, among other effects, created a hardship on those who were victims—women thrown out of their husbands' homes, leaving them without any social status.

I shall use the term *sexual deviations,* then, to mean deviations from biblical standards. And in discussing the question of how sexual deviations arise, I shall be more concerned with biblical than with psychological explanations—not that the two necessarily conflict. They provide answers to different questions. Psychological explanations are descriptive and generally attempt to answer the question *how.* Biblical explanations deal with the *why* of the deviations.

Deviations from God's norms occur because we are fallen and live in a fallen world. Our bodies and the ground we walk on reflect the Fall. Sin indwells us. The ground is under a curse. Our bodily tissues have been affected, making it impossible apart from grace for us to function as we were designed to function. Hence we may experience pulls in a sexually deviant direction.

Psychology attempts to show how the differences between deviations arise. Because our upbringings and our lines of inheritance vary, some of us will experience deviant sexual pulls that differ from those experienced by others. And the sinful environment around us, full of perverse stimuli, will make any deviant pulls stronger.

Our standards for human behavior must arise from our understanding of what we human beings are and of what we are meant to be, sexually and in every other way. However, certain details are lacking. Nowhere in Scripture do we find the kind of information found in sex manuals. Scripture is not concerned with sex techniques. It enjoins husbands and wives to mutual consideration but does not spell out what methods of intercourse are consistent with the purposes behind our sexuality. Hence controversies arise over issues such as whether there is any place for orogenital contact.

This paper will concern itself with obvious deviations that are contemporary concerns. The three we shall look at are homosexuality, child molestation, and incest.

### III. MAN AS A RELATIONAL BEING

#### A. Terms Used

Already I have used the term *pull* in relation to sexuality. Throughout this paper I shall try to avoid using the technical terms of the human sciences in relation to sexual expression. Psychoanalytic theories, for instance, speak of sexual *drives*. I cannot use such terms without their being understood in the deterministic sense of a particular theory.

To say that I have a sexual drive means more than that I feel like having sex. I shall therefore use terms like *pull* or *urge* which refer only to subjectively experienced inclinations.

In the Genesis 2 account God pronounces the man's aloneness as "not good." Man, like his Creator, is to be a social, relational being. Only so can human nature reach the potential for which it is designed. Only so can it truly reflect the Creator's own tripartite being.

Because we are physical and require bodily, physical sustenance, interpersonal relationships are physical, bodily relationships. Woman came from man. Children come from man and woman. Love is expressed primarily in physical ways (with the giving of food, shelter, comfort, service, touching, embracing, and coitus.) In a sense, the crucial relationship, certainly the starting point of all relationships, is the erotic relationship between husband and wife. In its physical exposure and tender accepting embrace can be found a profound sense of no longer being alone. From the Genesis passage we learn that:

1. The sexual relationship is *hetero*sexual—between a man and a woman (Gen. 2:24).
2. The relationship supercedes other relationships creating a new, living, permanent unity (Gen. 2:24).
3. The relationship serves not only to ensure the social nature of humanity but to subserve procreation. This had already become apparent in Genesis 1:28. Procreation is now seen to take place in the vortex of loving intimacy.

## B. Sexuality After the Fall

Following the Fall there were changes in human sexuality, the most significant being:
1. The shame of nakedness.
2. Painful childbearing.
3. Male sexual dominance.

## C. The Shame of Nakedness

Previously unaware of their nakedness (Gen. 2:25), our forefathers felt immediately compelled to cover their bodies (3:7). Nakedness symbolizes psychological exposure, the exposure of whatever we would prefer to hide—a condition we as sinners cannot stand. This same sense of shame made our forefathers hide from God (vv. 8–10). (Those primitive tribes that appear to be naked still experience the shame of nakedness—some symbolic fibrous string or decoration representing a covering whose absence they will not tolerate, except under conditions of sexual intimacy. Western nudity represents *shamelessness*—a pathological denial of the shame.)

The covering also symbolized an impairment of ordinary social intimacy, the intimacy now being necessarily confined to conjugal sexual relations.

God recognized the distress and spiritual danger of the nakedness of the fallen couple, confirming that their urge to clothe themselves was a proper one. In his mercy he clothed them in a manner that involved the shedding of blood (Gen. 3:21). Fallen human beings are meant to be clothed. Perhaps in a coming day we may be clothed *only* with righteousness—but if so, in that sense we shall indeed be clothed, our bodies being *covered* with God's righteousness.

## D. Painful Childbearing

The pain of childbirth reflects at once (1) God's judgment on sin (Gen. 3:16), (2) a consequence of the Fall, and (3) a manifestation of satanic rule on earth. And just as God mercifully provided for our shame with coverings of animal skins, so he has revealed to us ways of alleviating the pains that still afflict women in childbirth.

### E. Male Sexual Dominance

"Your desire shall be to your husband and he will rule over you." Opinions vary as to the meaning of the words. Some commentators focus on the word *rule*, seeing in the statement the origins of male headship. But the statement might be better understood simply as a divinely ordained result of sin and the Fall. In practice the dominance has both physical and social expressions. Physically there is the possibility both of rape and of forced intimacy in marriage. Most men are physically capable of it not only because of their strength but because of the rigidity of a sexually aroused penis. Lacking such a bodily "weapon," women cannot enforce their sexual desires.

God does not approve of rape (any more than he delights in a woman's labor pains), but it has become a tragic fact of life in consequence of the Fall. In addition, a woman with a godly husband may find herself desiring her husband's sexual approaches, even though they may result in an unwanted and painful childbirth. Her desire is to *her husband*. Nor can she force him to gratify that desire, however powerful it may be. As a result of sin and the Fall, she is the victim of her bodily urges to a greater degree than her husband.

But the shame of nakedness, painful childbearing, and the male sexual domination are but three of the many effects of the Fall on our sexual functioning. As a race some of us are subject to multiple deviant pulls, among which are homosexual desires, powerful temptations to molest children sexually, and incestuous urges.

### IV. HOMOSEXUALITY

In 1973 homosexuality became officially (for the American Psychiatric Association) part of normal human behavior—an acceptable variant of sexual expression. The only homosexual behavior calling for treatment eventually became *ego-dystonic* homosexuality—homosexuality the homosexual wished to change. However, it is interesting to find homosexuality still described as a *perversion* of psychiatry.[2] An approach to the subject is still marked by "a fundamental lack of consensus"[3] in the behavioral sciences.

Christian opinion on the topic has unfortunately polarized along unfortunate lines. On the one hand, there are those who are so concerned with the political issues that they have no time to reach out in Christian love to homosexuals; and on the other, there are the sentimentalists whose love and acceptance of homosexuals includes total acceptance of their sin. We lose sight of the homosexual's real needs in taking sides for or against humanism. For some years now a minority of evangelical counselors, influenced by changing climates of opinion, have encouraged counselees to accept their homosexuality as their particular sexual gift from God. It is taught that God made the homosexual so. The teaching is unacceptable for two reasons, one of which has already been discussed. We may have compassion on a murderer cursed with strong tendencies to violence, but we never accept murder as legitimate, nor would we view the proclivity to violence as a gift from God. Yet both arose in precisely the same way. Sexual deviations arise because we are a sinful, fallen race. God did not create us with sexual deviations.

Some "scientific" claims for the normality (if not the health) of the condition have been based on the allegedly greater creativity of homosexuals, but as Barnhouse points out:

> There is no evidence to support such claims. In fact, contemporary psychological research shows that on tests designed to measure creativity and divergent thinking, heterosexuals tend to perform better than homosexuals.[4]

Scripture makes it plain that homosexuality is deviant. "Do not lie with a man as one lies with a woman; that is detestable" (Lev. 18:22). Homosexual prostitution in heathen temples may have been particularly abhorrent, as was the defiant homosexual promiscuity of the Roman world described by Paul. But the proscription itself is general and absolute.

Christians have responsibilities toward homosexuals—to proclaim to them the forgiveness of sin, to provide for them a loving Christian community into which they can be integrated, and to pray effectively for their deliverance from bondage. For the Christian the term *homosexuality* should refer to behavior, not to the condition that renders someone specially vulnerable to the behavior. It is the behavior that Scripture condemns, not the condition, which, *as a condition*, is nowhere mentioned in Scripture. To focus on the condition is to be confused in one's thinking. A condition of special proclivity exists, but when we are trying to understand whether something is sinful or not, we must focus first on the behavior itself. The condition will naturally become more set as the behavior is practiced.

But a condition does exist that calls for Christian compassion. It varies in its severity and consists of sexual attraction to one's own sex, sometimes combined with absence of sexual arousal to the opposite sex. It is from this condition that men and women should be called on to flee and from which Christ offers deliverance.

## A. Immediate Antecedents of the Condition

The general cause of homosexuality is the Fall. Specific causes may be many, and theories are not wanting. Heredity cannot be ruled out, but specific evidence is lacking. No conclusive evidence exists for any one theory, but it seems likely that any factors in childhood which undermine children's future grasp of their own manhood or womanhood may be powerful determinants. Sexual molestation by a parent or by a trusted figure is one such antecedent. Sgroi writes:

> Sexual abuse is nearly always a profoundly disruptive, disorienting and destructive experience for the child. . . . There is interference with normal developmental tasks. The progression of mastery of one's self, environment and relationships with others is significantly disrupted.[5]

Parents who display disappointment over the sex of their child or who cross-dress their children "for fun" may also contribute to homosexual confusion, as may passivity and emotional withdrawal by a parent of the same sex.

Leanne Payne describes significant cures of homosexuals where she is able to discover the determining factor in individual cases.[6]

Christians who minister to homosexuals often use terms such as *the child within* or *the inner child,* phrases arising from the work of child psychiatrist Hugh Missildine.[7] They accept the psychoanalytic view that damage to the person in childhood arrests development at certain points. Some form of healing of the wounds of the past is seen as necessary if deliverance is to take place. Comiskey writes:

> One might say that adults who struggle homosexually possess an inner child that was never sufficiently affirmed in its gender through consistent, loving relationships with the same sex. Many of us can recall the rejection of same sex peers on the basis of our being "different," or the conditional, detached love of a parent whose approval we so badly wanted. The majority of my counselees attest to the fact that gay sex wasn't really the motivating factor while same sex intimacy was an emotional as opposed to an erotic one. And those needs are legitimate.[8]

Once the proclivity to homosexual temptation is established, it can be strengthened and reinforced by masturbation with homosexual fantasies and by the use of homosexual pornography. Statistics are not easy to come by, but there is some evidence that in males masturbation continues longer and more frequently in homosexuals than in heterosexuals. Most homosexuals also agree that their homosexual behavior is further stimulated by pornography.[9]

## V. PEDOPHILIA—THE MOLESTATION OF CHILDREN

Pedophilia means the erotic love of children by adults. Pedophilia has become an element in pornographic literature. It probably represents the offense against children that Jesus denounced in Matthew 18:6. The gravity of the problem and its widespread nature in Christian circles has only recently been coming to light. It is unlikely that we will ever have accurate statistics. But from both my former clinical practice and my more recent ministry in churches and conferences, I know that it has been common throughout my own lifetime.

As boys in England, my friends and I learned to protect one another from child-molesting Christian youth workers. Currently I frequently come across older women whose lives and marriages have been permanently scarred because many years ago as young girls they were victims of sexual abuse by a church elder, a pastor, or a Christian leader. Rarely was the matter ever brought into the open. Any attempts to deal with it in later life ran into a solid wall of indignant denial and counteraccusation.

Children are ashamed of what happens to them and rarely mention it to anyone. They are almost invariably cut off from adult help, often totally alone in their problem. Sometimes, too, they are threatened by their molester. The threat may simply be, "I'll tell your parents what we've been doing if you don't let me go on." Children, not realizing the threat will never be carried out, continue to be victimized. Often the threat is a threat of physical violence.

The effects on the child's emotional and sexual development are considerable. Usually the child is sexually roused and is confused and ambivalent about what is happening. Vulnerable children may also have an unsatisfied longing for closer physical affectional contact so that part of what is happening meets a deep and legitimate longing for an unmet need. On the other hand, they may be terribly afraid of certain aspects of the molestation yet be forced to encounter repeats of whatever they hate and fear. Female children who are induced to take an adult penis into their mouths are terrified when they feel it swelling and becoming rigid inside their mouths. Some have nightmares about snakes and fears of suffocation. Terror and pain may accompany attempts at anal and vaginal rape by male molesters.

Already we have quoted from Sgroi. The child is left with various mixtures of fear, guilt, a feeling of cheapness and worthlessness, sexual identity confusion, and distorted feelings about the nature of sex as well as confusion about the self and the environment.

A number of problems thus arise. How can we help children to avoid being molested? How can we help those who are molested? How should we deal with molesters?

## VI. INCEST

The passage that deals most with incest is Leviticus 20:11–21. With one exception, incest is seen as initiated by men, though both parties are seen to be equally to blame. In all cases the law has adults in mind.

Incest can involve only two adults, but much more commonly it involves an adult and a child, or else an older and a younger sibling. Its effects on the victim are similar to those of other forms of child molestation, with the addition that the victim learns that the home is not a safe place. In general they are more severe. Psychosis occasionally follows. In addition where a parent is involved, sexual relationships in adult life will almost invariably be distorted. A child learns how to relate to the opposite sex in the context of a healthy family. Where normal family relationships are disturbed, particularly in this way, groundwork is laid for the disturbance of future heterosexual and social relationships.

Crowded sleeping conditions, drinking, depression, and poverty all contribute to the likelihood of incest. Offending adults commonly give a history of having been molested themselves as children. The perpetrator is more likely to be a man than a woman in a ratio of about five to one, and the molestation itself more likely to be heterosexual than homosexual, though both types occur.

The wife or husband of the perpetrator frequently prefers not to know what is happening. Sometimes there is a pretence not to know. At other times if a child appeals for help to the other parent, he or she will be indignantly rebuked or even punished and told not to say "such terrible things." Not infrequently a grandparent will be approached for protection, and the grandparent will also molest the child. A profession of faith in Christ seems to make no difference to the incidence of incest.

The family situation is difficult to deal with once the condition comes to light. The relationship between the spouses is usually unsatisfactory. Denial is often hard to break down. The collaboration of both spouses will be necessary if changes are to take place, and such collaboration is usually given only reluctantly. Understanding discipline and support from the church is rarely available.

## VII. THE GOSPEL AND SEXUAL SINNERS

The inerrant Scriptures are not only law; they are also gospel. Therefore we must address ourselves to the question of how the church (to which the gospel has been entrusted) shall fulfill her commission to sinners enslaved by sexual sin. Unless we do so, our consideration will be at best an academic, and at worst, a Pharisee-like attempt to define a self-righteous position.

Gospel is good news for those who are oppressed and enslaved by their sin and by the powers of hell. Gospel involves a proclamation of *Christus Victor,* who by his death and resurrection redeems and rescues. That proclamation will rightly be perceived as defective if there is no evidence of Christ's delivering power and no true concern for the captives.

If our attempts to proclaim truth focus primarily on a protest to the corrupt and humanistic community surrounding us and on an effort to reform defective laws, we shall have failed. I am convinced that in this respect the church as a whole is failing sadly at the moment. One or two renewal-oriented churches, upon whom many of us look down, seem to be the ones who are devoting themselves to problems of this nature.

While we protest the malign influence of humanism in Western society, we turn to counselors whose methods spring from scientific humanism where sexual problems arise in the church. Always our first thought is to seek professional help. Sadly, too, counselors on the staff of many local churches have failed to think through the issues involved and rely more on imperfectly evaluated psychological theory (the theory being by no means devoid of value) than on the power of Christ.

Homosexuality, incest, and child molestation involve two problems. The first has to do with helping wounded captives. The second has to do with the discipline of offenders. Both problems involve considerations far too extensive to deal with effectively here. The two are really aspects of one problem—the problem of sin and its effects on individuals and on the people of God.

Ken Blue and I have dealt with the church disciplinary issues in the book, *Healing the Wounded.*[10] It is our conviction that the traditional approach to an understanding of the *aims* of church discipline reflects only a part of the biblical teaching. It is also our conviction that ultimate corrective disciplinary measures depend not on the precise nature of the sin being dealt with but on the more serious wrong of refusing to acknowledge the right of the church to intervene and of refusing the help proffered. As for helping wounded captives, whether those captives be molested children, incestuous adults, or practicing homosexuals, it is probably true that in practice their help must come simultaneously from two human sources—a loving Christian community and experienced godly counsel made effective by the power of the Holy Spirit. It is not enough for us to "pass the buck" by referring sinners to professional counselors, most of whom cannot and do not deal with issues such as forgiveness, Christ's acceptance, redemption, sanctification, the need of the sinner also to forgive, etc.

Churches are (or should be) the "loving Christian communities" necessary for deliverance of personality-damaged sinners. It is in the context of a local church that Paul gives the instruction, "Brethren, if a man be overtaken in a fault, you who are spiritual, restore such a person in the spirit of meekness, lest you also be tempted. Bear one another's burdens, and so fulfill the law of Christ" (Gal. 6:1–2). Comiskey writes:

> Man emerges within a disordered world, and must rely upon God's grace to reveal true order to him. That order is upheld and progressively realized through human relationships within the Church. Disorder in human lives can then be realized and redeemed within the Church's context of grace and truth.[11]

One example of such a church with a truly effective role in the redemption of homosexuals is the West Hollywood Vineyard Christian Fellowship, which works in collaboration with Desert Stream, a Christian organization devoted to the healing and redemption of homosexuals, in nearby Santa Monica.

West Hollywood, on the other hand, is a city devoted to the upholding of gay rights, whose council is dominated by practicing homosexuals. It is a community in which approximately fifty percent of the population has a homosexual lifestyle. It thus represents "hard core" resistance to the idea that homosexual behavior is sinful. Nevertheless, a team from Vineyard regularly goes onto the "strip" and into bars there to bear witness of Christ to gays.

The proclamation of the gospel, largely in personal conversation, focuses on the deep need experienced by homosexuals for relatedness. Repentance is presented in general terms and in the context of the acknowledgement of God's mercy and his sovereign right to control but does not focus specifically on the issue of homosexuality.

Homosexuals themselves, many of whom come from Christian backgrounds, are deeply aware of the moral issue and begin to come to painful grips with it once they find themselves accepted in the Christian community. It is at this point that they are referred to Desert Stream in Santa Monica, where through expert, experienced counsel and prayer, many homosexuals eventually emerge into a changed experience, ongoing deliverance from homosexual sin. I have had the privilege of interviewing a number of them personally. Some live celibate lives; others are able successfully to enter into heterosexual marriage.

Examples of loving church discipline rightly understood and of this sort of ministry to sexual sinners are rare. Yet without such a ministry our proclamation of liberty to the captives of sexual sin will be hollow. If the Word of God is true, then we are charged with a responsibility we are fulfilling only inadequately and in part. We are called on to repent as a community, and to ask God how we as a church at large may obey our Lord's commission.

# ENDNOTES

[1] William A. Heth, "Divorce and Remarriage," in *Applying the Scriptures*.

[2] William W. Meisner, "Theories of Personality and Psychopathology: Classical Psychoanalysis," in *Comprehensive Textbook of Psychiatry*, ed. Harold I. Kaplan and Benjamin J. Sadock, 4th ed. (Baltimore: Williams and Wilkins, 1985), p. 401.

[3] John K. Meyer, "Ego-Dystonic Homosexuality," in *Comprehensive Textbook*, p. 1056.

[4] Ruth Tiffany Barnhouse, *Homosexuality: A Symbolic Confusion*, p. 26.

[5] Suzanne M. Sgroi, *Handbook of Clinical Intervention in Child Sexual Abuse* (Lexington: D. C. Heath & Co., 1982), p. 35.

[6] Leanne Payne, *The Broken Image* (Westchester, Ill.: Crossway, 1981).

[7] Hugh Missildine, *Your Inner Child of the Past* (New York: Simon & Schuster, 1963).

[8] Andy Comiskey, "Healing the Child Within" in the Desert Stream *Newsletter* (Santa Monica), January/February 1985, p. 3.

[9] Andy Comiskey, "Hot Thoughts: The Effect of Pornography on Male Homosexuals" (unpublished paper).

[10] John White and Ken Blue, *Healing the Wounded: The Costly Love of Church Discipline* (Downers Grove: InterVarsity, 1985).

[11] Andy Comiskey, "Homosexuality and the Church: Relational Problem, Relational Solution" (unpublished paper, 1984).

# A Response to Sexual Deviations

**Lawrence J. Crabb**

Dr. White, reflecting his commitment to biblical authority and inerrancy, properly resists the strong trend to define deviancy in terms of the socially or personally offensive or the unusual. One of the most telling failures of secular social science is its inability to agree on a standard by which to define normalcy.

When the Scriptures are recognized as the accurate statement of our Creator, then biblical prescription for human behavior becomes normative. Any deviation from those norms is rightly regarded not as a preferred alternative but as a sinful perversion of God's good design. Dr. White's comments on sexual deviation build on this solid foundation.

When his discussion shifts from establishing biblical norms as the basis for *defining* deviancy to questioning the *causes* of deviation, he carefully remains within a biblical framework by putting fundamental blame for all deviation on the fall of man into sin. To quote Dr. White, "deviation from God's norms occurs because we are fallen and live in a fallen world."

His thoughts on a Christian *response* to sexual deviation again reflect a strongly biblical perspective. In my mind he strikes just the right balance between two opposing errors, compassionate compromise on the one hand and unfeeling orthodoxy on the other. The church is uniquely called and equipped to reach into the messy details of people's lives with rich involvement and wise counsel. Folks enslaved to sexual sin—whether homosexuality, transvestism, or child molesting—and those who have been victimized by the sexually deviant, including rape victims, adults with memories of incest, and children exposed to pornography from their earliest years, have a real battle on their hands. The shame is that professional counselors are assigned the primary

role in helping while the Christian community is viewed as a
benign but largely useless spectator.

When a body of believers armed with the Word of God and
indwelt by the Spirit of God is set aside in the struggle to help
sexually deviant people be restored to righteous and joyful living,
something is wrong. Dr. White puts it this way:

> While we protest the malign influence of humanism in Western
> society, we turn to counselors whose methods spring from
> scientific humanism where sexual problems arise in the church.
> Always our first thought is to seek professional help. Sadly, too,
> counselors on the staff of many local churches have failed to
> think through the issues involved and rely more on imperfectly
> evaluated psychological theory (the theory being by no means
> devoid of value) than on the power of Christ.

In my response to Dr. White's excellent paper, I want to focus
attention on why this situation exists. Why is the church so rarely
an instrument of healing and change for the exhibitionist and the
voyeur? A pastor recently confided in me that for years he has
struggled with powerful urges to exhibit himself. In his desire for
help, he faced not only the real dilemma of embarrassment and
rejection but also the realization that no one in his church,
including himself, had the slightest idea what to do about the
problem.

Why is the church known more for decrying what is wrong
with people than for effectively ministering to them? Most
Evangelicals would agree that we should be able to move into the
lives of sexually deviant people with real answers rooted in the
gospel. Why, then, do exhortations to make the church into a vital
agent of change typically arouse either short-lived enthusiasm or
uncomfortable retreat?

Certainly part of what is wrong involves our dislike of
anything different and our strong but subtle commitment to keep
church fellowship warmly comfortable, at least in appearance. We
naturally back away from conflict and tension, even at the expense
of developing real relationships. Too often a church's existence is
maintained by denying much of the disturbing reality of what
really goes on in people's lives and by implicitly requiring our
fellow worshipers to cooperate with the pretense.

But lack of integrity and failure of love may be more symptom
than cause. Perhaps a more central deficiency is our lack of
understanding of how the inerrant Word speaks to the realities of
deviant urges and behavior. Many people who have settled the
issue of *inerrancy* in their minds still entertain serious doubts about
the *sufficiency* of Scripture in speaking comprehensively to the
questions of social science. In discussing sexual deviancy from a
biblical perspective, we easily agree that whatever the Bible says

about the subject is authoritative. But does it say enough to guide the church in understanding sexual deviancy and in helpfully responding to it? Or do we depend on psychological insights and wisdom of experience to *really* explain and treat sexual deviation? Something seems terribly wrong if the inerrant Bible is reduced to essential irrelevancy in guiding us in the task of practically helping people who compulsively violate God's pattern for sexuality. After handing out a few spiritual prescriptions about making no provision for the flesh and spending more time in God's Word, coupled with encouragements to trust in God's power, many Christian leaders who know the Bible well have no idea what to do with the homosexual wanting help.

Without entering the debate about whether the Bible is a counseling text, let me suggest a few thoughts about biblical hermeneutics which for me have opened up the Scriptures as a framework for thinking through every nonorganically rooted problem in living, including sexual deviancy.

We must begin, I submit, by viewing the Bible not only as the inerrant statement of truth (which it is) but also as a framework for thought within limits imposed by the statements. Just as theologians reflect on the attributes of God and the nature of man in their efforts to define a theology of Christianity, so we must think about sexual deviancy (and all other personal problems) within the framework of carefully studied texts, expecting to find, at least in outline form, all that we need to know to adequately minister God's life-changing truth to the deviant.

Dr. White asserted that homosexuality and all other deviations can be accounted for in general terms by the Fall. Without sin there would be no deviation from God's standards.

But all fallen people are not sexually deviant. The *general* explanation must therefore be supplemented by a *specific* explanation which tells us why one fallen person is morally heterosexual and another is driven by seemingly irresistible homosexual urges.

Dr. White adds the important point that masturbation, exposure to pornography, and engaging in the deviant act all *strengthen* the sexually perverted urge.

With regard to specific causes, Dr. White indicates that something deeply internal occurs in which a person's sexual identity as male and female is significantly threatened. Poor role models, sexual trauma, overt or covert rejection for one's sex, forced cross-dressing, and the like may contribute to threatened identity. Threatened sexual identity seems to play a large role in creating vulnerability to perverted sexual desire. Specific arousal opportunities (for example, homosexual seduction) then direct urges in definite directions.

We have then a three-tiered model for thinking about sexual deviancy:

1. *the Fall* as *general cause*
2. *threatened identity* as *specific cause*
3. *arousal opportunities* as *shaping* and *strengthening cause*

The first part of the model is clearly derived from Scripture. The third part is also easily seen to emerge from biblical warnings that the practice of sin leads to enslavement to sin (Rom. 6:10). The second part, the idea that threatened sexuality is at the core of sexual deviancy, seems more to depend on psychological observation and theorizing than on biblical study.

But if the Bible is sufficient to equip us for every good work, including restoring the sexually deviant to righteous living, then we should expect to find help in the text in defining not only general and strengthening causes but also specific causes. Perhaps the key to our study is found in Dr. White's assertion that "the concepts found in Genesis 2:18–3:21 form the foundation for all our understanding of sexual normalcy. . . ."

Briefly consider the implications of some of the material in those two chapters regarding maleness and femaleness. When God declared that it was not good for man to be alone, he immediately proceeded to parade all the animals in front of Adam for naming. One would have expected that after commenting that man's aloneness was not good, God would have next created Eve. The text (2:20) tells us that among all that had been created to that point, Adam could not find a suitable partner. Apparently, whatever was *male* about Adam required *human femaleness* to resolve aloneness. Reflection on this data suggests that maleness can be enjoyed most deeply in the presence of femaleness.

Notice, too, that sin brought disruption between Adam and Eve: they now wanted to hide from each other. Intimacy became more threatening than fulfilling. Whatever was male about Adam and female about Eve could no longer be fully enjoyed in the intimacy God intended. The beginnings of threatened sexual identity are evident.

Notice further that when God confronted our first parents, Adam ran from the role of responsible initiative and shifted blame onto his helper. Eve avoided dealing with her failure to be the complement to Adam by blaming the serpent. They both felt uniquely uncomfortable with who they were as male and female and handled God's confrontation by running from their identities.

One of the major legacies left to us by Adam and Eve is, I submit, threatened sexual identity. No male is fully comfortable with his responsibilities. We all fear failure somewhere. No woman is totally at ease in a vulnerable position—and understandably so. Rather than giving to others what we have, we are committed to protecting ourselves from (1) exposure of our inadequacies and (2) rejection by people who matter to us.

Threatened sexuality is a universal fact of human existence

since the Fall. Some, however, feel far more threatened than others. Perhaps the third factor in our model can explain the degree to which any one person feels threatened. The *degree* to which we are threatened depends largely on parental and other environmental input. If the concept of threatened sexuality is biblically based, then reflections *within the framework* of that concept can rightly be called biblical.

The more someone is threatened, the stronger will be his tendency to avoid normal heterosexual relationships. It is in that relationship where he must uniquely give what he fears he does not have. Marriage requires substantial intactness of one's sexual identity if it is to function according to God's design. When the required intactness is perceived as largely absent, marriage becomes an opportunity to fail, a risk (for most) not worth taking.

Sexual perversion, I suggest, represents compromising solutions to the problem of a desire for male-female intimacy when the wherewithal to develop that intimacy is perceived as lacking. Most people, suffering from only limited threat, remain normally heterosexual, *but* they retreat from the opposite sex until a safe, comfortable distance is established. The overriding commitment to protecting oneself from exposure of inadequate maleness or femaleness explains much of the staleness in marriage today.

People with greater levels of threat run *further* from heterosexual relationships in their pursuit of relational satisfaction without risk of exposure. Homosexuality provides the chance for meaningful relationship without the requirement to be as fully male as a female partner would require—or as fully female as a male partner would require.

Child molestation offers a similar opportunity for felt closeness (undeniable longing within each of us) without the need for mature involvement. Pornography stimulates people with counterfeit feelings of consuming satisfaction without imposing the fearful demands of relationship. Transvestism gives temporary relief from the pressure always to be the man whom the transvestite fears he may not be.

Perhaps the point to be underlined is that sexual deviation has far more to do with the problem of threatened sexual identity than with the pursuit of physical pleasure. That point is obvious. But some of its implications may warrant further thought. Let me close this paper by discussing a few implications of this line of thought.

Perhaps our inerrant Bible is sufficient for more than we think. The root cause of sexual deviation may be explainable by the biblical idea of threatened sexuality. Further reflection on that concept may lead to specific directions we can take in helping people find release from the chains of sexual bondage. Maybe more is required than exhorting abstinence from sexual sin.

Perhaps we can help people learn to recognize how committed they are to protecting themselves from exposing their inadequacies and then teach them to label their pursuit of self-protection as sin. As they learn to take hold of their worlds as men and women, encouraged by a loving community of God's people, the degree to which they feel compulsively drawn toward their sexual perversion decreases.

Dr. White's call to the church to repent of her distance from the sexually deviant and to plunge into the realities of their lives with *biblical* understanding and compassion must not go unheeded. With confidence in an inerrant and sufficient Bible as our guide, we may respond to the challenge of bringing the gospel to every person regardless of the severity of their struggles.

# A Response to
# Sexual Deviations

### Earl D. Wilson

I appreciate very much the opportunity to respond to Dr. White's paper on "Sexual Deviations" because I believe it to be a very timely and well-researched article. Thank you, John, not only for this work but also for your applied theological contributions over the years, particularly as they relate to sin, Satan, and sexuality.

Dr. White puts things in proper perspective by reminding us that God's standards regarding deviation are different from those of the world in which we live. He is right in insisting that deviation be defined in terms of God's norm and not by the norms established by human sciences.

> The man without the Spirit does not accept the things that come from the Spirit of God, for they are foolishness to him, and he cannot understand them, because they are spiritually discerned (1 Cor. 2:14).

I also appreciate very much the emphasis upon mercy which appears in the paper in both explicit and implicit form. Such an emphasis serves to keep us in touch with the Christian responsibility to hate sin while loving the sinner. Our loving response to the sinner must include preventative measures such as social involvement and political action. It also needs to include redemptive measures such as evangelism and discipleship among sexually deviant populations, and Christian counseling with those who are seeking victory in Christ. James 4:17 helps us to focus on the merger of mercy and responsibility. "Anyone, then, who knows the good he ought to do and does not do it, sins."

I want to underscore the importance of the discussion of man as a relational being, because I believe that without this foundational truth we cannot really understand the tremendous tragedy of sexual deviation. If social and psychological research has told us anything about those who practice sexual deviation, it is that they are lonely people, unattached, and desperately in need of relationships. They live in this unrelated state while at the same time practicing sexual behaviors which move them away from rather than toward intimate relationships. Sexual deviation either violates or disregards God's response to loneliness, which is a one-man/one-woman relationship and strong relationships within the body of Christ. "The LORD God said, 'It is not good for the man to be alone . . .'" (Gen. 2:18a).

Sexual deviation has proven inadequate to meet man's relational needs and therefore proves itself to be both sinful because it violates God's norm and maladaptive because it contributes to even greater human problems. The scriptural emphasis of Ephesians 5:18–33 is important in understanding man's relational needs as they relate to sexuality. The "one-flesh" relationship of husband and wife is presented as a picture of the "profound mystery," the relationship between Christ and the church. Fidelity and intimacy are the key issues—the ideals. Leaving and cleaving are the means to reaching these ideals. The only thing closer relationally than the one-flesh relationship of husband and wife is the relationship between Christ and the church. It is a marvelous picture which underscores the great provision of God for man's relational needs.

Sexual deviation today is justified on the basis that mankind has needs which cannot be met by normal husband-wife relationships. Mankind has chosen to search for alternative ways of meeting those needs rather than to pursue the plan which God has outlined. This is another aspect of sexuality after the Fall which I feel needs to be emphasized along with those things which Dr. White highlighted. Romans 1 clearly ties the practice of sexually deviant behavior to sinful disobedience.

> They exchanged the truth of God for a lie, and worshiped and served created things rather than the Creator—who is forever praised. Amen.
>
> Because of this, God gave them over to shameful lusts. Even their women exchanged natural relations for unnatural ones. In the same way the men also abandoned natural relations with women and were inflamed with lust for one another. Men committed indecent acts with other men, and received in themselves the *due penalty for their perversion* (Rom. 1:25–27).

Is it possible that the "due penalty for their perversion" referred to here is at least in part continued unmet relational needs? I think so. Sexual deviation is a choice, not just a response to unmet needs. Mankind is victim to the choices which are made, not to the fact that needs are present.

## I. CONCERNS FOR THE CHURCH

Sexual deviation presents two major battlefields for the church and theologians. The first is political and economic, while the second is social-psychological.

Sexual deviant practices support the multimillion-dollar pornography industry and have become focal issues in human rights debates. The scriptural response to issues must be sounded loud and clear. God has spoken, and we must stand ready to answer such statements as, "God created me homosexual." If a Christian suffers from heterosexual temptation, we tell him that he must abstain. I see no reason why we should accept any lower standard for those who claim to be "gay."

In my judgment the gay rights political movement is committed to gaining soldiers at the expense of individual rights and personal well-being. When persons are told that they cannot change and therefore must live out the way God made them to be, they are being asked to commit themselves to a cause which leads only to self-destruction. I sometimes feel that when it comes to the gay rights movement, misery loves company. Scripture condemns homosexuality for the same reason it condemns heterosexual practices outside of marriage. They both lead to dehumanization and loss of personal self-esteem. We dare not desert the political and economical battle.

On the other battlefield are those who struggle socially and psychologically. They must not be forgotten. Christ is our hope, and he is the hope of those caught in sexual deviation. We must reach out in love just as our Lord reached out to all types of sinners. It is not enough to condemn sinful practices. We have a responsibility as believers to present a better way.

Does Christ offer hope for those caught in sexual deviation? I believe the answer is yes. I also believe that the hope has either not been presented—probably out of fear that we will pollute our fellowships with deviants—or we have misrepresented the hope by suggesting that deliverance from sexual deviation comes with salvation.

## II. WHAT IS THE NATURE OF DELIVERANCE?

Deliverance is a result of obedience and must not be presented as an automatic consequence of receiving Christ. Deliverance from sexual deviation does not come as a door prize when you enter the family of God. Persons who are taught that it is become disillusioned and hopeless.

Jesus told sinners to go and sin no more. He did not say that because of their new life they would not sin. New life in Christ brings with it new resources with which sexual deviation can be combated. The Spirit of God dwells within and encourages us to do the right and avoid the wrong. The Word of God provides new concepts around which life can be restructured and new equipment for fighting battles of sexual temptation (Eph. 6:11–13). The church provides new relationships and new support in fighting sin.

The victory comes as the result of a process, not as a product of the atonement. We must preach perseverance, not "magic," while at the same time never failing to stand in awe of our powerful, miracle-working God. "Let us not become weary in doing good, for at the proper time we will reap a harvest if we do not give up" (Gal. 6:9).

## III. IMPORTANCE OF PREVENTION

If an impact is to be made on sexual deviation, we must do more than restate the biblical position against inappropriate sexual practices. We must come to grips with the fact that truth does not prevent evil and changes do not come about by injunction. For example, Dr. White has suggested that "a profession of faith in Christ seems to make no difference to the incidence of incest." I believe this statement can be applied to other forms of deviation as well. One secular writer has suggested that Christianity is part of the problem rather than a potential solution.

I believe we have created a climate in the Christian community where we have encouraged people to deny their sexuality and the fact that they have sexual urges rather than to recognize them as a reality of living in a fallen, sexually saturated society and supporting each other in the battle to overcome the urges or pulls. We have denied that lust exists until it has arisen with such great force that it has destroyed individuals and injured the testimony of Jesus Christ.

In the process of trying to deny the urge to commit sexual sin, we have created a new form of legalism, which has a distorted view of sin. For example, one pastor preached strongly that it was sin for a man to touch a woman other than his wife. At the same time he categorized fondling his daughter as non-sin because penal penetration did not occur. Another believer said, "I never thought of homosexuality as true sex. Sex is something you do with women. It was just a way to release my tension and find a little pleasure."

Repression of sexual feelings and denial of the nature of our sexuality will result in greater sexual deviation. We must confess the problem and support one another in making choices regarding our sexuality that are consistent with the teachings of Scripture. We spend too much time condemning homosexual lust while condoning heterosexual lust. Lust is lust. To deny either is to be vulnerable to disobedience. When the believer begins to relabel behavior or to rationalize feelings or behavior, sexual deviation is likely to follow. We need to heed the teachings of James.

When tempted, no one should say, "God is tempting me." For God cannot be tempted by evil, nor does he tempt anyone; but each one is tempted when, by his own evil desire, he is dragged away and enticed. Then, after desire has conceived, it gives birth to sin; and sin, when it is full-grown gives birth to death" (James 1:13–15).

I believe that Christian fellowship is another important aspect of prevention. We are to meet together in order to encourage one another to love and good deeds (Heb. 10:23–25). Fellowship will not eradicate sexual deviation, but it does provide for some of man's basic relational needs, and it can provide support and encouragement for the believer who struggles with disobedience.

Particularly important is the need for the formation of strong, nonsexual, same-sex relationships. The friendship of David and Jonathan recorded in detail in 1 Samuel is a model which should be encouraged. Although some homosexuals have tried to convince themselves that this relationship was sexual, the evidence is to the contrary. Both had children afterward, and certainly David struggled with heterosexual, not homosexual lust. There seems to be a tendency to discredit examples of strong intimate relationships, i.e., David and Jonathan are accused of homosexuality, and Jesus and Mary Magdalene are portrayed as physical lovers in *Jesus Christ Superstar*. Mankind desperately wants normal intimate relationships, yet does not seem to be able to accept their validity when in fact they do exist.

Another aspect of prevention is sound teaching. There is a need for a reinterpretation of the sex act as an interpersonal relationship. Most forms of sexual deviation result in either coersion and intimidation, which destroy interpersonal relationships, or in anonymous sex, the antithesis of interpersonal relationships. One homosexual stated, "All I want is a relationship. All I get is sex."

Sexual deviation persists not only because of mankind's propensity for disobedience, but also because of the erroneous belief that sex is a cure for loneliness. Anonymous sex and masturbation are not solutions for loneliness. They maintain loneliness because they deny the intended purpose of sex— oneness of relationship—spirit and soul, not just body.

## IV. REFLECTION ON SEXUAL OBSESSION

In my book, *Sexual Sanity*, I have described what I consider to be one of the greatest social ills of our time, sexual obsession. Sex and sexual deviation have become a god. The greatest idolatry in America is not materialism. It is sexual obsession.

Scripture makes it clear that "as [a man] thinketh in his heart, so is he" (Prov. 23:7 KJV). In our sexually explicit society thinking is pushed toward sex. I believe this preponderance of thoughts turns to obsession, which leads to deviant behavior. We must accept sexual obsession as a fact and counteract it with Scripture just as we speak out on abortion, murder, and witchcraft.

Calvin Miller has hit the nail on the head in his very important book, *The Valiant Papers*.

> The entire planet celebrates its common appetite. They make every possible use of this omnipresent urge. Sex sells soap and autos, hand cream, and clothing. From highway billboards half-naked forms, gargantuan in size, gaze out over eighteen lanes of traffic. These titan nudes smile down in bronze skin to sell the products they espouse. Seductive mouths smile with an intrigue across the void, begging tourists to lust, if only for an instant, as they hurtle down the freeways.

SEX, SEX, SEX. It must be said three times to make three syllables. Yet this silent, screaming inner drive drives men![3] Mankind is caught in the pleasures of sin for a season. The longer the season the deeper the obsession seems to become. Sexual deviation when not challenged leads to deeper entrenchment in deviant patterns. Who will stop to ask the question, "Where will this all end?" Ultimately it will lead to death—spiritual death as the result of separation from God, and physical death as the result of disease and dissipation.

Is there life after sexual deviation? Is there hope? I find a solid answer in God's response to the sinful and often sexually deviant children of Israel:

> This day I call heaven and earth as witnesses against you that I have set before you life and death, blessings and curses. Now choose life, so that you and your children may live and that you may love the Lord your God, listen to his voice, and hold fast to him. For the Lord is your life, and he will give you many years in the land he swore to give to your fathers, Abraham, Isaac and Jacob.

# THE STATE UNDER GOD

## Charles W. Colson

The earth is the LORD's, and everything in it,
the world, and all who live in it;
for he founded it upon the seas
and established it upon the waters (Ps. 24:1–2).

"Teacher," they [the disciples of the Pharisees] said, "we know
you are a man of integrity and that you teach the way of God in
accordance with the truth. You aren't swayed by men, because
you pay no attention to who they are. Tell us then, what is your
opinion? Is it right to pay taxes to Caesar or not?"

But Jesus, knowing their evil intent, said, "You hypocrites,
why are you trying to trap me? Show me the coin used for
paying the tax." They brought him a denarius, and he asked
them, "Whose portrait is this? And whose inscription?"

"Caesar's," they replied.

Then he said to them, "Give to Caesar what is Caesar's, and
to God what is God's."

When they heard this, they were amazed. So they left him
and went away (Matt. 22:16–22).

## I. INTRODUCTION

"When they heard this, they were amazed." Could there be a
more appropriate response to this teaching of Christ? I doubt it.
Here we have the King of Kings clearly acknowledging the rights
of another ruler, one who had a leading part in the rebellion of
mankind against heaven. Were they not so familiar to us, these
words would be utterly astonishing.

How can it be that Christ spoke as he did? This question leads
us into an area of theological dispute which has unsettled the
Christian church since the beginning: understanding the proper

role of the state in God's design. This has been so, in part, because the Scriptures do not address this subject as a central focus of concern. Though we who affirm the inerrancy of Scripture "deny that biblical infallibility and inerrancy are limited to spiritual, religious or redemptive themes, exclusive of assertions in the fields of history and science (including political)," we have no embarrassment about agreeing heartily with Calvin when he counsels, ". . . express declaration of this matter is not to be sought in the writings of the apostles; for their purpose is not to fashion a civil government, but to establish the spiritual Kingdom of Christ."[1]

The Scriptures that do address directly the question of civil government are principally concerned with the responsibility of individual Christians as citizens, not with the development of a theory of government. Developing a theology of state is a bit like trying to work out a theology of clothing. Especially in the New Testament, the Scriptures seem to assume the existence of the thing and address very general questions of its proper use. But despite the paucity of biblical data, Christians, sometimes out of practical necessity, sometimes out of corrupt hope of gain, have never been slow to offer definitive and elaborate schemes outlining the nature of government.

Though there have been diverse opinions on this subject in the past, I doubt that there has ever been such widespread confusion as is evident in the United States today. Even among the proponents of inerrancy there is a breathtaking diversity of opinion. There is a great need for informed dialogue among Christians to resolve as far as possible the confusion.

This paper is an effort to begin such a dialogue; in it are highlighted what seem to be several major themes in Scripture which must be taken into account for any comprehensive view of the subject "The State Under God."

## II. GOD IS KING

The classic New Testament text on government, the first six verses of the thirteenth chapter of Paul's letter to the Romans, is the appropriate point of beginning.

> Everyone must submit himself to the governing authorities, for there is no authority except that which God has established. The authorities that exist have been established by God. Consequently, he who rebels against the authority is rebelling against what God has instituted, and those who do so will bring judgment on themselves. For rulers hold no terror for those who do right, but for those who do wrong. Do you want to be free from fear of the one in authority? Then do what is right and he will commend you. For he is God's servant to do you good.

But if you do wrong, be afraid, for he does not bear the sword for nothing. He is God's servant, an agent of wrath to bring punishment on the wrongdoer. Therefore, it is necessary to submit to the authorities, not only because of possible punishment but also because of conscience.

This is also why you pay taxes, for the authorities are God's servants, who give their full time to governing. Give everyone what you owe him: If you owe taxes, pay taxes; if revenue, then revenue; if respect, then respect; if honor, then honor.

Paul's claim that "there is no authority except that which God has established" (v. 1) obviously presupposes one of the central declarations of Scripture, that God is the sovereign King of all creation. By virtue of his acts of creation and preservation, God is declared to have the right of ownership over what he has made. He exercises this right in his moral government of the world wherein he orders all things according to his infinite power, wisdom, and goodness.

The doctrine of God's rule is taught throughout the Scriptures. It is perhaps most dramatically and existentially attested in the Psalms. It is evident in Psalm 24, a portion of which is cited at the beginning of this paper. Psalm 24 begins by talking about God the Creator, moves on to praise God the righteous Judge, and ends with a hymn to God, the King of glory.

Who is he, this King of glory?
The LORD Almighty—
he is the King of glory (v. 10).

The author of this psalm was a king, a man familiar with power and its capabilities for good and evil. But he was also David the shepherd, who knew of the wonders of God's creation and of man's frailty in the hand of the one who made all and could destroy all. David grasped clearly the association between God's identity as creator and his role as ruler and judge. Many psalms, including those not by David, repeat this theme: Since God is the Creator and Sustainer of all, God is rightfully the Ruler of all.[2]

"Rightfully the ruler" is a phrase our contemporaries may choke on. We may sometimes stumble over it ourselves, because we have become so committed to the autonomy of every individual. But unless we begin our thinking about the state by asserting God's absolute rule over all things, we are inviting tyranny and wickedness. God's sovereignty is the first point of reference for all thinking about government.

## III. GOD APPOINTS SUBSIDIARY AUTHORITIES

But the second point is equally important: that God establishes authorities under him to effect his will. The old word often used to label this appointment, a word which has fallen out of fashion in our egalitarian times, is vice-regent.

God has chosen to rule the world through mediators, agents who perform certain tasks and who thus possess certain authority, all for the sake of accomplishing God's will. When Pilate confronted Jesus with a just claim that he had the power of life and death, possessing the authority to free Jesus or to crucify him, Jesus countered not by disputing the legitimacy of Pilate's claim to authority but with a lesson about the source of Pilate's authority: "You would have no power over me were it not given to you from above."

Paul refers specifically to the idea of subsidiary authority in Romans 13:4 when he calls the civil ruler an "agent" of God. The civil authorities do not possess power merely by virtue of some human contract; they are instead appointees entrusted with responsibility from God.

Of course, the state is not the only such appointee. There are at least two other institutions of government, the family and the church, that are also established by God. All three institutions are examples of the principle of divine conferral of authority.

One of the important corollaries of this principle is that certain rights and responsibilities are established in these institutions that are not identical with the rights and responsibilities of individuals before God. It should be obvious that, for example, I cannot legitimately require the residents of my community to pay taxes to me. Private citizens, no matter how admirable their motives or how powerful their henchmen, cannot rightfully demand goods from their fellow citizens. Such behavior is called extortion. The state on the other hand has the right under God to collect taxes, a right specifically noted by Paul in Romans 13 and confirmed by Jesus in his encounter with the Pharisees in Matthew 22. There is, therefore, a legitimate difference between taxation and extortion.

Similarly, the state may punish citizens for certain wrongdoing, just as a parent may punish his child or the church a member for certain wrongdoing. In each case the institution is exercising a right (in fact, a duty) that individuals do not have, though the punishment must be appropriate to the offense and to the sphere in which it is adjudicated. The elders of a church, for example, would not be allowed to use physical force to administer spiritual discipline (physical force is in the sphere of the state). Similarly, the state does not have the right to prevent someone from the Lord's Table for some civil offense (that discipline is for the church). And as an individual, I may restrict a child's actions but may not abuse a child in the nature of parental authority.

In each of these examples, proper jurisdiction is spelled out by biblical principles. And in each of them, authority is conferred not to an individual as such but to an officer of an institution.

Every father is an officer in his family, having certain duties because of that office, not merely by virtue of being a Christian person.

It has been noted that Romans 12, the great passage on brotherly love, on not taking revenge, on overcoming evil with good, immediately precedes Romans 13, which pronounces the civil ruler as the agent of God's wrath who does not bear the sword for nothing. The authority of the state is obviously not in conflict with the personal ethic of love in the mind of Paul, because he knew that the responsibilities of the state are not identical with the responsibilities of individuals. There are in a sense two sets of rules. What is wrong for an individual may not be wrong for a state. This is a point that must be strongly upheld, as many Evangelicals today are insisting that the responsibilities of the state are somehow identical with those of individual believers.

Summing up, these two facts—that God is sovereign and that he establishes subsidiary authorities—are the basic points to keep in view as we sketch our picture of the state under God. The first refers to the purpose of all government, the second to the means of God's rule.

## IV. ALL GOVERNMENT MUST RESPECT GOD'S LAW

With the authority under God to punish wrongdoing, the state must pursue its calling by establishing laws and sanctions for civil behavior. God rules the universe by his providence, his omnipotent preservation of all creatures and their actions. But he has also provided precepts for his rational creatures, laws which are evident in the natural order and revealed and maintained verbally in special revelation. God's revealed laws are an expression of his holy will.

It is useful to note that God gave his own people laws shortly after they were called out of Egypt—not just the Ten Commandments, but laws governing numerous aspects of civic life. It is often forgotten that, according to the account in Exodus, just prior to the legislative session on Mount Sinai Moses was spending his time in judicial activity. In Exodus 18:13 we read that Moses "took his seat to serve as judge for his people, and they stood around him from morning till evening." Apparently the courts were clogged from the very beginning. Jethro, Moses' father-in-law, was the first judicial reformer. He told Moses he would wear himself out if he did not appoint some lesser judges to take care of some of his case load. While he kept the difficult cases for himself, routine matters were settled in lower courts.

Why did this nomadic tribe need judges in the first place? The text treats the need for this aspect of government in a rather matter-of-fact manner. The people of Israel had disputes among themselves. We are not told the precise nature of these disputes. Moses tells Jethro that "the people come to me to seek God's will. Whenever they have a dispute, it is brought to me, and I decide between the parties and inform them of God's decrees and laws" (vv. 15–16). We also are told that "dishonest gain" may be a temptation for the new judges (v. 21), so we can assume that whatever the disputes were, they had enough significance to invite the possibility of bribery.

The fact of such disputes, whatever they were, did not seem to surprise or trouble anybody. Ever since Cain killed his own brother in a family argument (which also concerned God's will), it has been a given of human society that disagreements would develop and that for violence to be averted some settlement was necessary. Furthermore, it seemed appropriate to seek third-party arbitration. That would guarantee some equity in the settlement as well as prevent constant outbreaks of violence.

But it is most interesting to see that the desired goal in those settlements was to seek God's will, specifically, to understand and implement the significance of God's decrees and laws that have a bearing on the matter in question. The judicial role of the earliest biblical forms of government was understood not as a mechanism for achieving some ideal state of social equilibrium but for enacting God's revealed will.

As an agent of God, the state is generally under God's authority (as is all creation) and is specifically charged with the task of forming laws that conform to God's rule for just societies. It is the difficult task of the church to articulate which principles of God's law apply to all societies and which apply only to his "holy nation," as Peter calls the church (1 Peter 2:9). Note that just prior to the giving of the law, God tells Moses to speak this word from him to the Israelites: "If you obey me fully and keep my covenant, then out of all nations you will be my treasured possession. Although the whole earth is mine, you will be for me a kingdom of priests and a holy nation" (Exod. 19:5–6).

In this passage, God asserts his lordship and rule over all the earth but proclaims a special relationship with his people because of the covenant he has established with them. No other nation could or would enjoy the consecrated status that Israel enjoyed. Since Christ's coming, only the scattered "nation" of the church enjoys such a high calling.

But this special status does not mean that Israel is the only nation whose laws have anything to do with God's will. When Paul exhorts the Roman Christians to "do what is right" and the civil authority "will commend you" (v. 3), he is not just enjoining obedience to some morally neutral legislation. He validates his argument by saying that the civil authority is "God's servant to do you good" (v. 4). In context, "doing what is right" seems to be the equivalent of obeying the laws of the land which are assumed to be just because they are framed by God's servant.

## V. WHEN THE STATE IGNORES GOD'S LAW

Of course, a state may choose to ignore God's law for its own convenience, but by so doing it becomes corrupt and introduces disorder. It is in effect playing the role of Satan by setting itself up as an alternative authority to God. Satan, tempting Jesus in the wilderness, attempted to introduce standards of behavior that were at odds with God's revealed will. Jesus, quoting that revelation, reasserted God's unique authority. In the Book of Revelation[3] the state becomes the Beast, following its evil tendencies to their logical extreme.

Any representative of God who violates the term of his commission will reap the evil he has sown. When the state betrays its calling by trying to assume the role of God, by pretending in effect to be the very kingdom of God, it is the obligation of the Christian to obey God rather than man. The story of Daniel's refusal to submit to an evil law is a dramatic example of the obligation of God's people to resist evil. Peter and John were following the same principle when they refused to stop preaching the gospel.[4] In that case, the state as an institution was exceeding its authority, impinging on the authority of another institution, the church.

The Christian cannot afford to act precipitately in this area. He must be certain that a law is in fact in violation of God's law and not simply awkward to keep. We must always be sensitive in our interpretation of God's law lest we become too rigid, seeing conflicts where there are none. Every effort should first be made to change questionable or clearly unjust laws. Since in this fallen world, in which man's disposition is to evil, we can never give preference to anarchy over the rule of law, defiance can be considered only as a last resort.

If God's eternal law is not violated by a particular statute, the Christian is obligated to obey it, even though it may create hardship. Of all people, the recipients of God's saving grace must show their respect for God's order by obeying government. In 1 Peter 2:13–14, Peter commands believers:

> Submit yourselves for the Lord's sake to every authority instituted among men:[5] whether to the king, as the supreme authority, or to governors, who are sent by him to punish those who do wrong and to commend those who do right.

It is significant that this passage comes immediately after the section of his letter in which Peter calls believers "a holy nation," language that might be misinterpreted as meaning that our citizenship in God's kingdom exempts us from trivial worldly allegiances. But Peter believes no such thing. In fact, he goes on in verse 17 to spell out a remarkable threefold program of Christian social behavior: "Show proper respect to everyone: Love the brotherhood of believers, fear God, honor the king." Not many of us would group those things together, perhaps because we fail to appreciate the relationship between God's rule and human government.

With all of these cautionary qualifications in mind, we nevertheless assert that human laws must submit to God's law. There will be some cases where no allowances for disagreement can be made. The taking of innocent human life is one clear and current example. The first great crime was fratricide. It was understood by the criminal to be justly punished by God. Cain suffered worse than capital punishment; he was hidden from the presence of God because of his crime (Gen. 4:14). The sanctity of human life, violated in the first crime, is the cornerstone of all civil law.

While some laws rest in unalterable absolutes, there are other cases in which it is appropriate to adjust temporal laws to suit particular needs of time and place. Some laws that are good for certain times and places might have disastrous consequences in another setting. In another context, Paul establishes a principle which certainly applies to the task of legislation: " 'Everything is permissible'—but not everything is beneficial. 'Everything is permissible'—but not everything is constructive" (1 Cor. 10:23). Paul introduces this principle in an attempt to enjoin wisdom about matters of personal behavior, but it has relevance to the conduct of statecraft as well. There is need for much wisdom in the framing of laws. There may be laws that violate no standard of God's but which are still unwise. In this instance Christians should obey the unwise law while seeking to reverse it, in order to demonstrate that God's law is our only ultimate authority but that human prudence and discretion is nonetheless significant.

Finally, in keeping with the biblical concern for the weak, temporal laws must always be framed with the weakest in mind, not only those weak in physical or social power but the morally weak as well. Some laws, although they do not intend it, may nonetheless invite corruption. Wisdom requires that the weaker brother not be so tempted.

## VI. THE JUSTICE ADMINISTERED BY THE STATE IS REAL BUT LIMITED

At one time or another, each of us is, of course, a weaker brother. Each of us will be tempted to sin at some point, and some of those sins will be public and visible sins over which the state has a right to adjudicate.

This is clearly the case when the God-given rights in the temporal realm of one person have been violated by another. Murder would be an obvious example, in which the right to life is taken by another. The articulation of exactly what these rights are is an important task for today's Christians, as we live in a time when just about everything is seen as a right. The inevitable effect of this trend is to bring all aspects of life under the authority of civil government. This is rightly labeled "totalitarianism." If the state were the only means by which God ruled the world, totalitarianism might be an option. It is, after all, a neat and holistic model. But it is not the biblical model.

The biblical model has a much more limited role for the state, serving both positive and negative functions. Its negative function, the restraint and punishment of sin, we have already examined briefly. It is quite prominent in Romans 13, and I will return to it soon. The positive function might be summed up as the pursuit of the common good in the ordering of social relationships. This is more than the restraint of sin; it is the promotion of justice and concord, the arranging of society so that people can live together in relative harmony.

Paul, in 1 Timothy 2:1ff., urges prayer "for kings and all those in authority, that we may live peaceful and quiet lives in all godliness and holiness." The civic order established by the state, the opportunity for peaceful and quiet lives, is here seen as providing the context for the pursuit of holy living by the saints. Some Christians today seem to despise the goal of peaceful and quiet lives. They seem to believe that the Christian commitment to social justice must be characterized not by peace, but by "the struggle." No one knew of struggle better than Paul. He wrestled against evil, fought it, resisted it, donned armor to attack it, and preached against it so strongly that he landed in prison. But even in the midst of the turmoil of the Roman Empire of the first century, even in the midst of his persecutions, Paul taught an ideal of domestic tranquility.

## VII. LAW AND THE MORAL ORDER

In Titus 3:1–2 Paul spells out a summary of Christian obligation in society, emphasizing the theme of civility and domestic order. "Remind the people to be subject to rulers and authorities, to be obedient, to be ready to do whatever is good, to slander no one, to be peaceable and considerate and to show true humility toward all men." Such a civic order is an end in itself, a natural good. But it also has a further end and a most surprising one: the maintenance of civil order introduces unbelievers to the idea of *moral* order.

Paul is quite clear in the following verses of Titus 3 that the ability to do such things as required by civic order is a product of God's mercy exercised in the lives of sinful men and women. The good news of salvation and its effects cannot be stated more clearly than this:

> He saved us through the washing of rebirth and renewal by the Holy Spirit, whom he poured out to us generously through Jesus Christ our Savior, so that, having been justified by his grace, we might become heirs having the hope of eternal life. This is a trustworthy saying. And I want you to stress these things, so that those who have trusted in God may be careful to devote themselves to doing what is good.

By juxtaposing the obligations for civic duty with this lucid summary of the gospel, Paul seems to be enjoining civic morality as a Christian good work. When done by believers, civic good, as promoted by a good state, is good works that prove the reality of faith.

Peter follows a similar line of reasoning in chapter 2 of his first letter. Beginning at verse 13, he explains that in the economy of God even evil magistrates serve his purpose. After enjoining submission to kings and other lesser civil authorities "for the Lord's sake," he defines civil governors as those sent by God "to punish those who do wrong and to commend those who do right." This accords with Paul's teaching in Romans 13:3, where he tells his readers that if they are leading good lives, they have nothing to fear from the civil authorities: "Do what is right and he will commend you. For he is God's servant to do you good."

This, of course, represents the ideal of the state that is functioning properly. Such a state commends good behavior, and by so doing—even unwittingly—praises all of those good works that follow from faith. The good state might not preach the gospel and must not administer the sacraments and spiritual discipline, but it must promote good works, that is, the consequences of the power of the gospel working through redeemed men and women. By so doing, the state indirectly serves what we might call a preevangelistic purpose, by predisposing men to see the propriety of certain good behavior. In Peter's explanation of this function, he adds in verse 15 that "it is God's will that by doing good you should silence the ignorant talk of foolish men." Even the unregenerate recognize at some level the propriety of good works. They may hate the good works, they may hate the God who enables such good works, but their mouths are stopped. So the state, by encouraging good behavior, promotes a sort of moral argument for God's existence. Such a moral argument, used with such success by C. S. Lewis in *Mere Christianity*, depends on the background of a society that encourages virtuous behavior.

If for believers the laws of the state provide an opportunity for doing good works, for nonbelievers as well as believers the state serves as an agent enforcing behavior that God requires of man as man, not man as a regenerate child of God. God expects (and effects) good works from his redeemed people, his holy nation, but he also maintains a standard of behavior for people not in covenant relationship with him. God sent the Flood to destroy the wickedness of men and women who lived outside of any special redemptive covenant relationship. Sodom and Gomorrah were destroyed not because the people were disobedient to special revelation but because they ignored general revelation. They were not measured by the standard of redemption; they failed to live up to the lesser standard of creation.

This lesser standard remains the norm for the state today. The state does not have the authority or the ability to bring in the full justice of the realized kingdom of God. It cannot effect the perfect justice of the kingdom because true righteousness requires that the right things be done for the right reasons with the right motives. Many will do mighty works, even in Jesus' name, but they are tares nonetheless, and they will be commanded to depart from the presence of Jesus. The mystery of the kingdom is that the wheat and the tares will coexist until the cataclysmic movement of God's judgment in the coming of Christ. The state does not have the duty or the ability to make wheat out of tares.

## VIII. THE INEVITABILITY OF INJUSTICE

The wickedness of men will often block the establishment of even a minimum of justice. Christians must face up to this and accept this inevitability. Men in government and outside of it will pursue and promote evil rather than good. In so doing the state then serves the interests of Satan. In the death of Socrates the philosophers were confounded with a shocking dilemma: How could one of the best states kill one of the best of (unregenerate) men? In the death of Christ is an even more shocking dilemma, when one of the best of states killed the perfect man.

One might expect this outrageous travesty, this intolerable injustice, to have made anarchists out of the apostles and the early church. Yet these were the same people urging others to obey the magistrate and to live quiet and peaceful lives. How could this be? Because the Resurrection demonstrated that the work of temporal government is not ultimate. It is, in fact, a lesser pursuit. Politics cannot satisfy the deepest needs of man, they cannot solve his most pressing problems, and they cannot answer his most perplexing questions. Politics will continue to produce crucifixions. Only God can produce resurrection. The early church did not reject the legitimate role of the state, because they recognized its limited role.

In fact, the most helpful contribution that the church may offer the world concerning political philosophy is to let politics be politics and not a religion, to insist that the state is only the state and not the kingdom of God. Politics may be onè of the most tyrannical and blasphemous of religions and one that is most attractive and tempting to our contemporaries.

But this fact dictates a crucial role for the church. While it cannot rule society, the church can and should play the role of the conscience of society. As such, it is to hold the state accountable for its commitments and obligations. Just as the church can preach to the unconverted in her reach, reminding them that God requires certain standards of behavior even from those outside the "holy nation," the church must also remind the state of the standards to which it must be accountable. It must remind the state of the promises it has made to its people, explicitly in laws and constitutions and implicitly by accepting the responsibilities of power delegated by God (even when that state fails to acknowledge such delegation).

## IX. JUSTICE AND JUDGMENT

While the state's laws are limited and often corrupt, the institution of the state still serves in the providence of God to teach men of the expectations of God. By being an agent of judgment, it reminds men that evil will not go unpunished. God will judge evil. We should be terrified.

The theme of judgment must be reattached to the idea of justice. In today's intellectual climate justice has been linked principally to redemption, especially redemption understood as liberation. But redemption and liberation are better understood as corollaries of God's mercy and grace. We ought to be slow to demand justice from God; we might get it. We easily and conveniently forget that justice is seen in the Scriptures as relating to God's judgment. It is because God is a righteous judge who hates sin and will punish it that the state is the agent of wrath.

Paul does not refer to the state as an agent of mercy. The state, even less than the church, as understood by the Reformers, has no repository of grace to dispense to sinful men, enabling them to live good lives. But the state must nonetheless recognize the reality of mercy and not get in the way of the church as it proclaims and embodies the good news of the grace of God in Jesus Christ. Only the grace and mercy of God can effect lasting righteousness in society. One of the tragedies of our time is the increasing trust in the capability of institutional change to usher in personal change. We must not allow our concern for straightening out structures, whether governmental or otherwise, to supplant our concern for straightening out the lives of men and women.

This is not to privatize the gospel, merely to recognize the inherent limits of social change by government decree.

## X. FORMS OF CIVIL GOVERNMENT

These, then, are some of the principles of Scripture that should guide our thinking about government. There have almost always been differences of opinion among Christians about the structure and responsibility of government. Today disagreement still exists between Anabaptists and Reformed Christians, between dispensationalists and postmillennialists.

But I believe all of us ought to be able to concur on certain points, and one of those is that there is no master blueprint for the state in the Scriptures, no clearly defined pattern for a form of government. Following the lead of Scripture, the great thinkers throughout the history of the church, men of the stature of Augustine and Luther and Calvin, have tended to be modest in suggesting specific forms of government. Calvin, for example, says, "This question admits of no simple solution but requires deliberation, since the nature of the discussion depends largely upon the circumstances." Calvin ends up preferring some blend of aristocracy and democracy, mainly because such a system would check the excesses of sinful men. He also believed that a moderated freedom was an important asset in a society.

> I freely admit that no kind of government is more happy than one where freedom is regulated with becoming moderation and is properly established on a durable basis, so also I reckon most happy those permitted to enjoy this state; and if they stoutly and constantly labor to preserve and retain it, I grant that they are doing nothing alien to this office. Indeed, the magistrates ought to apply themselves with the highest diligence to prevent the freedom (whose guardians they have been appointed) from being in any respect diminished, far less be violated. If they are not sufficiently alert and careful, they are faithless in office, and traitors to their country.[6]

Perhaps all we can add is that the best form of government is one that resists the tendency to becoming an ultimate authority and one that encourages systems and habits of self-criticism and correction. Since all governments will go astray, sometimes with disastrous consequences, it is in the best interest of governors (who will have to answer before God for their performance of duty) to allow for checks and balances on the exercise of power. Caesar should have realized that he was merely Caesar and that his image existed only on ephemeral things such as coins and buildings. Those coins are mostly lost today. But God is still God; and Jesus Christ, the perfect image of God, retains his authority untarnished. He is still the King of Kings, waiting for the day of justice when all will give an account.

# ENDNOTES

[1]John Calvin, *Institutes of the Christian Religion*, 2 vols. (Grand Rapids: Eerdmans, 1953), 4.20.12.

[2]See, for example, the series of psalms that proclaim God's reign in God's universe: Psalms 90, 93–99

[3]Ch. 13.

[4]Acts 4:19–20; 5:29.

[5]Literally, every human institution.

[6]Calvin, *Institutes*, 4.20.8.

# A Response to
# The State Under God

### John W. Whitehead

In "The State Under God," Charles Colson provides a clear analysis of the responsibilities and boundaries of the civil government, particularly in relationship to the two other governments—the family and the church—which God has established. In reading his examination of Scriptures relating to this topic, one is reminded that here is a former government official who was himself party to a scheme to overstep the limits of the law and who, as a consequence, faced the authority of the state as the punisher of wrong. It was during this juncture that Colson recognized Jesus Christ's rightful claim to absolute authority in his own life, and his life was dramatically transformed. Colson is a man well acquainted with the responsibilities and perversions of power.

Early in his article Colson affirms God's absolute claim as ruler of all, who has established authorities under him to effect his will. As he accurately states, civil authorities "do not possess power merely by virtue of some human contract; they are instead appointees entrusted with responsibility from God."

Unfortunately, the modern state has often ignored the source of its authority and, consequentially, the explicit limited scope of its power. As Colson also rightly points out, the civil government has been granted its authority in relationship to the authority and responsibilities conferred upon the church and the family. Each one has been entrusted with a specific jurisdiction and is not to impinge upon the jurisdiction of the others.

The proper jurisdiction of the civil government, as Colson correctly derives from the Scriptures, is to be an agent of wrath against wrongdoing and a promoter of good. That is, it restrains sin by punishing the wrongdoer, and it promotes justice and order by arranging society in such a way that people can live together in relative harmony.

These general roles allow for more specific functions, such as collecting taxes to carry out its responsibilities and creating courts to resolve disputes. Colson cites the example from Exodus 18 in which Moses appointed judges to handle many of the lesser disputes erupting between the people. But as he clarifies, the desired goal in settling these disputes was *to seek God's will*—to understand and implement God's decrees and laws as they had bearing on the specific matter in question. Following that principle today, man's laws and the implementation of those laws are to conform to God's just rule.

Colson's major premise, with which I fully concur, is that the state, in order to fulfill its legitimate functions, must recognize three facts: (1) its dependency on the ultimate sovereignty of God; (2) its own limited jurisdiction in governing the actions of men; and (3) its goal of conforming its laws to the revealed will of God.

Colson is direct in issuing the bottom line for the state that has ignored God's claim to ultimate authority. Such a state is in effect "playing the role of Satan, by setting itself up as an alternative authority to God." This is a strong but deserved pronouncement, for whatever seeks to replace God is an enemy of God.

The state that attempts to usurp the role and authority of God forfeits its claim to obedience. When it enacts laws that conflict with God's revealed will or violate the rightful jurisdictions of the church or the family, then the Christian, like the apostle Peter, has the duty to obey God rather than men.

Specifically, the state is not to hinder the church's obligation to preach the truth of God's redemption, which will restore men to fellowship with God and enable them to straighten out their lives through the transforming power of Christ. Too often, however, as Colson notes, instead of seeing itself primarily as an agent of wrath—appointed by God to administer justice and punish the wrongdoer—the state claims the role of agent of *mercy*, attempting to redeem man through institutional structures.

Along with his admonition that Christians must obey God rather than men when men's laws conflict with God's, Colson wisely cautions Christians to be sure that a law does in *fact* violate God's law and is not merely awkward or burdensome to keep. This is a valid caution. As I have discovered from my own experience as an attorney, many Christians are far too anxious to rebel against *all* state authority because of *some* illegitimate laws, an extremist reaction that clearly contradicts God's command to submission in Romans 13.

In general I concur with Colson's scriptural analysis of the state's roles and responsibilities as designated by God. He is obviously a man who studies the Word prudently, seeking to extract God's accurate meaning and application.

Unfortunately, I found him weak in his conclusions of how Christians should respond to the state when it violates its divine appointment. It is one thing to say how the state *should* be. It is another to deal with it as it *is*. How should Christians react when it is obvious that the state, as a general institution, has denied the ultimate authority of God in its actions? How do we deal with a state that has trampled upon the jurisdictional rights of the family and the church and has deliberately suppressed rather than encouraged the proclamation of God's standards and the furtherance of his kingdom? In understanding the ideal, we must effectively confront the flawed realities, seeking to bring them back into line with the absolute standard.

For example, while it is true that the state has been given the authority to punish wrongdoing, it has increasingly claimed for itself the right to determine *what* is right and wrong—arbitrary judgments which are often in direct opposition to what God has established. One all too pervasive example is the state's seizure of jurisdiction over children's education, which properly rests with the parents. Rather than being commended for fulfilling their God-given responsibility to direct their children's education, parents who have chosen to teach their children at home have instead been forced into court under charges of neglect or even child abuse.

As for the exhortation not to hinder the proclamation of God's will, one only has to read the daily newspaper to discover numerous efforts of the state to restrict or even oust religious expression from public areas—particularly the public schools, the so-called *purveyors* of truth and knowledge.

To cite merely two recent examples: Last year the U.S. Supreme Court ruled that it was unconstitutional for Alabama legislators to allow school children a moment of silence for voluntary meditation *or prayer.* And in April a court of appeals denied the right of some Indiana teachers to meet on school property before class to study the Bible and pray. Teachers *are* permitted, however, to meet together to discuss any other topics.

Colson states that "the most helpful contribution that the church may offer the world concerning political philosophy is to let politics be politics and not a religion, to insist that the state is only the state and not the kingdom of God." Part of this contribution involves playing the role of the conscience of society. According to Colson, this involves holding the state accountable for its commitments and obligations, reminding the state that its authority is delegated by God, and that its actions must thus conform to God's standards.

But what does Colson have in mind when he calls the church

to "remind" the state of its responsibilities? To me, a "reminder" has the connotation of a mild stimulant—a gentle jogging of the memory of one who has merely forgotten what he is supposed to do. But the state has not *forgotten* its obligations; it has *defied* them by consciously setting itself up as the adjudicator of right and wrong, with no sense of accountability to a higher authority.

Surely it takes more than a *reminder* to reform such a state. More often it takes direct and aggressive *confrontation* to repudiate illegitimate claims to authority and to knock down unjust laws. The forms of this challenge may range from staging public protests, to speaking up at open legislative hearings, to initiating aggressive court action.

While the Christian is always to maintain an attitude of civility and respect for his opponent—who has value because he too is created in the image of God—he must be firm in standing for what is true and just as revealed in God's Word. The apostle Paul himself, when arrested for preaching the gospel, insisted that he had done no wrong, and he appealed to Caesar—in effect, demanding a hearing with the land's highest court.

At one point Colson presents the admonition of 1 Timothy 2:1–4, that we are to pray for all those in authority in order to live peaceful and quiet lives. He then adds that some Christians "seem to despise the goal of peaceful and quiet lives. They seem to believe that the Christian commitment to social justice must be characterized not by peace but by 'the struggle.'"

While I agree that we should pray for our authorities toward the *goal* of living peaceful and quiet lives, we again must deal with the reality of the world as it *is*. The Bible states very clearly that Christians are engaged in continuous spiritual warfare against the enemies of God, and warfare demands constant vigilance and defense strategies against an enemy that seeks to devour us (1 Peter 5:8). Since this spiritual warfare is often implemented through the temporal agencies of the state (which, as Colson states, plays the role of Satan when it severs itself from the authority of God), the Christian who stands for God against a rival authority should indeed expect a massive struggle. At that point the peace and tranquility comes from the inner assurance that he is acting according to the true dictates of God and can thus move forward with the confidence of his convictions.

In summary, I found Charles Colson's distinctions of jurisdictional responsibilities and his appraisal of the state's relationship to God to be clear-cut and scripturally sound. I would, however, have preferred more emphasis on our *response* to the modern secular state, since that is what we are clearly up against. To speak of the ideal without addressing the reality gives reasons for the current conflict but little resolution.

# A Response to
# The State Under God

### Kenneth S. Kantzer

Mr. Colson's excellent piece, "The State Under God," represents a splendid foundation for the development of an evangelical approach to politics.

For two generations American Evangelicals have withdrawn from the political marketplace. To borrow a phrase from Richard Neuhaus: They have abandoned their calling as Christian citizens and left America with a "naked public square."

Now many Evangelicals are moving back into the political arena. But they are doing so without a clearly thought-out view of politics. In his article Mr. Colson poses a basic framework which Christians sorely need as they move back into public life. In outlining this basic framework, he naturally leaves many crucial areas untouched.

While Mr. Whitehead chides him for failing to provide solutions to many problems currently facing Evangelicals, this omission may have been a happy stroke of genius. Had Mr. Colson pursued these avenues, he would have moved into areas where contemporary Evangelicals have not done their home-work—areas, it must be noted, that are not only highly controversial but on which Evangelicals themselves are violently in disagreement. For example, Mr. Whitehead's attempt to supplement Mr. Colson's article by a Christian view of the state relative to education immediately runs into a buzz saw of controversial opinion, each vigorously supported by Evangelicals equally committed to the inerrant authority of Scripture.

It is true that Mr. Colson's presentation cries for development in many areas. A solid commitment to the framework he sketched out, however, will go a long way toward helping us to work out these supplements on a sound basis.

What are some of these pressing issues—each usually addressed only obliquely, if at all, in Holy Scripture?

Most serious is the problem presented but not solved by Mr. Colson: Of all that a Christian by special revelation knows is good for humankind, how much should he seek to write into law? One traditionally evangelical answer is that we should seek to enforce the second table of the law (Ten Commandments) but not the first. For example, we should have a law against stealing, but not against the making of idols. This is an intensely practical issue for all who live in any community blessed with a significant portion of evangelical Christians. In the past, so-called "Blue Laws" have fallen on the boundary between what should or should not be written into law. On this issue Moral Majority and its supporters have never articulated a clear-cut theological or philosophical basis for their "evangelical agenda," but Evangelicals desperately need some clearheaded biblically grounded thinking on this matter.

A second area needing development by Evangelicals is the role of the Christian in the exercise of the sword. This in turn poses the role of the Christian attitude toward war. Can he approve nuclear war? Or just wars? Or is there some legitimate sense in which a Christian defers certain moral decisions to the government because of its right to use the sword? However that may be decided, the Christian cannot surrender his conscience. In the last analysis he must obey God rather than the state.

One of the related problems faced by Evangelicals is that of the boundary between nonviolent and violent opposition to bad laws. When, if ever, is a Christian justified in simply keeping quiet in the face of bad laws? And what should the Evangelical do about opposition to a government that not only passes unwise and unjust laws but refuses generally to support the good and put down evil?

When, if ever, does the Christian have the duty to resist violently or to engage in seditious or rebellious acts? Many Evangelicals defend the American Revolution as a just war, but quite inconsistently argue that a Christian ought always to obey his government except when it requires him to disobey God.

Another pertinent issue for our day is that raised by Mr. Whitehead: The role of government in education. Here I should have to disagree with Mr. Whitehead's premise that education must be left exclusively in the hands of the family. A government has a valid interest in the education of its young just as do parents and church. Parents have rights under God; but so does a government have rights under God. And the state has the duty to enforce these rights in the education of its young.

Again Evangelicals have never solved, even to their own satisfaction, what is the responsibility of the church as over against the responsibility of individual members of the church functioning as private citizens. And if we assume that the church as an organization has any responsibility to speak on some issues, what sort of issues should be its concern, and what should be the province only of the individual Christian citizen?

Mr. Colson wisely points out that no government is free from sin, and none is a panacea for the ills of mankind. This is a very necessary warning to Americans, who often latch on to democracy as the ultimate political solution in ways quite similar to the communist faith in communism. Either response is idolatry.

Yet biblical principles also give us the best rationale for the wisdom of democracy as the form of government best suited to a fallen human race. An evangelical commitment to democracy is not based upon any naïve faith that the democratic process always results in good laws and a just society. Nor does the Evangelical necessarily hold that democracy is the best government for all peoples at all times. Democracy, rather, is the best of the evils. Though all governments are liable to corruption and, therefore, are inherently dangerous, for most people democracy is the least dangerous of the available alternatives. It is based not only on the biblical doctrine that each human being is created by God with inalienable rights and possesses infinite value. It also recognizes that man becomes his best through moral choices and decisions for which he must take responsibility. And a key factor in the evangelical defense of democracy is the doctrine of human depravity that takes into account the fact that each sinful human being is the best guardian of his own rights. Much biblical wisdom was written into the American Constitution with its (often inefficient) checks and balances and its protection of minorities. Perhaps the best test of a truly just government is the degree to which it safeguards the rights of unpopular minorities within its jurisdiction.

On these and many similar political issues, the Lutheran and Calvinistic Reformers worked out slightly different theoretical and practical answers, building on the foundations laid down by Augustine and his successors. Later the English Puritans worked out still another view of the proper relationship between church and state. Throughout this period the Anabaptists had their own understanding of biblical teaching about church and state.

American Evangelicalism inherited from all of these strands as well as from nonevangelical political theory stemming from the Enlightenment and other sources.

Since Woodrow Wilson, no Evangelical or near-Evangelical has worked out a political viewpoint that has made any significant impact on the practical political life of the nation. The only exception could be Reinhold Niebuhr, who, though definitely not an Evangelical, absorbed many traditional biblical principles into his practical political insights that he never really worked into a system.

The development of a theistic and evangelical world view with a consistent understanding of politics is a necessary *desideratum* if Evangelicals are to assume a responsible role in our society for the coming generation.

# LAW AND JUSTICE

## John Warwick Montgomery

In his discussion of "Law As the Will of God: The Heritage of the Old Testament," Carl Joachim Friedrich observed that "Yahweh, the God without name of Israel, was clearly distinguished from surrounding gods of other peoples by His preoccupation with law."[1] If the Bible is what it claims to be—not a collection of fallible ancient New Eastern opinion but the inerrant written revelation of the God of the universe—what does this scriptural "preoccupation with law" mean in the sphere of human jurisprudence? It is the contention of the present essay that a divinely given, biblical philosophy of law offers two overarching contributions to the human search for justice: explicit eternal norms against which positive law can and must be judged and a redemptive perspective for all juridical activity.

## I. BIBLICAL JURISPRUDENCE AND THE QUEST FOR NORMS

Is human law no more than a sociological product of the *Zeitgeist*, the spirit of the age? If so, the truly clever man is the one who can "get away" with violating it in order to achieve his purposes; after all, law observance is then only a question of the values of some over against the values of others. In W. H. Auden's words,

> . . . Law-abiding scholars write:
> Law is neither wrong nor right,
> Law is only crimes
> Punished by places and by times,
> Law is the clothes men wear
> Anytime, anywhere,

Law is Good-morning and Good-night.[2]

These lines point to the single most important conceptual battle in modern philosophy of law: the struggle between natural law theorists on the one hand and the legal positivists or realists on the other.

The most influential contemporary representative of legal positivism or realism is H. L. A. Hart, a thinker schooled in the best traditions of the analytical philosophy movement. Hart has raised to a level of considerable sophistication the rather simplistic nineteenth-century view that law and rights are no more than products of the commands of a sovereign (John Austin) or the results of judicial decision (John Chipman Gray). In Hart's view, law requires a social dimension (rules have an "internal aspect") and can only function by way of "shared morality."[3]

But, as Rosenbaum well observes, Hart's "community" approach to rights does not tell us "how to obtain universal agreement on the essentials of a community" or "how it is possible to experience the sense of community when the competing views around the world on the nature of community seem to thwart the development of a unified concept of human rights."[4] The force of these criticisms becomes particularly evident when we note that for Hart the ultimate "rule of recognition" on which any given legal system is founded is *unjustifiable* outside of the system itself.

> We only need the word "validity," and commonly only use it, to answer questions which arise *within* a system of rules where the status of a rule as a member of the system depends on its satisfying certain criteria provided by the rule of recognition. No such question can arise as to the validity of the very rule of recognition which provides the criteria; it can neither be valid nor invalid but is simply accepted as appropriate for use in this way. To express this simple fact by saying darkly that its validity is "assumed but cannot be demonstrated," is like saying that we assume, but can never demonstrate, that the standard meter bar in Paris which is the ultimate test of the correctness of all measure in meters, is itself correct.[5]

We are thus left—as in the case of sociological and anthropological relativism—with no single, unified, justifiable legal standard.[6]

The single gravest problem with all forms of legal realism or positivism is their restriction of the idea of justice to the confines of particular legal systems or jurisprudential orientations. No overriding standard of law and justice is brought to bear on the human situation. As the great Belgian philosopher of law, Ch. Perelman, succinctly puts it:

> This conception of juridical positivism collapses before the abuses of Hitlerism, like any scientific theory irreconcilable with

the facts. The universal reaction to the Nazi crimes forced the Allied chiefs of state to institute the Nuremberg trials and to interpret the adage *nullum crimen sine lege* in a non-positivistic sense because the law violated in the case did not derive from a system of positive law but from the conscience of all civilized men. The conviction that it was impossible to leave these horrible crimes unpunished, although they fell outside a system of positive law, has prevailed over the positivistic conception of the grounding of the law.[7]

In the nineteenth century, legal positivism or realism replaced a much older juridical philosophy, the theory of natural law. And today, the overwhelming difficulties with all varieties of realism are producing still another pendulum-swing in the history of ideas—a swing back to natural law thinking.[8] But the most influential representatives of the current natural law revival do no operate theologically as did their medieval predecessors; rather, they attempt philosophically to establish a ground within human nature for absolute legal norms, a ground allegedly surpassing positive law and cultural relativity.

The most impressive contemporary effort to rehabilitate natural law is provided by John Finnis, fellow of University College, Oxford. Finnis is Roman Catholic and much concerned with the interpretation of Thomas Aquinas vis-à-vis the arguments he presents, but Finnis's great work, *Natural Law and Natural Rights*, is not disguised theologizing. He is thoroughly trained in analytical philosophy and attempts to show in the most general sense that "practical reasonableness" in ordering human affairs requires an approach to the state, law, and justice that will preserve and extend human goods (specifically: life, knowledge, play, aesthetic experience, friendship or sociability, religion, etc.). "There are human goods," he writes, "that can be secured only through the institutions of human law, and requirements of practical reasonableness that only those institutions can satisfy."[9]

What Finnis is trying to show is how any common enterprise of human beings, aims at achieving a common good, and hence demands something which can only be called political or governmental authority. Nor is the function of such authority to be understood exclusively, or even primarily, in terms of any mere exercise of coercive force. No, it is rather for the necessary and indispensable coordination of the efforts of the different agents of the community that the authority is instituted in the first place; and it is only through the exercise of such a directing and coordinating authority that the common good of the community can even be concretely determined, much less achieved. And as for law—human law or positive law—it is nothing if not the indispensable instrument of such a public or governmental authority, aimed at the attainment of the good of the community. Moreover, since the good of the community is not any literally collective good, or even an addictive good, but simply the well-being of each and all of the members of the community individually, the law needs to be so constituted as to respect the rights of the individual members of the community. And here again, in his discussion of the rights, i.e. the natural rights, of citizens, Finnis is very careful to construe such rights—e.g. common law rights, such as the right to property, to a fair trial, to protection against self-incrimination, to safeguards against violence—not as absolute rights, in the way in which this term is so often understood nowadays, but rather as rights that are justified in terms of the natural needs and requirements of the individual, if he is ever to be able to live the life of a truly moral and autonomous human person.[10]

Finnis's commendable attempt to establish standards of justice in terms of practical reasonableness and the common good of the community suffers from great difficulties, however. Bankowski has pointed out that, of the several "human goods" Finnis sets forth, only "knowledge" is effectively justified by his retorsive argument that one cannot argue against it without cutting the ground out beneath one's own feet. And even in the case of knowledge the vital question is still left open: "what items of knowledge we should seek."[11] Indeed, Finnis "is better at showing how law needs to be grounded in ethics, than he is at showing how the principles of ethics are discoverable right in the very facts of nature and reality."[12]

Like every natural law thinker, Finnis must solve the problem of defining what man's nature really is. As Aristotle well observed: "In order to find what is natural we must look among those things which according to nature are in a sound condition, not among those that are corrupt."[13] Granted, man frequently desires knowledge, life, and friendship; but it is equally the case empirically that human beings have often sought to deceive, kill and subjugate their fellows. After all, Hobbes—and Machiavelli before him—built his totalitarian social theory strictly on the natural law basis that human life is "nasty, brutish and short"! A successful natural law theory must be able to say whether the good or the bad in human life is truly "natural" and to what degree—for otherwise no one can determine what values are justly to receive legal sanction in society.

And this dilemma connects with the related quandary for natural law thinkers as to how, even if we know what human nature actually consists of, we can justify deriving an "ought" from the "is." The great analytical ethicist G. E. Moore termed this difficulty the "naturalistic fallacy": the false idea that once you know what is natural you will have justified it as a positive value.[14] In reality, even as the natural fact of murder or torture *does not* justify killing or inhuman punishment, so the natural fact of self-preservation or truth-seeking *does not* vindicate the alleged right to life or civil liberties.

A fatal error is therefore committed when well-meaning religionists (not excluding some Evangelicals) try to solve the root problems of legal philosophy by rejecting positivism in favor of a return to natural law thinking. In reality—though this is almost never recognized—jusnaturalism and legal positivism have correlative strengths and weaknesses which point directly to the need for *biblical jurisprudence.* Consider the two essential defining elements of all natural law theories with their corresponding advantage and disadvantage, and the parallel defining elements and strength/weakness of legal positivism or realism:

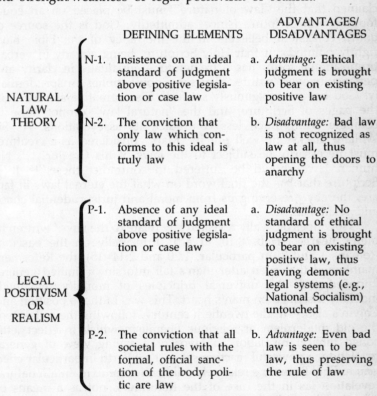

| | | DEFINING ELEMENTS | | ADVANTAGES/ DISADVANTAGES |
|---|---|---|---|---|
| **NATURAL LAW THEORY** | N-1. | Insistence on an ideal standard of judgment above positive legislation or case law | a. | *Advantage:* Ethical judgment is brought to bear on existing positive law |
| | N-2. | The conviction that only law which conforms to this ideal is truly law | b. | *Disadvantage:* Bad law is not recognized as law at all, thus opening the doors to anarchy |
| **LEGAL POSITIVISM OR REALISM** | P-1. | Absence of any ideal standard of judgment above positive legislation or case law | a. | *Disadvantage:* No standard of ethical judgment is brought to bear on existing positive law, thus leaving demonic legal systems (e.g., National Socialism) untouched |
| | P-2. | The conviction that all societal rules with the formal, official sanction of the body politic are law | b. | *Advantage:* Even bad law is seen to be law, thus preserving the rule of law |

What is needed for a sound jurisprudence is a *combination of defining element (N–1a) of jusnaturalism with defining element (P–2b) of legal positivism*—and the rejection of the corresponding disadvantageous elements of the two positions ([N–2b] and [P–1a]). *This is precisely what the biblical jurisprudence offers.*

Thus Romans 13 plainly asserts that "the powers that be are

ordained of God," that "whosoever resisteth the power, resisteth
the ordinance of God," and that we are to be subject to constituted
authority "not only for wrath, but also for conscience sake" (vv.
1b–2, 5 KJV). Scripture clearly holds that even bad law is
nonetheless law and that there is something worse even than bad
law—namely anarchy. The positivist concern with the preservation of the rule of law (P–2b) is thus vindicated.

Even more important, Holy Writ provides from cover to cover
innumerable declarations of God's normative standards for human life. These norms are exactly what natural law theory gropes
for (N–1a) but is unsuccessful in defining apart from a clear and
unambiguous Word from God. In the Genesis-versus-evolution
area of evangelical discussion, where the noninerrantists have
claimed that the "law of nature" must be placed on an equal
footing with Scripture (since, admittedly, God is the source of
both), consistent believers in the inerrancy of the Bible have
rightly pointed out that Holy Scripture, being already in verbal,
propositional form, has a tremendous advantage in clarity and
perspicuity over "nature." The same point applies jurisprudential-
ly: God has unambiguously set forth his normative standards in
the pages of Scripture, and the "natural law" cannot hope to
compete with, much less contradict, its asseverations. As Sir
William Blackstone well put it: "Man, considered as a creature,
must necessarily be subject to the laws of his Creator. . . . No
human laws should be suffered to contradict these."[15] It is
Scripture that has the final word on what the eternal laws in fact
are, thereby preserving us from moral and jurisprudential chaos
and relativism.

How does biblically revealed law relate to the laws "written in
men's hearts" (Heb. 8:10; et al.)? Principally on the basis of
Romans 1 and 2 (in particular, 1:20 and 2:14–15), the Reformers
maintained that even after man's fall into sin, a limited general
knowledge of the universal principles of morality remained,
indelibly inscribed on man's heart. This was Luther's position and
Calvin's also.[16] In the twentieth century, following the collapse of
the old modernism or religious liberalism which in effect jetti-
soned biblical revelation in favor of a saving view of general
revelation, a powerful reaction set in. Karl Barth in particular cried
*nein* to Emil Brunner's relatively mild endeavor to maintain natural
revelation (as in the case of the Reformers, not as a means of
salvation, but only as a partial and imperfect knowledge of divine
standards for human life and thus an objective judgment on man's
sinful conduct toward his fellows).[17] Brunner's position was in
fact little more than a restatement of the classic Reformation
doctrine of the *Schöpfungsordnungen* (Orders of Creation), declaring on the basis of Scripture that even after the Fall, God in his
grace structured human life through government, the family,

education, etc., to prevent sinful man from destroying himself through unrestrained selfishness.[18] The weight of evangelical scholarship has concluded that Barth's total rejection of natural theology—and, with it, natural law theory—is scripturally unwarranted.[19]

But even if a biblical natural law theory is accepted, does it provide the necessary grounding for human jurisprudence? Norwegian theologian Einar Molland contends that:

> It is enough to believe in the value of man and in a written law which is valid for all mankind at all times, that is, in the law which ancient thinkers called the natural law. This is not what the natural sciences understand by natural law, since the law they refer to raises us above nature. The law in question here is concerned with man and corresponds to man's nature. For human coexistence, it is enough to believe that such a natural law exists and that we can all more or less clearly discern it.[20]

We doubt very much that this is "enough for human coexistence." The problem is not that formal natural-rights structures or orders are absent from human society. The trouble is that, though ubiquitously present, they *are* "formal," lacking in universal or justifiable substantive content. Perrott's theory of fundamental rights highlights the root difficulty when he concludes that "there are what may be called Natural Areas of Legal Concern rather than Natural Law principles with a specific content," and that "the precise content of the rules, within limits, does not matter very much; what does matter is that legal discriminations should be drawn and then generally adhered to. We *do* need to decide which side of the road to drive on; the choice of sides is, within limits, arbitrary."[21]

With respect, this is simply inadequate. In a footnote to the quoted passage, Perrott states that "of course, it [the choice of substantive legal content] matters enormously from an evaluative or emotional point of view." Does it only matter emotionally? Is it just an arbitrary question of which side of the road one drives on? A little earlier in his essay, Perrott declares that "a number of different definitions of murder may be equally acceptable"! In point of fact, the substantive definition of legal standards is all-important, and it is these clear definitions which natural law fails to provide. Carl Joachim Friedrich noted that the formula of the Justinian Code is so "imprecise" that it does little more than to underscore the need for "some kind of equity."[22] I observed at the Buchenwald death camp in East Germany that the *Digest's* vague expression, "Give to each his own" was inscribed in German translation (*Jedem das seine*) on the metal doors leading into that place of horror.

This is not in any sense to deny the reality of natural rights: it is only to say that their content is left undefined by natural law thinking, and it is precisely their content which is essential to solve the jurisprudential dilemma. C. S. Lewis is correct that all human societies operate—and must operate—with ethical values;[23] but in order effectively to oppose the myriad variations of man's inhumanity to man, we must be able to determine *which* ethical values are good, bad and indifferent. (Is torture wrong? What about cannibal environmentalists cleaning their plates?) The Orders of Creation are a reality; but it is not enough to know that the family has been instituted by God: one must be able to determine whether polygamy and polyandry are an asset or a liability to human dignity.

The best that can be said of religious natural law theories is that, like John the Baptist, they point beyond themselves. They point to God's special revelation of himself in the living Word (Jesus Christ) and the written Word (the Bible). God's inerrant special revelation yields concrete eternal norms of divine law by which human laws can and must be evaluated and judged.[24] This is the first of the two great contributions of biblical religion to man's quest for law and justice. The second is no less important, and we now turn our attention to it.

## II. BIBLICAL JURISPRUDENCE AND THE CENTRALITY OF REDEMPTION

An inerrant catalog of divine norms for jurisprudence is of incalculable value, for it makes fundamentally impossible the reduction of human law to mere sociological consensus—to

> . . . the clothes men wear
> Anytime, anywhere.

But revealed norms are not enough, for the profoundly practical question remains: granting that we know or are in á position to learn God's will in the sphere of normative jurisprudence, *what is law supposed to accomplish?* What are its proper functions? What is it supposed to do, and what is it incapable of doing? Without an answer to this basic functional question, we are like workers who have been given a perfect tool but are unclear as to what the tool should properly be used for.

The God of the Bible has not left us in such a quandary. The Scriptures make clear what the law's proper functions are and what they are not. Here is a summary expression of biblical teaching on the subject in terms of the classic doctrine of the "three uses of the law":

> The Law has three uses, the Political, the Elenchtico-pedagogical and the Didactic. By the Political use is meant the use of the

law as a curb to hold in check wicked men, and to protect society against their aggressions. By the Elenchtico-pedagogical use is meant its use to convict men of sin and thus indirectly to lead them to Christ (Gal. 3:24). This use of the Law refers primarily to the unconverted. But there is an Elenchtico-pedagogical use of the Law even for the regenerate, inasmuch as the Christian's life should be a daily repentance, and the Law enables him to see his daily shortcomings and his need for Christ more and more clearly. The Didactic use of the Law is its use as a guide for the Christian mind and conduct.[25]

Politically, the law is regarded as a restraint for the wicked, not as a means of building the "perfect society." Christian faith has no illusions about man: "there is none that doeth good, no, not one" (Ps. 14:1, 3 KJV; 53:1; Rom. 3:12). To be sure, the Christian should strive to maximize good through the existing legal system and employ all legitimate efforts to change that system for the better where it falls short; but no legal system will be perfect, for it is administered by imperfect men, and even if it were perfect, it could not make men good. Is the lawyer's task therefore an unimportant one, viewed politically? Hardly, for without it society would literally explode, since the conflicts of self-interest among sinful men will be resolved either within an ordered, legal framework or in an anarchical conflict. But the attorney or judge must see his work in this respect as more analogous to that of the policeman (ponder the double meaning of the term "lawman") than to the endeavors of the social reformer.

At the same time, the Christian in the legal sphere has a positive role of the most powerful nature—one far more significant than the (often naïve) role of the social activist. The pedagogical use of the law, which Luther regarded as its primary function, is that of "schoolmaster [Greek, *paidagogos*: the slave who took the schoolchild to his master] to bring us to Christ." The law shows us where we fall short and therefore continually reminds us of our need for Christ's redemptive work on the cross. Lawyers and those who administer the law have, not so incidentally, an ideal vantage point from which to drive home to others this central truth of the gospel. They are constantly in contact with those in trouble—whether because the latter have personally displayed a *mens rea* or because they are caught in the machinery of a sinful world. What better time or opportunity to help them to see that Christ is the only ultimate answer?[26]

As for the third, or didactic, use of the law, the most important thing to note about it is that, unlike the political and pedagogical uses which apply to non-Christian and Christian alike, it has meaning solely for the believer. Only those who have experienced the forgiveness of sin in Jesus Christ can look at the law (revelational or civil) as something more than a threat. Only the Christian believer can say *ex corde:* "O how I love thy law" (Ps. 119:97, 113 KJV) and "Thy law is my delight" (vv. 77, 92, 174 KJV). Christ's presence alone is capable of transmuting law from a terror (*lex semper accusat*) into an expression of God's loving will.[27]

Having seen what law is from the standpoint of biblical revelation, we must now state with equal precision what it is *not.* As noted in our comments on the political and pedagogical uses of the law, law is *not gospel.* Indeed, the proper distinction between law and gospel can be regarded as the key to all sound theology and Christian life.[28] In his great New Year's sermon of 1532 on Galatians 3:24–25, Luther—who had read law for a year before taking up theological studies—declared:

> The difference between the Law and the Gospel is the height of knowledge in Christendom. Every person and all persons who assume or glory in the name of Christ should know and be able to state this difference. . . .
>
> . . . To be sure, both are God's Word: the Law, or the Ten Commandments, and the Gospel; the latter first given by God in Paradise, the former on Mount Sinai. but everything depends on the proper differentiation of these two messages and on not mixing them together. . . .
>
> Therefore place the man who is able nicely to distinguish the Law from the Gospel at the head of the list and call him a Doctor of the Holy Scripture, for without the Holy Spirit the attainment of this ability to differentiate is impossible. . . .
>
> . . . . By "Law" we should understand nothing but God's Word and command by which He tells us what we are to do and not to do and demands our obedience or work. . . .
>
> The Gospel is such a doctrine or Word of God as does not demand our works or command us to do anything but bids us simply receive the offered grace of the forgiveness of sins and eternal salvation and be satisfied to have it given to us as a free gift.[29]

The essential difference between law and gospel is not that gospel comes from God while law comes from man; both have their origin in the Divine will. The distinction between them is not genetic but functional: law *commands,* while gospel (Old English *godspel,* "good news") *bestows a gift.* Law and gospel are differentiated on this basis throughout the length and breadth of Scripture, but the distinction can be seen with particular clarity when the Bible speaks of the way of salvation or provides salvatory examples. When the people asked our Lord, "What shall we *do,* that we might *work the works* of God?" (thereby confusing gospel with law in thinking that salvation comes by fulfilling the law), Jesus answered in terms of pure gospel: "This is the work of God, that ye believe on him *whom he hath sent*" (John 6:28–29 KJV, italics mine ). Similarly, Jesus with the rich young ruler (Matt. 19:16–22), and Paul with the Philippian jailer (Acts 17:29–34).

The apostle states this principle in formal terms again and again; indeed, it constitutes the very theme of his epistles to the Romans and to the Galatians. For example, in Romans 3:20–22 he draws the line between law and gospel with surgical precision:

> By the deeds of the law there shall no flesh be justified in his sight: for by the law is the knowledge of sin. But now the righteousness of God without the law is manifested, being witnessed by the law and the prophets: even the righteousness of God which is by faith of Jesus Christ unto all and upon all them that believe. . . (KJV).

Why is this distinction between law and gospel so vital? Simply because the whole message of salvation turns on it. A sinful human race wants above all to prove its worth by saving itself—by demonstrating that it can create and maintain ideal legal and ethical structures and thereby satisfy the most exciting cosmic demands. But Scripture depicts such activity as a Tower of Babel—an impossible effort to scale the heights of heaven. "The fear of the LORD is the beginning of wisdom": man needs to recognize that the first step in salvation is to admit that he cannot save himself by the deeds of the law—however impressive the deeds or however commendable the law. "No man hath ascended up to heaven, but he that came down from heaven, even the Son of man" (John 3:13).

This endemic fallacy of egotistic fallen man—turning law into gospel—is evident whether one looks back into history or gazes across the expanse of the present. Contemporary political theorist Eric Voegelin, in his epochal series, *Order and History*, has identified the theme of "metastatic gnosis" in the human drama: the Promethean urge to create on earth a millennial perfection which only God is in fact capable of achieving. Voegelin charts the appalling evils produced by this Nietzschean transvaluation of all proper value, and correctly stresses that its result is always the very opposite of true order.[30]

In the Marxist East, one observes a religious conviction (a genuine opiate of the people?) to the effect that if the structures of society are altered, human perfection is attainable: eliminate by revolutionary action the inequities in the ownership of the means of production, recast law so that it no longer favors a ruling caste of capitalists, and a millennial "classless society" will arise.[31] In the capitalist West the means of social engineering are different, but the theory is the same: Change the structures, and you will save mankind. Somehow no one asks the painfully obvious question: How can a self-centered Skinner build a Skinner box that will provide an environment capable of yielding non-self-centered future generations? Our craze for environmental works-righteousness disregards C. S. Lewis's perceptive observation that "man's power over Nature is really the power of some men over other men, with Nature as their instrument."[32] And in the Third World, whether we observe the lamination of a modern European civil code on a medieval Ethiopia or seek to comprehend mystical socialism in Tanzania, it becomes plain that law is regarded as a prime weapon of social change.[33]

No Christian, much less the Christian lawyer, can justify otherworldly indifference to social amelioration or to the importance of law revision in achieving worthwhile societal goals. But the way of salvation does not lie along that path. Law must be rigorously distinguished from gospel. "The law was given through Moses; grace and truth came through Jesus Christ" (John 1:17 KJV).

Confusion of law and gospel is possible in two directions. Law may be invested with the quality of gospel, thereby deceiving men into thinking that they can save themselves through personal or societal efforts. But gospel may also try to replace law, producing what Bonhoeffer has classically phrased "cheap grace." In the one case, law swallows up gospel, and the result is *legalism*; in the other, gospel absorbs law, yielding *antinomianism*. The gravity of dispensing with law for any reason—even on the alleged ground that grace renders it no longer necessary—is suggested by the New Testament use of the Greek word *anomos* ("lawless one") for the Antichrist (2 Thess. 2:8).

In contemporary theology the antinomian error is rife. Among modern theologians Paul Lehmann argues that not law or moral rules but rather "believing contexts" should guide our actions; what we should do will be discovered dynamically as we participate in the believing community.[34] A more radical variation on this new morality is Joseph Fletcher's "situation ethics," where we learn that "only one thing is intrinsically good, namely love," and that "love's decisions are made situationally, not prescriptively."[35] Such views fail to recognize that law and principle are unavoidably present—implicitly if not explicitly—in personal and societal decision-making and are far more dangerous when implicit; that love is a motive, incapable of charting specific action apart from a structure of values; and that to depend on situations to yield their own answers is to engage in a most perilous form of magic, since what bubbles up from the caldron of sinful situations has no guarantee whatever of ethical purity.[36]

The late James A. Pike, a lawyer before he entered the Episcopal priesthood, declared in his 1962 Rosenthal Lectures at the Northwestern University School of Law that though the Ten Commandments "give us a very good rule of thumb as to standard situations," they are "pregnable to the assault of a higher

claim:" "rules, whether they be traffic regulations or commandments from Mount Sinai, do not exhaust the full moral dimensions
of things." And where is the "higher claim" to be found? In the
dynamics of the existential situation. "In these pages," wrote
Pike, "it will become apparent that I am an existentialist." As an
illustration, he commends the heroine of the apocryphal Book of
Judith for her willingness to operate with a "higher claim" than
the sixth commandment in being willing to commit adultery so as
to kill a political enemy of her people.[37] Here, as in situation
ethics, the sinful human existential moment is invested with
revelatory quality: immediate, individual situations are naïvely
supposed to be able to "reveal" what neither human law—the
product of far wider and deeper reflection—or even Holy
Scripture—which claims to be and is the very Word of God—can
adequately provide.[38]

The belief that the world of law is capable of being humanisti-
cally replaced by a climate of love, peace, and joy has been
expressed by Charles Reich, formerly of the Yale law faculty, in
*The Greening of America.* There he declares that the hippie
exuberance—turning on and dropping out—of the 1960s heralded the dawn of a new consciousness: "Consciousness III,"
representing no less than "the beginning of the development of
new capacities in man" and positing "a community of a very
different sort, based upon love and trust." The conquest of
scarcity has made literally possible a "change in human nature,"
since "man no longer needs to base his society on the assumption
that all men are antagonistic to one another." As for legal
structures, Reich grudgingly concedes that "perhaps democracy,
law, and constitutional rights will still be wanted in a new
society"; but he quickly adds that, if so, "they cannot be based or
justified any longer on assumptions" such as that "man is a wolf
to man."[39]

And yet that is precisely what man continues to be. The
Christian must never make the mistake of thinking that in his
personal life or in the life of his society law is dispensable. If he
does, the wolf within him and others will gnaw away his very soul
and that of society. Concretely, the Christian will recognize that
Romans 13 makes any violation of positive law an evil, even if in
particular instances the law is not wise or just, and even if the
subject matter prohibited by it is not *malum in se.* (Thus revolution
is always an evil—though in some instances it may admittedly be
a lesser of evils—and alcohol or marijuana, even if not inherently
harmful to the body, cannot be used with moral impunity where
prohibited by law.)

In sum, the Christian will test all positive law by the
pronouncements of Holy Scripture, endeavoring by every legitimate means at his disposal to bring man's temporal law into

conformity with God's eternal law.[40] Such a practical recognition that law is indispensable will serve the highest purpose of all: It will remind the individual and the society how far short of God's standards of justice they fall and will, as a schoolmaster, point them to Christ's perfect salvation.[41]

# ENDNOTES

[1] Carl Joachim Friedrich, *The Philosophy of Law in Historical Perspective*, 2d ed. (Chicago: University of Chicago Press, 1963), p. 8.

[2] W. H. Auden, "Law Like Love" (From *The Collected Poetry of W. H. Auden*), reprinted in John Warwick Montgomery, ed., *Jurisprudence: A Book of Readings*, 2d ed. (Strasbourg, France: International Scholarly Publishers; Anaheim, Calif.: The Simon Greenleaf School of Law, 1980), pp. 4–5.

[3] Hart has presented his philosophy of law systematically in *The Concept of Law* (Oxford: Clarendon, 1961). J. W. Harris offers a helpful interpretation of Hart's ideas with a good bibliography (*Legal Philosophies* [London: Butterworths, 1980], pp. 105–14).

[4] Alan S. Rosenbaum, "Introduction," in his *The Philosophy of Human Rights: International Perspectives* (Westport, Conn.: Greenwood, 1980), p. 33.

[5] Hart, *The Concept of Law*, pp. 105–6.

[6] For a more detailed treatment of legal positivism with an examination of the views of Hans Kelsen, Ronald Dworkin, et al., see my *Human Rights and Human Dignity* (Dallas: Probe; Grand Rapids: Zondervan, 1986), ch. 4.

[7] Ch. Perelman, "Can the Rights of Man Be Founded?" in *The Philosophy of Human Rights*, ed. Rosenbaum, p. 47. See also M. J. Detmold, *The Unity of Law and Morality: A Refutation of Legal Positivism* (London: Routledge & Kegan Paul, 1984).

[8] Cf. C. G. Haines, *The Revival of Natural Law Concepts* (Cambridge: Harvard University Press, 1958).

[9] John Finnis, *Natural Law and Natural Rights* (Oxford: Clarendon, 1980), p. 3. Finnis's list of human goods is based upon Germain Grisez, "The First Principle of Practical Reason," *Natural Law Forum* 10 (1965): 168–96.

[10] Henry B. Veatch, review of *Natural Law and Natural Rights* by John Finnis, *American Journal of Jurisprudence* 26 (1981): 253.

[11] Z. K. Bankowski, review of *Natural Law and Natural Rights* by John Finnis, *Law Quarterly Review* 98 (July 1982): 474.

[12] Veatch, Review of *Natural Law and Natural Rights* by Finnis, p. 250.

[13] Aristotle, *Politics*, 1.5.

[14] G. E. Moore, *Principia Ethica* (Cambridge: Cambridge University Press, 1903), ch. 1. For a more extended discussion and critique of contemporary natural-law theories, including the Neo-Kantian approaches of Rawls and Gewirth, see my *Human Rights and Human Dignity*.

[15] Sir William Blackstone, *Commentaries on the Laws of England*, ed. Stanley N. Katz, et al.; 4 vols., facsimile ed. (Chicago: University of Chicago Press, 1979), 1:39, 42.

[16] On Luther, see Philip S. Watson, *Let God Be God! An Interpretation of the Theology of Martin Luther* (London: Epworth Press, 1947), pp. 73–85, 105–16; and Marc Lienhard, "Luther et les droits de l'homme," *Revue d'Histoire et de Philosophie Religieuses* 54/1 (1974): 15–29 (English translation in *A Lutheran Reader on Human Rights*, eds. Jorgen Lissner and Arne Sovik: *LWF Report* 1–2 [September 1978]: 66–80). Paul Helm of the University of Liverpool's Department of Philosophy, in delivering the third Finlayson lecture, provides an excellent overview of "Calvin and Natural Law:" *The Scottish Bulletin of Evangelical Theology* 2 (1984): 5–22.

[17] See the celebrated debate between Barth and Brunner, *Natural Theology: Comprising "Nature and Grace" by Professor Dr. Emil Brunner and the Reply "No!" by Dr. Karl Barth*, trans. Peter Fraenkel (London: Geoffrey Bles, 1946).

[18] John Warwick Montgomery, "Karl Barth and Contemporary Theology of History," in his *Where Is History Going? Essays in Support of the Historical Truth of the Christian Revelation*, reprint ed. (Minneapolis: Bethany, 1972), pp. 104–5; and Montgomery, "A Critical Examination of Emil Brunner's *The Divine Imperative*, Bk. III," in his *The Shape of the Past*, rev. ed. (Minneapolis: Bethany, 1975), pp. 358–74.

[19] See, for example, Alan F. Johnson, "Is There a Biblical Warrant for Natural-Law Theories?" *Evangelical Theological Society Journal* 25/2 (June 1982): 185–99; and Bruce A. Demarest, *General Revelation* (Grand Rapids: Zondervan, 1982). Professor Demarest (p. 244) rejects on biblical grounds the entire—predominately Dutch hyper-Calvinist—tradition which maintains that "no knowledge is mediated by general revelation in nature and providence" (Demarest refers specifically to Abraham Kuyper, G. C. Berkouwer, Cornelius Van Til, Gordon Clark, T. F. Torrance, and Donald Bloesch—as well as Karl Barth). Jacques Ellul, as one would expect, follows Barth in unqualifiedly rejecting natural theology: see his *The Theological Foundation of Law*, trans. Marguerite Wieser (New York: Seabury, 1969); and cf. John Warwick Montgomery, "Technology and Eschatology," in his *Faith Founded on Fact* (Nashville: Thomas Nelson, 1978), pp. 155–59.

[20] Quoted in Marc Lienhard, "Protestantism and Human Rights," *Human Rights Teaching* [UNESCO] 2/1 (1981): 30.

[21] D. L. Perrott, "The Logic of Fundamental Rights," in *Fundamental Rights*, eds. J. W. Bridge, D. Lasok, et al. (London: Sweet & Maxwell, 1973), pp. 13–15.

[22] Friedrich, *Philosophy of Law in Historical Perspective*, p. 33. See also John Warwick Montgomery, *The Law Above the Law* (Minneapolis: Bethany, 1975), pp. 38–40.

[23] C. S. Lewis, *The Case for Christianity* (New York: Macmillan, 1943), reprinted in his *Mere Christianity* (New York: Macmillan, 1953); and cf. his *Abolition of Man* (New York: Macmillan, 1947).

[24] For a systematic presentation of the scriptural norms governing positive law, see, for example, H. B. Clark, *Biblical Law*, 2d ed. (Portland, Ore.: Binfords & Mort, 1944).

[25] Joseph Stump, *The Christian Faith* (Philadelphia: Muhlenberg, 1942), pp. 309–10. This basic conceptualization is found in all the standard works of classical dogmatics.

[26] This theme is further developed in my book, *Law & Gospel: A Study in Jurisprudence* (Oak Park, Ill.: Christian Legal Society, 1978).

[27] See John Warwick Montgomery, "The Law's Third Use: Sanctification," in his *Crisis in Lutheran Theology*, 2 vols., rev. ed. (Minneapolis: Bethany, 1973), 1:124–27.

[28] C. F. W. Walther, *The Proper Distinction Between Law and Gospel*, ed. W. Dau (St. Louis: Concordia, 1928).

[29] *WA* (the standard, critical Weimar edition of Luther's writings), 36:25, 29–31.

[30] See Montgomery, *Shape of the Past*, pp. 131–37. Norman L. Geisler has recently pointed out similarly disquieting tendencies in the Calvinist "Reconstructionist" camp ("A Premillennial View of Law and Government," *Bibliotheca Sacra*, July–September 1985, pp. 250–66), though the true source of the Reconstructionist error would appear to lie not in their rejection of premillennialism or dispensationalism but in their acceptance of the Calvinist view that the pedagogical use of the law is to be subordinated to the third or didactic use. Such triumphalism opens the door to postmillennial naïveté.

[31] See John Warwick Montgomery, "The Marxist Approach to Human Rights: Analysis & Critique," *The Simon Greenleaf Law Review*, vol. 3 (1983–84), passim.

[32] Quoted in P. H. Sand, "The Socialist Response: Environmental Protection Law in the German Democratic Republic," *Ecology Law Quarterly* 3 (1973): 485.

[33] H. C. Dunning, "Land Reform in Ethiopia: A Case Study in Non-Development," *UCLA Law Review* 18 (1970): 271; R. B. Seidman, "Law and Stagnation in Africa," *Zambia Law Journal* 5 (1973): 39.

[34] Paul Lehmann, *Ethics in a Christian Context* (New York: Harper and Row, 1963), pp. 159–61.

[35] Joseph Fletcher, *Situation Ethics: The New Morality* (Philadelphia: Westminster, 1966).

[36] Joseph Fletcher and John Warwick Montgomery, *Situation Ethics—True or False; A Dialogue* (Minneapolis: Bethany, 1972), pp. 25–48.

[37] James A. Pike, *Beyond the Law* (New York: Doubleday, 1963), pp. xii, 14–16.

[38] For my critiques of Pike's theology, in dialogue with him and in print, see John Warwick Montgomery, *The Suicide of Christian Theology* (Minneapolis: Bethany, 1971), pp. 17–61, 231–32.

[39] Charles A. Reich, *The Greening of America* (New York: Bantam, 1971), pp. 379–430.

[40] For guidelines in those difficult situations where the implementation of divine norms in a secular legal climate conflicts with the Christian's primary evangelistic task, see John Warwick Montgomery, *The Shaping of America* (Minneapolis: Bethany, 1976), pp. 152–58.

[41] Noteworthy as contemporary illustrations are Charles Colson and Jeb Magruder, who came to Christ as a direct result of seeing their lives in shambles because of their participation in the Watergate illegalities.

# A Response to
# Law and Justice

## Gleason L. Archer

John Montgomery's discussion of the proper relationship between human law enacted by men and the law of God set forth in Holy Scripture serves to bring out very clearly the basic principle that human legislation must ultimately rest on those concepts of right and wrong which are set forth in the Bible. This paper comes as a solemn reminder to the courts and legislative bodies established by mankind that they are finally responsible to the Lord of Justice himself for a faithful administration of their trust. In his opening section, "Biblical Jurisprudence and the Quest for Norms," he points out that valid human law must rest on a firmer foundation than the spirit of the age, a mere sociological product of the *Zeitgeist* that happens to prevail in modern times. The now popular view of the legal positivists, that human governments are answerable to no higher power than their own, fails to take stock of the operative principle upheld by the Nuremberg trials conducted against the leaders of the Nazi Reich. What seemed warranted and proper within Hitler's Germany between 1935 and 1945 with its unbridled tyranny and systematic genocide was completely rejected as an unpardonable offense against the human race. The condemnation of those surviving members of Hitler's high command were not condemned on the basis of the disapproval of the victorious allied nations themselves but on a much higher authority than that of men. The underlying assumption behind these judicial proceedings was that mankind as a whole is answerable to a standard of right and wrong imposed on the human race by the Author of creation.

We must, therefore, recognize from the outset that the very basis of commitment to a moral order, to which we all as human beings are unanswerable, stems from the understanding set forth

in the very first chapter of the Bible, that man has been created in
the moral and spiritual image of God. After the destruction of the
great Flood, when Noah and his family are given the assignment
of beginning a new race of men governed by a sense of
responsibility toward God, the Lord himself is quoted as charging
Noah with governmental authority on this basis: "From every
man, from every man's brother, I will require the life of man.
Whoever sheds man's blood, by man his blood shall be shed, for
in the image of God he made man." This can only mean that he
who transgresses against his fellow man or unjustly takes his life
must pay for that murder with his own life, precisely because he
has transgressed against God himself. It further implies that
human courts are finally answerable to Almighty God if they fail
to carry out capital punishment for justifiable homicide. This is a
mandate which cannot be altered to a term of years in jail or the
payment of monetary damages or be altogether forgiven on the
basis of a spurious plea of insanity. The divine mandate is one of
justice, of recognizing the worth of the victim who has been slain,
acknowledging him as one born in the image of God.

Montgomery rightly observes, concerning John Finnis, that
his attempt to find a secure base for the "natural" rights of man on
the inherent worth of man as a created species, even apart from
his status as a son of God under the covenant that God made with
Adam, turns out to be less than compelling. A view of man such
as reflected in the Declaration of Independence, with an inherent
right to "life, liberty and the pursuit of happiness," may be taken
as a mere self-flattering delusion on the part of the human
species—unless it is based on the presupposition expressed in the
Declaration itself. The context affirms that man has "by his
Creator" been endowed with these inalienable rights. Without the
decree of God the human race has no objective foundation for
claiming any such status at all. Apart from the revealed decree of
the Lord Almighty in Genesis 1 and 2, there is no solid basis for
asserting such natural rights, as over against the rights of the rat
or the tiger or of any other animal with aims and goals quite
contrary to the good of mankind. For the human race to proclaim
any kind of inherent worth or set of privileges over against the rest
of the animal world is unjustified arrogance incapable of logical
justification.

From the foregoing considerations concerning the divine
image decreed by the personal God who first created man, it
inevitably follows that the human race is not at liberty to spell out
the implications of life, liberty, and happiness according to its
preferences or desires. These so-called natural rights, bestowed on
us by God, must be exercised only in accordance with the will of
God as revealed in his written Word, the Bible. This has been
almost universally acknowledged by various races of mankind

from the beginning of recorded history. Even the most idolatrous nations, like the ancient Egyptians, understood that their entire pantheon sponsored and enforced the moral law as represented by Ma'at, the goddess of "truth," against whom the heart of each deceased person had to be weighed on the scales of judgment in the presence of Osiris, the king of the dead. They understood full well that this moral order was divinely ordained rather than being manufactured by any sort of organized human government or human authority. The inherent rights of men had been given them by the gods themselves rather than by human legislation based on some sort of "social contract." Even the Pharaoh, though regarded as a divine son of Re', the sun god, was subject to the guidelines and the penalties of Ma'at, no matter how much he would have had it otherwise.

From this standpoint, then, the humanistic assumptions which seem to underlie some of the recent decisions of the United States Supreme Court, which understands the mandates of basic morality to depend on the majority opinion of contemporary culture, are altogether unsound. While public opinion must be taken into consideration of legal decisions, it must be clearly understood that popular sentiment is altogether incompetent to abrogate or set aside the basic principles embodied in the Ten Commandments. What God has established, man may not validly annul. As we read in Isaiah 5:20-23:

> Woe to those who call evil good, and good evil;
> Who substitute darkness for light and light for darkness; . . .
> Woe to those who are wise in their own eyes,
> And clever in their own sight! . . .
> Who justify the wicked for a bribe,
> And take away the rights of the ones who are in the right!
> NASB).

These pronouncements from the God of Isaiah make clear the wickedness and the folly of human judges and human teachers in our public schools who advocate the right of any mother-to-be to have her unborn child butchered in an abortion clinic, the right of all murderers to escape the penalty of death even though they have snuffed out the life of another who has been created in the image of God. Those who have given themselves over to the depravity of homosexual pollution or who brutally abuse their wives and defile their children by incest, those who make a business of prostitution or who indulge in the sordid practice of fornication and adultery—all of these stand under the judgment of God. No changing values in modern society, no new approaches to sexual morality or to the stewardship of the human body, have the slightest validity to overturn the standards of the past which were derived from the guidelines of Holy Scripture.

The tragic history of the northern kingdom of Israel, which failed
to honor even the most basic moral principles of God's law (Hos.
8–10; Amos 3–4) and was completely destroyed and exiled by
Assyria in 721 B.C. serves to demonstrate that divine retribution
ultimately overtakes any nation that settles for a man-made set of
values in preference to the standards appointed by the Lord. The
judgment imposed on the heathen neighbors of Israel for disre-
garding the basic requirements of humanity and justice is similarly
declared against Damascus, Gaza, Tyre, Edom, Ammon, and
Moab in Amos 1–2. The surrender of Judah to crass materialism
and brutal disregard of the rights of God and man led to the total
destruction of Jerusalem and its temple in 587 B.C. There can be no
reasonable doubt that a similar fate awaits the nations of
Christendom, Islam, and the Marxist powers of our present day
unless their people repent of their wicked folly in abandoning the
standards of the moral law and return to moral sanity.

Dr. Montgomery suggests that biblical jurisprudence combines the emphasis on an ideal standard of judgment over against
positive legislation or mere case law (characteristic of the natural
law theory) together with the stress of legal positivism on the duty
of obedience even to laws or regulations which seem to be
defective or ill-conceived. It should perhaps be added that the
cultural framework of the Old Testament, reflecting a divinely
appointed body of law intended for the guidance of the entire
nation of Israel, presented a clearer case for unquestioning
obedience (apart from tyrannical decrees by wicked Hebrew
kings), than would have been true for the New Testament age
when the Gentile power of Rome was in control with Nero at its
head, for example. But whether the government was in the hands
of Jews or Gentiles, the duty of obedience to God over against the
evil mandates of unjust rulers is clearly maintained by the refusal
of Daniel's three Hebrew comrades to bow down to Nebuchadnezzar's golden image (Dan. 3:16–18) and by the firm insistence of
the apostles before the Sanhedrin in Acts 5:29: "We ought to obey
God rather than men" (KJV). It might be profitable to comb
carefully through the specific instances in the record of both
Testaments in order to establish a clear definition of when such a
conflict arises. But in general it may be observed that there is a
qualitative difference between modern perceptions of the advocates of "social justice" (so called), who identify their policies of
radical activism with the will of God; and those clear-cut confron-
tations between the divinely established moral law and the
decrees of brutal opponents of the Lord such as Pharaoh in the
time of Moses, or of Ahab and Jezebel in the time of Elijah, and of
Nebuchadnezzar in the time of Daniel. The courageous stand of
the Hebrew midwives against infant abortion, of Lot against the
Sodomites who tried to attack his angelic visitors, of General

Obadiah in shielding the prophets of Jehovah against the bloody
persecution of Queen Jezebel, the absolute refusal of Nebuchadnezzar's Jewish civil servants to join in an act of idolatry—all of
these examples serve as guidelines of a far different character than
the sitdown strikes and the harboring of illegal aliens in the
present-day sanctuary movement espoused by certain liberal
churches in open defiance of the duly enacted legislation of our
national Congress.

Another important area that needs to be explored with greater
precision is the feasibility in injecting factors of Christian compassion into the theory of criminology. A dangerous element of
confusion has been introduced into the administration of justice in
such a way as to favor and protect the wrongdoer as against his
victims. A false sentimentalism which injects primary concern into
psychological or environmental factors which led the criminal to
commit his crime tends to obscure the just and proper rights of
those whose lives he has unjustly taken or ruined, has made a
travesty of much of American criminology. A drunken sailor may
tie up, rape, and strangle eight nurses in a single night for a lark,
and the U.S. Supreme Court may void the verdict of the jury
which found him guilty, solely because no person was allowed to
sit on the jury who rejected the whole concept of capital
punishment. Or a businessman of such sanity as to carry a good
deal of influence in local politics can engage in the practice of
murdering twenty or thirty young men after he has sodomized
them, and still be shielded from the death penalty on the ground
that he is mentally deranged. A high-strung young man may
attempt, and nearly succeed, in murdering the president of the
United States in order to gain the attention of some Hollywood
actress who hardly knows of his existence. But if his attorney is
clever enough to convince the jury that the poor boy was in a
highly disturbed state of mind, he may be let off from the capital
punishment that his crime deserves. The right of our chief
executive to head the government of our nation is thus set aside in
order to give the frustrated gunman free room and board for the
rest of his limited life term. It is doubtful how long any nation can
endure that devotes its courts and legal process to the grossest
miscarriages of justice, often upheld by a Supreme Court that feels
free to manipulate and profoundly alter the Constitution of the
United States away from the intention of the framers of that
document and the congresses and state legislatures that enacted
the subsequent amendments. We live in an age when the judicial
branch of our government usurps the functions of the legislative,
handing down decisions tantamount to new law, in which the
voting public and the legislative bodies elected by them have not
the slightest say. The benevolent endorsement of any expectant
mother to have her baby murdered by an abortionist has rendered

our Supreme Court indirectly responsible for the execution of well
over 13 million totally innocent American citizens. The only higher
tribunal left to bring such heinous guilt to a proper trial is that of
the Lord God Almighty before whom each of those justices who
voted with the majority in *Roe v. Wade* will some day have to give
account.

A closely related misconception implicit in the present-day
sentimentalism is the completely unfounded and unbiblical notion
that the primary purpose of imprisonment is psychological
rehabilitation. The futile expectation implied in the heart-wringing
appeal of the defense attorney is that his unfortunate client should
be viewed not as an enemy of society deserving of punishment
but as a misguided victim of his environment or heredity who
needs psychological counseling and a brief term in prison in order
to straighten out his thinking and emerge from incarceration as a
newly productive and exemplary citizen. It is, of course, most
blatant in the typical humiliation and sneering innuendoes leveled
against the women who are victims of forcible rape that the
criminal is to be justified in our American courts, and the objects
of their brutality are subjected to public shame without the
achieving of any kind of justice. But in general it should be
pointed out that all too often the compassion of judge and jury is
directed toward the rapist or the robber or the perpetrator of incest
who has psychologically ruined his children for the rest of their
lives. Little or no concern is shown toward the objects of their
brutality or lust, and no provision is made to help them through
the consequences of the injustice perpetrated against them. It is
high time that these grave abuses are called to the full attention of
our American electorate while there is still time to replace the
present breed of judges and justices with those who believe that
the real purpose of our courts is to administer justice rather than
injustice.

Dr. Montgomery is to be commended for his sturdy Lutheran
emphasis on the need of distinguishing between law and gospel.
This is, of course, a specifically religious concern that pertains
more particularly to our churches rather than to our citizenry as a
whole. But it is of utmost importance to make clear that there is no
necessary connection between moral living and a state of redemption. It is safe to say that no class of sinners is so hard to convert to
a saving knowledge of Christ as those who are religiously
uncommitted but who maintain a high moral standard in their
actual lifestyle. They are the hardest to convince that they are still
nothing but guilty sinners worthy of eternal hell. They fail to
comprehend that only the righteousness of Jesus Christ and the
blood he has shed for their atonement can avail before God. In this
sense the law has no redemptive value at all but only serves to
demonstrate that they too have "come short of the glory of God"

(Rom. 3:23 KJV). But this emphasis on the second use of the law, the pedagogical, must not obscure the first use of the law, the political, which has a binding force on all men, whether believers or not.

There remains only one other observation to make in regard to the Montgomery paper. The closest and most careful attention needs to be devoted to the distinction between the general and universally binding provisions of the moral law of God and those of a ceremonial or ritual character, which served to train and prepare God's ancient people for the coming of Christ. Helpful guidelines may be found in Acts 10:9–15 (Peter's vision of the great sheet), Acts 15:22–29 (the Gentiles excused from circumcision and the ceremonial law), Colossians 2:16–23 (matters of diet and the observance of Jewish feasts), Hebrews 8:7–13 (the New Covenant by which the law is written on the hearts of true believers) and Hebrews 9:9–10. Passages of this sort should be studied with great care in order to bring out those guidelines of holy and morally responsible living which are contained in the Hebrew Scriptures and are applicable to the context of the present world. Admittedly there may arise highly defensible differences of interpretation in this whole investigation, but surely there will be many a principle or standard of justice or equity that can be appropriated in our modern jurisprudence. All of this process must be carried on with a solemn sense of responsibility before the Author of liberty whose gracious providence made possible the kind of life and polity which we presently enjoy in this favored land. Legislators, judges, and lawyers are responsible not only to their human electorate but also to their divine Sovereign before whose tribunal all men shall some day stand in order to give an account of the deeds done in the body, whether good or bad. "It is appointed unto men once to die, and after this the judgment" (Heb. 9:27).

# A Response to
# Law and Justice

## William N. Garrison

Dr. Montgomery has set before us well a foundation for our discussion on the Christian and his relationship to law and justice. He has demonstrated that neither the theory of natural law nor positivism can, in and of itself, provide a sufficient basis for law. His development of this brings to mind the wistful words of James M. Wall, editor of the *Christian Century*, as he writes concerning his encounter with an intellectual fundamentalist, "It is the curse of liberalism that we have to start over again with each issue, searching for right and wrong and defending our conclusions against a *backdrop of relativity*. The fundamentalist who is also an intellectual (and there are some) continues to probe the nature of evil, but always within the perimeters of a moral universe." All of us here are in editor Wall's frame of reference "Fundamentalist," and we are here probing the nature of evil within the perimeters of a moral universe. We are also here in a common conviction that God has revealed himself in a divinely superintended written account of his intervention in the affairs of creation and mankind, culminating in the incarnation, death, resurrection, and ascension of his Son, Jesus Christ; and we believe that that written Word is inerrant, subject to the caveats and qualifications of understanding which are included in the 1978 Chicago Statement. We are also here in substantial agreement that that inerrant document can be understood sufficiently well so that its message is clear. Our task on this occasion is to address the "So What?" which is unavoidable in that line of thought. If this be the Word of God, and we are in agreement as to how it should be understood, what impact should, and shall, it make on our lives? Our subject is the Christian and his relationship to law and justice, and in that connection I would like to ask for discussion under three headings.

## I. SECULAR LAW, OR THE LAW OF NATIONS

We think it is essential to recognize and distinguish the Mosaic law from the secular law, that is, the law of Romans 13. When the theologian speaks of the law he instinctively thinks of Sinai and the elaborate commands and instructions which were there given to Israel in connection with worship, with diet, and with the relationships between men. We believe that Sinai was and is a distinctive in history, an event when God brings into existence the nation which he has ordained in a unique way as a portion of his program of self-manifestation. Albright has commented on the uniqueness of the recorded origins of that nation, beginning as it does with a lowly sheepherder, passing through a protracted family experience, then through the nomadic and tribal multitude of descendants of that family and finally being transformed into a nation with its elaborate laws and with its distinctive ownership and possession of the land. This sequence of events is so unique that we must be careful lest we attempt to extrapolate it into something normative for all men for all ages and for all societies. We do not know of any biblical authority commanding us to impose the Sinai law on any nation other than Israel, nor are we aware of any statement that any other nation will be judged according to that law.

To speak to the application of law and justice insofar as the Christian is concerned requires that we address secular law in the same way that the apostles Peter and Paul encountered it and learn from their and other illustrations in the Scriptures. It is the Roman secular law, which exclusively benefited its citizens, that Paul appealed to in Acts 16 and 21; and that his appeal was utilitarian is obvious. He sought the protections accorded him by that law for his life and safety. But I am certain that he had no illusions that it was "holy and righteous and good" in the sense that he spoke of in Romans 7:12. Nevertheless, that is the law to which he referred in Romans 13, declaring that it is of God. It is particularly significant that by the time of his writing, the Roman Empire had begun to take notice of the Christian sect within Judaism and was responding with an accelerating degree of persecution.

It is interesting to note that when the Jews set out to destroy Jesus they were scrupulous in their recognition of their limitations in the carrying out of capital punishment. They were careful in the fabrication of the stories concerning Jesus and presented him as a threat to the Roman Empire, thereby attempting to incite Pilate and Herod to view him as an insurrectionist, posing great danger to the empire for which he could be executed. This attitude on the Jews' part seems to have been unique for this one occasion, and beyond their knowing, important in the eternal scheme to bring to pass the insidious religious hatred joining forces with Gentile indifference and callousness for the execution of the Son of God. A short time later the Jews were not nearly so fastidious in the stoning of Stephen, nor is there any evidence that the Romans were at all disturbed about this happening. Nowhere else in the Book of Acts does the Gentile power take offense at the Jewish excesses of this nature, the attitude of Gallio in Acts 18:17 being a case in point. In Acts 21 the Jews would have killed Paul but for intervention by the Roman commander upon learning that Paul was a Roman citizen.

Paul enjoins Timothy from prison that prayers are to be offered for the people in power in government, and the reason is given that it facilitates godly living and the spread of the gospel. The question of application is just as relevant for us today as it was for Peter in Acts 4 and later in Acts 12 after the execution of James by the Romans; and the history of the church is, in large measure, a record of the believer's struggle with secular law.

## II. MAKING OF LAW AND ITS ADMINISTRATION

There has been debate recently about the evangelical commitment of the fathers of our country. There is no doubt, however, that their frame of reference was greatly shaped by the philosophy of the Protestant Reformation, which acknowledged the sinfulness of man, the accountability to a sovereign God, all of which resulted in a respect for government and our need for it. The making of our early laws, however, was not spontaneous, nor was it a consensus of all of those involved. The following quote concerning the Massachusetts Bay Colony illustrates the diversity expressed.

> It must also be remembered that the principal leaders of early Massachusetts—Cotton, Winthrop, Dudley, and Endicott in particular, were overly zealous in their efforts to prevent and suppress any manifestation of independence in religious or political matters. They considered democracy in any form to be at variance with the will of God and the good of man and hence were violently opposed to any democratic innovations. Suspicious of a common people and distrustful of the motives and intentions of ordinary men, they inaugurated a stringent policy, which in some instances, amounted to spiritual, intellectual and political repression.

By contrast today the function of law making, that is government service, has been abdicated by the Christian community until very recent efforts to reinvolve the Evangelical. In the early part of this century the Evangelicals retreated, for reasons which are too complicated to speculate here, and they did not train and encourage their children with a view to public service. How we love to discover evangelical Christians in government, but all too often we discover that they are converts in later life. Since politics and government are viewed as essentially dirty and suspect, this is a convenient attitude because we are spared the process of political advancement and only have to deal with people who are already "winners" in that arena—that is, already in office.

There probably is a lack of awareness that law in the secular sense has developed dramatically over the years, and that development is a response to the needs of society. A simple tribal society has a simple set of laws. Commerce and financial activity carry with them the necessity for a sophistication of law. The early English common law was simple in the extreme by comparison with our laws today. An expanding economy inevitably leads to an expanding sophistication of the law. It is also essential to notice that an expanded view, or an enlightened view, of human rights and the protection of those rights by the law best occurs in an expanding and dynamic economy. Political power that exists in a poor and deprived economy will very seldom produce significant human rights advancement except superficially.

British common law was a development of law based on the doctrine of *stare decisis,* meaning law is an accumulation of all the opinions which have been rendered by the courts down through the years and decades. This law in England tended to be arbitrary, and it functioned on the proposition that all wrongs which a person experienced could be compensated for in a pecuniary sense. This law is the "legal" system of thought, but as the economy of Britain expanded, it became apparent to the Crown that monetary judgments were not sufficient in all cases. There developed from this an expression of the king's conscience, through his chancellor, a whole new body of law which came to be known as "equity." In the first instance equity knew no tradition, and the chancellor simply looked at each situation and made a determination as to what was right. The subjectivity was without bounds, and there developed a series of statements characterizing this new form of relief. The courts of equity were separate from the courts of law, and in them a man who "seeks equity" must "do equity." It was further said that a man "must seek equity with clean hands." "Equity is the King's conscience." After a good many years equity began to build its own volume of reported cases, and when jurists held the post of chancellor there began to be more system in the matter. In the American courts today, both federal and state, the courts sit at law and in equity without advertising to the public the distinction. In Deuteronomy 19:14 is the command "You shall not move your neighbor's boundary mark, which the ancestors have set, in your inheritance which you shall inherit in the land that the LORD your God gives you to possess" (NASB). There is no penalty prescribed, but presumably the remedy would be equitable—that is, forcing the offender to move the boundary mark back to its rightful place. The legal remedy would simply be monetary damages for the offense. That the concept of equity in England took shape as late as the sixteenth century illustrates that the law of the land, the secular law, is a developing, evolutionary thing which reflects the complexity of civilization and is an indicator of the economic dynamics of the sovereign as well as its concern for the protection of individual rights.

The last several decades have witnessed a phenomenon in American law which is unprecedented in previous history, and that is the concept of affirmative action. You will notice in the Decalogue as the commandments speak to the relationships among men only (Exod. 20:12), which is "Honor thy father and mother," is an affirmative command. All of the others are negative. Think if you will the difficulty of monitoring and measuring obedience to an affirmative commandment. If the question were asked here today, "Do you honor your father and your mother?" the answer will be "Yes," but in your mind, "Compared to what?" None of us are completely comfortable that we have done all we could in the honoring of our parents, and we will look instinctively to relative standards to which we can compare ourselves. The American jurisprudence system has entered an era of almost overwhelming complexity as the legislatures have commanded us not only to refrain from evil in regard to our relationships to our fellow man, but also to pursue and do what is right. As a result, we have burgeoning federal and state agencies to make employers be reasonable and kind to their employees. We have agencies to make us be kind to our environment. We have agencies that monitor our biases so that we will not engage in subjective hiring practices and thereby discriminate against anyone because of age, sex, race, or religious persuasion. The businessman knows today the demands which are placed on him to make sure that he "does right" in all matters. Those of us who are white, Protestant males in middle America, sometimes wish for an agency that would attend to our own self-perceived suffering as we comply with all these mandatory requirements that we "be nice." In our treatment of the application of the Christian in his relationship to law and justice, we must take into account the enormous complexity of life and business in a world which has gone mad in the creation of paper and computer memory storage.

The question before us is: "How do John Q. and Mary C. Christian live for Jesus Christ in this environment of the Western world?" The spiritual prosperity of religious freedom has dulled our Christian sensibility to the fact that true spirituality has always been in conflict with secular government insofar as ultimate goals are concerned. The biblical records of men of God living in hostile environments are Daniel in the Babylonian/Persian captivity and Joseph in the patriarchal days of Israel in Egypt. What can be learned from these men is that they functioned in an exemplary manner in environments completely hostile to the Jewish way of life. Their advancement in offices is not a direct product of their spirituality but of their efficiency and competence in performing the tasks which were placed before them. We have little but imagination to tell us the nature of these tasks, but it can be safely assumed that on a daily basis over the period of years involved, these were not tasks that were dear to their Jewish hearts. It cannot be assumed that the democratic experiment is a given for all time; and as secularization occurs, it will be increasingly incumbent upon church leadership to prepare people for the task of significant and authentic Christian living in a society which may elect to become more and more secularized.

In this section we have dealt with the involvement of the individual Evangelical in the making of law and its administration, but there is another aspect to be considered, and this is the role of the institutional church in government. Perhaps a brief overview of the church and its relationship to the state in New Testament times would be helpful. In the instances which have already been noted in Acts, particularly in Acts 4, 12, and 16, it can be seen that politically the church is perceived as powerless, and the state is indifferent to it. Organized religion—that is, Judaism—constantly appeals to the state for power and authority to make the early church conform to religion's view of society, under the guise that the religious view was also the state's view. This did not continue indefinitely. Whereas the early church was, in the words of British historian Paul Johnson, "charismatic and eschatological," after the elapse of several centuries it became institutional, political, and confrontational.

After the Edict of Milan and in the fourth century Augustine made his presence felt in many ways, including his view of the church. Under him the church took on the ways of the state. It became institutional, it became confrontational, and the ministry was defined by the clergy. Note the evaluation by Peter Brown, biographer of Augustine:

> The Catholicism of Augustine, by contrast, reflects the attitude of a group confident of its powers to absorb the world without losing its identity. This identity existed independently of the quality of the human agents of the Church: it rested on "objective" promises of God, working out magnificently in history, and on the "objective" efficacy of its sacraments. This Church was hungry for souls: let it eat, indiscriminately if needs be. It is a group no longer committed to defend itself against society; but rather, poised, ready to fulfill what is considered its

historic mission, to dominate, to absorb, to lead a whole Empire. "Ask me, and I shall give the uttermost parts of the earth to Thy possession." It is not surprising, therefore, that Africa, which had always been the home of articulate and extreme views on the nature of the Church as a group in society, should, once again, in the age of Augustine, become the "cockpit of Europe," for this, the last great debate, whose outcome would determine the form taken by the Catholic domination of the Latin world until the Reformation.

The church, having found its expression in Augustine, that the Catholic church in its empirical form was the kingdom of Christ, from that time forward found itself in interaction and conflict for power with the state wherever they coexisted. The lives of Calvin, Luther, Knox, Kuyper, and Cromwell all have their dimension of theonomy as the church has as its goal the imposition of God's law as it understands it on the state. Nevertheless, with the exception of the United States, all of the Western countries have the continuing experience of a state church inextricably bound up with the secular system itself.

The American system is a unique experiment in history, and after slightly over two hundred years it can still not be considered too much more than an experiment. The early settlers came to the thirteen colonies primarily from Britain but all from Northern Europe, and they brought with them varying reactions to the church they had experienced in their homelands. In some colonies, such as Massachusetts, there were strong expressions which we would recognize as theonomic today and which are cited by current theonomists as normative for where the church and state should be in their relationships. While the attitude varied in the thirteen states when the Constitution was finally hammered out, a unique concept of separation of church and state had been incorporated. This we know today as the establishment clause of the First Amendment which states simply that "Congress shall make no law respecting an establishment of religion, or prohibiting the free exercise thereof." In reading the writings and statements of the men who drafted that document and considering the deliberation that attended it, it is highly unlikely that any of them would conceive that religion, of all forms, would be relegated completely in the minds of the secular government to a matter only of private concern. The statement that the state would create no church has in two hundred years of interpretation by the courts created polarization, a secularization which is exceeded by no other nation of Northern European extraction. Whereas the United States experiment has furnished a matrix for a very virile and expansive form of evangelical Christianity, it has dismayed itself with its capacity for fracturing the unity of the church and its ability in this century to assert itself through the conscience of men on the government itself. The current politics of the New Right are an expression of frustration on the part of millions of American citizens who are weary of that secularization process which is occurring.

In our first section we stated our persuasion that Christians are, by the examples of both Testaments and the expressed commandments, to be subject to the secular laws of their environment. In this section it is our conclusion that Christians must be responsible citizens wherever they live; and this consists, at a minimum, of obeying the law, paying taxes, and exercising the privileges of vote to the extent that that is possible. In addition, the vocational call of politics and government service is just as valid as any other vocational call; and the evangelical world should treat it accordingly. Such a call to the making of law and its administration in society must be respected as much as any other, and it will be to a pattern of day-by-day activities of government in the same spirit which motivated Daniel and Joseph. They both functioned as sojourners in the eschatological sense but were exemplary in their day-to-day performance. Too often the Christian thinks of involvement in government as exclusively being a concern over single issues. God has left his people, those whom he has redeemed, in the world to interface with society; and we believe it is to be a pervasive, persistent, patient encounter with all of legitimate society which includes participation in the making of law and its administration.

Insofar as the individual Christian is concerned, we would conclude that his command is to represent a pervasive influence of redemption in the society in which he lives. On the other hand, we are not persuaded that the Bible, either Testament of it, furnishes any basis for a theonomic mandate to the institutional church. There is no evidence of that mind-set in the first-century church, and the above quotation concerning Augustine places the origin of that theological view in the fourth century, long after the canon was completed.

## III. BAD LAW, JUSTICE, AND REVOLUTION

Dr. Montgomery pointed out in his paper that bad law is still law and must be obeyed by the Christian, although he would, I think, by rationalization conclude that the American Revolution was God ordained. From the Romans passage in chapter 13 it is evident when seen in the context of Paul's own experience that he would concur that bad law is nevertheless the law. Although there is bad law in connection with business and commerce which usually fails to give proper redress for wrongs which have been perpetrated, we normally think of bad law as it provokes criminal injustice. Injustice, in fact, occurs when the law is bad and when good laws are not properly administered.

A cursory review of slavery provides a good insight on man's inhumanity to man. The idea of ownership of the person and all the rights of another individual goes so far back in history that its roots are uncertain. It prevailed in Greek and Roman cultures, to say nothing of the Assyrians, Persians, and the Egyptians before them. In considering this matter, one must give pause to the fact that Jesus never spoke out on this particular form of brutish behavior, nor did the apostle Paul condemn it in his letter to Philemon. And yet we know that the dignity afforded the individual by the message of the Gospels, the divine fiat that man is created in the image of God, is ultimately the basis on which slavery has come to an end in history.

In eighteenth-century England there appeared a popular Wedgwood ceramic cameo which depicted a black man on his knees with the prayer, "Am I not a man and a brother?" The literature defending the slave trade in those days reveals the horrible fact that men, for mercantile and commercial reasons, convinced themselves that the blacks of Africa were subhuman if they were human at all. Wilberforce offered his first resolution in Parliament in 1792 for the abolition of the slave trade, and it was finally in 1833 when Parliament abolished the practice of slavery throughout the empire. His resolutions enjoyed parliamentary support from Pitt, Burke, and many others of great stature in the British government; yet it required more than forty years to affirmatively answer the question of "Am I not a man and a brother?"

How do Christians respond to injustice from bad law or from improperly administered law? It would seem that they must register their protest, and there is shame for all of us as we realize those great issues of our day in which we were absent or late in arriving on the scene to make our expression. God makes it abundantly clear that true religion works itself out in care and compassion in the pursuit of justice. Fortunately, the "law of widows and orphans" is tacitly recognized in most of our courts, which guard their rights with a diligence not shown in other matters. The prophets of the Old Testament are pointed in their indictments that a true and proper relationship with God will work itself out in the doing of justice.

What of revolution? Is it ever appropriate? Those of us who are beneficiaries of the American Revolution wish desperately for a biblical rationale for justification for that great event in the course of our country's history. Dr. Montgomery infers that he has that all worked out, but the question persists. Is it different from any other revolution which at best is an expression of rebellion against the law, even though it is a bad law? Perhaps the most sobering thing about revolution is that it rarely achieves what it promises to the masses, and it depends a great deal on demagoguery. That they get out of control is amply illustrated by the French Revolution in the death on the guillotine of Robespierre, an event which terrified the British aristocracy to move toward a democratic procedure that avoided a civil war of a like kind in Britain. In this century we have long debated the role of the church and the ministry in the fascist state of Nazi Germany. It is to the embarrassment of many of the clergy and the church leaders that no outcry was made on the awful destruction of society which was being conducted in Germany on the rise of the Third Reich. Out of that era came Bonhoeffer, who posthumously became a hero to much of the Christian world. On the occasion of his impending death he stated beautifully for all of us the ambiguities inherent in the decision to resist or acquiesce. In his *Letters and Papers from Prison* we read, "It is therefore impossible to define the boundary between resistance and submission on abstract principles, but both of them must exist and both must be practiced. Faith demands elasticity of behavior."

To those of us in this country, our forefathers assumed by implication a formidable task when they wrote that *all* men everywhere are created equal and have the right to the pursuit of happiness. We have yet in this society to translate that into reality even within our own borders. Our efforts to export our principles by which the stated goal can be achieved have met with more failures than successes. The test of our own relationships to these issues will be in terms of our obedience to the will of Jesus Christ for our lives. The history of the development of law, the dealings of mankind with his own injustices to the rest of mankind, are warnings to us of our ultimate inability to properly self-govern and our inability to create any sort of utopian state of affairs. The kingdom that we profess to long for will only be established under the personal reign of Jesus Christ when he makes his appearance for that purpose on this earth. The task for every Christian in the meantime is to be obedient to all of the implications of the incarnation of Jesus Christ and the revealed and stated will of God. There is nothing in history to encourage us to believe that we are upon any final solution in this matter, and, in fact, we can know that our perception of our failings and shortcomings will be as imperfect as our forefathers were imperfect in their evaluation of their own days and times. But of this we can be sure, that God has redeemed us and called us to be his own and has decreed that we are to interface with the society, in time and space if you will, in real and meaningful terms. And in our relationship to him, he has scripturally furnished us with sufficient eschatological data that we should serve him as sojourners in the here and now with an eye on the eternity which he has prepared for us.

# DISCRIMINATION AND HUMAN RIGHTS

## Gretchen Gaebelein Hull

"I am not an animal! I should be treated like a human being!" This was the cry of a woman who had been subjected to the pain of incest as a child and was now being abused by her husband. Something deep within her cried out: "I am human and I have human rights."

This self-consciousness of the human being defies explanation apart from scriptural revelation. Those who would discount or ignore the biblical account of the origin of life cannot get around the fact that such denial leaves humanity on a purely animal level. There is no "in between." As G. Campbell Morgan wrote, "To deny that man is a mysterious mingling of dust and Deity by the will and act of God is necessarily to be compelled to think of him as the last product of animal evolution; and therefore as himself an animal, and nothing more."[1] Yet people do indeed constantly affirm their instinctive belief that human beings are "a breed apart." Such familiar judgments as "People were packed in like animals" or "People acted like animals" indicate that the animal level is not considered the norm for human beings.

Humanity's self-awareness is today expressed most noticeably in the proliferation of various rights movements, in the desire to define and protect civil rights, and in the perception of terrorist acts as a new threat to human rights. Our instinctive response to the cry "Help!" indicates our conviction that human life is to be preserved and to be treated with respect, and even among persons with little or no interest in God's Word, there is a consensus that the uniqueness of humanity carries with it certain basic rights.[2]

We who believe the Bible to be God's inspired and utterly trustworthy Word find in Scripture the foundation for any meaningful study of humanity and therefore of human rights. We

333

begin with the affirmation of God as Creator of all things.[3] We believe that his creative activity not only included the creation of all the world and all life[4] but also that the creation of human beings was the culmination of the creative act.[5] It is only after the creation of humankind in his image that God saw that all that he had made was "very good."[6] The final and deliberate setting apart of man and woman as created "in the image of God" is what determines that human beings cannot be treated as merely the highest of many animal species.

Even a superficial reading of the Bible shows that God's Word affirms the worth and dignity of all men and women. The genealogies, the two censuses of Numbers, the individual names of real people in real situations which God caused to be recorded, all show his interest in human individuals. Human life is not cheap but is precious in God's sight, so precious that he entered our world himself[7] to offer us a second chance to be all we were created to be.[8]

Therefore the fact of the Incarnation (God come in the flesh) also supports the uniqueness of human life. Because Christ was fully human, he bestowed worth upon human life from its very conception.[9] Because Christ interacted with fallen humanity, he gave dignity to humankind.[10] Because Christ died for our sins, he placed the highest possible value on human life.[11] Because Christ rose again, he makes possible the re-creation of all who believe in him and gives to them new spiritual life.[12]

When this re-creation is consummated in the completion of the redemptive act,[13] the Bible tells us that the created world will also experience the fullness of redemption. Further evidence of the uniqueness of humanity but also great cause for our humility is the fact that the re-creation of a world marred by our sin hinges on the culmination of the completed redemptive process in humankind.[14]

Until that day, we look to the Bible for guidelines as to how to treat God's precious gift of life. The fact that God delegated to humanity the authority to govern the earth and to have power over both plant and animal life[15] does not give liberty to abuse those life forms. Scripture directs us to treat our environment with care.[16]

Guidelines for the treatment of human life are particularly emphasized. These guidelines indicate that human beings should enjoy certain rights on the natural (physical and mental) level and also on the spiritual level. To divide human nature this way is not an endorsement of all kinds of dualism or to open up the dualistic/holistic controversy[17] but rather to recognize as a practical matter that human beings without God are operating on a plane that is incomplete.[18] To become what they were created to be they need the re-creating power of God to renew their lives so that all aspects of their nature come into harmony with their created purpose. Further, even persons indifferent to God experience the feeling that "there must be more to life than this." Scripture puts it that "He has also set eternity in the hearts of men"[19] and goes on to tell us that all our yearnings find their answer in Christ, in whom all the promises of God are "Yes."[20] As will become evident, recognition of both the natural and spiritual aspects of human beings is important in any discussion of human rights.

In current usage a "right" denotes something to which we have a just claim. Most civilized countries today consider that to preserve and enhance life human beings can claim certain rights, and the United Nations has set forth the Universal Declaration of Human Rights enumerating various rights and indicating how these rights should be protected and implemented.

However, just as apart from Scripture there is no basis for the uniqueness of human life, so also apart from Scripture there is no basis for human rights either. Article 1 of the United Nations Declaration states: "All human beings are born free and equal in dignity and rights. They are endowed with reason and conscience and should act towards one another in a spirit of brotherhood."[21] This begs the question: Endowed by whom or what? But, in fact, the very wording of this article bears out the truth of Romans 1:20 and 2:14–15 that human beings do instinctively recognize the authority of a higher power and that God's laws are indeed written on their hearts.[22] As Carl Henry puts it, "Biblical theism alone provides adequate intellectual struts for . . . human rights, whereas nontheistic views render such rights merely postulatory and problematical. . . . The evangelical view is that human rights are grounded in the revealed will of God, that religious liberty and political liberty are alike based on the Bible."[23]

Psalm 146 warns us not to put our trust in political structures which come and go but to look to God as champion of our rights. Because societal acceptance of rights will vary, it should be recognized that civil rights are not necessarily synonymous with human rights.[24] Therefore in any examination of human rights there is a need to distinguish between unchanging rights, those derived from Scripture, and apparent or provisional rights, those derived from the philosophy of a particular state or societal group (which may or may not be biblically oriented.) The former, rights derived from Scripture, will be unalterable, while the latter may be altered or redefined by the state or societal group.

There are two scriptural strands to trace in discovering the biblical basis for human rights. The first strand is the sanctity of life, from which we deduce the right to life and from which flow rights on the natural (physical and mental) level. These include rights germane to the preservation and enhancement of life, such as the right to just and humane treatment; the right to adequate food, clothing, and shelter; the right to medical care; the right to enter into the marriage relationship and the right to procreate within marriage; the right to work; and the right to education.

The second strand is the self-revelation of God (in the Word of God written, in the Word made flesh, and to individuals). From the self-revelation of God we deduce the right to know God, and from that general right flows the right to freedom of religion, which incorporates the right to act on knowledge of God (including the right to reject the biblical revelation), the right to learn about God, and, once a person is regenerate, the right to serve God as he calls.

From both these general strands societies (and especially societies influenced by the Judeo-Christian tradition) have extrapolated additional civil rights. One example would be the right to vote, which can be thought of as an extension of the basic right to "choose for yourselves whom you will serve"[25] and also the right to self-government.[26] Another would be the right to travel freely, based on God's command that humanity move out to fill the earth and his subsequent scattering of peoples to insure that happening.[27] Included in this right would be the right to travel to fulfill religious obligations.[28]

An extention of the right to know God and the right to choose whether or not to serve him would be the right to speak freely. The Bible abounds with illustrations of honestly questioning persons who interact with God.[29] Human beings have free will, and Scripture encourages free speech.

However, with this as with all rights, comes responsibility. Rights must be viewed in the context of society and their use balanced by the need to be sensitive to the rights of others. Thus free speech is balanced by responsibility for the words uttered.[30] The Bible makes it clear that all human rights must be exercised responsibly and with a view toward accountability to those in governmental authority and ultimately to God.[31]

Recognizing that rights must be used responsibly also requires us to take into account the principle of the good of the many. We were not created to be isolated beings but to be components of society.[32] We do have a right to be members of society, but we are not to act in ways that infringe on the rights of others or unjustly harm them.[33] The biblical challenge is to work for the good of the many. Paul wrote to the Corinthians, "For I am not seeking my own good but the good of the many, so that they may be saved. Follow my example, as I follow the example of Christ."[34] And what was Christ's example? Although he had the right to command all power and receive all homage, he gave up those rights so that he could give himself up as a ransom for many.[35]

Now in cases where, for the good of the many, a person's rights are involuntarily limited, there is a need to investigate whether this limitation has been fairly imposed. For example, someone who has contracted a virulently contagious disease will experience certain restrictions or even be isolated from general society. However, the most usual reason for restricting rights is to discipline antisocial behavior. If individuals or groups misuse their rights by exercising their rights in such a way as to defy God's laws or to violate the rights of others, they may expect discipline or punishment.[36]

God-given principles of government indicate that one function of government is to make guidelines for harmonious behavior and then to make judgments as to whether or not individuals or groups have lived according to those rules of society. Similarly God's Word gives guidelines for his people and also sets forth sanctions if these guidelines are perverted or ignored.[37]

In this context discipline must be distinguished from discrimination. As has been noted, misuse of rights will eventually lead to their restriction. Such restrictions will always be imposed perfectly fairly by God: "Will not the judge of all the earth do right?"[38] However, since human justice will be imperfect, human discipline must not become a cloak for discrimination, as when there is unequal or even abusive treatment of offenders. Certainly when rights are limited or denied in the name of the good of the many it must be clear that this is not being done because of some discriminatory bias such as racial prejudice (as in apartheid), political preference (as in imprisonment of nonviolent dissidents), or paternalism (as in treatment of the American Indians), or out of some unfounded fear (as in the incarceration of Japanese-Americans during World War II), but is viewed objectively for the good of the many. Further, Scripture teaches us to avoid unjust application of societal safeguards and also to abhor inhumane actions and cruel methods of punishment.[39]

Because God's Word always inveighs against injustice and inhumane actions, it is clear that humanity is not so to be treated. Over and over again passages about justice are undergirded by "It is the Lord who speaks" or "This is the word of the LORD." Scripture tells us that God's throne is founded on righteousness and justice and that the Lord loves justice and hates wrongdoing.[40] Intrinsic to any discussion of human rights is the realization that God is deeply concerned with justice issues and expects his people to be so also. Because God demands fair treatment of humanity, so may we. God's tremendous challenge to all human beings is found in Micah 6:8:

What does the LORD require of you?
To act justly and to love mercy

and to walk humbly with your God.

The Old Testament gives specific commands about just actions which indicate that God not only expects us in all situations to treat our fellow human beings impartially and compassionately but also that he expects us to give special care to those who are not able to help themselves. It is most significant that the Bible language repeatedly emphasizes the need to preserve the rights of the widow, the orphan, the alien, the poor, and the oppressed.[41]

We see the divine ideal of justice embodied in the life of Jesus. In his own announcement of his mission, by quoting Isaiah 61:1–2, he indicated that the Good News incorporates the ending of injustice and oppression. Although the Incarnate Christ lived in a society dominated by discrimination, he himself showed none. He said, "Whoever comes to me I will never drive away."[42] He treated all persons with respect, regardless of their race, sex, age, physical condition, political preference, economic status, or educational level. By touching the untouchables and interacting with "the least of these" he told all persons, "You have worth and value, and there is rejoicing in heaven when you as an individual become part of my family."[43]

Jesus overturned the social and cultural mores of his day and challenged legalistic traditions.[44] He came to meet human need, whether that need was embodied in a hated tax collector, an alien Roman, a mixed-race Samaritan woman, an outcast leper, a homemaker, a lawyer, or a dying girl. He mingled with "sinners" and accepted the homage of a prostitute. He offered his deepest teachings to the scholars of his day, to fishermen, and to women, treating both the educated and uneducated as intelligent and responsible human beings. He did not seek to curry favor with the powerful and influential but constantly called to account those in authority with words like Matthew 23:23: "You have neglected the more important matters of the law—justice, mercy and faithfulness." When questioned about the most important commandment, Jesus joined belief with compassion and reinforced this with the parable of the Good Samaritan to teach us that the criterion for social concern is human need and not discriminatory practices.[45] Such was Christ's view of the sanctity of human life that he did not discriminate in picking his disciples but offered himself freely to the "worst case" when he said: "Have I not chosen you, the Twelve? Yet one of you is a devil!"[46]

The record of the early church continues to underscore the fact that God does not discriminate against any person.[47] Old Testament and New Testament join in telling us that God is no respecter of persons, with the supreme revelation of this truth in the Person and work of Jesus Christ and in his new commandment that we love others as he has loved us.[48] Therefore no person who desires to be obedient to Scripture can engage in or condone discriminatory acts.

In seeking to apply these truths, the scriptural affirmation of the worth and value of the individual human being must always be the standard by which to evaluate whether or not acts are discriminatory. Discrimination is treating oneself or one's group as entitled to certain human rights and others as unentitled or not entitled to the same degree, and basing this unequal treatment on the proposition that the unentitled have different characteristics or belong to a different group from the entitled. Discrimination is usually practiced by the societally empowered against the societally unempowered. Groups experiencing forms of discrimination are women, children, and minorities (including racial, religious, and political minorities), the aged, the disabled, and the economically disadvantaged.[49]

Some human beings experience an added weight of discrimination because they belong to more than one of these groupings, such as Amerasian children, migrant workers, or the disabled poor. The plight of women in some Third World countries is particularly poignant.[50]

Overt discrimination is evidence of injustice. It has many causes and can take many forms, from denying someone equal opportunity because of a physical characteristic (e.g., race, sex, disability) to outright segregation. Discrimination can be institutionalized, as in apartheid or the caste system. It can be the result of political expediency, as in violations of the rights of political prisoners. It can be the result of public apathy, as in disparate educational programs or inequitable public housing. Particularly troubling to Americans should be a recent report by the Department of Health and Human Services that "significant health inequities still exist for members of racial and ethnic minority groups."[51] But whatever its cause or whatever its form, discrimination depersonalizes and marginalizes human life. As a South African black described his experience: "Apartheid shatters you. It leaves a wound in your own humanity."[52]

Discrimination "with its gloves off" is manifested in cases of rape, wife abuse, child molestation, callous treatment of the disabled, police brutality, and inhumane prison conditions, including physical and psychological torture. These violations of human rights are the ultimate discrimination by the empowered against the unempowered and are saying, "The unempowered is a throw-away, to be manipulated, used, abused, or even tortured as suits the purpose of the empowered." Persons who willfully violate human rights have made the ultimate discriminatory act in favor of themselves and against all others. Such an act treats the unempowered as less than human.

In practice, therefore, discrimination is any action that restricts or abrogates natural rights and therefore harms or diminishes the physical and/or mental life of this unique individual, the human being, who was created in the image of God and for whom Christ died. The Bible inveighs against such discrimination: God commands that all human beings be treated justly and fairly and that they be given equal opportunity to enjoy human rights.[53]

But, as earlier noted, those human rights also include spiritual rights: the right to know God, the right to choose to believe in him, the right to learn more about him from his Word, and the right to serve him. Therefore, just as discrimination in the area of natural rights is contrary to God's will, so also is discrimination in the area of spiritual rights. All persons have the right to religious freedom, which not only will include the right to worship as they choose but also the right to reject biblical revelation. Thus no form of religious persecution can ever be justified. Furthermore, the damage done to the cause of Christ by pogroms such as the Inquisition is incalculable.

However, affirming the right of all persons to religious freedom does not mean that God's people are to be indifferent to the spiritual welfare of others. Here it is appropriate to highlight another area of discrimination to which Christians must be particularly sensitive—namely, lack of concern for evangelism. As evidenced by the Word of God written and also the Word made flesh, human beings have a right to know God's plan of redemption. Whenever we Christians are indifferent to our part in proclaiming that right we are guilty of discrimination. We cannot excuse our indifference on the ground that those who reject God's plan are accountable for that rejection. Indifference to the lost is as good as saying: "You are sub-human; your soul does not matter." Such discrimination ignores Christ's commission to be his witnesses and is the height of selfishness, ignoring the fact that as we received the free gift of new life so also we are to offer that free gift to others as yet outside God's family.[54]

Viewed in the context of human rights, the best evangelistic tool is not necessarily what Christ has done *for* you or me but what Christ can do *through* us. A hurting world is not so much interested in our personal testimonies but in whether we offer some means to heal the hurts. W. E. Sangster wrote, "A Church boldly challenging this present social order, and giving visible evidence of our Lord's power to reshape it nearer to His own desire, would open to evangelism millions of people to whom the offer of changed feelings seems a well-intentioned but pitiful irrelevance."[55] So we see that part of our task in combating discrimination is to affirm the worth and value of all persons by working to uphold their natural rights, thereby creating a climate in which they will be receptive to exercising their spiritual right of knowing God and choosing to accept his free gift of new life in Christ.[56]

Then, once a person has been born again, discrimination is also any act that restricts that person's spiritual rights and thus in this world harms or diminishes that person's position as a new creature in Christ Jesus or limits the person's opportunities to serve God as he calls.

The guarantee of the Christian's spiritual rights is the finished work of Jesus Christ. The wonder of the substitutionary atonement is that he gives all who believe in him the power to become children of God.[57] Based on the miracle of the resurrection, the biblical principle is "as with Christ, so with the believer." Paul's exposition of this truth in Romans 6:1–14; 8:11, 15–17; and 2 Corinthians 5:14–21 clearly shows that we who are born again are no longer to be thought of in worldly terms—that is, in terms of our old human nature or our physical "houses." Rather we are now in God's family, heirs of God and joint heirs with Christ, and his ambassadors. As such we are also entrusted with a new mission, the ministry of reconciliation. Christ commands his own to love others as he loves us and to be his witnesses to those as yet outside his family. Therefore no born-again believer should ever, on the basis of extrabiblical requirements, be denied full fellowship in the body or, on the basis of extrascriptural distinctions, be denied full opportunity to use his or her God-given gifts in the service of the Master.

The Bible teaches that we are engaged in a spiritual warfare and warns us to be alert against attacks of the devil.[58] In warfare an effective strategy is to divide and conquer, and Satan will use the sin of discrimination to divide believers. But Scripture also tells us that Christ destroys all barriers between believers, because in him we are now members of one body, one spiritual family, one temple of God.[59] Concentrating on our unity in Christ will help us guard against the divisiveness of discrimination. Yet how sad when the Enemy can trick fellow believers into artificial divisions and thus into the sin of discrimination. We cannot ignore the fact that many members of the body are being hurt by practices that restrict or even deny their spiritual rights to full personhood as God's children.[60]

As we consider the tragedy of division within the body, we must remember that nowhere does Christ teach that gender, race, age, physical condition, social or economic factors, or political affiliation hinder our salvation or bar us from serving him. In John 10:16 Jesus said, "I have other sheep that are not of this sheep pen. I must bring them also. They too will listen to my voice, and there shall be one flock and one shepherd." Certainly a perusal of those persons Jesus called to himself during his earthly ministry supports this truth. Jesus also warned against discrimination when he rebuked the disciples for wanting to exclude from ministry those who did not do things exactly as did the disciples.[61] The continuing record of the Book of Acts shows the inclusiveness of the early church, which Paul reinforced with his call to unity in Galatians 3:26-28.

Yet one of the most emotionally charged areas of discussion today is that of discrimination against women in ministry.[62] Again we need to remember that just as the basis for natural (physical/mental) rights is God's Word, the basis for spiritual rights is God's Word also. Both men and women were created in the image of God. Neither sex needs any other mediator than Christ Jesus.[63] Women as well as men are included in the concept of the priesthood of all believers[64] and share what Jude 3 calls our common salvation. Regenerate women as well as regenerate men are included in the spiritual principle of "sonship" and have the right to act as "sons of God" and to claim their full inheritance rights as fellow children of God.[65] Denying women the full privileges of sonship discriminates against women by restricting their opportunities to co-administer their spiritual inheritance and also violates their right to abundant life that is guaranteed by Jesus in John 10:10 because it limits the full use of their spiritual gifts.[66]

Thus many sincere Christians are puzzled that some today would discriminate against women who seek to serve as fellow soldiers in the salvation army, and those women themselves are genuinely and deeply hurt. At the heart of the matter is the question: Since 2 Corinthians 5:21 tells women as well as men that they have now become the righteousness of God, then how can women still not "measure up"? Women (and indeed any Christians whose spiritual rights are restricted and full employment of spiritual gifts denied) have every reason to ask: "Is this verse for us, or not? If it is, then we, too, are full ambassadors for Christ; and to us, too, is committed the privilege of proclaiming the message of reconciliation." In the light of the full humanity of women and the full redemption of women, the burden is not on women to prove that they should be allowed to use their gifts in all areas of God's service; but rather the burden is on those who would restrict the spiritual rights of women to prove that they are not discriminating against their sisters in Christ.[67]

Protecting and upholding both the natural and the spiritual rights of all human beings is an ongoing task. However, good will alone is not an adequate weapon to combat discrimination. It is sad that we use adjectives like "civilized" or "Christian" for nations, yet the world continues to experience persistent violations of human rights. Persons of good will deplore the Holocaust as one of the most awful violations of human rights ever known; and yet forty years later many seem unwilling to face the fact that there are similar violations in places such as Cambodia and Afghanistan. Agreements like the Helsinki Accords are ultimately only as good as the self-interest of the parties involved, because even the pressure of "world opinion" is an inadequate lever to force compliance if a powerful nation refuses to honor the terms of such an agreement. Amnesty International reports that "almost half the governments of the world held political prisoners in 1984, and many tortured inmates as an instrument of state policy or jailed citizens without charge or trial."[68] Even in the climate of American democracy constant efforts are needed to combat racism; sexism; child abuse; inhumane prison conditions; discriminatory programs for the disabled, the elderly, and the poor; and discrimination in matters of foreign policy. In addition, the Christian church worldwide must forcefully combat all varieties of religious persecution while at the same time continuing to examine itself for discriminatory practices.

It is evident that while an appeal for justice can and should be made to persons of good will to treat all human life with care and respect, nevertheless good will alone is insufficient to deal with the magnitude of the human rights problem. Only affirming the biblical truth of the worth and value of each human being as made in the image of God and practicing a Christlike attitude of servanthood will be the ultimate means of combating any form of discrimination and the resulting violations of human rights.

In the Olivet Discourse Jesus warned: "As lawlessness spreads, men's love for one another will grow cold."[69] Then after the Last Supper he gave his followers the new commandment: "Love one another. As I have loved you, so you must love one another. All men will know that you are my disciples if you love one another."[70] In today's lawless and loveless climate we realize that we need this new commandment more than ever before.

We need to see that any system that encourages one person to feel entitled to be over another is not biblical.[71] Entitlement is the antithesis of servanthood; and if we have any sense of entitlement, not only will our relationship with Christ suffer but so will all our human relationships as well. A sense of entitlement smothers the grateful heart and stifles any appreciation of common grace.[72] God's Word tells us that it is the pride of our hearts that deceives us into thinking: "We are better than others, and thus we have a right to discriminate against them." The prophecy of Obadiah warns us that unchecked pride will lead to the grossest violations of other persons' human rights.

In contrast Jesus came to proclaim the worth and value of all human beings and to show us that in his sight no one of us is better than another. Calvary is both the great leveling agent and the great unifying agent: we are all the same at the foot of the cross. Regardless of any positions we may be privileged to hold or any blessings we may experience, we are never to "thank God that we are not as other men."[73] Rather we are all fellow sinners for whom Christ died; and when, by his grace, we receive new life, we become part of a diplomatic corps whose members are all servants. Our equality and our unity in Christ show us that any sense of entitlement to place or position is inimical to Christ's call to servanthood.[74] Therefore just as to Christianize slavery is to end it (as Paul's beautiful letter to Philemon shows) so also to Christianize paternalism, patriarchalism, and elitism are to end these.

It is sobering to ask: Has the "white man's burden" really been the heavy weight of entitlement, and does that burden need to be exchanged for a servant lifestyle where the yoke is easy and the burden is light?[75] This is not to excuse anyone from similar self-examination. We remember that when Sarah was given power over Hagar she misused that power. The Sermon on the Mount exposes the fact that we each need to see the planks in our own eyes.[76]

Leon Morris calls us all to account with these challenging words:

> It is a matter of profound sorrow that the track record of the Christian Church in this matter is far from uniformly good. In our thinking about minorities we are too often all too representative of the communities in which we live. The lines have sometimes been drawn as hard in the churches as anywhere. It is not difficult to find examples of professing Christians who have shown anything but love to the underprivileged in their area. All too often we have been just as ready as anyone to ostracize our minorities and to make them the scapegoats for the ills in our midst.[77]

Those who are politically, societally, economically, or clerically empowered must see themselves simply as stewards and caretakers of God's gifts. Only then will they be freed from the grip of entitlement. Rights are gifts from God, and true discipleship means giving those rights back to him. Oswald Chambers wrote, "The stamp of the saint is that he can waive his own rights and obey the Lord Jesus. . . . Are you willing to obey your Lord and Master whatever the humiliation to your right to yourself may be?"[78] This will be the true measure of freedom in Christ Jesus because the test of freedom is not only the ability to choose how to act but also the ability voluntarily to limit these actions.

In this, as always, our highest example is that of Christ. He gave up every right to power and majesty and for our sakes underwent horrible injustice and experienced the most dreadful violations of human rights. Yet in giving himself up for us who were his enemies he prayed, "Father, forgive them, for they do not know what they are doing."[79] Therefore we see that as Christ gave up his rights in order to redeem humankind, in order to show his love today, we his disciples must use our rights redemptively also. We must be dedicated to upholding the rights of others while being willing to relinquish our own rights for the good of the many or for the good of the weaker brother or sister.[80] In so doing we will undoubtedly face some difficult choices (in line with Acts 4:19–20 and 5:29). We will risk being misunderstood and/or censured by secular society and possibly by the institutional church.

But as we reach out to others in obedience to Christ's command to love our neighbor as ourselves we realize that from the beginning of time the answer to the question "Am I my brother's keeper?" has been "Yes." God's Word says, "The righteous care about justice for the poor, but the wicked have no such concern."[81] And God's Word commands: "Speak up for those who cannot speak for themselves, for the rights of all who are destitute. Speak up and judge fairly; defend the rights of the poor and needy."[82] Scripture warns us that lack of concern for the rights of others cannot be excused as ignorance[83] or overcome by additional religious observances.[84] Not bending every effort to protect and uphold the natural and spiritual rights of others is a discrimination because such lack of concern is really telling them, "You don't matter."

It is significant to note that Jesus used concern for the disadvantaged and unempowered as one measure of recognizing his followers.[85] Surely we who are his disciples today should not miss any opportunities to show that concern. Only sacrificial examples of Christ's love flowing through us will combat the evils of self-centered entitlement and arrogant elitism which, as manifestations of pride, are at the heart of the sin of discrimination.

In our responsible and even redemptive use of rights we Christians have the tremendous opportunity of combating discrimination and thus advancing the cause of Christ. In so doing, we are to exhibit the freedom and joy that are the result of giving over all our rights to our Lord and Savior so that he can use us as his ambassadors to bring his message of reconciliation to a hurting world.

If we fail to seize this opportunity, not only will we lose our witness to the secular world, but we will also risk alienating the unempowered in our midst and driving them out of the church. As David G. Horner has pointed out: "Our generation may not be responsible for the prejudice and oppression that have tormented the minorities, but if we don't redress the wrong, the judgment of God will fall on us."[86]

# ENDNOTES

[1] G. Campbell Morgan, *Living Messages of the Books of the Bible,* 4 vols. (New York: Revell, 1912), 1:18.

[2] See, e.g., *United Nations Universal Declaration of Human Rights* (1948); *Multilateral Protection of War Victims, Geneva Convention* (1949); *Helsinki Accords* (1975).

[3] Genesis 1:1; John 1:1–2; Colossians 1:16.

[4] Genesis 1, 2; Isaiah 40:12–28.

[5] Genesis 1:26–27; 2:7, 21–22; Zechariah 12:1; Malachi 2:10.

[6] Genesis 1:27, 31.

[7] John 1:1–18.

[8] Second Corinthians 5:14–21.

[9] Luke 1:30–35.

[10] A reading of the Gospels shows this clearly.

[11] Mark 10:45; 1 Corinthians 6:20; 2 Corinthians 8:9; Philippians 2:8.

[12] Romans 6:1–14.

[13] First Corinthians 13:9–10; Hebrews 9:28; 1 John 3:2.

[14] Romans 8:19–22.

[15] Genesis 1:28–30; 9:2–3.

[16] The Old Testament laws give many instances of humane treatment of animals and of the need to care for the environment. Verses like Jonah 4:11; Habakkuk 2:17; and Luke 12:6 give further evidence of God's concern for "lesser" life forms.

[17] See, e.g., John Cooper, "Dualism and the biblical view of human beings," *The Reformed Journal,* September 1982, p. 13; and October 1982, p. 16.

[18] John 3:36; Romans 8:8.

[19] Ecclesiastes 3:11.

[20] Second Corinthians 1:20.

[21] United Nations, General Assembly, December 10, 1948, *Universal Declaration of Human Rights* (DPI/15–14792), art. 1, p. 3.

[22] This is a truth that was recognized by the signers of the American *Declaration of Independence,* which states, "We hold these truths to be self-evident, that all men are created equal, that they are endowed by their Creator with certain inalienable rights. . . ."

[23] Carl F. H. Henry, "Religious Freedom: Cornerstone of Human Rights," *Christian Legal Society Quarterly,* 5/3 (1984): 7.

[24] Persons living in a Western democratic society often tend to confuse human rights with civil rights. Because these people are so accustomed to various civil rights, they may tend to forget that there are many people who have lived without these, including people living in Bible times. In a free society people may confuse privileges with rights and may also try to claim the status of rights for social trends or even personal desires. However, when there are accepted civil rights, these must be protected and upheld without discrimination. In an article in *Eternity* (June 1981, p. 19) Case Hoogendoorn pointed out:

> The term "civil rights" technically refers to the rights of citizens to participate in and benefit from the civil order embodied in governmental structures and the political process. Government and political process do not exist solely for the benefit of citizens who belong to a particular religious persuasion, race, nationality, or language group. Nor does it exist only for the benefit of those who live up to certain minimal moral standards. Government must protect and provide justice for the worst sinners as well as the best saints.

[25] Joshua 24:15

[26] Genesis 1:26–28; Psalm 8.

[27] Genesis 1:28; 9:1; 11:1–9.

28 Exodus 5:1.

29 See, e.g., the speeches of Job, Psalm 73, Habakkuk's questions, and the fact that Jesus encouraged dialogue.

30 Matthew 12:36–37; Luke 12:2–3; James 3:5–10.

31 Matthew 10:28; Romans 13:1–5; 14:10–12.

32 Genesis 2:18; Psalm 68:6a.

33 In situations where the rights of different parties are in conflict, governmental bodies may be required to make difficult judgments in order to prioritize those rights. For example, if a parent wishes to withhold necessary medical treatment from a child, the parental right to authority over the child must be subordinate to the child's basic right to life. This situation can be compounded if the parental action is dictated by religious conviction, because now the parent's right to religious freedom is also colliding with the child's right to life.

34 First Corinthians 10:33; 11:1.

35 Matthew 26:53–54; Mark 10:45; Phil. 2:5–8.

36 See, e.g., the disciplinary aspect of the wilderness wanderings as explained in Numbers 14 and as commented on in Deuteronomy 8:2–6; and see also Daniel's comment on the Captivity in Daniel 9:1–19.

37 Deuteronomy 4:1–40. In addition, Jeremiah 7:3–15; 22:1–23; and Micah 3:1–12 clearly associate God's discipline of Israel with its violations of human rights.

38 Genesis 18:26. See also Nehemiah 9:33; Psalms 9:8; 11:7–8, 119:75; Jeremiah 9:24.

39 See, e.g., the judgment on Haman in the Book of Esther, Proverbs 12:10; Nahum 3:1; and the woes of Habakkuk 2:15–17.

40 Psalms 37:38; 89:14; 97:2; Isaiah 61:8.

41 See, e.g., Deuteronomy 10:17–19; Isaiah 58:6–12; Zechariah 7:9–10; James 1:27; and the account of treatment of widows in Acts 6:1–14.

42 John 6:37.

43 Luke 15:1–10.

44 See, e.g., Mark 7:1–13; John 2:12–17; 4:27.

45 Matthew 22:36–40; Luke 10:25–37.

46 John 6:70.

47 See the Book of Acts, especially 10:1–48; 15:7–11.

48 John 13:34–35.

49 With almost numbing repetition, news articles give constant evidence of discrimination and violations of human rights worldwide. The following news items are a sampling of this tragic situation:

"Human Rights Question Revives as Summit Nears," *U.S. News and World Report*, October 28, 1985, p. 30.

"In Nicaragua, Rights Curbs Bring Uncertainty and More Censorship," *New York Times*, October 24, 1985, A–1.

"U.N. Finds Widespread Inequality for Women," *New York Times*, June 23, 1985, p. 10.

"Brazil's Battered Women Find Haven From Abuse," *New York Times*, September 14, 1985, p. 2.

"Life, Death, and the Rights of Handicapped Babies," *New York Times*, June 18, 1985, C–1.

"Argentine, Where Kids Are War Booty," *Newsday*, September 11, 1985, p. 13.

"Poverty: Suffer the Children," *Time*, June 17, 1985, p. 37.

"White Supremists Voice Support of Farrakhan," *New York Times*, October 12, 1985, p. 12.

"Racist Aryan Nations Group Inducts New Disciples," *New York Times*, October 20, 1985, p. 31.

"Can South Africa Avoid Race War?" *U.S. News and World Report*, August 26, 1985, p. 20.

"Apartheid Foe Says Protest in White Areas Is Inevitable," *New York Times,* September 7, 1985, p. 6.

"Intellectuals Silent on Global Intolerance of Religion," *Wall Street Journal,* June 10, 1985, p. 22.

"Justices to Ponder Extent of Rights of the Disabled," *New York Times,* October 22, 1985, A–21.

"The Twilight of Forced Retirement (of the Aged)" *U.S. News and World Report,* August 19, 1985, p. 66.

The evangelical press echoes this litany in articles such as these:

S. Thomas Nicolls, "Human Rights: A Concern for the Righteous," *Eternity,* May 25, 1979, p. 23.

Karen King and Chris Moss, "Human Rights in Nicaragua," *The Other Side,* May 1984, p. 24.

"Rights Abuses Increase in El Salvador," *Sojourners,* November 1985, p. 9.

Lloyd Billingsley, "Scheduled Slavery: The Misery of India's Untouchables," *Eternity,* November 1984, p. 39.

Marshall Shelley, "The Death Penalty: Two Sides of a Growing Issue," *Christianity Today,* March 2, 1984, p. 14.

"They Know Not What They Do: A Christian Call for the Abolition of Torture," *The Other Side,* June 1984, p. 19.

Joyce Hollyday, "An Epidemic of Violence: Manifestations of Violence Against Women," *Sojourners,* November 1984, p. 10.

Kenneth W. Petersen, "Wife Abuse: The Silent Crime, the Silent Church," *Christianity Today,* November 25, 1983, p. 22.

Lucille Travis, "Are There Battered Women in Your Pews?" *Eternity,* November 1981, p. 32.

Beth Spring, "The Rationalization of Racism," *Christianity Today,* October 4, 1985, p. 18.

Barbara R. Thompson, "Can Blacks and Whites Ever Work Together in South Africa?" *Christianity Today,* July 15, 1983, p. 22.

Verne Becker, "The Counterfeit Christianity of the Ku Klux Klan," *Christianity Today,* April 20, 1984, p. 30.

James C. Dekker, "Religious Persecution in Latin America," *The Reformed Journal,* February 1983, p. 16.

John Bookser-Feister, "The Struggle for Work-Place Justice," *The Other Side,* April/May 1985, p. 46.

Daryl Borgquist, "Empowering the Poor," *Eternity,* June 1984, p. 21.

"Black Children Face Increased Poverty," *The Other Side,* September 1985, p. 4.

Rodney Clapp, "Vanishing Childhood," *Christianity Today,* May 18, 1984, p. 12.

"Elderly Abuse: A Close Second to Child Abuse," *U.S. News and World Report,* quoted in *Christianity Today,* June 12, 1981, p. 24.

[50]Evelyn Miranda-Feliciano makes this observation in her article "Requiem for Renata," *The Other Side,* November 1985, p. 19:

In fact, women's status has gotten worse in the last ten years, according to the *Alternative Country Reports,* written by some sixty women from fourteen Asian countries who recently met in Davao, Philippines. . . . Three trends have surfaced in the past ten years, according to the summary of the reports: the commodification of women ("women are being sold"), the pauperization of women ("women are poor"), and the domestication of women ("women have no rights"). Commodification includes prostitution, mail-order brides, sex tours, pornography, rape, sexual harassment, and wife beating, as well as the increase of migrant women workers searching for a means of survival. Pauperization is typified by the Philippine situation where hunger, poverty, and landlessness have increased tremendously. In poverty, women receive leftovers. Cultural values, religious dogma, and a patriarchal dictatorship nullify or weaken whatever is gained legally by women. Religion has been a key to the perpetuation of women's oppression through the ages, a majority of the delegates agreed and that includes Christianity. A devastating statement—but all too painfully true.

[51]"Minorities Seen as Still Lagging in Health Status," *New York Times,* October 17, 1985, A–16. A report on how poverty affects minority children had this to say:

> According to Children's Defense Fund President Marian Edelman, the plight of black children has worsened dramatically compared with that of whites since 1980. Black children, said Edelman, are now twice as likely as whites to die before their first birthday, three times as likely to live in an impoverished or female-headed family, four times as likely to live with neither parent and five times as likely to be dependent on welfare (quoted in "Poverty: Suffer the Children," *Time,* June 17, 1985, p. 37.)

[52] Ernest Makhetha, quoted in "Four Faces of Conflict in South Africa," *U.S. News and World Report,* October 14, 1985, p. 35.

[53] See, e.g., Deuteronomy 16:18–20; Proverbs 20:10; Ezra 45:9; Amos 2:6–8; 5:7, 10–15, 24; Zechariah 8:16–17; James 2:1–12. The Book of Esther is also one of the greatest indictments of discrimination of all time.

[54] Matthew 28:19–20; Acts 1:8. Jesus' words in Luke 6:27–32 and 14:12–14 also tell us that we are to reach out with no thought of being "paid back." In addition we are to reach out regardless of the response of those to whom our compassion or our evangelism is addressed. For example, there are those who refuse food, clothing, and shelter and insist (for whatever reason) on living as "street people." This rejection of social service programs does not mean that such programs should be discontinued. So there will be those who refuse their spiritual rights as well, but again this rejection does not relieve Christians of the obligation to protect those rights and uphold the basic right of all human beings to hear the gospel. A comparison of a church's or an individual's support of programs addressed to those who have already heard the gospel to support of programs for those who have not yet heard can be the most revealing of what is for most persons an unconscious discrimination.

[55] Frank Cumbers, ed., *Daily Readings from W. E. Sangster* (London: Epworth, 1966), p. 271.

[56] However, in this there is a *caveat,* as John Stott pointed out at the 1983 Leadership Luncheon following the 1983 National Prayer Breakfast in Washington, D.C. Stott said:

> Sharing the good news of Jesus is not to be the hobby of a few eccentric enthusiasts. Mission is the concern of every follower of Jesus. But there is a precaution that I need to add. To proclaim the uniqueness of Jesus is one thing; to proclaim the superiority of Western civilization or ecclesiastical culture is something quite, quite different.
>
> It is particularly important that as we interact with the Third World that we avoid that variation of discrimination which is paternalism.

[57] John 1:12; 5:24; Romans 6:23; Ephesians 2:8–10; Titus 3:4–7.

[58] Ephesians 6:11–12; 1 Peter 5:8–9.

[59] First Corinthians 12:12–13; Ephesians 2:11–22; 1 Peter 2:5, 9.

[60] Again the media reflects these hurts, with the following articles being only a sampling:

Robert L. Niklaus, "Can Christian Colleges Mix with Minorities?" *Christianity Today,* November 6, 1981, p. 44.

Steven Snook, "Forgiveness and Justice in South Africa," *The Reformed Journal,* September 1985, p. 18.

Joseph Bayly, "Saved, Single, and Second-Class," *Eternity*, March 1983, p. 23.

"An Interview with Joni Eareckson," *Eternity*, May 1981, p. 23.

"Bishops Seeking Larger Role for Black Catholics," *New York Times*, September 10, 1985, B–3.

61 Luke 9:49–50.

62 The column "Foretaste" in *Eternity*, May 1984, p. 4, showed this tension by commenting: " 'Ordination of women': This is perhaps best *fought* within each denomination . . ." (italics mine).

63 First Timothy 2:5.

64 First Peter 2:4–5.

65 Romans 8:15–17.

66 Those who say that it is a scriptural truth that women have a restricted role and cannot serve in teaching or leadership capacities appear to be in conflict with the fact that the Bible says that God uses women in those very ways. See, e.g., Miriam (Exod. 15:20; Mic. 6:4), Deborah (Judg. 4–5), Huldah (2 Chron. 34:19–28), Esther, Priscilla (Acts 18:26), Junia (Rom. 16:7). How can prohibition of women in teaching or leadership be a timeless truth when Scripture itself not only gives "exceptions" but commends the women for their actions? A timeless truth cannot have exceptions. Rather God's Word teaches that every believer's mission in life is to serve God, and the case histories in his Word demonstrate that he chooses and equips the servant who is best suited to the particular job that needs to be done. We must never forget that God is Creator and that his co-opting use of us, his creatures, is infinitely creative.

67 While ordination undoubtedly figured in church order in some way, no New Testament text tells us exactly what ordination is, and there is no New Testament text that mandates ordination before a person can go out to preach the gospel. In the New Testament ordination was not a prerequisite to proclamation or to the exercise of certain spiritual gifts such as prophesying, pastoring, teaching, or administering. It is discriminatory to use ordination as a device to limit women's full use of their God-given gifts. More and more women are asking those who would restrict ordination to men only, "Who are you to judge someone else's servant?" (Rom. 14:4). Persons with a high view of Scripture should be cautious about narrowing a concept or procedure that the Bible does not spell out in detail. Certainly Paul warns us in 1 Corinthians 4:6 not to go beyond what is written.

68 "Rights Unit Reviews 123 Nations," *New York Times*, October 9, 1985.

69 Matthew 24:12 (New English Bible).

70 John 13:34–35. David H. C. Read, pastor of the Madison Avenue Presbyterian Church, New York City, has pointed out that this is still the new commandment because it has so rarely been practiced.

71 See, e.g., Isaiah 14:11–17; 57:15; Mark 9:35; Luke 9:23–25; 14:7–11; James 4:6. Over and over again in the Old Testament we read that God told his people that they had no cause for pride or elitism (e.g., Deut. 7:7–8). Scripture warns both Jew and Gentile of the danger in feeling entitled to a preferred position (Luke 3:8; Rom. 2:17–3:19; 11:17–21). "For God does not show favoritism" (Rom. 2:11).

72 Jesus' interchange with the Jewish leaders in John 8 and 9 shows that their sense of entitlement blinded them from hearing Jesus Christ's message and from showing any compassion to someone less fortunate than they.

73 Luke 18:9–14.

74 Matthew 20:24–28; Mark 8:34; Luke 9:46–48; John 12:24–26; 13:14–17.

75 Matthew 11:28–30.

76 Matthew 7:1–5. In this self-examination we must keep uppermost an awareness of our creation in the image of God. As Frank Gaebelein pointed out, this

> sets our lifestyle in the perspective of the human dignity inherent in our creation. It compels us to see whether anything in the way we live tends to diminish or degrade the humanity of our fellow image-bearers. It

forces us to grapple with the relation of our lifestyle to the needs of the poor and hungry and oppressed—those whom God Himself is especially concerned about (quoted from "Old Testament Foundations for Living More Simply" in Ronald J. Sider, ed., *Living More Simply* [Downers Grove: InterVarsity, 1980], p. 27.)

[77] Leon Morris, "The Boat People," *Christianity Today,* October 20, 1978, p. 71.

[78] Oswald Chambers, *My Utmost for His Highest* (New York: Dodd, Mead, 1964), pp. 268, 270.

[79] Luke 23:34.

[80] See, e.g., 1 Corinthians 9:12, 19–22; Romans 9:3; 14:13–21; Galatians 6:2. This does not mean that we will always or should always agree with the other person's position. In this connection Case Hoogendoorn perceptively comments:

> The evangelical community must fight to maintain the right to shape the moral character of its institutions and its members. It must never give up the power of social censure and ostracism even though the force of those powers has weakened considerably in recent years. Yet, as a reconciling force in a pluralistic society, it must lead the way in issuing the call for civil rights and justice for all people and groups regardless of race, religion, saintliness, or sexual preference. Only then will its actions support the witness of the Word it proclaims (Case Hoogendoorn, "Gay Rights and Wrongs," *Eternity,* June 1981, p. 19).

[81] Proverbs 29:7.

[82] Proverbs 31:8–9.

[83] Proverbs 24:11–12.

[84] Isaiah 1:1–27; Matthew 5:23–24.

[85] Matthew 25:31–46.

[86] David G. Horner, past President of Barrington College, as quoted in an article by Robert L. Niklaus, "Can Christians Mix with Minorities?" *Christianity Today,* November 6, 1981, p. 44.

# A Response to Discrimination and Human Rights

**Anthony T. Evans**

Mrs. Gretchen Gaebelein Hull addresses the subject of "Discrimination and Human Rights" well. Careful grounding of her definitions and conclusions in accordance with biblical and theological foundations gives her arguments potency and credibility. For example, Mrs. Hull shows definitely that the human rights issue is essentially, at its core, a biblical theological issue for, "just as apart from Scripture there is no basis for the uniqueness of human life, so also apart from Scripture there is no basis for human rights either." Mrs. Hull then proceeds to argue from what she calls the "two scriptural strands"— namely, the sanctity of life and the self-revelation of God—that human rights must find their basis from a sound theological perspective.

A second crucial contribution of Mrs. Hull which, in my opinion, provides the most significant contribution of her work, is what might be termed "delicate distinctions." Rather than simply using and defining terms generally, Mrs. Hull does a wonderful job of not assuming the reader will make certain distinctions himself. She makes crucial distinctions between human rights and civil rights, the latter referring to rights societies have extrapolated from principles of human rights (i.e., the right to vote). Another distinction that was made was between discipline and discrimination, since the misuse of rights will and should lead to their restriction. Such restriction should not be viewed as discrimination if justly enacted. This distinction then places the factor of responsibility alongside of rights. It is the responsibility of those arguing for their rights that such rights are exercised with sensitivity to the rights of others and accountability to those in authority; and it is the responsibility of those who execute justice and discipline to make sure that such discipline is not "a cloak for discrimination." Other good distinctions made by Mrs. Hull are between secular and sacred discrimination, and institutional and noninstitutional discrimination.

Particularly helpful was Mrs. Hull's identification of the lack of Christian evangelism as discrimination, because it says in essence to the lost that they are subhuman and that their souls are insignificant. This is clearly seen in Jesus' willingness to go through Samaria and share the truth regarding himself with a woman to whom his disciples would never have witnessed (John 4).

One area where Mrs. Hull does not go far enough in making delicate distinctions is the application of her thesis to the discrimination against women in ministry. She uses the Scripture to argue for the equality of women with men and that such equality prohibits the denying of women "the full privileges of sonship" and is thus discriminating in that it restricts their opportunity to coadminister their spiritual inheritance which impedes their enjoyment of the abundant life. It is not that Mrs. Hull's antidiscrimination call against women is not correct and biblical; it is rather that the distinction made between spiritual gifts and spiritual roles is not made. Mrs. Hull's implication is that because women are equal to men, and they are, there is to be no distinction in spiritual functions. However, such distinctions are regularly made in Scripture. In the family there are distinctions of roles made between husbands and wives even though there is equality of essence (Eph. 5:23–24). Even within the Godhead this is true, because Jesus, who is equal to God, could not be said to have been discriminated against by the Father since it was the Son, not the Father, who became incarnate. In other words, every believer is gifted by God, but not every believer can function in the same role with that gift. There is no indication, for example, that women could be elders. Distinctions of function then should not be termed as discriminatory.

At this point a crucial question arises which is a natural outgrowth in Mrs. Hull's discussion: How does the church function to address the human rights issue, and in what priority? This question is crucial in light of the fact that the human rights issues and their attendant sociological repercussions have reached national and international proportions and that the church is constantly bombarded with a call to correct all the wrongs that exist. So central has sociology become to the doing of theology (particularly in light of the international rise of liberation theology) that it has become the new integrating point for theology as opposed to philosophy which has historically held that position.

It is my view that the church's primary responsibility is to the church, and then as an overflow to the world, not vice-versa. In our attempt to right the wrongs of the world, we have tragically missed the human rights and discrimination issues in our own households. This grave reality results in the society at large not having a significant model of God's righteousness and justice for it to emulate. Thus people can and do argue for national human rights issues and still maintain eleven o'clock Sunday morning as the most discriminating hour in America.

The Scripture is clear that the church is first obligated to itself if it, in fact, will have anything to offer the world at large. Galatians 6:10 expressly makes this point when it says, "So then, while we have opportunity, let us do good to all men, and especially to those who are of the household of the faith." Another important passage in this regard is John 13:35 which says, "By this shall all men know that you are My disciples, if you have love for one another" (NASB). There are two important things to note here; first, that the reality of Christ is demonstrated by the unselfish nature of the members of Christ's church toward one another; and secondly, this love is being demonstrated in the sphere of the world where it can be witnessed by the world. The point is that when the church functions as the church should function, the message of Christ is uniquely proclaimed.

A corollary passage to this is Matthew 5:13 which says, "You are the salt of the earth; but if the salt has become tasteless, how will it be made salty again? It is good for nothing anymore, except to be thrown out and trampled under foot by men" (NASB). Here again, the influence of the salt upon the world is related to whether the salt is salty. Saltless salt on meat is useless. This is why the New Testament epistles are written to the church about the church. In fact, very little is said about making changes in the world when compared with making changes in the church, so that the world will have something to see. The tragic reality is that the failure of the church locally, nationally, and internationally is made "twice worse" by the reality that within its own ranks discrimination and violation of human rights run rampant, many times being far behind the progress made in secular society. This is blatantly seen, as Mrs. Hull says, in the denial of women in the use of their gifts in the church (gifts must be distinguished from roles). This is also seen in the racial prejudice shown by black and white Christians toward one another, as well as in political discrimination between members of the body who do not line up with what one group would consider as the "proper Christian party line." Another very prominent Christian discriminating action is of the rich over the poor. Poor Christians are regularly unwelcome in the more middle-to-upper-class church bodies. Such economically based discrimination is condemned by the apostle James. He says that it is sin to have economic discrimination in the local church, and it is also simply illogical since, "Did God not choose the poor of this world to be rich in faith and heirs of the kingdom which He promised to those who love him?" (James 2:5 NASB). For James discrimination is an insult to God's value system.

Cultural or racial discrimination is also specifically condemned by God, as seen in Paul's confrontation with Peter. Peter's decision, in Galatians 2:11–21, to withdraw from the Gentiles was a racially, as well as culturally, motivated one.

Peter earlier had exhibited a racial problem in being able to relate to Gentiles. It took a direct revelation from God to get him to recognize his racial prejudice and begin the process of dealing with it (Acts 10:9–23). However, this vision did not fully correct his Jewish pride and prejudice. In Antioch people had at least begun to associate with Gentiles (Gal. 2:12). However, when James sent some Jews to the church at Antioch, Peter withdrew from the Gentiles. The reason for this withdrawal was Peter's "fearing of the party of the circumcision" (v. 12). Thus Peter conformed to the racial prejudice of his brothers in the flesh, so as not to lose his own acceptance among them. Thus race, as well as culture and religion, took priority over truth. So all-encompassing was this decision that "the rest of the Jews joined him in hypocrisy, with the result that even Barnabas was carried away by their hypocrisy" (v. 13).

Paul, however, in addressing this problem, makes it quite clear that ethnic distinctions that contradict the unified nature of the church are to be categorically condemned. Thus Paul opposed Peter personally (Gal. 2:11), publicly (v. 14), and biblically (vv. 14ff.). The theological reason for Paul's condemnation of the Jews was because "they were not straightforward about the truth of the gospel" (v. 14). The point was that racial preferences are never to interfere with the unifying nature of the gospel. Nor is the Bible to be used to place requirements in race that are not consistent with the unifying nature of the body of Christ (vv. 15–16).

As the church practices justice, it then is a drawing card to those who desire justice. This means that the church becomes a magnet, since the world at large has no internal basis for promising or guaranteeing justice in society.

In conclusion, the presentation by Mrs. Hull is excellent in its scope and specificity. She gives a pragmatic call for the issue of discrimination and human rights to be addressed from a biblical perspective. Finally, she successfully makes a call for the attitude of servanthood to rule supreme if the attitude of entitlement is to be overcome, thus providing the kind of mind-set that will prompt the kind of Christian behavior that will address the need for citadels of righteousness, justice, and human dignity that our world so desperately needs.

# A Response to
# Discrimination and Human Rights

## Michael E. Haynes

Discrimination and denial of human rights is one of the major issues of this age on an international and local level.

Mrs. Hull approaches this complex subject with candor, clarity, conviction, and courage. In precise statements and in general intimations she is more forthright than many of her male counterparts in the evangelical world.

Her litany of rights needs to be examined individually and carefully. Among them are: right to life; just and humane treatment; adequate food, clothing, and shelter; adequate medical care; marriage; procreation; work; and education.

In a second category she lists the right to know God; the freedom of religion; freedom to learn about God and to serve God; and the right to vote, travel, and speak freely.

Essentially, she directly or indirectly touches upon every area where a human is discriminated against. She provides an adequate agenda for discussion and resolution, particularly for the evangelical community at large.

As a black American who maintains a solid evangelical position in regard to Scripture, my final response was "Amen and Amen!" Now Evangelicals, let us apply God's truth and change the atmosphere of our own nation and the world at large.

A "high view" of Scripture demands a high view of the uniqueness and dignity of all of God's human creation. This in turn commands an utter obedience to God's Word in relation to how we perceive all other people and how we treat all other people.

The study and the analysis is fine. The rhetorical conclusions are exciting. The personal and institutional application of God's command on the treatment of "the least of these" is "where the rubber meets the road"!

In her introductory page, the writer states that there is an "instinctive response" and conviction "that human life is to be preserved and to be treated with respect."

Mrs. Hull then follows with a truism which embarrasses and indicts many professing so-called Evangelicals and evangelical institutions, stating that "even among persons with little or no interest in God's Word there is a consensus that the uniqueness of humanity carries with it certain basic rights."

In this age many of the persons who have taken the fore in the struggle for human rights would be regarded by Evangelicals as liberals, radicals, militants, agnostics, atheists, and leftists. Oppressed people often follow them because they act like they care.

The late Martin Luther King, Jr., with whom I had the privilege to be associated at Twelfth Baptist Church during the period of his doctoral studies, often stated that "Jesus calls the Church to be the headlight in this world, but we are usually the taillights."

In recent generations the majority of the evangelical world has not been on the cutting edge nor on the front line in defending human rights, or in combating discrimination.

More recently, however, a number of Evangelicals have taken aggressive stands against certain issues, such as abortion, pornography, and homosexuality.

Albeit, we nevertheless appear more than hesitant to be as aggressive in following other biblical mandates which cry out against racism, oppression, and injustice. Political expediency, economics, and popularity oftentimes cause us to be less than biblical in our stand.

The writer suggests two scriptural stands which need to be traced in discovering the biblical basis for human rights.

The first is *the sanctity of life*. From this, she says, emerges the right to life and other *natural rights*. There are ramifications from this issue that get little attention or emphasis; e.g., adequate medical care, quality education, job training, and jobs.

It is biblical to be prolife. But it is hypocritical to allow those "grown babies" to struggle and suffer later for an education, a decent home, decent job, adequate medical care, and a sense of self-worth. We must be equally aggressive to maintain the right to life from the cradle to the grave—and yes, even on to glory!

The writer's second scriptural stand is the *self-revelation of God*, from whence comes "a right to freedom of religion," etc. This particular area in all of its ramifications also needs to be expanded.

The news media has unofficially declared this to be the age of the evangelical. Our prominence in some of the most vital areas of American life cannot be denied. We have made great strides in the areas of television, radio, publishing, government—including access to the White House—medicine, education, etc.

Jesus, in his servant parable recorded in Luke 12:48, establishes a principle of servanthood, stewardship, and sacrifice, saying, "For unto whomsoever much is given, of him shall be much required: and to whom men have committed much, of him they will ask the more" (KJV).

The "gospel" we proclaim to the world is often tainted, slanted, distorted, miscolored, watered-down, or invalidated by the stand we take or *do not* take on issues of human rights and discrimination. "What we do [or do not do] speaks so loudly they [the world—the hurting] cannot hear what we say!"

Eleven o'clock on Sunday morning is still the most segregated hour of the week. The gathering hour of the "body of Christ" still reflects rank discrimination by reason of race, sex, national origin, culture, economic status, and educational ability.

The following statements of biblical truth, emphasized by the writer, demand serious consideration and action.

1. "The criterion for social concerns is human need and not discriminatory practices" (p. 338).
2. "No person who desires to be obedient to Scripture can engage in or condone discriminatory acts" (p. 339).
3. "A hurting world is not so much interested in our personal testimonies but in whether we offer some means to heal the hurts" (p. 340).
4. "[Create] a climate in which they will be receptive to exercising their spiritual right of knowing God and choosing to accept his free gift of new life in Christ" (p. 341).
5. "We are also entrusted with a new mission, the ministry of reconciliation" (p. 341).
6. "Therefore no born-again believer should ever, on the basis of extrabiblical requirements, be denied full fellowship in the body or, on the basis of extrascriptural distinctions, be denied full opportunity to use his or her God-given gifts in the service of the Master" (p. 341).

The too-often distinct lines between color, class, and culture continue to be the special focus of the forces of sin and Satan in order to weaken the mission of the church of Jesus Christ, divide the saints, discredit our message, invalidate our testimony, and relegate so-called evangelical Christians to the level of "sounding brass and tinkling cymbals."

Mrs. Hull rightly emphasizes that Satan uses "the sin of discrimination to divide believers"!

How do we gain the strength to recognize these evils; confess the same; repent of the same; and move to the speedy eradication of every vestige of discrimination, exploitation, and oppression on the part of Evangelicals in America and in the world. Think of the glory the Lord would gain if "We [were] not divided, all one body we"!

The writer understandably shows a bias in her deep concern for women's rights. I undoubtedly reflect the same on the issue of racism. Others may indicate sensitivity in specific areas where they sense or know that God-given rights have been denied.

In reviewing all these exciting, hope-inducing, biblical injunctions to eradicate Satan's work of discrimination and denial of human rights, as a minority person who has felt intensely the sting of being discriminated against within the very heart of the evangelical world, I find hope in this summary presented in the words of Malbie Babcock:

> This is my Father's world,
> O let me ne'er forget,
> That though the wrong,
> Seems oft so strong,
> God is the Ruler yet.
>
> This is my Father's world,
> The battle is not done,
> Jesus Who died
> Shall be satisfied,
> And earth and heaven be one!

The statements on entitlement (p. 344) and empowerment (p. 345) are most important. God has granted some the privilege and responsibility of a stewardship which allows them to administer his resources to humankind and to his church for his glory and honor. History has proven that in almost every instance those in power never relinquish any of that power voluntarily.

Mrs. Hull presents a universal biblical mandate that needs to be heard and heeded when she says, "Those who are politically, societally, economically, or clerically empowered must see themselves simply as stewards and caretakers of God's gifts."

A New York-centered Kosher advertisement says that a certain company is putting the best ingredients into its product to produce excellence for the consumer, not because the city, state, or federal government requires it, but because they have to "Answer to a higher authority."

Those who adhere to biblical orthodoxy, those who dare take a stand for biblical inerrancy must also answer to a higher authority for how we fulfill our mandates of faith and practice.

James 4:17 says, "To him that knoweth to do good, and doeth it not, to him it is sin" (KJV).

The wise man of the Old Testament says, "Withhold not good from them to whom it is due, when it is in the power of thine hand to do it" (Prov. 3:27 KJV).

The extent to which Bible-believing Christians fall short individually and institutionally in practicing the love of God in relation to human rights and discrimination oftentimes makes part of Paul's sermon on Mars Hill applicable to us: (1) We worship in superstitious ignorance a God whom we really do not know; (2) we act elitist and arrogant as if he needs us and we do not need him and his mercy; (3) we forget that all we have is his free gift to us; and (4) we belittle his sovereignty, ignoring the fact that he "hath made of *one blood* all nations of [people] to dwell on all the face of the earth, and [he] hath determined the times before appointed, and the bounds of their habitation" (Acts 17:26 KJV).

To those who have the power and influence of office, rank, riches of land, gold, patronage, authority, etc., the words of the prophet Micah ring out as a mandate and a warning from Jehovah God: "He hath shewed thee, O man, what is good; and what doth the LORD require of thee, but to do justly, and to love mercy, and to walk humbly with thy God?" (Mic. 6:8 KJV).

Throughout America, in South Africa, in other nations across the world, there are "huddled masses yearning to breathe free." God calls us to help them—not to pussyfoot, rhetoricize, justify, rationalize, nor procrastinate—but to help, to heal, to set free! He has loaned us the resources. All we need to do is submit our will to his will, and we can make this sinful world a better place to journey through as we lead lost souls to God's eternal "kingdom of love and light."

"Let us hear the conclusion of the whole matter: 'Fear God, and keep his commandments: For this is the whole duty of man. For God shall bring every work into judgment, with every secret thing, whether it be good, or whether it be evil" (Eccl. 12:13–14 KJV).

# WAR

## Kurt E. Marquart

The divine commands not to kill and to turn the other cheek are quite straightforward and not the least bit obscure. Nor is there any doubt about the deadly potential of nuclear weapons. Given this rare clarity on both the question of law and the question of fact, the case seems open and shut: the very existence of nuclear weapons, not to mention any possible use of them, is an affront to Christian morality. This perception has become practically self-evident for many of our contemporaries both inside and outside the churches. Yet its appealing simplicity is thoroughly misleading. Such plausible perceptions habitually short-circuit real moral reasoning for they are charged with the powerful, primal currents of popular culture, which in our time and place includes goodly doses of utopianism and sentimentality.[1] A valid transition from biblical teaching to the nuclear-weapons issue is, in fact, far from direct or obvious. I propose first to examine some reasons why this should be so and then to see whether and how biblical ethics offers any guidance in respect of nuclear weapons.

## I. BIBLICAL DISTINCTIONS

Our Lord rejects out of hand any resort to self-serving distinctions and technicalities designed to evade the clear claims of moral duty (Matt. 23:16–22). This does not mean, however, that moral distinctions as such are wrong. On the contrary, if we are to "stop judging by mere appearances, and make a right judgment" (John 7:24), moral distinctions are indispensable. Distaste for such moral "discrimination" owes more to modern cultural egalitarianism than to the Savior, who said that "from everyone who has

been given much, much will be demanded" (Luke 12:48), and that
on Judgment Day Sodom and Gomorrah would fare better than
those who had despised the messengers of the Son of God
Incarnate (Matt. 10:15). Circumstances do alter cases. It is wrong,
for instance, to take one's own life (e.g., Judas). But giving it up
for the sake of others is admirable not only in a military code of
honor but in Christian ethics itself (John 15:13).

A most important question about every biblical command is:
"To whom is this addressed?" One cannot simply add a "Go and
do thou likewise" to every divine command in Scripture. So, for
instance, Abraham but no one else was told to sacrifice his son.
And the genocidal commands of Deuteronomy 20:16–17 were
given to ancient Israel, not to us nor to the modern Zionist state
for that matter.

It is also possible that quite opposite commands are addressed
to the same persons but in different capacities or roles. Under the
Pentateuch legislation, for example, murder—that is, the taking of
human life by private individuals at their own discretion—was of
course strictly forbidden. On the other hand it was a public duty
to impose and carry out the death penalty for a whole catalogue of
capital crimes (Lev. 20). This private/public dichotomy is by no
means abolished in the New Testament. As a human being,
particularly as a Christian, I must love and forgive those who
wrong me. But as a citizen, policeman, judge, juror, prison guard,
or executioner, I am duty-bound to help catch, convict, punish,
and sometimes even execute criminals—regardless of my personal feelings about them (Rom. 13:1–5). Pacifism risks moral
incoherence by collapsing this vital distinction between private
and public duty or between person and office.[2]

Important as the differences between the Old and New
Testaments are, they do not amount to a moral evolution. It is not
true, for instance, that Old Testament morality required "an eye
for an eye" and that Christ upgraded ethics from this primitive
level by his command to turn the other cheek (Matt. 5:38–39). The
contrast in Matthew 5 is not between the Old and the New
Testaments but between traditional misinterpretations of the Old
Testament (see Matt. 3:43) and its genuine authentic sense (5:17).
The "eye for an eye" maxim is civil, not moral law in the Old
Testament (Exod. 21:24; Lev. 24:20; Deut. 19:21) and is in principle
endorsed by Christ (Matt. 26:52; cf. Gen. 9:6). The basic moral law,
also in the Old Testament, is not "an eye for an eye" but "Love
your neighbor as yourself" (Lev. 19:18; Matt. 22:39). The Ten
Commandments themselves cannot simply be identified with the
moral law—that is, with the ethical duties of all men everywhere.
Since the Ten Commandments in their original form (Exod. 20;
Deut. 5) include elements of the ceremonial law and are embedded in the civil, theocratic code of ancient Israel, they must pass

through the "filter" of their proper, New Testament interpretation (Matt. 5; Col. 2:16–17) in order to function as moral law today.

Most important of all for our purposes is the radical "separation of powers" instituted by the New Testament. In Christ the provisional Old Testament theocracy is fulfilled, transcended, and abolished. The church, the true Israel (Rom. 2:28; 9:6–9; Eph. 2:19–22), is truly universal now, no longer tied to or bounded by national, geographic, racial, or political particularities of any kind. Christ's kingdom is not of this world (John 18:36), and the church's weapons and warfare are entirely spiritual, not political or military (Eph. 6:10–18). Civil and spiritual authority, therefore, are strictly distinct. The church is sent to transmit to lost mankind that supernatural, divine life and salvation which "is in his Son" (1 John 5:11). This transmission happens through the faith-creating gospel, including baptism and the Holy Supper (Matt. 28:19–20; Rom. 1:16; 1 John 5:8). While the state, or civil society, too, is God's servant, God rules in that realm not through the revealed gospel of his grace but through reason, conscience, natural law (Rom. 2:14–15), and a coercive power based on these (13:1–5).

Although some established churches in Europe manage to dodder on better than others, the real challenge today is to shake off entirely the fateful Constantinian state/church embrace as a "kind of collective experience of the far country in which the prodigal spent his inheritance with harlots."[3] Freed of these illusions, we may catch a glimpse again of the New Testament vision of the church as the humble bride of Christ, gloriously endowed by her divine Bridegroom with all the treasures of salvation. The caricature of the church as a moral policewoman patroling the public square arises ultimately out of an alien abyss (Rev. 17:8). The New Testament church meets in public assembly for the solemn transaction of the salvific, evangelical "mysteries of God" (1 Cor. 4:1; 10:16–17; 11:23ff.), not to conduct pep rallies for social causes, however worthy.

The Savior himself refused to act as arbiter of social justice (Luke 12:14) and solved a moral dilemma about controversial taxes by differentiating sharply between God and Caesar (Matt. 22:21). As the promised messianic King he offered liberation from sin, death, and hell. Preferring something more practical, official Jerusalem got the crowds to shout instead for the Liberation Front terrorist Barabbas (27:21). The same political frenzy agitates contemporary churches[4] as they huff and puff against social, military, economic, nuclear, and all other temporal oppressions. The agendas of modern church conventions, ever anxious to be "relevant,"[5] compete with the United Nations Organization in concerning themselves with everything from Afghanistan to Zambia. The apostolic church's agenda in Acts 15 seems modest,

even petty, by comparison. Ignoring all the grave social ills then
bedeviling the Roman Empire, the Jerusalem Council debated and
settled the implications of the gospel for circumcision and Jewish
dietary regulation! Concentrating all its energies on the alone-
saving gospel of Christ (Gal. 1), the apostolic church had not yet
made the category mistake which seemed so self-evident to the
World Council of Churches in Amsterdam (1948) when it spoke in
the report on "The Church and the Disorder of Society" of "the
responsible society" as "the goal for which the churches in all
lands must work."

The church's marching orders are to make disciples of all
nations by baptism and Christian instruction (Matt. 28:19–20). As
the reference to baptism shows, the church's teaching function is
controlled entirely by her missionary command. There is no God-
given basis for civics lessons on the side. The object of the
church's teaching mission is not general uplift but that "repentance and forgiveness of sins [be] preached in his name to all
nations, beginning at Jerusalem" (Luke 24:47). States can neither
repent nor believe nor receive forgiveness; nor, thank Heavens,
are they capable of eternal life. Therefore, while the church indeed
addresses all mankind with the message of God's judgment
against sin and his mercy in Christ, the church as church has
nothing at all to say to any state as state. That legally incorporated
bodies called "churches" may make use of their civil and social
standing to express some public concerns of their members as
citizens is another matter altogether and has no direct basis in the
church's mission as such. The concerted action of Christians as
citizens should not be called even a "secondary" duty or function
of the church, as if Christ had said: "My kingdom is not *primarily*
of this world."

Has Christian ethics then any guidance at all to offer the
Christian citizen or public official? Yes, of course it has. But in
light of the foregoing we can now appreciate the full import of the
question with which we began: "To whom is this addressed?" If
the nuclear-weapons discussion among Christians is to be rescued
from the flaccid moral murkiness in which at present it largely
flounders, then some such delimiting preliminaries as the following must be nailed down first:

1. The Bible is not a handbook for all and sundry on good
behavior, but it is the book about Jesus Christ (Luke 24:44–45;
John 5:39).

2. To unbelievers and believers alike the church preaches the
law in order that the knowledge of sin (Rom. 3:19–20; 7:7) might
prepare the way for the gospel of the Savior.

3. To Christian believers the church explains the law also as a
guide—though not the motive power (Rom. 12:1)—for the good
works which flow out of a genuine life in Christ and which cannot
exist apart from him (John 15). Biblical ethics addresses Christians.

4. To unbelievers the church has in principle nothing to say except: "Repent and believe the gospel." Apart from this evangelical mission the church has no warrant to prescribe the behavior of non-Christians (1 Cor. 5:12), be they government officials, basketball players, or candlestick makers.

5. Since the Old Testament theocracy has been abolished, no country today is or can be in the special position of ancient Israel. States and civil societies are to be ruled not with the written Word of God—which offers no divine blueprint of statecraft—but with the justice and common sense resting on natural law (Rom. 2:14–15; 13:1–5).

6. While there are Christian politicians, farmers, chemists, and the like, there is no such thing as Christian politics, biblical farming, or evangelical chemistry. Laws can be just or unjust, furrows can be straight or crooked, and laboratory procedures can be competent or incompetent, but it is a category mistake to replace such terms with the words "Christian" or "non-Christian." Civil society is to be "humanized" not "Christianized."

7. Christians must be taught that it is their duty to employ also their political, social, and economic power and influence in the best interests of their fellow human beings. But how such goals are best implemented in practice, i.e., prudential judgment, must be left to the conscience of individual Christians themselves in their various callings. Ministers of the Word exceed their authority and competence when they make pronouncements beyond the scope of the written Word of God. As citizens of course they are entitled to their own opinions like everyone else.

## II. NUCLEAR WEAPONS: MORAL DIMENSIONS

One's first impulse is to say that Christian ethics is opposed to all weapons. Such a pronouncement, however, would reflect secular sentimentality more than Christian morality. Optimistic utopians (including Marxists) see evil as residing not in human nature but in unjust systems, institutions, and structures, which, when smashed, will release humanity's native goodness. Also, contemporary cultural relativism is loath to speak of "good" and "evil" in relation to "alternative lifestyles." It is easier to focus on symptoms and to crusade against "violence," guns, and bombs generally. Thus there arises the utterly amoral perception that guns in the hands of the police and in the hands of the criminal "community" are somehow equivalent. Christianity, on the other hand, knows that good and evil reside not in things but in persons—that is, in the wills of moral agents. Biblical ethics therefore focuses on the moral nature of purposes and actions, not on weapons as such, which are simply a function of a morally neutral technology. Barring devices designed for senseless cruelty (e.g., dumdum bullets), modern weapons are inherently no worse than swords and spears. And once it is admitted that killing is ethically permissible in some circumstances, then a weapon's capacity for killing more people does not in and of itself render it immoral. Or else jumbo-jets would be much more immoral than oxcarts because they place many more lives at risk.

Paradoxically, biblical ethics has less to say about nuclear bombs than about swords, and this not for the trivial reason that bombs are only a recent invention. The point is rather that unlike swords, nuclear bombs are, for the present at least, the prerogative of states, not of private individuals. Nuclear weapons thus virtually by definition comply with one of the traditional criteria of a just war—namely, that it is to be started and prosecuted by lawful authority and not at the whim of private persons. The main interest of biblical ethics in swords is that private individuals should not wield them (Gen. 9:6). States, on the other hand, must wield the sword (Rom. 13:4), and this largely to insure that individuals do not. When the state's sword-bearers are Christians, they must, of course, be motivated by love and therefore seek genuine justice, mitigate severity, protect the weak, and the like. But there is no specifically Christian way of governing a state or of fighting a war.

The crux of the nuclear-weapons issue today is not nuclear war but nuclear deterrence. No one advocates nuclear war. The main question is whether given the danger of nuclear war it is ethically acceptable to prevent nuclear war by threatening potential nuclear aggressors with nuclear retaliation. (I accept the distinction urged in this connection by the Anglican Bishop of London, Graham Leonard, between the morally acceptable and the morally good.[6] The latter sounds too much like approving something as ideal. In the real world statesmen often face nonideal options, *e.g.*, terrorists holding hostages. The operative moral principle here is to minimize harm and evil, not to expound abstractly good nonoptions.)

Most American churches which have spoken to the issue grudgingly allow deterrence,[7] the Roman Catholic bishops more grudgingly than their West European counterparts.[8] The World Council of Churches, with Iron Curtain participation, takes the purist view that nuclear deterrence "is to be rejected as morally unacceptable and as incapable of safeguarding peace and security in the long term."[9]

The usual argument against the morality of deterrence is that if it is wrong to do something, then it is also wrong to threaten to do it. Although this sounds plausible in the abstract, it fails to take account of the fact that if injustice or bloodshed can be averted by a judicious use of bluff, then such bluffing is the morally indicated policy. In any case the alleged principle is refuted by a celebrated biblical counterexample: King Solomon's threat to cut a baby in half could not have been carried out ethically. But since the threat issued happily in justice being done, it has always been taken as evidence that Solomon "had wisdom from God to administer justice" (1 Kings 3:28). Thus "wisdom is proved right by her actions" (Matt. 11:19).

What is remarkable about the whole case against nuclear deterrence is that it is short on moral argument and long on political and ideological judgments—surely not what one would expect from churches. How does the WCC's central committee know, for instance, that nuclear deterrence is "incapable of safeguarding peace and security in the long term" and that its own prescriptions, such as renunciation of the "first use" option and disarmament efforts, including "unilateral initiatives leading to the relaxation of tensions and building of mutual confidence," are likely to have the desired effects? Most of the ecclesiastical pronouncements, in fact, seem to assume that disarmament is the basic key to peace. Edward Norman put it very charitably when he pointed out that Christian leaders "tend to amateurism" in the political realm and "are permanently liable to absorb seemingly any account of world conditions which exploits their generosity."[10]

The fact is, of course, that responsible decisions about how to keep World War III at bay involve many hard questions about military, historical, technological, political, and other matters about which it is simply inappropriate for churches to pontificate. Let the churches tell their statesmen and citizen members that it is their duty to prevent nuclear war if possible. But the statesmen and citizens must decide for themselves, in light of the best information available to them, what actual policies can most realistically be expected to achieve the desired results. It is in fact arrogant and unethical to suggest that those who on prudential grounds favor disarmament as the best way to avoid war are for peace, while those who seek the same end by means of deterrence are for war.

It is refreshing therefore to see books like Jerram Barrs's *Who are the Peacemakers?* (1983) and the splendid symposium by Francis Schaeffer, Vladimir Bukovsky, and James Hitchcock entitled *Who Is For Peace?* (1983). These very titles challenge the disarmament advocates' exclusive claims to the "peace" banner. Both Barrs and Schaeffer show that biblical morality requires the responsible use of force in the civil realm and that to shrink from this use is to abandon the weak to the tender mercies of the Hitlers and Stalins of this world. Love for the neighbor requires our best efforts in his behalf against his oppressors.

Schaeffer quotes Jacques Ellul to the effect that in the era leading up to World War II "the Christians, full of good intentions, were thinking only of peace and were loudly proclaiming pacifism! In matters of that kind, Christian good intentions are often disastrous."[11] No less an authority on strategic analysis than Captain Basil Liddell Hart has concluded that one of the main causes of World War II was the long period of Western complacency which encouraged Hitler's aggressiveness.[12] Korea and the Falklands provide perhaps even clearer examples of wars brought about directly by a perceived unwillingness to defend the areas in question. On January 12, 1950, United States Secretary of State Dean Acheson had given a speech in which he had forgotten to mention Korea in defining the American defense perimeter. Later Acheson recalled

> that he had actually been rebuked by the then Soviet Ambassador to the UN for delivering a speech which permitted the Soviet Union to deduce that Korea did not matter to the United States, then changing his mind and, by reason of this blunder, involving both nations in a war which neither wanted.[13]

Likewise, Argentina's ex-President Galtieri has stated that Argentina would never have attacked the Falkland Islands had a minimal deterrent force there made clear Britain's intention to defend the Falklands.[14]

I am not suggesting that the World Council of Churches, having taken to heart these lessons, should now reverse itself and urge nuclear deterrence as the best way to avoid nuclear war. The point is rather that churches are not competent to determine just what sort of measures are most likely to prevent war. Nor is that the function of biblical ethics. That is why it would have been better, in my view, had Barrs's valuable little book mentioned above been subtitled "The Moral Deterrence." There simply is no "Christian case" either for or against deterrence. While the Christian citizen will be motivated differently from his non-Christian neighbor, he will reason about nuclear deterrence very much like any other person of good will and common sense.

Ethics supplies the principles, but valid applications depend on correct and realistic perceptions of the facts of the case. In this respect ethics is like a computer: put garbage in, and you get garbage out. The finest principles can, if the facts are misread, result in gross miscarriages of justice. It is therefore the Christian statesman's supreme ethical duty to know as many of the relevant facts as well as he possibly can. It would be an unethical and fanatical illusion on his part to believe that his Christian faith itself provides him with privileged information about statecraft or that his good Christian intentions excuse him from the rigors of attaining competent understanding. Biblical ethics does not seek to impose on the conscience of the Christian citizen or statesman a set of ready-made case law, or of one-dimensional idealisms.

Instead it seeks to discipline that conscience to pursue the freedom and responsibility innate in the utmost sobriety and realism, for the neighbor's need requires nothing less. (Given the biblical realism about human sin, it is strange to read in Chaplain [Major] Davidson's rather fair analysis of the major American churches' attitudes to nuclear weapons that, unlike governments, "Churches tend to be optimistic in their views of human nature").[15]

In this context the constant clamor for "negotiations" as an alternative to effective weapons needs to be seen as spurious— that is, pseudoethical. Diplomacy has been defined as the art of saying "nice doggie" while one is reaching for a stick. It is fatuous to suggest that it is the Christian diplomat's duty to throw away his stick in order to say "nice doggie" more sincerely! Negotiations and force are not alternatives in the sense that the former could work by itself without the latter. Bishop Leonard provides a good discussion of the point and states: "Not only does the power remain [in negotiations], even if hid in the velvet glove. It may be that negotiation has only become possible because the existence of that power has previously been made evident in an exemplary and limited way."[16]

It might be thought that the nuclear-arms discussion is so sobering that the participants in this discussion need not reality therapy but a strengthening of their ideals. It is useful, therefore, to remind ourselves of just what is being urged by some in the name of Christian duty. The following sentences are taken from a contribution to a recent British symposium by Lord MacLeod (The Very Reverend Doctor George Fielden MacLeod, M.C.):

> Is the Christian Church never to trust her enemy? Is Christ's commandment that we *must* trust them something for us to disregard? . . . I trust Russia. . . . There is sufficient evidence of the constancy with which they have tried to convince America and the West of their efforts to prove the sincerity of their desire for peace.[17]

Lord MacLeod gives a glowing report of the 1982 "World Conference: Religious Workers for Saving the Sacred Gift of Life from Nuclear Tragedy" in Moscow, in which he participated. "Five hundred and ninety eminent representatives of Buddhism, Christianity, Hinduism, Islam, Judaism, Sikhism, Shintoism and Zoroastrianism met to discuss" how to erect "an insurmountable barrier on the road to nuclear war." He concludes, "Is it conceivable that all this could take place in Moscow if the hierarchy [sic] was secretly opposed to peace and disarmament? No!"

Few would articulate this position in as clear-headed and candid a manner as did Lord MacLeod. Similar assumptions, however, influence the whole discussion in various degrees. The moral duty of geopolitical sobriety requires Christian citizens, before endorsing naïve "peace" efforts, to assess the strategic aims of the Soviet Union. How do the Soviets themselves understand "peaceful coexistence," and how do they regard treaties and international law?[18] What are the implications of the Soviet Strategic Plan and its "aim of 'global peace' following final Soviet victory,"[19] as described in detail by the former chief-of-staff of the Czech Communist minister of defense? Is it true, as former Soviet U.N. diplomat Arkady N. Schevchenko writes, that "There is *no* disagreement among Soviet leaders—political or military, young or old—as far as their ultimate goals are concerned"?[20] And not only citizens but church leaders must prick up their ears at the report (Michael Binyon *The Times* [London], November 8, 1981) that Boris Ponomaryov himself, an alternate member of the Politbureau and chief orchestrator of "peace" campaigns for the Soviet Union globally, "urged Communist parties to work more closely with religious organizations."[21] This took place a few months before Lord MacLeod's antinuclear "peace" conference in Moscow.

The moral justification of deterrence policies, then, must rest largely on considerations of the prudential, strategic sort. And the proper forum for that sort of discussion is not the church but the political arena. This leaves unsettled the question whether Christians could ever regard the actual use of nuclear weapons as morally acceptable. Although the mind boggles at the potential for destruction, it would be irresponsible to strike an ostrich pose and pretend that nuclear war is simply unthinkable. We may begin with an observation by Bishop Leonard. He notes that just when the general trend is to recognize ever fewer moral absolutes, the prohibition of nuclear weapons is being made into such an unqualified moral absolute. This simply sweeps aside the competing moral claims of other legitimate human values, such as liberty, truth, and human dignity. Bishop Leonard continues:

> It is, I believe, not consistent with the moral nature of man to proclaim one principle of such moral rigidity that these other fundamental moral issues become secondary. Nor do I believe that for a Christian who believes that man is made for eternal communion with the living God who is just and holy can the principle of survival take precedence over all other moral claims.[22]

If there were, as pacifists maintain there is, one single biblical maxim directly applicable to war and, therefore, to nuclear war, the case would be simple. But there is no such single directly applicable maxim. To guide Christian office-bearers in their civil duties, the Christian love ethic must be "refracted" through a complex grid of social and political interdependences. Human goods and moral obligations are many and various, and their claims often appear in the hurly-burly of life in a fallen world to compete in such a way that while self-sacrificing love for the neighbor is always the overarching duty, the exact apportionment of this duty among conflicting claims and claimants is by no means always clear. Simplistic panaceas like "nonviolence," therefore, are bound to be false. As Paul Ramsey put it, "Jesus did not teach that his disciples should lift up the face of another oppressed man to be struck again on the other cheek."[23] Pacifism and holy war are simply two sides of the same false coin, that of the confusion of the church with civil society. (Lord MacLeod's impression, quoted above, that the "Christian Church" has "Christ's commandment that we *must* trust" the communist enemy, goes well beyond the common confusion in forgetting that not even within the church itself is it the duty of shepherds to bring up their lambs to trust wolves [John 10:12]).

Since neither holy war nor holy peace is an authentic biblical directive for politics, what is left? What is left is precisely the traditional just-war doctrine. Adapted by Saint Augustine and others from pre-Christian considerations of natural justice, the just-war concept establishes constraints which decent people must observe in waging war. It must be noted, however, that these moral limitations on war, as Paul Ramsey has said so well,

> arose not from autonomous natural reason asserting its sover-
> eignty over determinations of right and wrong (and threatening
> to lead Christian faith and love, which are and should be free,
> into bondage to alien principles), but from a quite humble moral
> reason subjecting itself to the sovereignty of God and the
> Lordship of Christ, as Christian men felt themselves impelled
> out of love to justify war and by love severely to limit war.[24]

Given this nature of the just-war doctrine refracted through many-sided civil obligation, and given that in the realm of civil power love expresses itself as justice, it is clear that the just-war "doctrine" is not a singular measuring rod but a bundle of criteria with variable relative weightings. For instance, in the past much was made of the necessity of a formal declaration of war—something which in some imaginable circumstances, given modern military technology, might well be an unaffordable luxury. But surely a formal declaration of war cannot as a criterion of ethical warfare have the same weight as, for instance, the importance of avoiding unnecessary civilian casualties. Just-war doctrine then is not a rigid monolith, but a mosaic taking into account several different goods. It is even more important not to treat the just-war criteria as if they were pedantic bureaucratic regulations or scholastic subtleties. Legality, when separated from morality, decays into legalism, as Solzhenitsyn reminded us in his Harvard speech.[25] And nothing is more unjust than a legalistic insistence on the letter of the law against its spirit. To pursue justice is to seek real equity—not abstract formalisms—and this cannot be done without attending to those significant moral features and their unique "mix," which distinguish one case from another.

Hard cases make bad law, and nuclear war is so hard that many take it to be beyond all law, including the law of just war. Paul Ramsey in particular is noted for having argued credibly for some, strictly limited, resort to nuclear weapons as justifiable within the just-war framework.[26] It cannot be our purpose here to review the several just-war criteria in detail. Some concluding observations may be in order, however, regarding the two criteria (discrimination between combatants and noncombatants, and proportionality) which are widely held to prohibit the use of any nuclear weapons outright.

Discrimination between combatants and noncombatants rests ultimately on the moral principle that not even lawful authorities have the right to punish the innocent (Exod. 23:7; Rom. 13:3). In war, of course, it is usually not possible to prevent all civilian deaths. The moral requirement means not that civilian casualties must be avoided at all costs—else even peacetime automobile traffic would have to be forbidden since a statistically predictable number of people die every week in road mishaps—but the destruction of civilians may not be directly intended. Civilian deaths may occur as a foreseen and unavoidable consequence of justified attacks on military targets. This means that (1) it is immoral to attack civilian populations even with "conventional" bombs, and (2) it may be moral to attack an enemy's nuclear arsenals, say, with minimum all-out weapons like the neutron bomb.

Just-war doctrine therefore condemns obliteration bombing like that of Dresden in World War II, in which perhaps more people died than in Hiroshima. Hiroshima, however, was the military headquarters for southern Japan and may therefore be regarded as a proper military target. This cannot be said about Nagasaki, however, which was bombed because the primary target, Kokura, happened to be covered by clouds on 9 August 1945. The official British observer of the Nagasaki bombing, Group Captain Leonard Cheshire, VC, makes a persuasive case that this second bombing was justified and, indeed, that the scourge of world war "was buried there forever."[27] The action saved millions of lives, both Japanese and American, which would have been lost had the war continued, and was necessary to break the Japanese war cabinet's five-to-one determination, even after Hiroshima, to continue the war. Under just-war doctrine, however, saving many combatants' lives by directly and deliberately killing fewer noncombatants is not as such defensible and smacks rather of terrorism. The same would be true of massive retaliatory obliterations of civilian populations, as envisioned in the old policy of "Mutual Assured Destruction." It is virtually certain, however, that Hiroshima and Nagasaki could happen only because Japan lacked the capability of nuclear retaliation against, say, San Francisco and Kansas City.

On the other hand, the present counterforce rather than counterpeople nuclear strategy would be defensible in just-war terms if the weapons and target selection were designed only to cripple the enemy's military capabilities while minimizing his civilian losses. What is odd is that some Christian spokesmen actually prefer "Mutual Assured Destruction" to the new emphasis on limited weapons and strategies.[28] Given that "slogans and [e]motive imagery are at times substituted for factual data"[29] by churchmen in this context, Christian ethicists cannot be indifferent to the possibility that should the slogans and emotive imagery succeed in creating a public mood hostile to the development of effective nuclear weapons and defense strategies, the result may well be nuclear war. That is one implication of the chilling scenario projected by the "father" of the neutron bomb, physicist Sam Cohen,[30] on the basis of the known reliance of Soviet military doctrine on surprise, deception, and a massive first strike.[31]

Finally there is the principle of proportionality, which states that the evil of a war must not outweigh the good which can reasonably be expected from it. This principle of weighing anticipated benefits and damages is basic to the very idea of equity but is very difficult to apply because, like apples and oranges, different public goods are difficult to compare. (For example, if one of two major presidential contenders took a good stand on abortion but advocated disastrous policies on national security, while the other was good on national security but wrong on abortion, for whom would it be the conscientious Christian citizen's duty to vote?) The church's real task here is to form good Christian consciences in those who will later face moral dilemmas but not to bind their consciences to particular solutions without a clear Word of God. Ethicists should not rush to where conscientious judges and generals fear to tread. By the same token of course, if a Christian citizen is convinced that his government's directives to him are morally wrong, he must obey God rather than men (Acts 4:19).

Nuclear pacifists argue that nothing, not even Soviet domination, could be worse than nuclear war itself, and that such war must therefore be avoided at all costs. This may be true, but it cannot be assumed in advance without a tough-minded moral appraisal of many complex human factors. A disturbing feature of much supposedly Christian sentiment on this subject is the unseemly haste with which all moral issues are simply smothered under what looks like an atavistic obsession with physical survival. In a veritable zoo of obscene mockeries of the Creator's purposes, is The Bomb really convincing as the *summum malum*? The pitiless official indifference of Western Christendom to the unspeakable torments of the Marxist inferno, and the compulsive anxiety to stifle the cries of the oppressed lest they irritate the oppressors and prevent "relaxation of tensions," suggest not Christian compassion and morality as the real engines of nuclear "peacemaking" but rather the essentially secular urgencies of self-indulgence. And clearly something other than morality is at work when Stalinist international socialism is, however, subtly, painted as ethically superior to Hitlerite national socialism.[32] Apart from a serious moral misjudgment of communism, based perhaps on wishful thinking, it is difficult to account for the hostility of many Western churchmen toward their own governments, combined with the same churchmen's relatively benign evaluation of Soviet policies and intentions.[33]

The "even-handedness" which treats the West and the Soviets as moral equals because both are guilty of ultimate evil in possessing nuclear weapons rests on a shallow, bureaucratic "conflict management techniques" model. A genuinely ethical model would, with Solzhenitsyn,[34] assert the radical moral assymetry of the two systems without in the least glossing over the serious flaws in Western society. It is not only political but moral nonsense to play "global village" while shutting one's eyes to all evidence suggesting that half the "village" is an armed concentration camp scheming to subdue the rest.

Especially if one takes into account the hopes and aspirations of the millions of innocent victims languishing in the Gulag,[35] it is by no means self-evident, under the principle of proportionality, that the defense of Western civilization's values of freedom, justice, and human dignity—however flawed, necessarily, in application by and to sinful human beings—is not worth the risk even of nuclear war as a last resort. Much depends on whether one holds to Bertrand Russell's "Better Red than Dead," or to Solzhenitsyn's reply: "Better to be dead than a scoundrel. In this horrible expression of Bertrand Russell's there is an absence of all moral criteria."[36]

Not to fear those who can kill only the body is a prime imperative of biblical ethics (Luke 12:4). What of the cosmic fear of the grand medieval *dies irae*?

> Day of wrath, O day of mourning!
> See fulfilled the prophet's warning,
> Heaven and earth in ashes burning.

Physical destruction is not the worst of it:

Oh, what fear man's bosom rendeth
When from heaven the Judge descendeth
On whose sentence all dependeth!

Here no ethics, not even biblical ethics, can help, but only the biblical evangel: "Thanks be to God! He gives us the victory through our Lord Jesus Christ" (1 Cor. 15:57)!

## ENDNOTES

[1] Bernice Martin, "Invisible Religion, Popular Culture and Anti-nuclear Sentiment," in David Martin and Peter Mullen, eds., *Unholy Warfare: The Church and the Bomb* (Oxford: Blackwell, 1983), pp. 108–40.

[2] A valuable treatment of the issue is John Helgeland, Robert J. Daly, and J. Patout Burns, *Christians and the Military: The Early Experience* (Philadelphia: Fortress, 1985).

[3] Fr. Robert Adolfs, quoted by Bishop Graham Leonard in *Unholy Warfare*, p. 192.

[4] Edward Norman, *Christianity and the World Order* (Oxford: Oxford University Press, 1979).

[5] For a perspective discussion of this fatal "relevance," see James Turner, *Without God, Without Creed: The Origins of Unbelief in America* (Baltimore: Johns Hopkins University Press, 1985).

[6] Graham Leonard, "The Morality of Nuclear Deterrence," in *Unholy Warfare*, p. 186. This of course is the old distinction between the good and the right.

[7] Donald L. Davidson, *Nuclear Weapons and the American Churches: Ethical Positions on Modern Warfare* (Boulder, Colo.: Westview, 1983), pp. 203–4 and passim.

[8] At least the French and the German bishops were much more concerned with justice.

[9] Paul Abrecht and Ninan Koshy, eds., *Before It's Too Late: The Challenge of Nuclear Disarmament* (Geneva: World Council of Churches, 1983), p. 384.

[10] Norman, *Christianity*, pp. 18–19.

[11] Francis Schaeffer, Vladimir Bukovsky, and James Hitchcock, *Who Is for Peace?* (New York: Thomas Nelson, 1983), p. 28.

[12] *News Weekly* (Australia), January 12, 1983, p. 6.

[13] Ibid.

[14] Ibid., p. 12.

[15] Davidson, *Nuclear Weapons and the American Churches*, p. 186.

[16] Leonard, *Unholy Warfare*, p. 189.

[17] Lord MacLeod, "But What About Russia?" *Unholy Warfare*, p. 224.

[18] Bernard A. Ramundo, *Peaceful Coexistence: International Law in the Building of Communism* (Baltimore: Johns Hopkins Press, 1967).

[19] Jan Sejna, *We Will Bury You* (London: Sidgwick and Jackson, 1982), p. 103. For the classic Red Chinese strategic analysis see Lin Piao, "Long Live the Victory of People's War!" *Peking Review* (September 3, 1965), pp. 9–30.

[20] Arkady N. Schevchenko, *Breaking with Moscow* (New York: Knopf, 1985), p. 369.

[21] B. A. Santamaria, "Fighting for Peace—Moscow Style," *News Weekly*, April 28, 1982.

[22] *Unholy Warfare*, pp. 187–88.

[23] Paul Ramsey, "The Case for Making 'Just War' Possible," in John C. Bennett, ed., *Nuclear Weapons and the Conflict of Conscience* (New York: Scribner, 1962), p. 145.

[24] Paul Ramsey, *War and the Christian Conscience* (Duke University Press, 1961), p. 59. Quoted in Colin Fletcher, *Banning the Bomb? An Argument from the "Just War" Position* (Bramcote, Notts.: Grove, 1982), pp. 13–14.

[25] A. Solzhenitsyn, *A World Split Apart* (New York: Harper and Row, 1978), pp. 15–19.

[26] See the good historical overview in Davidson, *Nuclear Weapons*, pp. 1–67.

[27] Leonard Cheshire, "How the Bomb Brought Peace," *The Sunday Times*, August 4, 1985.

[28] Davidson, *Nuclear Weapons and American Churches*, pp. 121–22.

[29] Ibid., p. 142.

[30] Sam Cohen, *We Can Prevent World War III* (Ottawa, Ill.: Jameson, 1985).

[31] Viktor Suvorov, *Inside the Soviet Army* (New York: Macmillan, 1982), *Inside Soviet Military Intelligence* (New York: Macmillan, 1984).

[32] "But the changes in the Soviet Union may lead us to judge that it is in the long term not as absolutely destructive of all values as Nazism was with its gas chambers. . . ." (Bennet, *Nuclear Weapons and the Conflict*, p. 117).

[33] Davidson, *Nuclear Weapons and American Churches*, pp. 142, 182–83, passim.

[34] Solzhenitsyn, *A World Split Apart*.

[35] See Julius Epstein, Operation Keelhaul: *The Story of Forced Repatriation* (Old Greenwich: Devin-Adair, 1973), for an insight into the attitude of many Soviet citizens toward their regime. And among South East Asian refugees today hardly anyone would support the view that the present "peace" in their countries is preferable to the Vietnam War, which so distressed the Western intelligentsia.

[36] A. Solzhenitsyn, *Warning to the West* (New York: Farrar, Straus, and Giroux, 1976), p. 119.

# A Response to
# War

## S. Craig Glickman

A war that includes nuclear weapons will likely be a war that includes biological and chemical weapons as well. The effects of the latter may be as hideous as those of the former. The cumulative destruction of "NBC"—nuclear, biological, and chemical—weapons, plus the effects of awesome new "conventional" weapons, will introduce a war unprecedented in history. And it will encompass land, sea, air, and outer space. It will be more than nuclear war. We must call it *superwar*.

"I am become Death, the shatterer of worlds," Krishna, lord of the fate of mortals, uttered in the Bhagavad-Gita. Small wonder they were also the words remembered by Robert Oppenheimer when he saw the culmination of his work on the Manhattan Project in the first nuclear blast in the sands near Alamogordo in July 1945. He was stunned. Other scientists were speechless.

As awe gripped those men then, how much more must it grip us now. We contemplate not one or two small nuclear weapons but a superwar with thousands of greater ones deliverable from practically anywhere.

But we are Christians. We know of something more awesome still. Mr. Marquart has admirably focused our attention beyond the awe of nuclear power to the greater awe of the power of God. He has also reminded us of our priorities. The distinctive Christian message is the power of God that is greater than any shatterer of worlds. As great as megadeath may be, God has defeated it in and through his Son. Superwar may destroy millions with deadly virus, chemicals, blast, heat, and radiation, but God will raise us all in resurrection, some to life with him, and others to eternal punishment. No shatterer of worlds will have the final word.

Mr. Marquart has also carefully pointed out what the

distinctive Christian message is not. As God has not given special revelation (at least to anywhere near the same degree) about farming, chemistry, or the sciences, he has not given special revelation about particulars of politics. We do not live in a theocratic state like Israel of old. We have only principles from which to derive counsel on government. Christians must be careful not to claim divine authority for their application of general biblical principles to complex political and social realities.

Mr. Marquart thus offers a timely preface to his comments on war. Weak men with weak reasons have often resorted to their positions of authority to justify their opinion; Christians can be no different, except for the added hypocrisy of claiming divine authority where it has not been given.

I not only appreciated Mr. Marquart's prefatory remarks to his position on nuclear war, but I concur with his fundamental positions against pacifism and for just war and nuclear deterrence. My disagreements with a couple of particular points are, I suspect, of interest only to a few and, in a way, challenge his basic conclusions.[1]

I would like, however, to build a bit upon Mr. Marquart's solid foundation with conclusions I have reached since studying nuclear-war issues. When I first began my study of these topics in 1978, I synthesized my research around six questions about superwar: How would it begin? Would the Soviets initiate it? Can the United States prevent it? Does justice allow it? Does prophecy predict it? Can anyone survive it?

I would like to summarize my answers to these questions and direct the reader to sources which I believe best substantiate and develop these positions.

## I. HOW COULD IT BEGIN?

I believe all scenarios fall into two major categories: accidental or intentional. The accidental scenarios from computer malfunction seem less likely to me, but any movement toward "launch on warning" makes it more likely. The shorter the fuse, the more likely a hasty response.

The intentional scenarios seem more likely. But even here I would bet on a scenario that develops not cooly and calmly, but one that escalates beyond the original intentions of the combatants. This came within a blink of an eyelash of happening during the Cuban missile crisis.

Although it may seem unnecessary or trite to say, the intentional scenarios of any kind, I would judge most likely to develop over Western Europe or the Middle East.

## II. MIGHT THE SOVIETS INITIATE IT?

Yes, if it were in their best interests to do so. That is their official military policy. If they do not initiate a superwar, it will not be because of ethical reasons. The Communist government has tortured and killed more of its own people than it has of its enemies, and it treats its enemies ruthlessly. In Afghanistan they have dropped small bombs in the form of toys for the purpose of maiming children to demoralize the population.

Everything I have learned convinces me I must discipline myself to recognize the moral asymmetry between the free world and the Soviet Union. I am naturally prone to project the good will I have for others upon all citizens everywhere. But especially with the Soviets I must resist that temptation. I firmly believe that nothing could be more harmful in global politics than to minimize the inherent evil in all men but especially in the rampant institutionalized evil of the Soviet Union.

## III. CAN THE UNITED STATES PREVENT IT?

Not absolutely. But certain policies may encourage war more than others. The sloganeering of nuclear freeze advocates, for example, reflects only the ignorance of its supporters. For years the total megatonnage of weapons on both sides has been steadily decreasing in favor of smaller, more accurate counterforce weapons.

Disarmament, for another example, would more likely initiate a war than prevent it. The only countries which have been attacked with nuclear, chemical, or biological weapons since 1940 have been those countries which could not strike back with the same.

The Strategic Defense Initiative, referred to often as SDI, or more popularly as the Star Wars Defense System, will receive my full support. It is far better, as Reagan said, to save lives than to avenge them. I am convinced it is technologically feasible and strategically necessary.

I said eight years ago and will reaffirm it now that a plan of this sort will be the most attacked plan by the KGB active measures program and general Soviet propaganda of anything this country has ever sought to do. So far their efforts have lived up to my expectations.

Nevertheless, no efforts should be withheld in the pursuit of this objective.

## IV. DOES JUSTICE ALLOW LIKE RESPONSE?

This question is made more difficult to answer if one does not know the possible effects of a superwar. If like response brings global suicide, then an answer is more difficult than if nuclear response brings the destruction only of the enemy's military and political structure.

One may argue, for example, that one may execute a murderer, but does one have the right to destroy the murderer's family, the block on which he lives, and the rest of the human race?

I personally believe the consequences of a nuclear war need not be an apocalyptic global suicide. If, on the contrary, a more selective response is possible, as I believe it is, then the response with nuclear weapons is as justifiable as a response with conventional ones.

## V. DOES PROPHECY PREDICT IT?

Not necessarily. I believe that much of the apocalyptic visions of the Old and New Testaments are still awaiting fulfillment in a global destruction that will be unprecedented. But I do not believe that an all-out superwar approximates the destruction described in those visions. The "end times" will likely include nuclear war, but a nuclear war will not necessarily mean the "end times" are upon us.

I would like to add that I believe many Christians hypocritically use their answers to the questions of justice and prophecy as excuses to bury their heads in the sand from harsh realities, and they shirk their responsibilities to protect those entrusted to them.

Many pacifists most vocal today, for example, haughtily and childishly refuse to participate in civil defense measures, and many "end-time specialists" claim to count on a rapture to deliver them. Yet neither group has faced up to the possibility of a war that would needlessly kill millions of people because of a leadership that has not done its duty to protect the innocent.

## VI. CAN ANYONE SURVIVE IT?

Yes. For starters, most of the citizens of Sweden and Switzerland would survive it, because these countries have provided excellent blast and fallout shelters for all their countrymen.

Apart from shelter, the United States will likely lose 80 percent of its people; with shelter, we might lose only 5 percent. Shelters that protect from nuclear effects can easily be designed to protect from biological and chemical weapons as well.

The nuclear weapon's lethal effects are its blast, its heat, and its radiation. All of these effects can be avoided in simple affordable shelter. A properly equipped basement-like structure four feet below the ground would protect from all three.

The radiation from fallout is a longer-term problem but not as long-term as is popularly believed in this country. The Swiss wisely prepare for four to six weeks in shelter. This is because the radiation from fallout decreases by one-tenth for every sevenfold increase in time. The 700 Roentgens/hour measured at three and one-half hours after the blast will decrease to 70 in twenty-four hours, and to 7 in seven days.

For protection until the radiation dissipates, every one foot of dirt reduces the radiation by one-tenth. So four feet of dirt over a shelter would allow only one-ten thousandeth of the radiation to enter the shelter, probably less radiation than one would receive in sunlight.

The possibility of emergence from the shelter into a "nuclear winter" was popularized by Carl Sagan and his colleagues just before the Pershing missiles were about to be placed in Western Europe. For what it is worth, the timing of his press releases on nuclear winter coincided perfectly with a widely recognized effort on the part of the KGB to prevent the implacement of those missiles.

But whatever the dubious political motives of the nuclear winter advocates, the scientific conclusions have been soundly criticized as, at best, premature and, at worst, ill-conceived.

The population that emerged from the shelters would nevertheless find a country absent its vital industrial infrastructure and much of its residential shelter. That prospect simply underscores the need to press on with the Star Wars Defense Systems.

I recommend the bibliography that follows the endnotes.

## ENDNOTES

[1]Speaking as a colleague, I might ask, for example, if he would consider recasting his commentary on "Thou shalt not kill." He writes: ". . . it is also possible that quite opposite commands are addressed to the same persons but in different capacities or roles" (p. 362). A more streamlined response might simply be that the command is literally, "Thou shalt not murder" (Hebrew *harag*). Murder is the unjust taking of a life. Execution is the just taking of life by the proper civil authority. So it is not that opposite commands are given to the same person in different roles. The command not to murder applies to all in every role; the command to justly execute applies to all in every role, too, as either a representative or citizen of the state. One avoids a peculiar dualism with this clarification. The Christian does not have one set of morals for public duty and a different set for his private life.

# 382 S. Craig Glickman
The explanation for turning the other cheek, loving one's enemy, and leaving vengeance to God may be explained in harmony with all this. In both testaments the commands are the same: one is not to take private vengeance with vigilante response but rather leave such vengeance to God, which is to say, with the state. Thus Leviticus can both authorize capital punishment but also command the people to not take vengeance (Lev. 19:18). Paul can tell the Roman Christians the same: "Do not take revenge, my friends, but leave room for God's wrath" (Rom. 12:19), he writes; but then a few verses later it is clear that the state "is God's servant, an agent of wrath to bring punishment on the wrongdoer." (Rom. 13:4). The wrath of God is to be mediated through the wrath of the state, not the wrath of individuals.

I understand the passages in the Sermon on the Mount similarly. The commands to refrain from personal vengeance were likely particularly necessary in light of the Zealot's pressure to initiate guerilla action against the Romans.

In any event, the impression Mr. Marquart inadvertently leaves, which I am sure he by no means accepts, that there may be a fuzzy distinction between murder and execution, leads to another place in his paper that might merit recasting. He notes that a common argument against deterrence is that if it is wrong to do something, then it is also wrong to threaten to do it. He challenges this by pointing out that if bluffing avoids bloodshed, then bluffing is morally acceptable. I agree with his response, but I believe a challenge of the suppressed premise gets more to the heart of the debate. The suppressed premise in "if it is wrong to do something, then it is also wrong to threaten to do it," is that the things being done are the same. But unjustified attack with nuclear weapons is no more the same thing as justified defense with nuclear weapons than unjustified murder of the innocent is the same as justifiable execution of a murderer. The premise thus makes the absurd assumption of a moral symmetry between aggression and defense, between evil and retribution for evil. It may be wrong to unjustly attack with any weapons, including nuclear, but it is not therefore wrong to justly punish the attacker with weapons, perhaps including nuclear (if it can be shown they can be used justly, that is, without disproportionate harm to the innocent). There is a difference between murder and execution, between aggression and retribution.

# BIBLIOGRAPHY

## Introduction

The Harvard Nuclear Study Group. *Living with Nuclear Weapons*. Cambridge: University Press, 1983.
Lefever, Ernest W., and E. Stephen Hunt, eds. *The Apocalyptic Premise*. Washington, D.C.: Ethics and Public Policy Center, 1982.

## Weapons Effects

Glasstone, Samuel, and Philip J. Dolan, eds. *The Effects of Nuclear Weapons*. 3d ed. Washington, D.C.: United States Department of Defense and the Energy Research and Development Administration, 1977.
Macabee, Howard. "Nuclear Winter: How Much Do We Know?" *Reason* May 1975, pp. 26–35.

## Civil Defense

*The Journal of Civil Defense*. The American Civil Defense Association (P.O. Box 910, Starke, FL 32091–0910).

Robinson, Arthur, and Gary North. *Fighting Chance*. Fort Worth: American Bureau of Economic Research, 1986.

Royal United Services Institute for Defense Studies, *Nuclear Attack: Civil Defense*. New York: Brassey's Publishers Limited, 1982.

## Just War

American Catholic Committee. Robert R. Reilly and Rev. James V. Schall, et al. *Justice and War in the Nuclear Age*. Lanham, Md.: University Press of America, 1983.

Novak, Michael. *Moral Clarity in the Nuclear Age*. Nashville: Thomas Nelson, 1983.

## Soviet Intentions

Barron, John. *KGB Today: The Hidden Hand*. New York: Reader's Digest Press, 1983.

Beilenson, Laurence W. *Survival and Peace in the Nuclear Age*. Chicago: Regnery/Gateway, 1980.

Shevchenko, Arkady N. *Breaking with Moscow*. New York: Ballantine Books, 1985.

# A Response to War

**Wallace E. Johnson**

In general I agree with most of the subject of Mr. Marquart's paper. I have really enjoyed his discussions and am excited about the prospect of meeting him.

The subjects on which I totally agree with Mr. Marquart are listed below:

1. Of how circumstances alter cases; i.e., it is wrong to take one's life, but to lay down his life for his friends is admirable. We must love and forgive those who offend us—but we are duty bound to catch, convict, and punish, and even execute criminals—regardless of our personal feelings toward them.

2. His discussions of how strictly distinct civil and spiritual authority are, and its application are very interesting.

3. His thoughts on how feeble a foundation that Christians have concerning arms control and nuclear weapons were done very thoroughly. His discussions on probable causes for World War II, the Falkland Island invasion, and the British lack of indication to defend the Falklands are very interesting.

4. His comments on what some people are urging in the name of Christian duty are interesting but very frightening to me.

5. His comments on how some Christians are so quick to condemn U.S. actions but fail to point out the atrocities and wrongs committed by Russia are certainly true.

6. Mr. Marquart's discussion on the moral dimensions of nuclear war is very complete. I fully agree with most of his statements, with the exception that it is inappropriate for churches to pontificate on the hard questions about military, historical, technological, and political matters as they relate to keeping World War III at bay. His discussion on the just-war theory is excellent.

The following discussion relates to those ideas set forth by Mr. Marquart where I may not agree:

1. For instance, he is too hard on the organized church as far as staying out of the arena and trenches of life. We, the church, need to be where the action is if we are to apply the teachings of the Gospels. The church must be concerned about not only the spiritual life of our neighbors but their social and political needs.

2. I cannot reason how he can justify the statement that the New Testament church is not to conduct pep rallies for social causes, however worthy (Rom. 15:27), and that the concerted action of Christians as citizens should not be called even a "secondary" duty or function of the church. I fully realize the church's commandment (Matt. 28:19–20) as being top priority, but to sit and watch the world and people go down the tube is not our right.

Please, I want to differ but in a loving way.

3. Another statement that I am not in full agreement with is where he states that "Modern weapons are inherently no worse than swords and spears." The effects of nuclear war will be much more devastating, perhaps very slowly and agonizingly. The effects of a nuclear bomb not only affect the present generation but the generations to come. The fires generated by nuclear explosion can cause severe burns, and our entire medical staff in the United States can probably handle only one thousand cases at any time. Now that certainly is not true of wars with swords and spears.

What about the nuclear winter scenario?

I will now share my personal feelings concerning nuclear war and the possibilities of preventing World War III.

The just-war theory assumes that a war would be started by persons who are in lawful authority. What about individuals such as Kadafi and other terrorists who have assumed authority?

We talk about making peace and treaties with Russia. What about the Third World countries who have nuclear weapon capabilities, such as Israel, India, Pakistan, South Africa, and Argentina?

Deterrence has kept the United States and Russia from blasting each other apart, but what do we do with the other nuclear countries?

The just-war theory says nothing about slowing down the arms race.

A comprehensive test ban (CTB) would slow down the arms race. A complete test ban would really slow down the arms race, in that, if we cannot test a device, we will not stockpile it either. With improvements in verification, we will be able to confirm that both parties are adhering to the test ban.

We all have the tendency to relate our position to numbers. Only two hundred nuclear devices are required to end it all.

The manufacture of nuclear weapon material is difficult or impossible to monitor.

We must do something—the powder keg is set to blow up!

The arms race will bankrupt many countries. The Star Wars concept will require such sophisticated software and hardware that we may not be able to develop, and may not work—the end result may be the biggest WPA program in history.

What then? Can it be that we need to resort to prayer—the type of prayer power exhibited by the Philippine people, resulting in the overthrow of Marcos? This could be more significant than the discovery of the nuclear power—the second chapter of the Book of Daniel perhaps coming true in our time (Ps. 102:16–22).

# ECONOMICS

## Ronald H. Nash

Discussions of what is called "Christian economics" are increasingly easy to find. While several years ago these presentations often took the form of attempts to deduce or "prove" capitalism from the Bible, a remarkable shift has occurred. In the last fifteen years the Bible has become an important weapon in the hands of those who seek a Christian justification for economic and political positions that regard capitalism as an evil sub-Christian or anti-Christian theory. The drift to the political and economic left is obvious. For the American Catholic bishops, it appears, God is a very liberal Democrat. For the more radical liberation theologians, God is a Marxist. This desire to find a biblical justification for economic and political collectivism has become increasingly obvious among the theologically conservative Protestants known as Evangelicals.

This attempt to identify the Christian gospel with left-wing economics is apparent in a recent book by Andrew Kirk.[1] Kirk thinks the traditional evangelical definition of the gospel—God's good news of the salvation available to those who believe in the crucified and risen Savior—is too narrow. Following earlier proponents of the social gospel and liberation theology, Kirk claims that there is an *essential* political and economic dimension to God's kingdom and to the gospel. Jesus died, it seems, so that we might all become socialists. While Kirk attempts to put it more delicately than this, he insists that his peculiar brand of socialism is an inseparable component of the gospel. Clearly, this is serious business. If one accepts Kirk's thesis (and a growing number of Evangelicals do), it follows that anyone who disagrees with Kirk's economic and political views cannot simply be treated as an erring brother or sister who needs instruction in basic economics; he or she must be regarded as a heretic.

Kirk's book is only one example of a growing extremism on the part of many Evangelicals who have embraced a left-wing economic and political ideology and who seek to identify it as the only proper Christian view. I do not mean to ignore right-wing extremists who have their own problems. But it seems clear that the major threat to a balanced, sane, and reasoned evangelical discussion of Christianity and economics comes from extremists on the left like Kirk.

This chapter is intended as a prolegomenon to Christian thinking about economics. It is designed to clear out some ground before the more systematic work of attempting to build a Christian economics begins. My work presupposes that a complete economic system cannot be deduced from the Bible. Those writers who may believe that they have deduced an economic system from Scripture appear simply to have read their preconceived opinions into their proof texts. What passes as Christian economics today is often little more than comments about a few selected subjects: help for the poor (certainly an important Christian concern), criticisms of economic freedom, pleas for greater governmental intervention in the economy, and condemnations of money and wealth. However important it may be for Christians to say relevant things about selected economic subjects, this activity hardly qualifies as Christian economics. And when the judgments are mistaken (as they often are these days), they can turn out to be neither Christian nor economics.

Even though I reject the view that the Bible can be approached as a textbook on economics, it does not follow that the Bible is silent in economic matters. My approach to reconciling economics with Scripture is inductive, not deductive. Once a Christian has a clear picture of the Christian world view,[2] he should put his best effort into discovering the truth about economic and political systems. He should try to clarify what capitalism and socialism really are (not what various propagandists say they are); he should try to discover how each system works or whether it can work. He should identify the strengths and weaknesses of each system. And then he should compare his economic options to the standard of biblical morality and ask which system is more consistent with the entire Christian world view. Obviously, a short essay like this can only make a start on this very complex enterprise, which is why I regard it as a prolegomenon to Christian thinking about economics.[3]

## I. WHAT IS ECONOMICS?

It is a mistake to think that economics deals only with the making, spending, saving, and investing of money or with the creation, development and management of wealth. Economics per se covers a much larger territory. *Economics is the study of human action with regard to scarce resources.* The two central notions in this definition are *scarcity* and *human action*. As we know, scarcity is an unavoidable feature of human existence. Since human wants and desires are always greater than available resources, we can never have everything we want. Therefore, human beings have to rank things and make choices among available options. The human actions that are the subject of economics are conscious human choices with regard to certain goals.

Economic decisions often have nothing special to do with money. Imagine a very busy person faced with many demands on his time. Suppose further that this person is given the opportunity to do several new things that he regards as more important than some of his other tasks. Since this person can only do so much in the time available to him, he begins to rank his new and old opportunities. He then uses his scarce time to pursue those goals that he has ranked highest. In this example, the person is engaged in a typically economic activity. Because of scarcity (in this case, scarcity of time), he has been forced to make conscious choices.

Economics is best regarded, not as a set of doctrines, but rather as a *way of thinking*. Economists James Gwartney and Richard Stroup point out seven guideposts to the economic way of thinking.[4]

(a) Among economic goods there are no free lunches. Someone must give something up if we are to have more scarce goods.

(b) Individuals make decisions purposefully, always seeking to choose the option they expect to be most consistent with their personal goals. Purposeful decision-making leads to economizing behavior.

(c) Incentives matter. People will be more likely to choose an option as the benefits expected from that option increase. In contrast, higher costs will make an alternative less attractive, reducing the likelihood that it will be chosen.

(d) Marginal costs and marginal benefits (utility) are fundamental to economizing behavior. Economic reasoning focuses on the impact of marginal changes.

(e) Since information is scarce, uncertainty will be present when decisions are made.

(f) In addition to their initial impact, economic events often alter personal incentives in a manner that leads to important secondary effects that may be felt only with the passage of time.

(g) The test of an economic theory is its ability to predict and to explain events of the real world.

These seven principles constitute a necessary starting point for any sound reflection on economics.

Principle *f* is especially important to the economic way of thinking. It suggests that one way of asserting any economic proposal is to ask what its long-range consequences will be. Many economic policies have been enacted because they appeared to produce desired consequences *in the short-run*. This has often been true of policies designed to help poor people. But measures that appear beneficial when viewed in the short term often look quite different after a few years. One reason this happens is because the policies produce incentives that lead people to modify their behavior in ways that turn the short-run success into a long-term disaster. Many recent proposals made in the name of "Christian economics" are bad economics in the sense that they are counterproductive. While Christians have an obligation to help the poor and disadvantaged, a number of important recent studies document the claim that antipoverty programs in the United States have actually increased poverty.[5] According to economist James Gwartney:

> Seeking to promote the welfare of the poor, the disadvantaged, the unemployed, and the misfortunate, well-meaning citizens (including a good many evangelical Christians) have inadvertently supported forms of economic organization that have promoted the precise outcomes they sought to alleviate. For too long, socially concerned Christians have measured policies by the intentions of their advocates, rather than the predictable effectiveness of the programs. Put simply, in our haste to do something constructive, we have not thought very seriously about the impact, particularly in the long-run, of alternative policies on the well-being of the intended beneficiaries.[6]

Sound economic thinking looks beyond the present and calculates the long-range consequences of recommended policies. Sound economics will accord as well with the other six guideposts of the economic way of thinking. Proponents of economic views that they want recognized as "Christian economics" should make certain that their positions are examples of sound economics.

## II. THREE ECONOMIC SYSTEMS

Three economic systems compete for attention: capitalism; socialism; and, somewhere between, the hybrid known as interventionism or the mixed economy. The presence of interventionism among these options is a source of much confusion. For one thing, many interventionists attempt to blur the important differences between their approach and capitalism as they attempt to persuade people that the mixed economy is simply a variant (or even the most plausible version) of capitalism. However, interventionism should be distinguished both from capitalism and socialism. Many economists have argued that interventionism contains fatal flaws that make it a hopeless attempt to stop on a slippery slope where no stop is possible. The only way the half-hearted economic controls of the interventionist can work is if they become the *total* controls of the socialist.[7]

Evangelical author Herbert Schlossberg is one writer who recognizes the difference between capitalism and interventionism as it is practiced in the United States. To the question, Should Christians support capitalism? he replies:

> If by capitalism one means the present system of statist manipulation of resources and people for the benefit of those who run the political system and their adherents [i.e., American interventionism], the answer is no. If it [capitalism] means the free and responsible ownership of resources by all who give value for what they receive, without the application of coercive power, then the answer is yes.[8]

It is important to recognize that the economy of the United States is interventionist, not capitalist. Many complaints about the economic policies of the United States are justified. But when the programs and policies that cause problems result from interventionist theory, it is hardly fair to blame capitalism. This is especially true in the case of Third World nations that attack the "capitalism" of the United States and other Western nations in order to justify their own drift toward more severe forms of statism and collectivism. While capitalism may well have problems of its own, there is something bizarre in blaming it for the problems of a distinct economic system.

Much confusion results from the fact that *capitalism*, *socialism* and *interventionism* actually function as umbrella terms that cover a variety of positions along a continuum. Generally speaking, as one moves along the continuum from socialism to interventionism to capitalism, one can find the following: the more freedom allowed by a socialist economy, the closer it is to being interventionist; the more economic freedom allowed by an interventionist system, the closer it is to being capitalist. The real issue in the dispute among these three positions is the degree of economic freedom allowed by each. The crux is the extent to which human beings will be permitted to exercise their own choices in the economic sphere of life.

## III. CAPITALISM AND SOCIALISM

One dominant feature of capitalism is economic freedom, the belief that people have the right to exchange things voluntarily, free from force, fraud, and theft. Socialism, on the other hand, seeks to replace the freedom of the market with a group of central planners who exercise control over essential market functions. There are degrees of socialism as there are degrees of capitalism in the real world. But basic to any form of socialism is distrust of or contempt for the market process and the desire to replace the freedom of the market with some form of centralized control.

Capitalism should be understood as a voluntary system of relationships. It utilizes what is sometimes called *the peaceful means of exchange* which may be summed up in the phrase, "If you do something good for me, then I'll do something good for you." When capitalism is understood correctly, it epitomizes the peaceful means of exchange. The reason people exchange in a real market is because they believe the exchange is good for them. They take advantage of an opportunity to obtain something they want more in exchange for something they desire less.

But exchange can also take place by means of force and violence. In this *violent means of exchange*, the basic rule of thumb is: "Unless you do something good for me, I'll do something bad to you." This turns out to be the controlling principle of socialism. Socialism means far more than centralized control of the economic process. It entails the introduction of coercion into economic exchange in order to facilitate the attainment of the goals of the elite who function as the central planners. One of the great ironies of Christian socialism is that its proponents in effect demand that the state get out its weapons and force people to fulfill the demands of Christian love. Even if we fail to notice any other contrast between capitalism and socialism, we already have a major difference to relate to the biblical ethic. One system stresses voluntary and peaceful exchange while the other depends on coercion and violence.

Some Christian socialists object to my account of socialism. They profess contempt for the more coercive forms of state socialism on exhibit in communist countries. They would like us to believe that a more humane, noncoercive form of socialism is possible. They would like us to believe that there is a form of socialism not yet tried anywhere on earth, where the central ideas are cooperation and community and where coercion and dictatorships are precluded. But they provide very little information about the workings of this more utopian kind of socialism, and they ignore the fact that however humane and voluntary their socialism is supposed to become after it has been put into effect, it will take massive amounts of coercion and theft to get it started.

Andrew Kirk tries mightily to disguise the coercion necessary to effect his own version of a Christian socialism.[9] Kirk is totally opposed to economic freedom. He claims it is inconsistent with the gospel to allow people's holdings to result from the natural outworkings of free exchange. The state must determine (presumably with Kirk's advice) when people have accumulated too much. When that point is reached, the state should take any excess and redistribute it among the poor, in the meantime skimming off enough to keep the agents of the state from worrying about their own standard of living. According to Kirk, the Bible teaches that any accumulation of wealth above that absolutely required for the necessities of life must result from violence, fraud, bribes, or theft. No one in Kirk's universe ever prospers honorably.

In Kirk's just society, someone (he does not say who) will fix both minimum and maximum pay for every job. In other words, the state will forcibly prevent anyone from working at a particular job at less than the official salary. Fortunately, any pain resulting from this coercion will be eased by the comforting knowledge that unemployment benefits will match this minimum pay. All money earned above the maximum wage set by the state will be "given" to charity. Of course, before it is given to charity, the state will have to take it away. This take-away will be aided, Kirk tells us, by "steeply progressive" tax rates. While Kirk recognizes that lots of people may resist the statist tyranny he proposes, he studiously avoids telling us what will be done to those who resist.

The massive problems connected with Kirk's so-called Christian socialism go far beyond its restraints of personal liberty and its enhancement of statist power. It would be difficult to think of a set of economic recommendations more in conflict with principle $f$ of the economic way of thinking noted earlier. Of special interest is the fact that Kirk is totally silent about formerly poor nations like Taiwan, Singapore, and Hong Hong that have achieved the highest rates of economic growth in the world. Perhaps he ignores them because they have succeeded by consciously rejecting his socialist model and following a free market approach.

Capitalism is not economic anarchy. For one thing, capitalism recognizes several necessary conditions for the kinds of voluntary relationships it recommends. One of these is the existence of inherent human rights, such as the right to make decisions, the right to be free, the right to hold property, and the right to exchange what one owns for something else. Capitalism also presupposes a system of morality. It does not encourage people to do anything they want. There are definite limits, moral and otherwise, to the ways in which humans should exchange. Capitalism should be regarded as a system of voluntary relationships within a framework of laws which protect people's rights against force, fraud, theft, and violations of contracts. "Thou shalt not steal" and "Thou shalt not lie" are part of the underlying moral constraints of the system. Economic exchanges can hardly be voluntary if one participant is coerced, deceived, defrauded, or robbed.[10]

One of the more important features of the market process is

the way fluctuating prices provide information to those smart enough to look for it.

> Market prices communicate information, coordinate the actions of buyers and sellers, and provide the incentive structure that motivates decision-makers to act. The information provided by prices instructs entrepreneurs as to (a) how to use scarce resources and (b) which products are intensely desired (relative to their opportunity costs) by consumers. Market prices establish a reward-penalty system, which induces individuals to cooperate with each other and motivates them to work efficiently, invest for the future, supply intensely desired goods, economize on the use of scarce resources, and utilize efficient production methods.[11]

Profits and losses give people incentives to act in ways that turn out to benefit society. Wise entrepreneurs will divert resources from less profitable goods and services towards goods and service that more people want. A market system makes people accountable for their economic activities. When individuals or businesses act in ways that waste resources, they will be penalized by lower wages or profits (or perhaps by even larger losses). In an economic system that concentrates decisions in a group of central planners, accountability too easily gets lost in the system. Under socialism, British economist Brian Griffiths explains,

> Rewards are not related to effort and commercial risk taking, but to party membership, bureaucratic status, political fiat and corruption. As a consequence, the legitimate commercial entrepreneurial spirit is killed, for perfectly understandable reasons, people devote their resources to hacking a way through the political and bureaucratic jungle of their economies.[12]

Capitalism does more than make it possible for a few people to make money. It provides the basis for a social structure that encourages the development of important personal and social virtues such as community and cooperation.

## IV. WHY SOME CHRISTIANS HATE CAPITALISM

Throughout his life, theologian Paul Tillich maintained that "any serious Christian must be a socialist."[13] Evangelical Andrew Kirk insists that biblical principles are incompatible with capitalism.[14] Many contemporary Christians have an aversion toward capitalism that borders on hatred. However the grounds on which such Christians reject capitalism illustrate how confused they are about economics in general and about capitalism in particular. Capitalism may indeed prove to be incompatible with important Christian concerns. But reasons that might support that conclusion have yet to appear in the writings of Christian collectivists. At least five faulty arguments support contemporary Christian rejections of capitalism.

1. Many times Christian critics of capitalism demonstrate that they have no idea what capitalism is. The capitalism they attack is a caricature, a straw man. The stereotype of capitalism that is the target of most attacks often results from an incorrect association of the word with existing national economies that are in fact interventionist. More attention needs to be given to the inappropriateness of regarding the interventionist economic policies of the United States as a paradigm of capitalism.

2. Capitalism is attacked on the ground that it exploits poor people and poor nations. On this view the only way some people can become rich is by exploiting others. Poverty is always the result of exploitation and oppression by someone else who profits from the poverty of others. According to Andrew Kirk, the reason some nations are poor is because they have been exploited by richer and more powerful nations.[15] The West is guilty for the persistent poverty of lesser developed nations. This exploitation model of poverty is simplistic. It is also an excellent example of the ease with which some Christians insist on reading Marxist theories into the Bible. It is certainly true that Scripture recognizes that poverty *sometimes* results from oppression and exploitation. But sometimes, Scripture teaches, poverty results from misfortunes that have nothing to do with exploitation. These include such things as accidents, injuries, and illness. And of course, the Bible also makes it plain that poverty can result from indigence and sloth.[16]

3. The myth about exploitation lends support to a related claim. Capitalism is denounced because of the mistaken belief that market exchanges are what is called a *zero sum game*.[17] A zero sum game is one where only one participant can win. If one person (or group) wins, then the other person (or group) must lose. Baseball and checkers are just two examples of zero sum games. If A wins, then B must lose. The error here consists of thinking that market exchanges are a zero sum game. On the contrary, market exchanges illustrate what is called a *positive sum game*. A positive sum game is one in which both players may win. We must reject the myth that economic exchanges necessarily benefit only one party at the expense of the other. In voluntary economic exchanges both parties leave the exchange in better economic shape than would otherwise have been the case.[18] Both parties to a voluntary exchange believe that they gain through the exchange. If they did not perceive the exchange as beneficial, they would not take part in it.[19]

4. Capitalism is also despised, because it is thought to encourage a number of character traits that are incompatible with

Christian values. Two of the traits supposedly encouraged by capitalism are selfishness and greed. Scripture clearly *does* condemn selfishness. But selfishness should never be confused with the quite different characteristic of self-interest. When Jesus commanded us to love our neighbor as ourself (Matt. 22:39), he gave implicit approval to self-interest. When a person is motivated by selfishness, he seeks his own welfare with no regard for the welfare of others. But when a person is motivated by self-interest, he can pursue his own welfare in ways that do not harm others. There is nothing sinful in caring about what happens to one's family and self. In fact, the New Testament condemns those who lack such concern (1 Tim. 5:8). Since the kinds of voluntary exchanges that characterize the market are mutually beneficial (in other words, are a positive sum game), selfishness is not an inherent element of capitalism. People who exchange on market principles engage in activities that benefit themselves and others. The conditions of a genuine free market oblige people to find ways of helping themselves at the same time they help others.

It is no more true to claim that capitalism encourages greed. The mechanism of the market actually neutralizes greed as individuals are forced to find ways of serving the needs of those with whom they wish to exchange. There is no question but that market exchanges often bring us into contact with greedy people. But so long as our rights are protected, the possible greed of others cannot harm us. As long as greedy individuals are prohibited from introducing force, fraud, and theft into the exchange process, their greed must be channeled into the discovery of products or services for which people are willing to exchange their holdings. Every person in a market economy has to be other-directed. The market is one area of life where concern for the other person is required. The market does not pander to greed. It is rather a mechanism that allows natural human desires to be satisfied in a nonviolent way. The alternative to the peaceful means of exchange is coercion.

5. Capitalism is rejected by many Christians because of a faulty understanding of what Scripture teaches about money and wealth. A good example of such confusion is Jacques Ellul's book, *Money and Power*.[20] Ellul's selective and often tortuous reading of Scripture leads him to three bizarre conclusions: (1) The New Testament condemns wealth; (2) the Bible hates the rich; and (3) Christians sin if they save money for their future. Such extreme claims are clearly incompatible with the teachings of Jesus, who saw nothing inherently evil in money, wealth, or private ownership. While Jesus clearly condemned materialism and the compulsive quest for wealth, he never condemned wealth per se. Jesus did not teach that being rich means necessarily being evil.[21] Jesus did not see anything sinful in the ownership of

houses, clothes, and other economic goods. Jesus had wealthy friends and followers (Luke 14:1); he stayed in the homes of wealthy people and ate at their tables (Luke 11:37).

A number of Jesus' parables provide insights into his views on wealth. In Luke 16:9 and the accompanying parable, Jesus taught that his followers should use their resources with the same dedication and keen judgment as the unjust steward. In the parable of the rich farmer (Luke 12:16–21), Jesus did not condemn the farmer for making money but rather for his single-minded concern with his own wealth and happiness. The man was a fool because he was a self-centered materialist who had forgotten God, not because he was a successful businessman. The parable of Lazarus and the rich man (Luke 16:19–31) does not teach that a person's eternal destiny is determined by his possessions in this life. It is clear that the rich man went to hell because of a godless and self-centered life, a fact made evident by the way he used his wealth and by his indifference to the poor. The parable also implies that Lazarus was a believer. Any interpretation of the parable that suggests the poor man entered heaven because of his poverty would contradict everything the New Testament teaches about regeneration.

Even gospel passages that stress our obligation to use our resources for God's purposes presuppose the legitimacy of private ownership.[22] Other obligations made clear in Jesus' teaching require that one first have certain financial resources.[23] Jesus often spoke about wealth without condemning it.[24] When Jesus did call on people to renounce their possessions, his demands reflected special conditions, for example, situations where people had made their possessions their god (Luke 18:22–24). Instead of condemning wealth, then, Jesus' teaching offered an important perspective on how people living in materialistic surroundings should view the material world.

What should concern the believer is not money (something necessary for many economic exchanges) but wrong attitudes toward money. Similarly, it is not wealth per se but the improper use of wealth along with wrong attitudes toward wealth that deserve condemnation. Every Christian, rich or poor, needs to recognize that whatever he or she possesses is his temporarily as a steward under God. Wealth that is accumulated in a dishonest way or that becomes a controlling principle in one's life is subject to condemnation. Wealth resulting from honest labor and wise investment, handled by people who recognize they are God's stewards is not.

## V. SOME BIBLICAL PRINCIPLES

I have argued that it is wrong to think that a full-blown system of Christian economics can be deduced from the Bible. But this does not mean that the Bible is silent on such matters and has nothing important to say about economic matters. In fact, I have already noted a number of significant biblical observations that falsify some of the more extreme views advanced by the Christian left. It is now time to take a careful look at some other biblical principles. In this connection, it is important to distinguish biblical principles from policies. As Brian Griffiths points out:

> Jesus was concerned with enunciating principles, not policies. He was not concerned directly with the creation of wealth or the removal of poverty. He did not examine in any detail the causes of either wealth or poverty or any connection which there might be between them. He did not explore at all the relationships which might have existed between the inequality of wealth and poverty in his own day and the structures of his own society.[25]

1. One economic principle discernible in Scripture is that Christians have a mandate to create wealth. This principle is consistent with my earlier observation that Scripture does not regard money or wealth as inherently evil. Brian Griffiths observes that since the world is God's creation and since God placed us in such a close relationship to the material world,

> the business of creating and using wealth is a natural activity for mankind. Life itself demands that we be continually involved in the process of wealth creation. The basic necessities for living are not provided like manna; the land has to be cultivated, the sea has to be harvested, minerals have to be extracted, the city has to be supplied with services. God created us with the capacity and the desire to do all these things. Life itself, therefore, demands that we use what God has given us to provide the necessities.[26]

God placed us in his world to "cultivate it, improve it and harness its resources for our own use. Man has been created to have dominion in this world. The urge to control, direct, and manage the resources of this world is part and parcel of man's nature and vocation. Idleness is at root alien to human personality."[27]

While the Christian left is quite vocal in its insistence that wealth be redistributed, it is noticeably silent when it comes to explaining how wealth will be produced. It also ignores the obvious truth that before wealth can be redistributed, it must first be produced. Advocates of economic redistribution frequently mention the miracle when Jesus fed the five thousand. They refer to Jesus' obvious compassion and pity for the hungry and how he proceeded to feed them. However, the redistributionists always drop their analogy at just this point and move on to other subjects. I suggest they should stay with the analogy a bit longer. It is certainly important to note that Jesus took pity on hungry people and fed them. But we should follow the story to its conclusion and observe that Jesus performed a miracle by actually *producing* wealth, in this case the food. If Jesus' compassionate feeding of the hungry is to be taken as an analogy of how Christians today are to have a natural interest in the needs of the poor, his miracle of producing wealth (the bread and the fish) should also lead us to ask by what means we should seek not just to distribute wealth but also to produce wealth.

The creation of wealth does not happen by accident. On the contrary, it results from human action and social cooperation. Proper attention must be given to the forces that underlie the production of wealth.

> Goods and services are not like manna from heaven. Individuals must be motivated to produce them—to acquire the skills, take the risks, invest in the machines, and supply the human energy and creativity essential for the creation of wealth. . . . Whether we Christians like it or not, mere mortals are much less willing to make the sacrifices involved in the production process when the fruit of their labors are redistributed to others. After-tax income—income that can be expended on not only personal desires but also on the needs and desires of family members and others about whom one cares—motivates producers to action. Weakening the link between productive behavior and individual reward is a recipe for economic stagnation, not social progress.[28]

When proper attention is given to the necessary role that the creation of wealth must play, it is clear that capitalism offers the poor their only real hope of economic deliverance. Socialism can only increase the misery of the masses while encouraging the growth of tyranny.

2. While there is nothing inherently evil about money or wealth and while the creation of wealth is a legitimate concern for Christians, the Bible clearly warns that money can and often does have a negative effect on people's character and spiritual relationships. Money can be hazardous to a person's spiritual health. While neither the parable of the rich farmer (Luke 12) nor of Lazarus (Luke 16) condemns wealth per se, they both demonstrate the extent to which the pursuit of wealth can damage a human soul. In Matthew 13:22, wealth was one of the things that choked the growing seed. The rich young ruler could not bring himself to renounce his wealth in order to follow Jesus.

> The mere fact of owning wealth tends to produce a spirit of arrogance and self-reliance. Success tends to breed a philosophy

of possessiveness: things become mine, my money, my property, my company, my work force. Wealth gives people a false
sense of security: it deadens the life of the spirit; it makes people
unresponsive to the good news of the gospel.[29]

Without question, then, Jesus warned that the pursuit of
money can become an obstacle that can make it difficult or even
impossible for some to enter the kingdom of God (Mark 10:25).
Concern with wealth can encourage the development of such
character traits as arrogance, selfishness, self-satisfaction, materialism, and a total indifference to the plight of the needy. Money
has the potential of becoming a god that competes for our
devotion and commitment.

3. Human beings are only stewards of their possessions. Since
God is the Creator of all that exists, he ultimately is the rightful
owner of all that exists (Job 41:11; Ps. 24:1). Whatever possessions
a human being may acquire, he holds them temporarily as a
steward of God and is ultimately accountable to God for how he
uses them. Human beings are accountable to God in every area of
their lives, including the economic. We are accountable to God for
how we acquire our wealth as well as for how we use it. Christians
have a duty to use their resources in ways that best serve the
objectives of God's kingdom (Matt. 25:24–30; Luke 19:11–27).

This doctrine of stewardship is not inconsistent with the
human right to private property. In fact, the biblical norm for
society is not collective or state ownership, but private ownership.
Many who note that God ordered the land of Israel to be divided
among Jewish families somehow miss the point that this entails
that property rights within Israel were private. While God is the
ultimate owner of all that exists, in the Old Testament he passed
on delegated ownership rights to families. The Old Testament
contains many laws designed to protect property rights (Exod.
20:15; Lev. 25; Deut. 23:19–20).[30]

The biblical defense of property rights holds important
implications for market exchanges.

> The freedom and ability to exchange rights to private property
> constitutes the definition of a free market. A free market is
> nothing more than an opportunity for property owners to
> exchange their titles to ownership. Any economic system
> therefore which involves private property rights also involves to
> a greater or lesser degree reasonably free markets. From this it
> follows that markets are likely to be features of all societies,
> ancient or modern, which allow some degree of economic
> freedom.[31]

Unfortunately, the doctrine of Christian stewardship has been
misused by Christian leftists in an attempt to justify the aggran-
dizement of the state, a necessary step in the implementation of

their political ideology. In their view, the enhancement of social justice requires the transfer of increasing authority, power, and money to the government, which alone has the compassion and knowledge to take care of the poor. Hence, Christian stewardship is perverted into a doctrine that obliges Christians to surrender their judgment, will, and resources to the state, which, in the view of the left, becomes God's surrogate on earth.

4. The followers of Jesus should share. Christians are responsible for those they can help (Matt. 25:31–46). Jesus' disciples were to demonstrate a constant willingness to share their possessions with others (Luke 6:29–30). However, the New Testament says nothing about this "sharing" being coerced by the state.

Christians do have an obligation to care about the poor. But once this is admitted, the next question concerns the best means to help the poor. By "best means," I have in mind—among other things—actions and programs that will work not just in the short run but in the long run. Certainly there are times when the poor do require help in the form of cash and noncash benefits *now*. But a welfare system that encourages people to become dependent on the dole, that robs the poor of any incentive to seek ways of helping themselves, that leads the poor into a poverty trap, is hardly a model of genuine compassion or of wise public policy. As black economist Walter Williams states, "It is clear that we do not help the less fortunate person by destroying his *best* alternatives, no matter how unattractive that alternative may seem to more affluent observers. . . . Many assume that just because a policy *intends* to help the disadvantaged it will in fact have the intended *effect*."[32] Exception must be taken to those Christians who insist that the only approved means of easing poverty is a welfare state, especially when such measures are now known to be so counterproductive. Roman Catholic theologian Michael Novak argues that the poor in America have been victimized by "wrongly designed theories" that led "to wrongly designed systems; such systems hurt the poor they are supposed to help."[33]

The debate between those Christians who denounce and those who defend a free market system is not a dispute between compassionate altruists and selfish materialists who are too busy making money to care about the poor. Economically informed Christians who oppose the various forms of collectivism do so because they believe that liberal programs end up doing far more harm than good to the poor.[34] Christians who do not care about the poor are defective in spiritual matters. But Christians who believe that helping the poor requires coercive policies aimed at redistributing wealth or curbing economic freedom are defective in economic matters. Herbert Schlossberg finds little in the allegedly prophetic voice of Christian leftists save constant bellyaching without any necessity for discrimination, reason, or knowledge. In general, radical Christian left has been a shrill scream, indiscriminately labeling everything it dislikes as idolatrous. . . . Moreover, its hasty identification with the prophetic writings that denounce those who oppress the poor lead it to divinize the poor and to cooperate with the policies of social democracy that turn poverty into a permanent condition. Imposing helplessness on poor people, it works to ensure the triumph of . . . policies that condemn the poor to perpetual dependency. Having lost the power of discrimination, this type of radicalism mindlessly associates itself with any expression of antiestablishment feeling and so substitutes a shabby anti-Americanism for a truly radical gospel. Its denunciations of the establishment leadership coexist with steadfast support for the destructive humanitarian redistributive policies that mark the establishment for what it is.[35]

The apparent harshness of Schlossberg's words seems justified when viewed in the context of the positive harm that such views do to the poor.

## VI. CONCLUSION

From the fact that I described this paper as a prolegomenon to Christian thinking about economics, it should be clear that I do not regard it as the final word on the subject. However, I believe some important progress has been made in unmasking some of the serious confusions that have led many Christians to embrace several varieties of economic and political collectivism. I have not deduced an economic system from the Bible. What I have done is describe accurately the major economic options and compared them with biblical concerns, Christian values, and the principles of the economic way of thinking. What seems clear is that the widespread Christian rejection of economic freedom not only involves a serious distortion of capitalism but also lacks any biblical or economic justification.[36]

## ENDNOTES

[1] Andrew Kirk, *The Good News of the Kingdom Coming* (Downers Grove: InterVarsity, 1985).

[2] The Christian world view includes the basic views about God, humankind, morality, and society that are taught or implied by Scripture.

[3] Many things that must be left unsaid in this short chapter have been discussed in some of my other writings: *Freedom, Justice and the State* (Lanham: University Press of America); *Social Justice and the Christian Church* (Milford, Mich.: Mott, 1983); *Liberation Theology* (Milford, Mich.: Mott, 1984); "Socialism, Capitalism and the Bible," *Imprimis*, July 1985; "Biblical Ethics and Economics and Political Freedom," *Fundamentalist Journal*, July–August 1985; and "The Christian Debate

Over Economic Freedom," *Journal of Private Enterprise Education* 1 (1985). My most complete and most important discussion of these issues can be found in *Poverty and Wealth* (Westchester, Ill.: Crossway, 1986).

4James D. Gwartney and Richard Stroup, *Economics, Private and Public Choice,* 3d ed. (Orlando: Academic, 1983), p. 16.

5See James Gwartney and Thomas S. McCaleb, "Have Anti-poverty Programs Increased Poverty?" *Cato Journal* 4 (1985): 1–16; Charles Murray, *Losing Ground* (New York: Basic Books, 1984); George Gilder, *Wealth and Poverty* (New York: Basic Books, 1981); and Thomas Sowell, *Race and Economics* (New York: David McKay, 1975).

6James Gwartney, "Social Progress, the Tax-Transfer Society and the Limits of Public Policy" (unpublished paper, Department of Economics, Florida State University), p. 3.

7A detailed investigation of interventionism's serious difficulties is not possible in this short essay. The classic analysis can be found in Ludwig von Mises, *Human Action* (New Haven: Yale University Press, 1949). For a less technical discussion, see Ronald Nash, *Social Justice and the Christian Church,* ch. 9.

8Herbert Schlossberg, *Idols for Destruction* (Nashville: Thomas Nelson, 1983), p. 318.

9Kirk, *The Good News of the Kingdom Coming.*

10Compare this with the biblical concern for just weights and measures (Deut. 25:15–16).

11Gwartney and Stroup, *Economics: Private and Public Choice,* p. 61.

12Brian Griffiths, *The Creation of Wealth* (Downers Grove: InterVarsity, 1985), p. 26.

13See J. Philip Wogaman, *The Great Economic Debate* (Philadelphia: Westminster, 1977), p. 133.

14Kirk, *The Good News of the Kingdom Coming,* p. 71.

15Ibid., p. 80.

16Proverbs 6:6–11; 13:4; 24:30–34; 28:19.

17For example, Andrew Kirk thinks that if one person maximizes his advantage, it must inevitably be at the expense of someone else. It never occurs to Kirk that society can be arranged in such a way that one person's success can produce an advantage for the other person. See Kirk's *The Good News of the Kingdom Coming,* p. 82.

18Of course, it is still true that economic exchanges *may* be marred by exploitation. The question is whether this possible exploitation is necessary and unavoidable. It is not.

19An exchange can also be regarded as beneficial if it is the lesser of two evils.

20Jacques Ellul, *Money and Power* (Downers Grove: InterVarsity, 1984). Upon learning that Ellul's book teaches that money is evil, many readers inquired if InterVarsity was giving it away free. They were not. Much of Ellul's confusion results from his failure to draw a clear distinction between money (anything that may be used as a means of exchange) and Mammon (which is money personified and deified). Ellul is right in saying money often assumes a sinister power over human lives. But whenever this happens, money (something ethically neutral) has become Mammon.

21For the Old Testament view on this subject, see Ecclesiastes 5:19.

22See Luke 16:1–13; 19:11–27; Matthew 25:24–30. These parables also commend those who demonstrate their ability to increase their wealth.

23For example, Jesus taught that children have an obligation to care for their parents (Matt. 15:3–9) and that his followers ought to be generous in their support of worthy causes (Matt. 6:2–4). It is rather difficult to support parents or charities unless one has certain financial resources.

24Matthew 13:44–46; 21:33–46.

25Griffiths, *The Creation of Wealth,* p. 45.

26Ibid., pp. 60–61.

[27] Brian Griffiths, *Morality and the Market Place* (London: Hodder and Stoughton, 1982), p. 92.

[28] Gwartney, "Social Progress," p. 9.

[29] Griffiths, *The Creation of Wealth*, p. 48.

[30] The notion of the Jubilee Year discussed in Leviticus 25 deserves attention. For my views of this subject, see Ronald Nash, *Social Justice and the Christian Church*, pp. 78–79.

[31] Griffiths, *The Creation of Wealth*, p. 58.

[32] Walter Williams, "The Minimum Wage and Minority Employment Opportunities," *National Federation of Independent Business Public Policy Discussion Series*.

[33] Michael Novak, "Helping the Poor," *Center Journal* 2 (Summer 1983): 37.

[34] For works supporting this claim, see n. 5.

[35] Herbert Schlossberg, *Idols for Destruction*, p. 256.

[36] For a more complete discussion of all the points raised in this paper, see Ronald Nash, *Poverty and Wealth* (Westchester, Ill.: Crossway, 1986).

# A Response to
# Economics

## David W. Breese

In discussing economics in the world of the 1980s, we find ourselves dealing with a subject which has moved from an obscure and "dismal science" to a position near to center stage in the considerations relevant to the life of the world. Economics has become a matter so important that it can no longer be trusted to the economists. The leaders of the nations are preoccupied with it, and its importance is the daily consideration from the halls of government down to the last country kitchen and the last harried housewife. So pervasive are the economic considerations of our time that many have become economic determinists, having decided that the abundance of the things which we possess has become that in which life itself consists.

The pervasive nature of the subject of economics was pressed upon the world anew by the seven-nation economic summit conference which took place in May of this year. The actual agenda which developed illustrated that one cannot discuss economics in our time without quickly considering politics, trade, protectionism, terrorism, and even, believe it or not, global religious influences. If there is a subject which pervades the meditations of the men of power, that subject is economics.

The pervasive importance of this theme is also to be noted in the current economic situation in the United States. Our national debt has now moved up to the level of $2.1 trillion. It takes nearly $200 billion a year to pay the interest on this staggering sum, which works out to about $4 billion every week. This means we are spending $800 million every working day, or $100 million each working hour to service the present debt structure of the nation alone. When we add to this the impossible obligations of the Third World, in fact virtually every nation of the world, we see that we

407

have a staggering and nearly incomprehensible economic problem. It is not surprising, then, that there is no economist and no politician (except Jack Kemp) who has a believable answer to the economic cul-de-sac in which the world now finds itself.

Considering the complexity and the urgency of this problem, we can expect that hopeful planners for the future will soon be looking for new, unprecedented economic solutions. Coupling this with the present emergent influence of Christianity and its frightening new visibility, we suggest that it is not beyond the realm of possibility that anxious managers of economic things may well soon look in the direction of Christianity. They may soon be asking Christian thinkers for their opinions, their touted solutions to the unstable equations which now characterize national and global economic thinking. Today's economic seers, for instance, look at the new anomaly of a *rising* stock market in the midst of *declining* basic industry. *Stagflation* is a word indigenous to this generation. Indeed, a nation which sees videotapes going up and agriculture going down is facing an uncertain future. So uncertain, so mystical is the scene today that we may soon see the world disposed to listen to theological answers for economic questions. The crystal ball and the tea leaves may give way to the question, "What does the Bible say?" Stranger things than this have happened.

Ronald Nash is, therefore, to be commended for his most excellent presentation on the subject of "Christianity and the Economic Way of Thinking." Showing himself to be commendably aware of the big picture, Nash has resisted the temptation to think of economics merely in terms of dollars and cents. He sees his task as a "very complex enterprise" and quickly reminds us of that complexity by presenting economics as a study of human action; human emotions; human interaction which involves the fears, hopes, dreams, and burning ambitions of diversely oriented individuals. Human beings are making choices every hour of every day, and the choices they make as to matters of value issue in this amorphous thing called "economics." Nash's suggestion as to the necessity of individual human beings exercising their will in the matter of choice is a helpful and, I believe, Christian interpretation of the realities of life.

In the light of this truth we must also commend Nash on his insistence that government coercion, i.e., socialist economics, is certainly to be considered less Christian than a free enterprise system. Indeed, socialist economics is not economics at all. It is merely a method by which individuals are enslaved by an elite group which uses the power of money as a club to coerce human beings into a pattern which they, if free, would not have chosen. "Socialism" and "economics" are two words which ought not naturally to find themselves in the same sentence. The same, as Nash would suggest, is also true about Christianity and socialism.

We commend Nash as well for pointing out that a growing number of "Evangelicals" are disposed toward a leftist oriented economic and political ideology. He then helpfully reminds us that the deadly virus of liberation theology is moving upon the church in what appears to be an ever-mounting fashion. Liberation theology was, in fact, the point-counterpoint discussion at this year's convention of the National Association of Evangelicals. Within the evangelical spectrum, books sympathetic to the liberationist point of view vastly outnumber those which properly present the true economic implications of historic Christianity. In this regard, Nash helpfully perceives that many economic suggestions made by those who tout a pseudo-Christian point of view are those with short-run consequences. Christians are very prone to push programs that seem to offer immediate salutary (and reportable) results while ignoring long-run consequences which are depressing and even disastrous. The needed attitude among Christians has to do with a longer view—in fact, the eternal consequences. Mocking the idea of the longer view, Keynes spoofed it by saying, "In the long run, we are all dead." But, of course, Keynes was not a Christian. Still, he is one of the seven men who rules the world from his grave.

In my view there are a score of immensely valuable points in Nash's paper on which he needs to be commended. These include the truth that capitalism is a voluntary, peaceful means of exchange; that socialism can only "succeed" with massive amounts of coercion and theft; that capitalism is particularly respectful of human rights, especially the right to freedom; that Christian rejection of capitalism is based on faulty arguments; that under free enterprise everybody wins; that a Christian is a steward of his temporary possessions; that we should be concerned about the *production* of wealth and not just its *redistribution*; that the welfare state does not solve the problem of poverty and that any Christian rejection of economic freedom is without biblical or economic justification. Nash's presentation should be read by all in these days of fuzzy Christian economic thinking.

Reluctant suggestions might also be made concerning the paper in the form of a sympathetic critique. The first is that *the sources of intervention in an otherwise free economy are more than just government.* Government intervention is indeed a heavy hand of inhibition upon an economy which weighs the balances in favor of coercion and against freedom. In the realm of economics "He who governs least governs best" is a commendable slogan.

But the economy is also intervened upon by other entities, not the least of which is the advertiser. How many millions of people have had their minds warped by the unscrupulous promoters of things without value or even ruinous things. The unscrupulous promoters on Madison Avenue (the economic determinists!) are preying daily upon the unwary to traduce them to drink, smoke, play, travel, dissipate their youthful energies in nugatory or pernicious pursuits. Will you truly have fun if you drink Miller Lite? Will Seagram's liquor really make you a man of distinction? Are Virginia Slims the real reason why you have come a long way, baby? Does everyone really drive a Stingray, and are you really out of it if you do not have one? Will a bikini neo-swimsuit really get you a Hollywood contract? Can you learn a language in two weeks in Berlitz? Will "My Sin" perfume put you in a class with Zsa Zsa Gabor? The ruthless promotion of lust is economic intervention, producing an "unnatural" influence on the economy.

Is the eternal expansion of a "consumer society" really worth the subversion of the imaginations and delicate sensibilities of our young people? The economy is intervened upon by the promoter who warps it in a sub-Christian direction.

Intervention, the weighting of an otherwise free economy, also comes from the criminal and the corrupter. The criminal takes $80 billion a year out of the economy in the awful, murderous business of drug trafficking. The corrupter has produced an underground economy of perhaps $100 billion a year in America.

The gambling "industry" brings on its ruinous influence as well as reducing thousands from prosperity to penury by inflaming their lusts for instant riches. There is no doubt that the corrupters have produced an immense drag (intervention) upon the economy.

Which brings us to a second suggestion concerning the paper. It affirms, but could greatly emphasize, the fact that *the basis of a "free" economy must be ethical behavior on the part of the citizenry.*

The individuals who, by the millions within our society, pursue economic success find it to be, for the most part, still an illusory thing. Prosperity continues to escape most individuals and society in general for a deeper reason than is stated by those who analyze economic failure. There is no doubt that things run in the red because of poor ideas, insufficient planning, lack of diligence, inefficiency, employee dishonesty, and a dozen other definitive inhibitions to success. Behind these, however, there is a deeper reason. The Scripture teaches that society, the natural man, is in "the bondage of corruption." Because of original sin, the scales are tipped against economic profit and human progress. Anything, therefore, that is not the object of the fierce attention and intrepid effort of diligent stewards will be subject to deterioration and dissolution. Apart from tireless, positive effort, the farm will grow high with weeds, the rust will displace the paint, the engines will expire, and the towers with their beacons illuminating the future will topple. Therefore, we must both face and announce the fact that, in the last analysis, society is built upon moral foundations. It is ethical diligence which produces the effort, the ability to endure tiresome repetition, the honesty, and the intrepidity without which the economy grinds to a halt. The engine of any limited progress which humanity may know must come from a core of moral sensitivity and ethical action.

From whence shall come this moral sensitivity and ethical action? Within the answer to this question is the only hope for society, economically, or any other way. It is at exactly this point that the Christian thinker comes to the fore. He is able to make not only the best speech in response to this question but the only speech possible. He is able to announce that moral discernment, ethical activity, comes alone from the transforming consequences of faith in Jesus Christ and belief in the gospel. It is possible that the world has yet to see because the church has yet to announce and exemplify the full meaning of the awesome promise, "If any man be in Christ, he is a new creature" (2 Cor. 5:17 KJV). As a consequence of the gospel, the Christian has been delivered from the bondage of corruption, he has "escaped the corruption which is in the world through lust" (2 Peter 1:4). Unless one has escaped human corruption by the virtue of the cross, he will lose all that he may ever gain. The coins of gold and silver which he temporarily controls will slip through his fingers like dry sand on a seashore, and it will all be gone. Therefore, no discussion of profit or loss is relevant which does not take into account the glorious gain of the cross.

Let us then consider a possibility, perhaps a necessity concerning the future. In his excellent paper, Ronald Nash has said, "My work presupposes that a complete economic system cannot be deduced from the Bible." Because of the diverse and contradictory economic systems which have already been touted as biblical, all of us will probably agree. To distill from Scripture the last details of an economic system would be a difficult pursuit, indeed.

Nevertheless, a new condition has come upon us. In 1976 George Gallup announced that there were 50 million believers in America. As an inevitable consequence of this astonishing statistic, organizations have developed in America which have escalated the Christian community into a level of visibility and external influence which has not been known in recent times. In this very year, Christians may indeed propel many of their articulate men and women into positions of political leadership. They may even raise one of their number to the level of being the chief occupant of the White House. Such a suggestion was merely amusing to the kingmakers in the past, but now the possibility of Christian political leadership in America causes the secular community to pause, consider, and even tremble.

Therefore, we are in a new condition. The condition is that of *potential leadership* which soon could lead to *actual leadership*. Soon, therefore, may well be pressed upon us great responsibility.

One can easily imagine the scenario. A known evangelical Christian is escalated to the presidency. He chooses a cabinet, a majority of which are of similar disposition. On his coattails ride a number of successful candidates who are now in the House and Senate. Corresponding successful campaigns on the state and local levels bring to believers a new visibility and new pressures. The white lights are turned upon these individuals and are quickly followed by the question, "You have promised to lead, now what do you intend to do? What is your answer to problems in the realm of the economic, the military, the social, the political, the global?" That is the time when our reputed Christian wisdom will be put to the test. In that moment we will be called to put up or shut up.

Should we not, therefore, be seriously thinking about "a Christian economic system"?

History is not without its testimony of ideologies and philosophies that were held by minority groups that then rose to the ascendancy. These groups were then called upon to codify their notions into systems of economic interaction. In the eighteenth century Rousseau gave us his classic *Social Contract*. His ideas concerning human interaction were to become an instrument in the hands of Napoleon Bonaparte for the transforming of France. So came the *Code Napoleon*, which was highly economic in content.

To illustrate further the principle that an ideology often issues an economic system, the world continues to suffer under Marxism. *The Communist Manifesto* is really about money, and *Das Kapital* is nothing if not economic.

We, therefore, suggest the strong possibility of an earnest call being issued for a Christian economic system. The fact is that this call is already coming. *Money* magazine of June 1986, in an article about a "Christian economist," begins to use the word "Christianomics." It appears, therefore, that the fat is already in the fire.

We may even decide that "Christianomics" is too simple a description and elect to go to something more complicated like "compassionometrics." This should certainly help complicate the picture.

Again, the high probability is now upon us that Christian thinkers of an economic bent, along with those with an expertise in economically related things (which are all things) would do well to meet and do some thinking now. An "Economic White Paper with Suggestions for the Future Western Civilization in the Light of the Teachings of the Word of God" would surely be received with consummate interest by politicians and the press. For good or bad, it would not be without influence.

Such a presentation should at least keep in mind the following principles:

1. The ability to get wealth comes from God.
2. Society must be built on a moral base, i.e., a disposition to conform to the will of God.
3. Government must inhibit those things which produce economic and moral dissolution—crime, vice, gambling, etc.
4. Individuals who exercise initiative and competence which benefit others should be rewarded.
5. Discretional individual philanthropy should be given status, prestige (by contrast to the government dole).
6. Various economic levels among individuals are inevitable. These should be protected and made the object of aspiration.
7. Responsible individuals should be given a greater voice and influence than irresponsible ones.

Winston Churchill said, "We must beware of trying to build a society in which nobody counts for anything except a politician or an official—a society where enterprise gains no reward and thrift no privileges."

A note of urgency may well be sounded in the call for a Christian economic view. This because strident religious voices are already being raised by other than evangelical religionists calling for economic change. Among others, these include the Roman Catholic bishops. This year they have published their third pastoral letter with pronouncements concerning poverty, wealth distribution, economic rights, jobs, military reduction, and welfare reform. Apart from an evangelical voice in this regard, the voice of the bishops may well prevail.

The evangelical left is already becoming vocal, as Ronald Nash has reminded us in his excellent paper. He has referred to *The Good News of the Kingdom Coming* by Andrew Kirk (InterVarsity) as being a strong voice from the left. Scores of such books are now out, going all the way to *Christians and Marxists*, in which Bonino says:

> It is my thesis that, as Christians, confronted by the inhuman conditions prevailing in the continent, they have tried to make their Christian faith historically relevant, they have been increasingly compelled to seek an analysis and historical programme for their Christian obedience. At this point, the dynamics of the historical process, both in its objective conditions and its theoretical development, have led them, through the failure of several remedial and reformist alternatives, to discover *the unsubstitutable relevance of Marxism.*

No wonder the book is subtitled *The Mutual Challenge to Revolution.*

Considering these many alternative voices, we do well to commit ourselves to further economic thinking lest a distorted economic view prevail. The world today is thirsting for new answers. Historic Christianity must not be without its own thoughtful economic presentation in response to that thirst.

# A Response to Economics

**Herbert Schlossberg**

There is a certain sadness in the fact that such a paper as Professor Nash's had to be written. It reminds me that Mickey Cohen, in between prison sentences, made a profession of faith in Christ but showed no evidence of change in his life. He is reported to have said when confronted about this, "If there are Christian doctors and Christian lawyers, why can't there be Christian gangsters?" Apparently the adjective "Christian" can be used to modify any noun, and when it is, it can be given any content. Hence, people feel free to describe a system of state coercion, confiscation, and redistribution as "Christian economics."

There is another sadness in that people such as Professor Nash and I are called upon to address Christians on a subject such as this. Normally those who are trained in the humanities are completely without competence in economics, a bad reflection on the quality of their training; and are uninterested in it, a bad reflection on their good sense. A friend of mine, trained as a literary scholar but in the business of publishing Christian books, prides himself on his ignorance of economics, and that is part of the reason that Professor Nash has to write, in order to refute the books my friend publishes. We seem to have a dearth of Christian economists who see any relationship between economic freedom and productivity, on the one hand, and biblical principles on the other; and so others have to stand in the breach.

If you have read much of what is being published in this field, Professor Nash's paper comes as a breath of fresh air. He actually talks about the production of goods in an environment of scarcity, and, therefore, about the importance of incentives; that is another way of saying that in a discussion of economics, he discusses economics. That only sounds tautologous to those who do not know the quality of so much of the debate. The people he is critical of do not have much to say about such things. The societies they construct have a scarcity of productivity combined with an abundance of scarcity. They are not interested in incentives, because they depend on coercion. In other words, as F. A. Hayek put it, they substitute politics for economics.

Part of the reason we so badly need to talk about economics is that our opponents will not, and that includes numerous opponents who earn their livings as economists. If you think that is an exaggeration, look at John Kenneth Galbraith's work some time, especially such books as *The New Industrial State* and *The Nature of Mass Poverty*. The irony in all this, as Nash points out, is that the anticapitalist policies that are motivated by concern for the poor, bring us more poverty and more virulent poverty. For now we confront not only the wretchedness of people who do not have enough of life's necessities but also the obscene culture of poverty with its sickness of soul, a creation of the welfare state that this species of "Christian economics" has helped fasten on us. The studies are starting to pile up now. George Gilder's *Visible Man* (1978) was followed by his *Wealth and Poverty* (1981). And more recently we have been given Charles Murray's *Losing Ground* (1984). Interspersed have been Professor Nash's various studies and also the works of angry blacks like John Perkins, Thomas Sowell, and Walter Williams, incensed about the disaster that the welfare state has created for their people.

My own opinion is that the case is virtually airtight against the argument for redistribution from a Christian perspective. I base this on more than the normal predilection for my own point of view. I get it largely from the refusal of the other side to argue the case. In 1984 Professor Ronald Sider, whose book *Rich Christians in an Age of Hunger* is almost the Bible of redistribution on the evangelical campuses, came out with a second edition, intended, as he said, to respond to his critics. The trouble is that he *did not* respond to his critics. The most important of those to whom he did not respond was P. T. Bauer of the London School of Economics, whose studies in development economics have knocked into a cocked hat the tendentious positions of the redistributors. But still those treatises keep coming, and Professor Nash is called upon to do the same job once again. Will they listen this time? Can they be induced to answer the arguments that are directed at their position? Do not hold your breath.

Yet I am not at all as devoid of hope as you may infer from that remark; rather I suggest that we have a lot more plowing and sowing to do before we will detect any noticeable harvest. Professor Nash says the trend is still against the acceptance of a more biblical approach to economic life in place of the current interest in leftist critiques. He does not provide any evidence for that, and I assume that it is based on his impressions. I have no more scientific conclusion than he has given us, but I would like to give a few impressions of my own.

One reason I think I see light at the end of the tunnel—which I trust is not affixed to the front end of a freight train—is that much of the former leftist intelligentsia has been mugged by reality and has changed its tune. The French left, almost uniformly Marxist until very recently, seems to have turned decisively toward economic freedom, probably largely as a result of the disasters visited on their country by the socialist government now in control. The neoconservative movement in the United States is led largely by former socialists. The unmitigated calamity of socialist regimes all over the world is becoming so obvious that even intellectuals are taking note of it. And we are now being given academic work that demonstrates that social welfare destroys the poor. It remains to be seen when the Evangelicals in academia will learn the appropriate lessons from all this and reassess their position. I am also encouraged by the gradual fading of the false theology that says the Christian faith is a purely interior thing with no relevance to the institutions of society. Finally, we ought to recognize that our hope is not in historical trends but in the sovereignty of God, which is stronger than all our arguments and efforts.

To the end that Professor Nash's efforts might bear fruit more quickly, I suggest that the following items be included on an agenda by which we advance our point of view among Christians.

## I. A QUESTION OF TERMINOLOGY

I have referred to our present "mixed" system as *social democracy*, which is a term commonly used by those who favor it. It comes from the idea that political democracy is not enough if it does not have the social and economic dimension. Professor Nash uses the term *interventionism* to mean what I believe is the same thing. One reason I do not like his term is that it is likely to be misunderstood as favoring a libertarian type of individualism which sees no role for government at all, indeed, which sees government action as the root of all evil. We ought to be very clear that we are not interested in replacing one antibiblical formulation with another. "Social democracy" is not without its own flaws, and perhaps we need to do some more thinking about what to call the system we oppose.

## II. IS THERE A SYSTEM TO BIBLICAL THINKING ON ECONOMICS?

Professor Nash says the answer to that question is no. If by "system" we mean the complex interaction of monetary and fiscal authorities, securities, and commodity markets, legal foundations, wholesaling and retailing networks, transportation systems, and numerous other facets of the economy, he is undoubtedly right. On the other hand, to say there is no economic system in the Bible tempts us to think there is only a number of discrete "principles," very broad and very vague, that can conveniently be turned into moral platitudes and thereby tacitly disregarded. But if we could drive all preconceptions out of our thinking and wonder what our economy would look like if we were to structure it *de novo* from studying the Bible, would we not end up with a structure containing the following elements: free exchange of goods and services by mutual agreement; hard work as a moral imperative; truthful dealing; no theft; honest money, probably commodity-based; productivity; capital in the hands of the family, which exercises stewardship over it and is not permitted to dissipate it; generous help for the poor, including loans to be given freely without interest and including something analogous to gleaning; no charity for those who will not work. That list comes from only a few minutes' reflection and is not intended to be exhaustive. It probably does not constitute a "system" as the term is usually used but is a lot more specific than many people think or would be led to think by the statement that there is no economic system in the Bible.

## III. FREEDOM

By their nature, all socialist and quasisocialist systems, such as the ones Professor Nash criticizes in this paper, restrict our freedom and put our destiny in the hands of politicians and bureaucrats. There is still a rich tradition in this country of belief that that is bad. The Declaration of Independence expressed it in this way, speaking of George III: "He has erected a multitude of new offices and has sent hither swarms of officers to harass our people and eat out their substance." Those who disagree with us seize the moral high ground by contrasting their "compassionate" position with our "individualist" one. These labels are illusions which we seldom counter effectively. We ought to brand those positions rather as freedom and oppression, and we ought to do it with a more sophisticated and biblical doctrine of freedom than we are accustomed.

## IV. PRODUCTIVITY

The Achilles heel of all forms of leftism is that they cannot produce. I do not think this is a problem that is amenable to solution. They cannot produce because they are based on materialisms that assume they can manipulate people by compulsion. Thus productivity remains low, and these societies persist only by taking their sustenance from the hides of others: by conquest, by foreign aid, by living off capital, or some such device. The societies that practice compulsion are all in trouble; the evidence mounts with each passing year, and we ought to help others understand why that is so. The reason this is fatal for the various socialist theories is that their materialism requires successful economic performance, since they have nothing else to recommend them. If people are in bad shape economically in these countries, then what else is there to serve as validation for the ideology?

## V. THE MAKING OF ALLIES

We have in the midst of the body of Christ a serious division on this subject. It is natural for people like the ones participating in this symposium to regard those with whom we disagree as enemies. *Natural*, but surely we, of all people, do not confuse what is natural with what is right.

In our educational institutions in particular, students are learning that economic freedom is a form of oppression and that earthly bliss—and, indeed, biblical justice—is found in collectivism. Can we hope that this teaching will change any time soon? I have a friend who has forgotten more about this subject than most of us will ever know who believes that this generation is gone, that we will have to wait for all the tenured faculties to die or retire, and that we should concentrate our efforts only on the next generation. He cites the work of Thomas Kuhn who, in *The Structure of Scientific Revolutions*, concluded that widespread changes of thinking necessarily take place without the old scientists, who cannot find it within themselves to repudiate what they have taught for years, the ideas on which their reputations were built, and that therefore only the younger ones can carry out a successful revolution in thinking. But Kuhn reckoned without the doctrine of sanctification, without the knowledge that God can change people rather quickly if it suits his purpose.

If we are to take advantage of that fact, then I think it is imperative for us to do more than talk to ourselves. We should be publishing in the journals whose readers do not agree with us. In that, Professor Nash serves as a good guide. You do not do that without cost, as he can attest. We have to be willing to stand on level ground with the others, without special pleading, and we have to be willing to take our lumps when we do so. We should be attending the same conferences, and speaking in them, as those who disagree with us. I think there are a lot of people who are silently waiting for some leadership that they are not getting now.

Finally, we ought to be on the lookout for better labels than we commonly use, better than I have used in some parts of this paper. If people get the idea that we are fostering American conservatism as opposed to American liberalism or radicalism or socialism, then they will be right to turn a deaf ear to us. I believe that if we give American political conservatives their way, they will belly up to the trough with as much shamelessness as their opponents do. In fact, they are doing it now. They are against all special interests, except, as it happens, their own. Those who disagree with us often say that we are just fostering a civil religion. Let us not prove them right.

# WORK AND LEISURE

## Walter A. Henrichsen

## I. WHY GO TO WORK?

"Labour not for the meat which perisheth, but for that meat which endureth unto everlasting life . . ." (John 6:27 KJV).

The purpose of labor and leisure is a strategic question for the conscientious believer. A large part of most days is given to one's work. If Christianity is relevant, it must address how eight to five Monday through Friday is used to the glory of God. Many people would rather be doing something other than their vocation. There is no sense of eagerness or excitement about heading to work on Monday morning. The prospect of retirement looms as a far more exciting possibility than continued labor. These same people, however, tend to feel guilty when they engage in leisure.

The question, "Why go to work?" profoundly influences their whole perspective on life and thus how they live.

The Genesis account seems to indicate that God brought to creation a sense of rhythm. He created in six days and rested the seventh (Gen. 2:2–3). It is an example of work and rest and the introduction of rhythm. Although God did not at this time command that mankind emulate him in this one-to-six ratio, a sense of rhythm is nonetheless present, even after the Fall. In Genesis 3:17–19 Adam is to work hard to harvest. The concept of things being seasonal is ubiquitous in Scripture (e.g., Deut. 23:2; Eccl. 3:1–8; John 9:4). Thus we see night and day, springtime and harvest, summer and winter, living and dying, etc. Work and leisure is understood in the context of rhythm.

Still, the Scriptures appear to give mixed signals regarding labor. Prior to the Fall, God placed Adam in the Garden of Eden "to till it and keep it" (Gen. 2:15 RSV). On the one hand God gives man work to do, but on the other hand we read that man toils and travails in his labor (3:17–19).

It is before the Fall that God gave man labor. From this we can conclude that work is good. Even after the Fall it is easy to see that man is fortunate in having work. How terrible it would be if man had to live his "three score and ten years" in boredom with nothing to do. Work is an expression of God's grace.

After the Fall, man was opposed in his labor. With it came pain and frustration, but work itself remained good.

One of the great themes in the Book of Ecclesiastes is that all the labor of man's hands is vanity on the one hand, but man is to enjoy his work on the other (cf. Eccl. 2:18–24; 3:12–13; 5:18). The frustration that Solomon senses from the toil of his labor is balanced by the joy which labor produces.

A biblical mind-set regarding one's vocation requires understanding God's rhythm along with keeping these "mixed signals" in balanced tension. Remembering certain principles or axioms will assist in this endeavor. This paper will identify nine such principles, five dealing with work and four with rest.

## A. You Do Not Work to Earn a Living

The Bible gives two fundamental reasons for going to work: first, God commands it; and second, it is an environment (not the only environment) in which the believer can represent Jesus Christ. The Christian does not work to earn a living. It is God who provides for his needs. The Bible is abundantly clear on this issue, as illustrated by the words of our Lord Jesus in the Sermon on the Mount (cf. Matt. 6:25–34).

The Greek word *merimnao* appears nineteen times in the New Testament, and six of them are found in the Matthew 6:25–34 passage. Kittel defines it, "to care for something or someone." In Matthew 5 it is translated "take no thought for" (KJV) and "do not be anxious" (RSV, NASB). It is contrasted with verse 33 where the believer is urged to concentrate his attention on "the kingdom of God and his righteousness," confident that God will provide needs such as food, drink, and clothing.

The apostle Paul summarized Jesus' admonition in Matthew 6 with the words, "My God shall supply all your needs according to his riches in glory by Christ Jesus" (Phil. 4:19).

Supposing a pastor said, "The reason I do the best job I can in my sermon preparation is in hopes that the church board will give me an increase in salary. I am a pastor because I need to earn a living. When I have speaking opportunities outside of the church, I make my selection as to where I will go on the basis of who will pay the highest honorarium. As a matter of fact, I hope to become well known so that I can raise my speaking fee." In hearing this you would no doubt conclude that he is in the wrong vocation, preaching the Gospel for "filthy lucre" (1 Peter 5:2 KJV).

All believers are in full-time Christian work. The only difference between the pastor and the laity is how the ministry is funded. If it is wrong for the pastor to view his pulpit as the means for earning a living (and it is), so also for all of God's people irrespective of their vocation.

A frequently heard objection to this is the apostle Paul's counsel in 2 Thessalonians 3:10, " . . . if any would not work, neither should he eat" (KJV). Paul is not arguing that we work to eat, otherwise he would be taking exception with his own words as well as Jesus'. Rather he is saying that God gave labor to man, and if he refuses to work, provision should not be made for him. God may use one's job to provide for him, but that is entirely different than saying that he looks to his labor for provision. It is to God, and God alone, that he looks for the meeting of his needs.

There are a number of what may be called "one-way streets" in the Bible. For example, 1 Corinthians 6:9–10 says drunkards (among others) will not inherit the kingdom of God, but this does not mean that if one does not get drunk he will inherit the kingdom of God. So also 2 Thessalonians 3:10 says that the person who does not work does not eat, but this does not mean that a person works to eat.

Ephesians 4:28, like 2 Thessalonians 3:10, is dealing with those who tend to be indolent. Paul warns that they are not to steal but rather to work so that they can contribute to the meeting of other people's needs.

There are numerous tensions or seeming contradictions in the Bible. The most familiar is the sovereignty of God and the responsibility of man. It is analogous to the tension seen here.

Suppose someone argues, "I am not a Christian, but I have read the Bible and understand that God elects whom he will. According to the apostle Paul, this was decided from before the foundation of the world. Therefore, if God elects me, I will be saved, and if he does not, I am going to be lost, and there is not a thing I can do about it."

A correct response would be, "The Bible also says there is a well-meant offer of the Gospel. You have heard God's offer of redemption, and if you do not believe, it is your problem, not God's. The responsibility rests squarely on your shoulders."

On the other hand, someone may say, "I am a Christian because of my own effort. The reason I am going to heaven and other people are not is because I live a better life than they do. Jesus died for the world. The reason I am saved and others are lost is because of what I did and what they failed to do. In the final analysis I am going to heaven because of my response to the offer of Jesus."

A proper response to this would be, "The Bible is very clear in pointing out that an individual does not go to heaven because of what he does but because of what Jesus does for him. It is 'not by works of righteousness which we have done, but according to his mercy that he saved us.' Again Paul reminds us, 'For by grace are ye saved through faith; and that not of yourselves: it is the gift of God: not of works, lest any man should boast' (Titus 3:5; Eph. 2:8–9 KJV)."

In the above illustration dealing with the sovereignty of God and the responsibility of man, differing sermons are preached to different needs. So also in the matter of labor. If an individual is slothful and says, "I do not have to work; God will provide my needs," and that individual refuses to labor, insisting on living on welfare, then he needs Paul's message in 2 Thessalonians 3:10, ". . . if any would not work, neither should he eat" (KJV). If, however, he argues that he labors in order to earn a living and that his income is a product of his own work, then he needs the opposite sermon. Some Christians may be lazy, looking to others to work for them, but most are hard-working and conscientious folks, trying to serve God in the context of their vocation. *People should feel as uncomfortable saying that they work to earn a living as in saying they work to go to heaven.*

If the believer does not understand this and concludes that providing for his needs is in the final analysis his own responsibility, then his attitude toward others in the marketplace will be to use and manipulate them rather than to minister to them. He cannot use people and minister to them at the same time!

Some no doubt argue that the people to whom they minister are different than the people with whom they work. They use some people in their endeavor to earn a living and minister to still others. If they embrace this argument, they end up compartmentalizing their lives. Eight to five, Monday through Friday, becomes secular rather than spiritual. Secular work is not full-time Christian service for people arguing thusly; it is secular work.

Hard work is encouraged in both the Old and New Testaments. In the Sermon on the Mount Jesus makes it an issue of focus. His followers work hard but for a different reason than the world. They do not work to earn a living. Rather they are motivated in their work by God's kingdom and righteousness.

## B. There Is No Correlation Between How Hard You Work and How Much You Make

In one sense this is merely a derivative of the first point. If it is God who provides, then there is obviously no correlation between how hard one works and how much he makes. The perception of most people is that this simply is not so. Most businessmen feel that they can out-earn their needs, that there is a direct correlation between how hard they work and how much they make. A given amount of work produces a given result. Such reasoning does not take Providence into consideration. Again and again God calls attention to this fact (e.g., cf. Deut. 28:38–42; Ps. 75:6–7; Hag. 1:6).

A stockbroker with an MBA from one of the prestigious graduate schools in the country said that an experiment was run on how to best select stock purchases. The *Wall Street Journal* was pinned on a board, and a monkey threw darts at it. The stock hit by the darts was purchased, and the success rate using this method was found to be as good as that obtained by scientific analysis.

The wheat farmer of Kansas understands this, as does the skilled laborer from a closed steel mill now working for minimum wage at Burger King. Or ask the man from the ghetto or from Indonesia who works hard and earns little. One real estate broker hits it big; another goes broke. One family buys a home, and it appreciates so that in five years they have tripled their money. Another family purchases a home only to find that it is in a depreciating neighborhood, and they lose their savings. Some people are born into wealth, some into poverty. All people everywhere understand that this is how life is lived.

This is not to suggest that people are not to work hard but rather to work because God commands it. The apostle Paul says, "Whatsoever ye do, do it heartily as unto the Lord, and not unto men" (Col. 3:23 KJV). The believer does quality work as unto the Lord because God commands it and because his credibility as an ambassador of Jesus Christ is at stake.

The application of this principle affects planning. There are two basic approaches to business planning. It is done according to priorities or according to income. In the latter the planner determines beforehand how much he wants to make in the year and then orders his priorities accordingly. In the former he determines before God his priorities and on that basis how many hours God wants him to spend in his vocation each week.

Both approaches are subjective. If, however, he plans according to income, he will allow the marketplace to dictate the level of his commitment to Jesus Christ. When he perceives that his needs are not being properly met and that he is not reaching his financial goals, instead of looking to God he will begin to work harder. Family priorities, time with the Lord, and ministry commitments will give way to the pressing need of meeting financial goals.

For example, if Bill owns an office building that is 90 percent vacant and has established priorities on the basis of income rather than time, he will sacrifice other commitments in order to work long hard hours in hopes of leasing the building. The level of his commitment to Christ will wane as the pressures of the market-place increase.

The marketplace will dictate his level of commitment to Christ in yet another way. Jim, a committed Christian, is called into the presence of his superior and told, "You have a great future with this company. But leave your Christianity at home. I do not care if you pray, go to church, and preach about your Jesus, but do not bring it to work with you. If you do, this company will terminate its relationship with you."

If Jim feels that he works to earn a living and that there is a correlation between how hard he works and how much he makes, he will follow the advice of his superior and leave his commitment to Christ at home. When the environment is friendly he will integrate his faith with his vocation; when it is unfriendly he will not.

These are the predictable consequences of those who believe that there is a correlation between how hard they work and how much they make.

## C. There Is No Intrinsic Value in the Product of Work

The word to underline in this axiom is *product*. The product of work may have utilitarian value, but it has no intrinsic value. It may have value in helping someone do what he wants to do, but the object has no value in and of itself. An automobile, for example, has value in that it helps one get from point A to point B, but there is no intrinsic value to the automobile. It is nothing but a piece of decaying rot which will eventually be relegated to the junkyard. Peter reminds us that this is the fate of all "things" in 2 Peter 3:10.

Work does have value in that it is used by God to determine reward in heaven and is drawn to the believer's attention in passages such as 1 Corinthians 3:10–15. So also God may assign value to what he does because of a love relationship that exists between them, but this does not mean that there is any intrinsic value in the product produced.

For example, when my children were young, they brought home their art work in varying colors. After talking about them, they ended the same place I am sure your children's drawing ended—on the refrigerator door. Here they were in prominent view for all who passed through the kitchen. They were exceedingly important to my wife and me because they were drawn by *our* children. But they would never qualify for the National Art Gallery, and we would get nothing for them if we included them in a garage sale. So it is in God's relationship with his children. Because he loves them, he may assign value to what they produce, but that does not mean that the things produced have value in and of themselves. They are going to "burn"!

Labor's value as viewed from the worth of the product is equal in importance for all people from God's perspective. Since the product is going to burn, it is the focus of the labor that is important to God. The product of the coal miner is as important as the product of the anarchist. The man in the gulag in solitary confinement for his faith is as productive for God, if the focus of his life is correct, as the great evangelist. It is one of the great equalizers of the human race.

Man's labor may be directed toward creating wealth, such as the farmer in the field or the bricklayer constructing a building. It can be in terms of self-improvement, such as the mastering of a skill or the learning of a language. Such accomplishments receive recognition from man, but note the apostle Paul's evaluation of his own accomplishments. "Yea doubtless, and I count all things but loss for the excellency of the knowledge of Christ Jesus my Lord: for whom I have suffered the loss of all things, and do count them but dung, that I may win Christ" (Phil. 3:8 KJV).

If this is not clearly understood by the believer, he will labor for the temporal rather than the eternal. It is the thing Jesus warns against in John 6:27. He will perceive greatness in terms of what he is able to create or accomplish. Feedback in terms of recognition and the accolades of man encourage this tendency, and his focus becomes riveted on the temporal rather than the eternal.

As he labors on behalf of the eternal, it is not the fault of the labor that produces significance but the *focus* of that labor. For example, two individuals can be doing the same thing, one participating in the program of God while the other is not. The fruit of the labor is the same, but the focus is different. The individual who works on the lathe in the factory is engaged in spiritual labor when the focus of his life is "the kingdom of God and his righteousness." Conversely, an individual can be a missionary for the gospel in a foreign land and be engaged in secular work if the focus of his life is someday becoming president of the mission.

Thus the secular is spiritual when the focus of a person's life is eternal. Conversely, the spiritual is secular when the focus of one's life is temporal. The slave in the salt mine is just as important in his labor as the pastor or missionary, assuming both are laboring for the glory of God and his kingdom.

There is an unequal distribution of gifts and opportunities. Some people are marginally gifted; others are multigifted. Some are able to labor in God's vineyard for may years, others for only a short period of time. Thus it is not the amount of fruit which an individual produces that pleases God, but the degree to which he is faithful to the opportunities God has given him. All of this is blurred if Christians do not have a firm grip on the fact that there is no intrinsic value in the product of work.

## D. Significance Is Not Found in the Kind of Work You Do

The last half of twentieth-century America has been marked by an identity crisis. People in a state of disorientation are looking desperately for a sense of self-worth and purpose. The entrance of women into the marketplace is a vivid example of this phenomenon. Not infrequently is heard the argument that the home does not produce an environment conducive to a sense of self-worth. Women want more out of life than dishes and diapers. Men have all the fun. It is competing in the marketplace that gives challenge to living. To exercise one's gifts in the context of a vocation is to sense one's significance. This is one of the great lies of our age!

Significance and a sense of personal worth are found in a person's relationship with God. In Jeremiah 9:23–24 God identifies three areas in which people look for significance: wealth, wisdom, and power. The world defines greatness in terms of these three factors. People are led to believe that they are important to the degree that they excel in one or more of them. In the economy of God, however, one is able to boast not in any of them, but solely in the fact that he knows and understands God.

People are not significant because they got their Ph.D. or reached the top of the corporate ladder or any one of a thousand worldly standards of success. Such things Paul calls "dung" (Phil. 3:8). God's children are significant because they are created in the image of God. He has declared them to be of eternal worth. He has made them "heirs of God and joint heirs with Christ" (Rom. 8:17 KJV).

Significance is not found in the exercising of one's gifts. Gifts differ both as to kind and intensity. Two people may have the same gifts, yet one may be more gifted than the other. When people look to their gifts for fulfillment, they invariably compare themselves with others. They feel inferior in the presence of those more gifted than they are. Even the highly gifted fear from what may be called "the fastest gun in town" mentality. They know that someday another will "ride into town" who is more gifted than they are.

Nor is significance and the value of labor found in one's vocation. If he looks to his vocation as the source of his fulfillment and receives negative feedback from those with whom he works, he develops a low self-image. Conversely, the greater the recognition of man, the greater his sense of self-worth. When a person's significance is a derivative of his vocation and he loses his vocation, he loses his reason for living.

Steve, a Christian politician, served in the United States Congress for many years. When his district was gerrymandered, he lost the election. For years his life was wrapped up in his vocation, and when it came to an end, he became disoriented, lost his reason for living, and died a frustrated man.

Joseph was as significant in God's economy when in prison as when prime minister of Egypt. Moses was as significant during the second forty years of his life in the desert region of Midian as in his last forty years as God's deliverer. Significance is not to be found in the kind of work one does nor in the gifts he has but in being part of the family of God.

## E. You Can Contribute Nothing to the Work of God

Again and again God reminds his people that his work was finished before the foundation of the world. He created it; he set it in motion; he sustains it. From start to finish it is his work (cf., e.g., Ps. 115:3; Isa. 46:9–10).

His children can participate in the work of God, but they can contribute nothing. To contribute is to give something, to furnish or to supply. Webster defines it as "to give a part to a common fund or store; to lend assistance or aid to a common purpose." It has the idea of helping or meeting a need. To participate, on the other hand, has the idea of sharing in something, or as Webster says, "to possess some of the properties, qualities or attributes of something; to take part in something; to have a part or a share in something." It connotes the idea of privilege—the privilege of having a slice of the action.

God in his love and grace gives his own the privilege of participating with him in what he is doing. They are deceived, however, if they believe that they can contribute anything to what he is doing.

The conversation between Esther and Mordecai in Esther 4:13–14 draws attention to this truth. Esther was queen when Haman, the king's prime minister, devised a plot whereby the Jews were to be exterminated. When Mordecai draws Esther's attention to this plot, he suggests that she can participate in the solution, but if she elects not to, God will bring deliverance from another quarter. God's promises to Israel will not be altered by the diabolical intentions of Haman. Esther is invited to participate in the solution.

By way of illustration, suppose you had access to an unbelievable real estate deal and came to me with the following offer: If I invest $5,000 with you, you will guarantee a return on the investment of $5,000,000 within six months. Not only so, but you are willing to sign a note to the effect that if the profit is not forthcoming, you will return the $5,000. You point out that you do not need my money to consummate the deal; it is an offer you are making out of the generosity and goodness of your heart.

Six months later I receive from you $5,000,000. I respond by saying, "Aren't you glad I helped you put the deal together?" If you were incredulous over such a remark, you would be justified.

I did not help you. Out of your generosity you allowed me the privilege of participating with you in that which would ultimately benefit me. So it is with God. We do not help him in the ministry. He helps us by allowing us to minister.

Those who do not understand that they can contribute nothing to the work of God's will: (1) establish goals; (2) make them of primary importance; and (3) ultimately compromise the commandments of God in an effort to accomplish them.

This can be seen on an individual level. A man said, "I want to serve God. My wife is not a believer and hinders me in everything I endeavor to do for God. She resents the money I give and the time I spend in the ministry. She is a millstone around my neck. I have decided that I will divorce my wife so that I can serve God better." Unfortunately this is not an uncommon attitude. Because this gentleman feels that he can actually contribute something to the work of God, he concludes that the contribution is important. The making of that contribution becomes all important, leading him to break the commandment of God in an endeavor to accomplish it.

It can also be seen on an organization level. When leaders of an organization feel that they can contribute to the work of God, they end up using people rather than ministering to them. What is best for the organization takes precedent over what is best for the person. This can be particularly noted in Christian organizations whether it be church or parachurch. Leaders who feel that they can contribute something to the work of God, in their endeavor to build men and women of God, end up using people to build their organization.

The person who believes he can contribute something to the work that God is doing will define the ministry in terms of how he perceives God is leading him. In this view God becomes dependent on his contribution, anxiously holding his breath waiting for him to accomplish his task. Others, perceived as an obstacle, are run over, and he competes for the limited resources of men and money with those equally eager to make their contribution.

## II. LEISURE

In one sense leisure is different from rest. Leisure is what gives a person rest, but what is leisure for one may be work for another. For example, mowing the lawn may be leisure for one person and work (possibly his vocation) for another. Leisure tends to turn into work when one feels there is something he needs to accomplish. For this reason many find that their hobbies turn into work.

Although there are these subtle differences between rest and leisure, to pursue them would be to derail the purpose of this paper. Therefore, in this presentation rest and leisure are considered synonyms.

Leisure brings balance to work in the rhythm of life. The Bible in general and the New Testament in particular does not say much about rest or leisure. In the Genesis account of creation God rested the seventh day, but from Adam to Moses there is no command to the effect that man should emulate God in this regard, and the need for rest is not mentioned.

During the Exodus (Exod. 16) the idea of man participating in a sabbath rest is first introduced. In Exodus 20 it is stated as the fourth commandment of the Decalogue. From Moses to Christ the sabbath observance became an important issue in the nation of Israel with dire consequences meted out for their failure to keep it.

From the death of Christ on there is no command to the effect that God's people should rest or that they should set aside any particular day as holy or sacred. In Romans 14 Paul argues that all days are alike in the sight of God and that it is up to the individual to decide if one is more holy than another. In his Epistle to the Colossians he says, "Therefore do not let anyone judge you by what you eat or drink, or with regard to a religious festival, a New Moon celebration or a Sabbath day" (Col. 2:16). Many commentators who favor the argument that the Decalogue is applicable today reason that these two statements by Paul refer to special religious days of the Old Testament and not to the keeping of the fourth commandment.

Even if it is accepted that the fourth commandment is applicable for the New Testament in the form of the Lord's Day, it still leaves unanswered questions such as, how many hours a day should a person work vis-a-vis leisure, how many days a year should be taken for vacation, and when (if at all) should an individual retire?

To further complicate the problem, there is no mention of how free time should be spent. In Ephesians 5:16 Paul says, "Redeem the time," and in 1 Timothy 5:13 he reasons that women should not be idle. Thus there is more to say about not abusing rest than there is about what to do with rest.

Hebrews 4 is a great chapter on "The Rest of God," but it deals with unbroken fellowship with God on a day-by-day basis rather than how the believer's leisure time should be spent. *Eukireo*, the Greek word for "leisure," is mentioned but a few times in the New Testament. For example, in Acts 17:21 it is used negatively regarding the Athenians; in Mark 6:31 they wanted to rest, but there was "no leisure." Numerous places mention that they "rested on the Sabbath" (e.g., Luke 23:56).

Although the evidence for leisure and rest is far skimpier than that for work, biblical principles can be deduced which are helpful as a guide for determining how to handle this important aspect of life. Because they are directly related to work and in some cases are a corollary to the principles on work, their exegesis will be somewhat shorter.

## A. Leisure Is Not Mandated by God in the New Testament

There are examples in both the Old and the New Testament of God's people resting from their work, but there is no command to this effect in the New Testament. A fundamental rule of hermeneutics is, "An example is not a precept." This leaves the believer on his own to determine before God what he should do.

The body wears out and demands leisure. The New Testament implies that this is understood and responds with a caution not to move toward excess (e.g., Eph. 5:16; 1 Tim. 5:13). Some people fear leisure; others are on a quest for leisure. Often this is reflected in an individual's age. Young people are often motivated to work hard and fear that they are not doing enough. Not infrequently elderly people long for retirement and look forward to the days when they can be freed from the necessity of working.

It is important for the believer to realize that it is an issue of stewardship. There will always remain a tension between work and leisure, i.e., how much time he should spend working and how much time he should rest. The absence of a New Testament mandate regarding leisure means that he is dependent on God to be led by the Spirit in this matter. Legislation regarding leisure tends to legalism.

## B. Leisure Can Be an Act of Worship

In the Old Testament there was a frequent link between rest and worship (e.g., Lev. 16:29–34). Deuteronomy 14:22–26 speaks of a "second tithe," adding to this link the spending of wealth. Each year the children of Israel were to take 10 percent of their increase for that year and bring it before the Lord as an act of worship to spend on themselves "that thou mayest learn to fear the LORD your God always" (v. 23 KJV).

This is not to suggest that believers are obligated to keep these Old Testament laws today. They are, however, illustrative of how God feels about leisure. Regarding wealth, there are two things God hates and two things he loves. He hates hoarding and stinginess, for they are expressions of man's independence. He loves extravagance and generosity, for they are expressions of dependence. God wants his people in a posture of perpetual dependence. Thus we have God calling upon his people in Deuteronomy 14 to squander 10 percent of their yearly gain—as an act of worship. The extravagant expenditure of part of the believer's wealth in a time of leisure may be as meaningful an act of worship as generously giving to alleviate the needs of others. Dependence is the highest form of worship.

With society becoming increasingly materialistic, the tendency is to push the pendulum to the opposite extreme. Many in the body of Christ would like to marry the biblical admonition of generosity with a socialist philosophy. Believers are taught that they should feel guilty if they extravagantly spend God's blessings on themselves. Balance is obviously needed here, but leisure and the spending of resources in the pursuit of leisure is not wrong in and of itself.

Work, leisure, and wealth, along with life itself, are all gifts of God. There will always be well-intentioned people telling others how to invest them. Many fall prey to these kinds of people in an endeavor to eliminate the need to walk by faith. As already mentioned in principle 6 above, it is an issue of stewardship. Most conscientious Christians would love to have someone eliminate the tension of determining how much of their leisure and wealth they should spend on themselves vis-a-vis others and yet would resent anyone telling them what to do.

In the struggle to maintain the balance, remember that leisure may be an act of worship.

## C. Leisure Contributes No More or Less Than Work in the Economy of God

This principle is the flip side of principles 3–5. Leisure is valid because Christians can produce nothing of significance for God. The product of their labor has no intrinsic value, and they can do nothing to contribute to the work of God.

Abraham, Isaac, and Jacob illustrate this principle. From a worldly perspective they produced nothing. They built no cities, conquered no lands, wrote no books. "Abraham believed the LORD, and he credited it to him as righteousness" (Gen. 15:6). One can believe God in leisure as easily as in working.

If the man or woman of God feels work is more important than leisure because he can contribute something of significance in the program of God, then when through illness or some other circumstance he is denied a chance to work, he will feel cheated. Furthermore, he will be motivated to work much, even to the detriment of other priorities. This is a uniquely subtle trap for vocational Christian workers. If they feel their work is important in its contribution to God's cause, the wife and children run the risk of being neglected. Possibly this is the reason the phrase "PK" carries a negative connotation.

If the Christian could contribute to the work of God, he would not be able to handle it. He would burn out trying to reach that last person whose salvation is dependent on his contribution.

Again, the Bible argues for the avoidance of excess. In this regard leisure is analogous to eating. The New Testament does not teach how much to eat nor how much to rest. In both eating and resting excess is to be avoided. Because the Bible does not argue against working excessively, it is easy to conclude that God places a higher priority on work than he does on leisure. The Scriptures simply do not substantiate this.

Many feel rest is a *means* to productive work, i.e., "I can do more if I take time to rest." This thinking will lead to a repudiation of principles 3–5 along with the negative consequences. Leisure is not valid because it is a means to accomplish labor. Nowhere in the Bible does God teach that a man should rest in order to work, nor that he should work in order to rest. Each are valid in and of themselves. Leisure contributes no more or less than work in the economy of God.

## D. Leisure Is Not Related to Finances

Leisure is a gift of God and not the fruit of financial gain. Time and wealth are both a gift of God (e.g., 1 Cor. 4:7). Those born into wealth have no more *right* to leisure than those born into poverty. The rich and poor alike are responsible to God for the stewardship of their time and money.

The perception of most is that the poor are where they are because of a lack of hard work. This may or may not be true. We have already established that there is no correlation between how hard people work and how much they make. This axiom is balanced by 2 Thessalonians 3:10, ". . . if you don't work, you don't eat."

Most people also feel that the rich deserve leisure. Few question the wealthy squandering their lives on the golf course or in other pursuits of pleasure. This is unequivocally false. Since people do not work to earn a living and what they have is a gift of God, they are answerable to God for how they spend both their time and money.

The disciple of Jesus does not retire when he can afford it nor when he reaches a certain age. Since a person's vocation is an environment given by God in which to be an ambassador of Jesus Christ, to retire is to leave one's pulpit. A person may feel the need to retire for health reasons, and even possibly because of advanced age, but it should never be related to finance.

Some in the body of Christ believe that in order to serve God you need leisure, and that requires money. These people are identified by statements like, "When I put this deal together, I will have the time to serve God."

Others feel that if they have less wealth than they want, they should work more and rest less. Biblical priorities tend to be neglected as they look to the arm of the flesh rather than to God for the meeting of their needs.

"Leisure is not related to finances." This axiom, along with the others dealing with rest and leisure, is inextricably related to those dealing with work. All of them are merely facets of a biblical understanding of work and leisure.

## III. CONCLUSION

Today's culture has developed a deeply embedded, nonscriptural concept of work and leisure. A biblical perspective on this important aspect of life cuts across the grain of what most of life teaches. These nine principles do not eliminate the tension in each Christian's life as he seeks to maintain a balance between work and leisure. Hopefully they will assist in keeping him from the extremes of legalism and being rudderless.

## ENDNOTES

[1] Goran Agrell, *Work, Toil and Sustenance* (Sweden: Verburn-Hokan Ohlsson, 1976).

[2] John Calvin, *Commentaries on the Bible,* 45 vols. (Grand Rapids: Eerdmans, 1956).

[3] John Calvin, *Institutes of the Christian Religion,* vols. 1, 2 (Grand Rapids: Eerdmans, 1964).

[4] D. A. Carson, ed., *From Sabbath to Lord's Day* (Grand Rapids: Zondervan, 1982).

[5] William E. Diehl, *Christianity and Real Life* (Philadelphia: Fortress, 1976).

[6] Paul Edwards, ed., *The Encyclopedia of Philosophy* (New York: Macmillan, 1967).

[7] Richard C. Halverson, *Between Sundays* (Grand Rapids: Zondervan, 1965).

[8] Tim Hansel, *When I Relax, I Feel Guilty* (Elgin, Ill.: Cook, 1979).

[9] Carl F. H. Henry, *Aspects of Christian Social Ethics* (Grand Rapids: Baker, 1980).

[10] Charles Hodge, *Systematic Theology,* vol. 3 (Grand Rapids: Eerdmans, 1952).

[11] Gerhard Kittel, ed., *Theological Dictionary of the New Testament* (Grand Rapids: Eerdmans, 1974).

[12] Gary D. Long, *The Christian Sabbath—The Lord's Day Controversy* (Sterling, Va.: Sovereign Grace, 1980).

[13] Paul Marshall, *Thine Is the Kingdom* (Great Britain: Camelot, 1984).

[14] Udo Middelmann, *Pro-exist-ence* (Downers Grove: InterVarsity, 1974).

[15] Rousas John Rushdoony, *The Institutes of Biblical Law,* vol. 1 (Philadelphia: Presbyterian and Reformed, 1973); vol. 2 (Vallecito, Calif.: Ross House, 1982).

[16] E. F. Schumacher, *Small Is Beautiful: Economics As If People Mattered* (New York: Harper and Row, 1973).

[17] Ronald J. Sider, *Rich Christians in an Age of Hunger* (Downers Grove: InterVarsity, 1977).

[18] Cornelius Van Til, *Christian Theistic Ethics* (Philadelphia: Westminster Theological Seminary Syllabus, 1958).

[19] Henry R. Van Til, *The Calvinistic Concept of Culture* (Philadelphia: Presbyterian and Reformed, 1959).

[20] Nelvin Vos, *Monday's Ministries—The Ministry of the Laity* (Parish Life, 1973).

[21] Bernard Adeney, "Work: Necessity, Vocation, Strategy," *Radix*, January–February 1984.

[22] Jack Buckley, "Calvin's View of Work," *Radix*, January–February 1984.

[23] Cheryl Forbes, "Dorothy L. Sayers—For Good Work, For God's Work," *Christianity Today*, March 4, 1977.

[24] David Gill, "Interview with Jacques Ellul," *Radix*, January–February 1984.

[25] Os Guinnes, *Recovering a Sense of Vocation*, audio tape of an address to InterVarsity Conference.

[26] S. Lewis Johnson, Jr., "Man and the Cultural Mandate," *Believer's Bible Bulletin*, October 22, 1978.

[27] William Kellogg, "Genesis 1:28 and the Meaning of Work," *The Chalcedon Report*, January 1981.

[28] David L. McKenna, "Toward a Theology of Work," *The Minister's Personal Library*, vol. 6, no. 2.

[29] Arthur F. Miller, Jr., and Ralph Mattson, "Find Your Niche," *Eternity*, November 1982.

[30] Leland Ryken, "Puritan Work Ethic: The Dignity of Life's Labors," *Christianity Today*, October 19, 1979.

[31] John R. Stott, "Creative by Creation: Our Need for Work," *Christianity Today*, June 8, 1979.

[32] John R. Stott, "Reclaiming the Biblical Doctrine of Work," *Christianity Today*, 1979.

[33] "Spending Your Time," *The Royal Bank Letter*, Royal Bank of Canada, July–August 1984.

# A Response to
# Work and Leisure

## W. David Beck

Henrichsen's essay provides an excellent analysis of the theology of work as it follows from a particular list of assumptions about the nature of God. I want to take a close look at some of its salient features and then indicate an alternate view of work that follows from a somewhat different conception of God's nature.

It will be helpful to begin simply by enumerating Henrichsen's nine principles. They basically outline the logic of the paper.

1. You do not work to earn a living.
2. There is no correlation between how hard you work and how much you make.
3. There is no intrinsic value in the product of work.
4. Significance is not found in the kind of work you do.
5. You can contribute nothing to the work of God.
6. Leisure is not mandated by God in the New Testament.
7. Leisure can be an act of worship.
8. Leisure contributes no more or less than work in the economy of God.
9. Leisure is not related to finances.

Seeing these principles together one cannot help but notice several key features of this solution. Surely its most commendable feature is its strong accent on the absolute sovereignty of God and man's total dependence. This dependence involves most obviously his physical well-being in all of its aspects. But beyond that, the very meaningfulness of his daily existence derives from God. Work itself, its rewards, its products, as well as the leisure with which it alternates, are all the magnanimous gifts of a gracious God. Meaning in life is found simply in obedience.

Another feature, however, is also noticeable, and it is closely related to the first. This solution has a strong note of arbitrariness to it. Nothing I do or am, none of my actions or productions, in relation either to myself or to God, has any intrinsic value. Whether I work or rest is in and of itself pointless and fruitless. Only as acts of obedience is there a value to work or leisure.

This view can only be understood against the backdrop of a particular concept of God. Given that view, it makes perfectly good sense and is surely correct. This view, as with any properly theistic conceptualization, begins with a notion of absolute sovereignty. The primary component of sovereignty, however, is the crucial feature. In this case it is the aspect of freedom. Hence, one might refer to this view as the voluntarist view, and it certainly has a long and distinguished past. Tertullian; to some extent Augustine; clearly Scotus and Occam who, in turn, influenced Luther mildly; and today positions like those of Van Til and Rushdoony all betray this characteristic.

It is precisely this emphasis on the absolute freedom of God that demands that only logic for any of God's actions, decrees, commands, choices, and so on, be just his will—sort of a divine existentialism. God wills solely in accord with his good pleasure to so will. Hence one cannot look any further for a rationale.

Since this voluntarism rules at the divine level, it must, of course, follow at the human level. My actions make no sense; they have no meaning, purpose, reason, or logic of their own—or of my own. They make sense because God wills that I should act as he acts and no more. And in so acting I have found my full meaning in obeying and thereby glorifying God.

Now it should be obvious why a certain arbitrariness follows for human actions: I want to point out just three ways in which this shows up in Henrichsen's essay. First, ethics itself cannot be strictly deontological. To say that an act is ethically right is only to say that God now wills it for me. Note that the desirability of work means only that God has commanded it (p. 422). Perhaps the most striking example is the morality of leisure. For the Old Testament believer it is requisite; for the New Testament believer it is not (p. 431).

Second, ethics cannot be a logical enterprise. One cannot expect to understand God's ways. Hence, one cannot predict them or subject them to some list of clear-cut principles. God's ways transcend ours, after all, and his will cannot be limited by finite human reason. Notice that all of Henrichsen's principles, except number 7, are negations. That is, they deny the existence of some simple correlation: between work and pay, intensity of work and reward, leisure and finances, and so on. In each case, they are to be replaced by a reliance on divine sovereignty and a commitment to obey. "This is not to suggest that people are not to work hard but rather to work hard because God commands it" (p. 425).

It shows itself as well in Henrichsen's description of revelation at "mixed signals" (p. 422), and as containing numerous tensions and "seeming contradictions" (p. 423). To be sure, he stops short of asserting actual contradictions, unlike some others. But the logic of this position shows itself primarily in the willingness to allow these tensions to remain as "differing sermons" for different situations (p. 424).

The third implication of this view of God in Henrichsen's paper is its egalitarian view of actions. Since the value of an action consists exclusively and entirely in God's desiring it, and since God desires perfectly (any theist must hold this, I assume), all good actions are equally desirable and, hence, equally valuable.

This is evident in Henrichsen's view that all work is equally ministry. There is no distinction between secular work and full-time ministry. "All believers are in full-time Christian work" (p. 423). Another example is the idea that any action, including leisure, can be worship. "The extravagant expenditure of part of the believer's wealth in a time of leisure may be as meaningful an act of worship as generously giving to alleviate the needs of others" (p. 433).

Again, Henrichsen's position follows quite consistently from a particular view of God, a view that has a venerable history and certainly exegetical support. Nevertheless, I want to argue that it has some serious liabilities. I will mention two briefly.

First, this view makes science impossible. The concepts and principles of work and leisure are currently hot topics in the social sciences. A whole new science, personnel management, is just now emerging. Much of this may well be due to the fact that social scientists have become less interested in doing ideology and more interested in doing real empirical science. In any case, we are just beginning to establish some genuine relationships, causal connections, historical consistencies, effective methods, and so on in relation to the various factors of work and leisure. So much of this already is very promising in demonstrating biblical truths. This makes it all the more tragic that Christians in general have remained virtually uninvolved in these areas and that theologians have, almost without exception, ignored them in working out a general theology of man.

I am convinced that much of the reason for this failure of Christians to do careful science in the twentieth century is the result of a widely held voluntarist view of God. To this view science will always appear irrelevant: it is much simpler to talk about God's action. It will also seem useless: It will always be easier to ask God to control or change events. Worse, it will make science into an enemy. It has to be seen as an attempt to give a naturalistic explanation of what is really supernatural action.

As a result, it ceases to be possible to say what conditions are due to natural causes and which to God's activity, since the former category does not exist. Hence, there really ought not to be science. What seems to me particularly damaging, however, is that this view cannot distinguish between the effects of sin and sovereignty. Note Henrichsen's examples for his second principle, that is, that there is no correlation between how hard you work and how much you make: the skilled steel worker now at Burger King, or the poor ghetto dweller who works hard and earns little. In what sense does this principle hold? Is it really a description of God's sovereign will and design, or is it a description of the actual state of affairs, one which is, in fact, counter to God's design and hence sinful. But I do not see that this view can make such a distinction.

A second problem with this view is that it makes work irrelevant. Now this is evident in several of Henrichsen's principles. In particular, neither work (p. 422), nor the product of work (p. 426), nor the reward of work (p. 425) is of any value. Having, in effect, eliminated all secondary causality, none of these tasks can be of any value.

Now I suppose it might be easy for some in professional careers who truly enjoy their work, especially a pastor, to recognize that their work is of no value except as an act of obedience. I find it hard to believe that this would be very compelling or satisfying to most workers who do what they do precisely to make a living for themselves and their families. This is not the place for a careful sociological analysis, except to say that this can only create alienation.

One cannot help but think of the teenager who, when she asks why she should do something, is told, "Because I said so." This produces real alienation between agent and action. In wanting to know why I should act, I am looking for its sense. How does this act "fit." That is just its value. And this view of God has no answer. This is, I think, not just a sociological and psychological difficulty but an exegetical one as well. Scripture seems clear that work does have value (Prov. 13:11; 14:23; Eccl. 3:13), that harder work deserves greater reward (Prov. 21:25; Eccl. 4:9), that the product of work has real value (Ps. 128:1–2), and even that human beings play a real role in God's work (1 Cor. 3:9; 15:58).

Finally, I want to suggest a different reading of the nature of God and indicate the difference it makes. Clearly one must begin with the sovereignty of God. But sovereignty does not need to be interpreted voluntaristically. Both the philosophical argument and the exegetical data imply that God is a person, in fact, three persons in relationship. Hence his sovereign will cannot be disassociated from his sovereign intellect or any other aspect of his character. Thus God is eminently rational, orderly, logical, and designing.

The system of creation is therefore seen not as the arena of God's arbitrary decisions but as his well-designed and orderly functioning handiwork. It is a structure so well done, and it contains a human language so carefully expressive that they can be revelation of God himself.

Now this makes for an important difference. Science is critical: both to understand and have dominion over the cosmos but also in knowing God. In particular, in the area of economics, including aspects like work and leisure, God has designed certain laws of human behavior. Their application is, of course, widely varied because human beings are each different. Furthermore, because the creation reflects God, and persons in particular are his very image, there is real value present. The corn and hogs the farmer grows are of value, as are the cars and computers rolling down the factory worker's assembly line. That is why it is so important to devise work methods and environments that do not alienate the worker from the product as well as systems that reward hard work. Even a pastor who neglects these factors is not being spiritually obedient but is just neglecting the real needs of his family (1 Tim. 5:8), his proper right as a person (Luke 10:7), as well as his church's need to act responsibly (1 Tim. 5:17).

It should be clear, then, that the principles of work and leisure will work out quite differently given this view of God's nature. In addition science will turn out to be a necessary and valuable ally in ascertaining these relationships and in clarifying and demonstrating revelational input. But this view will also be able to clearly identify the results of sin, and thus the principles will never be fully empirically testable. It is not God who discriminates, nor is it "life" that is unfair. The problem is that sinful human beings discriminate, are unfair, devise poor economic systems, fail to properly pay their employees, and so on. Thus it is true for all of us, as Henrichsen so well argues, that we are ultimately reliant on a sovereign and loving God.

Finally, this view also gives human beings a very real role in carrying out the work of God. We have an important part in the preserving and perfecting of the creation in general (Gen. 1:28) as well as in the specific work of reconciliation (Col. 1:28–29; John 4:36). Of course, we can add nothing to God's being or value, but God himself has created us persons with value not only in what we are but also in what we do. Thus there is value both in obedience itself as well as in what we obediently do.

# A Response to
# Work and Leisure

### Frederic R. Schatz

> Whatever your task, work heartily, as serving the Lord and not
> men, knowing that from the Lord you will receive the inheri-
> tance as your reward; you are serving the Lord Christ (Col.
> 3:23–24 RSV).

Mr. Walter Henrichsen has written a genuinely helpful paper
on work and leisure. He begins by pointing out the problems and
the importance of a Christian response to both work and leisure.
In his opening section he establishes the basis of his approach
through the concept of the rhythm of life beginning with creation.
He combines with this rhythm an emphasis on the stewardship of
all of life.

In the body of the paper Henrichsen proposes certain
principles for developing the Christian response to these two
critical areas of life. These principles are generally well supported
by Scripture and address some major questions and issues related
to both work and leisure. Through application of these principles
the author consistently and appropriately points out the nonscriptural concept of work and leisure which is embraced within our
modern culture in general, and sadly, within much of the
Christian community as well.

I am both honored and challenged in responding to Henrichsen's paper. My response is divided into two basic sections:
(1) areas in which I feel further comment proves useful, and (2) a
review of the specific principles which the author sets forth. My
additional material includes the biblical concept of God's calling, a
comparison of the secular and Christian views of work and
leisure, and a proposed definition of Christian vocation. In
reviewing the principles of Henrichsen's paper, I often find myself

in agreement with the basic point the author is making yet not always in agreement with the principles as they are stated and/or applied.

## I. HOW IT ALL BEGAN

In the opening section Henrichsen establishes the context of work and leisure through his discussion of the rhythm of life. The biblical understanding of the goodness of work and leisure is properly set forth based on the opening chapters of Genesis and the Book of Ecclesiastes. It should be clearly pointed out that the "mixed signals" and "frustrations" referred to are the result of the Fall and man's viewing life "under the sun" and apart from God.

Before beginning the response to the principles which the author sets forth, it is helpful to briefly consider the concept of God's call, the stark contrast between the Christian and secular views of work and leisure, and a definition of Christian vocation.

## II. GOD'S CALL

God's call lays claim to the entire life of the believer. Work and leisure are important parts of this call. As the believer matures in Christ the false barriers between the "religious life" and the "totality of life" are torn down. As maturity increases there is no longer a compartmentalizing of life into parts which are Christian and parts which are secular. Scriptures such as 1 Corinthians 3:5–9; 10:31; and 1 Timothy 6:1–2 show us that the believer should view both work and leisure as opportunities to: (1) apply Christian ethics (Amos 5:8; James 5:4–5), (2) use God-given gifts and skills (Rom. 12:6–8; 1 Cor. 12:28; Rev. 14:13), (3) build relationships and witness of Christ to those outside the body (Rom. 10:14–15), and (4) influence organizations for the kingdom (Matt. 5:13–16). Professor James H. Nichols summarized these thoughts on the relationship between calling and work when he noted that "the Protestant doctrine of 'vocations in the world' became the means of the greatest penetration of Christianity into culture which history or faith has seen."[1]

Understanding God's calling as the basis of life will greatly aid the believer as he/she is involved in both work and leisure as service to Christ.

## III. CHRISTIAN VIEW VERSUS SECULAR VIEW

In coming to a proper Christian perspective of work and leisure, it is important to understand the contrast between the secular and Christian views of these aspects of life. The secular view sees work as primarily a means to money, power, and self-fulfillment. The emphasis is on climbing the ladder to success, often without regard for people and with frequent compromises. Leisure is a means of self-gratification and is the product of the "good life." The secular view of work and leisure is basically self-centered in its desires, with self-fulfillment its goal. Others frequently become objects to be used toward this goal.

By contrast, the Christian view of work and leisure asserts that both are part of the Christian calling given by God's grace. As part of God's calling, work and leisure are integrated into a Christian world view which encompasses all of life. Both work and leisure are seen as opportunities to glorify God, serve others, and build God's kingdom.

## IV. WHAT IS A CHRISTIAN VOCATION?

Dr. Henlee H. Barnette offers a helpful definition:

> A Christian vocation is one which renders a genuine service to humanity; one which meets a real need of society; a job over which one can pray; a job in harmony with love, justice and human dignity; one which requires of the worker integrity, creativity, imagination, and social usefulness; and finally, it is one characterized by a sense of purpose.[2]

### A. You Do Not Work to Earn a Living

In this lengthy section Henrichsen points out some powerful truths to guide the believer. It is proper to emphasize that the Christian is to be dependent on God for meeting *all* needs, and the priority for one's life is the kingdom of God. A critical point is made that all believers are in full-time Christian work and, therefore, none are to be lazy. The author demonstrates that "compartmentalizing" has disastrous effects for the life and witness of the believer. A weakness in this section is that Henrichsen fails to make clear that God provides work as the vehicle for receiving his gracious provision—not manna from heaven. Man is *responsible* to use this provision as a statement of his obedience and dependence on God. It is God's responsibility to produce the "living," but it is man's responsibility to use the vehicle which God has provided—namely, work.

### B. There Is No Correlation Between How Hard You Work and How Much You Make

The author concludes that because God is the provider, there is no correlation between earnings and how hard one works. Support is provided through scriptural references to the providence of God and his actions, which result in blessings for some but not all. Henrichsen rightfully concludes that we are to work hard in order to be good witnesses. We are to set plans based on God's priorities and not on abundance or paucity of resulting income.

While it is true that there is rarely, if ever, a *direct* relationship between how hard one works and how much money is earned, I do not agree that there is *no correlation* between the two. If there is no correlation, then results are strictly random, and we would be forced to deny any meaningful providence of God. Within the context of God's grace and providence, Scripture points out that there is some relationship between effort and results, although not always a direct relationship (i.e., Prov. 6:6–11; 2 Thess. 3:10).

Ecclesiastes might be improperly used to support the no correlation position, but, in fact, this book supports the fact that there is some relationship between hard work and results. With respect to this issue, five additional points bear mentioning:

1. We cannot control life and its results through our own efforts alone.
2. Despite toil, all have a common lot (4:14–16; 9:13–16).
3. There is an indiscernible moral order (3:16; 7:15).
4. God is sovereign.
5. Life is to be lived in joy as God's gift (2:24–26; 3:12–13; 5:18–20).

The joyful living called for is only possible because God's providential control prevents randomness and chaos. We are called to yield control to God and to look to him for meaningful results from our efforts.

## C. There Is No Intrinsic Value in the Product of Work

As long as a clear distinction is made between the product of work and the focus of work, or the work itself, the point appears to be problematical but valid. Henrichsen properly points out that earthly "things" will pass away and that Paul counted all things as loss except for his knowledge of Christ (Phil. 3:8). Some apparent problems with the author's conclusion could include: (1) God's intention to "renew" the creation (Rom. 8) rather than to destroy it, (2) God's command to man to subdue and have dominion, and (3) the making of disciples. The impact of the "value" of these works on the principle set forth requires further discussion and thought.

Henrichsen makes a valuable point with his emphasis on the focus of labor rather than on the results. Properly understood, this will eliminate the need which many Christians feel to earn God's love through the results of their labor. This truth must be carefully applied so that believers do not become slothful on the one hand or fail to give God the glory for the results of their labor on the other.

## D. Significance Is Not Found in the Kind of Work You Do

The author makes a valid and important point in defining significance apart from the kind of work in which people engage. The crisis of identity which marks the lives of many people often finds them looking to their work for personal significance. The results are predictable: workaholism, sacrifice of family life, relentless drive to achieve, and great frustration and pain.

Henrichsen appropriately defines significance in terms of a person's relationship with God. This is a great equalizer without barriers of race, sex, position, power, wealth, or vocation. The author emphasizes the *position* of the person (created in the image of God and joint heir with Christ) as the only basis for significance. I find it difficult to define significance exclusively in these positional terms. Does not the believer's life within his position impact personal significance? The Scripture calls for a life of obedience and exercising of gifts as God's people fulfill their positions as the priesthood of all believers. I believe the "doing" of people in this sense impacts their relationship with God and, therefore, plays a role in defining their significance.

## E. You Can Contribute Nothing to the Work of God

Henrichsen boldly addresses a complex and emotional issue in this point. He strongly and properly defends the omnipotence and independence of God by eliminating any contribution on man's part while allowing for participation. When people conclude that God "needs" them to build his kingdom, the results do not often bring glory to God.

The author properly makes the "no contribution" point but fails to make clear that God *commands* participation (Acts 20:24; Rom. 10:10–14) of his people. Their participation *does* make a difference. God has chosen men and women to act on his behalf and graciously uses them as real participants.

Many of the problems pointed out by Henrichsen are attributed to the belief in "contribution" but these same problems can also occur if the believer misunderstands "participation." An example of the author's position is found in his discussion of goal setting and its negative predicted results. This is a broad and inappropriate attack on goal setting and planning. It is based on the author's view that these actions occur because people believe they can contribute to God's kingdom. God's people are called to strategize and plan *within* the framework of God's providence. They also are called to carry out those plans in a godly and submissive manner.

## V. LEISURE

Henrichsen gives a good overview of the biblical concept of leisure and treats rest and leisure as synonyms in his paper. It would be useful, however, to point out that a biblical study of the concept of rest is significantly different from the modern view of rest/leisure. Biblical rest is generally related to the Sabbath or fellowship with God rather than the modern view of rest/leisure which is simply taking time from daily routines.

As with the case of work, the author bases his principles for leisure on the concept of the rhythm of life and on the stewardship of life. Henrichsen correctly points out that the Bible gives us little propositional teaching about leisure; but on the other hand, he does not seem to appreciate the breadth of the examples associated with leisure that are found throughout the Bible (see my comments below in section A, "Leisure Is Not Mandated by God in the New Testament"). No detailed argument is set forth on the Sabbath, and although this is related to work and leisure, it should be treated as a subject of its own. Suffice it to say that there is significant diversity within evangelical Christianity on the meaning of the Sabbath. I would add as useful background material the following definition of the characteristics and benefits of leisure/play: "That activity which is freely and spontaneously entered into but which, once begun, has its own design or rules."[3]

### Characteristics

1. Concerns of earning a living suspended.
2. Volunteer to play.
3. Spontaneity of play.
4. Nonutilitarian as an end in itself—nevertheless proves productive beyond its own boundaries.

### Benefits

1. Continuing sense of delight.
2. Affirmation of one's united self.
3. Creation of common bonds with one's world.
4. Emancipation of one's spirit as it moves toward the sacred.
5. Relativization of one's work.

C. S. Lewis developed a theology of play which is a useful example of the Christian view and can be summarized as follows:
1. Play releases the imagination, senses, mind, and spirit.
2. Real joy in the fullest sense can be experienced.
3. "Joy" points to an otherness of man and signifies a relationship with a loving God.

4. Play produces joy which is related to holiness. Only through a Christian world view can work and leisure produce the joy, growth, and satisfaction which God intended.

## A. Leisure Is Not Mandated by God in the New Testament

Henrichsen rightfully points out that there is no explicit command that leisure be a part of the believer's life. The use of time in terms of both work and leisure is at its crux an issue of stewardship. In many cases Christians seem to place value on work and often see leisure as wasteful. In order to counterbalance the "wasteful" perspective, I offer the following as examples from Scripture which clearly point to the "value" of leisure:

1. The "rhythm" of creation pointed out by Henrichsen.
2. The beauty and diversity of the created order and God's purpose in such a creation.
3. The Hebrew practices of dance (Job 21:11–12; Jer. 3:13), feasting (Gen. 21:8; Luke 15), festival (Lev. 23:40; Deut. 16:9–15; Heb. 8:9–12), and hospitality (Judg. 19; Luke 10).
4. The symbolic use of oil represents gladness and celebration (Ps. 23:5; 45:7; Isa. 61:3).
5. Ecclesiastes teaches man to enjoy life (2:24–26; 3:12–13 5:18–20) under the providence of God.
6. Song of Solomon, which Karl Barth called the Magna Charta of humanity, is a frank and explicit celebration of love.
7. Jesus' celebration of events and people led his accusers to call him a glutton and a drunkard (Luke 7:34–38; 14:13; John 2).
8. Jesus took time to rest (Mark 6:30–34).
9. There is a calling of Christians to the expression of joy as part of the fruit of the Spirit (Gal. 5:22–23).
10. The potential use of leisure to build family relationships, broaden horizons, and strengthen our physical bodies.

In light of the principles and examples above, the Christian should see leisure as something which God has graciously given and which should not be dismissed as wasteful. Leisure is not mandated, but principles point to the value and need of leisure for all of God's people.

## B. Leisure Can Be an Act of Worship

The author rightly points out the strong relationship between leisure and worship. Believers are called to enjoy the worship of God and to celebrate his personhood and his works. Proper use of dollars in leisure is rightly pointed out as a matter of balance and stewardship. Henrichsen presents the concept of "squandering" resources as an act of worship. However valid this may be, it must be balanced by the difficult time most Christians have in committing all that they own or value to the lordship of Christ. The message of the world, "You've earned it," seems to have permeated much of the Christian church. Unfortunately this attitude has often destroyed a balanced use of resources which God mandates.

## C. Leisure Contributes No More or Less Than Work in the Economy of God

The author states that "leisure is valid because Christians can produce nothing of significance for God." I am troubled by this basis for leisure. I believe the validity of leisure is best established by applying the biblical principles and examples pointed out in section 6 above. As Henrichsen says later in this section, leisure is valid in and of itself. The author aptly points out the danger of vocational Christian workers "driving" to build God's kingdom and thus ignoring other responsibilities. In his book *Strengthening Your Grip* (chapter 10, "Leisure"), Chuck Swindoll points out that few Christians are able to relax and enjoy life, but many are marked by a sense of "driveness." Swindoll says that fatigue in the lives of Christian workers is seen as "next to godliness." He sets forth an attack on these practices and sees a consistent dose of leisure as a strong corrective.

The excesses of Christian workers mentioned by Henrichsen are not simply the result of believing that they "contribute" to God's work. The same problems arise when Christians view their "participation" without proper regard for God's purpose. Leisure does have value but only as priorities and responsibilities involving both work and leisure are properly set.

## D. Leisure Is Not Related to Finances

The author develops a strong case for correcting several falsely held views relating finances and leisure. If leisure is valid, as has been established, then it is valid for all of God's people, both poor and rich. The person who works hard in order to have time for leisure later in life is out of balance in the use of his time. Just as waiting for the "right time" to serve God is wrong, so also is waiting for the right time for leisure. Proper stewardship is again the crux of the issue.

## VI. CONCLUSION

Despite some disagreements on points of emphasis and detail, Henrichsen has done a fine job in pointing out some of the critical issues facing the Christian in understanding work and leisure. The Bible certainly speaks clearly enough on these topics to develop general principles and practices for the believer. The task of properly integrating these principles into the everyday life of the believer is critical if our faith is to be a "life to be lived" rather than simply a religion. As Dietrich Bonhoeffer wrote:

> I wonder whether it is possible (it almost seems so today) to regain the idea of the Church as providing an understanding of the area of freedom (art, education, friendship, play) so that Kierkegaard's "aesthetic existence" would not be banished from the Church's sphere, but would be reestablished within it? I really think that is so, and it would mean that we should recover a link with the Middle Ages. Who is there, for instance, in our times, who can devote himself with an easy mind to music, friendship, games, or happiness? Surely not the "ethical" man, but only the Christian (January 23, 1944, *Letters and Papers from Prison*).

His insight continues to inform the Christian community in its struggle to seek a biblical understanding of work and leisure.

## ENDNOTES

[1]James Nichols, *Primer for Protestants* (New York: Association, 1947), p. 138.
[2]Henlee H. Barnette, *Introducing Christian Ethics* (Nashville: Broadman, 1961), p. 157.
[3]Robert K. Johnston, *The Christian at Play* (Grand Rapids: Eerdmans, 1983), p. 35.

## PRINCIPAL RESOURCES

*Business Life*. Minneapolis, Minn. Various issues.

Douglas, J. D., ed. *The New Bible Dictionary*. Grand Rapids: Eerdmans, 1962.

*Focus on the Family*. Magazine of Dr. James Dobson's ministry.

Hodge, Charles. *Systematic Theology*. Vol. 3. Grand Rapids: Eerdmans, 1952.

Kittel, Gerhard, et al., eds. *Theological Dictionary of the New Testament*. 10 vols. Grand Rapids: Eerdmans, 1964–76.

Longenecker, Richard N., and Tenney, Merrill C., eds. *New Dimensions in New Testament Study*. Grand Rapids: Zondervan, 1974.

Murray, John. *Principles of Conduct*. Grand Rapids: Eerdmans, 1957.

Schaeffer, Francis. *How Should We Then Live?* Old Tappan, N.J.: Revell, 1976.

Sproul, R. C. *Ethics and the Christian*. Wheaton, Ill.: Tyndale House, 1983.
Vine, M. E. *An Expository Dictionary of New Testament Words*. Old Tappan, N.J.: Revell, 1966.

# WEALTH AND POVERTY

## John M. Perkins

The Scriptures have very few good things to say about the rich. As I research I find that the best thing Jesus says to the rich is that they should help the poor. All the Scriptures below can be summed up by declaring that our attitude to the poor and needy is what authenticates our faith. Our actions toward the disadvantaged in society show whether or not we are real in our relationship with Christ.

James 2:1 says, "My brethren, have not the faith of our Lord Jesus Christ, the Lord of glory, with respect of persons" (KJV). James is asking the question, "Do you have the faith of our Lord Jesus Christ and show respect to all people?" James goes on to say,

> For if there come unto your assembly a man with a gold ring, in goodly apparel, and there come in also a poor man in vile raiment; and ye have respect to him that weareth the gay clothing, and say unto him, Sit thou here in a good place; and say to the poor, Stand thou there, or sit here under my footstool: Are ye not then partial in yourselves, and are become judges of evil thoughts? Hearken, my beloved brethren, Hath not God chosen the poor of this world rich in faith, and heirs of the kingdom which he hath promised to them that love him? But ye have despised the poor. Do not rich men oppress you, and draw you before the judgment seats? Do not they blaspheme that worthy name by which ye are called? If ye fulfil the royal law according to the Scripture, Thou shalt love thy neighbour as thyself, ye do well: but if ye have respect to persons, ye commit sin, and are convinced of the law as transgressors (KJV).

In Luke 16:19 we read of Lazarus and the rich man:

There was a certain rich man, which was clothed in purple and fine linen, and fared sumptuously every day: And there was a certain beggar named Lazarus, which was laid at his gate full of sores, and desiring to be fed with the crumbs which fell from the rich man's table: moreover the dogs came and licked his sores. And it came to pass, that the beggar died and was carried by the angels into Abraham's bosom: the rich man also died, and was buried; and in hell he lifted up his eyes, being in torments and seeth Abraham afar off, and Lazarus in his bosom. And he cried and said, Father Abraham, have mercy on me, and send Lazarus, that he may dip the tip of his finger in water, and cool my tongue; for I am tormented in this flame. But Abraham said, Son, remember that thou in thy lifetime receivedst thy good things, and likewise Lazarus evil things: but now he is comforted, and thou art tormented. And beside all this, between us and you there is a great gulf fixed: so that they which would pass from hence to you cannot; neither can they pass to us, that would come from thence. Then he said, I pray thee therefore, father, that thou wouldst send him to my father's house: For I have five brethren; that he may testify unto them, lest they also come into this place of torment. Abraham saith unto him, They have Moses and the prophets; let them hear them. And he said, Nay, father Abraham: but if one went unto them from the dead, they will repent. And he said unto him, If they hear not Moses and the prophets, neither will they be persuaded though one rose from the dead (KJV).

Matthew 11:2–6 tells of Jesus' purpose to come and help the disadvantaged:

Now when John had heard in the prison the works of Christ, he sent two of his disciples, and said unto him, Art thou he that should come, or do we look for another? Jesus answered and said unto them, Go and shew John again those things which ye do hear and see: the blind receive their sight, and the lame walk, the lepers are cleansed, and the deaf hear, the dead are raised up, and the poor have the gospel preached to them. And blessed is he, whosoever shall not be offended in me (KJV).

Mark 10:17–22 tells of the rich young ruler:

And when he was gone forth into the way, there came one running, and kneeled to him, and asked him, Good Master, what shall I do that I may inherit eternal life? And Jesus said unto him, Why callest thou me good? there is none good but one, that is, God. Thou knowest the commandments, Do not commit adultery, Do not kill, Do not steal, Do not bear false witness, Defraud not. Honour thy father and mother. And he answered and said unto him, Master, all these have I observed from my youth. Then Jesus beholding him loved him, and said unto him, One thing thou lackest: go thy way, sell whatsoever thou hast, and give to the poor, and thou shalt have treasure in heaven: and come, take up the cross, and follow me. And he was sad at that saying, and went away grieved: for he had great possessions (KJV).

In Jeremiah 22:16, Jeremiah is speaking to Jehoakim and says,

He judged the cause of the poor and needy; then it was well with him: was not this to know me? saith the LORD (KJV).

In Micah 6:6, the prophet asks:

With what shall I come before the LORD, and bow myself before the high God? shall I come before him with burnt offerings, with calves of a year old? Will the LORD be pleased with thousands of rams, with ten thousands of rivers of oil? shall I give my firstborn for my transgression, the fruit of my body for the sin of my soul? He hath shewed thee, O man, what is good: and what doth the LORD require of thee, but to do justly, and to love mercy, and to walk humbly with thy God? (KJV).

Any ardent reader of Scriptures would come to the conclusion that God is concerned about the poor and that he has a very positive attitude toward the poor. It can also be seen that God has a very loving attitude toward the rich, however, he is constantly saying to them that they should help the poor.

Why would this God of creation be so concerned about the poor? I believe it comes from God's heart of righteousness and justice. God is the Creator, and he has provided these resources for the good of all men. It seems that God's highest call upon man is to love your neighbor as you love yourself.

A theme that is apparent to me throughout the Scriptures is how difficult it is for the rich to love their neighbors. It is an attitude of justice. I believe that justice is always an economic issue. It basically has to do with our understanding of who owns what. First, we must understand that God is the owner of the universe. The revelation that we have from God himself is that he is the God of creation, the God of the heavens and the earth. He is a God of love, righteousness, and justice. He wants all men to be recipients in the loving distribution of his provisions. He has made mankind into stewards or distributors of his resources.

God, then, has created the earth and everything that is a part of life. He now wants man to subdue the earth, turning his knowledge into technology, and then to use the products of his resources for the good of all humanity. Injustice, then, is to deprive a man from open access or full participation in God's creation. I define justice as: "Helping mankind to come to know this great God of provision, love, and creation. Then to help them to be able to become workers together with God, to scratch into God's earth to enjoy the fruit of their labor, and then to raise their hands in praise to God."

God's call upon man is for man to use his own free will to use these resources for the highest good. Injustice then is to deprive man of that opportunity.

The process begins by understanding God's total love for the whole of humanity. Christ's death on the cross is the ultimate proof of God's love. The Bible says, "For God so loved the world, that he gave his only begotten Son, that whosoever believeth in him should not perish, but have everlasting life" (John 3:16 KJV), and "Greater love hath no man than this, that a man lay down his life for his friends" (15:13 KJV). Jesus' life on this earth was a life of showing that he had been loved by the Father. It was his love that he had received from the Father that he was sharing with the world. His encouragement to his disciples was, "I have loved you, the Father has loved me, and I want you to continue in this sharing of love with your fellow man."

To practice justice is to distribute God's resources in a way that exemplifies God's love. People who have great wealth often do not know how to use their wealth in a very creative way. Often in America we develop such an imperialistic attitude in our own minds that we have lost our sense of stewardship in the world. The American people might be the greatest benevolent and sharing people in the world, yet we still need to learn how to help the poor. That is the big question. Maybe we have already patronized the poor to such an extent that this benevolent system itself is causing further dehumanization of the poor.

The rich need to take the responsibility of finding ways to share their resources in a way that affirms the dignity of the poor and creates motivation and incentive for people to participate fully with their hands in God's creation. This might be why the apostle Paul said to the disciples as they go out, "To teach them to work with their own hands so that they may be able to give to people in need."

As I travel around the country, people ask me lots of questions about wealth and poverty. The big question raised sometimes is concerning Jesus' statement about "The poor we will have with us always." I believe that the poor will indeed be with us always as an opportunity for us to understand our own stewardship as God's people.

Another question often asked is whether or not God calls us to be poor or whether he calls us to be rich. It seems that God's call upon us is to be obedient. I think we then follow that obedience wherever it leads. Abraham, being the father of our faith, heard the voice of God and responded to it. He understood God's will through him, which was to build his nation. The nation would not be an end; it would become a blessing to all other nations. So through Abraham, all the families of the earth would be blessed. As Abraham moved out with an attempt to live in obedience to God, the by-product of that obedience was wealth and success.

There is a passage where God speaks of Abraham and says, "I know that Abraham will do right." Not only will Abraham do right, but he will raise up his offspring to do right. God understood Abraham's desire to be a good steward of God's resources, and it was on that basis that God made Abraham a success in life.

I believe that we can find many examples in the Scripture of people whom God saw as good stewards. We can take this argument to Job.

> There was a man in the land of Uz, whose name was Job; and that man was blameless and upright, one who feared God, and turned away from evil. There were born to him seven sons and three daughters. He had seven thousand sheep, three thousand camels, five hundred yoke of oxen, and five hundred she-asses, and very many servants; so that this man was the greatest of all the people of the east (1:1-3 RSV).

What we have here is a key to understanding the Book of Job. Can God trust Job with all of his resources to be a good steward? Was Job serving God to reap the glamorous benefits, or was he serving God out of his love and obedience to God?

As we read on, Job is stripped of all his wealth, family, and health. Throughout all of this Job maintained all of his integrity before God. Here is an example of a rich man who maintained his integrity toward God. In the end we see that because of Job's heart his wealth was restored fully. We can understand Job's heart in his statement, "Though he slay me, yet will I trust him" (15:15).

Job makes a strong testimony to justify himself because of his concern for the poor. In 29:12 he declares to his friends,

> Because I delivered the poor who cried,
>     and the fatherless who had none to help him.
> The blessing of him who was about to perish came upon me,
>     and I caused the widow's heart to sing for joy.
> I put on righteousness, and it clothed me;
>     my justice was like a robe and a turban.
> I was eyes to the blind,
>     and feet to the lame.
> I was a father to the poor,
>     and I searched out the cause of him whom I did not know
>     (RSV).

It seems to me that the greatest claim that the rich can make upon God is in their attitude. This may be why God said that it is harder for a rich man to enter into the kingdom of heaven than it is for a camel to get through the eye of a needle. But God then turns around and says what is impossible with man is possible with God.

Zacchaeus was a rich tax collector. Jesus visited Zacchaeus, and before Jesus left, Zacchaeus was declaring "Half of my goods I give to the poor, and if I have defrauded anyone, I restore it by four times" (Luke 19:8). Again I say, the evidence of our Christian faith is our attitude toward the poor.

James says that "true religion, undefiled before God the Father is this, to visit the fatherless and the widows in their affliction and to keep one's self unspotted before the world" (James 1:27). The underlying theme of Jesus' life was to share that one's attitude toward the poor holds the secret to authentic faith. I do not know whether or not Jesus calls upon everyone to sell all that he has as he did the rich young ruler. The rich young ruler asked a particular question: How can he enjoy the kingdom of God? Jesus showed him how he could enjoy the kingdom of God without possessions, through his relationship with him. Zacchaeus made a disinvestment of some of his resources, but this does not seem to be the requirement of all rich people who come to Jesus. I think that it all has to do with their attitude toward the poor in relation to their possessions. Our creative sharing is our identity as God's people.

The great pushing of Jesus to his own disciples was to get them to acknowledge him as Messiah and Lord. At Caesarea Philippi when Jesus asked his disciples, "Who do men say that I am?" Simon Peter answered saying, "You are the Christ, the Son of the living God." Jesus then said, "Upon this statement I will build my church and the gates of hell will not prevail against it" (Matthew 16:13–18). The fact that we believe that Jesus Christ is the Son of God is the criteria for salvation.

When the disciples came and asked, "Are you the Messiah or look we for another?" (Matthew 11:3). The Bible says that Jesus was grieved and that he went into the streets and began to heal the sick, raise the dead, and give sight to the blind. And he said, "Go back and tell what you have seen, the poor have the Good News preached to them" (Matthew 11:4).

I cannot stress enough that it is our attitude toward the poor that is the evidence of the Christian faith. It seems as though God has special spiritual lessons for those who follow him in obedience. God rather makes them his servants in society. If we will serve him and those in need, he will provide for us. Matthew 25:35–40 is the final judgment when Jesus says,

> "For I was hungry and you gave me food, I was thirsty and you gave me drink, I was a stranger and you welcomed me, I was naked and you clothed me, I was sick and you visited me, I was in prison and you came to me." Then the righteous will answer him, "Lord, when did we see thee hungry and feed thee, or thirsty and give thee drink? And when did we see thee a stranger and welcome thee, or naked and clothe thee? And when did we see thee sick or in prison and visit thee?" And the

King will answer them, "Truly I say to you, as you did it to one
of the least of these my brethren, you did it to me" (RSV).

Again, it seems like it is our attitude toward the little people,
the poor in society, that determines our attitude toward God.
We need to close by asking the questions, "What is my
attitude? Who are the poor? And how do we help the poor?" I
think that we can conclude by saying that we help the poor when
we feed, clothe, and do those things that affirm their dignity. We
must let others know that they have been created in God's image,
by affirming them as we approach them.

My approach to helping the poor can be summed up in "the
three Rs of development": *relocation, reconciliation* and *redistribution.* I am convinced that participating in these three Rs is a way
that affirms the dignity of my brothers and sisters in Christ.

The first R is *relocation.* In order to minister effectively to the
poor, Christians need to become accessible to the community of
need as part of a local body of believers. By living as neighbors
with the poor, the needs of the neighborhood become one's own
needs. Shared needs and friendships become a bridge for
communicating the good news of Jesus Christ and working
together for better conditions in the community.

The second R is *reconciliation.* The love and forgiveness of the
gospel reconciles us to God. The gospel also calls for reconciliation
with our neighbors. The local church is to be a force and a forum
for reconciliation across all racial, cultural, social, and economic
barriers.

The third R is *Redistribution.* Christ calls us to share with those
in need. This means redistribution of more than our goods. It
means a sharing of our skills, technology, and educational
resources in a way that empowers people to break out of the cycle
of poverty and become able to meet their own needs.

# A Response to
# Wealth and Poverty

## Ted W. Engstrom

It is not difficult for me to express my heartfelt appreciation for both the work and person of my friend, Dr. John M. Perkins. I have known John Perkins for almost two decades of faithful service to his Lord. In addition, he has faithfully served as a valued contributor to the board of World Vision for the past seven or eight years.

I have the deepest respect for the effective ministry he has had of making the poor productive and helping to restore their dignity. It is a privilege for me to respond to a paper by a man who is a seasoned practitioner in ministry among the poor.

## I. STRENGTHS OF THE PAPER

There are several strong points taken in John's paper. I would like to highlight just a few.

1. His insistence that *faith in Christ should have a link to compassion to the poor.* There is indisputable evidence in the Scripture that Jesus felt that faith in him naturally, or at least eventually, led to concern and involvement with the unmet needs of the poor.

It is not inconsequential that the vast majority of the evangelized people in our world today are also among the poverty-stricken poor. It is no longer possible for a Christian to ignore this reality and to miss the plain fact that God is thrusting us who name his name into intensive involvement with the poor as we obey his command to go to every nation with the gospel.

Although this point merits strong emphasis, there are some things mentioned about it in the paper with which I disagree, which I will briefly cover in a later section.

2. *God is very concerned about the poor.* This is part of the Good News to the poor! They have not been abandoned nor forgotten nor cursed by their Creator. Rather the poor are given special attention throughout the Scriptures.

Although God is not a respecter of persons, nor does he favor partiality to the poor nor deference to the wealthy in matters of justice (Lev. 19:15), it is unmistakable that God has his eye on the poor and cares very deeply for their needs. His anger is particularly riled toward those who abuse or even ignore the poor.

This is not to say that the poor have not sinned or that they are not in need of a personal Savior. But Dr. Perkins's reminder to us from the scriptural passages which he has shared reveal to us much of the tender and watchful concern of God toward the poor.

3. *God owns the earth; we are stewards.* Jesus gave to us several parables to remind us of this important reality. The parable of the wicked tenants is one found in Matthew 21. He concludes the parable with the sobering question, "When therefore the *owner* of the vineyard comes, what will he do to those *tenants*?" (v. 40 RSV, italics mine). Here we are reminded that we are merely tenants in a world whose property and goods rightfully belong to the Owner who entrusted them to us for a short while.

John challenges us to "become workers together with God . . . to use his resources for the highest good." John moves on from this point to the natural conclusion that proper stewardship leads to proper economics and the healthy handling of wealth for the benefit of others.

4. *Americans need to learn how to help the poor without dehumanizing them.* Here John confronts us with his important insight that "people who have great wealth often do not know how to use their wealth in a creative way." It is rather ironic that the wealthiest nation in the world is also one of the world's most generous nations, yet in many ways its wealth has been misused to create a benevolent system which so often dehumanizes the poor.

John includes the rich in the quest for effective ways of helping the poor. He asks that the rich take the responsibility of finding ways to share their resources in a way that *affirms the dignity of the poor* and *creates incentive* and motivation for people to participate fully with their hands in God's creation.

5. *Our primary call is to be obedient, not rich or poor.* This is John's very wise response when asked by audiences, "Does God call us to be poor or rich?" Here John is teaching us that there is no neat little formula which can help us solve the dilemma of justifying our individual wealth compared with the graphic descriptions of miserable poverty, both domestically and in other nations.

We are reminded of the importance of an intimate walk with the Lord and of learning to obey the promptings of his Holy Spirit that affect every realm of our life—including our wealth.

I can still recall with deep soul searching my signing of the Lausanne Covenant having to do with an altered lifestyle. The Lord has brought this to my mind on numerous occasions, and I am reminded of the personal and practical application which following Christ makes on my lifestyle choices.

## II. AREAS OF POSSIBLE DISAGREEMENT

1. "Justice is *always* an economic issue." I do not believe that strictly speaking it is accurate to say that justice always has to do with producing and distributing income and wealth (economics).

It seems to me that some injustices are not primarily economic but are social or political injustices. For example, the injustices of prejudice toward ethnic people who are Jewish, or some other cultural distinctive, is more a social injustice than an economic one. There are economic consequences to the unfair treatment unjustly given, but the realm of economics does not appear to be the dominant motivation in all issues of justice.

In both personal and societal relationships, such as in a marriage or in stereotyping various segments of society, the question of income and wealth does not seem to be the main issue in all cases of reconciling injustice and seeking justice. I believe that generally John's point is well taken that injustice has to do with depriving a person from open access or full participation in God's creation and in enjoying the fruit of his labor. I just become nervous when one single issue, in this case economics, is identified as the sole contributor in problems or solutions of justice.

2. "Our attitude toward the poor is *the* evidence of Christian faith." As mentioned earlier, it is clear that we cannot contest that our attitude toward the poor is a crucial "fruit" of faith in Christ.

I am fearful that a certain smugness and pride can enter in, however, even among those sacrificing for the poor if we make *the* evidence of Christian faith this important attitude. This makes our attitude toward the poor a "litmus test" or "supreme fruit" of genuine faith in Christ. I disagree with this conclusion.

From Jesus' statement about the *Great Commandment*, we must be clear that loving God with our whole being is the primary call and highest goal of the Christian. We must guard against any substitutions to this *highest call to worship and love God*, and give him our undivided loyalty, devotion, and adoration. We know that what follows this highest call is to love our neighbor as ourself; and certainly love for the poor is part of that overall love for others that is the fruit of genuine faith in Christ.

As much as we need to increase our involvement and as much as we need to identify more wholeheartedly with the poor, I do not believe that we should claim that the evidence of faith in

Christ is that identity and proper attitude toward them. For one thing, we can often burn ourselves out in service to others, including the poor, if we believe this; and we reserve no quality strength or energy for *our first love* and adoration: the Lord Jesus Christ.

## III. AREAS NOT MENTIONED IN THE PAPER

1. Let me suggest the relationship of political power to wealth and poverty. Especially in a democratic society a discussion of wealth and poverty at some point leads to consideration of addressing injustices and accomplishing goals to help the poor through the use of political power. Perhaps Dr. Perkins is so well acquainted with the limitations of political power in developing the poor that he purposely chose to deemphasize it. However, I believe that it is still worth mentioning that in American society we have attained a certain equilibrium in economic life and in the relationship between wealth and poverty by setting organized power against organized power. And sometimes the more broadly based political power available in our land has been useful in redressing disproportions and imbalances in economic society.

The thrust of John's paper concerns itself with challenging and motivating those who seek to follow Christ to begin or continue to be closely identified with the poor. But perhaps the paper would be strengthened by John explaining how believers committed to helping the poor can more effectively utilize American political power as checks and balances against injustice.

What is heartening in John's paper is the utter lack of bitterness or resentment. Anyone who knows John's pilgrimage as a Christian and as a man who has suffered terrible injustice and prejudice, knows that he is a living testimony of one who has not been overcome by evil but rather has overcome evil with good. In his struggle for justice he has not succumbed to the divisive notion that it is time for a new group or race to be "top dog" in this nation. Rather he is advocating that there be no "dog-fight" at all and that there be mutual respect and mutual responsibility among all races and peoples.

2. *Further elaboration could be given to the point that people of great wealth do not know how to use their wealth in creative ways.* Many sincere people in this nation would welcome some practical suggestions in this area. Although suggestions for voluntary redistribution of wealth, and the importance of simplifying one's lifestyle, are helpful, the greatest impact for helping the poor seems to be in creatively using wealth to make the poor more productive and self-sufficient.

The old adage applies here: "If you give a man a fish, he will eat for a day; if you teach a man to fish, he will eat for a lifetime."

Ultimately it is much better to create something the poor can use long term.

I believe that John would agree that the main growth in productivity has to come out of the resources of the poor. *Aid* can be a catalyst which releases local energies, but done improperly it can (and certainly will) destroy the *incentive* of the poor to improve their life and livelihood.

Also, aid can tend to flow toward only the *problems* among the poor rather than also flowing toward the *opportunities* among them. But there is little development potential in focusing only on problems. The best this can do is to possibly prevent collapse. But unless a vision for creatively using wealth for opportunities occurs, we will not help build the *new* changes that are needed.

Let me share an example that I have read in a book by Peter Drucker entitled *The Age of Discontinuity:*

> . . . In one of our worst ghettos in Oakland, California, there is a small group who first obtains definite jobs. It obtains a contract to service electric typewriters at the university or the cars of the telephone company. Then it goes out and trains unemployable and unemployed young men for those already existing jobs. This way it can both guarantee a job and demand high performance standards.

This seems to me to be an example of using wealth, information, and know-how in a creative way to help the poor. I would like to know of several more examples of how people are using wealth to greater opportunities, a modern-day example of the parable of the talents.

3. *Some reflection on the debate between capitalism and communism.* A discussion of wealth and poverty often leads to comments on the debate between these two major economic systems in the world. Both systems ostensibly address questions concerning wealth and poverty, adopting rather opposite views and methodologies to achieve their ends.

Perhaps John has some convictions about these two systems that relate to helping the poor. Also, he may have some views on how a capitalist system provides opportunities (and perhaps hinders in some cases) to empower the poor, and enables them to break out of the cycle of poverty and to meet their own needs.

Of course, the remarkable thing about John's ministry is that he not only has definite views on this matter but that he is a practitioner and entrepreneur who makes things happen among the poor. He is not a "sour grapes" bystander, complaining about the system; he is "out in the arena" rescuing people and improving their circumstances.

# IV. CONCLUSION

I want to conclude by again saying that it is a privilege to know John Perkins and to be associated with his ministry for these years. Any critique I have concerning his paper on "Wealth and Poverty" is simply in the interest of slight improvements on a topic to which John has devoted the major portion of his adult life. I highly respect and salute his practical common sense and vast experience in ministering to the poor and needy of our land in the name of our Lord Jesus Christ.

# A Response to
# Wealth and Poverty

## Jay Alan Sekulow

In his paper, "Wealth and Poverty," Dr. Perkins has set forth an accurate interpretation of the biblical commands relating to the obligations of the wealthy to the poor and less fortunate. I am in complete accord with many of the major aspects of the paper. The cry of the poor for social reform has been heard around the world far too long. The time has come for the issues to be addressed and actions taken in light of the biblical mandates. Perhaps Jesus' own words recorded in Matthew 25:35–40 represent the most powerful statement which establishes the responsibility of the wealthy to the poor:

> "For I was hungry and you gave me something to eat, I was thirsty and you gave me something to drink, I was a stranger and you invited me in, I needed clothes and you clothed me, I was sick and you looked after me, I was in prison and you came to visit me."
>
> "Then the righteous will answer him, 'Lord, when did we see you hungry and feed you, or thirsty and give you something to drink? When did we see you a stranger and invite you in, or needing clothes and clothe you? When did we see you sick or in prison and go to visit you?'
>
> "The King will reply, 'I tell you the truth, whatever you did for one of the least of these brothers of mine, you did for me.' "

Yet, as Dr. William D. Taylor[1] states in his essay "The Cry for Justice and Liberation," "No human social justice and liberation will solve the fundamental spiritual separation between God and man." The separation can only be bridged by faith in Jesus Christ. As the apostle Paul said in Romans 3:21–25:

> But now a righteousness from God, apart from the law, has been made known, to which the Law and the Prophets testify.

This righteousness from God comes through faith in Jesus Christ to all who believe. There is no difference, for all have sinned and fall short of the glory of God, and are justified freely by his grace through the redemption that came by Christ Jesus. God presented him as a sacrifice of atonement, through faith in his blood. He did this to demonstrate his justice, because in the forebearance he had left the sins committed beforehand unpunished—he did it to demonstrate his justice at the present time, so as to be just and the one who justifies those who have faith in Jesus.

Truly, justice will reign supreme in heaven. As we explore the obligation of the wealthy toward the poor, it is important to keep the words of the apostle Paul and Dr. Taylor in mind. Our precepts concerning helping the poor and less fortunate are derived in large part from the themes contained throughout the Scriptures. Yet no matter how much assistance any individual or group provides to the poor, nothing can serve as a substitute for the saving power and grace found in our Lord Jesus Christ.

As Dr. Perkins has established, a prevalent theme carried throughout the Scriptures concerns man's required obedience to God. Undoubtedly, within the context of obedience to God, the obligations of the wealthy to the poor are firmly established. "The righteous care about justice for the poor, but the wicked have no such concern" (Prov. 29:7).

Fulfillment of our obedience to God in this realm encompasses fairness, compassion, love, and mercy to the poor. The sharing of financial resources; skills; and, most importantly, the sharing of God's saving grace all serve as evidence of being obedient to God. Yet within this context of being obedient to God, the Scriptures also tell us that we all must learn to serve God in the situation he has put us in, be it rich or poor.

In 1 Corinthians 7:20–24 the apostle Paul confirms this biblical truth:

Each one should remain in the situation which he was in when God called him. Were you a slave when you were called? Don't let it trouble you—although if you can gain your freedom, do so. For he who was a slave when he was called by the Lord is the Lord's freedman; similarly, he who was a free man when he was called is Christ's slave. You were bought at a price; do not become slaves of men. Brothers, each man, as responsible to God, should remain in the situation God called him to.

If we are able to improve our circumstances in this lifetime, that is fine. However, as individuals we must learn contentment at every stage we find ourselves in. Rather than being overly concerned with our particular station in life, we need to concentrate our efforts on being obedient to God. Admittedly, in order to be truly obedient to God, the wealthy must be cautious of greed, but the poor must not become more preoccupied with what they do not have and thereby bring about envy and covetousness.

In order to understand the obligations of the wealthy to the poor, it is important to study the way in which God deals with the wealthy throughout the Scriptures. God does show a very loving attitude toward them. However, Dr. Perkins's premise that the Scriptures have very few good things to say about the wealthy needs to be placed in a proper context. Jesus did say it is harder for a rich man to enter the kingdom of heaven than it is for a camel to get through the eye of a needle. Yet a survey of the Scriptures points out that the patriarchs, as well as Job, Nicodemus, and Joseph of Arimathea—all wealthy men—were used by God in a powerful way in order to advance his kingdom. Furthermore, as a blessing to obedience, God promised Israel prosperity: "The LORD will grant you abundant prosperity—in the fruit of your womb, the young of your livestock and the crops of your ground—in the land he swore to your forefathers to give you" (Deut. 28:11).

However, Israel was to be cursed if the people did not obey God. Thus I cannot overemphasize the need for both the rich and the poor to be obedient to God, regardless of their circumstances.

With regard to the wealthy, what the prophets and Jesus rebuke is riches being placed before God. As the apostle Paul said in 1 Timothy 6:10: "For the love of money is a root of all kinds of evil. Some people, eager for money, have wandered from the faith and pierced themselves with many griefs."

Thus in a true biblical context, the problem of the wealthy can be that unbelief and unrighteousness, mixed with the love of money, cause disobedience to God. In 1 Timothy 6:10 it is not the *possession* of money that causes the problem, but rather the *love* of money.

Another excellent illustration of the potential problem the wealthy have regarding the love of money is found in Jesus' parable of the rich fool as recorded in Luke 12:16–21:

> "The ground of a certain rich man produced a good crop. He thought to himself, 'What shall I do? I have no place to store my crops.'
>
> "Then he said, 'This is what I'll do. I will tear down my barns and build bigger ones, and there I will store all my grain and my goods. And I'll say to myself, "You have plenty of good things laid up for many years. Take life easy; eat, drink and be merry.'"
>
> "But God said to him, 'You fool! This very night your life will be demanded from you. Then who will get what you have prepared for yourself?'
>
> "This is how it will be with anyone who stores up things for himself but is not rich toward God.'"

It is interesting to note what made the rich man a fool. It was
not wealth that made him a fool; rather it was wealth placed
before God. Similarly, the Scriptures do emphasize that riches
have a tendency to corrupt. But this corruption is not because of
wealth per se; it is man's sinful nature which allows riches rather
than the Redeemer to be the focal point. Yet I also can imagine a
parable which might be called the parable of the poor fool. In fact,
I am confident there are probably as many poor fools as rich fools.
The parable of the poor fool goes something like this:

> There was a poor man who had met the rich fool. The poor man
> spent his whole life craving and desiring the wealth of the rich
> fool. Rather than being productive for himself and society, he
> spent his days imagining how happy he would be if he had the
> riches of the rich fool. He did not like the rich fool, not because
> of the rich fool's failure to give to God, but rather because the
> rich fool did not give anything to the poor man. The rich fool
> died, and the poor man went to his funeral dreaming that he
> would one day be in the place of the rich fool, with abundant
> wealth. But you see, the poor man was really a poor fool. He
> was a poor fool because the powers of hell had already captured
> one fool that day. Both the rich man and the poor man were
> fools when they acted unrighteously toward God.

The temptation for some is to be like Tevye in *Fiddler on the
Roof*, who, if he were rich as portrayed in the song "If I Were a
Rich Man," would buy a new house, eat great food, and sit in the
prestigious place in the synagogue. Yet Tevya did not express any
concern with regard to the poor. In a sad way Tevya was much
like the poor fool who, if he received wealth, would become the
rich fool. Thus the wealthy must not be preoccupied with wanting
more for the sake of pleasing themselves.

There is little question that the possession of wealth is a large
responsibility and is filled with temptations, but it is not intrinsically evil. With the large responsibility of wealth comes the
freedom to assist others not as fortunate as themselves, which
surely will be pleasing to God. As G. K. Chesterton wrote in his
book *All Things Considered*, "The honest poor can sometimes forget
poverty—the honest rich can never forget it."

While the biblical mandate to render assistance to the poor is
firmly established, it is important to understand the motivations
for our actions in light of our responsibilities. It is important not to
act to glorify ourselves. Jesus said in Matthew 6:1–4:

> "Be careful not to do your 'acts of righteousness' before men,
> to be seen by them. If you do, you will have no reward from
> your Father in heaven.
>
> "So when you give to the needy, do not announce it with
> trumpets, as the hypocrites do in the synagogues and on the
> streets, to be honored by men. I tell you the truth, they have

received their reward in full. But when you give to the needy, do not let your left hand know what your right hand is doing, so that your giving may be in secret. Then your Father, who sees what is done in secret, will reward you."

Our motivation for helping the poor must be out of love, compassion, and most importantly, reverence and obedience to God. In his essay Dr. Taylor points out that man lives by two breads—the primary Word of God bread, and the material, nourishing bread necessary for human sustenance. We must be cautious of the dangers of promoting social justice and thereby concealing the true meaning of the gospel. To bring about more equality and justice, as well as improving the overall living conditions of oppressed people, without giving those people a basis for forgiveness, love, peace, and everlasting life would not improve the oppressed people's conditions at all. Eternally, they will still be caught in the grips of sin and hell. While a significant aspect of Jesus' ministry was helping the poor and afflicted, it is the preaching of the Word of God to all people—wealthy and poor—which must take biblical priority to the establishment of a proper and just social program.

Providing assistance for the poor and afflicted is an expression of our Christian commitment, yet the method by which we provide assistance is also of utmost importance. Dr. Perkins correctly states that the poor will always be with us. Yet Jesus did not say there *should* be economically poor people; rather there always *would* be. Since the poor find themselves in this predicament, we can develop a clear understanding of our stewardship responsibilities. The poor must come to the realization that there is dignity in their calling, just as the wealthy need to seek means by which to dignify the poor in giving help. As Tevye from *Fiddler on the Roof* said, "It's no shame to be poor, but it's no great honor either. . . ." We must seek to honor the poor, not shame them.

In rendering assistance it is important not to be patronizing. If we are at all concerned about the dignity of the poor, then our desire to help must go past providing food and clothing. If we desire real change for the less fortunate, education, job training, and providing work opportunities may very well be as important as providing food and clothing. We must seek to encourage the poor to productivity and thereby rebuke laziness. The Scriptures clearly state in Proverbs 10:4: "Lazy hands make a man poor, but diligent hands bring wealth."

I am certainly not taking the position that all poor people are lazy, any more than I would say that all wealthy people are unrighteous. Rather it is our responsibility to help the poor and less fortunate to reach for realistically obtainable goals in order to improve their position.

Although sharing our resources with those less fortunate is important, the concept of redistribution, as stated by Dr. Perkins, might well be overlooking a very real human element. Granted, as has been true throughout the ages, there is an unequal distribution of wealth and much injustice in the world. Yet the redistribution of wealth and resources, in and of itself, will not negate these injustices. I am quite confident that, even if the world's riches were equally divided among all people, there would still be rampant unfairness. Often, revolutionary movements focus on redistribution, yet rarely does this action result in increased righteousness. As Dr. Emilio Nunez[2] states, "There will always be poor people because of the evil of the human heart."

The bottom line of the economic and social injustice comes to rest with the issue of the sinful nature of man. In the final analysis it is the hearts of men and women which must be changed in order to achieve social justice, fairness, and equality for all people. Through obedience to God in faith in Jesus Christ, all people—the least and the wealthy—will find their rewards in the kingdom of heaven, not at all based on merit, but upon grace.

## ENDNOTES

[1] Dr. William D. Taylor was formerly an associate professor of Latin American Missions and Crosscultural Christian Education in the School of World Mission and Evangelism at Trinity Evangelical Divinity School and continues as a visiting professor of Mission at Trinity and as pastor of the Fellowship Church, Russellville, Arkansas.

[2] Dr. Emilio Nunez is a professor at Central American Theological Seminary in Guatemala.

# STEWARDSHIP OF THE ENVIRONMENT

## Carl F. H. Henry

The human role in respect to the environment is best seen in threefold biblical context. First, the creation account depicts the first human as fashioned in God's image and as designated God's deputy ruler over the cosmos and its creatures (Gen. 1:26, 28–29; Ps. 8:5–8). Second, Jesus teaches in parables about the wise steward (Luke 12:42ff.) and the unjust steward (Luke 16:1–14) of his master's things. Finally, numerous passages speak of the ultimate subjection of all things to the dominion of Christ (Heb. 2:8) who even now exercises divine lordship in a hidden way (Rom. 14:9) and will do so openly in the end time (Eph. 1:20f.; Col. 2:6, 10).

If Scripture makes anything crystal clear, it is that God the Creator is the human species' most permanent and universal environment. The most awesome aspect of mankind's stewardship therefore consists primarily in the relationship to the divine Creator of all and not simply to human or to cosmic nature. Human beings, despite their fallen condition and sullied image of God, have a continuing responsibility to learn what God thinks of himself and of human selves in their present state, and what our fixed duties are under God.

This reminder is doubly important in a day when moderns hurriedly reduce the theme of "stewardship of the environment" to cosmological concerns only, or even more restrictedly to creaturely concerns that focus on subhuman species of life. The human environment is dramatically personal, for under God humanity has crucially important duties to all mankind as well as to the Creator.

"Am I my brother's steward?" asked Cain (Gen. 4:9), and indeed he was. Genesis 9:6 stipulates capital punishment for the murder of a human being, since mankind even after the Fall retains remnants of the divine image. The Bible views all humans as God's stewards (cf. Jer. 22:3, 13); not even rulers of nations are excluded (cf. Rom. 13:6, "they are God's servants").

Humanity's own earthly existence is so intertwined with the organic and physical orders that human survival in this life is inconceivable in total separation from these. Human beings incorporate a part of nature in themselves so that human incursion of nature is not simply a matter of impacting on the exterior cosmos. To be sure, man in his totality, psychic and physical, belongs to the created universe. But man is not, contrary to some pagan religions, immersed in nature or a mystical participant in it. Still, nature is not, as man is, the image of God. Yet God nonetheless reveals himself ongoingly in nature (Ps. 19; Rom. 1), and the misuse of nature is a demeaning of that revelation. But the tendency to use the term environment only of what completely encloses one, or of that which lies outside, overlooks the fact that in some sense mankind is an aspect of the larger world of nature—that is, of created reality—even if his being involves a distinctive relationship to the divine image and his body is ideally the temple of the Holy Spirit.

But this important consideration in no way minimizes the critical issue of human responsibility touching the nonhuman cosmic environment. The modern world view encourages mankind to regard nature as something beneath man, and as distinct and inferior, since man is presumed to have accidentally evolved and emerged from nature. This readily encourages the human manipulation and exploitation of nature. For nature then exists simply for the sake of mankind. Humans are free to play God— and a quite irresponsible deity at that—in relation to it.

By contrast, nonbiblical religions of the ancient Near East tended to view nature itself as divine. Worship of the heavens, correlation of earth's seasons with fertility gods, and much else that Judeo-Christian theism demythologized, underlay the popular beliefs of the ancient world. One need not share Conrad Hyers's notion that the Genesis creation account is simply a symbolic negation of primitive polytheistic myths to share his conviction that it counters the idolatry of sun, moon and star gods, of sky gods and earth gods and water gods:

> Each day dismisses an additional cluster of deities, arranged in a cosmological and symmetrical order. On the fist day the gods of light and darkness are dismissed; on the second day, the gods of sky and sea. On the third day, earth gods and gods of vegetation; on the fourth day, sun, moon and star gods. The fifth and sixth days take away any associations with divinity from the animal kingdoms. And finally human existence, too, is emptied of any intrinsic divinity—while at the same time *all*

human beings . . . and not just pharaohs, kings and heroes, are granted a divine likeness. And in that divine likeness, all human beings are given the royal prerogatives of dominion over the earth, and of mediation between heaven and earth.[1]

Some recent expositions of the divine image have moved away from classical emphasis on the spiritual likeness (rational-moral capacities and volition) to a more corporal understanding. Gerhard von Rad locates the *imago* in man's entire historical bodily function as divine representative to enforce God's claim to dominion over the earth.[2] Some scholars contend (Bernhard Anderson, for example) that the Genesis depiction is a recension of Near Eastern religious myth. In contrast with the Egyptian reference of the *imago* to Pharaoh alone as the divine king, Genesis "democratizes" the *imago* by referring it not only to Adam but to Eve as well, and to all mankind as a social collective. But this view depends on quite vulnerable assumptions, such as that the Genesis narrative motif comes from Egyptian sources. The Old Testament represents Yahweh alone as divine King, and is reluctant to speak approvingly of any earthly divine king except in messianic terms. The Old Testament ban on visible images would exclude human beings as a corporeal image of Yahweh. If what we have in the creation story is simply a countermyth, moreover, it would in any case seem difficult indeed to attach any literal truth to man's endowment with the *imago Dei*.

Some critical commentators note that the divine command that man "subdue" (*rada*) the earth and have "dominion" (*kabash*) over its creaturely life accommodates the possibility of nonbenevolent rule, or Pharaoh-like dominion, since sometimes the former term means "to trample" and the latter term "to rape" (cf. Num. 24:19; 1 Kings 4:24; Neh. 9:28; Ps. 72:8). If critical scholars exclude moral and rational categories from the *imago*, no objection can in principle be mounted against thus placing the text in the service of an unbenevolent "trampler." The one-sided connection of the *imago* only with the dominion passage thus pays a high penalty for tendential exegesis.

Many contemporary scholars formulate ecological concerns in a way that minimizes nature's importance and exaggerates man's importance over both creaturely and inanimate existence. The crucial issue then becomes human survival. Given the economic preoccupation of the current generation, it should be no surprise that humans regard as dispensable all lower forms of life lacking an identifiable economic value or potential. Pollution or destruction of cosmic reality is seldom confronted except in the context of the future of humanity. The implication is not simply that the cosmos has less value than man, but rather that apart from man nature is valueless. Humanity itself imposes upon nature whatever values nature carries, if any.

Technocratic scientism has encouraged the notion that man is the mastermind of nature, and that technology is simply the means of controlling and remodeling it for man's benefit. In stark contrast to the African medicine man who claims to apply the healing power of nature for the recovery of man, the contemporary naturalist presumes to remake the earth to serve the whims of its human manipulator. A recent CBS network news program discussing the projected inclusion of an academician in a missile flight crew spoke of "teachers with a shot at space." Contemporary mankind has forfeited a sense of awe in the presence of earthly existence and life. We view ourselves, and especially the frontier scientists among us, as "the masters" of nature and the manipulators of life. After all, have we not advanced in less than a century from horses to space missiles?

Although pollution problems reach back into antiquity, environmental issues have become an especially critical concern during the second half of our century. The conviction that human neglect of environmental problems will jeopardize the natural resources that make possible mankind's own physical survival has stimulated a wide stream of literature.[3] What is new to our generation, as Rowland P. Moss observes, is a sense of urgency over addressing the issues, the enlarged role of political decision and public planning, and the evident need for a comprehensive ethical approach.[4]

The lengthening litany of ecological horrors—toxic pollutants, fertilizer and lead poisoning, radioactive miscarriage of nuclear plants, impending oil depletion—alongside estimates that the global population will double every fifteen years—led to massive protests. The 1970 Earth Day teach-in at the University of Illinois had echoes on 12,000 high school and college campuses, with many politicians scrambling to get aboard the movement. Typically, such protest involved speculative exaggerations. Julian Simon challenged future population estimates and called for an approach that would enlist human beings rather than limit their numbers, while projecting an equally debatable view that the earth could carry 30 billion people as readily as 3 billion.[5]

But on any reading an ecology crisis had dawned, and modern technology and population growth had accelerated its problems. While technology can produce highly effective responses to environmental problems, the problems which it addresses are often of its own making. Technology devours natural resources on a colossal scale, and its ever improving methodology is seldom without costly side effects. Yet the desire of the multiplying population for ever improved living standards simultaneously increases the demand for more efficient technologies. The modern mass media stimulate materialistic aspirations not only in developed but also in developing countries, although the media, to be sure, can also create an awareness of environmental issues and publicize possibilities of coping with them. Jacques-Yves Cousteau warned that disregard for an environmental code of conduct has no stopping place: "After the fish, the birds, the forests, the wolves and foxes and elephants and dolphins."[6] Others protested polluted streams, burning forests, poison air and acid rain, wanton killing of wildlife, strip mining the earth, coating the land with DDT, using our planet as a dumping ground for atomic waste, and turning outer space into a disposal site for missile junk.

Some theorists have blamed the Judeo-Christian ethic for the ecological crisis. They contend that the Old Testament's emphasis that man is the divinely appointed lord of nature encourages human exploitation of nature and a disregard of environmental concerns. Lynn White gave currency to this calumny in 1967.[7] White asserted that Christians hold that human beings are nature's rightful masters to manipulate nature as they wish, that as made in God's image they consider humans to be—like God—transcendent over nature, that their emphasis on historical progress encourages an exploitation of nature, that science and technology are a manifest extension of that commitment, and that these views—assertedly anchored in Scripture—have gifted the modern world with a legacy of environmental unconcern.

But it is not the biblical view,, as the present writer elsewhere emphasizes,[8] that "man alone matters to God." The human species is not the final cause of the universe. R. P. Moss shows that the biblical ethic is essentially conservation oriented.[9] Mankind at creation was given the vocation of keeping and dressing the Garden (Gen. 2:15). The conservation and preservation of nature are Christian imperatives. The modern humanist aspiration to control the cosmos and to establish a technological paradise in which man exercises transcendent sovereignty is but the extension of the rebellion in Eden that questioned any moral direction transcendent to man himself. The view of Genesis, that man is the divinely delegated steward (even if in this respect some Christians, like non-Christians, have shown a callous indifference to environmental concerns) is not the source of ecological insensitivity.

Charges that biblical theism is to blame for ecological insensitivity are laid to rest by cautious observers of the history of ideas and of the cultural influence of Christian conviction. John Black refutes the effort to lay the modern ecological crisis at the door of Scripture.[10] Christopher Derrick also replies to the complaint.[11] What really makes the biblical ethic unacceptable to its modern critics is not its supposed inadequacy but the high moral and spiritual demand it exerts.

Moss affirms, cogently, that a middle way exists between the technomania of contemporary society and the recent countercultural rejection of science and technology and the mystical-ecological subculture. "The middle way is feasible, however," he emphasizes, "only if science and technology are incorporated into a rational scheme of responsible values like that provided by the biblical concept of moral responsibility and its associated system of binding ethical principles."[12]

In the biblical view nature is a space-time reality fashioned by God *ex nihilo*. Nature is neither essentially divine nor self-subsistent, nor is it without beginning. The Hebrews disavowed the ultimacy of the processes of nature and rejected the Canaanite divinities identified with these. Nature is the creation of a sovereign, rational, moral God who continually reveals himself in nature. God who speaks in and through nature declares not alone that nature is dependent on him but also that he is the one Sovereign on whom mankind also depends. He has fashioned nature as an environment in which humans have responsible dominion over inanimate and animal existence in the service of God and for the implementation of his moral purposes. The Creator declared nature to be "good" prior to the creation of the human species. Mankind is to worship the God of nature. He is to be grateful that God has provided nature to contribute to the satisfaction of human needs and to promote understanding. He is to enjoy nature, to preserve it, and to enhance it.

Due to the fall of the first parents into sin, nature in its present state is imperfect and unbalanced, although it shares in the promise of a full future redemption. Mankind now copes with a terrain cursed because of Adam; into the tragedy of that rebellion nature itself is drawn. Humanity's misuse of nature is wicked and calls for repentance and divine forgiveness. Nature has purposes beyond those exhausted in its subordination to mankind. It is to be valued independently of its value for humanity. To squander nature for the sake of human greed and affluence is immoral.

Luther emphasized how man's fall into sin warped the divinely-intended human relationship of dominion under God:

> What we achieve . . . is brought about, not by the dominion which Adam had but through industry and skill. Thus we see the birds and the fish caught by cunning and deceit; and by skill the beasts are tamed. Those animals which are most domesticated, such as geese and hens, nevertheless are wild so far as they themselves and their nature is concerned. Thus, even now, by the kindness of God, this leprous body has some appearance of the dominion over the other creatures. But it is extremely small and far inferior to that first dominion, when there was no need of skill or cunning, when the creature simply obeyed the divine voice because Adam and Eve were commanded to have

dominion over them. Therefore we retain the name and word "dominion" as a bare title, but the substance itself has been almost entirely lost.[13]

Luther's focus on dominion largely in terms of animate creation is significant. Human life, as we have already stressed, does have a sanctity not shared by animal and plant life. Yet although animals have no "human rights" (or duties), God's moral purpose nonetheless embraces them. The desire to preserve an endangered species is not without moral basis, even if the benefits may accrue not to humanity but to animals.

Adam originally named the living creatures (Gen. 2:19–20) and knew the nature of the animals. The Bible contains references to the main orders of mammals, birds, and reptiles as well as lower animals; more animals are in fact mentioned in Scripture than a casual reader might think. The fish of the sea are mentioned first in the assignment of dominion, suggests U. Cassuto, "either because the different categories of animal life are enumerated here in the order of their creation, or in order to emphasize that man would hold sway even over those creatures that were blessed with special fertility."[14]

After the fall of man, animals live in fear and dread of humans (Gen. 9:2–3), and man seems confused about their nature. Luther notes the development from Genesis 2:19–20, where the creatures are put under man's rule, to the condition reflected in Genesis 9:2–3, where the beasts shun and fear man in sin as their slayer and consumer. Luther thinks that prior to the Flood "man had used animals solely for the tasks for which they were suited and for sacrifices, but not for food and nourishment."[15] But God approved man's supplementing of his food supply by the eating of the flesh of beasts, birds, and fish. Some vegetarians have criticized the use of animals for food, but it is apparent from Genesis 9:2–3 that the use of fish, fowl, and beasts for food was part of the Noahic covenant. A distinction between clean and unclean animals had already been made (Gen. 7:2), differentiating those that could be eaten or offered as sacrifices. But even the slaughter of animals was not to be wanton, whether for sacrifice or for human consumption, but was to be done with ethical sensitivity. Nor were humans to eat raw flesh (Gen. 9:4).

Egyptians and other ancients worshiped the ox, the sheep, and the ichneumon. Pagan religion had its sacred hippopotamus and sacred serpents. Totemism assigned spiritual powers to animals. Hinduism views animals as participants in the cycle of reincarnation and considers cows sacred. The ancients designated special lands for sacred animals, and keepers paid with their lives for killing any. Vast sums were spent on animal funerals.

Modern secular society, by contrast, often implies the worth-

lessness of the animal world except as it serves humanity's interest
to preserve, destroy, or consume animals. Does man's mandate to
have dominion give license for exploitation of animal life, whether
the slaughter of seals for coats, alligators for hides, elephants for
tusks? Is a disregard for wildlife even on camping trips a matter of
ethical indifference?

It is the case, of course, that medical understanding has been
promoted by animal experimentation, a practice that some animal
lovers assail as cruelty. Are mice or monkeys only a divine
provision for the furtherance of scientific experiments?

Were animals divinely destined to be caged in a zoo or to be
killed for sport in quest of trophies or to be domesticated for work
that man cannot do?

On the other hand, were they destined to be cherished as
children in a world of orphans and lavished in luxury in a world of
human poverty? Some women will abort a fetus bearing the *imago
Dei*, yet cuddle and pamper an animal pet. In a world of famine
and destitution some Americans carry major medical and comprehensive insurance coverage on pets who are fed better than
impoverished humans. Yet by no means are pets to be deplored as
necessarily an extravagance. For many persons animals provide
necessary security and companionship.

But are animals to be valued only for what services they
provide human beings, or do they, no less than inanimate nature,
have independent value? Even the sentiment sometimes voiced
that we should promote the survival of endangered species like
polar bears and buffalo because they are "brother animals" seems
to value such species for the wrong reason. The earth and its
fullness are not man's, but God's, and man is to value the created
order as a responsible trust. The biblical reminder that "the cattle
on a thousand hills" are God's affirms not only that the Creator is
owner of the cosmos but that God attaches specific value to
creature life. God tells Jonah of his desire to spare Nineveh not
only because of its 120,000 inhabitants, but because of "much
cattle" (Jonah 4:11). While humans have more value than spar-
rows and lilies, the subhuman species were declared "good" at
their divine creation and retain value in God's sight. Amid the
modern concentration on inanimate nature as a stewardship
concern, the whole issue of man's relationship to the animal world
stands as an equally important priority that needs to be recan-
vassed.

The biblical ethic can best challenge and arrest the misuse of
nature. For scientific naturalism cannot sustain objective ethical
claims. It provides no real sanction for ecological morality. The
temptation to confront environmental problems only in terms of
self-interest—whether the individual's relation to his neighbors or
to the community, or the corporate economic requirements for

conserving natural resources and avoiding pollution, or the importance of constructive international relations—has achieved less in the way of solution than it has in gaining publicity for the issues. Protest groups like Friends of the Earth and Greenpeace have attracted media coverage, but discussion has focused more on objectives than on controlling principles. Ecological concerns are voiced by spokesmen who hold radically different metaphysical, sociological, and moral assumptions, but whose differing world views imply distinct forms of ethical justification for concerted action.

If the human species is but an evolutionary accident, and if all ethical imperatives are man-made, then neither rational nor volitional restraints exist for repelling a selfish misuse of the environment. Evolutionary humanism seeks unavailingly to transcend scientistic limits by promoting universal values that, in fact, cannot be sustained by naturalistic processes. While sophisticated elaborations of evolutionary environmental ethics are now appearing, their cogency is being challenged.[16] Even if the human species were in some respects the most intricate species yet to emerge on earth, that would not establish mankind's greater worth than other species, nor would it preclude the emergence of a future superhuman species. The effort of secular humanism to superimpose an ecological ethic on naturalistic evolution is unpersuasive. Humanism reduces all social imperatives to community consensus. The evolutionary world view disallows any transcendent unchanging norms and cannot provide an objective principle of duty. It replaces faith in the self-revealed transcendent Creator by faith in moral abstractions that a naturalistic metaphysics cannot really sustain.

Even less effective as a restraint on ecological misbehavior is romantic mysticism, whether in the form of Oriental religious philosophy or of Western pantheism, both of which blend man and nature into a universal All. The theory cannot rise to an *ought* that transcends the *is*. Not only does it fail to articulate a real concept of responsibility, but it tends to individualize whatever ethical imperatives it advances by suspending them on inner mystical conviction.

The argument that nature should be honored because it is divine leads to an equally excessive reaction, one that views all nature as entirely unrelated to the supernatural and as wholly explicable by empirical methodology. The instability of secular philosophy and ethics is apparent from its accommodation of wide swings of conviction, such as that nature, if not inherently spiritual, is therefore totally unrelated to spiritual reality. Without much success, recent process philosophy has sought to promote ecological concern on the premise that evolutionary nature is an expression of God's becoming.

Ecologists more and more acknowledge that without an emphasis on self-interest the appeal for secular sensitivity to environmental concerns lacks motivational power. Unregenerate humanity is usually more interested in immediate self-advantage than in the future of the human species. A metaphysical and moral perspective is required that confronts inordinate self-interest. The basic issue in environmental concerns, as in all else, is the character and will and judgment of God. The ethical referent for human relationships to the cosmos, therefore, is not military preparedness ("the Soviets are doing it") and self-survival, or social consensus, or aesthetic sentiment, or property values, but God's purpose for his creation.

The Amish seem in our century like museum-piece people who live without television, radio, and telephone, and who are content to travel routinely by horse and buggy. But among them thrives the Christian confidence that the earth is a sacred trust and that harnessing it and cultivating it require diligent and devout work. The Amish believe that one can more easily live a Christian life in a rural atmosphere. Merle Good writes:

> For the Amish preacher, the Bible bursts with images and parables of nature. . . . There are different kinds of soils, . . . each with its own potential, some more conducive to good seed, some more encouraging to weeds. . . . Depending on weather teaches dependency on God. Nature teaches constancy in hardship. Even though crops fail one year, the soil holds out promise of another harvest. . . . The two most important lessons learned from nature and the soil, perhaps, are central to the faith of these people. First, . . . a seed, placed into the earth, must die before it can give birth. The images of death and resurrection surround the farmer. And secondly, . . . sooner or later, one reaps what one sows.[17]

Yet everywhere the modern world encroaches on the Amish communities. The Three Mile Island nuclear accident, for example, occurred only some twenty miles distant from the Amish community in Lancaster County, Pennsylvania. Mankind will not reverse the scientific revolution, nor will most Christians seek to escape it. Christianity, after all, was a shaping force in the rise of Western science; the task now facing Christians is to challenge its unethical deployment and to project and practice it in a better way.

Christianity is not a matter of isolated piety but of convictions shaped by God's revelation of his purposes that order one's daily life both internally and externally through a distinctive lifestyle. Christians are to be salt, light, and leaven even in ecological matters. The Bible reinforces the value of all human life; the right of all humans to basic survival needs; respect for other created life forms and for the cosmos itself; the importance of preservation of air, water, lands, forests and the biosphere; and the further importance of such commitments not alone for ourselves but for future generations also.

Scripture does not set forth specific lines of ecological action, which may indeed vary with time and place. But it does adduce fixed principles that indicate that God was not content to create a chaotic wasteland but rather a habitable universe and that he expects his designated stewards to maintain it that way. No less than to the commission to preach redemptive good news world-wide, the believer must respond to the divine call to apply to the world the doctrine of God's creation and preservation of the universe and of mankind's stipulated role of stewardship.

Christian engagement at ecological frontiers need not involve a politicizing of the church in the interest of particular ideological perspectives—whether unilateral disarmament, opposition to nuclear power for energy, hostility to international corporations per se, and other causes that are readily attached to environmental concerns. Many misjudgments, from an absolute world government to a technological utopia shaped on behaviorist lines, have been promoted as the preferred way of fulfilling human steward-ship of the earth. But the promise of significant international cooperation and peace and justice can be fulfilled only when human beings and nations define their interests under God in a context that honors and deepens human rights and duties. Some contend that because the earth is the Lord's and the Bible sees the human race as a corporate organism, we must share the world's resources in common, and that equal redistribution of property is a demand of justice. Some insist that income differences are evidence of injustice and exploitation and that citizens should be disproportionately taxed to aid the less fortunate or that govern-ment should stipulate at what price an owner may rent his property. Others emphasize that a reliance on bureaucratic omniscience and enforcement usually postpones solutions and often even worsens conditions, and they call for maximal freedom of choice within the limits of a stable society, provided that freedom is exercised responsibly. After World War II many scholars pursued sociology as if it were simply a natural science whose interests could be wholly quantified, and they excised references to religion. Terms derived from biblical theism—such as covenant, stewardship, and salvation—were completely secu-larized, even if religious rhetoric was exploited in the context of a pragmatic sociology of the community or of the individual.

After reciting the sorry record of human misuse of earth's resources, Wesley Granberg-Michaelson calls for a piety that turns not simply inward but that expresses itself in a spirituality that includes a manifest stewardship of the earth.[18] Instead of exercis-ing a lordly dominion our role should be that of caretaking.

Granberg-Michaelson proposes lifestyle changes. Emphasizing that the New Testament envisages a new creation, he urges the people of God to anticipate it in their attitude and relation to nature. He considers genetic engineering and nuclear warfare incompatible with belief in God's creation of the world.

Christians should neither fall into ideological traps, nor on the other hand should they shun the need to engage in public policy debate to indicate and promote desirable legislation. But the quest for practical alternatives requires of Christians first and foremost that as God's people they exemplify in their lives and activities what genuine environmental concern implies. Ecological concern will question indulgent lifestyles, the preference for air polluting automobiles, indifference to energy-saving devices, and much else. Almost a decade ago five professors and two student fellows, after engaging for an academic year in concentrated study at the Calvin Center for Christian Scholarship, issued a three-hundred-page work offering representative proposals.[19] These included family gardens; more use of public transit; car pooling; driving of fuel-saving, smaller automobiles; turning down home heating; avoiding energy-consuming appliances; recycling materials; avoiding prepackaged and over-packaged goods; reusing shopping bags; avoiding paper towels; assessing recreational activities for environmental impact; limiting family size; promoting ecological awareness among children; sponsoring hunger-awareness events; electing leaders with environmental sensitivities; allowing wild animals to live on institutional grounds; and exploring and encouraging solar and wind energy.

The church should be a model in its own use of resources and care of God's creation. It should faithfully proclaim what Scripture teaches about stewardship, and not confine the theme—as is so often done—to tithing and generous giving. A cursory examination of library listings in most evangelical seminaries will indicate the extensive ecclesiastical correlation of the subject of stewardship with financial concerns. Stewardship over nature, justice in the use of resources, and the call to obedience in all human activities should be as much a part of church proclamation of stewardship as is the interest in charitable giving.

Duncan Vere asks, "Does man's 'dominion' over nature include the natural world within himself?"[20] Speaking of human incursion into nature, he notes among other examples the ready resort to abortion to destroy unwanted fetuses, the use of drugs other than as effective medical therapies, and recent *in vitro* fertilization and brain surgery, and notes their ethical implications. The resort to plastic surgery simply to preserve the illusion of youth or to enhance one's sexual appeal also raises ethical questions.

Evangelical literature is now appearing more routinely to spell out implications of biblical theism for environmental problems,[21] sometimes indicating its relevance for such specific concerns as water pollution.[22] Such expositions provide a needed alternative to such speculative proposals as that of Dorothee Soelle, who opposes a distorted "masculine" domination of nature, but curiously asks for our "reconciliation with nature" in an erotic relationship with creation within a bond of mutuality.[23]

Social critics who look for ecological solution to the curtailment of technology, the extension of bureaucratic control, or the restriction of economic growth may in significant ways worsen the problem. Technology can ride roughshod over community concerns, and free enterprise can ignore legitimate counterclaims. More than two decades ago Jacques Ellul voiced trenchant criticism of the premise that technological innovation can resolve all human dilemmas and assure the betterment of mankind.[24] But without capitalism and without technology most of the developed world would be where the developing nations are now. The notion that the elimination of free market forces and the overthrow of right-wing governments will assure an ecological paradise is naïve. Only a moral program that enlists voluntary response can hope to cope with ecological dilemmas. What is needed is technological and social development in the context of a proper value constellation.

The Marxist confrontation of environmental problems[25] exhibits what may appear to be surface advantages over the approaches of secular humanism and of technological pragmatism. As Moss notes, it is "wholistic" or comprehensive, and its analysis is in terms of social structures (rather than of scientific or technological dilemmas), and it calls for present sacrifice for the sake of future achievement of the communist goal. But its approach is a fully materialistic cost-benefit assessment. Its sanction for environmental action shares with other atheistic views the inability to provide an objective "ought."[26] Planning by government bureaucracies is not invulnerable to the promotion of immediate party goals even if under the guise of long-term economic growth.

If God is revealed in nature, a technocratic society has no justification for the obliteration of nature by construction of towering concrete jungles and superhighways not only unrelieved by aesthetic considerations but also permanently clouding the heavens that are God's handiwork. The preservation of wilderness societies, the provision of public parks, the protection of clean water, are important goals.

Technology can advance under God and not simply at the expense of humanity. But the confidence that technology can of itself provide a "quick fix" of environmental problems is misplaced; its power needs to be harnessed and directed by ethical imperatives. Contemporary scholars more and more concede the need of moral norms yet question, as does Hans Jonas, whether technocratic scientism can of itself achieve these.[27]

Moss notes that God has given to mankind a special responsibility with respect to "our universe in general, our planetary system more particularly, and preeminently the earth on which we live."[28] The emphasis points far beyond a restricted view of human cosmic dominion, which in an earlier decade of space exploration prompted some Christians to question the propriety of launching missiles and moonshots. The sin in Paradise was not simply the disobedience of a divine command but also the rejection of Adam's creaturely answerability to the will of his Maker. That rebellion not only ruptured Adam's own relationship to God but also disturbed his relationship to nature. Nature no less than all humanity continues to be implicated in the Adamic fall and rebellion.

Only God's redemptive intervention spared this disruption from inescapable catastrophe. Salvific rescue by God aims at a final restoration of humankind and nature to its intended creational ideal, including the human treasuring of nature not merely for physical survival needs or for economic profit but as an arena primarily in which God will display not only his glory but also his moral purposes for his creation.

The Old Testament sabbath legislation, the Year of Jubilee, the prophetic correlation of the fruitfulness or barrenness of the land with the personal and national ethical obedience or turpitude of God's people, and the messianic vision of the final restoration of nature all looked ahead to the first and to the final stages of Christ's coming. The resurrection of the Crucified One occurs as the first fruit of a general resurrection which exhibits God, human nature, and physical nature in comprehensive moral harmony. The whole creation now, in this interim, groans and waits for this impending new creation as God's consummatory act of grace and judgment. The people of God never contemplate the future simply under the dread possibility of atomic destruction or universal environmental pollution. Christ is Lord of the environment and of its possibilities, and the universe will not be finalized without his triumph.

In Luke 12:42 Jesus asks his disciples, "Who then is that faithful and wise steward, whom his lord shall make ruler over his household . . . ?" (KJV). In the parable of the assessment of servants, he warns of judgment of "that servant, [who] knew his lord's will" and did not do it (Luke 12:47 KJV). It takes little imagination to view the cosmos as God's household in which humans have a responsible stewardship role. Of the deliberately ravaged natural world, Charles Babbage writes:

There exists, not alone in the human conscience or in the omniscience of the Creator, but in external material nature, an ineffaceable, imperishable record . . . of every act done . . . from the birth of our first parent to the final extinction of our race, so that the physical traces of our most secret sins shall last until time shall be merged in that eternity of which not science, but religion alone, assumes to take cognizance.[29]

The future assize, of which Babbage forewarns us, will focus attention on the Creator who will judge the self-appointed lords of the land and sea and sky, and assess the stewardship role of the human race to whom an ethical dominion was assigned. Both Old and New Testaments affirm that God alone has ultimate dominion, and they speak in luminous terms of his eternal rule (Job 25:2; Ps. 22:28; 145:13; Dan. 4:3, 34; 6:26; 7:26; Zech. 9:10; 1 Tim. 6:16; 1 Peter 4:11; 5:11; Jude 25; Rev. 1:6). The New Testament emphasizes that all things were made through Christ and for him, and that all things—mankind included—will be subject to him. The term *kyriotēs* (lordship, dominion) has its supreme application to the Deity (2 Peter 2:10; Jude 8) and especially to the risen and exalted Jesus who will rule over humanity (Rom. 14:9) as King of Kings and Lord of Lords.

## ENDNOTES

[1] Conrad Hyers, "Dinosaur Religion: On Interpreting and Misinterpreting the Creation Texts," *Journal of the American Scientific Affiliation* 36/3 (September 1984): 147.

[2] Gerhard von Rad, *Genesis*, Old Testament Library (Philadelphia: Westminster, 1961), p. 58.

[3] For a useful overview and extensive bibliography see R. Attfield, *The Ethics of Environmental Concern* (Oxford: Blackwell, 1983).

[4] "Environmental Problems and the Christian Ethic," in *Horizons of Science*, ed. C. F. H. Henry (New York: Harper and Row, 1978), pp. 63–86.

[5] Julian Simon, *The Ultimate Resource* (Princeton: Princeton University Press, 1981).

[6] Jacques-Yves Cousteau, foreword to Robert Cahn, *Footprints on the Planet* (New York: Universe, 1978), p. vi.

[7] *Science* 155/37 (1967): 1203ff.

[8] *God, Revelation and Authority* (Waco: Word, 1976), 2:91–103.

[9] Rowland P. Moss, *The Earth in Our Hands* (Leicester: InterVarsity, 1982).

[10] John Black, *The Dominion of Man* (Edinburgh: University of Edinburgh Press, 1970).

[11] Christopher Derrick, *The Delicate Creation* (London: Tom Stacey, 1972).

[12] "Environmental Problems and the Christian Ethic," in *Horizons of Science*, p. 79.

[13] *Luther's Works*, vol. 1, Lectures on Genesis, ed. Jaroslav Pelikan (St. Louis: Concordia, 1958), p. 67.

[14] U. Cassuto, *A Commentary on the Book of Genesis* (Jerusalem: Magnes, 1961), pp. 56–57.

[15] *Luther's Works*, vol. 2, Lectures on Genesis, ed. Jaroslav Pelikan (St. Louis: Concordia, 1960), p. 132.

[16] Cf. A. G. N. Flew, *Evolutionary Ethics* (New York: St. Martin's, 1968).

[17] Merle Good, *Who Are The Amish?* (Intercourse, Pa.: Good Books, 1985).

[18] Welsey Granberg-Michaelson, *A Worldly Spirituality: The Call to Redeem Life on Earth* (San Francisco: Harper and Row, 1984).

[19] Loren Wilkinson, ed., *Earthkeeping: Christian Stewardship of Natural Resources* (Grand Rapids: Eerdmans, 1980).

[20] Duncan Vere, "Does Man's 'Dominion' Over Nature Include the Natural World Within Himself?," *Faith and Thought*, vol. 3, no. 1 (1985), pp. 57–64.

[21] Cf. R. Elsdon, *Bent World: Science, the Bible and the Environment* (Leicester: InterVarsity, 1981); Rowland P. Moss, *The Earth in our Hands* (Leicester: InterVarsity, 1982).

[22] John R. Shaeffer and Leonard A. Stevens, *Future Water* (New York: William Morrow and Co., 1983). The authors contend that a circular configuration that recycles water and waste would not only eliminate pollution but produce energy, fiber, and food, and do so profitably.

[23] Dorothee Soelle, *To Work and To Love: Theology of Creation* (Philadelphia: Fortress, 1984).

[24] Jacques Ellul, *The Technological Society* (New York: Knopf, 1964).

[25] Cf. H. L. Parsons, *Marx & Engels on Ecology* (London: Greenwood, 1977).

[26] Roland P. Moss, "The Ethical Underpinnings of Man's Management of Nature," *Faith and Thought* 3/1 (1985).

[27] Hans Jonas, *The Imperative of Responsibility* (Oxford: Oxford University Press, 1984).

[28] Moss, "Ethical Underpinnings of Man's Management," p. 49.

[29] Quoted by David Ehrenfeld, *The Arrogance of Humanism* (New York: Oxford University Press, 1978), p. 191, from *The Ninth Bridgewater Treatise*.

# A Response to
# Stewardship of the Environment

## John W. Klotz

Dr. Henry's essay is of the quality we have come to expect from him. It is concise, thought provoking, incisive, and above all, scriptural. In a very objective and unemotional way he answers the secular humanists and the pantheistic environmentalists who wish to attribute all of our environmental problems to the biblical environmental ethic. He points out that the problem is not with the biblical approach to our environmental problems but rather with the lack of acceptance of biblical principles of stewardship of the environment.

Dr. Henry is quite right in attributing many of our environmental problems to the theory of biological evolution. His emphasis and his repeated references to this fact represent some of the strengths of the paper. Some years ago *Audubon* magazine carried a lengthy article attacking creationists and blaming them for the damage that our environment has suffered. The author, Peter Steinhart, wrote, "Many fundamentalists believe it is man's duty to develop and exploit nature, citing the biblical injunction to subdue the earth and have dominion over all living things. . . ." He then referred to some of my writings and activities and expressed surprise that I, a known creationist, should be so active in a conservation movement. He characterized me as a creationist who was the exception to his general rule that creationists advocate exploitation of the environment, saying,

> Not all . . . agree. John Klotz, a biologist at Concordia Seminary in St. Louis and one of the founders of the Creation Research Society, says, "Some people would argue that since man is the foremost of creatures, his rights and privileges take precedence. But I think it is a misinterpretation to say 'rule over and subdue' means to exploit. I don't think the rights of animals can be

ignored. We need to set aside places where other creatures can survive. It is very obvious that God cares not only for man but for beast and bird as well."

I wrote him a letter which was subsequently printed in *Audubon* in which I pointed out that I was an environmentalist *because* I was a creationist. I developed many of the points which Dr. Henry has developed in his essay, pointing out that because I believed in God the Creator, I recognized that I was only a steward, not the owner of creation. I have a responsibility to my Creator to care for what he has given me. Let me quote what I said.

Since Peter Steinhart quoted me in the September *Audubon*— accurately at that—let me respond. I do not accept evolution for a variety of reasons. I do not believe that the scientific evidence supports it as an explanation for the variety of living things we see on our time level. Nor do I believe that the question of origins lends itself to anything other than scientific speculation.

But let me come to the point in which you and your readers are interested. Steinhart's "Essay" does a disservice to the cause in which you and I are both interested. You see, it is because of my religious background that I am a conservationist or environmentalist or Auduboner or whatever you want to call me. My understanding of Scripture and my science agree. Because I believe that God made all that I see, it belongs to him and not to me. His command to Adam was that he was to till the garden and care for it (Gen. 2:15). God's concern extends to the birds and animals, for he provides them with food (Ps. 147:9). Not a sparrow falls to the ground without his knowledge and concern (Matt. 10:29). The eyes of all—plants, animals, and man—wait on him, and he gives them their meat in due season (Ps. 145:15–16). Because I take seriously what he tells me, I must act as a responsible steward of what he has made and what he owns. I cannot exploit it because it does not belong to me. I started my permanent career preparing teachers for Lutheran parish schools. I had a minor in ecology and it quickly became apparent to me that if these teachers were to be faithful to the Scriptures in their work, they would have to understand the created world and practice responsible stewardship over it. I served as president of one of the older Chicago conservation organizations, the Friends of our Native Landscape; and when I moved to Fort Wayne I became one of the founders of and first president of ACRES, Inc., a sort of regional Nature Conservancy. I have been active in the conservation movement for over thirty-five years now. It is my acceptance of the Bible at face value that has led to my position, a position which you will find elaborated in my book *Ecology Crisis*, published some ten years ago. Most creationists, I am convinced, will agree with my position. Steinhart is wrong in condemning creationism as it opposes evolution from a scientific point of view, and he is wrong, as Lynn White, Jr., was suggesting, that creationists advocate exploitation. Quite the contrary, if they are really consistent.

We are all aware of the effect that social Darwinism had during the last part of the nineteenth century and beginning of the twentieth century. We are aware of how capitalism lost face because of the excesses of ruthless money barons who argued survival of the fittest. But we are not always as aware as we should be of the effect that the theory of evolution has had on our environmental problems and how it has encouraged exploitation of God's creation. The repeated references to the damage that the theory of evolution has done in Dr. Henry's essay deserve serious consideration. The demon in our environmental crisis is not Scripture but the generally accepted theory of biological evolution. If you tell people they are animals, they feel justified in acting like animals. If you tell them that nature is red in tooth and claw and that survival of the fittest is the rule not only of the jungle but also of human society, they will have no scruples about destroying other species and other individuals of their own species and exploiting the entire evolved world for the benefit of the master race. Writing in the May 1986 issue of *BioScience*, Norman D. Levine says:

> Extinction is a normal part—indeed a necessary one—of evolution. . . . Shakespeare was right—man is the measure of all things. *Homo sapiens* is (at present, at least) the dominant creature on Earth. . . . Do we really need snail darters and condors and black lion tamarins? Let us not be disturbed at the loss of some species. Extinction is not evil; it is normal and necessary.

Another strong point in the essay is Dr. Henry's rejection of both secular humanism and of pantheism. Closely associated with this is his rejection of the materialism which characterizes our age. He points out that humanism reduces ethics and morals to human consensus; Christianity depends for its system of ethics and morals on God's absolute standards reflected in the Ten Commandments. It is very evident that consensus may change, and if we are to decide what is right by majority vote, we may very frequently be faced with changing standards. There was a time when medicine stressed the importance of preserving life. The Hippocratic Oath, the basic standard of medical ethics, pledges the doctor not to give a woman a substance which will bring about an abortion. As late as 1968, the American Medical Association Declaration of Geneva required the following pledge from the embryo doctor, "I will maintain the utmost respect for human life from the time of conception, even under threat, I will not use my medical knowledge contrary to the laws of humanity." But the general consensus, as reflected in the *Roe v. Wade* decision, has changed. Doctors now perform abortions. They argue that the human life, which they reluctantly recognize begins at the time of conception, does not necessarily imply human personhood, and they have no scruples against terminating the child's life at the wishes of his mother. It is clear that if ethics and morals are reduced to human consensus, ethics and morals may change, and we as individuals may be the victims of those changes. It is with this concept that creationists and Christian environmentalists take issue. Steinhart, in the article I have referred to, says, "What creationists have in common with the . . . past is . . . the conviction that we live in a moral universe and not a material one."

Secular humanism is another product of the theory of evolution; chance is the creator. Man is not only the master of his fate and the captain of his soul but also the master of the entire created world.

On the other hand, many environmentalists are pantheists. They recognize the need for a god as Paul points out in the first chapter of Romans (vv. 19ff.), and so they equate nature with God. They talk about the marvels that nature has accomplished, usually praising evolutionary developments. Their god is a force, not a person. They praise nature and worship nature rather than the Creator. They emphasize the unity and common ancestry of man and animals.

Dr. Henry deplores the maudlin approach of brother wolf and sister dove. He notes the irony of a situation where women cuddle dogs and cats and shower their affection on animal pets but have no scruples about killing fetuses. Pantheism is as old as man. Paul, in his Epistle to the Romans, tells us that the heathen had changed the glory of God and in the stead of their Creator worshiped the images which resemble not only men but birds, animals, or reptiles (Rom. 1:22). The God you and I worship is a personal God. He is not just a force, though he can certainly demonstrate his power. He is indeed immanent, for in him we live and move and have our being; but he is also transcendent, apart from his creation. So also, as Dr. Henry points out, man is a part of nature and yet is above it. He is subject to and limited by natural laws. In exploiting the environment, he damages himself. It is worth pointing this out to those who abuse their surroundings; some people are impressed with that sort of selfish appeal. But it is not nearly as effective as one based on the biblical approach which depends on a Creator-Owner/creature-steward relationship.

Dr. Henry's approach to environmental problems is a balanced one. He neither exaggerates nor minimizes the importance of nature. It is not God; it is not to control man. Rather man is to rule over the earth and subdue it. Still nature and natural laws are important. The world about us is God's creation, and it was created good. We must be very reluctant to seek to improve on this natural world which God has created. We sometimes forget that in spite of the corruption of sin, it is still the good world that our beneficent and all-wise God made. We are to manage it, not tinker with it. And in our management, we need to proceed slowly and cautiously. Our approach must not be that of arrogantly seeking to correct mistakes that a blind and blundering nature has made, but rather of respectfully managing a world that has been turned over to our care.

Dr. Henry, therefore, points out that it is not the biblical view but a distortion of the biblical view that has led to problems. The Bible standards are very high standards. The Scripture's emphasis on stewardship indicates that we have no right to exploit. The Creator is the owner; we are only the stewards. God made it; it belongs to him, not to us. We have it only on loan.

Dr. Henry points out that God is immanent as well as transcendent. I am convinced myself that the doctrine of preservation is one of the really neglected doctrines of Scripture. The controversy over creation has led us to ignore the importance of preservation. Indeed the initial scientific attacks were levied against preservation, not against creation. It was Newton's causal determinism and his watchmaker god that first attacked biblical teaching. Newton was very pious. He believed in absolute time and space, which he associated with God. He believed that the age of miracles was over. He developed the concept of the universe as a machine. He was a positivist who turned his back on metaphysics in favor of a small but growing body of exact knowledge. He believed that it was possible to acquire truth about things without presupposing any theory of their ultimate nature.

Newton's ideas of cause and effect led him to develop the concept of a watchmaker God. He accepted the miracles of the Old Testament and the New Testament, but he also believed the age of miracles was past. In effect, while he accepted creation, he denied the doctrine of preservation. He believed that God had indeed created the universe and that he had established the laws by which it is governed. In our modern era Newton believed that God had withdrawn from the universe which he created and that he operated solely through the laws which he had established at the time of creation.

This mechanistic approach reached its zenith in the work of Laplace, who believed that if there were a superhuman intelligence capable of knowing the position and momentum of every atom in the universe and capable of solving all mathematical equations, it could with precision state the minutest detail of every event "whether it be thousands of years in the future or remote in the past."

Newton's work and the work of Laplace led to a causal determinism in science. It made God philosophically unnecessary and irrelevant. There was no real point in debating whether God existed. If he did exist and was the watchmaker God, he did not interfere with the affairs of the universe. The role of science was determining what these laws were, rather than seeking to debate the existence of the God who had given them.

Causal determinism was philosophically devastating to theology, but somehow or other it did not attract the attention or opposition of churchmen. It led to logical positivism, which until recently was embraced by the majority of scientists. The implications of causal determinism for orthodox Christianity were indeed profound. This was certainly as significant a philosophical attack on Christianity as any, yet its significance was largely overlooked. Logically it led to deism and made agnosticism a reasonable approach. Dr. Henry makes a very important point when he emphasizes the doctrine of preservation and our Christian acceptance of the immanence of God. He is still very much involved in this world which he has created.

Finally, I liked Dr. Henry's emphasis on the fact that God still rules. This is closely associated with his emphasis on God's immanence, and it leads to a Christian optimism. In spite of the evil that we see in the world about us, final decisions are being made by God. If I were a scientist and not a Christian, I would be very pessimistic. I would be realistic enough to recognize the evil that is in the hearts of men. I would recognize that they are more likely to use the technology and the control over the environment for selfish purposes, that they are likely to exploit rather than protect for future generations. But I recognize that it is God who moves nations and people across the stage of history. It is he who is preparing the script. I have always been impressed with a plea issued by C. P. Snow in 1960. He pleaded for unilateral nuclear disarmament by Britain and the United States, predicting that if we did not disarm, the world would be involved in a nuclear war with all its horrors within ten years. While he proposed negotiations with Russia, he suggested junking nuclear weapons whether or not the Russians went along with the proposal. This is 1986, and a nuclear holocaust has not engulfed us. It is not that C. P. Snow was wrong in his understanding of what would follow a nuclear attack or was wrong in evaluating the likelihood of the evil use of nuclear power. What he failed to realize was that God was still in charge. It is still he who moves nations across the stage of history and controls its course. He loves me and loves his church, and he is going to protect me and his church.

There are just a few additional points that I would like to make. Dr. Henry emphasizes the spiritual corruption that has come by the Fall. I am sure that all of us subscribe to what he has said in this connection. I believe, though, that we ought to recognize that the Fall involves not only spiritual corruption but also the corruption of, and a limitation on, our mental powers. It is not only that we are selfish, we are also stupid. I tell my classes that compared to God, man has approximately the IQ of a chicken. Let me suggest that this is the reason why so often he "lays an egg."

I would, therefore, like to suggest that some of our environmental problems have come not as a result of man's selfishness but as a result of man's inability to anticipate the results of what he is doing. Even well intentioned, he may upset the balance of nature and regret the changes that he has made. We need to be very cautious in our efforts to improve on God's world. It is still a good world in spite of the Fall, and the changes we make are likely to cause damage. Most of our pests, both plant and animal, are exotics. They are animals and plants which have been introduced into an environment different from that in which God placed them. Some of these introductions have been accidental; some have been deliberate. In some cases we felt that we were improving on the natural world. We are not wise enough to anticipate all these effects of changes we bring about.

We need to be less cocky and less arrogant. We do not have the wisdom of God. We need to exercise real caution in the improvements we introduce into nature. Another result of the Fall is our inability to judge our own motives. Very often they are a mixture of altruistic and selfish motives. We can very easily persuade ourselves that we are acting in love as the situation ethicists do when basically we are selfish. Our consciences are corrupt. They tell us to do what God has not commanded, and they also suggest activities which he has forbidden.

We cannot overemphasize the result of the Fall, for as a result of this action of our first parents, even we Christians are in danger of becoming materialists. The things of this world seem more important and more attractive than spiritual things. We become oriented to this life instead of to the life to come.

I believe we also need to emphasize the fact that because we have greater control over our environment through technology, we who live in the twentieth and twenty-first centuries have greater responsibilities. This then equates with a greater hazard because of the limitations of man's mental powers. For example, today we can level mountains, fill in valleys, and reroute rivers. But can we anticipate the full effects of these changes? Is our technical skill itself not a hazard to our health?

I believe, too, that we need to recognize and emphasize Luther's doctrine of the two kingdoms. We are citizens not only of heaven but also of this world. We need to avoid confusing our citizenship. Christ's kingdom is ultimately a spiritual kingdom.

True, he rules this earth, but he does this through his powers. It is only in his church, the kingdom of the right hand, that he rules by his Word. Control over the environment is a part of the kingdom of the left hand.

Finally, I should like to call attention to the Jewish property laws and to Dr. Henry's comments on the Amish respect for the land. To me, it is very interesting that the Jews felt that their land was held in trust. They were only stewards, and they did not have the concept of property rights that we have. They could not sell their property; they could only lease it until the Year of Jubilee; and under the theocracy, in the Year of Jubilee, the land returned to the original owner. I believe this is a reflection of their stewardship concept, of their recognition that God is the Creator and Owner and of their emphasis upon the importance of caring for the land as stewards. It was not their property to dispose of as they saw fit.

# A Response to
# Stewardship of the Environment

## Loren Wilkinson

Dr. Henry comes to the question of the stewardship of creation from a magisterial command of the whole discipline of Christian ethics. So although many have written on environmental ethics (especially in these last two decades), few have done so with quite such a deliberate concern for the whole range of ethical questions involved. It is a particular privilege, therefore, to respond to a survey of environmental ethics that is so clearly set within the whole context of God's revealed purpose for his creatures.

My purpose in this response is first of all to suggest, by way of summary and appreciation, the solidity of the foundational ideas which Dr. Henry has laid out here. Those ideas can be described in terms of two well-worn theological terms, "transcendence" and "immanence." They can be used to describe aspects of both divine and human relationship to creation. (Henry uses only the idea but not the word *immanence*). My second purpose is to suggest the need for thinking yet more foundationally about God's immanence, or involvement in creation, and its implications for human attitudes toward creation.

The only legitimate starting point for Christian ethics is the fact of all creation's dependence on the transcendent Creator. Henry makes this very clear here: If there is no place to stand outside the flux of the world, there can be no ethics at all. Thus Henry criticizes recent attempts to formulate an "evolutionary environmental ethic" because of that lack of a transcendent viewpoint: "The evolutionary world view disallows any transcendent unchanging norms. . . . It replaces faith in the self-revealed transcendent Creator by faith in moral abstractions that a naturalistic metaphysics cannot really sustain."

Our action toward the creation, then, is guided first of all by our knowledge that it is a *creation*, and that the transcendent Creator has revealed himself to us. In Henry's words again: "Mankind is to worship the God of nature. He is to be grateful that God has provided nature to contribute to the satisfaction of human needs and to promote understanding. He is to enjoy nature, to preserve it, and to enhance it."

Our main impetus to care for creation is thus rooted not in what creation is, but in who the Creator has revealed himself to be: the God beyond both man and nature. Obedience to the Creator should be our primary motive. Thus the biblical doctrine of divine transcendence underlies not only environmental ethics but all ethics.

A similar kind of transcendence characterizes the human relationship to creation. As Henry puts it in his opening paragraph, "the creation account depicts the first human as fashioned in God's image and as designated God's deputy ruler over the cosmos and its creatures." Just as God the Creator is other than creation, so also the man the "deputy ruler," though himself a creature, also stands apart from the rest of nature. Human beings are not "immersed in nature or a mystical participant in it." They are rather to have dominion over it.

At this point Dr. Henry questions the interpretation, made popular by Gerhard von Rad, that the whole meaning of the *imago dei* is to be found in the exercise of dominion (after the practice of conquerors who erected an image to represent their presence in vanquished territory). Says Henry, recognizing the harshness of the verbs used to describe human dominion, "If critical scholars exclude moral and rational categories from the *imago* no objection can in principle be mounted against thus placing the text in the service of an unbenevolent 'trampler.'" While agreeing with Henry's rejection of that harsh concept of dominion—which is based on the analogy of human to divine transcendence—I would like to suggest that it would be better to base that softening of the harshness of *kabash* and *radah*, not on some conjectured "moral and rational categories" in the *imago*, but rather on a more profound capacity in the human creature for the same kind of empathetic immanence demonstrated by the Creator. I will return to this point in conclusion.

As Dr. Henry points out, many have seized on this biblical picture of human transcendence over creation (itself an image of divine transcendence over creation) as a cause for Western environmental destruction. Lynn White's 1967 article is widely quoted in this connection. Henry refers to it with the optimistic comment that such criticisms have been laid to rest. But the idea is far from dead. The belief that the Judeo-Christian tradition is the source of environmental degradation is a kind of environmentalist orthodoxy—so much so that when I present the full biblical view in a secular setting, people often respond with bewilderment and anger, as though I were making it up. Everyone "knows" that Christians, having thoroughly desacralized nature, regard it as a raw material for their own ends.

Sometimes this judgment that Christians do not care about creation is simply a convenient reason for not hearing the gospel. Nevertheless, it is important for us to hear it, for two reasons. The first is apologetic: it is a genuine barrier to belief. For many of our secular contemporaries, a wonder at creation has led to an unacknowledged hunger for the Creator. Yet they reject the God of the Bible because they mistakenly understand that God only in terms of a transcendent detachment from creation.

The second reason it is important to hear such contemporary caricatures of transcendence is that many Christians perpetuate them. Too many believers would have a hard time stating their understanding of God's relationship to creation—and their own as well—in ways that differ substantially from this deist-like detachment. In the understanding of many, God's concern with creation extends no further than saving humans out of it. (Another strength of Dr. Henry's paper is his reiteration of God's concern for creation quite apart from man.) This too-common view of a Creator concerned only with the human was expressed recently, for example, by Constance Cumbey. In a book that contained some good warnings against the pantheistic tendencies in the New Age movement, she criticizes the Calvin College study of Christian stewardship (from which Henry quotes some specific suggestions for lifestyle change). To the statements made in that book that God is concerned with the redemption of the whole creation, Cumbey replies: "If I read my Bible correctly, our peace was to be with God—not nature. The Calvin College position distinctly smacks of both Monism . . . and animism. God was going to make all things new—not redeem nature along with man."[1]

An encouraging thing about Henry's paper (in the face of this Christian tendency—both reputed and real—to stress only divine and human transcendence over creation) is its solid emphasis on human immanence. While not letting go of the truth that human beings are set over creation, Henry emphasizes that "man in his totality, psychic and physical, belongs to the created universe."

In one way this is quite obvious. But in an era when more and more human beings are living in a superficially manmade environment, it is ever more essential to be reminded of our embeddedness in creation. Apart from our own organic mortality, we have increasingly vivid reminders that we share life with the rest of creation. An obvious one is that we are linked in the present to the beasts and plants of the world's ecosystems which keep food, air, and water in their ceaselessly nourishing cycles.

Not so obvious, but more troubling to many Christians, is the inescapable evidence of our links in the past with other creatures. If fossil evidence were not enough, the remarkable similarity of genetic and chemical makeup between us and other living things suggests that God's forming man of the dust of the earth was a long process and one which roots us firmly in the rest of creation. Because ecological and evolutionary biology has often been used as an argument against the Creator, Christians have sometimes not listened closely enough to what creation itself has to tell us of our links with the rest of the planet. Yet Scripture itself reflects that human immanence. Not only are we mankind, *adam* from the earth, *adamah* ("humans from humus"), but we share a day of creation with the animals.

In a generation of Christians to whom the word "creation" is all too likely to mean only an action by the transcendent Creator in the past, we need this biblical understanding of man being nourished by God in a network of other creatures which live and move and have their being in him.

The phrase—"in him we live and move and have our being"—which Paul quotes on Mars Hill from a Stoic poet, points to the biblical teaching on divine immanence, on which Henry could lay more stress. In a striking statement early in his paper, Henry echoes the truth that "He is not far from each one of us": "God the Creator," says Henry, "is the human species' most permanent and universal environment."

Certainly this is a brilliant way of stating God's nurturing care for his creatures. But it is not quite clear whether Henry means by the statement that it is the transcendent God beyond creation who is our environment, or the immanent God in creation, upholding us through his gracious gifts of light, water, food, and existence itself. For we know that like ourselves, all these things "hold together in him."

It is this latter sense of the immanence of the transcendent Creator which Christians need to reaffirm. We ought indeed to point out the error of trying (as Dr. Henry puts it) to restrain ecological misbehavior by "romantic mysticism . . . whether in the form of Oriental religious philosophy or of Western pantheism." These ways deny the transcendence of the Creator, and there is a great deal of both around today. But we need to be careful lest, in avoiding that denial of transcendence, we fall into an opposite error of exaggerating transcendence.

There are abundant resources in Scripture for a proclamation of God's immanence. God is shown to be not only the transcendent Creator but the life-giving Spirit—as in Psalm 104:

When you send your Spirit,
    they are created (v. 30a).

This is no distant deist's God, setting up laws which blindly carry out his designs. Rather the Creator Spirit is intimately and immanently involved with each thing. Likewise the picture of God's wisdom in Proverbs 8 is an eloquent testimony to the divine delight in creation:

> I was filled with delight day after day,
>     rejoicing always in his presence,
> rejoicing in his whole world
>     and delighting in mankind (vv. 30–31).

Christians have long seen this Old Testament presence of Wisdom in creation to be a foreshadowing of the cosmic Christ, that Word of God without whom John says nothing was made, and of whom Paul says, "In him all things hold together."

Using such biblical resources as these we need to reflect, in the light of current cosmological, ecological, and biological understanding, on the immanence of God in creation. One way of doing so is to consider the doctrine of the Trinity as descriptive of God's simultaneous transcendence and immanence. In his 1984–85 Gifford lectures published as *God in Creation: An Ecological Doctrine of Creation*, Jürgen Moltmann speaks eloquently of some of these creatorly dimensions of the Trinity:

> In the free, overflowing rapture of his love the eternal God goes out of himself and makes a creation, a reality, which is there as he is there and is yet different from himself. Through the Son, God creates, reconciles and redeems his creation. In the power of the Spirit, God is himself present in his creation—present in his reconciliation and his redemption of that creation.[2]

Along these lines, while maintaining a strong sense of God's transcendence, we can recapture the biblical teaching on God's immanence in creation. Then we will perhaps be able to understand better both the process of creation across time—which is sometimes misnamed evolution—and the intricacy and interrelatedness of creation across space which (in the realm of living things) is the concern of ecology.

I suggested earlier that the harsh picture of human relationship to creation which comes from understanding the image of God solely in terms of an image of God's transcendence could be softened by thinking of that image in terms of the other revealed aspect of God's relationship to his creation, his immanence. There is, of course, much in the Genesis text itself which softens the harshness of autocratic dominion—particularly the verbs *radah*, "serve," and *shamar*, "guard," in Genesis 2:15. But if we are to argue from the *imago dei*, then we would do well to look not only at God's transcendent dominion but at his self-giving and redemptive involvement. Here Claus Westermann's comments on the *imago dei* are helpful. Westermann suggests that the meaning of the phrase is not so much in any specific content, but in God's determination to make a counterpart with whom he could enter into relationship: "human beings are created in such a way that their very existence is intended to be their relationship to God."[3]

But we have broken that relationship to our Creator, and consequently our relationship with creation is broken, a perversion of Godlike dominion. The biblical story concerns the restoration of that relationship with the Creator which is accomplished in Christ. We learn in Hebrews 2 that Christ, the perfect image of God, has restored as well the human relationship to creation, which the psalmist describes as "all things under [man's] feet." Jesus, among us as one who served, washing the feet of the disciples, showed how lordship was to be exercised. And Philippians 2 gives us the paradigm for all our uses of power. There we are told to "have the mind of Christ," who "grasped not" at dominion, but became a servant in the creation over which he is rightful Lord.

That picture of Christ does not deny his transcendence. But the transcendence becomes the basis for a redemptive immanence, a suffering for the world. This cannot be without relevance for our understanding of human dominion over creation. It is only through this kind of self-giving involvement with the created world, over which we are, through God's gift of the privilege of stewardship, "transcendent" that we will exercise our stewardship rightly.

Dr. Henry speaks of a "middle way" between the technomania of contemporary society (which is an exaggeration of human transcendence) and the "countercultural rejection of science and technology and the mystical-ecological subculture," which is an exaggeration of human immanence. Both the pattern and the power for that "middle way" are in the redemptive immanence of the transcendent God, who has made us for a relationship both with himself and with his creation.

## ENDNOTES

[1] Constance Cumbey, *The Hidden Dangers of the Rainbow: The New Age Movement and Our Coming of Age of Barbarism* (Shreveport, La.: Huntington House, 1983), p. 163.

[2] Jürgen Moltmann, *God in Creation: An Ecological Doctrine of Creation* (London: SCM Press, 1985), p. 15.

[3] Claus Westermann, *Genesis 1–11: A Commentary*, trans. John J. Scullion (London: SPCK, 1984), p. 158.

# GOD AND HISTORY

## James Montgomery Boice

It is appropriate that a summit conference on the application of the Bible to the great issues of contemporary life should end with "God and History," for implicit in this title are the convictions that there is a purpose to human history and that Christianity has something important to say about that purpose. Without these convictions there is little point in applying the Bible or anything else to our problems in the hope of achieving beneficial change.

Not everyone today is convinced that beneficial change is possible. In 1919 during his libel suit against the Chicago *Tribune*, Henry Ford, the inventor and industrialist, said, "History is bunk." On another occasion, when he was asked about history's meaning, Ford said, "History is the succession of one damned thing after another."[1] Most of our contemporaries would probably not be as forthright in their evaluation as Henry Ford, but most nevertheless sense that something has indeed gone wrong with the view that history has a clearly identifiable meaning and that progress is inevitable. During World War II and for a while after that conflict, the Time/Life corporation produced a series of cinematic newsreels called *The March of Time*. There was stirring "martial" music, the voice of an assured announcer, and a sequence of scenes from around the world that left the viewer dazzled with all that seemed to be happening in this fast-paced, modern age. What a vision! How inevitable the perfection of all things seemed!

Today it is difficult to maintain this optimism in the face of two world wars, numerous lesser wars, and epidemics of senseless death and violence that seem to sweep over our planet with startling frequency.

## THE FOCAL POINT OF HISTORY

What is history about? Historians turn to kings, queens, presidents, generals, inventors, nations, wars, battles, peace treaties, and geography as they struggle to bring meaning to a chaos of events. The Bible turns to the work of Jesus Christ and the church, which he founded. In writing to the Ephesians the apostle Paul, who was himself no mean historian, wrote, "His intent was that now, through the church, the manifold wisdom of God should be made known to the rulers and authorities in the heavenly realms, according to his eternal purpose which he accomplished in Christ Jesus our Lord" (Eph. 3:10–11).

Though brief, this sentence makes three points crucial for a Christian understanding of history:

1. *History has meaning.* Paul speaks of this twice, saying that God has a specific "intent" and "eternal purpose" in history.

2. *History is focused in the work of Jesus Christ.* The work is twofold. It concerns what Jesus did during the days of his flesh in providing for his people's redemption, and it concerns what he is continuing to do in his people, whose task is to make God's "manifold wisdom" known.

3. *The meaning of history is revealed in and through the church.* This statement is the most astonishing of all. It means that the Christian view of history is a 180-degree reversal of nearly all non-Christian views. John R. W. Stott says:

> Secular history concentrates its attention on kings, queens, and presidents, on politicians and generals, in fact on "VIPs." The Bible concentrates rather on a group it calls "the saints," often little people, insignificant people, unimportant people, who are however at the same time God's people—and for that reason are both "unknown (to the world) and yet well-known to God."

> Secular history concentrates on wars, battles and peace-treaties, followed by yet more wars, battles and peace-treaties. The Bible concentrates rather on the war between good and evil, on the decisive victory won by Jesus Christ over the powers of darkness, on the peace-treaty ratified by his blood, and on the sovereign proclamation of an amnesty for all rebels who will repent and believe.

> Again, secular history concentrates on the changing map of the world, as one nation defeats another and annexes its territory, and on the rise and fall of empires. The Bible concentrates rather on a multi-national community called "the church," which has no territorial frontiers, which claims nothing less than the whole world for Christ, and whose empire will never come to an end.[2]

## THE FIRST CONTRARY VIEW: THE GREEKS

Before considering the Christian view of history more careful-ly it will help to look at the two major contrary views competing with it. The first is the Greek or classical view.

It is sometimes said that the Greeks were not interested in history. This is not an entirely fair comment on a race that produced such eminent historians as Herodotus, who chronicled the rise of Greece, and Thucydites, who recorded its decline. But there is some truth in the statement despite these two figures.

What can be said of the Greeks is that their interest in history was directed to where their own race and its unique outlook on life had come from. But while they undoubtedly considered themselves to be a giant step beyond and above the barbarism that preceded them, they did not think of this as a stage in some unending upward movement of the race but rather as a peak which was inevitably to give way to poorer times again. The usual way of expressing this is to say that the Greek view of time was circular—that is, there was undoubtedly change in history. But it was change that constantly returned upon itself, just as the planets or seasons do. Nations had risen to power in the past and had then declined. They would do so again. But their citizens did not "get anywhere" by their rise, nor did others "advance" by their fall. The only meaning was in the circle itself, and the only salvation for a person caught up in such a circle was escape from it.

1. *The past is of little value* as far as studying it to seek reasons for why things are as they are. If the past has interest, it is only as an illustration of those characteristics of human thought and behavior also observable in the present.

2. *The future holds nothing new.* Epicurus said, "Nothing new happens in the universe if you consider the infinite time past" (*Fragments*, 55).

3. *Man's being bound to time through bodily existence is a curse.*

4. *Salvation is deliverance from this eternal circular course* and therefore from time itself. Plato gave a classic expression of this:

> The soul . . . is . . . dragged by the body into the regions of the changeable, and wanders and is confused. . . . But when returning into herself she reflects, then she passes into the realm of purity, eternity, immortality and unchangeableness, which are her kindred, and with them she ever lives . . . and, being in communion with the unchanging, is unchanging (*Phaedo*).

This ancient view of history has several modern expressions. The most obvious are the Eastern religions, which are making their way into Western life with increasing vigor. They stress the eternal circle and the need for escape from it. A less philosophical but equally escape-oriented view is contemporary Western materialism, particularly when coupled to an attempt to escape reality through the use of drugs.

## THE SECOND CONTRARY VIEW: INEVITABLE PROGRESS

Somewhere along the line the ancient, circular view of history passed over into the modern notion of inevitable historical progression. Christianity had a major role in that process.

One element Christianity brought to the picture was its doctrine of a God who revealed himself in history. Here was a God, on the one hand, utterly removed from the futile, half-human, half-divine gods and goddesses of the Greek pantheon and, on the other hand, equally far-removed from the unchanging and unchangeable First Mover of the Greek philosophers. This God grieved for his people, loved his people, and moved heaven and earth, as it were, for their deliverance. Another element Christianity brought to the picture was its view of the human being, not as a divine soul imprisoned in a perishable, evil body, as the Greeks thought, but as a union of body and spirit, created in God's image. In this view each part of the human being was important and valuable. Salvation was to be conceived, therefore, not as a salvation of the soul or spirit alone, but rather of the body as well through a final historical resurrection. Finally, Christianity introduced a heightened moral consciousness that required a balancing out of good and evil, rewards and punishments, at the last judgment.

During the Middle Ages Christianity mingled with Platoism and Aristotelianism to produce an other-worldliness that obscured Christianity's historical interests. But in the late sixteenth and seventeenth centuries—first through the budding scientism of Francis Bacon (1561–1626) and then through the philosophy of such thinkers as René Descartes (1596–1650) and Baruch Spinoza (1632–1677)—the value of knowledge, perceived by the Greeks, and the idea of a flow of history, derived from Christianity, were combined into a faith in inevitable scientific and social progress. This view flowered in the eighteenth century's rise of science and the nineteenth century's rise of industry—the industrial revolution. At the end of this period, when Charles Darwin (1809–1882) introduced the idea of an evolutionary progression among living things, the victory of the new outlook seemed complete.

According to the new philosophy:

1. *Progress is a natural process.* It has always been and will always be in operation.

2. *Progress occurs in all spheres.* There must be social, moral, religious, and philosophical improvement as well as scientific advance.

3. *Progress is inevitable.* This is necessary if it is truly a natural and universal law.

It was part of this philosophy that progress was thought to be achieved by: (1) the accumulation of knowledge, (2) political and social planning, and (3) biological evolution.[3] But each of these causes is today seen to be inadequate to sustain such optimism. The advance of scientific knowledge is inadequate for the reason that nothing in the scientific enterprise in itself determines how the discoveries of science will be used. Science can produce atomic energy, but the energy can be used to make a bomb as well as to provide for nuclear power stations—and even they are not unambiguously a step forward. Again, there is doubt whether political and social planning really solve problems; some believe that they actually create as many difficulties as they ease. As far as evolution is concerned it seems arrogant to assume that the human race is the epitome of biological advance when our "advance" has now made it possible for us to blow ourselves off the planet.

Where are we left today? Are we to say that the modern view of historical progress is entirely mistaken? Shall we conclude that history contains no meaning after all? That is not a correct conclusion from the perspective of Christianity. What is necessary is to return to the biblical view of history in which God, not man, is in control of history and in accordance with which his will, rather than man's will or some abstract principle, is done. The Christian expresses this confidence when he prays, "Your kingdom come, your will be done on earth as it is in heaven" (Matt. 6:9–10).

## THE CHRISTIAN VIEW OF HISTORY

The Christian approach to history may be traced by a review of the unique biblical doctrines that bear upon it: creation, providence, revelation, redemption, and judgment. When applied to history they teach that: (1) there is a comprehensive and universal history of the human race, (2) God controls history, (3) history has a pattern or goal, which God makes known to us, (4) God acts redemptively in history, and (5) people are responsible for what they do or do not do within history's flow.

1. *Creation.* The doctrine of creation teaches that the world is not eternal but rather that it came into being as an expression of God's will and through his explicit acts. It involves an ordering of creation according to which the natural world is rightly viewed as the backdrop for the world of men and women. This means that the human race is not an accidental part of the created order but is rather that specific and most valuable part of creation for which the other parts were brought into existence. Moreover, it is part of

Christianity's teaching that the race descended from one original pair, Adam and Eve, and is therefore one despite subsequent division into national and ethnic groups. In historical terms this means that the purpose of history must involve all groups and not merely Western or other "favored" ones.

There was no philosophy like this anywhere in the ancient world. Nor is there any truly like it today save through borrowings from Christianity. The Greek simply had no concept of creation; for him matter was eternal. Nor did he have anything like a universal outlook in which all human beings from all races are part of one grand pattern or design.

The interesting thing about this universal scope for history is that the need for it has been stressed only recently by secular historians. One thinks of the histories of Oswald Spengler and Arnold J. Toynbee, for what is unique about these authors is their desire to write a universal history of the race. Spengler in his monumental two-volume work, *The Decline of the West*, is critical of his predecessors at this point. He says that they have been provincial in thinking that Europe is the all-important center of history—simply because they happened to live there. They have neglected other peoples and areas. Far more serious than their provincialism, however, is the error of interpretation to which such provincialism leads, according to Spengler. By restricting one's concern to Europe it may be possible to devise the kind of progressive view of history the historians of recent centuries have provided, but when one looks beyond Europe to Asia and other previously neglected areas of the world one sees at once that history is not an upward linear process but rather a biological type phenomenon in which cultures are born, grow strong, deteriorate, and die. It was on the basis of this analogy that Spengler predicted the West's decline, hence the title of his book.

Toynbee is more optimistic than Spengler and also less pretentious. His well-acclaimed work is called merely *A Study of History*. That is, it is one interpretation among many and not *the* interpretation of history for all time. But although different in his attitude, Toynbee's object is the same as Spengler's—namely, to bring all history within one framework. In doing this he has isolated thirty-four civilizations, including thirteen "independent" civilizations, fifteen "satellite" civilizations, and six "abortive" civilizations, each characterized by a dominant motif.

Here is the interesting thing. Both Spengler and Toynbee seem alert to the fact that the human race is one and that the history of the race should therefore be a universal history, but their histories are remarkably different. In fact, it is striking how little overlap there is between them. What is wrong? Does this mean that desire for a universal history is misplaced, that no one history exists after all? Not necessarily. Significant divergence between such great scholars as Spengler and Toynbee shows how difficult it is for one mere human mind to grasp a subject of such proportions.

The point can be made even more strongly. Since the writing of history involves selection and interpretation of facts and since selection is always made at least in part on the basis of the subjective experience and judgment of the interpreter, it is actually impossible to write a purely objective history. Historical interpretations of this scope (or even of a more limited scope) differ and will *always* differ. The only way out of this problem is to receive an interpretation of history from outside history, as it were, from a being who perfectly understands history but who is above and beyond it and is therefore not affected by the distortions and prejudices that living and working in history introduce. In other words, the only way to have an objective and truly universal history is for God, the God of history, to provide it.

Christianity maintains that this is precisely what God has done. So even when we talk of a doctrine of creation and its implications for a universal view of history, we do so only because God has first revealed these things to us through the Bible.

2. *Providence.* The doctrine of providence follows naturally from the doctrine of creation, for the Bible reveals that, having created the world, God did not then abandon it, as if it were a large mechanical clock which he had wound up and was then allowing to run down. On the contrary, God guides the development of history through his eternal decrees and sometimes intervenes supernaturally both in nature and history to accomplish them.

This doctrine puts a Christian view of history into categories entirely different from those of naturalism. The naturalist believes that there are certain unalterable laws of history according to which it is possible to predict what is coming. Spengler is an example of this, for he has used laws of birth, growth, decline, and death to predict the fall of Western civilization. An even better example is Karl Marx (1818–1883) who reduced the laws of history to materialistic or economic factors. Marx's view was that of Ludwig Feuerbach (1804–1872), who taught by the use of a German pun that *"der Mensch ist was er isst"* ("man is what he eats"). According to this view, materialist factors are everything. Class struggle, revolutionary action, and eventually the classless society are the inevitable products of them.

Christians are not locked into such determinism. According to the Bible, God does have a plan in history, and history is following out that plan, but that does not mean that the outworking of that plan is mechanical.

Here we get into one of the great mysteries of the Christian faith: the relationship between the eternal decrees or will of God and contrary human wills. While we cannot always say precisely how that relationship works, we can say that each is real and that the flow of history is therefore wrapped up at least partially in man's obedience to or rebellion against God. The most important consequence of this in regard to God's plan in history is that the plan therefore does not unfurl itself with what we would regard as mathematical regularity. By contrast, it comes in fits and starts. There are periods of fast-moving spiritual events, but then there are periods in which the promises often seem delayed. This is true in regard to historical movements. For example, the deliverance of Israel from Egypt under Moses contrasted with the previous four hundred years of captivity. It is also true individually. At times God seems to be moving quickly in our lives. At other times we see little progress, and his acts of deliverance seem delayed.

With our twentieth-century penchant for tight schedules and regular progress, this usually seems frustrating. But it makes sense when we realize that God's purpose in history is not to build buildings (even churches) faster than anyone else or to run the trains or planes according to a tighter schedule but rather to develop Godlike character and conduct in his people. Moreover, since such conduct and character can come only from association with himself, God has arranged things so that we will inevitably be drawn to him in prayer and other forms of fellowship. Thus we pray for the coming of God's kingdom, and we ask for a revelation of his will where our particular lives are concerned.

3. *Revelation.* The doctrine of revelation is related to the first two doctrines, for it is only by revelation in the Bible that we know that this world has been created by God and is guided by him according to his own perfect plan.

God's revelation has both a general or objective character and a personal or subjective one. That is, there is a revelation of God's overall plan in Scripture beginning with the creation of the human race and continuing through the Fall, the calling out of a special people through whom a Redeemer would come, the appearance and work of Christ, the establishing of the church, and the promise of Christ's eventual return. This is the objective framework for the Christian view of history, but the revelation also has a personal or subjective side. For as we read the Bible God also speaks to us to call us into that framework through faith in and obedience to Christ. Christ is the focal point of history. Consequently, we become a part of God's work in history and serve his plan for it only as we come into a saving relationship to Jesus who is at the center of its workings.

4. *Redemption.* The doctrine of redemption introduces two new ideas: sin and God's unique act in Jesus Christ to save the sinner.

The first of these themes is important because it explains why no naturalistic or nonethical view of history can do it justice. Those who stand within the modern, progressive understanding of history are particularly vulnerable at this point, for the progress they envision is not pure progress, and in some cases it is questionable whether what they point to is progress at all. What is the problem? The problem is not that so-called "progressive" elements are not present. They are. It is that man's tragic flaw— what Christian theology calls original sin—mars these elements and at times perverts them for destructive rather than constructive ends.

Sometimes, particularly in the self-righteous climate of relatively modern times, it is assumed that this destructive element resides in institutions and can therefore be eliminated by social restructuring or revolution. But the problem is deeper than that. It is in the deep nature of men and women and therefore can be dealt with only by God for whom everything, even a restructuring of human nature, is possible.

If God did not act in history, there would be no solution. There would be only a continuing struggle with evil in which pessimism (the destruction of the race) or escapism (the solution of the Greeks) would win out. But God does act—decisively. And he acts not merely to guide history or to provide a moral framework in which the worst sins are somehow judged but to redeem those very sinners who are responsible for the evil. He redeems them through the work of Jesus Christ.

At the beginning of his influential book *Christ and Time*, Oscar Cullmann calls attention to the fact that in the Western world we do not mark time in a continuous forward-moving series of events that begins at a fixed initial point, but from a center from which time is reckoned both forward and backward. The Jewish calendar begins from what it regards as the date of the creation of the world and moves on from that point. We, by contrast, begin with the birth of Jesus of Nazareth—fixed within the space of a few years—and then number in two directions: forward in an increasing succession of years which we identify as A.D. (*anno domini*, "in the year of [our] Lord"), and backward, in a regression of years which we identify as B.C. ("before Christ").

This system did not always prevail. The custom of numbering forward from the birth of Christ was introduced in A.D. 525 by the Roman abbot Dionysius Exigius. The custom of numbering backward from the birth of Christ originated only in the eighteenth century. The interesting point is not so much the time at which these customs originated, however, but rather the testimony they give to the conviction in Christian hearts that Jesus is the dividing point of history.

A secular historian might judge that the coming of Jesus was pivotal because of his obvious influence on later history. But the

conviction, symbolized by the division of time, goes beyond this.
As Cullmann says:

> The modern historian may when pressed find a historically
> confirmed meaning in the fact that the appearance of Jesus of
> Nazareth is regarded as a decisive turning point in history. But
> the *theological* affirmation which lies at the basis of the Christian
> chronology goes beyond the confirmation that Christianity
> brought with it weighty historical changes. It asserts rather that
> from this midpoint all history is to be understood and judged.[4]

Christianity affirms that apart from Christ there is no way of
determining what history as a whole is all about, nor can we
legitimately weigh historical events so that one may be pro-
nounced better or more significant than another. However, with
Christ both these essentials for a true historical outlook are
provided. We affirm this by our division of time into the two great
halves of history.

5. *Judgment.* To make the Christian view of history complete
there must be added to the doctrines already considered—creation, providence, revelation, and redemption—the doctrine of
God's final judgment within but at the end of history. The
Christian expresses this belief when he confesses concerning
Christ each Sunday in the Apostles' Creed: "From thence [that is,
from heaven] he shall come to judge the quick and the dead."

In saying that Christ is to pass judgment on the dead as well
as on the living, the creed is saying that in the ultimate analysis
the meaning of history is not to be found only at the end of
history, as if everything has been building up to one final peak of
accomplishment which shall then be judged fit or not fit for glory.
It is rather to be found in any given moment in the choice or
choices made by any given individual, no matter who that one is,
where he or she has come from, or how important or unimportant
he or she may seem to be.

This means that the important moment in history is *now*.
Herbert Butterfield makes this point by some interesting analogies:

> History is not like a train, the sole purpose of which is to get to
> its destination; nor like the conception that my youngest son
> has of it when he counts 360 days prior to his next birthday and
> reckons them all a wearisome and meaningless interim, only to
> be suffered for the sake of what they are leading up to. If we
> want an analogy with history, we must think of something like
> a Beethoven symphony—the point of it is not saved up until
> the end, the whole of it is not a mere preparation for the beauty
> that is to be achieved in the last bar. And although in a sense
> the end may lack in the architecture of the whole, still in
> another sense each moment of it is its own self-justification,
> each note in its particular context is valuable as any other note,

each stage of the development having its immediate significance, apart from the mere fact of any development that does take place. . . . We envisage our history in the proper light, therefore, if we say that each generation—indeed each individual—exists for the glory of God.[5]

## GOD'S MANIFOLD WISDOM

I return to Ephesians 3:10–11, which speaks of God's "manifold wisdom," and I ask, How is the church to make God's manifold wisdom known? I offer this explanation.

When Satan rebelled against God and carried the host of fallen angels, now demons, with him into eternal ruin, God could have crushed the rebellion and annihilated Satan and his host forever. That would have been just and reasonable. It might even have been merciful; for if God had gone on to create Adam and Eve, as he had no doubt determined to do beforehand, Satan would not have been there to tempt them, the pair would not have fallen, and sin and death would not have passed upon the race. But this would not have shown God's "*manifold* wisdom." It would have revealed God's power and perhaps even something of his mercy, but it would not have shown that God's way, the way of truth and righteousness, is the only really good way and the only sure road to happiness.

So instead of annihilating Satan, God took an entirely different path. God said, "I have already determined to create a race called man, and I know in advance, because I know all things, that Satan will seduce man from my righteousness and plunge him into misery like his own. Satan will think he has won, evil triumphing over good. But while Satan is doing that—turning the human race against me and even against itself—I will begin to create a new people who will glory in doing what is right, even when it is not popular. I will create a race of those who will delight in pleasing me, even when they are made to suffer for it. Satan will say, 'Christians serve you only because you protect them, only because you provide for them materially.' But here and there in a great variety of ways I will allow my own to be greatly abused and persecuted, and I will show by their reactions that not only will they continue to praise me in their suffering, and thus bring glory to my name, but that they will be happier even in their sufferings than Satan's people will be with their maximum share of human prestige and possessions."

God lets history unfold like a great drama upon a cosmic stage. The powers of heaven are the audience. We are the actors. Satan is there to do everything he can think of to resist and thwart God's purpose. This great drama unfolds across the centuries as Adam and Eve, Noah, Abraham, Moses, David, and Isaiah, John the Baptist, Jesus, Peter, Paul, and all the other *dramatis personae* of the past, both the great persons and the minor persons, are brought on stage to play the part God has given them and speak words that come from hearts that love him. Adam proved that God's way is the best was as he repented of his sin and trusted in the Christ who was to come. So did Eve and Noah and all the others. All these endured as seeing him who is invisible. They looked beyond the distresses of this life to their reward.

You and I are players in this drama. Satan is attacking, and the angels are straining forward to look on. Are they seeing the "manifold wisdom" of God in us as we go through our part and speak our lines?

I close with this illustration. In William Shakespeare's tragedy *King Lear* there is a character who is not even given a name. He is a servant, and he is not even in the list of characters presented at the beginning of the play. In the text he appears only as the "first servant," one of three. This character has only four lines of dialogue, but they are spoken in this way. Two cruel characters are about to put out the eyes of the old Earl of Gloucester. There is no one to stop them. At the crucial moment, this servant rushes forward to do what he can and is then cut down from behind and dies. Then the villains go on and put out the eyes of Gloucester anyway.

If this were real life, the world would never pay attention to such an "unimportant" character. He had no name. He accomplished nothing. But if the Bible is correct, in the sight of God this "first servant," who did the right thing at the right time regardless of the consequences, was far more important than the kings and earls. In such decisions, patterned on the character of Jesus Christ, is the flow of history.

## ENDNOTES

[1] John Warwick Montgomery, *Where Is History Going?* (Minneapolis: Bethany Fellowship, 1969), p. 15.

[2] John R. W. Stott, *God's New Society: The Message of Ephesians* (Downers Grove: InterVarsity, 1979), pp. 127–28.

[3] See Gordon H. Clark, *A Christian View of Men and Things* (Grand Rapids: Eerdmans, 1967), pp. 46–49.

[4] Oscar Cullman, *Christ and Time*, trans. Floyd W. Filson (Philadelphia: Westminster, 1950), p. 19.

[5] Herbert Butterfield, *Christianity and History* (New York: Scribners, 1950), p. 67.